ATHEIST MANIFESTO

ATHEIST MANIFESTO

*The Case Against Christianity,
Judaism, and Islam*

Michel Onfray

Translated from the French by Jeremy Leggatt

Arcade Publishing • New York

Library of Congress Cataloging-in-Publication Data is available on file.

ISBN: 978-1-61145-008-8

Printed in the United States of America

The concept of "God" invented as a counter-concept of life — everything harmful, poisonous, slanderous, the whole hostility unto death against life synthesized in this concept in a gruesome unity! The concept of the "beyond," the "true world" invented in order to devaluate the only world there is — in order to retain no goal, no reason, no task for our earthly reality! The concept of the "soul," the "spirit," finally even "immortal soul," invented in order to despise the body, to make it sick — "holy"; to oppose with a ghastly levity everything that deserves to be taken seriously in life, the questions of nourishment, abode, spiritual diet, treatment of the sick, cleanliness, and weather! In place of health, the "salvation of the soul" — that is, a *folie circulaire* [manic-depressive insanity] between penitential convulsions and hysteria about redemption! The concept of "sin" invented along with the torture instrument that belongs with it, the concept of "free will," in order to confuse the instincts, to make mistrust of the instincts second nature!

— Nietzsche, *Ecce Homo*

Contents

CONTENTS

CONTENTS

Preface

1

Desert memory. After a few hours on the trail in the Mauritanian desert, I saw an old herdsman traveling with his family. His young wife and his mother-in-law rode camels; his sons and daughter were on donkeys. The group carried with them everything essential to survival — and therefore to life. The sight of them gave me the impression that I had encountered a contemporary of Muhammad. Burning white sky, scattered, scorched trees, uprooted thorn bushes blown by the desert wind across unending vistas of orange sand ... the spectacle evoked the geographical and psychological background of the Koran, in the turbulent period of camel caravans, nomad encampments, and clashing desert tribes.

I thought of the lands of Israel, Judaea and Samaria, of Jerusalem and Bethlehem, of Nazareth and the Sea of Galilee. Places where the sun bakes men's heads, desiccates their bodies, afflicts their souls with thirst. Places that generate a yearning for oases where water flows cool, clear and free, where the air is balmy and fragrant, where food and drink are abundant. The afterlife suddenly struck me as a counterworld invented by men exhausted and parched by their ceaseless wanderings across the dunes or up and down rocky trails baked to white heat. Monotheism was born of the sand.

It was nighttime at Ouedane, east of Chinguetti, where I had traveled to see the Islamic libraries long buried in the sand. Even today, sand dunes are patiently but inexorably swallowing up whole villages. Abduramane, our driver, unrolled his prayer mat under the stars in the courtyard of the house where we were staying. I was quartered in a small room with a makeshift mattress. As the full moon shone on Abduramane's black skin, the blue-gray light caused his flesh to appear purple. Slowly, as though impelled by the ancestral movements of the planet, he knelt, lowered his forehead to the ground, and prayed. Light from dead stars reached down to us in the hot desert night. I felt that I was witnessing a primitive ritual, similar to humankind's earliest act of worship. As we continued our journey next day, I talked with Abduramane about his religion. Surprised that a westerner, a white man, was interested in Islam, he challenged every assertion I made. I had just read the Koran, pen in hand, and I had memorized several passages word for word. But his unquestioning faith led him to deny that any verses in his holy book were contrary to basic Islamic principles of goodness, tolerance, generosity, and peace. Holy war? Proclamation of jihad against unbelievers? A fatwa issued for the execution of an author? State-of-the-art terrorism? Madmen did those things, certainly not Muslims . . .

Abduramane did not like it. There I was, a non-Muslim, reading the Koran and pointing out that, despite the many chapters that comforted him and supported his beliefs, there were just as many verses in the same book that justified armed fighters wearing the green banner of martyrdom, Hezbollah terrorists wrapped with explosives, the Ayatollah Khomeini condemning Salman Rushdie to death, the kamikaze attackers flying commercial aircraft into Manhattan's towers, and bin Laden's disciples beheading civilian hostages. I was skirting blasphemy. We lapsed into silence in that landscape devastated by the sun's fire.

2

Ontological jackal. After hours of silence and the same unchanging desert scenery, I returned to the Koran and the prospect of paradise. Did Abdou believe that the Koran's fantastic description of paradise was meant to be taken literally or as a symbol? Rivers of milk and wine, beautiful virgins, beds of silk and brocade, celestial music, magnificent gardens? Yes, he said, adding: *That is what it is like* . . . And hell? *Just as the Koran says it is* . . . What of Abduramane himself, a man of near-saintly ways — considerate, tactful, willing to share, ever mindful of others, gentle and calm, at peace with himself, with others, and with the world — would he one day experience those delights? *Yes, I hope so* . . . I wished it for him with all my heart. But deep down, I knew that he was wrong, that he was deceived.

After another silence, he went on to say that before entering paradise he would have accounts to settle. He was worried that his whole life as a pious believer would probably not be enough to make up for a certain error that he had committed, one that might well cost him peace and life everlasting . . . What crime? A murder? A mortal sin, as Christians say? Yes, in a way: once, in his car, he ran over a jackal. Abdou was driving too fast that night, over the speed limit. But it was a desert trail, and approaching headlights were visible from miles away. The road was clear, he saw nothing ahead . . . when suddenly a jackal leaped out of the shadows, and two seconds later it was dying under the wheels of his car.

Had he obeyed the rules of the road, he would not have committed that act of sacrilege — killing an animal when he had no need to eat it. Apart from the fact that the Koran makes no such stipulation, surely we cannot be held responsible for everything that happens to us! But Abduramane believed that we are. Allah is behind even the smallest of incidents. Allah used this event to demonstrate the necessity of submission—to the law, to rules, to order, because even the most trifling transgression brings us closer to hell. It can even lead us there directly.

The jackal long haunted his nights, keeping him from falling asleep, and he often saw it in his dreams, barring the road to paradise. As he spoke of it, his emotions resurfaced. His father, a wise old man in his nineties who had fought in World War I, was uncompromising: clearly, Abdou had failed to respect the law, and would have to account for his crime on the day he died. In the meantime, he must strive in his smallest actions to atone as best he could. The jackal would be waiting at the gates of paradise. I would have given anything for the animal to disappear and liberate the soul of this honest man.

It may seem truly remarkable that this good man with his humble aspirations should share the same faith as the September 11 pilots. One bore the burden of a jackal inopportunely thrown to the dogs, the others rejoiced in their annihilation of the greatest possible number of innocent people. Abdou believed that paradise might deny him entrance because he had turned a carrion-eater into carrion; the 9/11 terrorists believed they had earned eternal bliss by consigning the lives of thousands—including fellow Muslims—to ashes. Yet the same book inspired both types of men operating at opposite ends of the human spectrum, one aspiring to saintliness, the others carrying out an act of inhuman cruelty.

3

Mystical postcards. I have often seen *God* in the course of my life. There, in the Mauritanian desert, under a moon that repainted the night in blue and violet. In the cool mosques of

Benghazi or Tripoli, in Libya. On my trip to Cyrene, the home of Aristippus. Not far from Port-Louis on Mauritius, in a shrine dedicated to Ganesh, the colorful elephant-headed Hindu god. In a synagogue in Venice, with a yarmulke on my head. Hearing the choir of Orthodox churches in Moscow. Waiting at the entrance to the Novodevichy Monastery, while inside priests with magnificent voices, gold-robed and swathed in incense, prayed with grieving family and friends over an open coffin. In Seville, standing before the Virgin de la Macarena, among women in tears and men with ecstatic faces. In Naples, in the Church of San Gennaro, god of the city built at the foot of the volcano, whose dried blood is said to liquefy at set times. At the Capuchin convent in Palermo, filing past eight thousand skeletons of Christians all dressed up in their most splendid clothes. At Tbilisi in Georgia, where passersby are invited to share boiled, bloody mutton under trees fluttering with small votive handkerchiefs hung there by devout Christians. On Saint Peter's Square one day when I had neglected to check the calendar: I was there to revisit the Sistine Chapel, but it was Easter Sunday and John Paul II was projected on a giant screen. His miter had slipped on his head, and he might have been speaking in tongues as he mumbled his divine message into the microphone.

I have seen God elsewhere too, and in other forms. In the icy waters of the Arctic during the landing of a salmon caught by a shaman, damaged by the net and ritually returned to the cosmos from which it had been extracted. In a back kitchen in Havana, where a Santeria priest performed a ceremony that involved a crucified, smoked agouti and a handful of volcanic rocks and seashells. In a voodoo temple deep in the Haitian wilderness, among basins stained by red liquids, the air filled with the acrid smells of herbs and extracts, the walls decorated with drawings to gain the favor of the Loa. In Azerbaijan, at Surakhany near Baku, in a Zoroastrian fire worshippers' temple. In Kyoto in Zen gardens—excellent exercises in negative theology.

I have also seen dead gods, fossil gods, gods as old as time itself. At Lascaux, I was stunned by the cave paintings in that earthly womb where the soul ebbs and flows under vast layers of time. At Luxor, in the royal burial chambers, located deep underground, watched over by men with dogs' heads, by scarabs and inscrutable cats. In Rome in the temple of Mithras, who slew the cosmic bull and whose cult might have transformed the world had it possessed its own Emperor Constantine. In Athens, climbing the steps of the Acropolis on my way to the Parthenon, as my mind dwelled on the city below where Plato had met Socrates . . .

In none of those places did I feel superior to those who believed in spirits, in the immortal soul, in the breath of the gods, the presence of angels, the power of prayer, the effectiveness of ritual, the validity of incantations, communion with voodoo spirits, hemoglobin-based miracles, the Virgin's tears, the resurrection of a crucified man, the magical properties of cowrie shells, the value of animal sacrifices, the transcendent effects of Egyptian saltpeter, or prayer wheels. Never. But everywhere I saw how readily men construct fables in order to avoid looking reality in the face. The invention of an afterlife would not matter so much were it not purchased at so high a price: disregard of the real, hence willful neglect of the only world there is. While religion is often at variance with immanence, with man's inherent nature, atheism is in harmony with the earth—life's other name.

ATHEIST MANIFESTO

Introduction

1

Keeping company with Madame Bovary. In Flaubert's novel, Madame Bovary relieved her despair by pretending. Many people do the same. Without romantic daydreams, their lives would be utterly desolate. A man can certainly avoid facing tragic reality by imagining himself as somehow different from the being he truly is — but only at the cost of turning himself into something unrecognizable. I do not despise believers. I find them neither ridiculous nor pathetic, but I lose all hope when I see that they prefer the comforting fairy tales of children to the cruel hard facts of adults. Better the faith that brings peace of mind than the rationality that brings worry — even at the price of perpetual mental infantilism. What a demonstration of metaphysical sleight of hand — and what a monstrous price!

Having realized all this, I experience the feeling that always arises deep within me when I am confronted with the symptoms of indoctrination and deception: compassion for the sufferer, coupled with burning anger toward those who perpetuate the deception. No hatred for the man on his knees, but a fierce resolve never to collude with those who urge him to adopt this humiliating posture and keep him there. Who would not sympathize with the victims of fraud? And who would not approve of battling the perpetrators?

Spiritual poverty engenders self-renunciation; it is just as significant as other deficiencies, whether sexual, mental, political, or intellectual. How ironic that other people's credulity should bring a smile to the face of the man who is supremely unaware of his own! The Catholic who eats fish on Friday derides the Muslim who refuses pork—who in turn scoffs at the Jew for refusing shellfish. The Lubavitcher swaying at the Wailing Wall looks askance at the Christian kneeling on a prayer stool and at the Muslim laying out his prayer mat in the direction of Mecca. Yet none concludes that the mote in his neighbor's eye might be smaller than the beam in his own. No one reaches the opinion that the critical mind, so relevant and always so welcome when applied to others, would be put to good use in a scrutiny of one's own beliefs.

Human credulity is beyond imagining. Man's refusal to see the obvious, his longing for a better deal even if it is based on pure fiction, his determination to remain blind have no limits. Far better to swallow fables, fictions, myths, or fairy tales than to see reality in all its naked cruelty, forcing him to accept the obvious tragedy of existence. *Homo sapiens* wards off death by abolishing it. To avoid solving the problem, he wishes it away. Only mortals have to worry about death's inevitability. The naïve and foolish believer *knows* that he is immortal, that he will survive the carnage of Judgment Day.

2

Profiteers waiting to pounce. I cannot fault those who need a metaphysical crutch in order to bear their lot. On the other hand, I am diametrically opposed to those who preach the ascetic ideal—and who also care for themselves in so doing. We are on opposite sides of the existential barricade. The traffic in afterlives benefits the men who engage in it by providing them the means to bolster their faith, for they find in it the material essential for reinforcing their own need for mental help. Just as psychoanalysts often treat others in order to avoid questioning themselves too closely about their own weaknesses, so the vicars of monotheist gods foist their vision of the world on the faithful — and day by day their own convictions become more secure.

Masking one's own spiritual poverty while exaggerating the same weakness in others, avoiding the display of one's own shortcomings by dramatizing those of the world at large, are tactics crying out to be denounced. No one is faulting the believer. But with the man who claims to be his shepherd, the case is different. As long as religion remains a purely private matter, we contend simply with neuroses, psychoses, and other personal factors. We deal with what aberrations we can, provided they do not threaten or endanger the lives of others . . .

My atheism leaps to life when private belief becomes a public matter, when in the name of a personal mental pathology we organize a world for others. For between personal existential anguish and management of the body and soul of our fellow human beings, there exists a whole world in which those who profit from human anguish lurk in concealment. Redirecting their own death fixation toward the world at large neither saves sufferers nor alleviates their suffering — but it contaminates the universe. The attempt to avoid negativity merely spreads negativity around like manure — ushering in a wholesale mental pandemic.

In the name of Yahweh, God, Jesus, and Allah — those convenient excuses — Moses, Paul of Tarsus, Constantine, and Muhammad exploit the dark forces that penetrate them, that work so powerfully within them. By projecting their somber visions on the world they blacken it still further — and with impunity. The pathological grip of the death fixation does not heal

3

itself through chaotic and magical muckspreading but by philosophical work upon oneself. Well-conducted introspection dispels the dreams and delirium on which gods feed. Atheism is not therapy but restored mental health.

3

Rekindling the Enlightenment. This work on oneself requires philosophy. Not faith, belief, fables, but reason and properly directed thought. We must fight against obscurantism, that fertile loam of all religions, with the weapons of the Western rationalist tradition. Sound use of our understanding, rational ordering of our minds, implementation of a true critical will, general mobilization of our intelligence, the desire to evolve while standing on our own feet—all these are strategies for dispelling phantoms. In other words, we need a return to the spirit of Light, of Enlightenment, that gave its name to the eighteenth century.

There is certainly much to be said on the historiography of that luminous century. With the French Revolution fixed firmly in their memories, and writing in its wake, the historians of the following century gave retrospective preference to whatever seemed to have contributed to that still recent event. They invoked the ironic deconstructions by Voltaire, by Montesquieu with his separation of the Three Powers, by the Rousseau of the *Social Contract*, by Kant and the cult of reason, by d'Alembert the master builder of the *Encyclopédie*, etc. But these dazzling Enlightenment figures—respectable, indeed politically correct—are the boldest that nineteenth-century historians could stomach.

I prefer sharper, more direct, and much bolder shafts of light. For behind their seeming diversity, all the revered figures mentioned above were united in deism. They strenuously rejected atheism. And they added an equal and sovereign contempt for materialism and the sensual. In other words, contempt for a host of alternative philosophical options that effectively constituted a "left wing" of the Enlightenment, a pole of radicalism that was soon forgotten but which might be usefully invoked today.

Kant is a monument of timid audacity. The six hundred pages of his *Critique of Pure Reason* contain the ingredients for blowing Western metaphysics sky-high, but the philosopher ultimately shrinks from the task. His separation of faith and reason, of presiding deities and concrete phenomena, is a step in the right direction. A little more effort would have obtained for one of these two world — reason — the right to claim precedence over the other — faith. It would also have made possible an unsparing analysis of the whole question of belief. But Kant stops short. In declaring the two spheres separate, he allows reason to abdicate its powers: he lets faith go scot-free, and religion is saved. Kant can then *postulate* (why did he need so many pages in order merely to postulate . . .) God, the soul's immortality, and the existence of free will, three pillars (along with the death drive) of all religion.

4

Once again, what was the Enlightenment? We know that Kant wrote a 1784 essay entitled *What Is Enlightenment?* Is it still readable over two centuries later? Yes. We can and we must subscribe to the Enlightenment project, which remains as viable as ever. It aims to lift man out of his infantile condition and set his feet on the path to adulthood; to remind him of his own responsibility for his infantile state; to inspire him with the courage to use his intelligence; to give himself and others the capacity to attain self-mastery; to make public and communal use of his reason in every field, with no exception; and not to accept as revealed truth what emanates from public authority. A magnificent project . . .

Why then did Kant have to be so un-Kantian? For how can we permit the attainment of adulthood and at the same time prohibit the use of reason in the religious sphere, which prefers the faithful to have the minds of children? We may of course think, says Kant; we must have the courage to ask questions, including of the teacher and the priest. Why then should we stop there, having reached such an encouraging point? Full steam ahead, surely! Let's postulate the nonexistence of God, the death of the soul, the nonexistence of free will!

So a final push is needed to rekindle the flames of Enlightenment. A little more Enlightenment, more and more Enlightenment! Let's be Kantian in opposition to Kant, let us pick up the gauntlet of boldness he throws down — without daring to act boldly himself. His mother, an austere and rigorous pietist if ever there was one, must have been holding her son's hand when he finished his *Critique of Pure Reason*. It must have been Frau Kant who helped defuse the unparalleled explosive potential of Kant's argument.

5

Atheology's dazzling light. The luminaries who succeeded Kant are well-known: among others, Ludwig Feuerbach, Nietzsche, Marx, and Freud. The "age of suspicion" gave the twentieth century a genuine decoupling of reason and faith, and then redirected the weapons of rationality against the fictions of belief. At last the battlefield was cleared and a new space set free. On this virgin metaphysical terrain an untested discipline saw the light of day. It is time to introduce *atheology*.

The term is to be found as early as March 29, 1950, in a letter from Georges Bataille to Raymond Queneau. In it, Bataille wrote that he would like to see a new edition of his books, previously published by Gallimard. For the three-volume collection, he proposed the overall title *Summa Atheologica*. In 1954, Bataille embarked on another project involving several texts announced four years earlier but not yet written, others still in the outline stage, and the internal integrity of the whole in constant flux. A fourth volume was announced, *Pure Happiness*, and then a fifth, *The Unfinished System of Nonknowledge*. None would see the light of day in the form envisioned. These works exist today only as a collection of incidental writings and selections from his notebooks.

The unfinished state of this important body of work, the abundance of plans and projects, the obvious equivocations in Bataille's correspondence on architectonics, his fierce insistence that he really did not want to be a philosopher — all this is evidence of an abandoned construction site. Above all, he gave up the project — founding a new religion — that had inspired his early reading, thinking, and writings. Atheology was left an orphan. Yet it is a brilliant concept.

Gilles Deleuze and Michel Foucault understood concepts as instruments in a toolbox at the disposal of anyone aspiring to philosophical work. That being so, I am adopting Bataille's term "atheology" for my own use. I am not, however, advocating Bataille's version of atheology — especially since it would require a tremendous amount of painstaking research and would likely yield only unsatisfying results. I am proposing the concept of atheology as a countercurrent to theology, a channel to carry us past discourse on God and flow upstream to the source, where we may examine the mechanisms of theology up close. On a world stage saturated with monotheism, it is high time to expose the back side of the theological scenery. This is an opportunity for philosophical deconstruction.

Beyond this preliminary *Atheist Manifesto*, then, the effort requires a mobilization of multiple disciplines. *Psychology* and *psychoanalysis*: consideration of the mechanisms of the fable-generating function. *Metaphysics*: plotting the genealogy of transcendence. *Archaeology*: giving a voice to the substrata beneath the surface geography of religions. *Paleography*: establishing archival texts. *History*, of course: acquainting ourselves with the epistemologies and their development in the areas where religions were born. *Comparative psychology*: establishing fundamental principles of thinking, learning, and behavior in various time periods and widely separated regions. *Mythology*: research into the details of poetic rationality. *Hermeneutics, linguistics, languages*: stressing local idiom. *Aesthetics*: tracing the iconic propagation of beliefs. And then of course *philosophy*: for philosophy seems best fitted to preside over the organization of all these disciplines. And the stakes? A physics of metaphysics, a true theory of man's inherent nature (immanence), a materialist ontology.

PART ONE

ATHEOLOGY

I

Odyssey of the Freethinkers

1

God is still breathing. Is he dead or not? The question is still undecided. However, such glad tidings would surely have generated cosmic events — which haven't yet transpired. Instead of the fertile field such a death would have opened up, we seem confronted today by nihilism, the cult of nothingness, the passion for nonbeing, a morbid relish for the twilight of waning civilizations, a fascination with the abyss and with bottomless pits where we lose our souls, our bodies, our identity, our being, and all interest in anything whatsoever. A lugubrious picture, a depressing apocalypse . . .

God's death was an ontological gimmick, a conjuror's trick. It was consubstantial with a twentieth century that saw death everywhere — the death of art, of philosophy, of metaphysics, of the novel, of music, of politics. So let's announce the death of all these fictional deaths! Tongue-in-cheek obituaries that once served certain thinkers — before they turned their metaphysical coats — as a dramatic setting for the paradoxes they uncovered. The death of philosophy engendered works of philosophy, the death of the novel generated novels, the death of art produced works of art, etc. As for God's death, it has released an outpouring of the sacred, the divine, the religious. Today we swim in these purgative waters.

Clearly, the announcement of God's death was as world-shaking as it was false — trumpets blaring, news bellowed from the rooftops, drums thundering in an orgy of premature rejoicing. Our era staggers under the weight of revelations solemnly hailed as the authorized utterances of new oracles. Abundance holds sway, to the detriment of quality and truth: never have so many false tidings been celebrated as so many revealed truths. For God's death to be certified, irrefutable facts, clues, and courtroom exhibits should have been produced. Yet none has emerged.

Who has seen the corpse? Apart from Nietzsche (and even then . . .). Like that of the corpus delicti in Ionesco's *Rhinoceros*, we should have felt its presence, its dominion, it would have been all-pervading, defiling, malodorous, it would have fallen apart little by little, day by day, and we would have witnessed a process of real decomposition — in the philosophical as well as the physical sense of the term. Instead of which God, invisible while alive, has remained invisible even when dead. And we are still without proof of his death. But who could furnish it? What new lunatic for this impossible task?

For, *pace* Nietzsche and Heine, God is neither dead nor dying because he is not mortal. A fiction does not die, an illusion never passes away, a fairy tale does not refute itself. Neither hippogriff nor centaur is bound by the laws governing mammals. A wildebeest or a horse, yes; an animal from the mythological bestiary, no. And God too (listed somewhere between "Gnome" and "Golem") is of that mythological bestiary, like the thousands of other creatures enumerated in dictionaries with numberless entries. The oppressed creature's sigh will endure for as long as the creature itself, in other words forever.

Besides, where would he have died? In Nietzsche's *The Gay Science*? Murdered at Nietzsche's summer home in Sils-Maria by an inspired philosopher — tragic and sublime, haunted and haggard — in the second half of the nineteenth century? And what was the weapon? A book, books, a life's work? Imprecations, analyses, proofs, refutations (the cold steel of writers)? Was the killer alone? Did he lurk in ambush? Or was he one of a group, along with the Abbé Meslier and the Marquis de Sade as guardian forebears? If he existed, would God's murderer not himself have been a superior God? And doesn't this noncrime mask an Oedipal urge, an impossible desire, an irrepressible ambition powerless to carry through a task essential to the creation of freedom, of identity, and of meaning?

You cannot kill a breeze, a wind, a fragrance, you cannot kill a dream or an ambition. God, manufactured by mortals in their own quintessential image, exists only to make daily life bearable despite the path that every one of us treads toward extinction. As long as men are obliged to die, some of them, unable to endure the prospect, will concoct fond illusions. We cannot assassinate or kill an illusion. In fact, illusion is more likely to kill us — for God puts to death everything that stands up to him, beginning with reason, intelligence, and the critical mind. All the rest follows in a chain reaction.

The last god will expire with the last man. And with him fear, terror, anguish, those devices designed to create divinities. They include horror of death's void, the inability to integrate death as a natural process with which we must come to terms, in whose presence intelligence alone can have any effect. And there is denial, the absence of any meaning beyond what we ourselves have to offer, with absurdity as a starting point. These are the genetic bloodlines of the divine. A dead God would imply a vanquished void. We are light-years away from such ontological progress . . .

2

Seeking a name for freethinkers. Thus, God will endure for as long as the reasons that brought him into being; and so will those who deny him . . . All attempts at establishing a family tree are a sham: God has no date of birth. Nor does practical atheism (atheism in the abstract is another matter). The first man (yet another fiction) to affirm belief in God must simultaneously, or successively and alternately, not have believed in him. Doubt is coeval with belief. The religious impulse, along with uncertainty or denial, have probably coexisted in one and the same individual from the beginning. Affirming and denying, knowing and not knowing: a time for kneeling, a time for rebellion, depending on the need either to create or immolate a divinity.

God thus seems immortal. On this point his standard-bearers prevail. But not for the reasons they imagine, for the neurosis that impels men to forge gods results from the usual workings of the psyche and the subconscious. Creation of the divine coexists with terror of the void in a life that must end. God is born of the rigor, rigidity, and stillness of dead members of the tribe. At the sight of a corpse, the dreams and smoke clouds that nourish gods take on more solid substance. When a soul collapses before the cold body of a loved one, denial takes over and transforms this ending into a beginning. The completion of the cycle becomes instead the start of a new adventure. God, heaven, and spirits come forth to dispel the pain and violence of death.

And what of the atheist? Denial of God and of afterlives probably shared the stage with faith in the soul of the first believer. Revolt, rebellion, refusal of the evidence, rejection of the decrees of fate and of necessity: the genealogy of atheism seems just as simple as that of belief. Afterlives and denial of God no doubt shared space in the mind of the first believer. Even as he rejected the evidence and refused to accept the dictates of fate and necessity, the seeds of doubt were sprouting and rebellion was brewing: the development of atheism was simultaneous with that of belief. Satan, Lucifer the light-bearer (that emblematic philosopher of the Enlightenment), the one who says no and refuses to submit to God's law, was created in the same gestational period as God. The devil and God were opposite sides of the same coin, like atheism and theism.

Atheism rejects the existence of God as a fiction devised by men desperate to keep on living in spite of the inevitability of death. The word "atheist" entered the French and English languages in the sixteenth century. Thus the word itself and the position it came to stand for arrived late in the West. But the idea of "godlessness" is old. The Bible alludes to atheists: Psalm 10:4, Psalm 10:13, and Jeremiah 5:12 speak of the wicked who will not seek after God, who despise God, who belie the Lord. The Greek term "atheos" dates from the seventh century BCE, was later incorporated into Latin, and thus was in use throughout Greek and Roman antiquity. It was an expression of severe censure and moral condemnation. Sometimes, indeed often, "wrong belief" was equated with "unbelief." The accusation of atheist could be leveled not only at the man who did not believe in God, but at the man who did not worship the dominant deities of the moment, the local, socially prescribed forms of divinity. Even a person deeply committed to a god—if it was a foreign, unorthodox god—might find himself condemned as an atheist. The word described not the individual who emptied heaven of its inhabitants, but one who peopled it with his own fabrications.

Throughout history, the authorities of a particular time and place have pledged allegiance to God or gods in the interest of consolidating their power. "Atheism" has served politically to thrust aside, label, or castigate individuals who believe differently. God himself is invisible, inaccessible, and therefore silent about what he can be made to say or endorse, but he makes no objection when people claim to be vested by him with the right to speak, ordain, and act (for better or worse) in his name. God's silence enables his ministers to exploit and abuse that title. Whoever does not believe in their god, and therefore in them, automatically becomes an atheist. The worst of men: immoral, loathsome, unclean, the incarnation of evil. Someone to be locked up on sight or tortured or put to death.

It is dangerous in such circumstances to proclaim oneself an atheist . . . But others say it, and always from the deprecatory standpoint of an authority bent on condemnation. The word's very structure makes this clear: a-theist. An exclusionary prefix, implying a negation, a lack, a void, an antagonistic stance. We possess no positive term to describe the man who does not worship phantoms of the imagination. All we have is this linguistic construction suggestive of amputation: so we have a-theist, but also mis-creant, a-gnostic (but no a-dieu!), un-believer, ir-religious, in-credulous, a-religious, im-pious, and all the words that flow from them: irreligion, unbelief, impiety, etc. Nothing that conveys the solar, affirmative, positive, free, and healthy aspects of the individual standing beyond magical thinking and fables.

"Atheism" is thus the product of a verbal creation by the manufacturers of gods. The word does not flow from the deliberate and sovereign decision of a person who defines himself historically by this term. "Atheist" describes the Other, the man who spurns the local god when everyone else, or almost everyone, believes in him. (And is well-advised to do so—for theology exercised behind closed doors is always buttressed by armed militias, existential police, and ontological soldiers who exempt us from thinking and instead demand the swiftest possible transition to belief and very often to conversion.)

Baal and Yahweh, Zeus and Allah, Ra and Odin—but also Gitche Manitou, the Great Spirit of the Algonquin tribes—owe their names to geography and history. In accordance with the metaphysics that made their existence possible they simply assume different names for one and the same fantasized reality. Yet none of them is truer than another. They all live in a pantheon of fictitious revelers where Ulysses and Zarathustra, Dionysus and Don Quixote, Tristan and Lancelot of the Lake — so many magical figures, just like the Fox of the Dogon or the Loa of voodoo — sit down to feast together.

3

The fruits of antiphilosophy. Lacking the perfect word to express the inexpressible, to name the unnamable — the madman with the audacity not to believe in God — we must therefore make do with *atheist*. There are of course roundabout ways of referring to nonbelievers without using the word, but it was Christians who invented such circumlocutions, introducing them to the intellectual marketplace with the same disparaging intent. After Pascal's death a Memorial he had written was discovered sewn into the lining of his coat. It spoke of the "God of Abraham, God of Isaac, God of Jacob, not of the philosophers and scholars . . ." In that context, Pascal used the word "philosophers" to mean *deists*. Terms then used in place of nonbeliever included *freethinker* and *libertine*, not in the sense of one leading a dissolute life but rather in the sense of one who doubts or denies religious dogma. Today, Belgian authors have coined the phrase "partisans of free examination."

Antiphilosophy — that eighteenth-century school of thought located on the dark side of the Enlightenment medal — is a current we wrongly neglect, but one on which we should train the light of current experience. For it demonstrates how far the Christian community will go in deploying means (including the most morally indefensible) to discredit the thinking of inde-

17

pendent temperaments not blessed with belief in its fables. Indeed, antiphilosophy fights with unthinkable violence against freedom of thought and against all thinking that deviates from the path of Christian dogma.

Witness, for example, the work of Father François Garasse, the Jesuit who invented modern propaganda in the seventeenth century. His *Curious Doctrine of the Beaux-Esprits* [figures rightly or wrongly celebrated for their wit and learning] *of Our Times, or Those who Claim to be Such* (1623) is an overstuffed volume of more than a thousand pages. In it he heaps abuse on the lives of independent philosophers, depicting them as debauchees, sodomites, drunkards, fornicators, gluttons, pedophiles (poor Pierre Charron, Montaigne's friend), and other satanic labels in order to dissuade people from looking into their progressive works. The next year that same Jesuit propaganda minister published a *Justification for His Book against the Atheists and Libertines of Our Times*. In it, Garasse adds another layer along the same lines, equally full of lies, calumny, villainy, and ad hominem attacks. Love of one's neighbor knows no limits.

Garasse used character assassination to undermine the influence of freethinkers. His tactics were not new. In the fourth century BCE, Epicurus was vilified by bigots and by the great and powerful. Today, the same tactics are still being used against any philosopher who (often without rejecting Christianity) does not think the Bible represents the ultimate truth — God's word, wholly inspired and infallible. Certain philosophers attacked by Garasse have yet to recover: they languish in obscurity. Some have undeserved reputations as immoralists and social outcasts, and those labels also stick to their works. For centuries, atheist thought was not presented in a fair light, and atheists were prevented from making their mark on the world. In philosophy, the term *libertine* still carries derogatory and polemical implications and libertine works encounter closed minds.

Because of the dominance of antiphilosophy in the official historiography of thought, a vast number of philosophical works remain unknown even to professional philosophers (apart from a handful of specialists). Many of these works are vigorous, powerful, and compelling, but they remain unread simply because their authors were anti-Christian, irreverent, or outside the mainstream belief system. Who for example, in the case of the century of France's Sun King, has read Pierre Gassendi? Or La Mothe Le Vayer? Or Cyrano de Bergerac—the philosopher, not the fictional character? So few . . . Yet an understanding of Pascal, Descartes, Malebranche, and other practitioners of the official philosophy is inconceivable without some familiarity with these philosophers, who strove for the autonomy of philosophy in relation to theology—to the Judeo-Christian religion, as it happens.

4

Theology and its fetishes. This dearth of positive terms to describe atheism, and the refusal to consider possible substitutions, goes hand in hand with the wealth of the vocabulary surrounding believers. There is not a single variation on this theme lacking its descriptive epithet: theist, deist, pantheist, monotheist, polytheist, to which we might add animist, totemist, fetishist, and even, in the case of historically established forms, Catholics and Protestants, Evangelicals and Lutherans, Calvinists and Buddhists, Shintoists and Muslims, Shiite and Sunni of course, Jews and Jehovah's Witnesses, Orthodox and Anglicans, Methodists and Presbyterians—the catalog is endless.

Some worship stones—from the most primitive tribes to today's Muslims walking around the Black Stone in the eastern corner of the Kaaba. Others venerate the moon or the sun, some an invisible god who cannot be represented on pain of idolatry, or else an anthropomorphic figure — white, female or male, Aryan of course. Another, a thoroughgoing pantheist, will see God everywhere, while another, an adept of negative theology, nowhere. By some he is worshipped covered in blood, crowned with thorns, a corpse; by others in a blade of grass, Eastern Shinto fashion. There is no man-made foolery that has not been dragooned into the ranks of putative divinities.

For those who still doubt the possible excesses of religions on the question of support media, let us consider the urine dance of New Mexico's Zuni, the manufacture of amulets of excrement of the Great Lama of Tibet, the cow dung and urine used for ritual ablution among Hindus, the Roman cults of Stercorius, Crepitus, and Cloacinus — respectively the divinities of filth, farts, and sewers — offerings of manure to the Assyrian goddess Siva, the consumption of her own excrement by Sushiquecal, the Mexican goddess and mother of gods, Ezekiel's divinely ordained recipe for the use of human fecal matter to cook food, and so many other impenetrable pathways or singular means of maintaining a relationship with the divine and the holy.

Faced with these multiple names, these endlessly varying practices, the immense vocabulary available for describing the unbelievable passion of believers, the atheist must be content with this single weak epithet, tailored to discredit him! Those who worship anything and nothing (the very ones who, in the name of their fetishes, justify intolerant violence and unending war against the godless) are thus the ones who reduce the freethinker to the etymological condition of an incomplete being, truncated, fragmented, mutilated, an entity without God and therefore without real existence.

God's soldiers have even developed a whole discipline entirely devoted to the examination of his names, his deeds and gestures, his memorable sayings, his thoughts, his words — for God speaks! — and his actions. It is the discipline of discourse on God, the province of loyal (and salaried) thinkers, his professionals, his lawyers, his spear-carriers, his contract killers, his dialecticians, his rhetoricians, his philosophers (yes, even those!), his henchmen, his servants, his representatives on earth and their institutions, his ideas, his diktats, and other nonsense — in other words, theology. The discipline of discourse on God.

The rare moments in Western history when Christianity has been manhandled — 1793 for example — yielded a few new philosophical activities and therefore a handful of new terms (which were quickly consigned to oblivion). Admittedly, people still speak of *de-Christianization*, but they do so only as historians to identify that phase of the French Revolution in which citizens turned churches into hospitals, schools, orphanages, when revolutionaries replaced roof crosses with tricolor flags and crucifixes of dead wood with living, healthy trees. The *atheist* in Montaigne's *Essays*, the *attayists* of Monluc's *Letters* (chapter 137), and Voltaire's *atheistic* quickly disappeared. So did the *atheist* of the French Revolution.

5

Naming infamy. The poverty of the atheist vocabulary is rooted in the unshakable historical domination of God's liegemen. For more than fifteen centuries they have enjoyed undisputed political authority. Tolerance is the least of their virtues, and they use every weapon in their arsenal to make the phenomenon, and therefore the word, impossible. The word "atheism" dates from the middle of the sixteenth century. But "atheist" existed in the second century of the common era among Christians who denounced and stigmatized the *atheos*— those who did not believe in a god raised from the dead on the third day. It was but a short step to conclude from their indifference to children's fables that they worshipped no god at all. Thus pagans—who, as their name tells us, worship the gods of the countryside—were seen as defying the gods and therefore God. No god, the wrong god, too many gods . . . to early Christians, it made no difference. The Jesuit Garasse stamped Luther as an atheist (!), and the poet Pierre de Ronsard reserved the same treatment for France's Huguenots.

The word stands as an absolute insult: the atheist is the immoralist, the amoral, the unclean, further consideration of whose life and books becomes a crime once the epithet has been uttered. The word is enough to block access to the works. It functions as a cog in the war machine launched against everything that does not move in the purest register of Catholic, Apostolic, and Roman orthodoxy. Atheist and heretic: in the last analysis they are the same. Which amounts in the end to a great many people!

Epicurus was forced very early to face charges of atheism. Yet neither he nor the Epicureans denied the gods' existence. The gods of Epicurus and of his disciples were creatures made of subtle matter. They were numerous, they inhabited between-worlds, they were imperturbable, indifferent to men's and the world's fate, true embodiments of freedom from care. They well and truly existed . . . But they were not like those of the Greek *polis*, who through the mediation of their priests demanded compliance with communal and social norms. That was their only fault: their antisocial nature.

The historiography of atheism—rare, skimpy, and generally of poor quality—is thus wrong to date the phenomenon from the earliest days of humankind. Social crystallizations require transcendence — order and hierarchy (etymologically, the power of the sacred) ... Politics and the *polis* can the more easily function by invoking the vengeful might of the gods, officially represented on earth by the powerful (who happen most opportunely to wield the levers of political control).

Commandeered into an exercise designed to justify secular power, the gods — or God — are seen as privileged interlocutors of tribal chieftains, of kings, of princes. Those terrestrial figures professed to hold their power from the gods, who confirmed this through signs decoded by the priestly caste, itself equally interested in the benefits of exercising a power for which it claimed legal sanction. Thereafter, "atheism" became a useful weapon for consigning this one or that one — providing that he resisted or protested a little — to jails, solitary confinement, even to the stake.

Atheism does not begin with those condemned and identified as such by official historiography. The name of Socrates cannot be decently included in a history of atheism. Neither can Epicurus and his disciples, any more than Protagoras, the first and most famous of the Greek Sophists, who contents himself in his *Concerning the Gods* with saying that he can conclude nothing about them — neither their existence nor their nonexistence. Which at the very least identifies a kind of agnosticism, an uncertainty, even a skepticism — but assuredly not atheism, which implies a frank assertion of the nonexistence of gods.

The God of philosophers often enters into conflict with the God of Abraham, Jesus, and Muhammad. First because the former proceeds from intelligence, reason, deduction, argument, and second because the latter proposes instead dogma, revelation, and obedience — the fruit of collusion between spiritual and temporal powers. The God of Abraham tends to define the God of Constantine, and then the God of not very Christian popes and warrior princes. That God had little in common with the extravagant constructions cobbled together out of causes lacking causality, out of motionless prime movers, innate ideas, preestablished harmonies and other cosmological, ontological or psychotheological proofs.

Any philosophical attempt to think about God outside the dominant political framework is usually reduced to atheism. Thus when the church cut out the tongue of the priest Giulio Cesare Vanini, hanged him, then burned him at the stake at Toulouse on February 19, 1619, it was murdering the author of a work entitled *Amphitheatre of the Eternal Divino-Magical, Christiano-Physical and Nonetheless Astrologico-Catholic Providence against the Philosophers, Atheists, Epicureans, Peripatetics, and Stoics* (1615).

Unless we choose to consider the above title meaningless, we must acknowledge that Vanini's oxymoronic wording rejects neither Providence, Christianity, nor Catholicism—but firmly opposes atheism, Epicureanism, and other pagan philosophical schools. Yet none of that makes an atheist (a man liable to the death penalty). He is more probably a kind of eclectic pantheist. But in any case, he is a heretic because he is unorthodox.

Spinoza, himself a pantheist—and of unequaled intelligence—was also condemned for atheism, or rather for insufficiently rigid Jewish orthodoxy. On July 27, 1656, the *parnassim* in session at the *mahamad*—the Jewish authorities of Amsterdam—read out in Hebrew, before the ark of the Houtgracht synagogue, a text of appalling violence. They charged him with horrible heresies, monstrous deeds, dangerous opinions, and evil conduct, with the result that a *harem* was pronounced against him—and never rescinded!

The community used language of extreme brutality: excluded, hounded out, execrated, cursed day and night, sleeping and waking, leaving home or returning . . . The men of God invoked the wrath of their fiction and his explicit anathema in time and space. To round out this gift, the *parnassim* asked that Spinoza's name be erased forever from the surface of the planet. The request was never granted, as we know.

Whereupon the rabbis, theoretical supporters of brotherly love, added to this excommunication a ban on any contact, verbal or written, with the philosopher. No one could help him, approach within six feet of him, or be under the same roof with him. It was of course forbidden to read his writings: Spinoza at that time was twenty-three, and had published nothing. His *Ethics* appeared posthumously twenty-one years later, in 1677. Today he is read all over the world.

Where is Spinoza's atheism? Nowhere. We could scour his life's work in vain for one sentence asserting the nonexistence of God. Admittedly, he denies the soul's immortality and asserts the impossibility of posthumous punishment or reward. He advances the notion that the Bible is a work composed by diverse authors and a work of historical — and therefore not "revealed" — facts. He refuses to subscribe to the theory of a chosen people, and proclaims this clearly in his *Tractatus Theologico-Politicus* (*A Theo-logico-Political Treatise*). He taught a hedonist morality of joy beyond good and evil; he held no brief for Judeo-Christian hatred of self, the world, or the body. Although a Jew, he discerned philosophical qualities in Jesus. But none of all that made him a denier of God, an atheist.

The list of wretches put to death for atheism in the history of the planet — priests, practicing believers sincerely convinced of the existence of a one God, Catholic, Apostolic, and Roman — is endless. So also is the roster of supporters of the God of Abraham or of Allah, they too executed in unbelievable numbers for failing to profess a faith bound by the accepted norms. The list of anonymous people who did not even rebel against the powers identifying themselves with monotheism, people who were neither refractory nor fractious — all these macabre numbers bear witness. Well before it was used to describe the God-denier, the word "atheist" served to condemn the thinking of the man even marginally liberated from authority and social supervision in questions of thought and reflection. The atheist was a man free in God's eyes — and ultimately free to deny God's existence.

II

Atheism and the Escape from Nihilism

1

The invention of atheism. The Epicurean Christianity of Erasmus or Montaigne, that of Gassendi, canon of Digne, the Pyrrhonian Christianity of Pierre Charron, theologian of Condom, accredited teacher of theology at Bordeaux, the deism of the Protestant Pierre Bayles or the Anglican John Hobbes sometimes exposed them to charges of impiety, of atheism. Here again, the term does not fit. Unorthodox believers, freethinkers beyond a doubt, but Christians, philosophers set free yet Christian by tradition, this wide spectrum permits belief in God without the constraints of an orthodoxy supported by army, police, and established power. Montaigne an atheist? What of his pilgrimage to Our Lady of Loreto, his professions of Catholic belief in his masterwork, his private chapel, his death in the presence of a priest at the moment (or so it is said) of the Elevation? No. All these fine, respectable philosophers believed in God.

What we need is a missing link, a precursor, an inventor, a proper name, a milestone from which we may proclaim: this was the first atheist, the one who denied the existence of God, the philosopher who thought it and wrote it clearly, precisely, without embellishment and without a wealth of innuendo, of prudence, and of endless contortions. A radical atheist, outspoken, widely known! Even proud. A man whose credo — if I may be allowed the term — does not have to be inferred, is not a matter of speculation, does not proceed from the convoluted hypotheses of readers in search of documentary proof.

The precursor we seek might well have been Cristovão Ferreira, a Portuguese and former Jesuit who renounced his faith under Japanese torture in 1614. (Ferreira's faith must have been feeble indeed, to judge by the relevance of arguments that must have occurred to him well before he was forced to recant.) In 1636, the year Descartes was writing his *Discourse on Method*, Ferreira wrote a small, explosive, radical book entitled *The Deception Revealed*.

In just thirty pages, he asserted that God did not create the world and that moreover the world had never been created. Neither hell, paradise, nor predestination existed; stillborn children were innocent of original sin (which in any case did not exist); Christianity was an invention. The Ten Commandments were impracticable lunacy; the pope was immoral and dangerous; payment for masses and indulgences, excommunication, dietary laws, Mary's virginity, the Three Kings, were all so much twaddle. The Resurrection was a tale bereft of reason, ludicrous, scandalous, a hoax; the sacraments and confessions were nonsense; the Eucharist a metaphor; the Last Judgment an unbelievable delusion.

Could there be a more violent assault, a more concentrated barrage? And the Jesuit had not finished. Religion? An invention by men to ensure power over their brethren. Reason? The instrument permitting men to fight against such rubbish. Cristovão Ferreira dismantled all these crude inventions. Was he an atheist then? No, for at no point did he say, write, assert, or think that God did not exist. And then, as if to confirm that he was a spiritualist but nonetheless a believer, he abandoned the Christian religion — but converted to Zen Buddhism . . . So he will not be our first atheist. But we are no longer far short of our goal.

The miracle occurred shortly after Ferreira, in the person of another priest, Jean Meslier—at last an identifiable saint, hero, and martyr of the atheist cause! The parish priest of Etrépigny in the Ardennes, the soul of discretion (apart from a clash with the village seigneur) through the whole span of his ministry, the Abbé Meslier (1664–1729) has left us a voluminous testament. It is a scathing attack on the church, religion, Jesus, God, but also on the aristocracy, the monarchy, and the ancien régime. He violently denounces social injustice, idealist thinking, and the dolorist brand of Christianity that promulgates the value of suffering. At the same time he professes an anarchistic communalism, an authentic and brand-new materialist philosophy, and a surprisingly modern hedonistic atheism.

For the first time (but how long will it take us to acknowledge this?) in the history of ideas, a philosopher had dedicated a whole book to the question of atheism. He professed it, demonstrated it, arguing and quoting, sharing his reading and his reflections, and seeking confirmation from his own observations of the everyday world. His title sets it out clearly: *Memoir of the Thoughts and Feelings of Jean Meslier*, and so does his subtitle: *Clear and Evident Demonstrations of the Vanity and Falsity of All the Religions of the World*. The book appeared in 1729, after his death. Meslier had spent the greater part of his life working on it. The history of true atheism had begun.

2

Planned obscurity. The dominant historiography hides atheism from our sight. The Abbé Meslier is largely forgotten. Occasionally he is alluded to as a curiosity, a scholastic incongruity, a miscreant priest! Whenever he is honored with a passing mention, we look in vain for references to other authors worthy of being cited. The materialist philosophers come to mind. One was Julien de La Mettrie, who asserted in his *Natural History of the Soul* (1745) that psychic phenomena were due to organic changes in the brain. Or Nicolas Deschamps, a Jesuit also known as Dom Deschamps, whose work *Les Sociétés Secrètes* was published after his death, or the Baron d'Holbach, born Paul Heinrich Dietrich, who caustically derided religion in his book *The System of Nature*. Then there was Claude-Adrien Helvétius, who placed hedonistic emphasis on physical sensation and whose book *On the Mind* attacked all forms of morality based on religion. There was Sylvain Maréchal and his *Atheist Dictionary*. The ideologues of the French Revolution, such as Cabanis, Volney, and Destutt de Tracy, are also habitually ignored. By contrast, the bibliography of German idealism overflows with titles, works, and research.

Thus the work of Baron d'Holbach cannot be found in the university: no scholarly or scientific edition by any philosophical publisher worthy of the name; no works, theses, or ongoing research; no paperback edition, of course (whereas editions of Rousseau, Voltaire, Kant, or Montesquieu abound); no classes or seminars devoted to analytic examination and propagation of his thinking; not one biography ... Painful!

The university harps on the same old themes, invariably returning to the so-called century of Enlightenment: Rousseau's social contract, Voltaire's tolerance, Kant's critiques, or the separation of powers dear to the thinker of Brède — so many musical saws, so many pious philosophical icons. And nothing on d'Holbach's atheism, on his caustic readings of biblical texts; nothing on his critique of Christian theocracy, of the collusion of state and church, on the need for separation of the two; nothing on the equal and separate status of the ethical and the religious; nothing on the dismantling of Catholic fables; nothing on comparative study of religions. There is likewise nothing on the critiques of his work by Rousseau, Diderot, Voltaire, and the supposedly enlightened deist clique; nothing on his concept of a post-Christian morality; nothing on the uses of practical knowledge in combating belief; nothing on the innate intolerance of Christian monotheism; nothing on the necessary submission of the political to the ethical; nothing on his call to use part of the church's wealth for the benefit of the poor; nothing on feminism and his assault on Catholic misogyny—all of them Holbachian theses of surprising contemporary relevance.

Silence on Meslier the wielder of *curses* (*Testament*, 1729), silence on d'Holbach the *demystifier* (his *Contagion Sacrée* dates from 1768). Silence too on Feuerbach the *deconstructionist* — (*The Essence of Christianity*, 1841) — that third great moment of Western atheism, a substantial pillar of an atheology deserving of the name. For Ludwig Andreas Feuerbach proposes an explanation of what God is. He does not deny his existence, he simply dissects the chimera. No assertion that *God does not exist*, but a question: *Who is this God in whom the majority of men believe?* His answer: a fabrication, a creation by men, a fiction that obeys particular laws—in this case projection and hypostasis. Men create God in their own inverted image.

Mortal, finite, limited, suffering from all these constraints, haunted by the desire for completeness, human beings invent a power endowed with precisely the opposite characteristics. With their faults turned inside out, like the fingers of a pair of gloves, they manufacture characteristics at whose feet they kneel and finally prostrate themselves. I am mortal, but God is immortal. I am finite, but God is infinite. I am limited, but God knows no limits. I do not know everything, but God is omniscient. I cannot do everything, but God is omnipotent. I am not blessed with the gift of ubiquity, but God is omnipresent. I was created, but

God is uncreated. I am weak, but God is the Almighty. I dwell on earth, but God is in heaven. I am imperfect, but God is perfect. I am nothing, but God is everything. And so on.

Religion thus becomes the exploitation par excellence of man's vulnerability to deception. It asserts man's separation from himself and proposes the creation of an imaginary world falsely invested with truth. Theology, says Feuerbach, is a "psychic pathology," against which he opposes his own brand of anthropology. Not without humor, he invites us to engage in "pneumatic water therapy" — using the cold water of natural reason against religious, and particularly Christian, hot water and steam.

Despite his immense philosophical undertaking, Feuerbach remains a forgotten figure in a history written by the dominant philosophy. His name does come up. It resurfaced notably in the 1960s, the glory days of philosopher-teacher Louis Althusser, the "Crocodile" of France's Ecole Normale Supérieure. Althusser credits Feuerbach with influencing the ideas of young Marx (as opposed to mature Marx). Feuerbach's influence is evident in Karl Marx's early works, *Economic and Philosophical Manuscripts of 1844* and *The German Ideology* (1845). Althusser saw a profound difference between Marx's early views and his later opinions, which he characterized as an "epistemological break." He used Feuerbach as a tool to help sell his theory, and Feuerbach's own genius disappeared beneath the great Althusser's utilitarian concerns. Sometimes total obscurity is preferable to a lasting misunderstanding or false interpretation.

3

Philosophical earthquake. And then came Nietzsche ... First, the priest Meslier with his imprecations. Next, demythologization by the chemist (d'Holbach was a distinguished geologist and scientist). Eventually, deconstruction by the businessman. (Feuerbach was not a professional philosopher: the university blocked him from academic advancement after he published *Thoughts on Death and Immortality* [1830], an attack on the concept of personal immortality. But thanks to his marriage, he ended up the left-wing owner of a porcelain factory, beloved by his workers.) And now enter Nietzsche! At last the dominant thinking—idealist, spiritualist, Judeo-Christian, dualist—had good reason to be worried. Nietzsche's Dionysian monism, his logic of forces, his genealogy of morals, and his atheist ethic made it possible to envisage an exit from Christianity. For the first time, radical and well-thought-out post-Christian thinking appeared on the Western landscape.

Nietzsche was being facetious (or was he?) when he wrote in *Ecce Homo* that he was splitting history in two in the manner of Christ, with one half before and one half after him. The philosopher of Sils-Maria (the Swiss village where he spent many summers) had no Paul or Constantine to call on, no hysterical traveling salesman and no emperor to expand his personal epiphany into conversion of the entire world. Historically speaking, it is just as well that he didn't. The explosive nature of his thought represents too great a danger for the earthbound clods who play the leading roles in real-life history.

But on philosophical terrain, the father of Zarathustra was right. After *Beyond Good and Evil* and *The Antichrist*, it was no longer the same ideological world. Nietzsche had breached the Judeo-Christian edifice. Although he did not achieve the whole atheological task, he did make it possible. Hence the advantage of being Nietzschean. Definition? It is absurd to think that "being Nietzschean" means "being the same as Nietzsche." It does not entail subscribing to his major themes: resentment, eternal return, the superman, will to power, physiology of art, or any other aspect of his philosophical system. No need. What good would it do? To take oneself for Nietzsche, to don his mantle, adopt his ideas wholesale, and assume his thinking ... that is not Nietzschean, and only small minds could think it was.

Being Nietzschean requires one to think apart from him, starting from the spot where the "work in progress" that is philosophy was transformed by his passage. He called for unfaithful disciples who, by their betrayal, would prove their loyalty. He wanted people to obey him by following themselves and no one else, not even him. Particularly not him. In *Thus Spake Zarathustra*, the parable of "The Three Metamorphoses" tells how the spirit becomes first a camel, then a lion, and finally a child. This and other of his works teach a dialectic and theory of aesthetics that we can put to practical use. We must honor Nietzsche but go past him. Certainly we remember his work, but above all we lean on it the way one leans one's weight on a huge lever in order to move philosophical mountains.

Nietzsche launched a new building project that represents an advance for atheism. Meslier denied all divinity, Holbach dismantled Christianity, Feuerbach deconstructed God. Then Nietzsche introduced transvaluation: atheism is not an end in itself. Do away with God, yes, but then what? Another morality, a new ethic, values never before thought of because unthinkable, this innovation is what makes it possible to arrive at atheism and to surpass it. A formidable task, and one still to be brought to fruition.

The Antichrist narrates European nihilism—which is still with us—and proposes a pharmacopoeia for that metaphysical and ontological disease of our civilization. Nietzsche's solutions are known to us. They register more than a century of life and of misunderstandings. Being Nietzschean means proposing alternative hypotheses, fresh, new, post-Nietzschean, but assimilating his struggle on the mountain peaks. The various forms of contemporary nihilism call more than ever for a transvaluation that finally leaves behind it the religious and secular hypotheses born of the monotheisms. Zarathustra must return to the conflict: atheism alone makes an exit from nihilism possible.

4

Teaching the case for atheism. While September 11, 2001, as seen by the United States and therefore by the West, calls upon everyone to choose sides in the religious war that supposedly pits Judeo-Christianity against Islam, we might prefer to avoid choosing either side and opt instead for a Nietzschean position. That position would be neither Judeo-Christian nor Muslim, for the very good reason that these belligerents are continuing the religious war that began with the Torah bidding the Jews to do battle with their enemies. The book of Numbers, chapter 21, verse 14, refers to the "book of the wars of the Lord." The justification for bloody battle against one's enemies is an important part of the Torah. And the Koran is infused with recurrent variations on the same theme: slaughter of the enemy. In other words, nearly twenty-five centuries of calls *by both sides* to acts of crime! Nietzsche's lesson: we can choose not to choose. And a decision not to side with Israel and the United States does not automatically mean that one is a fellow traveler of the Taliban.

Talmud and Torah, Bible and New Testament, Koran and the Hadith offer insufficient grounds for the philosopher to choose between Jewish, Christian, or Muslim misogyny. Or to opt against pork and alcohol but in favor of the veil or the burka, to attend the synagogue, the temple, the church, or the mosque, all places where intelligence is ailing and where, for centuries, the faithful have practiced obedience to dogma and submission to the Law—and therefore obedience and submission to those who claim to be the elect, the envoys and the word of God.

At a time when the West is debating the teaching of religion in schools on the pretext of manufacturing social solidarity, of reuniting a community slipping out of its grasp (precisely, let us remember, because of a liberalism that daily generates negativity), of inspiring a new form of social contract, of rediscovering common sources (which all happen to be monotheistic), it seems to me that we might prefer the teaching of atheism. The *Genealogy of Morals* (1887) rather than the epistles to the Corinthians.

Today we are witnessing efforts to smuggle the Bible and other monotheistic bric-a-brac back through the window into the house after centuries of philosophical struggle to eject them through the front door. The struggle was led by the Enlightenment and the French Revolution, socialism and the Paris Commune, the left and the Popular Front, the libertarian spirit and May 1968, but also by Freud and Marx, the Frankfurt School, and the French left's mistrust of the Nietzscheans. This itch to restore the trappings of religiosity arises strictly and etymologically from willingness to accept reactionary thinking. Not in the manner of Joseph Le Maistre, Louis de Bonald, or Blanc de Saint-Bonnet but in the Gramscian manner of a return to the diluted, deceptive, travestied, and hypocritically reactivated ideals of Judeo-Christianity.

These days, it is true that no one openly vaunts the merits of theocracy or advocates doing away with rule by the people (the ideals of 1789). No one has written a book entitled *On the Pope*, extolling the supreme pontiff's political power. But we do denounce the individual, deny him rights, and heap him with duties by the shovelful. We celebrate collectivity over the singular, plead for transcendence, exempt the state and its parasites from explaining their actions on the grounds of their ontological extraterritoriality. We ignore the people and brand as populists and demagogues those who care about them. We despise the intellectuals and philosophers who go against the tide. The list could go on forever.

Never more than today has there been such evidence of vitality in what the eighteenth century called "antiphilosophy": the return of religious thinking, proof that God is not dead but that he was merely and briefly dozing, and that his awakening foretells great disenchantment. The trend has escalated to such an extent that we are now obliged to take up old defensive positions. We used to think that progress had rendered those positions out of date. But no. Atheism is forced to step into the breach once more. Religious instruction has put the fox back among the chickens. If professors cannot teach religion openly, they do it on the sly, claiming that the stories of the Old Testament, New Testament, Koran, and Hadith give students a greater appreciation and understanding of Marc Chagall, the *Divine Comedy*, the Sistine Chapel, and Ziryab's music.

But religions should be taught as a part of the existing curriculum — philosophy, history, literature, plastic arts, languages, etc. — the way the proto-sciences are taught: for example alchemy within chemistry courses, phytognomonics and phrenology within the natural sciences, totemism and magical thinking as a part of philosophy, Euclidean geometry within mathematics, mythology within history. Or in order to explain etymologically how myth, fable, fiction, and folly preceded reason, deduction, and debate. Religion proceeds from a primitive, genealogical, and outdated mode of rationality. Reactivating this prehistoric history means delaying and even missing altogether the history of today and tomorrow.

Presenting the case for atheism requires delving into the religious impulse. It stems from fear, misgiving, unease, inability to look death in the face, the feeling that something is lacking, and distress at the realization that human life is finite: the primary components of existential angst. Religion is a fabric woven with

fictions and metaphysical placebos. It calls for a systematic unraveling—just as in philosophy one investigates the occult and
the borderline of insanity during the search for the essential nature of reason.

5

Plate tectonics. We are still in a theological or religious stage
of civilization. But there are signs of movement, comparable to
the types of motion in plate tectonics: convergence, divergence,
sliding, collision, subduction, overriding, fracture. The *pre-Christian era* is clearly demarcated: from pre-Socratic mythology to
Roman Empire Stoicism; i.e., from Parmenides to Epictetus.
Next came a turbulent transition period, as early-stage Christianity overlapped late-stage paganism. The *Christian era* is easily
defined: it started with the church fathers, was spread in the second century by millenarian prophets (proclaiming that God is
about to destroy the world and only true believers will be saved),
and continued to the eighteenth century with the secular deism
of the Enlightenment. The beheading of Louis XVI in January
1793 marked the end of theocracy in France. Christianity, of
course, persisted.

We are now living in a new transitional phase, heading toward a third era, the *post-Christian era*. In some ways, our current
period is curiously similar to the transitional stage between the
pagan and Christian eras. Thus, the end of the pre-Christian and
the beginning of the post-Christian both exhibit the same
nihilism, the same anxieties, the same dynamic interplay between progressive and reactionary trends. Today we have conser-
vatism, reaction, yearning for the past, and rigid religion vying
with liberalism, progressivism, social reform, and movements

dedicated to building a better future. Religion is anchored in tradition and cashes in on nostalgia. Philosophy looks to the future.

The forces in play are clearly identifiable. It is not Western, progressive, enlightened, democratic Judeo-Christianity pitted against Eastern, backward-looking, obscurantist Islam. Rather, it is yesterday's monotheisms pitted against the atheism of tomorrow. Not Bush versus bin Laden. Instead, it is Moses, Jesus, Muhammad, and their religions of the book versus Baron d'Holbach, Ludwig Feuerbach, Friedrich Nietzsche, and their philosophical formulae of radical deconstruction of myths and fables.

Historically speaking, the post-Christian era will deploy its forces the same way the Christian era did: the monotheist empire can be toppled. The religion of an only God cannot become the fixed horizon of philosophy and of history itself—as communism once was for some people or as free-market liberalism is for others today. A Christian era once replaced a pagan era, and it will inevitably be replaced by a post-Christian phase. The turbulent period we live in suggests that change is at hand and the time has come for a new order. Hence the importance of an atheological project.

III

Toward an Atheology

1

Spectrum of nihilism. The age we live in seems atheistic, but only to Christians or believers. In fact, it is nihilistic. The true believers of yesterday and the day before have every interest in characterizing the worst and most negative aspects of contemporary life as products of atheism. The old idea of the immoral, amoral atheist, with neither faith nor ethical rules, dies hard. The phrase "if God does not exist, then everything is permitted" — a refrain picked up from Dostoyevsky's *The Brothers Karamazov* — continues to resonate, and people in fact associate death, hatred, and poverty with individuals who supposedly seek justification for their misdeeds in the nonexistence of God. This misguided notion needs to be thoroughly demolished. For the opposite seems to me to be true: "because God exists, everything is permitted." Let me explain. Thirty centuries, from the earliest texts of the Old Testament to the present day, teach us that the assertion of one God, violent, jealous, quarrelsome, intolerant, and bellicose, has generated more hate, bloodshed, deaths, and brutality than it has peace . . . There is the Jewish fantasy of a chosen people, which vindicates colonialism, expropriation, hatred, animosity between peoples, and finally an authoritarian and armed theocracy . . . There is the Christian image of the Temple moneylenders, or of a Pauline Jesus claiming to have come bearing a sword. This justifies the Crusades, the Inquisition, the French Religious Wars, the Saint Bartholomew's Day massacre of Paris's Protestants, the stake, the *Index*, but also worldwide colonialism, North American ethnocides, support for twentieth-century fascist movements, and the centuries-long temporal hold of the Vatican over the smallest details of daily life . . . And there is the clear exhortation on almost every page of the Koran to destroy unbelievers — but also the Jews and Christians of the book — their religion, their culture, their civilization, all in the name of a merciful God! So many pathways to entrench the idea that precisely because of God's existence everything is permitted — in him, through him, and in his name, without the slightest objection by believers, clergy, the masses, or the ruling spheres.

If the existence of God, independently of its Jewish, Christian, or Muslim form, had given us at least a little forewarning against hatred, lies, rape, pillage, immorality, embezzlement, perjury, violence, contempt, swindling, false witness, depravity, pedophilia, infanticide, drunkenness, and perversion, we might have seen not atheists (since they are intrinsically creatures of vice) but rabbis, priests, imams, and with them their faithful, all their faithful (which amounts to a great many) doing good, excelling in virtue, setting an example, and proving to the godless and perverse that morality is on their side. Let their flocks scrupulously respect the Commandments and obey the dictates of the relevant suras, and thus neither lie nor pillage, neither rob nor rape, neither bear false witness nor murder — and still less plot terrorist attacks in Manhattan, launch punitive raids into the Gaza Strip, or cover up the deeds of their pedophile priests. Then we would see the faithful converting their neighbors right, left, and center through the example of their shining conduct. But instead . . .

So let us have an end to this linkage of the world's woes to atheism! God's existence, it seems to me, has historically generated in his name more battles, massacres, conflicts, and wars than peace, serenity, brotherly love, forgiveness of sins, and tolerance. To my knowledge, no popes, princes, kings, caliphs, or emirs have excelled in the practice of virtue, so outstandingly did Moses, Paul, and Muhammad excel in murder, torture, and orgies of plunder — I call the biographies to witness. So many variations on the theme of loving one's neighbor.

The history of the human race unquestionably teaches the rewards of vice and the disappointments of virtue ... There is no transcendent justice any more than there is an immanent justice. Whether God is or is not, he has never made anyone pay for insulting, neglecting, despising, forgetting, or crossing him! Theists indulge in every kind of metaphysical contortion to justify evil in the world, while simultaneously affirming the existence of a God whom nothing escapes! Deists seem less blind, atheists more lucid.

2

A Judeo-Christian epistemology. So the times we live in are no longer atheist. Nor do they yet seem post-Christian, or barely. On the other hand, they are still Christian, much more so than first appears. Nihilism stems from the turbulence of this transit zone between still very present Judeo-Christianity and timidly blooming post-Christianity. The background is an atmosphere where the presence or absence of gods, their proliferation, their fantastic multiplicity, and their extravagances intersect. Heaven is not empty but on the contrary full of divinities manufactured from one day to the next. And the nihilism coexists with a flagging Judeo-Christianity and a post-Christian era still relegated to the sidelines.

While waiting for an outspokenly atheistic era, we must

plan for and be content with a Judeo-Christian epistemology pregnant with significance. Precisely because the institutions and the contract killers who have embodied and transmitted it for centuries no longer possess a readily identifiable style and visibility. The waning of religious practice, the apparent autonomy of ethics in relation to religion, the perceived public indifference at the prospect of a papal visit, churches empty on Sundays—but not for weddings and still less for funerals—the separation of church and state . . . all these give the impression of a period indifferent to religion.

But let's remain on our guard . . . Never before, perhaps, has this apparent eclipse so effectively hidden the strong, powerful, and decisive presence of Judeo-Christianity. The disaffection of the faithful does not mean a retreat from belief. To see a correlation between the two is to misinterpret the situation. We might even argue that the end of the official church monopoly over religious issues has liberated the irrational, generating a greater profusion than ever of the sacred, of religiosity, and of widespread acquiescence in religious folly.

The retreat of Judeo-Christian forces has not undermined their strength or their control over territories conquered, held, and administered by them for nearly two thousand years—testimony to their long-standing ideological, mental, conceptual, and spiritual control. Even after their physical departure the conquerors are still there, because they have subdued the bodies, souls, minds, and flesh of the majority. Their strategic withdrawal does not mean the end of their effective rule. Judeo-Christianity has left an epistemology, a platform on which all mental and symbolic exchanges still take place. Even without the priest, without the religious and their incense-bearers, their former subjects remain submissive, manufactured, formatted by two millennia of history and ideological domination. Hence the permanence and the current relevance of the struggle against this renascent force, all the more dangerous because it wrongly appears to be obsolete.

Of course, not many people still believe in transubstantiation, in Mary's virginity, the Immaculate Conception, papal infallibility, and other dogma of the Catholic, Apostolic, and Roman Church. The real, not symbolic, presence of Christ's body in the Host or the wine? The existence of hell, paradise, and purgatory, with their associated geography and their own logic? The existence of a limbo in which the souls of infants dead before baptism stagnate? No one still subscribes to such twaddle, even (and especially) those many Catholics who fervently attend Sunday Mass.

Where then does the Catholic substratum survive? And where the Judeo-Christian epistemology? Simply in the notion that matter, the real, and the world are not all there is. That *something* remains outside all the explanatory apparatus: a force, a power, an energy, a determinism, a will, a desire. And after death? Well, certainly not nothing. *Something* . . . And how can it be explained? By a series of causes, of rational and deducible linkages? Not altogether: *something* escapes the logical sequence. And the world — is it absurd, irrational, illogical, monstrous, senseless? Assuredly not . . . *Something* must exist to justify, legitimize, make sense. Otherwise . . .

This belief in *something* gives rise to a vigorous superstition suggesting that if all else fails the believer will still subscribe to the dominant religion — of his king and of his nanny, as Descartes put it — of the country where he sees the light of day. Montaigne maintains that one is a Christian the way one is Breton or a native of Picardy! And many individuals who consider themselves atheists profess — without noticing it — an ethic, a way of thinking, a vision of the world saturated in Judeo-Christianity. Between a sincere priest's homily on the excellence of Jesus and the praise of Christ offered by the anarchist Peter

Kropotkin in *Ethics*, we look in vain for a gulf, or even a small ditch.

Atheism implies the banishing of transcendence. With no exceptions. It also demands the transcending of Christian gains. Or at least it demands the right to take stock of them, to examine virtues presented as such and vices equally summarily asserted. A secular and philosophical reevaluation, from the ground up, of the Bible's values and the question of their preservation and their use, is not enough to produce a post-Christian ethic.

In *Religion within the Limits of Reason Alone* (1793), Kant proposes a secular ethic. Reading this book, of major historical importance in the construction of a Western secular morality, we again encounter the philosophical formulations of a seemingly inexhaustible Judeo-Christian spring. The book's revolutionary implications are evident in the form, style, vocabulary. But at what point do the Christian ethic and Kant's differ? Nowhere ...The Kantian mountain gives birth to a Christian mouse.

People laugh at the pope's words on the need to ban contraceptives. But a lot of people still get married in church—to please their families and in-laws, according to some. They smile when reading the *Catechism*—that is, if they even have the curiosity to consult it. But the number of registered civil funerals is tiny. They mock priests and their beliefs. But they seek them out for blessings, those updated indulgences that reconcile the pious hypocrisies of both sides: the consumers come to a compromise with their churchgoing peers, and by the same token, the providers find customers.

3

Vestiges of empire. Michel Foucault characterized epistemology as a device invisible but effective in discourse, in the envisioning of things and the world, in representations of the real. A device that locks in, crystallizes, and hardens an era in frozen postures. From the hysteria of Paul of Tarsus on the road to Damascus to the globally televised utterances of John Paul II on Saint Peter's Square, Judeo-Christian epistemology identifies a conceptual and mental empire pervading every component of civilization and culture. Two examples among a multitude of possibilities: the body, and law.

The Western body (including that of atheists, Muslims, deists, and agnostics raised in the geographic and ideological Judeo-Christian zone) is Christian. Two thousand years of Christian discourse — anatomy, medicine, physiology, of course, but also philosophy, theology, and aesthetics — have fashioned the body we inhabit. And along with that discourse we have inherited Platonic-Christian models that mediate our perception of the body, the symbolic value of the body's organs, and their hierarchically ordered functions. We accept the nobility of heart and mind, the triviality of viscera and sex (the neurosurgeon versus the proctologist). We accept the spiritualization and dematerialization of the soul, the interaction of sin-prone matter and of luminous mind, the ontological connotation of these two artificially opposed entities, the disturbing forces of a morally reprehensible libidinal humanity . . . All have contributed to Christianity's sculpting of the flesh.

Our image of ourselves, the scrutiny of the doctor or the radiologist, the whole philosophy of sickness and health — none of this could exist in the absence of the above-mentioned discourse. Nor could our conception of suffering, the role we allot to pain and therefore our relationship with pharmacology, substances, and drugs. Nor could the special language of practitioner to patient, the relationship of self to self, reconciliation of one's image of oneself with an ideal of the physiological, anatomical, and psychological self. So that surgery and pharmacology, homeopathic medicine and palliative treatments, gynecology and thanatology, emergency medicine and oncology, psychiatry and clinical work all obey Judeo-Christian law without any particularly clear understanding of the symptoms of this ontological contamination.

The current hypersensitivity on the subject of bioethics proceeds from this invisible influence. Secular political decisions on this major issue more or less correspond to the positions formulated by the church. This should be no surprise, for the ethos of bioethics remains fundamentally Judeo-Christian. Apart from legislation on abortion and artificial contraception, apart from these two forward steps toward a post-Christian body — what I have elsewhere called a *Faustian body* — Western medicine sticks very closely to the church's injunctions.

The *Health Professionals' Charter* elaborated by the Vatican condemns sex-change operations, experiments on the embryo, in vitro fertilization and transfer, surrogate motherhood, medical assistance with reproduction, but also therapeutic cloning, analgesic cocktails that suspend consciousness as life comes to an end, therapeutic use of cannabis, and euthanasia. On the other hand, the charter praises palliative care and insists on *the salutary role of pain*. These are all positions unanimously echoed by ethical committees calling themselves secular and believing themselves independent of religious authority.

Naturally, when practitioners in the West are confronted with a sick body, they are generally unaware that they think, act, and diagnose in the way they have been trained, that is, in the Judeo-Christian tradition. The conscience is not involved but rather a series of deeper, more ancient determinisms referring back to the hours that have gone into developing a temperament, a character, and a conscience. The therapist's and the patient's subconscious emerge from one and the same metaphysical bath. Atheism demands a study of these formattings, no longer visible but meaningful in the details of daily bodily living: a detailed analysis of the sexed, sexual body and related interactions would take up a whole book.

4

Garden-grown torture. Second example: the law. Our courthouses forbid the open display of religious symbols. A judicial decision cannot be handed down beneath a crucifix displayed on its walls, much less beneath a verse from the Torah or a sura from the Koran. The civil and penal codes supposedly assert the law independently of religion and the church. Yet there is nothing in French jurisprudence that fundamentally contradicts the prescriptions of the Catholic, Apostolic, and Roman Church. The absence of a cross in the courtroom does not guarantee a judiciary that is independent with respect to the dominant religion.

For the very foundations of judicial logic proceed from chapter 3 of Genesis. Hence a Jewish (the Pentateuch) and a Christian (the Bible) ancestry for the French Civil Code. The apparatus, the technique, and the metaphysics of the law flow in a direct line from what is taught in the fable of the original Garden — the story of a man who is free, and therefore responsible for his acts, and therefore potentially guilty. Because he is endowed with freedom, the individual may choose and prefer one option over another in his spectrum of possible choices. Every action thus proceeds from a free choice, a free will, informed and manifest.

The premise that human beings have free will is the key to the cause-and-effect relationship between crime and punishment. For eating the forbidden fruit, disobedience — the error perpetrated in the Garden of Earthly Delights — flow from an act of the will, and therefore from an act that can be reproved and punished. Adam and Eve could have refrained from sinning, for they had been created free, but they chose vice over virtue. So they can be called to account for their action. They can even be punished. And on that score, God in the Garden of Eden did not hesitate. He sentenced them and their descendants to perpetual shame, to guilt, to toil, pain in childbirth, suffering, aging, woman's subjection to man, the near impossibility of any sexual intersubjectivity. From then on, based on this model and in virtue of this principle laid down in the first moments of scripture, a judge could play at being God on earth.

When a court functions without religious symbols, it nevertheless operates in accordance with this biblical metaphysics. The child-rapist is free: he has the choice of engaging in a normal sexual relationship with a consenting partner or of inflicting horrifying violence on a victim he destroys forever. In his soul and conscience, endowed with a free will permitting him to prefer one option over another, he chooses violence — when he could have decided otherwise! So that he can be required to account for himself in court, listened to with half an ear or not even heard, and sent to spend years in prison. There he will probably be raped in a gesture of welcome before rotting in a cell from which he will be released after failing to confront the disease he suffers from.

Who would ever countenance a hospital locking up a man or a woman diagnosed with a brain tumor — no more of a free choice than a pedophiliac fixation — in a cell, exposing him to the repressive violence of a handful of cellmates imbued with the savagery of confinement before abandoning him, after a quarter of his life span, to the ravages of cancer, without care or concern, without treatment? Who? Answer: all those who set the machinery of justice in motion and operate it like a device found outside the gates of the Garden of Eden, without ever wondering what it is, why it has been left there, how it works.

That same machine, present in Kafka's penal colony, daily produces the same results in Western courts and their adjacent prisons. This collusion between the principle of free will and the voluntary choice of evil over good—which legitimizes the notion of responsibility, and therefore guilt, and therefore punishment—requires the workings of magical thinking. There is no place here for what Freud's post-Christian project illuminates through psychoanalysis, or the work of other philosophers who highlight the power of subconscious, psychological, cultural, social, familial, and ethological causes.

Body and law, even (and especially) when they think, believe, and call themselves secular, proceed from Judeo-Christian epistemology. So do analyses of teaching, aesthetics, philosophy, politics—all of these areas are influenced by biblical religious doctrine. Yet another push is needed before we can call ourselves truly republican.

5

On Christian ignorance. Our failure to recognize the workings of this logic of penetration can be explained if we stress that much of it takes place in the subconscious register, concealed from informed and lucid consciousness. Christian ideology is transmitted insidiously, without the medium of language or overt assertions. Apart from the case of self-acknowledged theocracies—political regimes openly inspired by one of the three books—the Judeo-Christian roots of secular practices go unnoticed by most people, including the practitioners, actors, and individuals concerned.

The invisibility of this process is not simply the result of its subconscious mode of propagation. It is also attributable to ignorance of Judeo-Christian teaching. This includes believers and churchgoers, often undereducated, informed only by the crumbs of information they are fed by the clergy. Sunday Mass has never glittered as a place for reflection, analysis, culture, or the spread and exchange of knowledge; nor has the *Catechism*; and the same could be said of their counterparts in the other monotheist religions.

Thus, no learning occurs while standing at the Wailing Wall or while the Muslim is performing his five daily prayers. He prays, he recites the responses, he exercises his memory but not his intelligence. For Christian Frenchmen, Bossuet's sermons constitute an exception in a twenty-century sea of platitudes . . . And for every Averroës and Avicenna, how many hyper-mnemonic but intellectually challenged imams?

Knowledge of their religion's structure, understanding of its disputes and controversies, injunctions to reflect and criticize, the clash of contradictory information and polemical debate are all resoundingly absent. The community is marked rather by the triumph of parrotlike repetition and the recycling of fables, with the help of well-oiled machinery that repeats but never innovates, which solicits not the intelligence but the memory. Chanting psalms, reciting, and repeating are not thinking. Nor is praying. Far from it.

Believers listen to a text by Saint Paul for the umpteenth time but have never even heard the name of Gregory of Nazianze. They set up the Infant's crèche each year but know nothing of the founding quarrels of Arianism or the Council on iconophilia. They commune with an unleavened Host but are ignorant of the existence of the dogma of papal infallibility . . . Nor is this all. Believers attend Christmas Mass but are unaware that the church picked this date in order to coincide with the winter solstice, when pagans honored *Sol Invictus*, the Unconquered Sun. They attend church christenings, weddings, and funerals but have never heard of the existence of the apocryphal angels. They remove their hats before a crucifix but have never learned that death by stoning and not by crucifixion was the standard punishment for the crime with which Jesus was charged . . . and so many other cultural blind alleys resulting from the fetishization of rites and practices. The prospects for enlightened exercise of one's religion are dim.

It all began with that ancient lesson from Genesis: man is forbidden to seek awareness; he should be content to believe and obey. He must choose faith over knowledge, suppress all interest in science, and instead prize submission and obedience. None of this helps raise the level of debate. The etymology of "Muslim," which according to the dictionary means *submissive* toward God and Muhammad, the impossibility of thinking or acting outside the Torah, which has laws regulating every tiniest detail of daily life — all these things militate against reason and in favor of submission . . . It's almost as if religion needs innocence, lack of education, and ignorance in order to thrive!

There exist, of course, men of the cloth who are highly educated in religion, history, and science. But they are dedicated to proving the validity of religious dogma; thus, they only add to a church arsenal already brimming with specious arguments. Centuries of rhetoric, a millennium of theological sophistry, whole libraries of scholastic nitpicking have promoted the use of knowledge as a weapon designed less for honest argument than for apologia. This was an art that Tertullian exercised brilliantly on behalf of Christianity, an art that required manipulating history to support the ideological agenda of the polemicist. (After all, the term "Jesuit" is also virtually synonymous with casuistry . . .)

Point out to a Christian that ever since the conversion of Constantine the church has chosen the camp of the powerful and neglected the weak and the poor. He replies triumphantly, "What about liberation theology?" — forgetting at the same time that liberation theology was condemned by John Paul II, leader and guide of the church. Suggest the obvious fact that Pauline Christianity, the official model, decries the pleasures of the flesh and despises women. He might retort, "'Mystical ecstasy' is on a higher plane than carnal ecstasy." There have been many cases of men seemingly possessed by the Holy Ghost who fall to the ground, flailing about in an orgasm of religious fervor. (Women too; notably Saint Teresa of Ávila.) But the speaker does not realize that in most cases the carnally inclined mystic was discredited during his lifetime (although after his death he may be welcomed back into the bosom of the faithful via beatification, canonization, and other ceremonies dedicated to the redemption of yesterday's lost sheep). Mention the massacres of the New World Indians perpetrated in the name of the most Catholic religion, the Spanish colonizers' denial of the soul and humanity of the Indians. The believer will laugh and say, "You're forgetting Bartolomé de Las Casas." But does he realize that Las Casas, theoretical defender of the Indians though he may have been, consigned every book written by the ancient Guatemalans to the flames? And that Las Casas (who believed that African blacks, soon to be swallowed up in the transatlantic slave trade, were endowed like the Amerindians with human souls) did not reveal his belief until after his death . . . in his will?

The same logic drives the interpreters — ayatollahs and mullahs — of Koranic law. They strive to give meaning and coherence to the contradictory texts in their holy book, juggling suras, verses, and thousands of hadith or fine-tuning abrogatory and abrogated verses! Should we point out to them the instances of hatred of Jews and non-Muslims that stuff the pages of the Koran? They would point to the practice of *dhimma*, theoretically intended to assure non-Muslim people of the book of their right to exist and be protected. But they would be careful not to add that this protection exists only after payment of a staggering tax, the *gizya*. Which aligns the professed Muslim tolerance with the Mafia's "protection" of an individual forced to finance the organization that persecutes him ... Another variant on the revolutionary tax!

These oversights, this defective information, this reliance on obedience rather than intelligence empties religion of its authentic contents, leaving only a pallid echo of the original, more or less compatible with every kind of metaphysical and sociological flavoring. Like Marxists who consider themselves Marxists yet deny the class struggle and reject the dictatorship of the proletariat, many Jews, Christians, and Muslims construct for themselves a made-to-measure morality. This implies selective borrowings (tailored to fit their needs) from their holy books in order to establish rules of play and participation by the community—to the detriment of all the other tenets of their faith. Hence a disappearance of outward religious practices alongside a strengthening of the dominant epistemology. Which brings us to Christian atheism.

6

Christian atheism. For too long, and on every point, the atheist has seen himself as the reverse of the priestly coin. Fascinated by his enemy, the God-denier has all too frequently borrowed a great many of his endearing idiosyncrasies. But this "clerical" atheism offers us nothing of interest. Chapels of free thinking and rationalist unions are just as bent on conversion as the clergy, while Masonic lodges modeled on those of France's Third Republic barely merit attention. Henceforth, we must aim for what Gilles Deleuze calls a *quiet atheism*—less a static concern with negating or fighting God than a dynamic method designed for postconflict reconstruction. Negation of God is not an end in itself, but a means of working toward a post-Christian or frankly secular ethic.

To draw the outlines of post-Christian atheism, let us stop for a moment at this obstacle we still have to cross: *atheist Christianity* — or Christianity without God. Yet another curious creature! The phenomenon exists: it characterizes one who denies God but at the same time asserts the excellence of Christian values and the incomparable virtue of evangelical morality. Its operation implies the disassociation of morality and transcendence: good has no need of God, of heaven, or of any intelligible anchorage. It is sufficient unto itself and arises from an immanent necessity — proposing a set of rules, a code of conduct among men.

Theology ceases to be the foster parent of morality, and philosophy takes over. Where a Judeo-Christian reading implies a vertical logic — from the low of human beings to the high of values — the Christian atheist hypothesis proposes a horizontal layout: nothing outside what can be rationally deduced, no design on any terrain but that of the real, tangible world. God does not exist, virtues do not flow from a revelation: they do not descend from heaven but proceed from a utilitarian and pragmatic viewpoint. Men give themselves laws and have no need to call on an extraterrestrial power to provide them.

The immanent ordering of the world distinguishes the Christian atheist from the Christian believer. But not their values, which remain identical. All operate on common ground — Priest and philosopher, Vatican and Kant, the Gospels and the *Critique of Practical Reason*, Mother Teresa and Paul Ricoeur, Catholic love of one's neighbor and the transcendental humanism of Luc Ferry as set out in *Man Made God: The Meaning of Life*, the Christian ethic and the great virtues of André Comte-

Sponville. Their concerns are charity, temperance, compassion, mercy, and humility, but also love of one's neighbor and the forgiveness of offenses, the injunction to turn the other cheek, indifference to the goods of this world, the ethical asceticism that rejects power, honors, and wealth as so many false values leading away from true wisdom. Those are the *theoretically* professed options.

Most of the time, this Christian atheism dismisses the Pauline hatred of the body, its rejection of desires, pleasures, drives, and passions. More in step with their period on questions of sexual morality than Christians on God, these advocates of a return to the Gospels—under cover of a return to Kant, even to Spinoza—consider that the cure for the nihilism of our period does not require a post-Christian effort but a secular and immanent rereading of the message left by Christ. Jewish philosophers provide some of the models for this Judeo-Christianity without God: Vladimir Jankélévitch (see *Treatise on the Virtues*), Emmanuel Levinas (read his *The Humanism of the Other* and *Totality and Infinity*), Bernard-Henri Lévy (*The Testament of God*), or Alain Finkielkraut (*The Wisdom of Love*).

7

A postmodern atheism. If we could get past Christian atheism, we might arrive at a true *atheistic atheism* (no redundancy implied). The term encompasses more than negation of God and of a part of the values derived from him. It calls for a different *episteme*, a Greek word used in philosophy to indicate the set of ideas, the science, the body of knowledge that makes it possible to separate the true from the false. *Atheistic atheism* would place morality and politics on a new base, one that is not nihilist but post-Christian. Its aim is neither to reconstruct churches nor to destroy them, but to build elsewhere and in a different way, to build something else for those no longer willing to dwell intellectually in places that have already done long service.

Postmodern atheism divests itself of its theological and scientific trappings in order to construct a moral system. Neither God nor science, neither intelligible heaven nor the operation of mathematical propositions, neither Thomas Aquinas nor Auguste Comte nor Marx. But philosophy, reason, utility, pragmatism, individual and social hedonism—these constitute so many invitations to maneuver on the terrain of pure immanence, in the interests of men, by themselves and for themselves, and not by God and for God.

Historically, two Englishmen were among the first to go outside the religious and geometric mold: Jeremy Bentham and his disciple John Stuart Mill. Bentham's *Deontology* merits reading over and over again. Both men turned their intellects to projects meant to serve society in the here and now. If German idealism envisioned immense cathedrals, beautiful but unlivable, Bentham and Mill built modest structures, practical and beneficial to the common man.

Good and evil continue to matter not because they coincide with religious concepts of belief and nonbelief, but simply as factors in the struggle to ensure the greatest possible happiness of the greatest number. The hedonist contract—nothing could be more immanent—legitimizes all intersubjectivity, conditions all thought and action, dispenses utterly with God, religion, and priests. With it, there is no need to brandish the threat of hell or dangle the glittering bauble of paradise, no point in establishing an ontology of posthumous reward and punishment to elicit good, just, and honest action. It is an ethic without transcendent obligations or sanctions.

8

Atheist Manifesto **takes on three challenges.** The book sets out to accomplish three objectives: deconstruction of the three monotheisms, deconstruction of Christianity in particular, and deconstruction of theocracy. Part two undertakes the first task: to analyze the three monotheisms and demonstrate how they are alike. Despite their historical and geographical divergences, despite centuries of the mutual hatred that has inflamed their supporters, despite the apparent irreconcilability of Mosaic law, Jesus's teachings, and the Prophet's words, the fundamentals remain the same. To adopt a musical metaphor, these three movements (elaborated over more than a thousand years) have different backgrounds and are played at different tempos, but they are variations on one and the same theme. Variations of degree, not of kind.

But what exactly are these shared fundamentals? First, a sequence of waves of hatred set in violent motion throughout history by men claiming to be the repositories and interpreters of God's word—the priestly castes. Second, hatred of intelligence, which monotheists reject in favor of submission and obedience; hatred of life coupled with a passionate and unshakable obsession with death; hatred of the here and now, consistently undervalued in favor of a beyond, the only possible reservoir of sense, truth, certainty, and bliss; hatred of the corruptible body, disparaged in every aspect, while the soul—eternal, immortal, divine—is invested with all the higher qualities and all the virtues; and finally, hatred of women, condemnation of liberated sexuality and sex for pleasure. Religion sets up the Angel, a bodiless archetype, in preference to real women. Chastity is a virtue common to all three religions.

All three monotheisms have a negative attitude toward the

joy of life and even toward some of the basic human drives. Once that has been established, this book will focus on one religion in particular. Christianity grew on the fertile soil of collective hysteria: a psychological term for the fears and volatile emotional state of the masses. It rooted itself in fallacious principles; it put forward lies, fiction, and myths, and then conferred on them the stamp of authenticity. The repetition of a sum of errors by the greatest number eventually becomes a corpus of truths that is sacrosanct. Questioning those truths could be dangerous for freethinkers — from the Christian bonfires of the day before yesterday to the Muslim fatwas of today.

To illustrate how a mythology is constructed, part three of this text offers a *deconstruction of Christianity*. We can pinpoint the moment in history when Jesus was forged; construction of his image proceeded over the next one or two hundred years. First-century Palestine under Roman occupation was a theater of unrest. A suffering, oppressed people needed a savior who could perform miracles. Jesus — a conceptual and in no way historical character — embodied the millenarian, prophetic, and apocalyptic aspirations of the times. His life, death, and message were embellished and promoted by Paul of Tarsus, who believed he had a mandate from God — when, in actuality, he was driven by a host of psychological problems. Paul converted his self-loathing into hatred of the world. His impotence and resentment took the form of revenge: the revenge of a weakling. Paul became the driving force behind a messianic cult that spread throughout the Mediterranean basin. This was one man's experience of masochism extended to the dimension of a sect. Furthermore, his was just one among thousands of sects active in that turbulent epoch. All of this becomes evident if we think about it just a little. It will require us to set aside obedience and submission in matters of religion and to reactivate an ancient taboo: tasting the fruit of the Tree of Knowledge.

Deconstructing Christianity entails an analysis of how the myth was fabricated and how Paul's neurosis was a contributing factor. But that is only the beginning. Promulgation of the myth had worldwide repercussions. We shall reflect on the historical implications of the emperor Constantine's conversion to the sectarian religion, motivated by pure political opportunism. In consequence of that conversion, the beliefs and practices formerly limited to a handful of visionaries expanded to encompass an empire. From a persecuted minority, the Christians became a persecuting majority, thanks to the intervention of an emperor who had become one of their own.

The thirteenth apostle, as Constantine proclaimed himself in the course of one church council, installed a totalitarian regime that enacted harsh laws against non-Christians and set out to systematically eradicate the ancient culture. It was an era of book burnings and autos-da-fé, physical persecution, confiscation of goods, forced exiles, assassinations, demolition of pagan buildings, desecration of shrines and objects of worship, library burnings, and architectural recycling: turning ancient temples into Christian churches or else using their rubble to build roads, etc.

Following several centuries of such unchecked power, the spiritual became confused with the temporal . . . Hence, part four: a *deconstruction of theocracies*. These forms of government exert a practical and political claim to power supposedly emanating from God. He himself does not speak (for good reason), but his priests and clergy lend him a voice. In the name of God, but through the agency of God's self-styled servants, heaven ordains what must be done, thought, experienced, and practiced on earth in order to please him! And the same people who purport to be bearers of his word also assert their ability to interpret what he thinks of the actions carried out in his name.

Theocracy's cure lies in democracy: the power of the

people, the immanent sovereignty of the citizens against the supposed dominance of God — or rather, the dominance of those claiming to speak in his name . . . In the name of God, as centuries of history attest, the three monotheisms have caused unbelievable rivers of blood to flow! Wars, punitive operations, massacres, murders, colonialism, the elimination of entire cultures, genocides, crusades, inquisitions, and today's global terrorism.

Deconstructing the monotheisms, demythologizing Judeo-Christianity and Islam, deconstruction of theocracy: these are three initial tasks for atheology. The next step is to formulate a new ethic and produce the conditions for a true post-Christian morality in the West — a morality in which the body is not a punishment; the earth ceases to be a vale of tears; this life is no longer a tragedy; pleasure stops being a sin; women, a curse; intelligence, a sign of arrogance; physical pleasure, a passport to hell.

With that behind us, we might then point to the advantages of a guiding principle less obsessed with the death wish than with love of life. The Other would no longer be considered an enemy, a "difference" to be suppressed, reduced, and dominated. Meeting the Other would be an opportunity to build interpersonal relationships here and now, not under the gaze of God or gods, but under the eyes of the protagonists only, a meeting of their minds and their inherent natures. In that event, paradise might function less as a fiction having to do with Heaven and more as a rational ideal here below. We can dream, can't we?

PART TWO

MONOTHEISMS

I

The Tyranny of Afterlives

1

Monotheism's somber vision. Animals, as we know, are un-contaminated by God. Excused from religion, they know nothing of incense and the Host, genuflections and prayers. We do not see them in ecstasy over celestial bodies or priests, they build neither cathedrals nor temples, and they are never caught praying to fictions. Like Spinoza, we imagine that if they created a god for themselves they would create him in their own image: long ears for donkeys, a trunk for elephants, a sting for bees. Just as men — when they take it into their heads to give birth to one God — do so in their own violent, jealous, vengeful, misogynistic, aggressive, tyrannical, intolerant image. In short, they sculpt their own death instinct, their own dark side, and make of it a machine hurled at breakneck speed against themselves.

For only men invent afterlives, gods, or a single God. Only men prostrate themselves, humble themselves, abase themselves, weave fables, and believe unquestioningly in the tales they have so painstakingly concocted in order to avoid looking their fate in the face. Only men extract from this fiction a delirium that draws in its train a welter of dangerous nonsense and of new ways out. They alone work passionately to bring about what they nevertheless hope more than anything else to avoid: death.

Does life, with death as its inevitable ending, seem unlivable to them? Swift to respond, they arrange matters so that the enemy governs their lives. They set out to die little by little, systematically, day by day, so that when the hour strikes death will seem less difficult. The three monotheistic religions call on their faithful to renounce life in the here and now because they will one day be forced to accept its loss. Their glorification of a (fictional) beyond prevents full enjoyment of the (real) here below. And what motivates them? The death instinct and unceasing variations on that theme.

An extraordinary paradox! Religion is a response to the ontological void apparent to everyone who learns that he will one day die, that his sojourn on earth is finite, that each life constitutes a brief interlude between the nothingness that came before it and the nothingness that comes after it. Fables only accelerate the process. They establish death on earth for the sake of eternity in heaven. In so doing, they spoil the only gift we possess: the living matter of a potential existence killed in the egg just because its life is finite! Fleeing life in order not to have to die is not a good bargain. It pays death twice, when once is enough.

Religion proceeds from the death wish. That strange dark force in the depths of our being works toward the destruction of what is. Wherever life begins to move, expand, vibrate, a countercurrent sets in, tending to arrest the newborn movement and immobilize its ebb and flow. As soon as life fights its way out of the tunnel, death is there, ready to start the clock ticking — that is its function, its modus operandi — and to collapse all life's hopes and plans. Being born starts the process of dying. Living for death means counting off one by one the days of our life while waiting to die. Religion alone seems to halt the mechanism. But in fact it speeds it up.

Turned against ourselves, the fixation with death generates every kind of risky behavior, suicidal impulse, and self-destructive conduct. Directed against others, it triggers aggression, violence, crimes, murders. The religion of the one God espouses these impulses. It seeks to promote self-hatred to the detriment of the body, to discredit the intelligence, to despise the flesh, and to prize everything that stands in the way of a gratified subjectivity. Launched against others, it foments contempt, wickedness, the forms of intolerance that produce racism, xenophobia, colonialism, wars, social injustice. A glance at history is enough to confirm the misery and the rivers of blood shed in the name of the one God.

Fired by the same inborn death drive, the three monotheisms share a series of identical forms of aversion: hatred of reason and intelligence; hatred of freedom; hatred of all books in the name of one book alone; hatred of sexuality, women, and pleasure; hatred of the feminine; hatred of the body, of desires, of drives. Instead Judaism, Christianity, and Islam extol faith and belief, obedience and submission, taste for death and longing for the beyond, the asexual angel and chastity, virginity and monogamous love, wife and mother, soul and spirit. In other words, life crucified and nothingness exalted.

2

Down with intelligence! Monotheism loathes intelligence, that sublime gift defined as the art of connecting what at first and for most people seems unconnected. Intelligence reveals unexpected but undeniable causalities; it produces rational, convincing explanations based on reasoning; it rejects every manufactured fiction. With its help, we can spurn myths and fairy tales. We need no posthumous paradise, no salvation or redemption of the soul, no all-knowing, all-seeing God. Properly and rationally directed, intelligence wards off all magical thinking.

The advocates of Mosaic law, Christian tale-spinning, and their Koranic clones share the same fable on the origins of negativity in the world. In Genesis 3:6 — common to the Torah and to the Old Testament of the Christian Bible — and in the Koran (2:29) we find the same story of Adam and Eve in a paradise where a God forbids them to approach a tree while a demon urges disobedience. In this monotheistic version of the Greek Pandora fable, a woman (of course) commits the irreparable, and her act spreads evil all over the world.

This story, in normal circumstances just good enough to earn a place in the roster of fairy tales or cautionary fables, has had incalculable consequences for human civilizations! Loathing of women and the flesh, guilt and desire for atonement, the quest for an impossible amends and submission to necessity, fascination with death and passion for suffering — all so many occasions for activating the death instinct.

What do the files on this story tell us? We find a God who orders the primal couple not to eat the fruit of the tree of knowledge. Clearly we are in the presence of metaphor. It took the church fathers to sexualize the story, for the text is clear: eating this fruit removes the scales from our eyes and allows us to distinguish between good and evil, and thus to resemble God. One verse (Genesis 3:6) mentions *a tree to be desired to make one wise.* Defying God's prohibition meant preferring knowledge to obedience, seeking to know rather than submitting. Or in different terms: opting for philosophy against religion.

What does this ban on intelligence mean? You can do anything in this magnificent Garden, except become intelligent — the Tree of Knowledge — or immortal — the Tree of Life. What a fate God has in store for men: stupidity and mortality! A God who offers such a gift to his creatures must be perverse ... Let us then praise Eve who opted for intelligence at risk of death, whereas Adam did not realize right away what was at stake. The bliss of ignorance!

What do the poor wretches learn, once the lady tastes the sublime fruit? They see reality. Reality and nothing else. Nudity, their natural state. And with their freshly acquired knowledge, they discover their cultural allotment: the choice of fig leaves (rather than grape leaves) to cover their nakedness was symbolic of a future cultural heritage. Worse: they discover the hardship of daily life, the sorrow in every destiny, the battle between the sexes, the gulf forever separating man and woman, the inevitability of backbreaking toil, the pain of childbirth, and the sovereignty of death. Once liberated from their state of ignorance, they avoid the additional transgression that would have given them eternal life (the Tree of Life grew next to the Tree of Knowledge), for the one true God — decidedly gentle, good, loving, generous — spared them that fate by expelling Adam and Eve from paradise. And we have remained outside ever since.

Lesson number one: if we lose the illusion of faith, the consolation of God, and the fables of religion, if we prefer seeking knowledge and intelligence, then reality appears to us as it is, tragic. But which is better? A truth that removes all hope of immortality yet saves us from losing our life altogether by living it only half alive? Or a story that briefly consoles us but makes us waste the only thing we really possess: life here and now?

3

Litany of taboos. God was not content with that one prohibition on the forbidden fruit. Ever since, he has revealed himself to us only through taboos. The monotheist religions live exclusively by prescriptions and constraints: things to do and things not to do to, say and not to say, think and not to think, perform and not to perform. Forbidden and authorized, licit and illicit, agreed and not agreed: the religious texts abound in existential, dietary, behavioral, ritual, and other codifications.

For obedience can be measured only by proscriptions. The greater their number, the greater our chances of falling into error, the fewer our chances of attaining perfection, the deeper our guilt. And it's a good thing for God — or at least for the clergy who identify with him — to be able to manipulate this powerful psychological tool. Everyone must at all times know that he must always obey, must conform, must do as he should and as religion demands. Not to behave like Eve but, like Adam, to submit to the will of the only God.

Etymology teaches us that *islam* means *submission* . . . And what surer way of renouncing intelligence than by submitting to the taboos of men! For we hear the voice of God only with difficulty, infrequently or not at all! How can he make plain his dietary laws, his dress codes, and his ritual preferences other than through a clergy that imposes bans and decides in his name between the licit and the illicit? Obeying these laws and rules may be submission to God, but it is much more certainly submission to the one who speaks in his name: the priest.

In the Garden of Eden, that blessed time of communication between God and his creatures, God spoke to Adam and Eve . . . But contact is broken after the expulsion from paradise. Hence the widespread belief that God sends us signs of his presence. He is manifest in every minor detail of daily life, in the most trivial act. God is not only up in heaven: he is everywhere, watching us and warning us. That means the devil, too, is lurking in his shadow.

Since God is in the details, the details acquire vital importance. For example, Jews do not allow themselves to eat shellfish because God recoils from aquatic creatures lacking fins or scales and wearing their skeletons outside their bodies. Catholics likewise abstain from meat on Good Friday — a day presumably notorious for its excessive levels of hemoglobin, And Muslims forgo the pleasures of pork sausage. All three are occasions, among many others, for displaying faith, belief, piety, and devotion to God.

The permitted and the forbidden play a leading role in the Torah and Talmud, are somewhat less important in the Koran, but are especially prominent in the Muslim Hadith. Christianity — all praise (for once) to Saint Paul! — does not weigh itself down with the whole list of major taboos that Leviticus and Deuteronomy invoke in order to coerce, forbid, and constrain in every field: table and bedroom behavior, harvesting, textures and colors of the wardrobe, the hourly employment of time, etc.

The Gospels forbid neither wine nor swine nor any other food, any more than they insist on particular garments. Membership in the Christian community requires adhesion to the Christian message, not to the details of lunatic taboos. It would never occur to a Christian to deny access to the priesthood to a deformed, blind, lame, disfigured, misshapen, hunchbacked, sickly individual, as Yahweh demands of Moses when he is selecting a candidate for the profession (Leviticus 21:16). On the other hand, Paul remains a stickler for the licit/illicit rule in the sexual domain. On this point, the Acts of the Apostles testify to an intimate link between Old Testament and New.

Jews and Muslims demand that we think of God in every waking second. From dawn to dusk, sleeping to waking, no aspect of behavior, even in principle the most trivial, is exempt from interpretation: observing the ritual prayer hours, what to eat and not to eat, how to dress. No personal judgment or individual choice is involved, just obedience and submission, denial of all freedom of action, insistence on the rule of necessity. The licit/illicit logic locks the believer into a prison where abdication of will signifies an act of allegiance and a proof of pious behavior. It is an investment repaid a thousandfold—but later, in paradise.

4

Obsession with purity. The marriage of licit and illicit works in parallel with the coupling of pure and impure. What is pure? Or impure? Who is? Who is not? Which individual decides these questions? Who authorizes and validates the decision? "Pure" designates the unmixed. Its opposite is the alloy. On the side of the pure are the one, God, paradise, mind, spirit. On the other side of the barricade are the impure: the diverse, the multiple, the world, the real, matter, body, flesh. The three monotheisms share this vision of an ideal world, and hold the physical world in low esteem.

Clearly, a series of impurities identified by the Talmud can proceed from practical wisdom. There is no question that a dead body, a rotting cadaver, the leaking of bodily fluids, leprosy all signify impurity. Common sense associates decomposition, putrescence, and disease with risks and dangers to individuals and the community. Catching fever, contracting an illness, causing an epidemic or pandemic, spreading sexually transmittable diseases, all these justify concern with prevention and an effective public-health response. Not allowing evil to take us by surprise is the first duty of virtue.

Impurity contaminates: place, location, life inside the tent, contact with other people of course, but also close personal proximity, uncovered vessels in the household, all may be implicated in contamination. The infected person in turn contaminates everything he approaches or touches until purification and ablution put an end to this state of collective danger. The health professional rightly sees such measures as steps designed to avoid the propagation of impurity. But for other kinds of impurity, the prophylactic argument does not answer. What do we risk in approaching a menstruating woman? Or one who has just given birth? Both are impure. Just as we may understand fear of abnormal flows that might point to hemorrhage, gonorrhea, or syphilis, so we must question ourselves about this horror of menstrual blood or of the woman who has recently given birth. Unless we advance the theory that in both these cases the woman is not fertile, and that she may therefore freely dispose of her body and her sexuality without risking pregnancy—a condition ontologically unacceptable to the rabbis, proponents of the ascetic ideal and of demographic expansion.

Muslims share many concepts with Jews, and in particular this fixation on purity. In a general sense, the body is impure from the simple fact of being. Hence a sustained and permanent effort to keep it pure through a series of precise steps: circumcision, cleaning and trimming the beard, mustache, and hair, paring nails, forbidding the ingestion of food not ritually prepared, proscription of all contact with dogs, naturally an absolute prohibition on pork and alcohol, and radical avoidance of all bodily matter—urine, blood, sweat, saliva, sperm, feces.

Once again, of course, all this can be justified rationally as prophylaxis, hygiene, cleanliness—but with never a hint of why pork rather than camel meat must be avoided. Some suggest that the pig is an animal emblematic of certain Roman legions, an unpleasant localized memory. Others point to the omnivorous nature of the animal, a consumer of public refuse ... Hatred of the dog may hark back to risks of bites and rabies; the ban on alcohol to the fact that hot countries seem favorable to indolence, siestas, and the urge to reckless slaking of thirst, in which case water or tea in quantity are preferable to alcohol because of its known effects. All this can be rationally explained.

But why not be content with a secular rationale? Why transform these sound, legitimate prohibitions into grounds for strict rules and inflexible laws, and then make eternal salvation or damnation dependent on their observance? No one questions the need for clean latrines, particularly in periods or places where sewage facilities, running water, flush toilets, septic tanks, and disinfectant products do not exist.

In the Hadith, there are detailed instructions regarding anal cleansing: no fewer than three stones to be used, no recourse to garbage (!) or to bones (!), and no urination in the direction of Mecca. There are also rules on one's state of preparation before prayer: no previous emission of seminal fluid, of gas, urine, feces, menstrual blood of course, but also — and this leads to a break in the link with Islam — no sexual relations during one's partner's menstruation nor anal penetration (here again because it means sex divorced from procreation) . . . It is hard to see the rational, reasonable connection.

5

Respecting the body. All the Jewish and Muslim taboos — so similar to each other — are due to associating the body with impurity. The body is dirty, unclean, infected, composed of vile materials. There are all sorts of bodies: libidinous, malodorous, sodomite, filled with nasty fluids and secretions. Some are infected, sick, bleeding. There are cadavers, bodies of dogs and women, made of garbage, made of filth. Stinking bodies, sterile bodies, barren bodies, loathsome bodies.

One hadith preaches the need to purify the body through the practice of ablution (ritual washing). It states that the more often ablution is performed, the greater one's chance of reaching heaven with a glorious (in the Christian sense) body. On Resurrection Day, the body is reborn, radiating light from the points where it contacted the prayer mat. A physical body of dark, black flesh is contrasted with a spiritual body, white and incandescent. Who among simple folk could love an earthly, sinful body when a beautiful, perfect, celestial one is guaranteed to every believer who abides by the licit/illicit rules in accordance with the pure/impure principle?

The purification ritual also furnishes an opportunity to treat the body with respect, as if it were not our own flesh but an entity unto itself. Every organ has its place in a process of organized, meticulously ordained prayer. Nothing escapes Allah's eye. He is concerned with: suitability of the materials utilized (water, stones, sand, soil), numbering the viscera, systematizing the steps of the ritual, the order of passing from one part of the anatomy to another during ablutions, choreography of the repetition of gestures. Fingers, the right wrist, forearms, elbows, do it three times, etc. Don't forget the heel; if you do, that omission leads to hell.

We can dispense with the notion that these rites are based solely on the desire for cleanliness. Some of the rules do promote cleanliness. For example, take care not to soil your garment with urine. In the toilet, do not wipe with the hand you eat with. But the argument does not hold up when we examine the hadith that authorizes *masah 'alal khuffain* (wiping wet hands over the tops of one's leather slippers) as a valid substitute for washing the feet. Some imams also permit performing *masah* on cloth socks, provided the cloth is very thick and sturdy. Either way, the feet get purified *without* getting washed! Can God's reasons be purely hygienic?

Training the body in the practice of purification goes hand in hand with training in the proper practice of prayer — the five daily prayers, all announced by the muezzin from the heights of his minaret. Organizing our time and even our bodies to suit our own needs is out of the question. Getting up and going to bed both depend on the muezzin's call, as does one's progress through the day, for everything comes to a halt for prayer. The schedule is rigid: it signifies order (the oldest go first), organization, and communal harmony. Prostration follows a very strict code: seven bones must be in contact with the ground—forehead, both hands, both knees, the extremities of each foot. (We will not quibble with the imam, but a single foot has five toes, two feet have ten, and, with a little help from chiropody, we have overshot the theoretical seven bones by a wide margin . . .)

Certain postures are prohibited because they do not conform to the rules. Certain ways of inclining the body or of prostration are also taboo: they too must be performed according to the rules. It is out of the question for the body to move with joyful spontaneity, for it must demonstrate its submission and obedience. One cannot be a Muslim without a zealous display of one's pleasure in observing the details. For Allah himself resides in the details. (One final word: the angels like neither garlic nor shallots. We therefore refrain from strolling in the vicinity of the mosque with those cloves in the folds of our djellabas, and even more from entering the sacred precincts with a burnoose redolent of garlic!)

II

Bonfires of the Intelligence

1

Producing the holy books. Hatred of intelligence and knowledge, the requirement to obey rather than think, the role of the licit/illicit–pure/impure coupling in eliciting obedience and submission rather than thinking for ourselves — all this is codified in the books. The three monotheisms are seen as the religions of the book — but their three books seem far from mutually supportive. Paulines have little liking for the Torah, Muslims do not really treasure the Talmud or the Gospels, upholders of the Pentateuch see the New Testament or the Koran as so much fraud ... Naturally, they all teach brotherly love. Thus from the very start it seems difficult to appear beyond reproach to our brethren of the Abrahamic religions!

The creation of these so-called holy books proceeded in accordance with the most elementary historical laws. We should approach the whole corpus from a philological, historical, philosophical, symbolic, allegorical (and every other qualifier) standpoint hostile to the belief that these texts were inspired and dictated by God. None of them is a work of revelation. Who would have done the revealing? Their pages no more descend from heaven than those of Persian fables or Icelandic sagas.

The Torah is not as old as tradition claims; Moses is improbable. Yahweh dictated nothing — and in any case, Moses could not have written down what Yahweh said unless he wrote in hieroglyphics, since the Hebrew script did not exist in the time of Moses! None of the evangelists personally knew the famous Jesus. The testamental canon arose from later political decisions, particularly those reached when Eusebius of Caesarea, mandated by the emperor Constantine, assembled a corpus stitched together from twenty-seven versions of the New Testament in the first half of the fourth century. The apocryphal writings are more numerous than those that constitute the New Testament proper. Muhammad did not write the Koran. Indeed, that book did not exist as such until twenty-five years after his death. The second source for Muslim authority, the Hadith, saw the light of day in the ninth century, two centuries after the Prophet's death. Hence we must infer the very active presence of men in the shadows of these three Gods.

2

The book's bias against books. To establish the authority of the definitive version of the Koran, the political authorities — notably Marwan, governor of Medina — began by collecting and then burning and destroying all existing versions in order to avoid historical confrontation and chancing upon vestiges of human, too human, manufacture. (One version indeed escaped from this auto-da-fé of the seven earlier versions, and still holds sway in certain African countries.) Marwan's act was a precursor of the many book burnings kindled in the name of the one book. Each of these three books claims to be "the only book that matters." Each of the three main religions claims that it alone possesses the one true holy book, which contains the whole of what needs to be learned and known. Like encyclopedia compilers, they have gathered the essentials, rendering it unnecessary to look in other books (pagan, secular, heretical) for wisdom that is already found.

The Christians set the tone with Paul of Tarsus, who called for the burning of dangerous books (Acts 19:19). The demand did not fall on deaf ears: Constantine and most subsequent Christian emperors sent philosophers into exile and persecuted polytheist priests, declaring them social outcasts, imprisoning them, and killing many. Hatred of non-Christian books resulted in an overall impoverishment of civilization. The establishment of the Inquisition and, later, the sixteenth-century creation of the *Index of Forbidden Books* were the climax of this campaign to eradicate everything that deviated from the official policy of the Catholic, Apostolic, and Roman Church.

The desire to be done with non-Christian books and the mistrust of unfettered thinking beggared philosophy, forcing its practitioners to give up the struggle, to remain silent, or to express themselves with extreme prudence. (The entire roster of important philosophers from Montaigne to Sartre, in a line including Pascal, Descartes, Kant, Malebranche, Spinoza, Locke, Hume, Berkeley, Rousseau, Bergson, and so many others — not to mention materialists, socialists, and Freudians — enjoys pride of place in the *Index*.) The Bible, claiming to contain everything, banned everything it did not contain. Over the centuries, the results were devastating.

Countless fatwas were proclaimed against Muslim authors even when they did not defend atheist positions, did not discredit the Koran's teachings, and did not indulge either in blasphemy or invective. It was enough simply to think and write freely for the thunderbolts to come crashing down. The slightest deviation came at a heavy price. Exile, prosecution, persecution, libel, even assassination, all these horrors were perpetrated by the likes of Ali Abderraziq, Mohammed Khalafallah, Taha Hussein, Nasr Hamid Abu Zayd, Mohammed Iqbal, Fazlur Rahman, Mahmoud Mohammed Taha.

In their implacable opposition to free expression, the priests of the three religions preferred to authorize the conjurers whose deft manipulation of language, verbal contortions, and jigsaw-puzzle formulations blew smoke in their readers' eyes. What did these schoolmen achieve over the centuries beyond a verbal repackaging of ancient fables and ecclesiastical dogma?

Jews, Christians, and Muslims love memory exercises, particularly in regard to the chanting of the faithful. Muslims memorize the suras of the Koran at a very early age and learn to chant them with the correct elocution (*tajwid*) and the correct delivery (*tartil*). Proper articulation and intonation of the Koran (*tajwid*) requires a slow, melodious declamation with rich flourishes, such as singing several notes to one syllable of text. *Tartil* is a slow, rhythmic, measured, and meditative delivery. Traditionally, theological schools teach seven ways of reciting the Koran, the differences between them being a matter of linguistic and phonetic variables: consonants stressed, unstressed, without overtones; dropped vowels; change in inflection; very soft tone of voice; or verbal ornamentation, such as deliberate repetition of a phrase at the beginning of successive verses. All this contributes to subordination of the spirit and message of the text in favor of pure literary style. The words lose their meaning, and their repetition becomes an artistic performance.

The litanies we hear in Koranic schools — madrassas, often centers of hostility to *falsafa*, or philosophy — bear this out. Students learn by reciting aloud, as a group, in cadence, in a collective and communal rhythm. Their dirges help them memorize the teachings of Yahweh or Allah. Jewish mnemonic technique also offers a method of apprenticeship in reading and the alphabet by an association of letters and contents that rests on Talmudic doctrine.

Thus, books aim paradoxically (after they have been memorized wholesale) at what virtually amounts to their own elimination! Rationally enough, students learn the Torah or the Koran by heart. Thus, when the danger of persecution raises its head or when conditions such as exile make it impossible to have the volume at hand, the believer still enjoys mental possession of the book and its teachings.

3

Hatred of science. This law of the one book, total and all-inclusive, coupled with the unfortunate habit of believing that "everything" can be contained within a single text, means that there is no recourse to nonreligious (which is not to say atheistic) books, such as scientific works. Monotheism does not really like the rational work of scientists. Clearly Islam embraces astronomy, algebra, mathematics, geometry, optics, *but only* to calculate the direction of Mecca more accurately by means of the stars, to establish religious calendars, to decree prayer hours. Clearly Islam values geography, *but only* to facilitate the convergence on the Kaaba when pilgrims from all over the world flock to Mecca. Clearly it prizes medicine, *but only* to avoid the impurity that mars one's relation with Allah. Clearly it esteems grammar, philosophy, and law, *but only* to enrich commentary on the Koran and the Hadith. This religious instrumentalization of science subjects reason to domestic and theocratic uses. In Islamic lands, science is not pursued for its own sake today but for the improvement of religious practice. Centuries of Muslim culture produced inventions, research, and important discoveries in the area of secular science, such as algebra and astronomy, as well as being responsible for the preservation of classical texts. One hadith indeed celebrates the quest for scientific knowledge as far afield as China, but always in the logic of its instrumentalization via religion, never for the human and immanent ideal of social progress.

Christianity too considers that the Bible contains all knowledge necessary for the effective functioning of the church. For centuries the Bible inhibited all research that scrutinized and questioned its contents (without ever contradicting its claims). Faithful to the lessons of Genesis (knowledge is not desirable, science distances us from the essential — God), the Catholic religion impeded the forward march of Western civilization, inflicting on it incalculable damage.

From Christianity's earliest days, in the beginning of the second century of the common era, paganism in all its aspects was condemned. Everything it produced was rejected, tied to false gods, polytheism, magic, and error. Euclidean mathematics? Ptolemy's maps? Eratosthenes' geography? Aristotle's natural sciences? Aristarchus's astronomy? Hippocrates' medicine? Herophilus's anatomy? They were simply not Christian enough!

The discoveries made by Greek geniuses — Aristarchus's heliocentrism, to take just one example — were obviously applicable independently of the gods and the religious systems of the day. What did the existence of Zeus and his kin matter when one had to determine the laws of hydrostatics, calculate the length of a meridian, invent latitude and longitude, measure the distance between us and the sun, argue for the revolution of the earth around the sun, perfect the theory of epicycles, elaborate the map of the heavens, establish the length of a solar year, link tides and lunar attraction, discover the nervous system, offer theories on the circulation of the blood, all of them truths of no interests to the denizens of heaven?

Turning one's back on the results of such research, acting as though these discoveries had never taken place, starting everything again from scratch is at best stagnation, evidence of a dangerous hostility to change. But at worst it means speeding blindly backward—while others forge ahead—to the darkness from which every civilization, by its nature and by definition, strives to free itself in order to be. Refusal of the Enlightenment characterizes the monotheist religions: they prefer mental night for the nurturing of their fables.

4

Negation of matter. In science the church has always been wrong about everything: faced with an epistemological truth, it automatically persecutes the discoverer. The history of science's relationship with Christianity yields a prodigious abundance of blunders and stupidity. Between the church's rejection of the heliocentric hypothesis of antiquity and its contemporary condemnations of genetic laws, twenty-five centuries of wasted opportunities for humankind are heaped up. We scarcely dare imagine how swiftly the West would have advanced without such sustained brutalization of science!

One line of force in this crusade against science is the church's prolonged, unbridled condemnations of materialist theories. In the fifth century BCE the genius of Leucippus and Democritus led them to discover the atom without possessing the material means to confirm their intuition. It was a stroke that never ceases to amaze. Lacking a microscope, a lens, indeed any enlarging instrument at all, they extrapolated from the motes of dust in a ray of light the existence of particles invisible to the naked eye—but nonetheless there! And on this basis they concluded that the existence of these atoms explained the makeup of all matter, and consequently of the world itself.

From Leucippus to Diogenes of Oenanda, passing via Epicurus, Lucretius and Philodemus of Gadara, the atomist tradition remained alive, lasting through eight centuries of Greek and Roman antiquity. Lucretius's *De Rerum Natura* (*On the Nature of Things*) proposes the fullest account of Epicurean physics: form, nature, weight, atomic constitution, behavior in a vacuum, the theory of declivity, generation and decomposition — everything necessary for a complete decoding of the world. And of course, if everything is made up of matter, soul, spirit, and gods as well share that makeup. So do men. With the advent of pure immanence, fictions and fables cease along with religions, and with their disappearance the means of circumscribing the body and soul of the city's denizens also disappear.

Ancient physics proceeded from a poetic method. Yet despite everything, time confirmed it. The centuries rolled by, but in the age of electronic scanning, particle accelerators, positrons, nuclear fission, and technological pathways into the very heart of matter, that Democritean intuition has been validated. The "philosophical atom" has received the stamp of authenticity from the scientific — and in particular the nuclear — world. Nevertheless, the church to this day persists in its idealist, spiritualist, antimaterialist position — that a reality irreducible to matter somehow exists in the human soul. It is no surprise, then, that materialism has been the fly in Christianity's ointment from the beginning. The church stops at nothing to discredit this coherent philosophy and its complete account of all reality. And in order to block access to atomist physics, what better means than discrediting atomist morality? So the Epicurean ethos must be condemned. The Epicurean defines pleasure as ataraxia — the absence of care. So we must transform this negative definition into sheer aberration, and say it celebrates bestial, crude, and casual congress with animals! With this achieved, we no longer need concede importance to a physics dangerous in the eyes of the Christian caste, because it proceeds from an Epicurean swine.

The church thus strikes everywhere a hint of materialism appears. When Giordano Bruno died, burned by Christians at the stake on the Campo dei Fiori in 1660, he perished less for atheism — he had never denied God's existence — than for materialism: he asserted the coexistence of God and the material world. Nowhere did he blaspheme, in no part of his work did he offer insults to the God of the Catholics. He wrote, thought, and stated that this God, who is, could not fail to be of the wider world. It was the extended substance of the language to come later, with Descartes.

Bruno, who was also a Dominican (!), did not deny the existence of the spirit. Sadly for him, however, he situated it at the physical level of atoms. He understood particles to be so many centers of life, places where the spirit manifests itself as coeternal with God. Divinity then exists, of course, but it comes to terms with matter, representing its mystery resolved. The church believed in God's incarnation, but only as the Son who is the offshoot of a virgin and a carpenter. It most certainly did not believe in atoms.

The same can be said about Galileo, the emblematic representative of the church's hatred for science and of the conflict between faith and reason. The legend focuses on the issue of heliocentrism, with the pope and the Inquisition condemning the author of *A Dialogue Concerning the Two Chief World Systems* (1632) because Galileo argued that the earth was a satellite of a sun located at the center of the universe. Charges, trial, retraction: we all know the story, which ends, according to Brecht, with Galileo muttering as he left the seat of justice, *Eppur' si muove (And yet it moves)*.

In fact, things happened differently. What did the Vatican *really* hold against Galileo? Not so much his defense of Copernican astronomy — although this was a thesis that contradicted the church's Aristotelian position — as his adherence to the materialist camp . . . Before the courts of the day, heliocentrism was punishable by lifelong house arrest, a relatively mild sentence. Defense of atomism, on the other hand, led directly to the stake! That being so, why not confess to the less damaging charge? In other words, acknowledge the venial sin of heliocentrism rather than the fatal atomic error.

5

Bakeshop ontology. But why was the church so bent on persecuting the advocates of an atomist conception of the world? First of all because belief in the existence of matter, to the exclusion of every other reality, leads logically to assertion of the existence of a material God. And thus to denial of his spiritual, timeless, and immaterial qualities, along with other distinguishing features noted in his Christian passport. And thus to demolition of the intangible God manufactured by Judeo-Christianity.

But there is another reason, relating as it happens to the bakery business. For the church believes in transubstantiation. It affirms, according to the words of Jesus at the Last Supper — *This is my body, this is my blood* (Matthew 26:26–28) — that the true body and the true blood of Christ reside in the unleavened Host and the wine. Not symbolically, not allegorically, but really . . . At the moment of the Elevation, then, the priest hoists Christ's real body in his hands.

By what extraordinary machinations of the Holy Spirit does the baker's bread produce the mystery of an infinitely divisible body and a flow of blood that has flooded the planet? At the very moment when the priests officiate, all over the globe, every single Mass *really* produces the flesh of a resurrected corpse, reappearing in its eternal freshness, unchanged by eternity. Clearly a staunch believer in linguistics, Christ moves into the performative mode, creating reality through his words: he makes what *he* says become fact by the simple act of saying it.

In its very earliest days the church believed firmly in this miracle. It still does. The *Catechism of the Catholic Church*—in its twentieth-century incarnation—still insists on the *real* presence of Christ in the Eucharist (Article 1373). In validation of this fiction, there follow references to the Council of Trent, to the *Summa Theologica* of Thomas Aquinas, to the Mysteries of the Faith—labeled number 9 by the church—and to other texts by Saint John Chrysostom, who, in his *First Homily Against the Antinomians*, very rightly approves the call of Paul of Tarsus. Paul had told the Corinthians, as if this were an occasion for celebration, that *as for knowledge, it will pass away* (1 Corinthians 13:8). Such an initial postulate seems a very necessary prelude to all the nonsense that ensued!

Thus the church still believes in the real presence of Christ's body and blood in the baker's bread and the vintner's nectar. But to make the patient swallow such an ontological pill, many intellectual contortions (major contortions) are required. And it was the conceptual toolbox of Aristotle, the Vatican's cherished philosopher, that facilitated this magnificent feat of legerdemain. Hence a series of magicians' turns using the metaphysical categories of the Stagirite.

The explanation: Christ's body is *veritably, really, substantially* —the official terms—present in the Host. The same holds true for the hemoglobin in the wine. For the bread's *essence* disappears once the priest has spoken, whereas its *perceptible characteristics*, its *accidents*—color, taste, temperature—remain. Those characteristics are preserved in miraculous fashion by the divine will. He who can do the maximum—create a world—can also do the minimum—play tricks with a bakery product. Of course it tastes like bread, but it is not (or is no longer) bread! You could just as well maintain that the wine has become bread: it is white as Christ's red blood and does not intoxicate (or no longer does). Say what you will, it's still sweet red wine!

We need all this juggling with substance and perceptible characteristics in order to make the faithful believe that what is (bread and wine) does not exist, and what is not (Christ's body and blood) truly exists! An incomparable display of three-card monte! Once theology takes a hand, gastronomy and the vintner's arts, and even dietetics and hematology, throw up their hands. Thus the fate of Christianity plays out in the pathetic farce of an ontological shell game.

6

Epicurus: not an enthusiast for Hosts. What about Epicurus in all this? He liked bread, since his banquet of a crust and a modest crock of cheese has come down through the centuries and left indelible memories in the history of philosophy. But he would have laughed at the Eucharistic rabbit pulled out of the Christian hat! Laughed very long and loud . . . For, in virtue of the principles laid down in his *Letter to Herodotus*, a Host is reducible to atoms. Lucretius would explain how, with wheat flour and water, and without yeast, we manufacture this white, bland, tongue-coating, melting wafer out of a small pinch of atoms, each linked to its kin. He offers nothing useful in support of the fiction of transubstantiation. Nothing but matter.

Therein lay the danger of atomism and materialism. It made a metaphysical impossibility of the church's theoretical twaddle! By the standards of modern atomic calibration, there is nothing to be found in the bread and wine but what Epicurus predicted: matter. The hedging made possible by blathering on about essence versus perceptible characteristics became impossible when confronted with Epicurean theory. That is why the disciples of Democritus had to be destroyed by discrediting their lives and by the travesty of labeling their ascetic ethos as licentiousness and immorality.

In 1340, Nicolas d'Autrecourt was bold enough to propose an extremely modern (but atomist) theory of light. He believed in light's corpuscular nature (modern science validates him), which implies an identification of substance with its characteristics. This was bad news for believers in the Aristotelian metaphysical broth! The church at once forced him to recant, and burned his writings. It was the beginning of a persecution of all scientific research proceeding through atomism — which the Jesuits banned as early as 1632, maintaining the prohibition for centuries. Materialism (Articles 285 and 2124 of the *Catechism*) is still on the prohibited list of the contemporary church.

7

Forever missing the boat. Since the hodgepodge of biblical knowledge was entirely sufficient for science, the church missed all the major discoveries of ten centuries. Throughout that time, the urgings of the intelligence were contained, but not halted, by the Catholic, Apostolic, and Roman authorities. Progress continued thanks to rebellious individuals, determined research, scientists who prized the truths of reason over the fables of faith. But a scrutiny of the church's reactions to scientific discoveries over the last thousand years reveals an astounding accumulation of missed opportunities!

They include rejection of atomism in favor of Aristotelianism. To this must be added opposition to any proposition that excluded the intentionality of a creator God (since Genesis reports that God began from nothing and created the world in a week, anything that contradicted this unleashed the Vatican's fury). What of rational causalities? Of rational sequences? Of claims verifiable from observation? An experimental methodology? A dialectic of reasons? And what else? God decides, wills, creates—period! Could there be an alternative to creationism? Absolutely not!

Is there anything to be said for scientific belief in the eternity of the universe? In multiple universes? (Both Epicurean theses, incidentally . . .) Absolutely not! God created the universe from nothing. Before nothing, there was . . . nothing. Darkness and chaos, but also, in this welter of nothingness, there was God and his itch to innovate. Light, day, night, the firmament, heaven, earth, the deeps—we know the whole story, right down to the beasts of the field, reptiles, animals both wild and human. That is the official history, its genealogy minutely dated. Multiple worlds? Absolutely not!

After precise and meticulous calculations, scientists confirmed Aristarchus's idea that the sun indeed sat firmly at the center of our world. The church's response: absurd. Creation by a perfect God could take place only in the center, the zone of perfection. And then of course the notion of a centrally placed sun came dangerously close to reviving pagan solar cults . . . To exist on the outer rim would be a mark of inconceivable imperfection, *therefore* it could not be scientifically demonstrable! The factual was wrong, the fictitious was right. Heliocentrism? Absolutely not!

Lamarck, followed by Darwin, published their discoveries. The former proposed that species change, the latter that they evolve according to the so-called laws of natural selection. The readers of the only book shook their heads: God created the dog and the wolf from whole cloth, the city rat and the country rat, the cat, the weasel, and the bunny rabbit. No likelihood whatsoever that a comparison of their bones might prove evolution or transformation. And then there was that notion that men descend from monkeys! An unbearable narcissistic wound, Freud suggested. The pope cousin to a baboon? Horrors . . . Transformation of species? Evolution? Absolutely not!

In the industrious atmosphere of their laboratories, scientists advanced the idea of polygenesis—the original and simultaneous existence of groups of humans at different geographical locations. A contradiction, thundered the church: Adam and Eve were indeed, factually and really, the first man and the first woman. Before them no one existed. The existence of the primordial couple, the couple who brought us original sin, buttresses the biblical logic of error, guilt, and redemption. What can we do with men and women existing before sin, and thus spared by sin? Pre-Adamites? Absolutely not!

Brushing dirt from stones and poring over fossils, geologists proposed a scientific dating of the world. Seashells found on mountaintops, strata and layers all attest to an immanent chronology. But there is a problem: their dating does not correspond to the sacred numerology supplied by the Bible. Christians insist that the world is four thousand years old, no more, no less. Scientists prove the existence of a world before that Christian world. Science is wrong . . . Is geology a science to be relied on? Absolutely not!

Men of goodwill cannot tolerate death and disease, and to be able to fight off epidemics and pathologies they need to open bodies and learn from the dead lessons useful to the living—using death in order to save life. The church absolutely opposes research on human bodies. There can be no question of rational causalities, simply theological reasons: evil and death flow from peccant Eve. Pain, suffering, and disease proceed from divine will and a divine decision to put the faith of men and their loved ones to the test. The ways of the Lord are impenetrable, and he moves according to a plan known to him alone. From material causalities to pathologies? A rational etiology? Absolutely not!

Sitting at the foot of his couch at the turn of the nineteenth century, a Viennese doctor discovered the subconscious and the mechanisms of repression and sublimation, the existence of the death instinct, the role of dreams, and a thousand other factors that revolutionized a psychiatry then in its prehistoric phase. He perfected a method for treating, relieving, and curing neuroses, mental abnormalities, and psychoses. It is true that along the way, in *The Future of an Illusion*, Sigmund Freud also demonstrated that all religion proceeds from an "obsessional neurosis" closely related to "hallucinatory psychosis." The church condemned him, duly issued its fatwa, and consigned him to the *Index*. Man is animated by a dark force located in his subconscious? But that contradicted the dogma of free will so necessary to the Christian obsession with making everyone responsible, thus guilty, thus punishable . . . And so useful in validating the logic of the Last Judgment! Freud and his discoveries? Come now . . . Psychoanalysis? Absolutely not!

And finally: twentieth-century researchers discovered the genetic blueprint. They had gently pushed through a door to a universe that promised astounding possibilities in diagnostics and disease prevention, greater precision in treatments and in the avoidance of pathologies. They were working toward the advent of a predictive medicine that would revolutionize the discipline . . . But the *Charter for Health Care Workers*, published by the Vatican, condemned them. Avoid pain and suffering? Believe ourselves exonerated from the price to be paid for original sin? Seek a human medicine? Absolutely not!

What an astonishing game of chess! On one side stood an unshakable determination to deceive (ourselves), to reject the truth, to maintain trust in the death instinct. On the other side stood the living impulse of research, the vitality of science, the dynamism of progress. The believers' condemnation of scientific truths — the atomist theory, the materialist option, heliocentric astronomy, geological dating, transformation of species, evolution, psychoanalytic therapy, genetic revolution — all loudly proclaimed the triumph of Paul of Tarsus, who had called for knowledge to pass away. It was a call successful beyond all expectations ...

Clearly, the church deployed extraordinary determination to attain this phenomenal rate of success in failing! Persecution, consignment to the *Index*, burnings at the stake, the instruments of the Inquisition, imprisonments, and trials have never ceased ... For centuries it was forbidden to read the Bible without priestly mediation. It was quite out of the question to approach the book with the weapons of reason, analysis, and criticism, as a historian, a geologist, a scientist. In the seventeenth century Richard Simon published the first Christian critical analysis of the Old and New Testaments. Naturally, Bossuet and the Catholic Church violently attacked him. The fruit of the Tree of Knowledge has left a lingering aftertaste of bitterness.

III

Seeking the Opposite of the Real

1

Inventing the afterlife. Monotheisms have no love for intelligence, books, knowledge, science. Preferring the ethereal over the material and the real, they have a strong aversion to man's instincts and basic drives. Thus not only do they celebrate ignorance, innocence, naïveté, obedience, and submission: the three religions of the book disdain the texture, forms, and forces of the world. The here and now is irrelevant, for the whole world, now and forever, bears the weight of original sin.

As a sign of their hatred of matter, the monotheisms cobbled together a world of antimatter. In antiquity the liegemen of the one God, embarrassed by these scientific questions, turned to Pythagoras (who was himself shaped by Eastern religious thought) and Plato to build their city of the spirit, where Ideas, surprisingly similar to clones of God, could flourish. Like God, these Ideas were eternal, immortal, without dimension, inaccessible to time, immune to growth and decomposition, resistant to all sensual, phenomenal, and corporeal conceptualization, requiring nothing but themselves to exist, endure, persevere in their being, and all the rest! Their identities were close kin to those of Yahweh, God, and Allah. On such stuff as this, the monotheisms built castles in the air intended to discredit all other habitation — real, concrete, or inherent.

Hence the schizophrenia of monotheisms. They judge the here and now by the standards of an elsewhere; they conceive of the earthly city only in terms of the heavenly city. They care about men, but only as a sideline to their preoccupation with angels; they give a thought to man's inherent nature if and only if it serves as a stepping-stone to transcendence; they are quite willing to turn their attention to the real world, but only to measure how well it corresponds to "intelligent design" theory; they are solicitous of earth only insofar as it offers an opportunity for heaven. Between these two contradictory concerns, a gap is created, an ontological wound impossible to close. Man can find no fulfillment there. An existential void gives rise to human malaise.

Here again, atomist monism (the atom is the universal substrate) and materialist unity (the only thing that can truly be said to exist is matter) permit us to circumvent metaphysical arguments that are full of holes. If a man considers the real to consist exclusively of matter, and if he concludes that reality has no manifestations other than earthly, sensual, worldly, phenomenal—such reasoning precludes mental wandering and keeps his feet on the ground, in contact with the one true world. Dualism, whether Pythagorean, Platonic, or Christian, does a disservice to those who subscribe to it. By aiming for paradise, we lose sight of earth. Hope of a beyond and aspiration to an afterlife engender a sense of futility in the present. If the prospect of getting taken up to paradise generates joy, it is the mindless joy of a baby picked up from his crib.

2

Birds of Paradise. This world outside the world produces two creations of fantasy: the angel and paradise. The angel functions as a prototype of anti-man. Paradise functions as antiworld, inciting humans to detest their condition and despise their reality in order to aspire to another essence and then to another existence. The angel's wing symbolizes the opposite of man's earthbound condition. In contrast to our own imperfect planet, paradise promises atopia, utopia, uchronia: that is, a land without territorial borders; an ideal society that lives in harmony, free of poverty, tyranny, and war; where time has no beginning and no end.

The Jews possess their own stables of winged creatures: the cherubim guarding the entrance to the Garden of Eden; the seraphim accompanying them (we recall the one who visited Abraham, or his colleague who wrestled with Jacob). Their job? To extol the Eternal One in a celestial Camelot. For although God disdains human trivialities, he does like his greatness to be celebrated. Both Talmud and Kabbala teem with angels. These are servants of God, but also protectors of the just and of the children of Israel. From time to time we see them leaving their heavenly abode to bear a message from God to men. (The pagan Hermes is never too far away; he too is feathered, but only on his hat and heels . . .)

Pure spirits of light—which in all logic does not exclude unarguably spiritual and luminous feathers and wings—the angels deserve our attention partly because they are without gender. Neither men nor women, androgynous, a little bit of each, even childlike, spared the throes of copulation. Happy creatures of the air, they are unaware of the sexual condition, for they are without desire, without libido. Seraphic poultry, they know neither hunger nor thirst, yet they feed on manna—the ambrosia of the pagan gods. But of course they do not defecate. Blissful avians, they know nothing of corruption, decrepitude, and death.

And then there are fallen, rebellious angels, untamed, undefeated. In the Garden of Eden the devil — "the slanderous one, the libeler" — teaches what he knows best: the option of disobedience, of refusal to submit, of saying no. Satan — "the adversary, the accuser" — breathes the wind of freedom across the dirty waters of the primal world where obedience reigns supreme — the reign of maximum servitude. Beyond good and evil, and not simply as an incarnation of the latter, the devil talks libertarian possibilities into being. He restores to men their power over themselves and the world, frees them from supervision and control. We may rightly conclude that these fallen angels attract the hatred of monotheisms. On the other hand, they attract the incandescent love of atheists.

3

Seeking the opposite of the real. As we might expect, these impossible bodies live in an equally impossible place — the walled-in Garden of Paradise. Pentateuch, Genesis, and Koran all affirm the existence of this hysterically conceived geography. But Muslims offer us its most perfect description. It is worth a visit! Streams, gardens, rivers, springs, budding meadows, magnificent fruit and drinks, great-eyed houris (always virginal), gracious young people, beds galore, superb garments, luxurious fabrics, extraordinary jewelry, gold, pearls, perfumes, priceless vessels ... Nothing is missing in this glossy brochure, the work of an ontological chamber of commerce.

And the definition of paradise? The antiworld, the opposite of the real. In the real world Muslims scrupulously respect their rites. They observe the same rigorous logic of the licit and illicit, accept the same drastic division of things into the pure and the impure. In paradise all that comes to an end — no more obligations, no more rites, no more prayers. At the heavenly banquet they drink wine (83:25 and 47:15), they eat pork (52:22), they sing, they wear gold (18:31) — forbidden here below — they eat and drink from plates and goblets of precious metal — illicit on earth — they wear silk — repellent on earth, silk being excreted by a worm — they fondle houris (44:54), they enjoy eternally virginal women (55:70) or caress beautiful youths (56:17) on couches of precious stones — in the tents of the desert their couch is a mere rug and they are allowed a maximum of three legitimate wives. In short, everything hitherto forbidden is now there for the taking ... ad libitum ...

In the desert camp, eating vessels are of earthenware, in paradise, precious stones and metals. In the tent, squatting on rough skin rugs, families share a modest subsistence that cannot be counted on every day — camel's milk, mutton, mint tea. In heaven, prodigious quantities of food and drink are served up, set out upon green satin and brocade cloths. Beneath the tribal awning the smells are coarse, strong, overpowering — sweat, dirt, leather, animal hide, smoke, suet, soot. In Muhammad's company there are only magnificent scents: camphor, musk, ginger, incense, myrrh, cinnamon. Around the tribal hearth, if by chance alcohol is consumed, drunkenness threatens. In the Islamic version of the Celestial Kingdom, intoxication is unknown (37:47) and so (not unimportantly) are hangovers. Moreover, unrestrained consumption does not induce the temptation to sin!

Still in the logic of paradise as an antiworld, desirable in the interests of making the real and often undesirable world tolerable: Islam was originally a religion of deserts and their brutal, hot, and violent climate. In paradise, an eternal springtime prevails, without sun or moon, just an eternal light, never day, never night. Does the desert sirocco tan the skin or the harmattan scorch the flesh? In the Islamic heaven, the musk-laden wind breathes gently over rivers of milk, of honey, of wine and water, spreading its balm far and wide. Gathering food in the desert is often a dangerous and chancy undertaking: sometimes you find nourishment, sometimes you find nothing, or very little — single dates, rare figs. In Muhammad's domain grapes are so big that a crow wishing to fly around a bunch needs more than a month to complete his circuit! In the vast expanses of desert sand the coolness of shade is extremely rare and infinitely welcome. In the mansion of Muslim Ideas, a horse takes a hundred years to emerge from the shadow of a single banana tree. On earth, caravans crawl endlessly across the dunes, their progress slow, each mile over the sand taking what seems like an age. The Prophet's stables possess winged horses created from red rubies, free of material constraints, moving at galactic speeds.

And finally, the same differences apply to the body. A troublesome partner on earth, constantly needing his water ration, his food quota, his libidinal satisfaction, so many occasions for distancing himself from the Prophet and from prayer, so many occasions for slavery to natural needs. In paradise, the body's immateriality shines forth: no more eating, except for pure pleasure. If ingestion takes place, digestion is not a problem — even Jesus, who ate bread, wine, and fish, never excretes . . . nor are flatulence or gas emissions an embarrassment, for in heaven smells that are revolting on earth become the musk-scented exhalations of moist, languid bodies!

No more need for procreation to guarantee one's lineage; no need for sleep, since weariness is unknown; no need to wipe one's nose or spit. Illness is unknown to the very end of time; sorrow, fear, and humiliation, so often overriding all else on earth, are erased from our vocabulary; there is no more desire — desire is pain and privation, says the Platonic tradition — it is enough for desire to make itself felt to be instantly transformed into pleasure; looking hungrily at a fruit is enough to savor its taste, its texture, and its fragrance in our mouths.

Who could say no? How totally understandable that countless Muslims, lured by the promise of these celestial dream vacations, should have left happily for battle, from the Prophet's first raid at Nakhla to the Iran-Iraq war all the way to the present day! How natural that Palestinian suicide bombers should unleash death on Israeli café terraces; that aircraft hijackers should hurl passenger planes against New York's Twin Towers; that Islamic radicals should detonate a string of powerful bombs on packed commuter trains in Madrid! These events represent blood sacrifice. Human sacrifice made at the altar of falsehoods so improbable as to stagger even the meanest intelligence.

4

Solving the woman problem. Should we discern the logical consequence of hatred for intelligence in the hatred for women common to Judaism, Christianity, and Islam? According to the holy books, original sin, error, the desire for knowledge, all stem from the decision of one woman, Eve. Adam was an innocent fool, content to obey and submit. When the serpent speaks — nothing wrong with that . . . don't all snakes speak? — he addresses the woman and starts a dialogue with her. (In the Koran, the tempter is called Iblis or Shaitan. For centuries, millions of Muslims have performed a ritual "stoning of the devil" as part of the annual pilgrimage to Mecca.) Seducing serpent leads to seduced woman leads to woman the eternal temptress. It is an easy progression.

Hatred of women is like a variation on the theme of hatred of intelligence. To which might be added hatred of everything women represent for men: desire, pleasure, life. Curiosity as well — many dictionaries confirm that inquisitive women are widely dismissed as "daughters of Eve." They generate desire; they also generate life. Original sin is perpetuated through women — that sin which, as Saint Augustine assures us, is transmitted from the moment of conception, in the mother's womb, via the father's sperm. The sexualization of sin!

The monotheisms infinitely prefer the angel to the woman. Far better a world of seraphim, of cherubim, of thrones and of archangels than a feminine or mixed-gender universe! And above all, no sex. Flesh, blood, libido, naturally associated with women, give Judaism, Christianity, and Islam welcome excuses for stressing the theme of the illicit and the impure. Thus they wage war against the desirable body, against the menstrual blood that briefly liberates women from the burden of motherhood, and against hedonist energy. Bible and Koran overflow with rapturous anathema on these themes.

The religions of the book detest women. They admire only mothers and wives. To rescue women from their consubstantial negativity there are only two solutions — in fact a single two-step solution — marrying a man, and then bearing his children. Caring for their husbands, cooking for them, handling household problems, feeding, caring for, and educating his children, they have no more time for addressing the feminine within. The wife and mother kill the woman — which is exactly what the rabbis, priests, and imams count on to ensure the male's peace of mind.

Judeo-Christianity promotes the idea that Eve was created secondarily, as an afterthought, from Adam's rib (Genesis 2:22)! An inferior cut off the prime beef, a humble sparerib. (As Adam's wife, of course, she appears in the Koran [sura 2:35]. But the fact that she is never named is revealing ... because the unnamed is unnamable!) The male came first, and only then, like a leftover fragment, a crumb — the female. Everything is against Eve, starting with her order of arrival. Her subordination to her husband set the pattern for womankind's existence. Above all, though, she was responsible for original sin. And she has paid heavily ever since.

Her body is cursed, and she is too, in her totality. The unfertilized egg emphasizes the feminine and negates the maternal; it is a sign of womanhood — but empty womanhood, divorced from motherhood. Therefore, a menstruating female is impure. The blood indicates periods when conception is not possible and is a reminder of the danger of infertility. For a monotheist there can be no more hideous oxymoron than a barren, sterile woman! And during menstruation she is at no risk of pregnancy, meaning that sexuality can be dissociated from fear and practiced for its own sake. The possibility of sex divorced from conception, and thus of sex alone, of pure sexuality — that is absolute evil.

In the name of this same principle, the three monotheisms condemn homosexuals to death (Leviticus 20:13). Why? Because their sexuality precludes (or precluded until very recently) the destinies of father, mother, husband, and wife, and clearly asserts the primacy and absolute worth of the free individual. The bachelor is only half of a person; he is incomplete without his female partner, says the Talmud. The Koran (sura 24:32) commands single men to marry. For his part, Paul of Tarsus saw in the solitary male the perils of lust, adultery, and free sexuality. Hence, given the impossibility of chastity, his endorsement of marriage — the least objectionable justification for the libido.

We find a similar horror of abortion in the three religions. The family functions as the fixed horizon, the basic cell of the community. It implies children, whom Jews consider to be the condition of their people's survival, whose number the Christian church wishes to see grow and multiply, whom Muslims see as a mark of the Prophet's blessing. Everything that disturbs this demographic metaphysics arouses monotheist anger. God does not approve of planned parenthood.

Yet immediately after childbirth the Jewish woman is considered unclean. Blood, always blood . . . If she gave birth to a boy, the ban on entering the temple lasts forty days; if she bore a

girl . . . sixty! Thus spake Leviticus . . . To the present day, Orthodox Jewish men in their daily morning prayer recite, "Praised be
God that he has not created me a gentile. Praised be God that he
has not created me a slave . . . Praised be God that he has not created me a woman" (Talmud, Menahot 43b). Not to be outdone,
the Koran does not explicitly condemn the pre-Islamic tribal
tradition that ascribed *shame* to a man who fathered a daughter
and legitimized his deliberations on whether to *keep* the child or
bury it beneath the dust (16:58).

As for our jovial Christian kin, delegates to the Council of
Mâcon in 585 submitted for discussion a book by Alcidalus
Valeus entitled *Paradoxical Dissertation in Which We Attempt to
Prove that Women are not Human Creatures.* Paradoxical? In what
way? We do not know if the attempt was successful; i.e., if Alcidalus won over his readers. But the Christian hierarchy was already sympathetic to his point of view: we need only recall Paul
of Tarsus and his countless misogynistic pronouncements. In any
case, the church's age-old prejudice against women remains to
this day an undeniable fact.

5

Celebration of castration. We know of the travails of Origen,
who took Matthew literally. The evangelist discusses eunuchs
(19:12) and establishes a typology for them—born without tes-
ticles, castrated later by others, or self-mutilated in honor of the
Kingdom of God—and concludes, "He who is able to receive
this, let him receive it." Crafty. Origen cut to the heart of the
matter, slicing off his genitals with a blade—probably before realizing that desire is less a question of one's sack than of one's
brain. But too late . . .

Monotheist literature abounds in references to the extinc-

tion of the libido and the destruction of desire: praise of continence, celebration of absolute or relative chastity. And since men
are neither gods nor angels but rather animals whose condition
we are forced to live with, monotheism encourages marriage
with fidelity to the spouse — or spouses in the case of Jews and
Muslims — and insists that all sexuality should be focused on
procreation. Family, marriage, monogamy, fidelity — all of them
variations on the theme of castration . . . Or how to become a
virtual Origen.

Leviticus and Numbers clearly state the rules on the question of Jewish sexual intersubjectivity: no sexual relations outside marriage; legitimization of polygamy; divorce at the
husband's discretion and without too many formalities (a letter,
a *guet*, to the repudiated spouse is sufficient); illegality of marriage to a non-Jew; transmission of Jewishness through the
mother (she has nine months to prove that she really is the
mother, the identity of the father being always uncertain); prohibition on women studying the Torah (mandatory for men); no
authorization for the daughters of Eve to recite payers, wear the
shawl, sport the phylactery, blow the shofar, build the ritual hut
(the *sukha*), or belong to groups of ten (the minimum necessary
for prayer); permission to own but not manage or administer her
own financial assets (the husband's role). Clear proof that God
made man in his own image, and not in the woman's.

A reading of the Koran shows the obvious kinship between
the two religions. Islam clearly proclaims the superiority of
males over females, for God prefers men to women (4:34).
Hence a series of diktats: prohibition on exposing the hair out of
doors — the veil (24:30) — or exposing bare arms and legs; no
sexuality outside legitimate relations with a member of the
community, who may himself possess several spouses (4:3); prohibition of polyandry for women, of course; praise for chastity,
of course (17:32 and 33:35); prohibition on marrying a non-

Muslim (3:28); prohibition on wearing men's clothing; no mingling of the sexes at the mosque; no question of shaking hands with a man unless wearing gloves; marriage mandatory, with no tolerance for celibacy (24:32) even in the name of religion; passion and love advised against in marriage, which is celebrated in the interests of family (4:25), tribe, and community; recommendation that the wife submit to all the sexual desires of the husband, who "*plows* his wife whenever he likes, for she is his tillage" — the metaphor is Koranic (2:223); permission to beat one's spouse on mere suspicion (4:34); the same ease of repudiation, the same existential minor status, the same legal inferiority (2:228), with a woman's courtroom testimony worth half that of a man, while a barren woman and a woman deflowered before marriage possess exactly the same value: none at all.

Hence praise of castration: women equal excess. Excessive desire, excessive pleasure, excessive wildness, excessive passion, excessive outbursts of ecstasy, excessive sexual delirium. They threaten the male's virility. The things women should strive for include God, meditation, prayer, performance of ritual, knowledge of the licit/illicit divide, awareness of the divine in the smallest details of everyday life. Heaven, not the earth. Still less the worst of what the earth has to offer—bodies . . . Woman, tempted long ago and long since transformed into eternal temptress, threatens the image man cherishes of himself, the triumphant phallus, borne like a talisman of his being. Terror of castration shapes every life led in the eyes of God.

6

Down with foreskins! Jews are not the only group to have a strong emotional attachment to circumcision. The Muslims followed their lead in this regard, as in so many others. It is no surprise that the issue enlivened the debates of the early Christians. On the question of whether to require Gentile converts to be circumcised, Paul of Tarsus (himself circumcised) declared that Gentiles could choose to spare the real flesh in favor of "circumcision of the heart" (Acts 15:1–9). Why not the lips, eyes, ears, and any other body part that might be useful? This "circumcision in spirit and not in the letter" (Romans 2:29) allows today's Christian (except for the Coptic Christians of Egypt) to sport a hood over his glans penis and shield it from the open air.

How strange that excision — female circumcision, with several languages using the same term for both kinds of mutilation — of little girls should revolt the westerner but excite no disapproval when it is performed on little boys. Consensus on the point seems absolute. But ask your interlocutor to think about the validity of this surgical procedure, which consists of removing a healthy part of a nonconsenting child's body on nonmedical grounds — the legal definition of . . . mutilation.

When Margaret Somerville, a Canadian philosopher, tackled the subject in a spirit free of polemical intent, with rational arguments, comparison, and analysis, when she provided genuine anatomical, scientific, neuropathological, and psychological information to support her charge of mutilation, she was subjected to a savage bombardment by her compatriots. Following this national cry of outrage, she stood by her conclusions, but withheld final judgment and later agreed to legitimize circumcision for . . . religious reasons. (For readers' information, 60 percent of Americans are circumcised, 20 percent of Canadians, and 15 percent of Australians on nonreligious, supposedly hygienic grounds.)

Chinese foot-binding, African stretching of the neck through the use of successive layers of rings, tooth-filing, piercing of nose, ears, or lips among Amazonian tribes, Polynesian scarification and tattoos, and Peruvian flattening of the skull proceed from the same magical thinking as African clitoridectomy or Jewish and Muslim circumcision. Marking the body for religious reasons, ritual suffering in order to earn integration into the community, tribal practices designed to attract the benevolence of the gods — there are a thousand reasons, even without the help of psychiatry.

We shudder at other people's strange practices. In Russia, the Skoptsi were a religious sect, active between the eighteenth century and the 1920s, whose members advocated voluntary castration. In some areas of Polynesia, young boys are not circumcised but superincised: a flat stick is pushed under the foreskin, then a single cut is made to split the foreskin on the top side of the penis. In Australia, the rite of passage for young male Aborigines is subincision, which entails cutting the underside of the penis along its full length from meatus to scrotum. But we have no right to shudder. Logic, assumptions about the nature of being, and magical thinking are not that far apart. We tend to judge as barbaric whatever is not our own custom. But how can we accept and justify our own surgical mutilations while castigating those of others?

For mutilation is a fact. First of all according to the law, which forbids any surgical procedure unsupported by medical evidence of a genuine pathology. And the foreskin is not of itself a pathology. Then on physiological grounds: the area removed corresponds to half or two-thirds of the skin covering the penis. In an adult, this thirteen-square-inch zone — external and internal skin — concentrates more than a thousand nerve endings, or two hundred and fifty feet of nerves. In other words, the resection of one of the body's most innervated structures.

Moreover, the disappearance of the foreskin — which primitive peoples bury, eat, dry, pulverize, preserve — produces a circumferential scar that becomes keratinized over time: permanent exposure to the rubbing of fabric acts abrasively on the skin, which hardens and loses its sensitivity. The drying of this surface and the disappearance of lubrication diminishes the sexual comfort of both partners.

7

God loves the maimed. The Koran does not require or encourage circumcision, but does not condemn it. However, tradition holds that Muhammad was born circumcised! The Koran does not recommend female circumcision or infibulation. On the other hand, such mutilations are practiced in the eastern Horn of Africa, involving the three types of female circumcision. (There is what is known as "gentle sunna" — *sunna* means "tradition" or "way of the Prophet" — which removes the head of the clitoris; moderate sunna, or clitoridectomy, which removes the clitoris and all or parts of the labia minora, infibulation, or total removal of the clitoris, labia minora, and labia majora, followed by sewing together of the remaining tissue, often with thorns, leaving a matchstick-caliber opening for urination and menstruation.)

The Jews too approve of this mutilation as a sign of full membership in their community. More or less the only such sign, so rigid on this point (so to speak) are the rules. God demanded it of Abraham, who submitted at the age of ninety-nine; he ordered it for all male members of his household, even slaves; he fixed it for the eighth day after birth; and he made of it the mark of God's specific Covenant with his chosen people. Circumcision is so important that if it falls on the Sabbath, all prohibitions on activity associated with that day are lifted. Even in the case of a child who dies before the foreskin's removal, the mohel performs his ritual task.

Montaigne describes a circumcision in his *Travel Journal*: the circumciser uses a knife placed beforehand on the mother's pillow in order to attract a maximum of propitiatory favor. He pulls the penis, grasps the foreskin, pushes back the glans, and cuts the flesh without anesthetic to remove the prepuce. After swallowing the wine he has been swilling in his mouth, he sucks the wound—this ritual aspiration is called the *meziza*—and then, says the Talmud, he draws the blood remaining in the wound into his mouth. He spits three times. And the child enters the community: he is given his name. The rite, *meziza* included, has remained unchanged since Montaigne.

Reams have been written and spoken about this primitive rite and its survival over the centuries. Followed by many other psychiatrists, Freud—whose biographers stress his bad memories of circumcision—has speculated about suppression of the feminine in the male (circumcision) as an echo of the suppression of the male in the female (excision). He proposed that the ritual could represent a paternal warning to male offspring against Oedipal urges via the threat of an even more drastic castration; or else the reenactment of the severing of the umbilical cord as the symbol of a new birth. Of course, such factors probably enter into play, in addition to the ritual's goal of establishing community membership and identity. But there is also—and significantly—the theory formulated by two Jewish philosophers, Philo of Alexandria in *Questions and Answers in Genesis* and Moses Maimonides in his *Guide for the Perplexed*. They hold that the procedure aims at weakening the sexual organ. It refocuses the individual on the essential—preventing his erotic inclinations from eroding an energy better employed in the celebration of God; it saps lust and facilitates mastery of desire. To which we may add that it adulterates sexual possibilities and precludes pure sexual fulfillment for its own sake; it carves into the flesh and with the flesh a hatred of desire, libido, and life. It implies the victory of the death-fixated passions at the very spot where the life force is located. It reveals one of the modalities of the death instinct turned against others — as always, for their own good.

With Christianity and the decisions arrived at by Paul, circumcision became a mental matter. No more need of a brand on the flesh; mutilation corresponded to nothing real. All that counted was "a circumcision of the heart." Achieving this meant stripping the body of all the sins resulting from carnal desire. Hence baptism, of course, but also and above all the daily asceticism of a life dedicated to the imitation of Christ, of his suffering and his Passion. With the man from Tarsus, then, the faithful kept his penis intact, but he lost the totality of his body. Henceforth the believer must separate himself entirely from his body, in the same way as the circumciser does away with the foreskin. With the advent of Christianity, the death fixation was ready to poison the whole planet.

PART THREE

CHRISTIANITY

I

The Construction of Jesus

1

Enter the forgers. Clearly, Christ existed—like Ulysses and Zarathustra, of whom it is hardly important to know whether they were flesh-and-blood people living at a precise time and in an identifiable place. Jesus's existence has not been historically established. No contemporary documentation of the event, no archaeological proof, nothing certain exists today to attest to the truth of a real presence at this meeting point between two worlds, abolishing one and naming its successor.

No tomb, no shroud, no archives, except for a sepulcher invented in 325 by Saint Helena, mother of Constantine. She must have been a woman of supreme gifts, since we are also indebted to her for the discovery of Golgotha and of the *titulus*, the wooden fragment bearing the charges brought against Jesus. Then there is that piece of cloth from Turin, which carbon-14 dating has situated in the thirteenth century CE, and which only a miracle could have wrapped around Christ's corpse more than a thousand years earlier! Finally, there are of course two or three vague references in ancient texts—Flavius Josephus, Suetonius, and Tacitus—but in copies made several centuries after the alleged crucifixion of Jesus and—significantly—after the success of his supporters was assured.

On the other hand, how can we deny Jesus's conceptual

existence? For the same reason as Heraclitus's Fire, Empedocles's Friendship, Plato's Ideas, or Epicurus's Pleasure, Jesus functions wonderfully as an Idea on which a vision of the world is articulated, a conception of the real, a theory of a sinful past and of future salvation. We must leave it to lovers of impossible debates to decide on the question of Jesus's existence and address ourselves to the questions that matter. What exactly is this construction named Jesus? What was its purpose? Its aims? To serve whose interests? Who created this fiction? How did the myth take shape? How did this fable evolve in the centuries that followed?

The answers to these questions require a detour via a hysterical thirteenth apostle, Paul of Tarsus (a "bishop of foreign affairs," as he called himself), the author of a successful coup d'état (the emperor Constantine), and his successors (Justinian, Theodosius, Valentinian) who incited Christians to despoil, torture, and slaughter pagans and burn pagan libraries. From Jesus the invisible ectoplasm to Jesus the absolute master of an empire and then of the world, history evolves alongside the family tree of our civilization. It begins in a historical fog in Palestine, continues in Rome, and then settles into the gold, pomp, and purple of Christian power in Byzantium. It thrives even today in millions of minds formatted by the unbelievable story—built on the wind, on the improbable, on contradictions that the church has invariably dispelled through bouts of political violence.

So we know that most existing documents are skillfully executed forgeries. Burned libraries, repeated orgies of vandalism, accidental fires, Christian persecutions and autos-da-fé, earthquakes, the media revolution that replaced papyrus with parchment and presented the copyists, sectarian zealots of Christ, with a choice between the documents to be saved and those to be cast into outer darkness . . . Then there were the liberties taken by monks who established editions by ancient authors to which they added what they considered (with the hindsight of the conquerors) to be missing. It all added up to a philosophical nightmare.

Nothing of what remains can be trusted. The Christian archives are the result of ideological fabrication. Even the writings of Flavius Josephus, Suetonius, or Tacitus, who mention in a few hundred words the existence of Christ and his faithful in the first century of our era, obey the rules of intellectual forgery. When an anonymous monk recopied the *Antiquities* of the Jewish historian Josephus (arrested and turned into a double agent, a collaborator with Roman power), when that monk had before him the *Annals* of Tacitus or Suetonius's *Lives of Twelve Caesars* (and was astonished to find no mention of the story he believed in), he added a passage in his own hand and in all good faith, without shame and without a second thought, without wondering whether he was doing wrong or committing a forgery. He could do it the more easily because in those days one did not approach a book with the eye of a modern reader, concerned with the truth and respectful of the authenticity of the text and the author's rights . . . Even today we read these writers of antiquity in manuscripts copied several centuries after they were written, and contemporaneous with Christian copyists who redeemed their contents by arranging them to swim with the flow of history.

2

Hysteria crystallized. The ultra-rationalists—from Prosper Alfaric to Raoul Vaneigem—were probably right to deny the historical existence of Jesus. The closed corpus of texts, documents, and information we possess has been pored over for decades without ever producing a definitive conclusion or winning general approval. From Jesus the fiction to Jesus the Son of God the spectrum is broad, and the number of theories advanced offers equal justification to the aggressive atheism of the Rationalist Union and to the beliefs of Opus Dei.

What can be said is that the period in which Jesus supposedly appeared teemed with individuals of his kind, fire-breathing prophets, exalted madmen, hysterics convinced of the rightness of their grotesque truths, heralds of apocalypse. A history of that incandescent century would include countless such examples. The Gnostic philosophers themselves proceeded from the millenarian effervescence and fiery lunacy which marked that period of anguish, fear, and change in a world nobody understood. The old was crumbling, splintering, threatening to collapse. And that threatened collapse generated fears to which certain individuals responded with frankly irrational proposals.

On the banks of the Jordan, a region familiar to Jesus and his apostles, a man named Theudas claimed to be Joshua, the prophet of promised salvation (and also an etymon, or earlier form, of the name Jesus) ... Arriving from his native Egypt with four hundred followers, all spoiling for a fight, he sought an end to Roman power and claimed the ability to divide a river with his words alone, thus allowing his men to advance and put an end to the colonial power. Roman soldiers beheaded this poor man's Moses before he could display his hydraulic talents.

On another occasion, in 45, Jacob and Simon, sons of Judas the Galilean — yet another place-name familiar to Jesus — began an uprising that ended as badly as that led by their father in the year 6. The Romans crucified the rebels. Menahem, grandson of a family prolific in freedom fighters, followed in his ancestors' footsteps and rebelled in 66, triggering the Jewish War that ended in 70 with the destruction of Jerusalem.

In this first half of the first century, prophets, messiahs, and bearers of good tidings abounded. Some invited their supporters to follow them into the desert, there to witness prodigies and manifestations of divinity. A visionary from Egypt with forty thousand followers occupied the Garden of Olives, another area associated with Jesus. He claimed that his voice alone could shatter the walls of Jerusalem and lay the city open to his men. Once again, the Roman soldiery dispersed them. Multitudes of stories describe this Jewish determination to unseat Roman power with the sole help of religious, mystical, millenarian, and prophetic discourse announcing the good tidings predicted in the Old Testament.

Their resistance was legitimate: the wish to eject occupying armies seeking to force their language, laws, and customs on the conquered always justifies resistance, rebellion, refusal, and struggle, even armed struggle. But to believe — spurred only by their belief in the impossible — that they could oppose the world's most battle-tested troops, hardened in all the major conflicts of the day, trained and professional, possessing impressive equipment and full powers, merely transformed their magnificent struggle into battles lost in advance. Brandished like a battle flag before the Roman legions, God was outmatched.

Jesus thus embodied the period's hysteria, its belief that with goodwill alone and with action undertaken in the name of God, one could conquer and triumph. Breaking down walls with one's voice instead of with battering rams and siege artillery, crossing rivers with a word and not in military craft worthy of the name, opposing battle-hardened troops with hymns, prayers, and amulets and not with spears, swords, or cavalry: there was nothing there to trouble the Roman army of occupation. Mere scratches on the Roman hide.

The name of Jesus crystallized the diffuse and disparate energies wasted against the imperial machinery of the day. It furnished the emblematic patronymic of all Jews who (armed only with their will and the belief that their God could miraculously free them from the colonial yoke) refused to accept Roman occupation. But if God's power and his love of his people were so great, surely he could have spared them from having to endure, even briefly, the occupiers' unjust laws. Why would he tolerate such injustice before encompassing its abolition?

Thus, whether Jesus really lived or not must be reduced to the status of a mere hypothesis. This Jesus may well have been the son of a carpenter and a virgin. He may well have been born in Nazareth, he may well have given lessons as a child to the doctors of the law and spoken as a grown-up to fishermen, craftsmen, and other humble folk working on the shores of the Sea of Galilee. He may well have had more trouble with Jewish communities than with the Roman authorities, accustomed as they were to these sporadic and unimportant rebellions. But he synthesized, focused, sublimated, and crystallized what roiled the period and the history of the first century of his era. Jesus gave a name to Jewish rejection of Roman domination.

Etymology supports this claim. "Jesus" means "God saves, has saved, will save." There could be no clearer expression of the name's symbolic freight: his very name pointed to his destiny. The patronymic heralded a future that was already known, and implied that the adventure ahead was written somewhere in a corner of heaven. Thenceforth, history was content to allow its revelation to unfold day by day. How could one imagine that such a given name did not mandate the fulfillment of these earlier prophecies and potentialities? Or what better way of saying that the construction of Jesus implies a forgery reaching down to the smallest details, itself serving as a pretext and an occasion for this ontological catalyst?

3

Catalysis of the miraculous. Jesus thus concentrated in his name the messianic aspirations of the period. In the same way, he epitomized the ancient term *topoi*, used to describe one who was miraculous. For to be born of a virgin mother told of her good fortune by a heavenly or angelic figure, to perform miracles, to possess a charisma that attracted passionate followers — all these were commonplaces scattered throughout the literature of antiquity. Obviously, if we consider the Gospels as sacred texts we have no need to undertake the comparative study that would set them in context — that would set what is miraculous in the New Testament squarely within the logic of what was miraculous in antiquity. Jesus, as characterized by Paul of Tarsus, shares some similarities with Homer's Ulysses and with Encolpius, one of the protagonists in Petronius's *Satyricon*. The writer Philostratus wrote a biography of Apollonius of Tyana, which some have seen as an attempt to construct a rival to Jesus Christ. In other words, Jesus is an epic hero among other epic heroes.

Who was the author of Jesus? Mark. The evangelist Mark, first author of the wonderful adventures of the said Jesus. Probably the companion of Paul of Tarsus on his missionary wanderings, Mark wrote his text around the year 70. Nothing indicates that he knew Jesus in person, and small wonder! An open and obvious acquaintance would have been legible and discernible in Mark's writings. But we cannot frequent a fiction . . . All we can do is credit it with an existence, just like the beholder of a desert mirage who honestly believes in the truth and reality of the palm tree and oasis he sees in the burning heat. The evangelist therefore relates, in the hysterically incandescent tones of the period, this fiction whose authenticity he attests to in all good faith.

Mark wrote his Gospel with conversion in mind. His audience? People who needed convincing, people essentially indifferent to the Christ message who had to be attracted, captivated, and seduced. His text is in the unmistakable register of propaganda — which routinely resorts to artifice in order to please, persuade, and convince. Hence Mark's recourse to the miraculous. How else could he interest his readers in the commonplace story of a simple man, a man just like the general run of mortals? The Gospels recycle the literary fashions of pagan antiquity, which took it for granted that one embellished, decorated, and dressed up a man one wished to transform into a crowd-inspiring herald.

To convince ourselves of this, let us read the best-known pages of the New Testament, as well as Diogenes Laërtius's work *Lives, Teachings, and Sayings of Eminent Philosophers*. And let us give both texts equal literary status, that of historical writings composed by men not inspired by the Holy Spirit but eager to reach their readers and persuade them that they speak of exceptional individuals, of great men, of remarkable people. Pythagoras, Plato, Socrates, and Jesus seen by the same eye, the eye of a reader of ancient texts. What do we find?

A homogeneous world, identical authorial literary devices, the same compulsion to give their subject the relief and brilliance necessary for their readers' edification. Mark wants Jesus to be loved, Diogenes Laërtius wants the same for his great philosophers of the ancient tradition. Does the evangelist recount a life full of supernatural events? So does the biographer, stuffing his text with astonishing, extraordinary adventures. For both paint portraits of exceptional men. How could they be born, live, speak, think, and die like ordinary mortals?

To be specific: Mary, the mother of Jesus, conceives in virginity through the working of the Holy Spirit. Nothing extraordinary there: Plato too was born of a mother in the prime of life but endowed with an intact hymen. The archangel Gabriel told the carpenter's wife that she would give birth without the help of her husband, a good-natured fellow who agreed without making a fuss? What of it? The same Plato was gratified when Apollo himself called in person! Joseph's son is essentially the

Son of God? No problem: so is Pythagoras, whose disciples take him for Apollo in person, coming in directly from among the Hyperboreans. Jesus performs miracles, restores sight to the blind, life to the dead? Just like Empedocles, who also brings a corpse to life. Jesus excels in prophecies? So does Anaxagoras, who accurately predicts meteor showers.

Nor is this all. Does Jesus speak with inspired fervor, lending his voice to those greater, stronger, and more powerful than he? What about Socrates, inhabited and haunted by his daimon? Does the man destined to die on the cross teach his disciples, converting them with his oratorical talent and rhetoric? All the philosophers of antiquity, from Cynics to Epicureans, deploy a similar talent. Jesus's relations with John, his favorite disciple? The same bond links Epicurus and Metrodorus. The man from Nazareth speaks metaphorically, devours symbols, conducts himself as an enigma? Pythagoras too . . . Jesus never wrote, except for one occasion, with a stick that immediately erases the characters traced on the sand? It was the same for Buddha and Socrates, philosophers of the spoken word and of healing speech. Jesus died for his ideas? So did Socrates. Did the Messiah suffer through a night of decision at Gethsemane? Socrates, while serving in the Athenian army, had raptures or out-of-body experiences on the battlefield of Potidea in Thrace. Did Mary learn of her destiny as a virgin mother through a dream? Socrates dreamed of a swan and met Plato the next day.

Anything more? Yes, there is more . . . Clearly Jesus's body ingests symbols, but it does not digest them: quite impossible to excrete a concept . . . What extraordinary flesh, impervious to every caprice: the Messiah neither hungers nor thirsts, he never sleeps, does not defecate or copulate or laugh. Neither does Socrates. Remember the *Apology*, in which Plato plays the part of a character ignorant of the effects of alcohol, of fatigue, of sleeplessness. Pythagoras too appears clad in an anti-body, in spiritual flesh, in ethereal, incorruptible matter, untouched by the agonies of time, reality, and entropy.

Plato and Jesus both believe in a life after death, in the existence of an immaterial, immortal soul. After the Crucifixion, the wise man of Galilee returns among men. Well before him, Pythagoras used the same tactic. But more gradually, for Jesus let only three days go past, whereas the linen-shrouded philosopher waited two hundred and seven years before returning to Greater Greece. And there are so many other fables at work, whether about Greek philosophers or the Jewish seer, when the author of the myth wishes to convince his reader of the exceptional nature of his subject and of the character he is describing.

4

Construction outside history. The miraculous turns its back on history. One cannot rationally do battle with downpours of frogs or anvils, any more than with dead men emerging from their tombs to dine with their families. As for the paralyzed or sufferers from dropsy or hemorrhoids, suddenly restored to health by the stroke of a magic wand, we should steer clear of such topics. A word that heals, speech that cures, a gesture that leads to physiological miracles, is beyond us if we stick to the terrain of pure reason. To understand them we must think in terms of symbols, allegories, stylistic effects. Reading the Gospels requires the same approach as the classical prose of antiquity or Homeric poems: surrender to literary effect and renunciation of the critical spirit. The labors of Hercules signify extraordinary strength, the pitfalls of Ulysses illustrate his cunning and intelligence. The same goes for Jesus, whose reality and truth do not reside in their connection with established facts but in what they signify: the extraordinary power, the enormous strength of a man participating in a world bigger than he is.

The Englishman John Langshaw Austin coined the term *performative utterances* for a class of statements that *perform* an action as opposed to merely reporting or describing it. The Gospel genre is performative (to borrow Austin's term): simply declaring something is true creates its truth. The testamental stories are indifferent to the real, the probable, or the true. On the other hand, they deploy a power of language that by dint of affirmation creates what it declares. The prototype of the performative is the priest who proclaims a couple married. By the very act of articulating a formula he makes the event correspond with the words that signify it. Jesus did not obey history but the performativity of the testaments.

The evangelists despise history. Their apologetic choice permits it. There was no need for their stories to have actually happened, no point in having the real coincide with the formulation of the narrative given to it. It is enough for the words to produce their effect — to convert the reader and elicit from him agreement on the character and his teaching. Were the authors of the New Testament conscious of this myth? I do not think so. It was neither conscious, nor deliberate, nor systematically thought out. Mark, Matthew, Luke, and John did. not knowingly deceive. Neither did Paul. *They* were deceived, for they said that what they believed was true and believed that what they said was true. None of them had encountered Jesus physically, but all credited this fiction with a real existence, in no way symbolic or metaphorical. Clearly they believed what they wrote. Intellectual self-intoxication, ontological blindness.

All of them credited a fiction with reality. By believing in the fable they told, they infused it with more and more substance. Proof of the existence of a truth is often reducible to the sum of errors repeated until they become received truth. Thus the probable nonexistence of an individual, about whom one spins details over several centuries, finally evolves into a mythology to which assemblies, cities, nations, empires, and a whole planet subscribe. The evangelists created a truth by harping on fictions. Paul's militant ardor, Constantine's coup d'état, and the repressions of the Valentinian and Theodosian dynasties did the rest.

5

Tissue of contradictions. Construction of the myth took place over several centuries, with the connivance of diverse and multiple writers. They recopied one another, added, subtracted, omitted, and travestied, wittingly or not. It finally added up to a considerable corpus of contradictory texts. This leaves us with the ideological challenge of distilling the material for an unambiguous story from this mass. The result: we retain some evangelists as reliable and we set aside those who obtrude upon the hagiography or the credibility of the project. Hence the synoptic Gospels and the Apocrypha, and even the intertestamental writings, on which researchers have conferred the curious status of metaphysical extraterritoriality!

Was Jesus a vegetarian, or did he resuscitate a cooked rooster at a banquet? Did the infant Jesus strangle little birds in order to take upon himself the noble role of reviving them? Did he redirect the course of streams with his voice, make birds out of clay and then transform then into real flying creatures, or perform other, similar miracles before the age of ten? What of Jesus curing snakebites by blowing on the spot where the fangs had buried themselves? What of the death of his father Joseph at the age of one hundred and eleven? And the death of his mother Mary? And Jesus roaring with laughter—and so many other stories set down on several thousand pages of apocryphal Christian writings? Why were they left out? Because they compromised the goal of an unequivocal narrative . . . Who put together this corpus and decided on the canon? The church, its councils, and its synods toward the end of the fourth century of our era.

Yet this culling has failed to remove an incalculable number of *contradictions* and *improbabilities* in the body of the text of the synoptic Gospels. One example: according to John, the wooden tablet on which the judges set down the reasons for Jesus's sentence—the *titulus*—is nailed to the wood of the cross, above Christ's head. According to Luke, it hung around the neck of the condemned man. Mark remains vague, offering no deciding opinion . . . And if we compare Matthew, Mark, Luke, and John on this *titulus*, the writing on it says four different things . . . On the road to Golgotha, says John, Jesus bore his cross alone. Why then do the others add that Simon of Cyrene helped him? Depending on which Gospel we consult, Jesus appeared after his death to a single person, to a handful, or to a group . . . And those appearances occur at different locations . . . There is no end to this kind of contradiction in the body of the Gospels themselves, even though those writings were retained by the official church in order to manufacture a single unequivocal myth.

Beyond these contradictions, there are also *improbabilities*. For example the verbal exchange between the condemned man and Pontius Pilate, an important Roman governor. Apart from the fact that in such cases the interrogation is never undertaken by the great man but by his underlings, it is hard to envisage Pontius Pilate conversing with a Jesus who was not yet the Christ nor what history would make of him—a planetary star. At the time, Jesus would have been merely a common-law defendant, like so many others in the occupying power's jails. It is thus hardly probable that an exalted official would deign to talk with a petty local jailbird. Moreover, Pontius Pilate spoke Latin and Jesus Aramaic. How could they have conversed as John's

Gospel says they did, back and forth, without an interpreter, translator, or intermediary? Sheer myth.

That same Pilate could not have been a procurator as the Gospels call him, for the title of procurator was first used around the year 50 of our era. Pilate's title was prefect of Judaea. And this Roman official could not have been the mild, affable man, benevolently inclined toward Jesus, that the evangelists describe, unless the authors of these texts were intent on blaming the Jews for their hero's death and (in a mild case of collaboration) flattering the Roman occupiers . . . For what history relates of this prefect of Judaea is rather his cruelty, his cynicism, his ferocity, and his taste for repression. Tinkering with the facts.

Another improbability: the Crucifixion. History again bears witness: at that time Jews were not crucified but stoned to death. What was Jesus accused of? Calling himself King of the Jews. The fact is that Rome could have cared less about this business of messiahs and prophecy. Crucifixion implied a challenge to the imperial power, which the crucified man never explicitly posed. But let us concede that he was put on the cross. In that case, like all other such victims, he would have been left hanging there, at the mercy of wild beasts and dogs that had no trouble tearing the body to pieces since the crosses were barely over six feet tall. Then the remains were thrown into a common grave. In any case, there was no question of bodies being laid to rest in tombs. Fabrications.

The tomb then. Another improbability. A secret disciple of Jesus, Joseph of Arimathea, obtained his master's body from Pilate for entombment. Without the ritual mortuary cleansing? Unthinkable for a Jew . . . One of the evangelists mentions aromatic herbs, myrrh, aloe — some seventy pounds of it — and swaddling bands, common in Egyptian-style embalmment. The three others omit these details . . . But the solution to the contradictions appears to lie in the meaning of the name of Joseph's birthplace: Arimathea, which means "after death." On the performative principle, then, Joseph of Arimathea names the man who appears after Christ's death and cares for his body, a kind of first among the faithful. Sheer invention.

A comparative reading of the texts leads to a host of other questions. Why were the disciples absent on the day of the Crucifixion? How can we believe that after such a thunderbolt — the death of their master — they returned to their homes without reacting, meeting, or continuing the mission begun by Jesus? For each of them resumed his old trade in his village. Why did none of the twelve carry on the work which Paul — who had never known Jesus — took upon himself: spreading the gospel, bearing the good tidings as far afield as possible?

What can be said about all this? What can be done about these contradictions, these improbabilities — some texts rejected, others preserved but full of inventions, myths, approximations, all signs of a later, lyrical and militant construction of Jesus's story? We readily understand why, for centuries, the church categorically forbade any historical reading of the so-called sacred texts. It was simply too dangerous to read them in the way contemporaries read of Plato or Thucydides!

Jesus was thus a concept. His whole reality resides in that definition. Certainly he existed, but not as a historical figure — unless it was in such an improbable manner that whether he existed or not is of little importance. He existed as a crystallization of the aspirations of his era and of the reverence for the miraculous common to the authors of antiquity, articulated in the performative register that creates by naming. The evangelists wrote a story. In it they narrated less the past of one man than the future of a religion. A trick born of the rational mind: they created the myth and were created by it. The believers invented their creation, then made it the object of a cult: the very essence of willing self-deception.

II

The Pauline Contamination

1

Ravings of a hysteric. Paul took hold of this concept, clothed him, and supplied him with ideas. The early Jesus hardly ever spoke out against the customs of everyday life. Two sentences (Mark 7:15 and 10:7) show him unopposed to marriage and indifferent to the appeal of the ascetic ideal. We seek in vain for rigid prescriptions concerning the body, sexuality, sensuality. This relative benevolence toward the things of everyday life went hand in hand with praise for and the practice of gentleness. Paul of Tarsus transforms Jesus's silence on these questions into a deafening hubbub thundering out hatred of the body, of women, and of life. Christianity's radical antihedonism proceeds from Paul — not from Jesus.

Initially Paul, a hysterical, fundamentalist Jew, had taken pleasure in the persecution and brutal treatment of Christians. When fanatics stoned Stephen to death Paul was one of their number. And on other such occasions, it seems. His conversion on the road to Damascus in 34 arose from pure hysterical pathology: he fell to the ground (not from a horse, as Caravaggio and the painterly tradition have it), was blinded by an intense light, heard the voice of Jesus, and remained sightless for three days, neither eating nor drinking throughout that time. He recovered his sight after the laying on of hands by Ananias — a Christian sent by God *in missi dominici* . . . Paul at once sat down to table, ate, and then set out on long years of fevered proselytizing all over the Mediterranean basin.

The medical diagnosis seems clear. Such crises are invariably witnessed and attested to by other people — and this was the case with Paul. His fall, the blindness which modern experts have diagnosed as hysterical (unless it was just a passing loss of vision), his deafness, his three-day loss of the sense of smell and of appetite, his tendency to mythomania (he claimed that Jesus spoke to him in person), and after all that his thirty-year mission to dramatize an imaginary character, the elect of God, chosen by him to transform the world . . . it all adds up to histrionics, to moral exhibitionism. Indeed his crisis reads unmistakably like a passage from a manual of psychiatry, chapter heading Neuroses, subsection Hysteria . . . This was true hysteria . . . a hysterical conversion!

2

Infecting the world with neuroses. How are we to live with our neuroses? By making them the model for the world to follow, by inflicting our neuroses on the world . . . Paul created the world in his own image. A deplorable image, fanatical, moving with a hysteric's irresolution from enemy to enemy — first Christians, then Gentiles — sick, misogynistic, masochistic . . . How could we fail to see in our own world a reflection of this portrait of a man so clearly controlled by the death instinct? For the Christian world eagerly experiments with such ways of being and doing — ideological brutality, intellectual intolerance, the cult of poor health, hatred of the vital body, contempt for women, pleasure in inflicting pain, disdain for the here and now in the name of a gimcrack beyond.

Small, thin, bald, and bearded, Paul of Tarsus provides no details on the illness he metaphorically describes. In 2 Corinthians 12:7, he confides that Satan gave him *a thorn in the flesh* — an expression later adopted by Kierkegaard. No details, except for one occasion when he draws attention to his haggard appearance while addressing the Galatians — after he had suffered a beating that left visible marks . . . So that for centuries critics have piled up theories on the nature of that thorn. It is hard to resist offering a solemn inventory of their diagnoses: arthritis, renal colic, tendonitis, sciatica, gout, tachycardia, angina pectoris, itchy rash, skin sores, boils, eczema, leprosy, shingles, plague, rabies, erysipelas, gastritis, intestinal cramps, kidney stones, chronic ear infection, sinusitis, bronchitis, bladder infection, urinary retention, Maltese fever, filariosis, malaria, pilariosis, ringworm, pilonidal cyst, headache, gangrene, suppuration, abscesses, chronic hiccups (!), convulsions, epilepsy . . . His joints, tendons, nerves, heart, stomach, bowels, anus, ears, sinus, bladder, head, all were involved.

All except the sexual register . . . The etiology of hysteria includes a weakened — if it exists at all — libidinal potential. Disturbances arising from sexuality, a tendency for example to see it everywhere, to indulge in extremes of eroticism . . . How can we not recall all this when Paul's pen drips ad nauseam a hatred, a contempt, a permanent mistrust for the things of the body? His loathing of sexuality, his praise of chastity, his worship of abstinence, his approval of the widowed condition, his passion for celibacy, his appeal to his listeners to conduct themselves as he did (clearly expressed in the First Epistle to the Corinthians 7:8), his reluctant consent to marriage, but only as the best of bad choices (he would have preferred renunciation of all things corporeal). These are all obvious symptoms of hysteria.

The above conclusions are borne out by a number of undeniable facts, foremost among them Paul's failure to acknowledge any kind of deep-seated pathology whatsoever. We can frankly admit to abdominal pain or arthritic joints. Rampant skin disorders are noticeable, as are repeated hiccups. It is less easy to admit to *sexual impotence*, which can however be very obliquely hinted at under the cover of metaphor (the "thorn" accomplished this). Sexual impotence or any fixation of the libido on a socially indefensible object — a mother, a human being of the same sex, or any other perversion in the Freudian sense of the term. Freud locates the roots of hysteria in the struggle against repressed terrors of sexual origin, and their partial realization in the form of a conversion — in the psychoanalytical sense, but the other meaning also fits.

There is a kind of law that appears to have held sway over the planet since the beginning of time. In homage to La Fontaine, let us call it the "fox and grapes complex": it consists in making a virtue of necessity in order to avoid losing face. Life inflicts sexual impotence or a problematic libido on Paul of Tarsus. His response? He gave himself the illusion of freedom, of autonomy and independence, by believing that he had freed himself from what defined him. Celibacy was not imposed upon him; it was a choice, a decision he had made. Unable to lead a sex life worthy of the name, Paul declares null and void all forms of sexuality for himself (of course) but also for the rest of the world. A desire to be like everyone else by demanding that everyone else emulate him, whence his determination to make all humankind bow to the rule of his own limiting circumstances.

3

A weakling's revenge. This logic is clearly apparent in a proclamation of the Second Epistle to the Corinthians (12:210), in which he affirms, "For the sake of Christ, then, I am content with weaknesses, hardships, insults, persecutions and calamities, for when I am weak, then I am strong." This comes close to a straightforward acknowledgment of the logic of compensation that held captive the hysteric who collapsed on the road to Damascus. From the starting point of his own dilapidated physique, Paul militated for a world that resembled him.

His hatred of self turned into a vigorous hatred of the world and all its concerns: life, love, desire, pleasure, sensations, body, flesh, joy, freedom, independence, autonomy. There is no mystery about Paul's masochism. He saw his whole life through the prism of difficulties: he loved problems, he rejoiced in them, craved them, longed for them, manufactured them. In the epistle in which he confirms his taste for humiliation, he makes a list of what he suffered in order to preach to the crowds: five floggings—thirty-nine strokes each time—three scourgings with rods, one stoning at Lystria in Anatolia—where he actually came close to dying, his body being left for dead on the ground—three drownings, one of them involving a day and a night immersed in icy water—without mentioning the dangers endemic to travel over roads infested with brigands, dangerous river crossings, the fatigue of marches beneath a leaden sun, countless nights without sleep, forced fasting, thirst, the cold of Anatolian nights. Add to those his prison terms, two years in a dungeon, exile...A masochist's dream!

Sometimes he found himself in humiliating situations. On the Agora in Athens, for example, where he tried to convert Stoic and Epicurean philosophers to Christianity by speaking of the resurrection of the body, sheer nonsense for Hellenes. The disciples of Zeno and Epicurus laughed in his face, but he took their insults without flinching ... On another occasion, to flee popular rage and the anger of the ethnarch of Damascus, he escaped in a basket lowered from a window down the city ramparts. Since ridicule never kills, Paul survived.

This hatred of self Paul transformed into hatred of the world—and of the need to be able to live with it, partly to dispel it, keep it at a distance. The opposite of what tormented him would henceforth haunt his reality. The contempt of the individual Paul for his body, so incapable of scaling the heights that it might have aspired to, became a discrediting of all flesh in general, of all bodies and of all people. In 1 Corinthians 9:27 he confesses, "I pummel my body and I subdue it," and he asks of men, "Pummel your body and subdue it. Do as I do . . ."

Whence, as we know, praise of celibacy, chastity, and abstinence. No Jesus in all this; just the revenge of the weak. In 1 Corinthians 15:8–9, Paul says, "Last of all, as to one untimely born, he appeared also to me," and he feels unworthy to be numbered among the apostles: "I am the least of the apostles . . . I am not meet to be called an apostle."

Unable to have women? He loathes them . . . Impotent? He despises them. An excellent occasion for recycling the misogyny of Jewish monotheism, later bequeathed to Christianity and Islam. The first verses of the first book of the Bible set the tone: Genesis radically and irrevocably condemns woman, the first sinner, the source of all the world's evil. And Paul embraced this disastrous, this infinitely disastrous idea as his own.

Hence the prohibitions rained upon them throughout the Pauline writings, epistles, and acts: fragile beyond repair, women's destiny is to obey men in silence and submission. Eve's descendants must hold their husbands in awe and refrain from teaching or from trying to control the supposedly stronger sex. Temptresses, seductresses, they may of course hope for salvation, but only in, through, and for motherhood. Two thousand years of punishments visited on women simply to exorcise the neuroses of a weakling!

4

In praise of slavery. Paul the masochist articulates the ideas with which Christianity will one day triumph. These include delight in the joys of submission, obedience, passivity, total subservience to the powerful on the false grounds that all power comes from God and that the social position of the poor, the modest, and the humble emanates from a heavenly will and a divine decision.

God, good, compassionate, etc., approves the diseases of the diseased, the poverty of the poor, the tortures of the tortured, the servility of servants. Addressing the Romans in the heart of their empire, Paul spoke with most timely enthusiasm of the need to obey magistrates, officials, the emperor. He called on everyone to pay his due: taxes to the tax inspectors, fear to the army, the police, and dignitaries, honor to senators, ministers, monarchs.

For all power came from God and proceeded from him. Disobeying the powerful was rebelling against God. Hence his extolling of submission to order and authority. Hence his injunction to flatter the powerful, legitimize and justify the destitution of the poor, respect those wielding the sword. The church now entered a partnership with the state, which from the start set it squarely on the side of tyrants, dictators, and autocrats.

Sexual impotence transfigured into power over the world, the inability to enjoy women turned into an engine of hatred for women, contempt for self transformed into love of one's tormentors, hysteria sublimated into the construction of a social neurosis — what wonderful material for a psychiatric portrait! Jesus took on substance by becoming Paul's hostage. Bland and without substance on questions of society, sexuality (and with good reason, for ectoplasm does not become flesh overnight), and politics, the man of Nazareth assumed ever clearer features. Construction of the myth went on apace, gaining ever greater precision.

Paul read no Gospel during its author's lifetime. He himself never knew Jesus. Mark wrote the first Gospel, either in the very last years of Paul's life or after his death. Beginning with the second half of the first century of our era, the teacher from Tarsus propagated the myth, visited multitudes of men, told his fables to thousands of individuals in dozens of countries: the Asia Minor of pre-Socratic philosophers, the Athens of Plato and Epicurus, the Italy of the Epicureans of the Campagna or the Stoics of Rome, the Sicily of Empedocles . . . He visited Cyrene, the city where hedonism was born with Aristippus. He also made a detour via Alexandria, Philo's city. Everywhere, he contaminated. Soon Paul's disease infected the whole body of the empire.

5

At war with intelligence. Hatred of self, of the world, of women, of freedom: Paul of Tarsus added to this deplorable roster hatred of intelligence. Genesis had already preached loathing of knowledge, for we must never forget that tasting the fruit of the Tree of Knowledge was the original sin, the unforgivable fault transmitted from generation to generation. Wishing to know, and not remaining content with the obedience and faith demanded by God — that was what was unforgivable. To rival God in knowledge, to prefer education and intelligence to the imbecility of the obedient, these were so many mortal sins.

And Paul's education? Nonexistent, or almost: the Old Testament and the certainty that God spoke through it . . . His intellectual training? We have no idea whether he was a bright student or undertook prolonged studies . . . Rabbinical training, in all likelihood . . . His profession? Maker and seller of tents for nomads . . . His verbal style? Heavy, derivative, complex, oral in fact. His Greek? Clumsy, graceless, possibly dictated to him as he went about his manual trade. Some have even concluded that he could not write . . . The opposite of a Philo of Alexandria, the philosopher and Paul's contemporary.

This uneducated man, openly scoffed at by the Stoics and Epicureans in the public square of Athens, faithful to his technique of making a virtue of necessity, transformed his lack of culture into a hatred of culture. He called on the Corinthians and Timothy to turn their backs on "the addled and foolish questionings" and "hollow frauds" of philosophy. The alleged correspondence between Paul and Seneca is clearly a forgery of the first order. Paul was not a learned man and he addressed not philosophers but his peers. His audience, throughout his wanderings around the Mediterranean, was composed of humble folk and never included intellectuals, philosophers, men of letters. In the second century, Celsus wrote *Alethes logos* ("True Discourse" or "The True Word"), a polemic against Christianity, in which he characterized Christians as tanners, cleaners, craftsmen, carpenters, and the like. So Paul did not need culture. Demagoguery was enough, and with it its perpetual ally: hatred of intelligence.

III

The Totalitarian Christian State

1

Hysteria (continued). Just as French rationalism was shaped on the basis of three dreams recalled by Descartes (!), so Christianity strode on to the historical stage with an event recalling the purest pagan traditions: astrological signs . . . The year is 312. Constantine is advancing on Rome. He is fighting his rival Maxentius, from whom he hopes to wrest Italy. His conquest of the north of the peninsula was lightning-fast: Turin, Milan, and Verona fell easily into his hands. The emperor was an old hand at direct contacts with the absolute: in the temple of Grand in the Vosges mountains of Gaul, Apollo appeared in person to promise him a reign of thirty years. At the time, paganism did not trouble him. Indeed he was a devotee of *Sol Invictus*, the Unconquered Sun.

But this time the message was transformed. Like Paul struck down on the road to Damascus, Constantine saw in the heavens a sign announcing that he would conquer in its name. And—a detail of some importance—his troops also witnessed the event: all of them saw the same holy talisman! Eusebius of Caesarea, the prince's house-trained intellectual, and furthermore a bishop, a peerless forger, an outstanding specialist in Christian apologia, gives us a detailed interpretation of this sign, which was in the form of a luminous cross above the sun. Moreover—

here Eusebius warms to his task — a celestial text promised that
the emperor would win his war against Maxentius by invoking
the sign. Two precautions are better than one: the next night Jesus appeared in a dream, teaching his protégé the sign of the
cross that would prove useful in winning every one of his battles,
provided he armed himself beforehand with the sign. We readily
understand that once he became the most Christian emperor,
Constantine, imbued as he now was with philosophical rationality, turned savagely on astrology, magic, and paganism. All that
philosophical rationality made him unreasonable.

A few days later, he won. Naturally . . . Maxentius was
drowned beneath the Milvius bridge on October 28, 312.
Helped by the ghost of the Nazarene, Constantine became master of Italy. He marched into Rome, disbanded the Praetorian
Guard, and gave Pope Miltiades the Lateran Palace. Admittedly,
the Christian kingdom was not of this world, but why should it
be neglected, especially when it offered the occasion for pomp,
gold, purple, money, power, dominance, all of them virtues naturally deduced from the messages of the carpenter's son?

And that sign? Was it a text message from Christ or a collective hallucination? A message from Jesus, riveted in celestial eternity but with a keen eye for the most trivial goings-on in the
here and now, or further proof that in this age of anguish a fis-
sured world was susceptible to communal neuroses and divinely
mandated hysteria? A proof of regeneration or a mark of decadence? Christianity's first step or one of paganism's last? The misery of men without God — and more miserable still with him.

Today this sign is interpreted in rational and even ultra-ra-
tionalist manner: not as astrology but astronomy. Contemporary
scientists propose a hysterical (and thus religious) reading of an
event reducible to the simplest of causalities. On October 10,
312, eighteen days before the glorious victory over Maxentius,
Mars, Jupiter, and Venus stood in the Roman sky in a configura-

tion that encouraged interpretation of the sign as a fabulous presage. Delirium completed the job.

While Constantine was not a monument of bookish culture, he is acknowledged to have been a cunning strategist, an astute politician. Did he really believe in the power of the sign from Christ? Or did he exploit it skillfully and stage-manage it for opportunistic ends? A pagan familiar with the workings of magic, a believer, like everyone else in this period of antiquity, in the claims of astrology, the emperor may also have counted on obtaining the maximum possible support from his troops, who included a large and loyal Christian contingent respectful of power and never questioning orders.

His father, Constantius Chlorus, had pursued a fruitful policy of tolerance toward Christ's faithful. Was Constantine (counseled by active Christian intriguers) emulating that politically astute policy? Did he have a visionary's glimpse of the possibilities inherent in exploiting this interesting force, annexing it to his cause through the award of timely and generous gifts that tied them to his project — let us call it Gramscian — of unifying the empire? In any event, in these early years of the fourth century, that unlikely candidate Jesus (his praises shouted from the rooftops by Paul) became the emblematic instrument in the fanfare of a new empire.

2

Constantine's coup d'état. Constantine's coup was masterly. We still live today with its fatal heritage. Naturally he understood what he could obtain from a people obedient to Paul's call for submission to the temporal authorities, for uncomplaining acceptance of dire poverty, for obedience to the magistrates and officials of the empire, for disapproval of temporal disobedience as an insult flung in God's face, for accepting slavery, deceit, and the existence of social disparities. Examples of Christian martyr-dom and Christian behavior in the relatively rare persecutions they endured were clear indications to the powerful of how useful this rabble could be to the legally untouchable figures at the summit of the state.

Constantine accordingly heaped them with assurances. To put it another way, he bought them. And the policy worked . . . He wrote into Roman law new articles that satisfied the Christians and made official the ascetic ideal. He enacted harsh laws against the degradation of social mores that marked the late empire, against unfettered sexuality, the triumph of the circus games, and the orgiastic practices of certain pagan cults. He made divorce procedures more difficult, forbade possession of concubines, made prostitution a crime, and condemned sexual dissipation. At the same time he abrogated the law forbidding the celibate to inherit. So, after a few timely demises, people of the church could now legally fill their pockets. He did not outlaw slavery, despite the wishes of Christ's sectarians, but mitigated some of its harshness . . . Magic, on the other hand, was banned, and so were gladiatorial combats. At the same time, Constantine ordered the building of Saint Peter's and of other, secondary basilicas. The Christians rejoiced: their kingdom was henceforth of this world.

At about this time Fausta, the new Christian's second wife, persuaded him that her stepson had tried to seduce her. Without waiting for proof, he sent his cutthroats to torture and then behead his own son, as well as a nephew also implicated in the "plot." When he realized the empress had deceived him, he sent the same gang in. They took advantage of Fausta's visit to her bath to release a flow of boiling water . . . Infanticide, uxoricide, homicide: the most Christian emperor bought his salvation and the church's silence with a host of gifts: tax exemptions for church landholdings, generous subsidies, and the creation of new churches — Saint Paul and Saint Lawrence. All variations on the theme of love for one's neighbor.

Thus benevolently disposed, afloat in gifts, fattened and enriched by gratuities from the prince, the clergy conferred full powers upon him at the Council of Nicaea in 325. The pope was absent, for reasons of what we would today call health. There, Constantine proclaimed himself the "thirteenth apostle," thus endowing Paul of Tarsus with a strong right sword arm. And what an arm! Church and state formed what Henri-Irénée Marrou, a historian scarcely to be suspected (being a Christian) of anticlericalism, atheism, or left-wing leanings, has called a "totalitarian state." The first Christian state.

While this was going on, Constantine's mother Helena, concerned for the salvation of the son who had authorized the axe and the boiling water, undertook a journey to Palestine. A devout Christian, and magically inspired, she discovered there three wooden crosses with one of the famous *tituli*, clearly Christ's. The site of Calvary was most opportunely buried under the temple of Aphrodite, which of course had to be destroyed .. . The eighty-year-old Helena spent the considerable sums given her by Constantine on the building of three churches: the Holy Sepulchre, the Garden of Olives, and the Nativity, where she put her relics on display. Even if those sites were "discovered" for that specific purpose, without a shred of historical justification or topographical evidence, their cult has endured . . . To repay the emperor for this major asset, and deciding that God had pardoned his crimes, the church made his mother a heroine of its mythology. As a result, Helena was canonized, becoming the first Roman empress to enter the thanatophilic Christian pantheon.

Constantine died on the day of Pentecost, May 22, 337. A few weeks before his death, he was baptized by the bishop of

Nicomedia, an ally of Arius. The Council of Nicaea had condemned Arianism as a heresy, yet the matter was not closed, and the disputes continued. Constantine's choice of an Arian bishop to perform the ceremony was a mark of the emperor's political genius. By this gesture, he reconciled Orthodox and Arian Christians, thus restoring the unity of the church. Even on his deathbed, he had an eye to the future, especially his post regnum. Even after death, he strove to preserve the unity of the empire.

Like many tyrants, Constantine was unable to settle the question of a successor. He left behind a power vacuum and a disorganized group of high officials of church and state. For more than three months at the height of summer, May 22 to September 9, the various ministers (civil, military, and ecclesiastical) reported daily to the imperial corpse as it lay in state. This neurotic behavior was a preview of the later cult of the dead, evidenced by Christian fascination with corpses and relics.

3

From victims to victimizers. Christians had admittedly suffered persecution, but it was not always as severe as the Vulgate claims. The figures for those devoured by lions in the arena have been substantially lowered by historians eager to leave the field of Christian apologetics and do their work conscientiously. Tens of thousands of dead, wrote Eusebius of Caesarea, Constantine's domestic intellectual. Modern estimates come closer to three thousand—by way of comparison, ten thousand gladiators fought to the death simply to celebrate the end of the war against the Dacians in 107.

What defines totalitarian regimes today corresponds point by point with the Christian state as it was constructed by Constantine's successors: use of constraint, torture, acts of vandalism, destruction of libraries and symbolic sites, unpunished murders, ubiquitous propaganda, the leader's absolute power, the remolding of the whole of society along the government's ideological lines, extermination of opponents, monopoly of legal violence and means of communication, abolition of the frontier between private life and the public sphere, overall politicization of society, destruction of pluralism, bureaucratic organization, expansionism—all signs of totalitarianism from its origins, as well as the totalitarianism of the Christian Empire.

The emperor Theodosius I proclaimed Catholicism the state religion in 380. Twelve years later he categorically banned pagan worship. Nicaea had already set the tone. In 449 Theodosius II and Valentinian III ordered the destruction of everything that might excite God's wrath or wound Christian hearts. That definition was apparently broad enough to include multiple exactions in every field. Tolerance, love of one's neighbor, and forgiveness of sins had their limits.

Constantine had previously been in contact with pagan intellectuals such as Nicagoras of Athens, Hermogenes, and Sopatros, but as of the year 330, he severed his relationship with them. That got the ball rolling. In 335, Sopatros was executed for witchcraft, and writings by the Neoplatonist philosopher Porphyry (who had died in 305) were burned. Such autos-da-fé came thick and fast, one much like the other. The emperor Theodosius I took severe measures against all heretics, including Montanists, Eumonians, and, above all, Arians. In 435, during the reign of Theodosius II, Nestorius the patriarch of Constantinople was exiled to Egypt and all of his writings were consigned to the flames, wherever they could be found in both the Eastern and Western Empire. Another symbol of the repression of rational thought by irrational religion was the murder of Hypatia of Alexandria, the first female mathematician known to history. A Hellenized Egyptian, she was a Neoplatonist, mathematician, astronomer, and teacher, one of the foremost intellects of her time. During an antipagan riot in 415, a Christian mob pulled Hypatia from her carriage and dragged her through the streets to a church. She was stripped naked, and the flesh was scraped from her bones with sharp oyster shells and broken tiles. After tearing her body to pieces, the mob burned her mutilated remains. A sterling example of the Christian belief in love of one's neighbor!

4

The name of the law. Lawmakers are quick to legitimize oppression and confer on it the force of law under the label of justice. Thus, legal formulas are devised to cover all manner of crimes and misdeeds, persecutions and assassinations. The reader should consult the Theodosian Code if he needs proof that the law *always* supports the ruling caste's domination over the masses. In United States history, the black codes (referring to laws enacted in the former Confederate states after the Civil War) were intended to assure the continuance of white supremacy. A review of the anti-Semitic laws passed by the Vichy government during the Second World War would dispel any remaining doubts.

To be specific: in 380 the law condemned non-Christians to "infamy," in other words rescinded their civic rights and therefore their chances of participating in the life of the city, for example in teaching or the law. It decreed the death sentence for all who threatened the persons or the goods of Catholic ministers and their places of worship. Meanwhile, Christians destroyed pagan shrines and confiscated, looted, and ravaged temples and their furnishings with the blessings of authorities backed by the legal texts.

The ban on pagan practices proceeded alongside a merciless battle against heresies, defined as what did not conform to imperial decrees. Meetings were forbidden, so of course was Manichaeism, and Jews were persecuted under the same heading as magic or dissolute morals. The law encouraged informers. It forbade marriage between Jews and Christians . . . It authorized the confiscation of non-Christian goods. Paul of Tarsus very early pointed down this path, for in the Acts of the Apostles (19:19) he admits his presence at a burning of supposedly magical books.

In keeping with the tactics of Constantine's mother, Catholic churches replaced the razed temples. Here and there, synagogues and Gnostic shrines went up in flames. Often-priceless statues were destroyed and broken up and their fragments recycled into Christian buildings. Places of worship were so utterly ravaged that their debris served for a time to repave roads and build highways and bridges. An index of how widespread the damage was: in Constantinople, the temple of Aphrodite served as a parking space for horse-drawn vehicles. Sacred trees were uprooted.

From the end of the eighth century BCE and for the next thousand years, the oracle of Apollo at Didyma near Miletus (on the west coast of Turkey) was second in importance only to Delphi. In 303 AD, the emperor Diocletian consulted an oracle to ask why his soothsayers' methods were not working. When he sought advice, the gods did not answer. The oracle said that the Christian God was too powerful and was preventing the Roman gods from communicating. Whereupon Diocletian initiated what was to be the last and greatest persecution of Christians by the Roman Empire. Ultimately, that sealed Didyma's fate. Its long history ended abruptly when Constantine the Great converted to Christianity and, blaming the oracle for the persecutions, retaliated by closing the temple of Apollo at Didyma and executing all the priests.

Subsequent emperors followed suit. A text dated February 19 of the year 356 decreed the death sentence for persons convicted of worshipping idols or participating in sacrifices. In consequence, Christians in Antioch seized a prophet of Apollo and tortured him. At Scythopolis in Palestine, Domitius Modestus conducted "interrogations" of the top officials and intellectual leaders of Antioch and Alexandria. His aim was to leave no educated man alive. Many Neoplatonist philosophers perished in this ferocious repression. In his *Homily on Statues*, Saint John Chrysostom condoned physical violence in certain circumstances and explicitly wrote that "Christians are the repositories of public order."

At Alexandria in 389, Christians attacked the Serapeum (temple of Serapis) and the Mithraeum (temple of Mithras). The idols inside were removed, publicly displayed, and mocked. The pagan faithful protested ("particularly the philosophers," according to contemporary sources), and riots ensued with many deaths on both sides. At Suffectum (Sufes in modern-day Sbiba, Tunisia) around 401, Christian monks destroyed a statue of Hercules, the patron god of the city, and sixty people died in the resulting riots. Encouraged by the aforementioned John Chrysostom, bands of monks ransacked the shrines on the Phoenician mountains. All this was the consequence of Paul's call to despise culture, knowledge, books, and intelligence.

5

Vandalism, autos-da-fé, and the culture of death. Like Paul of Tarsus, Christians were convinced that academic learning hindered access to God. All books (not just books by authors accused of heresy, such as Arius, Mani, and Nestorius) were at risk of being burned. Neoplatonist works were condemned as books of magic and divination. People who possessed libraries feared for their safety. In 370 the citizens of Antioch, terrified of persecution, preempted the Christian commissars and burned their own books in the public square. As for the Great Library of Alexandria, its daughter library was housed in the Serapeum, a temple dedicated to the god Serapis. In 391, by order of the bishop of Alexandria, the temple was leveled and the library went up in smoke.

In 591, the Neoplatonic school in Athens was closed, and the Christian Empire confiscated its holdings. Paganism had survived in the Greek capital for centuries. Plato's teachings could point to a thousand years of uninterrupted transmission. The philosophers set out on the road to Persian exile. What a triumph for Paul of Tarsus, once mocked by Stoics and Epicureans in the home of philosophy during his attempt at proselytization. The posthumous victory of God's weakling and his disastrous neuroses! A culture of death, of hatred, of contempt and intolerance . . . At Constantinople in 562, Christians arrested "Hellenes" — an insulting name — parading them through the city to the accompaniment of hoots and jeers. On Kenogion Square, Christians lit a huge bonfire and tossed the philosophers' books and the images of their gods into the flames.

Justinian hammered in the final nail, stiffening Christian legislation against the unorthodox. Non-Christians were forbidden to bequeath their wealth to pagans; it was forbidden to testify in court against the church's followers; forbidden to own Christian slaves; forbidden to draw up a legal deed; forbidden to profess freedom of conscience (!). And in 529 Justinian made it mandatory for pagans to take instruction in the Christian religion and then undergo baptism, on pain of exile and confiscation of their goods; he forbade those converted to the religion of brotherly love to return to paganism; forbade them to teach or to draw official pensions. For at least a thousand years, philosophizing became dangerous . . . Now—just as in every succeeding period—theocracy stood unveiled as the opposite of democracy.

PART FOUR
THEOCRACY

I

Selective Exploitation of the Texts

1

Historical extraterritoriality. Everyone knows of the existence of monotheism's three books, but very few know their dates of origin, their authors, or the ups and downs attendant on establishing the three texts — the absolutely final, immutable texts. For the Torah, Old Testament, New Testament, and Koran took an unthinkably long time to emerge from history and claim that their texts issued from God alone, that they had no need to explain themselves to those who entered their paper temples armed only with faith, unburdened of reason and intelligence.

One instance: in a library specializing in the history of religions, scholars face great problems hunting down dates of composition and origin for the body of texts that make up the holy books. As if even historians, men of reason, were indifferent to the conditions in which these texts were composed. Yet knowledge of those conditions is essential to our understanding of the texts. Take Genesis for example. It was contemporaneous with which book, which author? The *Epic of Gilgamesh* or the *Iliad*? Hesiod's *Theogony* (*Origin of the Gods*), the *Upanishads* or Confucius's *Analects*?

We address the opening texts of the Torah, the Old Testament, and the Bible knowing nothing more about them than their existence. We are not even aware of our lack of knowledge of the subject. For these pages, like all that follow, enjoy extraterritorial historical status. This methodological quirk confirms the pious in their belief that these books have no human author, no established birth date, that they fell from heaven one day in miraculous fashion or were dictated to an inspired man in a divine voice impervious to time and entropy, immune to growth and corruption. A mystery!

For centuries, the clerics banned direct reading of the texts. Questioning their historical veracity was all too human, they felt—and we still live more or less under the shadow of that veto. Those who serve religions know intuitively that direct contact and a reading that is both intelligent and imbued with common sense will expose the incoherence of these pages. They were written by a considerable number of people after centuries of oral transmission, extending over an extremely long historical span, the whole having been copied a thousand times. The scribes who copied them were often unscrupulous or foolish; they could even be genuine and outright forgers. When we cease to approach their work as sanctified objects we swiftly drop the illusion that they are holy. Hence the need to read them properly, pen in hand.

2

Twenty-seven centuries in the making. When we finally become aware of these facts, our surprise persists. For example, the French edition of the Bible produced by Emile Osty and Joseph Trinquet proposes a ten-century time frame for its composition—between the twelfth and second centuries before Jesus Christ. In other words, between the last Egyptian books of wisdom—the royal scribe Ani of Thebes, for example—and the

New Academy of the Skeptic philosopher Carneades. Jean Soler —an excellent demolisher of myths—gives us his own estimate: between the fifth and the first centuries before the common era, in other words between Socrates and Lucretius. And some historians shrink the time frame still further, proposing just the third and second centuries BCE . . .

This means that the estimated birth dates for the first book of the Bible are almost ten centuries apart! Which makes it difficult to think as a historian and perform a task of sociological, political, and philosophical contextualization. The labor of erasure (deliberate or not), traces or proofs of historicity, and the stripping away of the scaffolding mean that we no longer know which men made these books nor what immanent conditions made them possible. This being so, the road is wide open for the mythical fabrications of those who believe in a divine source!

The same vagueness clouds the origins of the New Testament texts. The oldest estimates date from a half century after Jesus's supposed existence. In any case, none of the four evangelists ever knew Christ in the flesh. At best, their knowledge of him stems from the mythological and fabulous account transmitted orally and then one day written down, some time between the fifties of the common era—Paul's epistles—and the end of the first century—the Apocalypse. Yet no copy of the Gospels exists before the end of the second or the beginning of the third. We date them with an eye to the supposed facts and with a prior belief in what those texts tell us.

Since they are by Mark, Luke, Matthew & Co., and since we are in those murky waters, the texts must naturally date from given periods—even if the oldest document we possess is a late arrival, contemporary with what some historians call the "forging" of Christianity, the notorious decades of the second century of our era. In 1546, the Council of Trent cut to the heart of the matter, deciding on the definitive corpus on the basis of the

Vulgate, itself manufactured from the Hebrew text and translated in the fourth and fifth centuries by a Saint Jerome not overburdened with intellectual honesty.

The Jews built their corpus equally slowly and over as long a span. While certain texts of the Torah are supposed to date from the twelfth century before Jesus Christ, we would have to wait until after the destruction of the Temple in Jerusalem (in around 70 CE) before the rabbis settled the details of the Hebrew Bible. In the same period, Epictetus lived the life of an emblematic Stoic in imperial Rome.

Early in the third century, they compiled and codified the Jewish oral laws (the Mishna) that supplement the laws in the Torah. At about the same time, Diogenes Laërtius collated his documents and began to write his *Lives, Teachings, and Sayings of Famous Philosophers*. Around 500, rabbis from Palestine completed the Babylonian Talmud, a commentary on the Mishna. By then, Boetius was writing his *Consolation of Philosophy* in prison. We would have to wait until about the year 1000 to see the definitive text of the Hebrew Bible established. At about this time, in his own corner of the old empire, Avicenna was trying to reconcile philosophy and Islam.

This was also the time when, from a handful of Korans — the "s" is mandatory — Muslims established their definitive version. In order to do this, they had to choose from among several texts, compare one dialect with another, standardize the spelling, separate abrogating and abrogated verses in order to avoid a too glaring incoherence. A genuine operation of textual but also ideological calibration. Time does its work on documents, and the meticulous history of this forgery has still to be written.

Conclusion: if we go upstream and take the most ancient Old Testament dating (twelfth century BCE) and then voyage downstream to the final establishment of the New Testament corpus at the Council of Trent (sixteenth century), the construction sites of the monotheisms were constantly at work for twenty centuries of action-filled history. For books directly dictated by God to his people, the opportunities for human intervention are numberless. At the very least, they call for and deserve serious archaeological spadework.

3

Monotheistic grab bag. What is certain is the staggering historical sweep we confront. We do not even possess an official date of birth for worship of a one God ... Some locate it around the thirteenth century BCE, but Jean Soler insists on the neighborhood of the fourth and third — in other words very late, and even here, fuzziness persists. But the family line is clear: the Jews invented it — even drawing inspiration from the Egyptian solar cult — to ensure the coherence, cohesion, and existence of their small, threatened people. The mythology they fashioned engendered belief in a warrior God, a fighter, bloodthirsty, aggressive, a war leader highly effective at mobilizing a people without a land. The myth of a chosen people founded the essence and existence of a nation thereafter blessed with a destiny.

Of that labor of invention, several thousand pages of canonical text survive — very few, considering their worldwide influence over the course of more than twenty centuries. The Old Testament boasts a total of three thousand five hundred pages, the New nine hundred, the Koran seven hundred and fifty, that is, a little more than five thousand pages in which everything and its opposite is said once and for all.

In each of these three founding texts contradictions abound. Every fact articulated is almost immediately confronted with its opposite. A given opinion appears to triumph — but so, immediately afterward, does its exact opposite. One value is given pride of place, only to be followed a little later by its antithesis. The labor of definitive dating and the construction of a definitive corpus make no difference, not even the decision to decree three synoptic Gospels in order that they may be read side by side. Jew, Christian, and Muslim may draw on the Torah, the Gospels, and the Koran as they wish: all three find material permitting them to justify black and white, day and night, vice and virtue.

Should a war leader need a verse to justify his action, he will find an unbelievable number to choose from. But a peacemaker, a hater of war, can just as easily brandish a sentence, a quotation, a word to justify the opposite! Does the former lift a few words from the texts to justify a war of total extermination? The books are there, and so are the texts. Does the latter call for universal peace? He too lifts the maxims he needs. Does an anti-Semite need justification for his hysterical loathing? Does a believer seek to establish his contempt for the Palestinians, Bible in hand? Or a misogynist need to prove the inferiority of women? An abundance of texts permits it . . . But another word lifted from this clutter authorizes the reader to arrive at the opposite conclusion. And the same applies if we seek a clear conscience on issues of hatred, murder, and contempt: there is just as much material to support vilifying one's neighbor as there is to extol undying love for him. Too many pages written over too many years by too many anonymous people, too much consolidation and too many second thoughts, too many sources, too much material: in the absence of a single source of inspiration (God) . . . The three so-called holy books offer us too many scribes, middlemen, and copyists. None of the books is cohesive, uniform, unequivocal. We are therefore forced to acknowledge the incoherence, lack of uniformity, and ambiguous nature of the books' teachings. A close reading, beginning with the beginning and aiming for the end by following a signposted path, is a simple but little-practiced method.

Who has really read the book of his religion from beginning to end? And who, having once read it, has directed his reason, his memory, his intelligence, and his critical faculties to the parts and the whole of what he has read? Reading does not imply thumbing through page after page, chanting their contents like an ecstatic dervish, consulting them like a catalog, selecting this or that story, here and there and from time to time, but taking the time to *meditate on the whole*. If we do that, we lay bare the incredible improbability, the tissue of incoherences that constitute these three books, which for more than two millennia have built empires, states, nations, and history.

4

Cherry-picking the scriptures. In this open-air archaeological dig, selective extraction is the order of the day. Since each of these books is held to have been inspired from or dictated by God, it cannot be anything other than perfect, absolute, definitive. God has mastered the use of reason, the principle of noncontradiction, the dialectic of consequences, and logical causality —or else he is no longer God. Since the whole is perfect, its constituent parts are equally perfect. Thus the book in its entirety reflects the perfection of every moment that goes into its construction: the Bible is true and thus each of its fragments is also true—and so is a word lifted out of context.

Starting from this principle, we meditate on the spirit according to the letter—and vice versa. Does one selected quotation say the opposite from its predecessor? Yes, but a third expresses the opposite of that opposite. And then we extract yet another phrase, which — offering us another contradiction — restores the first proposition. This game of justifying our thesis by use of a quotation taken out of context allows everyone to use the so-called sacred texts for his own purposes. Hitler defended some of his measures by invoking Jesus driving the moneylenders from the Temple. Martin Luther King validated his campaign of nonviolence by quoting from the Gospels ... The state of Israel invokes the Torah to legitimize its colonization of Palestine. The Palestinians quote the Koran to provide justification for the murder of innocents with the ultimate goal of eliminating Israel. Sophistry, convoluted dialectical skills, and relish for argument are enough to bestow blessings on vice and consign virtue to the pillory.

A Jewish example. We all know the story. Haloed in mist, surrounded by flames, and speaking with a mighty voice — hard to imagine him falsetto and unsure of himself — Yahweh intervenes in person on the mountain to deliver his Ten Commandments to Moses. The fifth on the list is the best-known: "Thou shalt not kill" (Deuteronomy 5:17). No sentence could be plainer: its subject, a personal pronoun; verb cast in the future tense; imperative mood; active voice; negative. God expresses himself in terms immediately accessible to the meanest intelligence: a ban on committing murder, on taking someone's life — an absolute, untouchable principle, requiring no adjustment, suffering no exceptions, no restrictions. The thing is said and understood.

Lifting these few words from the Ten Commandments is enough to define an ethic. Nonviolence, peace, love, forgiveness, mildness, an entire program rejecting war, violence, armies, capital punishment, battles, the Crusades, the Inquisition, colonialism, the atom bomb, assassination — all things that believers in the Bible have been practicing shamelessly for centuries in the very name of their holy book. Why then this blatant logical contradiction?

Blatant because only a few verses later in Deuteronomy 7:1, the same Yahweh steps in to justify the Jews in their extermination of certain peoples explicitly named in the Torah: the Hittites (settlers who came originally from Asia Minor), Amorites, Perizzites, Canaanites, Girgashites, Hivites, and Jebusites, no fewer than seven peoples, constituting most of the population of Palestine. Against these tribes, Yahweh authorizes anathema, racism — mixed marriage is forbidden — and a ban on contracts. Spurning compassion, he demands the demolition of their altars and monuments and legitimizes book burnings. His reasons: the Jews are the chosen people (Deuteronomy 7:6) singled out by God and exalted above all others and despite all others.

The injunction not to kill is very clear. But the vocabulary of the rest of Deuteronomy includes: smite, perish, destroy, burn, dispossess, and other terms straight out of the repertory of total war. Yahweh justifies the slaughter of every living thing. Men and beasts, women and children, the old, donkeys, bulls, the ox, the ass, and the sheep — the text recording them all faithfully — must perish by the sword (Joshua 6:21). The conquest of the land of Canaan and the taking of Jericho come at the price of all life there. The city of Jericho is burned. The gold and silver are spared the general destruction and dedicated to Yahweh in return for his greatness, his acts of generosity, and his complicity in what we may rightly call *the first genocide*: the extermination of a people.

What are we to conclude from this? Should we see an undeniable contradiction? Or should we read more closely, more subtly, leaving the beaten paths habitually taken in approaching this subject? For the imperative of not killing can seem to be made compatible with justifying the extermination of a people. In his own day, Leon Trotsky gave voice to the solution in his book *Their Morality and Ours*: a morality of combat, one ethic for one side, a different code for the other.

A hypothesis: the Ten Commandments are valid as a local,

sectarian, and communal recommendation. Understood is "thou, a Jew, shalt not kill Jews." The commandment plays an architectonic role in ensuring the life and survival of the community. On the other hand, when killing others, non-Jews, the goyim — the word itself connotes two irreconcilable worlds — killing is not really the crime, or at least it is no longer tied to the Commandments. The imperative of not taking life ceases to be categorical and becomes hypothetical. It does not found the universal but upholds the particular. Yahweh speaks to his chosen people and has no concern at all for the others. The Torah invented the ethical, ontological, and metaphysical inequality of races.

5

The whip and the other cheek. Another example, Christian this time, of possible contradictions or logical contradictions. The four Gospels apparently celebrate only gentleness, peace, and love. Jesus shines forth as a symbol of forgiveness of sinners, a figure gifted with words of consolation for the indigent and afflicted, for the poor in spirit, and other variations on the theme of charitable thinking. That is the usual panoply of the Messiah, as served up to small children and stage-managed every Sunday in sermons addressed to families.

A selected morsel to illustrate this aspect of the character: the parable of the other cheek. It is well-known. Matthew (5:39) reports it and Luke borrows it from him (6:29). Jesus taught that he was not supplanting the Old Testament but fulfilling it. On the question of the Jewish law of retribution, the *lex talionis*, he suggests that what he meant by "fulfilling" was overtaking. To those who practiced the principle of an eye for an eye and a tooth for a tooth, he proposed a new tactic: the man smitten on the right cheek must turn the other cheek (which will probably be smitten in its turn . . .).

Here again, as with the sixth commandment, the recommendation allows of no ambiguity. No prevarication, no close scrutiny of the parable that might justify returning the blow. One slap, and the Christian responds with an act of abstention that defuses the situation. No wonder the Roman Empire encountered no problems dispatching Christian martyrs to the lions! Turning the other cheek leads inevitably — and without striking a blow — to our own destruction as long as our adversary is a ruthless brute. Lying defiantly across strategically vital railroad tracks in one of their many acts of civil disobedience, Mahatma Gandhi and his followers could take heart from the example of the evangelists — in the knowledge that their adversary was not a Nazi battalion commander who would quickly have denied them the use of either cheek.

But the Gospels contain another story also validated by the church authorities, since it figures in the canon — the story of Jesus and the Temple moneylenders. According to John 2:15, he drove them all out with a scourge (or whip). It is useless to argue (as some are tempted to do) that turning the other cheek is an authentic reflection of the Messiah's teachings — whereas Christ's fury and violence in the Temple is inconsistent with his character, and therefore must surely be attributable to someone else, an apostle perhaps. The same Jesus who refused to return blow for blow violently ejected the vendors and moneylenders for selling oxen, sheep, and doves and changing money in the Temple! Gentle, peaceful, tolerant Jesus?

For believers who might find this episode too trivial to invalidate the image of a peaceable Christ, let us recall a few more passages from the New Testament in which their hero's conduct is not always genteel . . . For example, when he utters seven *curses* against hypocritical Pharisees and scribes (Luke 11:42–52); when he consigns to hellfire those who do not believe in him (Luke 10:15 and 12:10); when he *heaps abuse* on the cities north of Lake Genesareth for their failure to repent; when he predicts the *ruin* of Jerusalem and the *destruction* of the Temple (Mark 13); when he declares that whoever is not for him is *against* him (Luke 11:23); when he teaches that he has come not in peace but bearing the *sword* (Matthew 10:34); and many other instances.

6

Hitler, Saint John's disciple. Adolf Hitler thought highly of the story of the Temple moneylenders, taken from the Gospel according to John. A Christian who never renounced his faith, Hitler praised the Catholic, Apostolic, and Roman Church, marveled at its creation of an unrivaled civilization, and prophesied its continued vigor in the centuries to come.

For the moment, I shall merely note that in *Mein Kampf* (volume 1, chapter 11, page 307),★ he mentions Jesus's actions in the Temple and refers explicitly to the *whip* (*scourge*) — Saint John was the only evangelist to provide this detail. This was the kind of Christianity Hitler admired: *true Christianity* (*loc. cit.*) and *apodictic faith* (volume 2, chapter 5, page 454). Apodictic, the exact word Hitler used, meaning "expressing essential truth or absolute certainty."

A Christian who does not deny the dual message of his Bible can also draw on Exodus (21:23–25) to evoke the *lex talio-*

★The page numbers cited correspond to the paperback edition of *Mein Kampf*, American translation by Ralph Manheim, published by Mariner Books, a division of Houghton Mifflin.

nis. As we know, it calls on us to exchange an eye for an eye, a tooth for a tooth, but also hand for hand, foot for foot, burn for burn, wound for wound, bruise for bruise. And as we have seen, Jesus proposed turning the other cheek as an alternative to this ancient tribal formulation. But if we abrogate this Gospel parable and replace it with the vengeful Old Testament prescription, and couple this with the New Testament episode of the Temple moneylenders, the worst of excesses can easily be justified. With such a cargo of sophistries, we could justify Kristallnacht as a modern-day eviction of the moneylenders—let us remember that Jesus reproached them with transacting business and money-changing ... Then, pursuing the same hysterical line of argument and invoking the *lex talionis*, the Final Solution becomes the logical response to the National Socialists' nightmare of the racial and Bolshevik Judaization of Europe . . . Unfortunately, the metaphoric scourge permits the dialectician and the determined theoretician to legitimize the gas chambers. Moreover, Pius XII and the Catholic Church succumbed to the charms of these Hitlerian contradictions from the very beginning. Indeed the church continues to do so, if we accept as an admission of collusion its enduring unwillingness to acknowledge the error implicit in the Vatican's support for Nazism. I shall return to this later.

7

Allah's problems with logic. Hitler—Abu Ali in Arabic— admired the Muslim religion in its very essence, virile, warlike, conquering, and militant. And many of the Muslim faithful subsequently repaid that kindness: there was the pro-Nazi grand mufti of Jerusalem during the Second World War, of course, but there were also the eternally anti-Semitic and anti-Zionist militants who recycled former Nazis into the highest ranks of Middle Eastern military staffs and secret services after the Second World War, who protected, concealed, and cared for many of the Third Reich's war criminals in their territories — Syria, Egypt, Saudi Arabia, Palestine. Not to mention an unbelievable number of conversions of former Reich dignitaries to the religion of the Koran.

Pursuant to our examination of the Torah, New Testament, and Koran, let us consider additional contradictions and examples of selective borrowing from the sacred texts as a pretext for evil deeds. The Old Testament prohibits killing but simultaneously condones the annihilation of certain enemies of the Jews. Christian brotherly love is juxtaposed with sanction of violence, when dictated by God's anger. The Koran, too, is full of inconsistencies. The mixed messages in all three monotheistic books have the potential of leading to monstrous consequences.

A Muslim example, then: an extremely imprudent sura (4:82) states that the Koran issued directly from Allah. The proof? The absence of *contradictions* in the divine book . . . Alas! It takes no time at all to conclude that every page teems with contradictions! At several points, the Koran refers to itself with evident self-satisfaction: "intelligently exposed" (6:114) — just like Spinoza! — "coherently narrated" (22:16) — like a proposition by Descartes! — and with "no hint of tortuousness" — like a page out of Bergson! Except that the book abounds in contradictory statements. Figuratively speaking, you have only to bend down and gather them up.

The Koran consists of one hundred fourteen suras or chapters. Except for sura 9, each chapter begins by repeating the first line of the first sura: In the name of Allah, the Beneficent, the Merciful. Duly noted. According to Islamic tradition, God has ninety-nine names; the hundredth will be revealed only in a future life. Many of these names are variations on the theme of mercy and compassion. Al-Rahîm: the Most Merciful, the Most Compassionate. Al-Ghaffâr: the All-Forgiving, the Absolver. Al-Ghafûr: the Pardoner. Al'-Adl: the Just, Equitable, Impartial. Al-Latîf: the Subtle, Gracious, Refined. Al-Halîm: the Lenient, Clement, Most Serene, Most Kind and Gentle. Al-Karîm: the Generous, the Bountiful. Al-Barr: the Gracious Benefactor, the Source of Goodness. Al'-Afûw: the Eraser of Sins, the Remover of Error, Fault, and Wrong Action. Dhû'l-Jalâli wal-Ikrâm: the Lord of Majesty and Generosity.

"Mercy" may be defined as "forgiveness extended to those one might punish." The specifically religious definition is "the goodness through which God extends his grace to men and to sinners." In that case, how is it that, among the ninety-nine Beautiful Names of Allah, there is also Al-Mudhill: the Humiliator, the Degrader, Bringer of Dishonor and Disgrace. Al-Mumît: the Taker of Life, the Creator of Death. Al-Muntaqim: the Avenger, the Inflictor of Retribution. Al-Dârr: the Punisher, Bringer of Harm to Those Who Offend Him. Debasing, killing, avenging, harming—strange ways of showing mercy! But justified on page after page of the Koran.

8

Roster of contradictions. Allah is constantly presented in the Koran as a warrior immune to pity. Of course he can exercise his magnanimity: it is after all one of his attributes. But when? Where? With whom? There is much more putting to the sword, subjecting to the yoke, torturing, burning, pillage, and slaughter than love of one's neighbor. And all this as much in the deeds and gestures of the Prophet as in the text of the holy book. Muslim theory and Islamic practice are not shining examples of compassion.

For Muhammad himself did not excel in chivalrous virtues, as his story attests: the Muhammad of Medina was a great raider during tribal wars, rounding up captives, sharing out booty, sending his friends into the thick of the fighting to commit deeds of extraordinary violence. And again, slightly injured by a flying stone, he watches his demoralized troops seek refuge in a trench, entrusting close friends with the liquidation of this or that dangerous rival, happily slaughtering Jews, and so forth. Allah was great, no doubt about it, and so therefore was his Prophet. But it would not be wise to scrutinize the qualities of the emissary too closely, for God might suffer by comparison.

Magnanimous, then? Here is a listing of contrary qualities: Allah excelled in strategy, battle tactics, and *punishment* — including killing (8:30) — he deployed his *cunning*, that virtue born of cynicism, more closely resembling a vice than anything else, with flair. He resorted willingly to violence and decided on questions of life and *death* (3:156); he devised *ignominious punishments* for doubters (4:102); he was the *Master of vengeance* (5:95 and 3:4); he *annihilated* evildoers (3:141); indeed he practiced that sublime virtue so assiduously that he did not even tolerate a belief that diverged from his wishes; thus he punished those who conceived a *false idea* about him (48). Magnanimity — nothing like it!

9

Everything and its opposite. On one occasion the Prophet teaches that the reward for good is paradise (3:136), *but* on another he asks (55:60), "Is the reward of goodness aught but goodness?" He affirms that everything proceeds from the will of God, who knowingly leads men astray (45:23), *but* in a later chapter, he says the opposite: that every man is responsible for his own acts and deeds (52:21). Not for nothing is the Prophet the heir of Moses and Jesus.

Multiple verses in the Koran conflict with the notion that Allah is beneficent and merciful, as he is characterized in the invocation that opens each sura. However, the contrary is also true. There is the Koran's injunction to kill unbelievers (8:39) and polytheists (9:5), *but* praise in the very next verse for those who offer them asylum (9:6). We see (in 8:39) an order to battle violently against unbelievers, *whereas* Allah's advice to "pardon them and turn away" (5:13) could possibly be construed as an appeal for toleration and living in peace. Sura 7:199 reiterates the same idea, expressed as "forgiveness and turning aside." Many verses authorize mass slaughter (4:56, 4:91 and 2:191–94). But sura 5:32 (often quoted to refute charges that Islam has a zest for butchery) states that: killing a man who has committed no violence on earth is the same as killing all men, in the same way as saving one man means saving them all. The Koran endorses *lex talionis* (2:178); one example: cutting off the hands of thieves (5:38), *but* elsewhere (5:45) it tells us that renouncing that harsh law "shall be an expiation for him who forgoes it." In 5:51, the Koran says, "Do not take the Jews and the Christians for friends," *but* earlier in the same chapter (5:5) it permits a man to marry a chaste woman who follows one of the other two books! Two more suras that contradict the prohibition against friendship with those of other faiths: 49:10 proclaims the brotherhood of all believers, and 29:46 suggests that one should debate courteously with them. The Koran gives its stamp of approval to hunting down the impious (4:91), *but* another verse concerning those who have strayed from God recommends leaving them alone: "We have not sent you as a keeper over them" (4:80). Verse 13:5 refers to infidels with chains on their necks, *but* verse 2:256 (often cited as proof of Islam's tolerance) states, "There is no compulsion in religion . . ." Here of course we are dreaming . . .

One sura contains prayers to God for the extermination of Jews and Christians (9:30), *but* a later verse in the same chapter (9:71) says that the peoples of the book are guardians of each other. The Koran affirms the equality of all in the face of life and death (45:21), *but* describes a father on being told of the birth of a daughter: "his face becomes black and he is full of rage" (43:17). To say nothing of the inequality in store after death: inmates of fire versus dwellers in the garden (59:20). So in countless places the Koran contradicts the invocation of a Magnanimous One with which each sura begins.

The sura entitled "Women" teaches that the absence of contradictions in the Koran proves the book's divine origin (it was dictated over a period of twenty years, at Mecca and Medina, to a man who, as a sweeper-up of camel dung, could neither read nor write). If that is true, the number of contradictions accumulated and cursorily indicated above authorizes us to insist yet again on the human, all too human, origins of the book. Paradoxically, the Koranic thesis of an absence of contradictions in the text (itself contradicted by a scrutiny of the text, which teems with contradictions) means that the text is correct, validating the conclusion that its origins are human and not divine.

10

Contextualization and sophistry. Scholars are thus faced with an onslaught of truths, refuted by as many countertruths, in a disordered metaphysical laboratory where every assertion is promptly contradicted. Some pick and choose from the Koran, ignoring other passages, in an attempt to reduce the totality of Islam to the small portion of texts that they wish to put into evidence. Some try to justify the logic of their own selection from the texts to show that the totality of Islam is reducible to the small proportion of texts they choose. One approach results in a moderate Islam, another in a fundamentalist Islam, a third in a secular (!), open, democratic Islam.

Attempts have even been made to paint Islam as feminist— based largely on the biography of the Prophet who, blessings be upon his name, helped his wife Aïsha with her household chores. Supporters of this view, no slouches in the intelligence department, then superimpose their ideas onto an alien context. From the camel races that Muhammad and his wife participated in, they extrapolate the possibility, today, of coed soccer tournaments! Another has gone so far as to assert that the Koran predicted the conquest of space (15:33) and the invention of cybernetics! But perhaps this is the right place to stop.

Some endeavor to select material from the book in order to depict Islam as peaceable and tolerant. All they need do is isolate the verses in which the Prophet recommends giving sanctuary to unbelievers; practicing forgiveness, forgetfulness, and peace; rejecting violence and crime; renouncing the *lex talionis*; loving one's neighbor (whether Jew, Christian, nonbeliever, atheist, or polytheist); and tolerating different points of view. Unhappily, another will claim exactly the opposite with the same appearance of legitimacy, affirming the rightness and justice of crime, murder, violence, hatred, contempt . . . For there is no Koranic truth, no right reading—merely fragmentary interpretations, ideologically slanted to derive personal benefit from the authority of the book and the religion.

For example, what does it mean to contextualize a verse that calls for a massacre of the Jews? Does it mean explaining the call as a function of the period, of the historical context, of the reasons for writing and thinking such things in the tribal moment? And afterward? Does anti-Semitism disappear when we show that its roots reach down into a loam fertilized by its history and geography? Does the call to crime suddenly and magically cease to be a call to crime? Whatever we think of the context, we cannot alter the fact that the words were written down black on white. Even if a contrary injunction is to be found elsewhere in the text, anti-Semitism is also there, and is expressed with an equal sense of legitimacy.

Yet somewhat paradoxically, Muslim enthusiasts for contextualization consider their book sacred, divine, inspired, revealed, dictated by God. As a result, the Koran becomes rationally untouchable. But to serve their own interests, these enthusiasts shift registers and abruptly lean toward a historical reading. Depending on their dialectical needs, they seek both faith and reason, belief and documentation, fable and truth. At one moment navigating on mystical terrain, at another on the philosophical level, they are impossible to pin down, never on the same wavelength as a reader free of prejudices or convictions and determined on a real reading of the text.

I favor a pitiless historical reading of the three so-called holy books. I also argue for the need to consider their effective repercussions in the history of the West and the world. The Jewish fables about Canaan, the genocidal Mosaic utterances, the prospect of a communitary set of Commandments, the rule of *lex talionis,* the scourge wielded to expel the moneylenders, the parables of the blade and the sword, the "mercy" of a murderous, anti-Semitic, intolerant God, all help forge the monotheistic epistemology, despite the Torah's prohibition on killing, the Gospels' brotherly love, and the mixed messages sporadically delivered by the Koran. These three books all too often serve a death instinct consubstantial with the neurosis of the religion of a one God—now transformed into the religion of the only God.

II

In the Service of the Death Fixation

1

Selective bones of contention. The ability to select at will from all three monotheist books could have yielded the best of results. It would have sufficed to choose Deuteronomy's injunction against killing, transforming it into a universal absolute allowing not a single exception; to stress the evangelists' theme of brotherly love (excluding everything that contradicted that categorical imperative); to give unequivocal support to the Koranic sura which holds that killing one man means killing all of humankind ... Then the three religions of the book might have appeared to us as respectable, pleasurable, desirable.

If rabbis insisted that one could not be Jewish and at the same time slaughter, colonize, and deport whole populations in the name of their religion . . . if priests condemned everyone who did away with his neighbor . . . if the pope, first among Christians, always took the side of the victims, the weak, the poor, the lowly, the descendants of the humble folk who were Christ's first followers . . . if caliphs, imams, ayatollahs, mullahs, and other Muslim dignitaries pilloried the wielders of swords, the Jew-killers, the murderers of Christians, the impalers of the unfaithful . . . If all these representatives of their one God on earth chose peace, love, and tolerance, we would first and foremost have known of it and witnessed it, and next we would have been able to support the three religions on the basis of their principles. And finally we could have condemned the exploitation of those principles by the bad, the wicked. Instead of all this, these representatives of their one God do the opposite. They select the worst options, and, save for extremely rare, intermittent, particular, and personal exceptions, they have historically supported war leaders, saber-rattlers, soldiers, warriors, rapists, pillagers, war criminals, torturers, promoters of genocide, dictators (except for Communist ones) — the very dregs of the earth.

For monotheism is fatally fixated on death. It loves death, cherishes death; it exults in death, is fascinated by death. It gives death, doles it out in massive doses; it threatens death and moves from threat to action: from the bloody sword of the Israelites killing off the Canaanites to the use of airliners as flying bombs in New York, stopping off on the way to release an atomic cargo over Hiroshima and Nagasaki. Everything is done in the name of God, blessed by him, but blessed most of all by those claiming to act in his name.

Today, the Grand Rabbinate of Jerusalem castigates the bomb-clad Palestinian terrorist in the streets of Jaffa but remains silent when Tsahal missiles kill the inhabitants of a West Bank neighborhood. The pope thunders out against the pill, responsible for "the greatest genocide of all time," but actively defends the massacre of hundreds of thousands of Tutsi by the Catholic Hutu of Rwanda. The most exalted spheres of world Islam denounce the crimes of colonialism, the humiliation and exploitation visited on Muslims by the Western world, but rejoice in a worldwide jihad carried out under the auspices of Al-Qaeda. Fascination with the deaths of people, miscreants, and infidels — all three of them additionally convinced that atheism is their single common enemy!

Monotheist indignation is selective, with esprit de corps

working full blast. The Jews have their Covenant, the Christians their church, the Muslims their ummah. Three brotherhoods operating outside the law and enjoying an ontological and metaphysical extraterritoriality. Among members of the same community everything is permissible and justifiable. A Jew — Ariel Sharon — may order the killing of a Palestinian — the hard-to-defend Sheikh Ahmad Yassin — without offending Yahweh, for the murder is committed in his name. A Christian — Pius XII — has the right to justify an exterminator of Jews — Eichmann, exfiltrated from postwar Europe with the Vatican's help — without offending his Lord, for the Nazi genocide avenges the deicide attributed to the Jewish people. A Muslim — the Mullah Omar — may order the hanging of women accused of adultery, thus gratifying Allah in whose name the gallows are erected . . . Behind all these abominations stand verses from the Torah, passages from the Gospels, and suras from the Koran, legitimizing, justifying, blessing.

As soon as religion triggers public and political results, it substantially increases its power to harm. When we point to a phrase culled from one or another of the three books in order to explain the rightness and legitimacy of a crime, we automatically render the crime immune to attack, for how can we attack the revealed word, the utterance of God, the divine urging? God does not speak — except to the Jewish people and the handful of visionaries, virgins for example, to whom he occasionally sends messages — but the clergy has him talk his head off. When a man of the church gives his opinion, quoting pieces from his book, opposing him becomes the equivalent of telling God no in person. Who possesses the moral strength and conviction to refuse the word of (a man of) God? Every theocracy is a denial of democracy. Even better: the smallest hint of theocracy neutralizes the very essence of democracy.

2

The Jewish invention of holy war. Let us give credit where it is due. The Jews invented monotheism and everything that went with it. First divine right and its mandatory correlative: the chosen people exalted, other peoples discounted; a logical enough sequence. Then, more importantly, came the divine strength needed to buttress this heaven-sent right, because the sword arm is what guarantees its realization here below. God utters, speaks, and his prophets, messiahs, and other emissaries translate his otherwise not very intelligible speech. The clergy transforms that speech into orders upheld by iron-plated, caparisoned, determined troops, armed to the teeth. Hence the three founding pillars of all civilizations: the prince representing God on earth, the priest providing the prince with ideas, and the soldier guaranteeing the priest's brute strength. And the people, of course, *always* pay the costs of theocratic perfidy.

The Jews invented the temporal dimension of monotheist spirituality. Well before them, the priest acted in concert with the king: the association was primitive, prehistoric, antediluvian. But the chosen people adapted this skillful and very practical logic for their own purposes: the earth had to be organized in the same way as heaven. Theological schemas had to be reproduced on the terrain of history. Immanence had to demarcate the rules of transcendence. The Torah tells the story without beating about the bush.

On Mount Sinai, God spoke to Moses. At the time the Jewish people were weak, threatened with annihilation in wars with surrounding peoples. It badly needed God's backing to envisage the future with confidence. An only God, bellicose, mail-clad, merciless, fighting and giving no quarter, capable of exterminating the enemy without a twinge of conscience, galvanizing his troops: such was Yahweh, whose type — like Muhammad's — suggested a tribal war leader promoted to cosmic rank.

God promised a land that would be theirs "for an everlasting possession" (Genesis 17:8) to his people. They were the elect, the chosen, singled out from among all others, raised above the common herd, a "peculiar treasure unto me" (Exodus 19:5). Did some unassuming race already inhabit that land? Did people cultivate its fields? Did its soil nourish children and the aged? Did men of mature age tend herds of livestock there? Did women give birth? Did their young receive schooling? Did the people worship gods? But these Canaanites were of little importance, and God had decided on their extermination: "and I will cut them off," he declared (Exodus 23:23).

God deployed his heavy artillery to conquer Palestine. Let us say (to borrow modern strategic terminology) that he invented total war. He split the sea in two (why not, after all?), drowned a whole army in it (no half-measures!), stopped the sun in its tracks to give the Hebrews time to annihilate their Amorite enemies (Joshua 10:12–14) ("love of one's neighbor" in action, with God's help). Earlier, God had released a deluge of hailstones and frogs (a touch of whimsy), called up swarms of mosquitoes and horseflies (no point in skimping), turned water into blood (an injection of poetry and color), unleashed plagues, ulcers, and pustules (bacteriological warfare so soon!), to which he added what soldiers have always done best: killing everything that moved, women, the aged, children, livestock (Exodus 12:12). Clearly, scorched earth, fire, and wholesale slaughter of populations are not a recent invention.

Yahweh blessed war and those who waged it. He sanctified combat, led it, supervised it, although admittedly not in person — ectoplasm has trouble wielding a sword — but by inspiring his people. He sanctioned crimes, murders, assassination, gave his blessing to the liquidation of innocents, killed animals like men and men like animals. He could be humane (unless he was dealing with Canaanites). He proposed an alternative to battle, offering slavery — a token of goodness and love — in its place. To the indigenous population of Palestine, already living there when the Hebrews arrived, he promised total destruction — *holy war*, to use the terrifying and ultramodern expression of Joshua (6:21).

For two thousand five hundred years, no leading figure descended from the chosen people has declared that these pages are rooted in fable, in prehistoric and highly dangerous — because criminal — fictions and nonsense. Quite the contrary. There exist on this planet a considerable number of people who live, think, act, and conceive of the world on the basis of these texts that call for generalized butchery. And there isn't the slightest danger that they will be denied the right to publish on the grounds that they encourage murder, racism, and other incitements to breaches of the peace. Yeshiva students memorize these passages, no more inclined to change a single comma than to touch a single one of Yahweh's hairs. The Torah offers the first Western version of the many arts of war published in the course of the centuries.

3

God, Caesar & Co. The Christians themselves were not slow to enroll God in their misdeeds. There was no question for them of being a chosen people, nor any divine justification for the annihilation of a people who threatened to frustrate their destiny as history's favorites. But they firmly believed that God's word condoned the distinctly temporal actions of their religion (at first sight so distinctly spiritual). From the humiliation of Jesus to the humiliations carried out in his name, the process of Christian evolution was swift and easy, and the resultant mania enduring.

Here again, selective borrowing from the texts proved its usefulness. The Christians drew on John, for example, for the following: "My kingdom is not of this world" (18:36). But they reverted to Matthew for the opposite, as follows: "Render therefore unto Caesar the things which are Caesar's, and unto God the things which are God's" (22:21). One asserts the primacy of the spiritual and a professed indifference to earthly matters. The other, while admittedly asserting the separation of powers, also promulgates a de facto legalism—for rendering unto Caesar justifies payment of taxes to support the army of occupation, accepting the burden of financing the imperial forces, and submitting to the laws of the empire.

The apparent contradiction is resolved when we seek clarification from Paul of Tarsus. For as it evolved into Paulinism, Christianity distanced itself from Judaism. And the epistles to the different peoples visited by the Tarsiot furnish us with church doctrine on the question of relations between the spiritual and the temporal. Paul believed that Jesus's kingdom would be of this world: he wanted to achieve this and worked for its accomplishment in the here and now, hence his travels from Jerusalem to Antioch, from Thessalonica to Athens, from Corinth to Ephesus. The convert from Judaism, not content with a promised land stolen from the Canaanites, wanted the whole planet to march under the banner of a sword-wielding Christ.

The Epistle to the Romans states it clearly: "There is no power but of God" (13:1). So much for theory. What follows in practice is approval of submission to Roman authority. On the principle that those who wield power are first and foremost God's ministers, Paul efficiently wraps up his case. Disobeying a soldier, challenging a magistrate, resisting a prefect of police, standing up to a procurator—Pontius Pilate for example— constitute so many affronts to God. So let us rewrite Christ's words in the Pauline manner: render therefore unto Caesar the things that are Caesar's and to Caesar the things that are God's— in full settlement.

Armed with this ontological asset, the Christians very early began to sell their souls—no longer useful for practice of the gospel message—to the temporal power. They settled into the gilt and purple of palaces; they clad their churches in marble and gold; they blessed armies; they sanctioned expansionist wars, military conquests, police operations. They raised taxes; they un- leashed the soldiery against the discontented poor; they lit bon- fires—as early as Constantine's reign, in the fourth century of their era.

History bears witness: millions of dead in the name of God, millions on every continent and in every century. Bible in one hand, sword in the other: the Inquisition, torture, the rack; the Crusades, massacres, pillage, rape, hangings, exterminations; the African slave trade, humiliation, exploitation, serfdom, the trade in men, women, and children; genocides, the ethnocides of the most Christian conquistadors, of course. But also, and more re- cently, we see Rwanda's Catholic clergy hand in glove with Hutu exterminators; the Vatican a fellow traveler with *every* brand of twentieth-century fascism—Mussolini, Pétain, Franco, Hitler, Pinochet, the Greek colonels, South American dictators, etc. Millions of dead in the name of brotherly love.

4

Christian anti-Semitism. It is hard for a Christian to love his neighbor, particularly if the neighbor is a Jew . . . Saul-become- Paul channeled all his passion into dismantling Judaism—the same passion that (before the road to Damascus) he brought to persecuting Christians, helping mistreat them, and even hastening their encounter with the beyond. To sell the sect he had newly embraced, he had to persuade his listeners that Jesus was the Messiah foretold in the Old Testament, and that Christ had abolished Judaism by fulfilling the prophecy. Since Yahweh's faithful did not buy the nonsense about a Son of God who died on the cross to save humankind, Jews emerged as fundamental adversaries. Then, very quickly, they became the enemy.

It is said that the Wandering Jew was afflicted with his curse because the first of them refused to slake Christ's thirst on the path to Golgotha. For this failure to help the Crucified One, the curse fell upon him — not very charitable of Jesus — but also and above all on his kind, his descendants, his people. This was all the more portentous because the Christian version of Jesus's death assumes that the Jews were responsible — not the Romans . . . And Pontius Pilate? Neither responsible nor guilty. Paul affirmed it when speaking of the Jews who "killed the Lord Jesus" (1 Thessalonians 2:15). The Gospels abound in openly anti-Semitic passages. Daniel Goldhagen lists forty or so in Mark, eighty in Matthew, one hundred and thirty in John, one hundred and forty in the Acts of the Apostles . . . Jesus himself, gentle Jesus, described the Jews as being "of your father, the devil" (John 8:44). In such circumstances, loving one's neighbor was difficult.

From the first Christian transformation of the Jews into a people of God-killers to the long-delayed recognition of the state of Israel by John Paul II at the end of 1993 (and taking into account the church's long love affair with every manifestation of anti-Semitism in history, including most significantly the twelve years of German National Socialism), the picture is clear. The extreme expression of this hatred was the active collaboration between the Vatican and Nazism. And then — which is less widely known — that of Nazism with the Vatican. For Pius XII and Adolf Hitler shared a certain number of points of view, in particular the loathing of Jews in all their guises.

5

The Vatican admired Adolf Hitler. The love-marriage between the Catholic Church and Nazism cannot be denied. Instances — and they are not minor ones — abound. Their complicity did not reside in unspoken approval, explicit omissions, or calculations made on the basis of partisan positions. The facts are clear to anyone who approaches the issue by interrogating history: it was not a marriage of reason, determined by concern for the survival of the church, but a shared loathing of the same implacable enemies: Jews and Communists — most often packaged together in the same grab bag labeled Judeo-Bolshevism.

From the birth of National Socialism to the extrusion of the Third Reich's war criminals after the regime's collapse to the church's silence on these questions ever since, the domain of Christ's heir Saint Peter was also that of Adolf Hitler and his henchmen, German Nazis and French fascists, collaborators of the Nazis, Vichyites, fascist militias, and other war criminals. Even today, it is still impossible to consult the Vatican's archives on the subject.

The facts, then. The Catholic Church approved the rearmament of Germany in the 1930s, which was of course contrary to the spirit of the Versailles Treaty but also to a part of Jesus's teachings, particularly those celebrating peace, mildness, love of one's neighbor. The Catholic Church signed a concordat with Adolf Hitler as soon as the chancellor took office in 1933. The Catholic Church held its tongue over the boycott of Jewish businesses, remained silent over the proclamation of the Nuremberg racial laws in 1935, and was equally silent over Kristallnacht in 1938. The Catholic Church provided the Nazis with its genealogical records, which told them who in Germany was Christian, and therefore non-Jewish. (On the other hand, the Catholic Church did invoke the principle of "pastoral secrecy" in order not to communicate the names of Jews converted to Christ's religion or married to Christians.) The Catholic Church supported, defended, and aided the pro-Nazi Ustachi regime of Ante Pavelic in Croatia. The Catholic Church gave its absolution to France's collaborationist Vichy regime in 1940. The Catholic Church, although fully aware of the policy of extermination set in motion in 1942, did not condemn it in private or in public, and never ordered any priest or bishop to condemn the criminal regime in the hearing of his flock.

The Allied armies liberated Europe, reached Berchtesgaden, discovered Auschwitz. What did the Vatican do? It continued to support the defeated regime. The Catholic Church, in the person of Cardinal Bertram, ordered a requiem Mass in memory of Adolf Hitler. The Catholic Church was mute and showed no disapproval at the discovery of the mass graves, the gas chambers, and the death camps. Even better, the Catholic Church did for the Nazis (shorn of their Führer) what it had never done for a single Jew or victim of National Socialism: it set up a network designed to smuggle war criminals out of Europe. The Catholic Church used the Vatican, delivered papers stamped with its visas to fugitive Nazis, established a chain of European monasteries that served as hiding places for dignitaries of the ruined Reich. The Catholic Church promoted into its hierarchy people who had performed important tasks for the Hitler regime. And the Catholic Church will never apologize for any of these things, particularly since it has acknowledged none of them.

If there is ever to be repentance, we shall probably have to wait four centuries for it, the time it took for a pope to acknowledge the church's error in the Galileo affair. Chiefly because the doctrine of papal infallibility proclaimed at the first Vatican Council in 1869–70 (*Pastor Aeternas*) forbids challenging the church — for when the supreme pontiff speaks or makes a decision he does so not as a man capable of being wrong but as the representative of God on earth, constantly inspired by the Holy Spirit — the famous doctrine of "saving grace." Are we to conclude from all this that the Holy Spirit is fundamentally Nazi?

While the church remained silent on the Nazi question during and after the war, it missed no chance to act against Communists. Where Marxism is concerned, the Vatican has given proof of a commitment, a militancy, and a vigor better expended in fighting and discrediting the Nazi Reich. Faithful to church tradition (which, through the grace of Pius IX and Pius X, condemned human rights as contrary to the teachings of the church), Pius XII, the pope so famously well-disposed toward National Socialism, excommunicated the Communists of the whole world en masse in 1949. He asserted collusion between the Jews and Bolshevism as one of the reasons for his decision.

To recapitulate: no run-of-the-mill National Socialist, no Nazi of elevated rank or member of the Reich's staff was ever excommunicated. No group was ever excluded from the church for preaching and practicing racism or anti-Semitism or operating gas chambers. Adolf Hitler was not excommunicated, and *Mein Kampf* was never put on the *Index*. We should not forget that after 1924, the date Hitler's book appeared, the famous *Index Librorum Prohibitorium* added to its list — alongside Pierre Larousse, guilty of the *Grand Dictionnaire Universel* (!) — Henri Bergson, André Gide, Simone de Beauvoir, and Jean-Paul Sartre. Adolf Hitler never appeared on it.

6

Hitler admired the Vatican. A widely held notion that fails to stand up to the most rudimentary analysis, still less to a reading of the texts, represents Hitler as a pagan fascinated by Nordic cults, a lover of Wagnerian horned helmets, of Valhalla and of generous-breasted Valkyrie, an antichrist, the very antithesis of Christian. Apart from evoking the difficulty of being at once atheist and pagan — denying the existence of God or gods while at the same time believing in them — to believe this means that we must ignore Hitler's writings (*Mein Kampf*), his political action (the Reich's failure to persecute the Catholic, Apostolic, and Roman Church, as opposed, for example, to its treatment of Jehovah's Witnesses), and the Führer's private confidences (his published conversations with Albert Speer), in which he consistently and unambiguously expressed his admiration for Christianity.

Was it an atheist Führer who decided to stamp the words *Gott mit uns* on the belt buckles of the Reich's soldiers? Do people know that the slogan comes from the scriptures? Notably from Deuteronomy, one of the books of the Torah, which says, "For the Lord thy God is he that goeth with you" (Deuteronomy 20:4). These words were lifted from the speech Yahweh addressed to the Jews leaving to fight their enemies, the Egyptians, to whom God held out the promise of unspecified extermination (Deuteronomy 20:13).

Was it an atheist Führer who ordered all schoolchildren in the National Socialist Reich to begin their day with a prayer to Jesus? Not to God, which might have made a deist of Hitler, but to Jesus, which explicitly labels him a Christian. The same supposedly atheist Führer asked Goering and Goebbels, in the presence of Albert Speer who recorded the conversation, to remain within the bosom of the Catholic Church, as he himself would until his dying day.

7

Christianity and National Socialism: points in common.
The understanding between Hitler and Pius XII went far beyond personal compatibility. The two doctrines shared more than
one point of convergence. The infallibility of the pope, who we
should remember was also a head of state, could not have been
displeasing to a Führer also convinced of his infallibility. The possibility of building an empire, a civilization, a culture with a
supreme guide invested with full powers — like Constantine and
several Christian emperors who succeeded him — was something that fascinated Hitler during the writing of his book. The
Christian eradication of everything redolent of paganism? The
destruction of altars and temples? The book burnings (remember
that Paul recommended them)? The persecution of all who opposed the new faith? All excellent things, Hitler concluded.

The Führer admired the theocratic evolution of Christianity. He wrote (*Mein Kampf*, volume 2, chapter 5, page 454) that
it was only by virtue of "passionate intolerance" for pagan altars
that an "apodictic faith" could grow up — Hitler's term for "unshakable faith." He marveled at the church's determination to
give up nothing, even and especially in the face of science when
it contradicted certain of its positions or took its dogma to task
(page 459); the flexibility of the church, for which Hitler predicted a future well beyond what people might imagine (page
459); the permanence of the venerable institution (volume 1,
chapter 3, page 115) despite the occasionally deplorable behavior of clergy (which did nothing to affect overall church policy).
In all this, Hitler asked his readers to "take lessons from the
Catholic Church" (page 459, but also pages 114–20).

What is the "true Christianity" Hitler mentions in *Mein
Kampf* (volume 1, chapter 11, page 307)? That of the "great
founder of the new doctrine": Jesus, the same Jesus to whom

children in the schools of the Third Reich prayed. But which Jesus? Not the one who turned the other cheek, no, but the angry Jesus who ejected the moneylenders from the Temple with a whip. Hitler specifically mentioned this passage from John in his argument. Also, let us not forget what sort of people this most Christian whip served to drive out: unbelievers, non-Christians, vendors, merchants, money-changers — in short, Jews, the unspoken key word in this complicity between Reich and Vatican. John's Gospel (2:14) does not invalidate Hitler's philo-Christian and anti-Semitic reading; indeed, it makes it possible. Particularly if we take note of the many passages in the New Testament consigning the Jews to hellfire. The Jews were a race of deicides. Here lies the key to this fatal partnership: they use religion, said Hitler, in order to do business; they are, he adds, the enemies of any kind of humanity; he goes on to specify that it was the Jews who created Bolshevism. Let everyone make up his own mind. But to Hitler himself things were clear: "to the political leader, the religious ideas and institutions of his people must remain inviolable" (page 116). So the gas chambers could be operated in the name of Saint John.

8

Wars, fascisms, and other pursuits. The partnership of Christianity and Nazism is not an accident of history, a regrettable and isolated mistake along the wayside, but the fulfillment of a two-thousand-year-old logic. From Paul of Tarsus, who justified fire and the sword in turning a private sect into a religion contaminating the empire and the world, to the Vatican's twentieth-century justification of the nuclear deterrent, the line has endured. Thou shalt not kill . . . except from time to time . . . and when the church tells you to.

Augustine, a saint by trade, dedicated all his talent to justifying the worst in the church: slavery, war, capital punishment, etc. Blessed are the meek? The peacemakers? Augustine is no more enthusiastic than Hitler about this side of Christianity, too soft, not virile or warlike enough, squeamish about bloodshed—the feminine face of religion. He offered the church the concepts it lacked to justify punitive expeditions and massacres. These things the Jews had practiced to acquire their land, on a limited geographical scale, but the Christians drew from that local action inspiration for action across the face of the globe, for their goal was converting the world itself. The chosen people generated catastrophes that were *first of all* local. Universal Christianity created *universal* upheavals. Once it triumphed, every continent became a battlefield.

With the church's blessing, Augustine, bishop of Hippo, sanctioned *just persecution* in a letter (185). A choice formulation, which he presents in contrast to *unjust persecution*! What differentiates the good corpse from the bad? Flaying of victims—when is it defensible and when is it indefensible? All persecution by the church was good, because motivated by love; while persecution directed against the church was indefensible, because inspired by cruelty. We should relish the rhetoric and talent for sophistry of Saint Augustine, who preferred his Jesus to brandish the whip and not to suffer it at the hands of the Roman soldiery.

Which brings us to the concept of *just war,* itself formulated by the same church father, a man who decidedly never shrank from brutality, vice, or perversion. As the heir of the ancient pagan fable—Greek as it happened—Christianity recycled trial by ordeal. In a war, the victor was designated by God; so too, therefore, was the vanquished. By deciding in the conflict between winners and losers, God designates the true and the false, good and bad, legitimate and illegitimate. Magical thinking, to say the least.

9

Jesus at Hiroshima. Jesus and his scourge, Paul and his belief in power emanating from God, and Augustine with his just war together constitute a Trinitarian assault group capable of justifying every operation committed in the name of God over the last two millennia. They gave us the Crusades against the Saracens, the Inquisition against supposed heretics, the so-called holy wars against unbelievers — what glory! Saint Bernard of Clairvaux confiding in a letter (363): "the best solution is to kill them," or again, "a pagan's death is a Christian's glory" — the most Christian campaigns of extermination against peoples called primitive, colonial wars to evangelize every continent, the fascisms of the twentieth century, including of course Nazism, all of them furiously unleashed against the Jews.

Little wonder, then, that official Christianity in the era of postmodern war opted for the nuclear deterrent, defended it, and excused it. John Paul II accepted its principle on June 11, 1982, via a truly extraordinary logical fallacy: the atom bomb, he said, opened the road to peace! France's bishops followed close behind, armed with their own reasons, which included the need to struggle against "the domineering and aggressive nature of Marxist-Leninist ideology." Sweet Jesus! What power of decision, what lucidly stated positions! How we would have welcomed an equally clear and straightforward condemnation of Nazism during its twelve-year reign. We would even have been grateful for a similar moral assertion *after* the death camps were liberated.

When the Berlin Wall fell and the Bolshevik threat could at least be said to have diminished, the church upheld its position. In part III, section II, chapter 2, article 5, item 2315 of its latest *Catechism*, the Vatican expresses "strong moral reservations" about the arms race. Note the understatement! The accumulation of nuclear weapons is not an effective deterrent to war, but the Vatican condemns it not at all. In the same document, under the article heading "You shall not kill" — long live logic and coherence! — item 2267 states, "The traditional teaching of the Church does not exclude recourse to the death penalty." It is scarcely surprising that the index has no listing for "capital punishment," "death sentence," or "punishment." On the other hand, euthanasia, abortion, suicide, issues addressed in the same chapter, are fully referenced.

As we know, the crew of the *Enola Gay* dropped an atomic bomb on Hiroshima on August 6, 1945. In a few seconds the nuclear explosion caused the death of more than a hundred thousand people, women, the old, children, the sick, innocents whose only crime was being Japanese. The crew returned safely to base: the Christian God had protected these new Crusaders. We should add that Father George Zabelka had solemnly blessed the crew before its deadly mission! Three days later, a second atomic bomb struck Nagasaki and killed eighty thousand people.

10

Love of one's neighbor (continued). The Pauline texts, so useful in justifying submission to de facto authority, triggered results that went far beyond the legitimization of wars and persecution. In the field of slavery, for example, which Christianity did no more than the other two monotheisms to deter. Indeed, in later centuries the small-scale slavery resulting from tribal raids evolved into the slave trade pure and simple, the sale and deportation of whole populations for use as chattels and beasts of burden.

But give antiquity its due. Since the ancients preceded us, they must be accorded the honor of inventing—if not confirming and legitimizing—a host of evils, including slavery. The Commandments do not advocate any particular respect for one's neighbor if he looks different, if he is not branded in the flesh by the rabbi's knife. The non-Jew did not enjoy the same rights as members of the Covenant. So that, outside the confines of the book, the Other may be called on to account for himself, to be treated like an object, a thing: the goy by the Jew, the polytheist or animist by the Christian, the Christian by the Muslim, and the atheist, needless to say, by everyone.

The subject is introduced into the Torah from the outset, for Genesis (9:25–27) defends slavery. It would have been difficult to get off the mark much faster ... You bought people, they became part of the household, sleeping under the same roof as Jews, you circumcised them, yet they remained slaves. The curse that fell on Noah when he sobered up and realized that a son had caught him naked in his drunken slumber was extended to a whole people—Canaanites yet again—doomed to servitude. Elsewhere, many other passages codify the implications of the curse.

Leviticus, for example, carefully specifies that a Jew must avoid using one of his own kind as a slave (25:39–55). A Jew might work as an indentured servant, yes, but this was more or less a rental agreement that ended after six years, whereupon his freedom would be restored. A non-Jew, on the other hand, could remain in a state of serfdom until his death. The children of the Covenant had been slaves of the Egyptians before Yahweh extracted them from that condition and made of the Jews a free people, capable of submission but obliged to submit to no other power than God's. The rights of the chosen people ...

Christianity, which also condoned slavery, brought no change. As we may recall, all power came from God, everything proceeded from his will. Someone finds himself a slave? The ways of the Lord are mysterious, but there is always a reason to fall back on: original sin, an abstract concept, but each individual has a personal responsibility to atone for it. Augustine (back so soon?) encouraged the slave to toil with a zeal pleasing to God! Every slave was a slave for his own good (whether he realized it or not). God created the slave; a state of servitude is what suited the slave's inherent nature; God's plan would have it no other way.

Then came the ultimate sophistry. Since men were equal in the eyes of God, what matter that there existed on earth differences that were in the final analysis incidental? Man or woman? Slave or owner? Rich or poor? Of little importance, said the church — at the same time aligning itself throughout history with men, the rich, the propertied . . . Every man was as God willed. To rebel against this was to resist the divine plan, to insult God. The good slave who honestly played his part as a slave — like Sartre's café waiter — entered his (fictional) paradise thanks to his (real) submission . . . Saint Augustine's *City of God* (19, 21) — what a truly edifying work!

In harsh reality, Christianity showed a harder side. As early as the sixth century, Pope Gregory I banned slaves from the priesthood! Before him, Constantine forbade Jews to keep slaves in their households. In the Middle Ages, thousands of them labored in the agricultural domains of the supreme pontiff. Great monasteries exploited them unblushingly. In the eighth century, for example, the monastery of Saint-Germain des Prés employed no fewer than eight thousand.

Inheriting this, as they inherited all the rest, the Muslims practiced slavery and the Koran did nothing to suppress it. On the contrary: it legitimized slave- and booty-hunting raids, loot in gold, silver, women, animals, men. Indeed, we owe the invention of the slave trade to Islam. In the year 1000 there was a regular traffic between Kenya and China. Muslim law banned the sale of Muslims, but not that of other believers. Nine centuries before the transatlantic trade, trans-Saharan traffic began its dismal career. It is estimated that ten million men were deported over a period of twelve hundred years by the faithful of Allah, the Compassionate, the Most Great, the All-Wise.

One comment: at heart, the three monotheisms disapproved of slavery, since Jews and Muslims forbade it for members of their own community, while the Christians, who detested Jews, prohibited them from owning domestic slaves. Then they made it illegal for a slave to enter holy orders in order to serve the word of God. Torah, New Testament, and Koran justified enslaving their enemies as a mark of infamy, and therefore of humiliation, a destiny befitting the subhuman nature of anyone worshipping any other god than their own.

11

Colonialism, genocide, ethnocide. The logical sequence to justification of slavery was colonialism, which entailed exporting one's religion to the four corners of the world and the use of force, of physical, mental, spiritual, psychic, and of course armed constraint to achieve those ends. Exporting slavery and extending it to every continent was the work first of Christianity and then of Islam. As for the Jewish people, they have sought to establish their dominion over *only one* territory, their territory, without ever seeking further. Zionism is neither expansionist nor internationalist. On the contrary, the dream brought to fruition by Theodor Herzl implies nationalism, a centrifugal movement, the desire of a closed society existing for oneself alone — and not a desire for mastery of the whole planet, a desire shared by Christianity and Islam.

The Catholic, Apostolic, and Roman Church excels in the destruction of civilizations. It invented ethnocide, the spiritual rather than the physical extinction of cultures. The year 1492 does not merely spell the discovery of the New World but the destruction of other worlds. Christian Europe laid waste a considerable number of Amerindian civilizations. Soldiers, accompanied by the scum of society — jailbirds, petty criminals, strong-arm men, mercenaries — disembarked from the caravels. Once the ensuing ethnic cleansing was over, the priests followed at a safe distance in solemn procession, with crucifixes, ciboria, Hosts, and portable altars, all most useful in preaching brotherly love, forgiveness of sins, the sweetness of the angelic virtues, and other tokens of biblical joy — original sin, hatred of women, of the body and of sexuality, guilt. Meanwhile, Christendom gave the peoples it called savages its housewarming gifts of syphilis and other transmissible diseases.

The partnership of the church and Nazism likewise aimed at extermination of a race reconfigured for the purposes of the cause into a people of God-killers. Six million dead. To which we must add complicity in the deportation and murder of gypsies, homosexuals, Communists, Freemasons, left-wingers, laymen, Jehovah's Witnesses, antifascists, and other people guilty of not being very Christian.

The Christian passion for mass extermination is old and enduring. A recent example was the genocide of Tutsis by the Hutu of Rwanda, supported, defended, and covered up by the Catholic establishment on the spot and by the supreme pontiff himself. The pope was much quicker to ensure that priestly genocide-bent war criminals, monks, nuns, and other members of the Catholic community might escape the firing squads than to offer one word of compassion to the Tutsi community.

For in Rwanda, a country with an overwhelmingly Christian population, the church even *before* the genocide had practiced racial discrimination in accepting candidates for seminaries, in training, in the administration of Catholic schools, in ordination or promotion in the ecclesiastical hierarchy. *During* the genocide some members of the clergy played an active part:

purchase and delivery of machetes by members of the Catholic establishment, sniffing out the victims' hiding places, actively participating in orgies of brutality—people locked into churches, the churches burned down, their remains obliterated by bulldozers—denunciations, sermons to fire up the masses, exploitation of racial language.

After the massacres, the Catholic Church stayed on course. Convents were taken over to hide guilty Christians from justice, networks galvanized to help smuggle this or that criminal out to European countries, air tickets provided by Christian humanitarian organizations. Guilty priests were farmed out to provincial Belgian and French parishes, bishops implicated in the genocide were whisked from view. And the church resorted to public attitudes of denial—insisting, for example, on referring to "fratricidal war" in preference to "genocide."

Silent on the preparations, silent during the massacres— nearly one million dead in three months (between April and June 1994) — silent after the scope of the disaster (carried out with the blessings of French president François Mitterrand) was revealed, John Paul II emerged from his silence to write a letter to the president of Rwanda on April 23, 1998. Its contents? Did he deplore? Did he express compassion? Did he repent? Regret? Blame his clergy? Wash his hands of their actions? No, not at all: he requested a stay of execution for Hutus found guilty of genocide. Not a single word for the victims.

12

Repressions and the death fixation. The fixation of the three monotheisms on the death instinct can be explained. How can we escape the domination of that instinct after so effectively killing off the life urge both within and outside ourselves? Fear of death, of the void, horror at the idea of the emptiness that follows death, all help generate consoling fables, fictions that incite us to deny use of our full powers. The real is not. Fiction, on the other hand, is. This false world, which forces us to live in the here and now buttressed by hopes of a tinsel afterlife, leads to denial, contempt, or hatred of the here and now.

Hence countless opportunities for seeing this hatred at work: on the body, desires, passions, drives, on the flesh, women, love, sex, on life in all its forms, on matter, on the things that enhance our existence in this world, in other words, on reason, intelligence, books, science, culture. This suppression of everything living forces on us the celebration of everything that dies — bloodshed and war — of whatever kills, of those who kill. Whereas intelligent reading from the three books would let us select whatever confers maximum power on the life force, religion seeks out the death force in all its forms. Suppression of the living engenders love of death. And generally speaking, all contempt for women — we prefer virgins, mothers, and wives — goes hand in hand with a cult of death.

Civilizations are not founded on the death drive. Sacrificial blood, the scapegoat, laying the foundations of a society through an act of ritual murder — these are sinister social constants. The Jewish extermination of the Canaanites, the Christian crucifixion of the Messiah, the Muslim jihad of the Prophet all shed the blood that blesses and sanctifies the monotheist cause. Primitive, magical aspersion, disemboweling of the propitiatory victims — who happen to be men, women, and children. The primitive survives in the postmodern, the animal survives in man, the beast still dwells in *Homo sapiens*.

III

Toward a Post-Christian Secular Order

1

Muslim thirst for blood. A worthy synthesis of the two monotheisms that preceded it, Islam acclimatized them to an Arabian desert conditioned by the tribal and the feudal. It also adopted as its own the worst legacies of the above-mentioned Jews and Christians: a community of the elect, a sense of superiority, the local transformed into the global, the private expanded to the universal, submission of body and soul to the ascetic ideal, the cult of the death instinct, theocracy indexed to the extermination of everything different, slavery, raiding, total war, punitive expeditions, murders, etc.

Let us remember that Moses slew an Egyptian foreman with his own hands. And that Muhammad and his followers regularly slaughtered people, beginning with the killing of an unarmed merchant at Nakhla (Saudi Arabia) in 623. He continued to kill until the day he died on June 8, 632. It is not possible to list all of the wars, battles, raids, surprise attacks, sieges, and other feats of arms by Muslim warriors. Battle of Badr (March 624): three hundred and fifty Muslims from Medina defeated an army of nine hundred commanded by Amr ibn Hisham, one of the polytheist leaders in Mecca. Also known as Abu Jahl, meaning "father of folly and ignorance," he was the one who had killed the first Muslim martyr (an old woman named Sumayyah), and he was himself killed at the battle of Badr. Uhud (March 625): Muhammad wounded; a few dozen martyrs. East Medina (late 626–early 627): Jews slain. The battle of the Trench (627): a "Jewish plot." The conquest of the Khaybar oasis (May–June 628). The raid on Mu'ta (September 629). Readers of the Koran do not seem to be overly concerned with verse 32 of sura 5: "Whoever slays one soul, it is as though he slew all men." (Paraphrase: To kill one man is to kill all men.)

Nearly two hundred and fifty verses — of the six thousand two hundred and thirty-four of the book — justify and legitimize holy war, jihad. Enough to drown the handful of very inoffensive phrases recommending tolerance, respect for one's neighbor, magnanimity or nonrecourse to violence in questions of religion (!). In such an ocean of blood, who can still take the trouble to linger over two or three sentences that recommend tolerance over barbarity? Particularly since the Prophet's biography bears eloquent witness: murder, crime, the sword, and the punitive expedition constantly recur. Too many pages encourage anti-Semitism, hatred of Jews, despoiling and exterminating them, for a Muslim fighter not to feel justified in putting them to the sword.

The Muslim community thought like the children of the Covenant. They too proclaimed themselves the chosen people, singled out by Allah, preferred by him (9:19 but also 3:110). But two claimants to elite status are one too many! Believing that others are of inferior race, that subhumans exist, that God establishes a hierarchy among humans by distinguishing the small designated community from the rest of humanity, means that the Other may not claim the same status as ourselves. Yesterday's hatred of the Hebrews for the Canaanites generates today's hatred of the Palestinians for the Jews, each side believing itself summoned by God to dominate the other — the others — and thus seeing itself as empowered to exterminate them.

For Islam *in its essence* rejects metaphysical, ontological, religious, and therefore political equality. The Koran teaches it: at the top, Muslims, below them Christians, because they too are people of the book, and then Jews, who as monotheists are also members of the group. Finally, after the Muslim, the Christian, and the Jew, comes the fourth group, all lumped together in general disapproval, unbelievers, the infidel, miscreants, polytheists, and of course atheists . . . The Koranic law, which forbids killing, committing crimes against, or massacring one's neighbor, is strictly confined to members of the community of the book: the *ummah*. As with the Jews.

But at the very heart of the Muslim community of supposed equals, hierarchy still prevails: men dominate women, the clergy dominate the faithful, pious believers dominate the lukewarm, the old dominate the young. Male supremacy, theocracy, gerontocracy, the original tribal and primitive models have remained unchanged over thirteen centuries. Islam is *fundamentally* incompatible with the societies that arose from the Enlightenment. The Muslim is not brotherly: he is the brother of his coreligionist, granted, but not of the others, negligible or hateful quantities, counting for nothing.

2

The local as universal. Muslims divide the world in two: friends and enemies. On one side, brothers in Islam, on the other the rest, all the rest. *Dar al-islam* against *dar al-harb*: two separate and incompatible worlds, governed by savage and brutal relations—a predator and a prey, an eater and an eaten, a dominator and a dominated. As in the most elemental of jungles, the big cats keep to themselves while the rest wait to be conquered, enslaved, and possessed. The law that governs relations among animals.

It is a world vision not too distant from Hitler's, justifying the logics of branding, possession, administration, and extension of territory. The fox and the chickens, the falcon and its prey, lion and gazelle, weak and strong, Islam and the others. No law, no justice, no communication, no exchange of information — just muscles, instinct, strength, battle, war, and blood.

The universal? To paraphrase Miguel Torga, the local minus walls. Seventh-century tribalism, the feudalism of the Arabian desert, the primitive view of the clan, invariably transplanted unchanged into the civilization of the hour, including our own postmodern, hyperindustrial, and digital model. The desert village become world blueprint. The oasis, where nothing has penetrated for centuries (apart from nomad caravans laden with subsistence-level goods), functioning as social, human, metaphysical, and political archetype.

A book dating from the beginning of the 630s, theoretically dictated to an illiterate camel herdsman, regulates down to the smallest detail the daily lives of billions of people in the era of supersonic travel, space conquest, worldwide information networks, the real and universal time of generalized communications, the sequencing of the human genome, nuclear energy, the first glimpses of the post-human . . . The remark applies equally for the Torah- and Talmud-obsessed Lubavitchers, who share a similar ignorance of the passage of time.

As in the nomad tent of fifteen hundred years ago, the family constitutes the core. Not the national or patriotic community, and still less the universal or cosmopolitan entity, but that of the paterfamilias, owner of his two, three, or four obedient wives — for primitive polygamy survives in the Talmud as in the Koran (4:3) — surrounded by numerous children. The latter are a blessing from God, authority of course proceeding from Allah, but through the voice of father, husband, and spouse, figurations of God under the goatskin tent.

Every action occurs in the gaze of the tribe, which judges it by its degree of conformity to Koranic or Muslim rules. The father, but also — following pure male chauvinist logic, the senior brother, the brother, and other variations on the theme of the male — is the incarnate locus of religion and therefore of politics and theocracy. He is the basic cell of society. Neither Plato — in *The Republic* — nor Hegel — in *Elements of the Philosophy of Right* — nor Mussolini, nor Hitler, nor Pétain, nor any other kind of fascist had doubts on that score. They all knew that the beginnings of the community, the genealogy of the community, were rooted in the intimate space of the family — the primitive tribe. Read or reread Engels and *Origins of the Family, of Private Property and the State* if you need convincing.

3

Yellow stars and Muslim tattoos. Of equal importance to the communal logic of inclusion and exclusion was the distinguishing mark or sign. Wearing the distinctive color yellow — sometimes as a turban — on one's person initially resulted from a decree by an eleventh-century caliph in Baghdad (the usual way of characterizing that period is to speak of the golden age of Islam), who sought to distinguish Jews and Christians by an outward sign that swiftly became one of opprobrium.

Muslims have a concept known as *dhimma*, which originally referred to the pact of surrender between non-Muslims and their Muslim conquerors. Today, a *dhimmi* is a non-Muslim citizen of a country governed in accordance with sharia, Islamic law. At one time, the status of *dhimmi* was available only to people of the book (Jews and Christians), but later it was extended to include Zoroastrians and certain others. Muslims characterize *dhimma* as a contract that protects *dhimmis*, allowing them to retain their religion and guaranteeing their personal safety and the security of their property. In theory, Islam is a religion of peace and tolerance. In practice, *dhimma* imposes an extra tax on the Jew, Christian, or Zoroastrian for the privilege of living in Islamic territory. Forcing non-Muslims to pay for protection is financial extortion.

Armed with this protection (!), the dhimmi enjoys civic rights that are almost nonexistent. In a tribal society, where ownership of a horse makes it possible to exist, to travel, to fight, to display one's social rank, the non-Muslim owns no such thing. He is permitted to ride an ass or mule (degrading mounts), but he has to ride sidesaddle, woman-style. He may walk in the street, but is not allowed to overtake a Muslim. Bearing arms is of course categorically forbidden — more or less implying that, being disarmed, the *dhimmi* is at the mercy of the first bandit to cross his path. Sometimes, beyond wearing the yellow fabric of sinister memory, he has a lion tattooed on his forearm, just as a later generation of Jews sported a tattooed number there.

In theory, the abolition of dhimmitude dates from 1839. In fact it was not until the end of the First World War that the Ottoman Empire finally abandoned a practice whose observance it was no longer able to impose . . . Obviously, the famous protection guaranteed on paper was not invariably granted — not by a long shot — to non-Muslim believers, who nevertheless conscientiously paid the tax and consented to live as subhumans.

4

Against the closed society. Islam has evolved within its own hermetic set of assumptions — within a history of its own that in effect ignores and denies the overall sweep of history. This has generated a closed, static society, shut in upon itself, fixated on the immobility of death. Marxism once claimed to be fulfilling history by abolishing it: its adepts professed a quasi-religious cult of history the better to achieve that goal. In the same way, the Muslim ambition to rule the planet aims ultimately for a frozen system, a system running counter to the flow of history, abandoning the dynamic of the real and of the world in favor of a universe conceived in the manner of an afterlife. A society applying the principles of the Koran would give us a universal nomad encampment, astir with the distant echo of subterranean spasms and the song of the spheres, dead husks orbiting themselves in celebration of nothingness, emptiness, the meaninglessness of a long-defunct history.

Every theocracy that refers back to the model of a timeless, dimensionless fictional universe seeks to impose on an immanent world a carbon-copy reproduction of that conceptual archetype. For the blueprints of the city of men are stored in the city of God. The Platonic Idea, such close kin to the idea of God (with no date of birth, no expected time of death, without answerability of any kind whatsoever, impervious to time or entropy, flawless, perfect), engenders the mirage of a closed society, it too endowed with the attributes of the Concept.

Democracy lives on movement, change, on contractual agreements, flexible time frames, enduring dynamics, dialectical interplay. It creates itself and thrives at the behest of a will that stems from living forces. It relies on the use of reason, on dialogue among the parties concerned, on active use of communication, on diplomacy and negotiation. Theocracy lives by the opposite principle: it is born, lives, and thrives on immobility, death, and the irrational. Theocracy is democracy's most dangerous enemy — the day before yesterday in prerevolutionary Paris, yesterday in Tehran in 1978, and today every time Al-Qaeda gives violence a voice.

5

Muslim fascism. The question of fascism still exercises a handful of contemporary historians, unable to agree on a firm and final definition. Was French marshal Philippe Pétain fascist? He was certainly a nationalist, and according to some a patriot, but although his Vichy regime pursued extreme right-wing policies, they were not necessarily fascist . . . These are byzantine debates, for there were many brands of fascism in the twentieth century, each with its own specific attributes. Indeed, we could call the last hundred years the *fascist century*. Brown and red in Europe and Asia, military khaki in South America. But green as well, which we too often overlook.

For the overthrow of the shah of Iran in 1978 and the seizure shortly thereafter of all powers by the Ayatollah Khomeini (and by one hundred and eighty thousand mullahs) gave birth to an authentic Muslim fascism. A quarter century later, with the blessings of a silent and forgetful West, it is still in the saddle. Because far from heralding the emergence of the *political spirituality* so lacking in the West (as Michel Foucault wrongly believed in 1978), the Iranian revolution gave birth to an Islamic fascism never before associated with that religion.

We know that Foucault seriously misread the event. Not only because of an article he wrote in *Corriere della Sera*, on November 26, 1978, stating that "there will be no Khomeini party, there will be no Khomeini government." (He was cruelly contradicted by events four months later.) But because he identified the new Islamic government as "the first great insurrection against planetary systems, the most modern form of revolt" — without considering for a second the possibility of a government inspired by Islamic law, the sharia . . . What did Foucault really know about the Koran and Islam?

By the time he wrote those words for the Italian daily, Foucault had already meditated fruitfully on the issues of incarceration, madness, prison, homosexuality, and folly. He should have known better than anyone else that by its very nature an Islamic government would enlist the services of everything he had fought against: sexual discrimination, imprisonment of outsiders, leveling of differences, the logic of confessions, the prison system, disciplining the body, unchallenged biopower, the panoptical principle, the punitive society, and so forth. Knowledge of the Koran and the Hadith (the two sources of sharia) should have made it clear that, far from signifying a return to the spiritual in politics, an Islamic government marked Islam's entry into the field of postmodern politics. And this, in perfect accord with the theocratic principle, ushered in the Islamic fascism whose implications at first eluded this very skilled student of the microphysics of power.

6

An ayatollah speaks. Politicians theorizing about power usually bequeath to us dry, straightforward books that go right to the heart of the matter, summarizing either their authors' intentions or else their achievements. In Cardinal Richelieu's *Political Testament*, Lenin's *The State and Revolution*, General de Gaulle's *The Edge of the Sword*, Mussolini's *The Doctrine of Fascism*, and Hitler's egregious *Mein Kampf*, we encounter respectively a theory of monarchic legitimacy, a Marxist-Leninist manual for Bolshevists, a treatise on the theory of modern war, a fascist manual, and a National Socialist racial doctrine.

After his death the Ayatollah Khomeini left a *Politico-Spiritual Testament* that outlines the theory of Islamic government that so excited Michel Foucault in the first days of the Iranian revolution. The Shiite dignitary put into words, simply, even concisely, the political program of an Islamic republic. His book explained how to govern minds, bodies, and souls according to Muslim principles and with the help of the Koran and the Hadith (in other words on the basis of sharia). It is a breviary of Islamic theocracy—an undeniably fascist breviary.

Muslim theocracy—like any other—presupposes an end to the separation between private belief and public practice. The believer emerges from the private center of his being to take over every single area of the community's life. We no longer enjoy a direct relationship with God, based on a mystical intimacy touching us alone, but an indirect relationship mediated by the political community and regulated by somebody else. The end of religion for one's own sake; the beginning of religion for others.

At which point religion becomes the business of the state. Not of a restricted community, a limited group, but the whole of society. This extension of politics to the totality of the human sphere is the very definition of totalitarianism. The state serves an idea—racial, fascist, Islamic, Christian, etc. — and family, work, privacy, school, barracks, hospital, newspaper or publishing office, friendship, leisure, reading, sexuality, courts, sports are all controlled by the dominant ideology. And thus Islamic family, Islamic work, Islamic privacy, Islamic school, and so on.

7

Islam: structurally archaic. How can we legitimize the totalitarian and immanent use of the Koran? By claiming to possess the only legitimate reading of the holy book. Selective excerpting makes possible an Islam à la carte, with a broad range of offerings. Today we can profess allegiance to the Prophet yet drink alcohol, eat pork, refuse the veil, reject sharia, bet at the racetrack, root for our soccer team, espouse human rights, praise the

European Enlightenment. Or so it is claimed by those who aspire to modernize the Muslim religion and live a secular, modern, republican Islam, and similar untenable twaddle.

Following this same incoherent logic, one can be a Christian yet not really believe in God, scoff at papal bulls, mock the sacraments, refuse to subscribe to the mysteries of the Eucharist, spurn dogma, brush aside all church teachings! The practice of selective borrowing from the texts today allows us to worship a mere signifier, emptying it utterly of what it once signified. At which point we are worshipping an empty shell, prostrating ourselves before nothing — one of the many signs of the nihilism of our era.

At the other end of the spectrum we find the reverse: scrupulous respect for Koranic teachings. Hence the practice of polygamy, routine sexist and male chauvinist behavior, the denial of existential reality to all non-Muslims, justification for the killing of infidels — from monotheists to atheists — zealous observance of the rituals and obligations of churchgoers, condemnation of all use of reason, etc.

The Koran does not countenance à la carte religion. Nothing in the book permits us to dismiss every sura hostile to comfortable living, to middle-class integration into postmodernity. On the other hand, nothing forbids (in fact, everything authorizes) a scrupulous reading on whose basis all the duties specified in the holy book are justified. No one is obliged to be a Muslim, but when he professes to be one, he must adhere to the theory and teachings and practice his beliefs accordingly. It is a question of the pure and simple principle of coherence. Islamic theocracy illustrates the maximum coherence possible on this subject.

For Islam is structurally archaic, contradicting point by point everything the philosophy of the Enlightenment has achieved in Europe since the eighteenth century. In other words, condemnation of superstition, rejection of intolerance, abolition of censorship, resistance to tyranny, opposition to political absolutism, an end to state religion, proscription of magical thinking, extension of freedom of thought and expression, promulgation of equal rights, the notion that all law arises from contractual immanence, the wish for social happiness here and now, the aspiration toward the universal reign of reason. Sura by sura, the Koran clearly states its opposition to them all.

8

Fascist thematics. In Iran, the Ayatollah Khomeini was officially addressed as "Imam" rather than Grand Ayatollah. In Sunni Islam, an imam is the leader of worship in a mosque. But in Shiite Islam, an imam is a spiritual and political leader whose authority comes from Muhammad through his son-in-law Ali. Being divinely inspired, the imam has the same attributes as the pope — in other words, infallibility. Like the Führer, Il Duce, the Caudillo, the Conducator (Romania's Ceausescu), and the Great Helmsman (Mao), the imam's word is law: *performative logic.* He has a monopoly on correct interpretation of the Koran. He alone is qualified to select from the Koran whatever passages appear to support the creation of a total theocracy.

For everything is in the Koran. Reading it gives us every possible reply to every possible and imaginable question. Money? Trade? The law? Justice? Education? Sovereignty? Women? Divorce? Family? Diet? Ecology? Culture? Nothing is missing, everything is there. Western governments would find priceless policy guidelines in the Koran. The supreme leader thus possesses the supreme source, the holy text, and his utterances are therefore to be identified with justice and law. He embodies the theory of the man of destiny.

To which must be added a *binary logic* pitting friends against enemies. No quarter, no details, no subtlety. No need for hair-splitting to decide for whom and against whom to fight. In the logic of the Iranian revolution, the enemies are America, Israel, the West, modernity, the superpowers. Multiple names, all reducible to the same entity: Satan. The devil, the demon, the Prince of Darkness. Every brand of fascism proceeds in this manner, designating the enemy and demonizing him to the maximum in order to galvanize troops for battle. Embodiment of the scapegoat theory.

Then (a theme common to fascism and Islamism) we have the claim of a *postpolitical logic*. Meaning? Neither right nor left but elsewhere, beyond, or — in Iran's case — above. On God's side. So Iran will have no truck with the Marxist, Bolshevik, Soviet (in its day), atheist, materialist, Communist left, (Khomeini even broadened this concept to embrace women's communism!) nor with the American, consumerist, self-indulgent, corrupt, business-oriented, and capitalist right. The two systems are lumped together. Embodiment of the theory of the end of politics.

Thus a *transcendental logic*: God as the solver of contradictions. Yet this Islamic synthesis retains parts of the two spurned systems mentioned above. It borrows from the left a discourse of solidarity with the have-nots, it directs its words to the wretched, it verbally displays a genuine populist determination to do away forever with poverty in the world. And from the bosom of the right it selects small-scale private capitalism and land ownership. The sum of these two borrowed currents of political thought offers an apparent coherence, guaranteed by Allah, begetter of the union. Embodiment of the theory of the end of history.

Moreover, fascism and Islamism commune in a *mystical logic*. At the other extreme from reason in history, from rational linkages of causality or from any constructive dialectic, the ayatollah promulgates the law of the irrational. The triumph of the collective requires the sacrifice of the individual. All individuality must be swallowed up in the totality thus constituted. So that in return for its disappearance, individuality is compensated with a new melting-pot identity — participation in the mystic body of society and therefore in the community, in other words in God. Hence a (falsely) divine future for man. Embodiment of the theory of the end of reason.

The *pantheistic principle* of community entails sublimation of the self for the greater good of the collective political body. The sense of self is diminished, as the individual identifies with a cause and sees himself only as part of something bigger. Martyrdom permits the individual not to perish. Instead, he achieves a transmutation of his being, which survives in the mystic community in a form that is eternal, extrahistoric and transhistoric. Hence Muslim suicide bombers. Embodiment of the theory of existential eschatology.

Similarly, like every kind of fascism, Islamic theocracy rests on a *hypermoral logic*. God commands history, his plan is consistent with reality, his design remains immutable. Allah requires the ethical purification of the believer, hence hatred of the body, the flesh, free sexuality, desires, etc. The realization of moral order as an occasion for hypostasis leads toward the mystic empyrean. This implies condemnation of luxury, homosexuality, gambling, drugs, nightclubs, alcohol, prostitution, cinema, perfume, lotteries, and other vices denounced by the ayatollah. Embodiment of the theory of the ascetic ideal.

Finally, fascism and Islamism imply a *logic of compulsory service*. Nothing and no one may refuse to answer the call, hence total mobilization of every cog in the state machine. A tight rein is kept on all institutions, press, army, journalism, education, the judicial body, police, bureaucrats, intellectuals, artists, scientists, writers, orators (*dixit* the supreme leader), and research workers. Competence in one's field of activity passes into the background. Faith, fervor, religiosity, and zealous religious practice move into the foreground. Embodiment of the theory of the militarization of society.

Everything that usually defines fascism is reproduced in the theory and practice of Islamic government. The masses are directed by an inspired, charismatic leader. Myth, the irrational, the mystical are revamped as the motive forces of history. Law and justice are created by the leader's words. The dominant national ambition is to abolish an old world in order to create a new one — a new man, new values; a vitalist world vision coupled with a bottomless love of death; expansionist warfare experienced as proof of the nation's health; hatred of the Enlightenment (reason, Marxism, science, materialism, books); police terror; abolition of all separation between private and public spheres; construction of a closed society; dilution of the individual in the community; self-realization through the loss of self and salutary sacrifice; celebration of warlike virtues (virility, machismo, brotherhood, comradeship, discipline, misogyny); destruction of all resistance; militarization of politics; suppression of all individual freedom; fundamental hostility to the ideology of human rights; permanent political indoctrination; history couched in the language of negative slogans (anti-Semitic, anti-Marxist, anticapitalist, anti-American, antimodern, anti-Western); the family promoted to the position of first link in the organic whole . . . The above litany more or less constitutes a definition of the essence of fascism, of fascisms of every stripe. Theocracy is still embroidering variations on this theme.

9

Fascism of the fox, fascism of the lion. The twenty-first century has opened on a merciless war. On one side is a *Judeo-*

Christian West, liberal in the economic sense of the term, uncompromisingly capitalist, brutally mercantile, cynically consumerist, producer of false values, without virtue, viscerally nihilistic, strong toward the weak, weak toward the strong, cunning and Machiavellian toward all, spellbound by money and profit, prostrate before the gold that engenders all power, creator of every system designed to dominate the body and the soul. Under this dispensation everyone — in theory — enjoys freedom. In fact, freedom exists for a mere handful, for a very few, while the others, the majority, huddle in poverty, destitution, humiliation.

On the other side, a *Muslim world*, zealous, brutal, intolerant, violent, imperious, conquering. The fascism of the fox against the fascism of the lion, one creating its victims postmodern style with state-of-the-art weapons, the other by resorting to a hyperterrorism of box-cutter knives, hijacked planes, and homemade explosive belts. God is claimed by both camps, each trusting in the trial by ordeal of primitive man. Axis of good against axis of evil, with the front lines perpetually overlapping one another.

Monotheist religions are waging this war, with Jews and Christians on one side and Muslims, postmodern Saracens, on the other. Must we choose a side? Must we opt for the cynicism of one on the pretext of fighting the barbarism of the other? Must we really align ourselves with this or that world vision when we consider both of them to be dead-end streets? Michel Foucault once indulged in Manichaeism and let himself be caught in its trap. He initially welcomed the prospect of a spiritual politics during the Iranian revolution, because it offered an alternative to what he called "planetary systems" (in 1978 nobody yet spoke of globalization). But after that, Foucault observed that the issue of political Islam is vital not only to the present but also to the years ahead. Duly noted.

10

Against "religious" secularism. In this devastated landscape of a Western world at bay, the tactics of some secular figures seem contaminated by the enemy's ideology: many militants in the secular cause look astonishingly like clergy. Worse: like caricatures of clergy. Unfortunately, contemporary freethinking often carries a waft of incense; it sprinkles itself shamelessly with holy water. As clergymen of a church of atheist bigots, the players in this not unimportant movement seem to have missed the postmodern boat.

The freethinkers' struggles have admittedly worked wonders in advancing the cause of modernity. They have given us the deconstruction of Christian fables, the unburdening of consciences, separation of the religious and the judicial. They have given us secularization of education, public-health services, and the army, campaigns against theocracy on behalf of democracy, and — to name their greatest triumph — separation of church and state.

Yet secular catechisms, civil ceremonies (baptisms, communion!), youth congresses, campaigns against the tolling of church bells in villages, dreams of creating a new calendar, iconoclasm, and opposition to the wearing of priestly garb, all smell a little too much like the kindling heaped at the feet of Christian stakes . . . De-Christianization does not come about through the manipulation of such trinkets and baubles, but through hard work on the epistemology of a period, through the injection of reason into human consciences. The French Revolution's de-Christianizing phase was swiftly followed by the cult of the Supreme Being and other observances, just as clerically ludicrous and inappropriate.

Let us think in dialectical terms. These excesses can be explained by the bitterness of the struggle ahead, the stubbornness of a Christian enemy still possessing full powers over bodies, souls, and consciences, and his commandeering of all the controls of civil, political, and military society. Freethinkers stigmatize their adversaries by calling them lice and vermin (parasites), spiders and serpents (cunning), swine and goats (filth, stench, lubricity), owls and bats (obscurity, obscurantism), vultures (gluttons for carrion!), and crows (blackness). The clerics hurl back at them apes (Darwin!), pigs (indestructible Epicurean porcines), dogs (the barker copulating in public, so dear to Diogenes) . . . The spectacle becomes more colorful, but the debate deteriorates.

11

Substance and forms of the secular ethic. More disturbingly, militant secularism leans heavily on the Judeo-Christian ethic, which it is often content merely to copy. Immanuel Kant writing *Religion within the Limits of Reason Alone* often serves as a breviary for secular thinkers. The gospel virtues, the message of the Commandments, the testamental recommendations are all merely represented in a new guise. Preservation of the substance, modification of the form . . . This secularization of Judeo-Christian morality often corresponds to an immanent rewriting of a transcendent discourse. What descends from heaven is not erased but reacclimatized for earth. The French priest and the French schoolteacher, self-appointed defender of the secular Republic's values, continue to be at daggers drawn, as they have been for so long—but in the end both fight for an essentially similar world.

Moral handbooks in republican schools preach the excellence of the family, the virtues of work, the need to respect one's parents and honor the old, the rightness of nationalism, patriotic obligations, mistrust of the flesh, the body and passions, the beauty of manual labor, submission to political authority, duty to the poor. What could the village priest object to here? Work, Family, Fatherland: the holy secular Trinity of Christendom . . . and of Vichy France.

Secular thought is not de-Christianized thought, but immanent Christian thought. Couched in rational language, it nevertheless preserves the quintessence of the Judeo-Christian ethic. God leaves heaven to come down to earth. He does not die, no one kills him, no one spurns him, he is simply adapted to the terrain of pure immanence. Jesus remains the hero of both visions of the world: he is merely asked to discard his halo and avoid excessively ostentatious gestures.

Hence a relativist definition of secularism: while the epistemology remains Judeo-Christian, secularism acts as if religion no longer impregnates and imbues consciences, bodies, and souls. We speak, think, live, act, imagine, eat, suffer, sleep, and conceive as Judeo-Christians, constructed by two thousand years of formatting by biblical monotheism. At which point, secularism fights to allow everyone to think what he wishes and believe in his own god, provided he does not make it a matter for the community. But publicly, the secularized religion of Christ leads the dance.

This being the case, the secular have no problem asserting the equality of Jew, Christian, and Muslim but also of Buddhist, Shintoist, animist, polytheist, and atheist in the contemporary Western state. Everything can easily be made to seem equal to everything else, once experienced in the depths and intimacy of the individual conscience, since everything outside, at the level of public life, institutions, forms, powers—in other words the essential—remains Judeo-Christian!

12

Toward a post-Christian secularism. Let us then leave behind us a secularism still too imprinted with what it claims to oppose. We may sincerely applaud it for what it once was, offer homage for its past struggles, propose a toast to what we owe it. But let us push forward in dialectical mode. Today's and tomorrow's battles require new weapons, better forged, more efficient, weapons suited to present needs. We need yet another effort to de-Christianize the ethic, politics, and the rest. But also to de-Christianize secularism, which would benefit immeasurably by emancipating itself still further from Judeo-Christian metaphysics, and which could truly be of service in the wars ahead.

For by decreeing the equality of all religions and of those who reject them, as today's regnant brand of secularism recommends, we condone relativism: equality of magical thinking and rational thought, of fable, myth, and reasoned argument, of thaumaturgic discourse and scientific thinking, of the Torah and Descartes's *Discourse on Method*, the New Testament and the *Critique of Pure Reason*, the Koran and the *Genealogy of Morality*. We declare Moses the equal of Descartes, Jesus of Kant, and Muhammad of Nietzsche.

Equality between the believing Jew — convinced that God promised his ancestors that they were his chosen people, in token of which he divided the sea, stopped the sun, etc. — and the philosopher who proceeds according to the hypothetico-deductive model? Equality between the believer — convinced that his hero, born of a virgin, crucified under Pontius Pilate, risen on the third day from the dead, and whiling his life away ever since sitting at the right hand of the father — and the thinker who deconstructs the manufacture of belief, the building of a myth, the creation of a fable? Equality between the Muslim — convinced that drinking Beaujolais and eating a pork roast disqualifies him from entering paradise whereas the assassination of an unbeliever throws open its gates for him — and the scrupulous analyst who, on the positivist and empirical principle, demonstrates that monotheistic belief is no more valid than that of the Dogon animist believing that the spirit of his ancestors returns in the shape of a fox? If we say yes to these questions, then let's stop thinking.

This relativism is crushing. In its name and in the name of secularism, all discourse carries equal weight: error and truth, the false and the true, the capricious and the serious. Myth and fable weigh as much as reason. Magic counts for as much as science. Dream for as much as reality. But all discourse does not carry the same weight: the discourse of neurosis, hysteria, and mysticism proceeds from another world than that of the positivist. We can no more tolerate neutrality and benevolence toward every conceivable form of discourse, including that of magical thinking, than we can lump together executioner and victim, good and evil. Must we remain neutral? Can we still afford to? I do not think so.

At this hour when the final battle — already lost — looms for the defense of the Enlightenment's values against magical propositions, we must fight for a post-Christian secularism, that is to say atheistic, militant, and radically opposed to choosing between Western Judeo-Christianity and its Islamic adversary — neither Bible nor Koran. I persist in preferring philosophers to rabbis, priests, imams, ayatollahs, and mullahs. Rather than trust their theological hocus-pocus, I prefer to draw on alternatives to the dominant philosophical historiography: the laughers, materialists, radicals, cynics, hedonists, atheists, sensualists, voluptuaries. They know that there is only one world, and that promotion of an afterlife deprives us of the enjoyment and benefit of the only one there is. A genuinely deadly sin.

BIBLIOGRAPHY

Atheology

1

Atheist poverty. The bibliography of the atheist question is poverty-stricken. Threadbare in comparison with works devoted to religions: every possible variation on the religious theme boasts multiple subsections — but who has ever seen an "atheism shelf" in a bookstore? And the rare books on the subject are of the poorest quality. As though their authors were in the pay of the god-mongers! Henri Arvon fired the first salvo in 1967 with a work in the *Que sais-je?* (What Do I Know?) series entitled *L'athéisme* (Atheism). Half of this slim volume is devoted to the atheism of Democritus, Epicurus, Lucretius, La Mothe Le Vayer, Gassendi, Pierre Bayle, Thomas Hobbes, John Locke, Hume, and others who never denied the existence of God or gods . . . The same goes for Hegel — an atheist! Max Stirner is disposed of in a chapter focused on Nietzschean atheism, although his only book, *The Ego and Its Own*, dates from the year of Nietzsche's birth: a truly premature Nietzschean! Another deficiency is his failure to mention Freud, who was after all the author of *The Future of an Illusion* (Standard Edition: English translation overseen by Freud himself, by James Strachey, W. W. Norton), which, categorically dismantling religion, takes its place among the great deconstructions of the religious question. A historian of anarchism, Henri Arvon ended his life as a convert to libertarianism — an ultra-conservatism of the kind that delighted Ronald Reagan.

Virtually the same defects are to be found in Georges Minois's monumental *Histoire de l'athéisme* (A History of Atheism), Fayard, 1998, just two of whose 671 pages are devoted to Freud! Apart from the abusive extension of the term "atheist" to include polytheists, deists, unorthodox Christians — Epicurus, Rabelais, and Hobbes sharing the limelight with Sade, Nietzsche, and Sartre! — the introduction in which the author attempts to define atheism is better left unread. The rest of the book merits attention chiefly as a road map directing one to possible further reading material. Generally speaking, a card-index system in need of sorting.

2

God is dead . . . oh, really? To verify the circumstances surrounding his assassination, we of course have Nietzsche and the notorious paragraph 125 — *The Madman* — in *The Gay Science* (translated by Thomas Common, Dover Publications, 2006). Read, too, *Ecce Homo* (translated by Anthony Ludovici, Dover Publications, 2004) and *The Anti-Christ*, in *The Portable Nietzsche* (translated by Walter Kaufmann, Penguin, 1977). To reacquaint ourselves with this question — "God is dead, so everything is permitted" (a proposition worthy of a course in elementary philosophy) — see Dostoyevsky's *The Brothers Karamazov* (translated by Richard Pevear and Larissa Volokhonsky, Farrar, Straus and Giroux, 2002).

In the absence of a good history of atheism (a subject still in search of an author), we might consult two philosophical approaches to the question. First, Jacques-J Natanson's *La mort de Dieu: essai sur l'athéisme moderne* (God's Death: An Essay on Modern Atheism), PUF: Presses Universitaires Françaises, 1975, in which the author combines a lucid and intelligent reading of questions relating to atheism with a blend of information, analysis, and commentary. Eight pages of bibliography. Next, and in the same spirit: Dominique Folscheid, *L'esprit de l'athéisme et son destin* (The Spirit and Fate of Atheism), La Table Ronde, 1991. An exhaustive analysis of Nietzsche and Dostoyevsky.

3

The fruits of antiphilosophy. This idea is specifically addressed in what I think is the only work devoted to the question: Didier Masseau's *Les ennemis des philosophes: l'antiphilosophie au temps des Lumières* (Adversaries of the Philosophers: Anti-Philosophy in the Enlightenment), Albin Michel. With the enlightened eighteenth century already well advanced, Jesuits, Jansenists, their apologists, and militant Catholics directed their hatred at philosophers—Rousseau, Voltaire, Diderot—and at philosophy. Historiography has smoothed the rough edges of that century, repainting it as the exclusive playground of the Enlightenment—and forgetting that Christian tradition, vengeful, militant, and contentious, stood at one extreme while at the other stood those I shall call the ultras of philosophy—the atheists (La Mettrie, d'Holbach, Helvetius)—who were criticized and attacked in the name of deism by the upholders of safe Enlightenment values... Twenty-seven pages of excellent bibliography.

François Garasse's *Doctrine curieuse* (A Curious Doctrine, shortly to be republished in French by Encre Marine) had paved the way in the previous century. To confirm that Vanini had never been an atheist, but rather a pantheist and a Christian, see Adolphe Delahays's *Oeuvres philosophiques*, (Philosophical Works) published in 1856 (translation by X. Rousselot) and never reissued in French. See also Emile Namer, *La vie et l'oeuvre de J. C. Vanini* (The Life and Work of J. C. Vanini), Vrin, 1980.

As a pendant to antiphilosophy, see the collection of texts published under the direction of Patrick Graille and Mladen Kozul, *Discours antireligieux français du dix-huitième siècle: du curé Meslier au Marquis de Sade* (Anti-Religious French Discourse in the Eighteenth Century, from the Priest Meslier to the Marquis de Sade), L'Harmattan, Les Presses de l'Université de Laval, 2003, an invaluable anthology with equally precious introductory notes. A curative for enemies of philosophy, past and present.

The not-quite-first atheist, Cristovão Ferreira, wrote *La supercherie dévoilée* (The Deception Revealed), originally a Portuguese pamphlet of 1636. This text, some thirty pages long, is laboriously introduced by Jacques Proust, an academic pretentious enough to post his surname on the title page of the work, which he translated in collaboration with a Marianne bearing the same name. The reader thus believes him to be the author, since the very name of Ferreira is nowhere to be seen. What honesty, what impeccable manners! The book's subtitle is *Une réfutation du catholicisme au Japon au XVIIe siècle.* (A Refutation of Catholicism in Japan in the Seventeenth Century). Perhaps a differently worded title might have done something to mask the work's odor of academic sanctity...but let's not ask too much. (Published by Chandeigne.) The bibliography of course cites every article ever written by this couple from Hades.

4

High-born bowels and Catholic intestines. We recall the Abbé Meslier's famous plea in favor of hanging and strangling every nobleman with the intestines of priests. Those words are to be found in the three-volume *Oeuvres* (Collected Works) of Jean Meslier (Anthropos, 1970). For those likely to be intimidated by its two thousand pages, see an excellent compendium entitled *Mémoire* (Memoir), Exils, 2000. The indispensable and probably unsurpassable labor of Maurice Dommanget, *Le curé Meslier: athée, communiste et révolutionnaire sous Louis XIV* (Meslier the Priest: Atheist, Communist, and Revolutionary under Louis XIV), Julliard, 1965, encompasses everything we can ever hope to know about this work by an authentic philosopher — inevitably consigned to oblivion because everything about him was guaranteed to offend: his hatred of God, of Christianity, of idealism, of the ascetic ideal, and his championing of freedom, hedonism, and earthly life. Lovers of shortcuts would be well advised to consult Marc Bredel, *Jean Meslier l'enragé: prêtre athée et révolutionnaire sous Louis XIV* (Jean Meslier the Madman: Priest, Atheist, and Revolutionary under Louis XIV), Balland, 1983. Bredel's virtually identical repetition of

Dommanget's subtitle is probably a faithful reflection of his debt to the latter.

Another of the excellent Dommanget's works worth reading is his critical intellectual biography *Sylvain Maréchaux, "L'homme sans Dieu": vie et oeuvre du Manifeste des égaux*, (Sylvain Maréchaux, "Man Without God": Life and Work of the Egalitarian Manifesto), as well as his *Dictionnaire des athées* (Atheists' Dictionary), Spartacus, 1950. Here again, an unsurpassed survey of the work of another thinker who has disappeared from contemporary intellectual circulation.

5

The Holbachian clique. Divine d'Holbach! Thanks to the courage and sparkling imagination of Jean-Pierre Jackson — whose editorial flair is obvious in everything he sets his hand to — we possess an edition, still in the making, of his *Oeuvres philosophiques* (Philosophical Works). Three monumental volumes (Alive Publications). They include *Le christianisme dévoilé* (Christianity Unveiled), *La contagion sacrée* (The Holy Contagion), and *Théologie portative* (Portable Theology) in volume 1; *Essai sur les préjugés* (Essay on Prejudices), *Système de la Nature* (Nature's System), and the incredible *Histoire critique de Jésus-Christ* (Critical History of Jesus Christ) in volume 2, and in volume 3 *Tableau des Saints* (Table of the Saints), *Le bon sens* (Common Sense), *Politique Naturelle* (Natural Politics), and *Ethocratie* (Ethocracy) — all of them absolutely essential teaching material in any curriculum expounding the case for atheism! They pulverize Rousseau's affected deist simperings, the anticlerical plays of Voltaire (stout defender of religion for the masses), and Diderot's shilly-shallying over the God dilemma.

A selection of texts in a hard-to-find volume by René Hubert, *D'Holbach et ses amis* (D'Holbach and His Friends), André Depeuc, publisher, part of an anti-Christian series that also published Gourmont and Jules de Gaultier on Nietzsche. Then, by Pierre Naville, *D'Holbach et la philosophie scientifique au XVIIIe siècle* (D'Holbach and

Eighteenth-Century Scientific Philosophy), Gallimard, 1967. The re-publication of a handful of works by the philosopher in Fayard's excellent Corpus collection brings together a number of contributions on d'Holbach from the review *Corpus*.

6

Planned obsolescence. Feuerbach's absence from the philosophical marketplace is equally scandalous. Apart from the takeover of his legacy and thinking by Louis Althusser, translator from the original German of the *Manifestes philosophiques: textes choisis (1839–1845)* (Philosophical Manifestos: Selected Texts, 1839–1845) for PUF and then for 10/18 in 1960, or that of his epigone Jean-Pierre Osier, to whom we owe *L'essence du christianisme* (The Essence of Christianity), Maspero, 1982, and translated into English by George Elliot (Prometheus Books, 1989), we would seek in vain for anything else. Unless it were the 1864 translation by J. Roy of a volume entitled *La religion* (Religion) and in 1845 *L'essence de la religion* (The Essence of Religion), translated into English by Alexander Loos (Prometheus Books, 2004), *Mort et immortalité* (Death and Immortality), 1830 — and *Pensées diverses* (Random Thoughts) and *Remarques* (Observations), republished by Vrin in 1987. More recently, *Pensées sur la mort et l'immortalité* (Reflections on Death and Immortality), Cerf, translated by Charles Berner, 1991).

Not much on Feuerbach. From Henri Arvon — author of the mediocre *Que sais-je?* text on atheism — we have *Ludwig Feuerbach ou la transformation du sacré* (Ludwig Feuerbach or the Transformation of the Sacred), PUF, 1957, and a selection of texts written by the same author but aiming more specifically at synthesis: *Feuerbach* (PUF, 1964). Alexis Philonenko has published a survey entitled *La jeunesse de Feuerbach (1828–1841): introduction à ses pensées fondamentales* (Feuerbach's Youth, 1828–1841: Introduction to his Basic Thinking), Vrin, 1990. One would like to see the same titanic labor devoted to the philosopher's last thirty years...Jean Salem steps in briefly with *Une lecture frivole des écritures:* "*L'Essence du christianisme*" *de Ludwig Feuerbach* (Irreverent Approach to the Writings: Ludwig Feuerbach's "Essence of Christianity"), Encre Marine, 2003.

7

A Judeo-Christian epistemology. Foucault proposed his notion of episteme in *Les mots et les choses* (*The Order of Things: An Archaeology of Human Sciences*), Routledge, 2001, in 1966. In *Dits et écrits,* volume 2 (French-only anthology), he asserts that "all relational phenomena among the sciences constitute what I call the episteme of a period." Clearly, we can grasp the details of an episteme only in archaeological terms, and on most improbable terrain. Referring to the Christian body in my own *Féeries anatomiques* (Anatomical Sorcery), I proposed an approach to the question of the episteme that takes Western flesh as its starting point. Worth reading on this subject are Nicolas Martin and Antoine Spire in *Dieu aime-t-il les maladies? Les religions monothéistes face à la maladie* (Does God Love Diseases? The Monotheist Religions and Illness), Anne Carrière, 2004, which illustrates the extent to which Judeo-Christian ideology still permeates questions of health, sickness, and, alas, bioethics. A detailed survey of the Christian position on health questions is to be found in the *Health Professionals' Charter* drawn up by the Pontifical Council on health services, and published in 1995 by the Vatican City: horrifying evidence of the extent to which our bioethics mark time — and even march backward — because of the retrograde positions of a Church defended by laymen drunk on holy water.

On the question of law and its Judeo-Christian formatting, I have set out my position in "Proposal for an end to human verdicts" in *L'archipel des comètes* (Archipelago of the Comets), Grasset.

8

A Christian atheism! André Comte-Sponville does not reject my formulation, but prefers "atheist believer." He explains what he means by this in his *A-t-on encore besoin d'une religion?* (Do We Still Need a Religion?) Les Editions de l'Atelier, 2003: "Atheist because I believe in no God; but a believer because I perceive myself as participating in a certain tradition, a certain history, and in those Judeo-Christian (or Greco-Judeo-Christian) values which are ours" (page 58). Likewise Luc Ferry, who — more prudent in every way — rejects the atheist position in favor of the agnostic option. See *L'homme-Dieu* (Man-God), Grasset.

This more explicitly assumed Christian tropism is also to be found in contemporary philosophy, in the thinking of Michel Henry and Giovanni Vattimo. The former approaches Christianity as a phenomenologist in *Incarnation* (Seuil, 2000), *Paroles du Christ* (Christ's Words), Seuil, 2004, and *I Am the Truth: Toward a Philosophy of Christianity*, translated into English by Susan Emanuel (Stanford University Press, 2002). Vattimo's approach is from the standpoint of hermeneutics . . . See his *Espérer croire* (Hoping to Believe), Seuil, 1998, and *Après la chrétienté* (After Christianity), Calmann-Lévy, 2004. Or how to immerse the Bible in the purgative waters of Heidegger's *Being and Time* in order to find a miraculous — in the chemical sense — solution.

9

Enduring scholasticism. Worth reading (although not atheists at all but unashamedly Christian) are Jean-Luc Marion, *Dieu sans l'être* (God Without Being God), PUF, 2002, and René Girard, *Je vois Satan tomber comme l'éclair* (I See Satan Strike Like Lightning), Grasset, 1999. Then, in the Jewish tradition crossbred with Russian, Italian, Spanish, French (but most decidedly not German) philosophy, Vladimir Jankélévitch: fifteen hundred pages in multivolume form: *Le sérieux de l'intention* (Seriousness of Intent), *Les vertus et l'amour* (The Virtues and

Love), *L'innocence et la méchanceté* (Innocence and Malice). In the same tradition, but blended here with Heideggerian phenomenology, Emmanuel Levinas, *Autrement qu'être ou au-delà de l'essence* (Other Than Being, or Beyond Essence), Nijhoff, 1974. Whence it emerges that love is preferable to war, courage to cowardice, forgiveness to resentment. Unimpeachable on paper.

Monotheisms

1

The price of the One Book. In theory, each of the three monotheisms presents itself as the one religion of a One book. In fact, these One books are legion. The renowned Pléiade library at Gallimard takes a curious position: it publishes these works in mouse-gray binding, while it issues its ancient texts in green. Why not issue the Bible, the Koran, the Intertestamentary Writings, or the Christian Apocryphal texts in the same colors as Homer, Plato, or Augustine? For they are all exclusively historical writings.

I have used Emile Osty's and Joseph Trinquet's Bible (Seuil). I prefer it to the three-volume Pléiade edition because it facilitates search by incorporating subtitles into the text. On the other hand, its footnotes and cross-reference system are without any real interest. My Koran is the Pléiade version, translated by D. Masson — an Islamophile version as one might expect. Its footnoting also needs revision for much the same reasons.

On biblical historicity: Israël Finkelstein and Neil Asher Silberman, *The Bible Unearthed: Archaeology's New Vision of Ancient Israel and the Origin of its Sacred Texts* (Free Press, 2002). Their work teems with historical information on the myth-manufacturing production line that generated the book. Other basic works: the Pentateuch and the Talmud. There is no genuinely critical and atheistic edition of any of these works!

Also worth reading is the *Catechism of the Catholic Church*. The endurance and longevity of mythologies inherited from a thousand years ago! For those eager to familiarize themselves with the study of angels — a major linchpin of that remote past — see Pseudo-Dionysius the Areopagite's *Complete Works* (English version, long out of print, published by Richwood Publishing, 1976). And a masterly synthesis, *Les anges* (The Angels) by Philippe Faure (Cerf, Fides). On angelic dwelling-places: Soubhi el-Saleh, *La vie future selon le Coran* (Future Life According to the Koran),Vrin.

2

Books on the One book. Bookstores and libraries overflow with religious works. Their abundance is matched only by the rarity of books devoted to atheism! As time passes, these sections continue to proliferate in bookstores, cheek by jowl with those celebrating the New Age, self-improvement, astrology, Buddhism, Tarot cards, and other manifestations of the appeal of the irrational. Take a quick look at Adorno's book on horoscopes, *From the Stars Down to Earth and Other Essays on the Irrational Culture* (Routledge, 2001), in which a wealth of analysis serves to facilitate understanding of religious belief.

The question of dictionaries is of real interest. See *Le dictionnaire des monotheisms* (Dictionary of Monotheisms), issued under the direction of Jacques Potin and Valentine Zubert (Bayard): three sections, Judaism, Christianity, Islam, with alphabetical entries, a final index, and another at the end of each entry that conflates these three phases — enough to provide the reader with the needed minimum on a given subject. The *Dictionnaire de l'Islam: religion et civilisation* (Dictionary of Islam: Religion and Civilization), Encyclopaedia Universalis, Albin Michel, is remarkable. And with his *Dictionnaire des symboles musulmans* (Dictionary of Islamic Symbols), Albin Michel, Malek Chebel has produced what is surely his best work, or in any event his least partial. Useful footnotes to the suras, bibliography, and cross-references.

Reading the Talmud is extremely tedious! Timid readers might consult Adin Steinsaltz, *Introduction au Talmud* (Introduction to the Talmud), Albin Michel, and Abraham Cohen's *Everyman's Talmud: The Major Teachings of the Rabbinic Sages* (Schocken, 1995). Excellent historical syntheses in the former, a thematic approach, rich in quotations, in the latter. But hands-on knowledge of the text of the Talmud itself is indispensable, naturally for its ideas and substance, but also in order to grasp the economy of a logical system, a dialectic, and a way of thinking.

As for Islam, Rohdy Alili's *Qu'est-ce que l'Islam?* (What Is Islam?), La Découverte, is preferable to Malek Chebel's *Dictionnaire amoureux de l'Islam* (Loving Dictionary of Islam), Plon, which is both partial and skimpy: Islam, religion of peace and love (!), tolerant of wine ("There has never been any question of banning wine outright, simply of dissuading true believers from its consumption," page 617), one of many singular paradoxes in this truly amorous dictionary that avoids such subjects as war, raiding, battles, conquests, and anti-Semitism — all of which more or less defined the life of the Prophet and of Islam for centuries. On the other hand, there is an entry on the Crusades to compensate for the absence of an entry on the Jews... As for sex, the reader will be gratified to know that "Islam has liberated sexuality and made of it an area of extreme sociability" (page 561). Worth asking women who live under the sharia for their opinion, because Malek Chebel (see the entry for Women) believes that ill-treatment of women is the fault of backward governments and incompetent politicians, never of the text of the Koran itself.

3

The antidote to monotheistic fraud. Read Raoul Vaneigem's *De l'inhumanité de la religion* (On the Inhumanity of Religion), Denoël. But also his preface to *L'art de ne croire en rien* (The Art of Believing in Nothing), followed by the *Livre des trois imposteurs* (Book of Three Frauds), Payot-Rivages. These three frauds were Moses, Jesus, and Muhammad. Also of interest is Jean Soler's important and very wide-ranging book *Aux origines du Dieu unique: l'invention du monothéisme* (On the Origins of the Only God: The Invention of Monotheisms), eds. De Fallois, 2002, which offers some startling conclusions — the Jews, "this mental [as one might speak of 'conceptual' art?] people is a verbal creation" (page 118). In it, the author asserts that the Hebrews went from polytheism to monotheism in order to guarantee their ontological existence on the basis of a One book. But also that their message of love is directed only at their own kind — "God of all mankind or God of the Jews?" (pages 184–186) — not at their neighbor. This last point is developed in *La loi de Moïse*, (The Law of Moses, pages 66–74 and 106–111), same publisher, 2003. A book that also demonstrates (chapter 1) the restrictive interpretation we are required to give to the supposedly universal imperative of "Thou shalt not kill." (My thanks to Jean Soler for the invaluable advice he gave me on looking over my manuscript.)

4

Foreskins, refinements, and libraries. The same Malek Chebel has published his *Histoire de la circoncision des origines à nos jours* (History of Circumcision from the Origins to the Present Day), Le Nadir, Balland. In his introduction (page 11) he writes: "the information in this book is resolutely accurate and untainted by proselytism." On page 7, he clarifies the nature of this objectivity: "This book is dedicated to the 'surgeons of enlightenment': the circumcisers." And on page 30, still entirely neutral, and in the wake of a number of psychological reflections and considerations (for Malek Chebel also styles himself a psychoanalyst), he asks: "Can one truly consider the ablation of such paper-thin skin as a 'traumatic' or even worse a traumatological act?" Sigmund, where are you when we need you?

On circumcision, the reader will prefer analyses inspired by the utilitarian and pragmatic Anglo-Saxon method (in the best senses of all those terms) of Margaret Somerville's *The Ethical Canary: Science, Society and the Human Spirit* (McGill-Queen's University Press, 2004).

Particularly interesting is chapter 8, entitled "Operating on the body of the small boy. The ethical stakes of circumcision" (pages 201–216). These pages changed my mind on this question even before I read them, and then convinced me entirely. See also Moses Maimonides, *Guide for the Perplexed* (Dover Publications, 2000).

To return to the same Malek Chebel: he has given birth to a book with a most beautiful title, *Traité du raffinement* (Treatise on Refinement), Payot, in which he celebrates refinement as a Muslim art, when in fact it proceeds from pre-Islamic Arab culture. The fact that a few princely courts — Baghdad, Cordova, the Maghreb, Egypt — persisted (heedless of Koranic teachings) in their praise of perfume, jewels, precious stones, wine (again!), luxury, gastronomy, and homosexuality does not authorize us to conclude that Islam ever converted to hedonism! We might as well judge the nature of Marxist-Leninism solely on the basis of the daily life of Kremlin hierarchs during the Stalin years.

To gauge the extent of Islam's tolerant hedonism, induce shivers to run down your spine by reading *Jalons sur le chemin de la chasteté* (Landmarks on the Path of Chastity) by Abd Allah b.' Abd al-Rahman al Watban, followed by the work of 'Abd al'Aziz b'.' Abd Allah b. Baz, *Les dangers de la mixité dans le domaine du travail* (The Perils of Mingling the Sexes in the Workplace), al-Hadith Publications. And for Islam's tolerance of books that are neither the Koran nor religious, the reader will be gratified to consult Lucien X. Polastron's *Livres en feu* (Books in Flames), Denoël. There he will learn of the evolution of the Christian relish for autos-da-fé, from the fourth-century origins of the Christian totalitarian state to the (never abolished) *Index of Forbidden Books*. The Jews have endured countless book burnings throughout their existence, but have never initiated a single one. There is an admirable synthesis in Anne-Marie Delcambre's *L'Islam des interdits* (The Islam of Prohibitions), Desclée de Brouwer, 2003. We owe the same author and publisher an excellent biography of the Prophet, *Muhammad*, published in 2003.

On the Vatican's relationship to intelligence (and hence to books), see Georges Minois's *L'Eglise et la science: histoire d'un malen-*

tendu (The Church and Science: The Story of a Misunderstanding), Fayard, an extremely factual work, weltering in detail (two volumes where one would have sufficed . . .), totally free of theorizing or conceptualizing. To be read with an eye to Jean Steiman's *Richard Simon: les origines de l'exigèse biblique* (Richard Simon: The Origins of Biblical Exegeis), Editions d'Aujourd'hui. Richard Simon (seventeenth century) inserted intelligence into the reading of so-called holy texts, and in so doing angered Bossuet, the Oratorians, Port-Royal, the Benedictines, the Jesuits, the Jansenists, and the Protestants. All good reasons for making a hero of him. Also read Jean Rocchi, *L'irréductible: Giordano Bruno face à l'Inquisition* (The Diehard: Giordano Bruno Against the Inquisition), with a most bracing foreword by Marc Silbernstein, dynamic inspirer of the (militant-materialist) publisher Syllepse!

Christianity

1

Flesh of an ectoplasm. Obviously, there are thousands of stories about Jesus . . . Those that deny his historical existence and reduce this figure to the crystallization of a fiction are, on the other hand, extremely rare. Of course . . . The most famous of these is from the pen of Prosper Alfaric, *A l'école de la raison: étude sur les origines chrétiennes* (The School of Reason: A Study of Christian Origins), Publications de l'Union rationaliste. See in particular pages 97–200, "The problem of Jesus. Did Jesus exist?" The answer: no. Today, Raoul Vaneigem defends this position, making it his own in *La résistance au christianisme: les hérésies des origines au XVIIIe siècle* (Resistance to Christianity: Heresies from the Beginnings to the Eighteenth Century), Fayard. He mentions in particular, on page 104, "the Catholic and Roman fable of a historical Jesus." Unambiguous . . .

Others admittedly believe in his historical existence, but in their lengthy tomes they identify thousands of improbabilities, uncertainties, inconsistencies, and countertruths in the Bible. They assert so many reasons for rejecting certainties that one wonders what prevents them from crowding into the camp of the deniers. Caution? Inability to take responsibility for this major act of iconoclasm? Inability to leave behind them their intellectual training (often they are former seminary students or people with a solid theological background)? For there is the thickness of a cigarette paper between their conclusions and those of the ultras.

Thus Charles Guignebert, *Jésus* (La Renaissance du livre, 1933) and *Le Christ* (same publisher, 1943), to whom I am indebted for several examples I have quoted to stress the excesses of the New Testament — the *titulus*, the language used by Pilate, and so forth. Gérard Mordillat and Jérôme Prieur have made a synthesis of this labor, fleshed out by a few rare recent works, in their *Corpus Christi: enquête sur l'écriture des Evangiles* (Corpus Christi: An Inquiry into the Gospel Writings), five small volumes issued by Mille et Une Nuits in 1997: *Crucifuxion* (Crucifixion), *Procès* (Trial), *Roi des Juifs* (King of the Jews), *Pâques* (Easter), *Résurrection* (Resurrection), and *Christos.* Twelve films distributed by Arte were based on these works by Prieur, *Jésus illustre et inconnu* (Jesus, Illustrious and Unknown), Desclée de Brouwer, 2001, and Mordillat, *Jésus contre Jésus* (Jesus against Jesus), Seuil.

2

God's weakling. It was he who said it . . . Saint Paul . . . in the First Epistle to the Corinthians (15:8). For all the texts on or by Paul, Epistles, Letters, Acts, etc., see *La Bible* (the Bible), translated by Osty, Seuil, 1973. A rich bibliography of course. And not invariably partial . . . Fayard Publications have a reputation for seriousness. This being so, how can we take the work wholly seriously when we read (from the pen of Françoise Baslez) the following detail from the chapter on Paul's conversion on the road to Damascus: "he would never make the slightest allusion to the possibility of blindness" — and then read in the Acts of the Apostles (9:8): "and when his eyes were opened, he saw no man" (and this for three whole days)?

In his television mode (you hear him as you read him), Alain Decaux has committed *Un avorton de Dieu: une vie de Saint Paul* (God's Weakling: A Life of Saint Paul), Desclée de Brouwer, 2003. The historian does not hide his Catholic loyalties, but he performs an honest task of compilation, particularly on the diseases attributed to the Tarsiot (page 101). Useful because it relieves one of the burden of doing the necessary reading on one's own behalf. No criticisms, no reservations, no personal interpretations, but a good introductory narrative.

Alain Badiou, philosopher, mathematician, Lacanian, novelist, and playwright, and also an extreme left-wing militant, confesses in his *Saint Paul: la fondation de l'universalisme* (Saint Paul: The Foundation of Universalism), PUF, 1997, to his interest (which we share) in the religion-founder, the empire-builder. A shame that he considers Paul as standing alone in this role, without incorporating into his argument what Constantine added in order to make the planetary Church a possibility. The ectoplasm needed the hysteric in order to become flesh, but it was the dictator who managed the extension of Jesus's body to the whole empire.

3

Portrait of an era. To comprehend the psychological atmosphere of the Late Empire, its belief in mystery, the miraculous, in images, astrology, its religion, its structural flaws, its taste for the irrational, read E. R. Dodds, *Pagan and Christian in an Age of Anxiety* (Cambridge University Press, 1991). And consult H. I. Marrou, *Décadence romaine ou Antiquité tardive?* (Roman Decadence or the Survival of Antiquity?), Seuil, 1977, which establishes the survival of the ancient world into the early Christian period. It is in this book that we encounter the expression "Totalitarian State of the Late Empire" (page 172). Marrou, a Christian, wrote among other subjects about Augustine, Clement of

Alexandria, and the history of the Church. On the world and the workings of paganism under Christian persecution, read Ramsay MacMullen's *Paganism in the Roman Empire* (Yale University Press, 1983), and A. J. Fustigière's *Hermétisme et mystique païenne* (Pagan Alchemy and Mysticism), Aubier-Montaigne, 1967. Gibbon — the English Michelet — wrote with authentic relish about antiquity in his *History of the Decline and Fall of the Roman Empire.*

For downwardly adjusted figures on the number of Christian victims of martyrdom and other persecutions (before they themselves became the persecutors), see Claude Lepelley, *L'Empire romain et le christianisme* (The Roman Empire and Christianity), Flammarion, 1969. Catholic historiography has substantially inflated these figures for propaganda purposes — motivated in this case, as in others, by apologetic aims.

4

The soldier convert. For a portrait of the tyrant, read Guy Gauthier, *Constantin: le triomphe de la croix* (Constantine: The Cross Triumphant, France-Empire, 1999). He expounds at great length the hypothesis of an astronomical (and therefore rigorously scientific) interpretation of the apparition Constantine saw, and his arguments are convincing. Making no concessions, but free of recrimination, it is a work that takes every position into consideration. Oddly enough, the face of the first emperor converted to Christianity has inspired little writing in France. André Pigagniol's venerable book *L'Empereur Constantin* (The Emperor Constantine), Rieder, 1932 remains a mine of information that has not aged.

A *Que sais-je?* synthesis by Bertrand Lançon, *Constantin* (Constantine), PUF, 1998, is useful. And in the same collection one might profitably read Pierre Maraval's *L'Empereur Justinien* (The Emperor Justinian), 1999, on the continuation of the work of the emperor touched by grace.

5

Christian vandalism. I have long sought proofs of Christian persecution of pagans. Many works remain silent, deny the facts, and even transform the new wielders of power into tolerant, likable, genial figures, book lovers, builders of libraries . . . I say nothing about works (easily the most numerous) that actively promote such commonplace fantasies. To find real traces of persecutions, of autos-da-fé, destruction of temples, statues, sacred groves, and bonfires, I have delved into the following:

First the ancient authors. Julian, that paladin of paganism who resisted (in vain, alas) the Christianization of the empire, wrote *Against the Galileans: An Imprecation Against Christianity.* Celsus, another pagan standard-bearer, published *Against the Christians.* The book itself was destroyed but was immortalized by Origen, who refuted Celsus's arguments and quoted from the book so extensively that its essentials have survived! Louis Rogier's *Celse contre les chrétiens* (Celsus Against the Christians), Le Labyrinthe, 1997, also addresses the question of Christian vandalism. Porphyry's *Against Christians* went up in flames — we know nothing about the book, except that it was a major loss. And finally, there was Libanius's lamentation addressed to Emperor Theodosius I, *Against the Desecration of Pagan Temples.*

See also Julius Firmicus Maternus's *The Error of Pagan Religions* (XVI-XXIV), and Sozomen, Socrates, and Theodoret, *Histoire ecclésiastique tripartite* (Three-Part Ecclesiastical History), personal translation: Laure Chavel. And Saint John Chrysostom's *Homily on Statues* (1), in Robert Joly, *Origines et évolution de l'intolérance catholique* (Origins and Evolution of Catholic Intolerance), Ed. Université de Bruxelles, 1986. These texts (my thanks to Laure Chavel for her invaluable library work) describe Christian exactions in detail. Yet strangely, historians make no use of their labors in order to show how Christianity was really manufactured — by force, the sword, blood, and terror.

Nor does anyone read the *Codex Theodosianus.* Books XVI and IX, translated by Elisabeth Magnou-Nortier (Cerf, 2002), legitimize all Christian exactions against the pagans: executions, police brutality, creation of a class of citizens not shielded by the law, ban on employment in a judicial capacity, and withdrawal of all protection . . . A blueprint for America's future black codes and Vichy's anti-Semitic laws — or how justice may establish laws that exclude a section of the population — pagans the day before yesterday, American blacks and the Jews only yesterday.

See the passages describing these exactions in Pierre Chuvin's *Chronique des derniers païens: la disparition du paganisme dans l'Empire romain, du règne de Constantin à celui de Justinien* (Belles Lettres-Fayard, 1991), translated into English as *A Chronicle of the Last Pagans*, translated by B. A. Archer (Harvard University Press, 1990). See also Pierre de Labriolle's *La réaction païenne: étude sur la polémique antichrétienne du Ier au Vie siècle* (The Pagan Reaction: Study of Anti-Christian Argument from the First to the Sixth Centuries), Durand Publications, 1954. Read Robin Lane-Fox's *Pagans and Christians* (Penguin, 2006). These works salvage the honor of a profession otherwise unanimous in its silence on Christian vandalism.

6

Patrological mush. With the advent of Christianity, philosophy became the handmaiden of theology, and theology became a discipline of glossing and cross-glossing. Philosophizing now became a labor of commentary on biblical texts and of hairsplitting over details in the creation of a world of pure abstractions and disembodied concepts. When this was not the case, the authors of the Greek and Roman patrology constructed a morality based on the ascetic ideal, obsessed with hatred of the body, of desires, of passions and physical drives, and praise of celibacy, of continence, and of chastity.

C. Mondésert provides a good introduction to this world in his *Pour lire les Pères de l'Eglise dans les sources chrétiennes* (Reading the Church Fathers in Christian Sources), Foi Vivante, 1979, as does Jean-Yves Leloup in *Introduction aux "vrais philosophes." Les Pères grecs: un continent oublié de la pensée occidentale* (Introduction to the "True

Philosophers": The Greek Fathers — Forgotten Continent of Western Thought), Albin Michel, 1998. Indeed they do proclaim themselves "true philosophers," but ignorance of their names and their writings is equaled only by their real and effective penetration of daily life over the centuries. We live with a Christian body they themselves manufactured.

Theocracy

1

Totalitarianisms, fascisms, and other brutalities. Hannah Arendt's work is of course incontrovertible: see *The Origins of Totalitarianism* (Harvest Books, new edition, 1973). Then there is Emilio Gentile's *Qu'est-ce que le fascisme?* (What Is Facism?), translated by P. E. Dauzat (Folio). The original Italian title is closer to *Fascism: History and Interpretation*, but the formatting of this collection belies the naming of a work that functions less as an introduction than the publisher would have us believe. Perhaps we can now set aside the squabbling of historians — which even emboldens some of them to exclude Vichy from the roster — who are still unable to agree on a definition of the phenomenon.

Less conventional is Jean Grenier's excellent and premonitory book *Essai sur l'esprit d'orthodoxie* (Essay on the Spirit of Orthodoxy), Idées Gallimard, which as far back as 1938 said everything worth knowing on the subject, and which France's New Philosophers picked up forty years later — Nazism, Hiroshima, not to mention May '68 — without ever actually mentioning Grenier's book. An equally indispensable addition to the reading list is Karl Popper's *The Open Society and Its Enemies*, volume 1: *The Spell of Plato*, volume 2: *The High Tide of Prophecy: Hegel, Marx, and the Aftermath* (Routledge, 2002). Here again, France's New Philosophers were quick to jump on the bandwagon.

2

Specific terrors. Yves-Charles Zarka and Cynthia Fleury, *Difficile tolérance* (The Challenge of Tolerance), PUF, 2004. Read it for Cynthia Fleury's convincing analysis which concludes that "Islam possesses no real equivalent of tolerance" and for her highly pertinent demonstration of the Islamic institution of "dhimmitude." However, Zarka's concept of *structure-tolérance* is much less persuasive. Read also Christian Delacampagne's *Islam et Occident: les raisons d'un conflit* (Islam and the West: Grounds for Dispute), PUF, an analysis that assumes the military and political success of the Americans in Iraq. A fine example of the rhetoric of French intellectuals and their predictable conclusions. From the same author come two practical syntheses: *Une histoire du racisme* (A History of Racism), and *Une histoire de l'esclavage* (A History of Slavery), both from Livre de Poche. Terse and telling observations on slavery and the Old Testament, and then on Christianity. More worthwhile is Peter Garnsey's *Ideas of Slavery from Aristotle to Augustine* (Cambridge University Press, 1997). An unsurpassed and indispensable labor on colonialism is Louis Sala-Molins's *Le Code noir ou le calvaire de Canaan* (The Black Code or Canaan's Martyrdom), PUF Quadrige — shattering for the Church, the French monarchy, and for the West as a whole.

A most interesting and dense little work is strategic expert Jean-Paul Charnay's *La Charia et l'Occident* (Sharia and the West), L'Herne. By the same author: *L'Islam et la guerre: de la guerre juste à la révolution sainte* (Islam and War: From Just War to Holy Revolution), Fayard, 1986, and then volume 3 of his *Classiques de la stratégie: principes de stratégie arabe* (Classics of Strategy: Arab Strategic Principles), L'Herne, 1984. The possibility of change in Islam is most cautiously envisaged … for a few centuries hence.

To speed this process of change and avoid waiting for ten centuries, Malek Chebel proposes a *Manifeste pour un Islam des Lumières: vingt-sept propositions pour reformer l'Islam* (Manifesto for an Enlightened Islam: Twenty-Seven Proposals for Islamic Reform), Hachette. In a word: if Islam were not Islam it would be much easier to defend! For what else would a feminist Islam *be*—democratic, secular, egalitarian, individualistic, tolerant, acquiescent in the rules of the game, etc.—but the opposite of what it actually, fundamentally *is*? To defend the Western virtues listed above, we have no need of a book and a tradition that have always condemned them. Jettisoning references to the Koran and Hadith seems an infinitely preferable way to bring off Malek Chebel's Enlightenment project!

3

Christian crimes. Georges Minois, *L'Eglise et la guerre: de la Bible à l'ère atomique* (The Church and War: From the Bible to the Atomic Age), Fayard. Rather long, occasionally padded, losing itself in details, short on analysis, factual, even slightly partial in places. Nothing for example on the blessing bestowed by Father George Zabelka on the crew of the *Enola Gay* before it destroyed Hiroshima. I came across that detail in Théodore Monod's *Le chercheur d'absolu* (Seeking the Absolute), Actes Sud, page 89. I learned from the same Théodore Monod (page 93) that the Catholic Church only abandoned use of the Sedia—the royal and papal throne borne on human backs—during the papacy of John XXIII.

On colonialism, read Michael Prior, a priest trained by the Vincentians: *The Bible and Colonialism: A Moral Critique* (Sheffield, 1997). The question of colonialism, slavery, and the trade in African blacks as practiced by Muslims has generated little work. Read Jacques Heers, *Les négriers en terre d'Islam: la première traite des Noirs, VIIe–XVIe siècles* (Slave Traders in Islamic Lands: The First Enslavement of Blacks, Seventh to Sixteenth Centuries), Perrin, 2003. He offers justifications for this rarely mentioned historical episode that fit well with the French talent for self-flagellation and self-denigration. Surely there are better motives for the writing of history?

On Rwanda: Jean-Damiscène Bizimana, *L'Eglise et le génocide au Rwanda: les Pères blancs et le négationnisme* (The Church and the Rwanda Genocide: White Priests and Denial), L'Harmattan, 2001. A pity this publishing house does not take its editorial obligations more seriously: the few factual errors that crop up here and there could be exploited — wrongly — to invalidate the book's unimpeachable theses. Read also the excellent book by Jean Hatzfeld, *Une saison de machettes* (Seuil, 2003), translated into English by Linda Coverdale as *Machete Season: The Killers in Rwanda Speak* (Picador, 2006). It is a masterpiece to be classed alongside the work of Primo Levi or Robert Antelme. Note the chapter entitled "And God in All This?" By the same author: *Dans le nu de la vie: récits des marais rwandais* (Seuil, 2000), translated into English by Gerry Feehily as *Into the Quick of Life: The Rwandan Genocide — The Survivors Speak* (Trans-Atlantic, 2005).

The Inquisition has generated a substantial number of books. Among them: Joseph Pérez, *Brève histoire de l'Inquisition en Espagne* (Fayard, 2002), translated into English by Janet Lloyd as *The Spanish Inquisition: A History* (Yale University Press, 2006). Same proliferation for the Crusades: see Albert Dupront's two volumes, *Le mythe de croisade* (The Crusader Myth), Gallimard. On Christian-Muslim relations: John V. Tolan, *Saracens* (Columbia University Press, 2002).

4

Swastika and crucifix. We know of the relationship between the Vatican and National Socialism from the works of Saul Friedlander, *Pius XII and the Third Reich: A Documentation* (Knopf, 1966); and of Daniel Jonah Goldhagen, *Moral Duty: The Role of the Catholic Church in the Holocaust and Its Unfulfilled Duty of Repair* (Vintage, 2003). Unanswerable. Difficult for the Church to respond to this mass of proven facts, opinions, analyses, etc.

Less well known is Hitler's defense of Jesus, of the Christ, of Christianity, of the Church... A reading of *Mein Kampf* suffices to confirm the führer's fascination with the story of Jesus driving the moneylenders from the Temple, and his admiration for the Church's success in building a European and even a worldwide civilization. The book exists, but who reads this text that everyone talks about but no one has ever opened? (Mariner Books paperback, Houghton Mifflin, translated by Ralph Manheim). Pay special attention to page 307 in volume 1, and to pages 114–120, 307, 454, and 459 in volume 2.

These Hitlerian assertions are confirmed by the chancellor's private remarks. Albert Speer, for example, comments on Hitler's devotion to Christianity and its Church. He also notes the führer's frustration at having no one of high caliber at the head of the Church with whom he might discuss "making the evangelical Church the official Church." See Speer's *Inside the Third Reich* (Simon & Schuster, 1970).

5

Zionism: up front and backstage. Theodor Herzl's Zionist project is of enduring interest to contemporary readers. See *The Jewish State* (originally *Der Judenstaat*, translated by Sylvie D'Avigdor, Dover Publications, 1989). In it we learn that for Herzl, Palestine was not a fixation: he notes that the choice of a homeland could also have fallen on Argentina and that the Jews would have to take what was offered them. The social blueprint was impeccable: work (a seven-hour day), organization, constitution, language (not Hebrew but all languages, with one of them eventually emerging on top), legal system, flag (white with seven gold stars), armed forces (an exclusively professional army quartered in barracks), theocracy (absolutely not: religious leaders would be banned from political activities), tolerance, freedom of belief, of conviction, and of religious denomination. On the acquisition of land, no question of brutal invasion but the auctioning off of property. All this seemed idyllic indeed. Why then the persistent silence over his *Diary*? In particular over Herzl's entry for June 12, 1895: "We must use persuasion in expropriating the land granted to us. We must strive discreetly to send the poorer population into neighboring lands, procuring work for them in transit countries without providing it for them here. The landowners will be on our side..." Quoted by Michael Prior, op. cit.

6

The philosopher and the Ayatollah. The *Politico-Spiritual Testament* of the Ayatollah Khomeini is a manual for every Islamic government, every Muslim theocracy. Essential reading and material for reflection.

Michel Foucault commented on this Iranian revolution in a series of articles commissioned by the *Corriere della Sera*. These articles have been reprinted in *Dits et écrits* (Comments and Writings), volume 3, 1976–1979. The reader cannot fail to be struck by the pages in which he hails the ayatollah as the spirit of the Iranian people and the return of the spiritual element to politics (which he appears to welcome), the pages in which he refers to the abolition of a tainted regime (about which, on the contrary, he seems lucid and well-informed), and the pages in which he announces the birth of Islamic resistance to globalization — on whose looming implications he conjectures most presciently.

His texts deserve better than his polemics: blind Foucault/heroic Foucault; Foucault the ayatollah's henchman/Foucault the infallible. That a man like Foucault (who that same year was working at the Collège de France on the birth of biopower and who could excel in textual analysis) could at the same time be so wrong in the analysis of facts — that is something for historians of philosophy to consider! We will read with fresh eyes his famous text entitled "Les 'reportages' d'idées" (The Transference of Ideas) pages 706–707.

7

A post-Christian secularism. For an account of those pioneering moments of secularism in history, read Jacqueline Lalouette, *La libre-pensée en France, 1848–1940* (Free Thinking in France, 1848–1940), Albin Michel. A survey by a historian who brings to light a substantial number of facts on the subject. Reading this book encourages us to ponder the kind of secularism that may prove more effective in confronting the challenges of the twenty-first century — challenges that are no longer the purely domestic ones involved in the fight for separation of church and state. The work still has to be done — and it is now of planetary concern.

Whence the interest of postmodern (and therefore post-Christian) secular thinking. Among a timely range of works on the subject, see the labor of synthesis by Henri Pena-Ruiz, *Qu-est-ce que la laïcité?* (What is Secularism?), Folio. Since he advocates a definition of benevolent neutrality in the terms of France's Third Republic, yet simultaneously defends the notion that the concept of secularism is also part and parcel of republican values (page 97), it is hard to see how he can defend these values at the same time as he defends monotheism — which substantially contradicts them. His well-founded analysis of the sects he debars from secular tolerance (page 98) and of the "charlatans who promise happiness on the cheap and try to subject men to an almost infantile quest for readymade recipes and solutions" (a definition that strikes me as applicable to every religion without exception) could profitably be expanded. Which would contribute enormously to the definition of a post-Christian secularism!

New York Times bestselling author **Christine Feehan** has over 30 novels published and has thrilled legions of fans with her seductive and sensual 'Dark' Carpathian tales. She has received numerous honours throughout her career including being a nominee for the Romance Writers of America RITA, and receiving a Career Achievement Award from *Romantic Times*, and has been published in multiple languages and in many formats, including audio book, e-book, and large print.

For more information about Christine Feehan visit her website: www.christinefeehan.com

Praise for Christine Feehan:

'After Bram Stoker, Anne Rice and Joss Whedon, Feehan is the person most credited with popularizing the neck gripper'
Time magazine

'The queen of paranormal romance'
USA Today

'Feehan has a knack for bringing vampiric Carpathians to vivid, virile life in her Dark Carpathian novels'
Publishers Weekly

For Misty Valverde.
We hope your travels have been safe
and that you're well and happy.
You dream big and live life large.
We've missed you at FAN!

For My Readers

Be sure to go to http://www.christinefeehan.com/members/ to sign up for my PRIVATE book announcement list and download the FREE ebook of *Dark Desserts*. Join my community and get firsthand news, enter the book discussions, ask your questions and chat with me. Please feel free to email me at Christine@christinefeehan.com. I would love to hear from you.

DARK
LYCAN

A CARPATHIAN NOVEL

CHRISTINE FEEHAN

piatkus

PIATKUS

First published in the US in 2013 by The Berkley Publishing Group
A division of the Penguin Group USA (Inc.),
First published in Great Britain in 2013 by Piatkus

A CIP catalogue record for this book
is available from the British Library.

Hardback ISBN: 978-0-349-40217-8
Trade paperback ISBN: 978-0-349-40195-9

Printed and bound in Great Britain
by Clays Ltd, St Ives plc

Papers used by Piatkus are from well-managed forests
and other responsible sources.

 MIX
Paper from
responsible sources
FSC
www.fsc.org FSC® C104740

Piatkus
An imprint of
Little, Brown Book Group
100 Victoria Embankment
London EC4Y 0DY

An Hachette UK Company
www.hachette.co.uk

www.piatkus.co.uk

Acknowledgments

Dr. Christopher Tong wrote a beautiful song for Fen to sing to his lady, Tatijana. Thank you so much, Chris; the song was perfect in every way.

Many thanks to my sister Anita Toste, who always answers my call and has such fun with me writing mage spells.

I have to give a special shout-out to C. L. Wilson and Sheila English, who were gracious enough to include me in our power-writing sessions. We rocked it, didn't we?

There would be no *Dark Lycan* without Brian Feehan or Domini Stottsberry. They worked long hours to help me with everything from brainstorming ideas and doing research to edits. There are no words to describe my gratitude or love for them. Thank you all so very much!

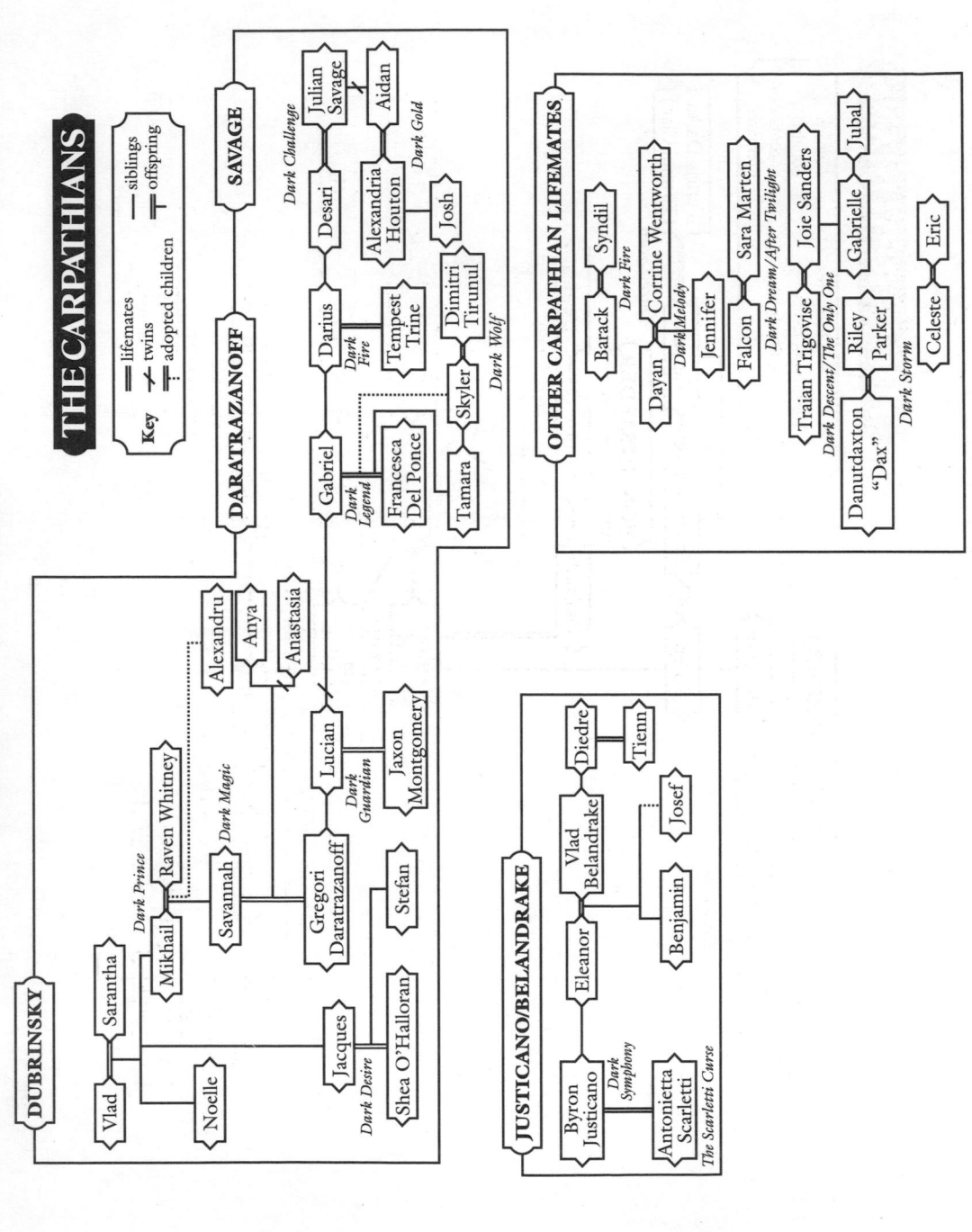

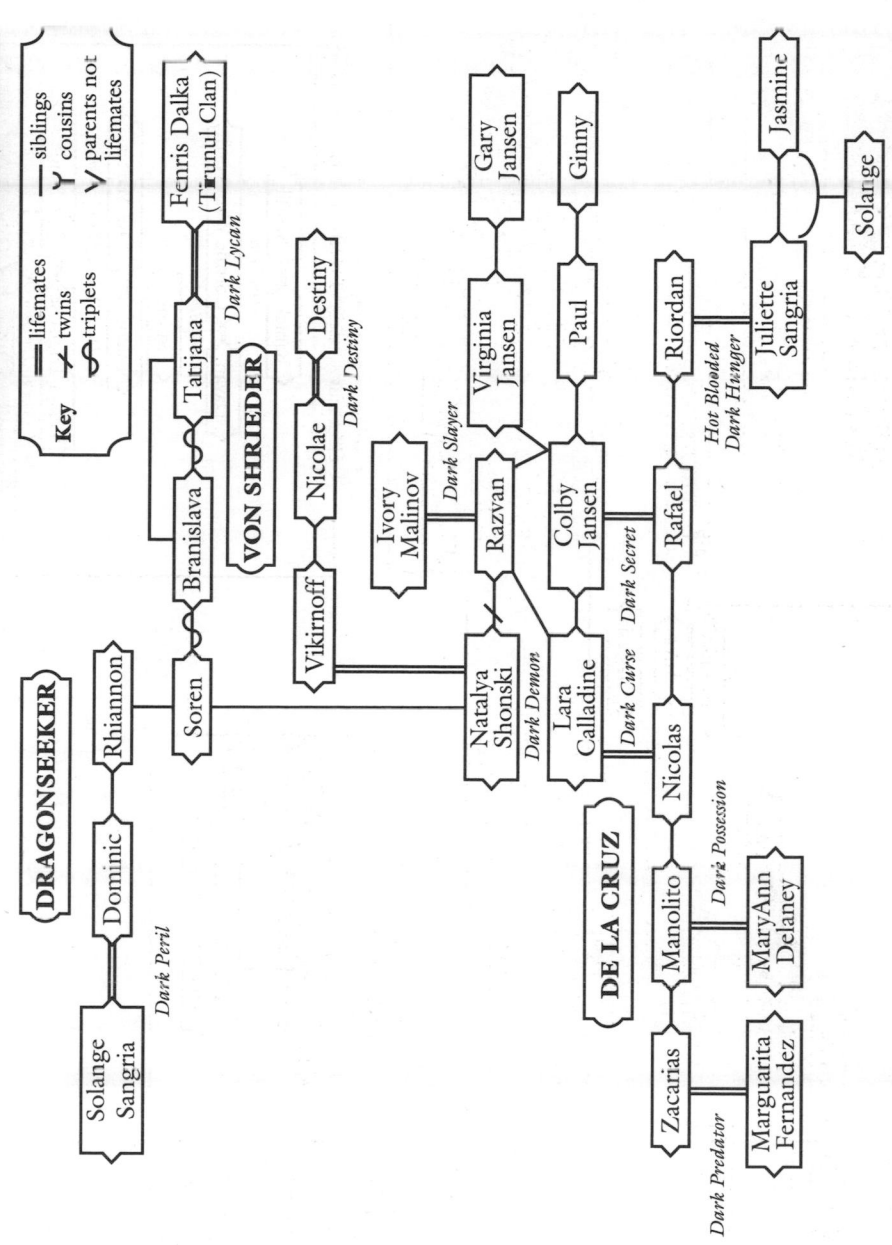

DARK LYCAN

I

Mist drifted through the trees. The moon, not quite full, was a yellow halo, dull and yet glaring. Around the moon a red ring gave off an ominous glow. A dangerous time, this cycle of the moon, especially when the mist came in thick and heavy, covering the ground a foot or so high, winding in and out of the trees as if alive. The mist muffled sound, dulled the senses, giving advantages to the shadowy figures that preyed upon the unwary.

Tatijana of the Dragonseekers woke beneath the earth with layers of dark, rich healing loam surrounding her. Vital nutrients, rich in minerals, cushioned her body. She lay for a long time, panicked, listening to her own heart beating, feeling too light, too trapped, too exposed. And hot. So hot. Above her, she sensed the guardians. Watching over her, they said, and it was probably true, but she'd been a prisoner for so long—she'd been born into captivity—and she trusted no one other than her sister, Branislava. Bronnie lay sleeping peacefully, very close to her, her only comfort.

Her heartbeat grew louder until it was thunder in her ears. She couldn't stand being trapped beneath the earth. She had to get out, to find freedom. To *feel* free. What was that like? She knew nothing of the world. She'd lived underground her entire life, deep in the ice caves, never seeing or speaking to anyone other than those who tortured and tried to terrorize her. She knew no other life, but that had changed—or had it?

Had Bronnie and she exchanged one cold, frightening prison for a silken cage? If so, their wardens had made a huge mistake putting them in the ground to recover. She hardly knew what it was like to be in her real form. She'd spent centuries in dragon form and dragons could move through earth fairly easily.

Bronnie, she whispered into her sister's mind. *I know you need your sleep. I will continue to explore our new world and come back at dawn with new information.*

Branislava stirred in her mind as if she might protest as she had each time Tatijana told her she was going.

I need to do this.

I will come with you, Bronnie answered, her voice far away, even though she was in Tatijana's mind.

Tatijana knew Branislava would force herself to awaken, although she wasn't truly healed inside, where they both needed it. They'd done everything together—been through the worst together. They'd never actually been apart, even when encased in ice, when they could only stare at one another. They still had telepathic communication.

Not this time, Bronnie, I need to do this for me. She whispered the words as she did on the occasions she awakened to explore their new world. She always gave Bronnie reassurance that she would be careful.

No one would ever imprison either of them again. Every rising she made that simple vow. She was growing stronger with each passing night. Power ran through her body and with it, confidence. She was determined they would stand on their own and be beholden to no one.

Tatijana didn't know how to tell her sister she didn't want to live under the rules of another. They were Carpathian. Dragonseeker. That meant something to the prince of the Carpathians and to all the others. The males were lining up in the hopes of claiming either Bronnie, or her. She could not live under the rule of another. She just couldn't do it. She didn't want anyone telling her what to do ever again, even if it was for her own good. She rose when she wanted and explored her new world on her own terms.

Tatijana made up her mind that she would find her own way, learn her own way, make her own mistakes. Bronnie was always the voice of reason. She protected Tatijana from her impulsive nature, but no more. As much as she loved Branislava, this was something Tatijana needed.

She sent her sister love and warmth and the promise she would return at dawn. Shapeshifting into the appearance of a blue dragon was easy—she'd been in the form for centuries and the structure and shape felt more familiar than her own body.

She burrowed deeper, going into the earth rather than rising where her guardians would see her. She'd already dug a tunnel, and she moved quickly through the packed soil. She'd chosen to exit several kilometers away from her resting place in order to ensure Branislava's safety and to make certain the guardians would have no idea she'd risen early. The blue dragon moved through the tunnel like a mole, digging when necessary, packing any dirt that had collapsed as she hurried steadily toward her goal.

Tatijana emerged in a deep forest. She was very careful to scan the earth above her before the blue dragon poked her wedge-shaped head out of the hidden entrance. She surfaced in the midst of a thick gray fog. Trees appeared as giant misshapen scarecrows with outstretched arms, swaying slightly, just enough to give them the appearance of monsters.

Tatijana had known real monsters and the dense forest of trees veiled in gray didn't alarm her in the least. Freedom was amazing. Her eyes were terribly sensitive, but other than that, the world felt as if it was hers and with the fog covering the ground, her eyes didn't even burn.

She shifted to her physical form, donning modern clothing, a pair of soft cotton pants that allowed her freedom of movement. She'd chosen a blouse she'd seen on a woman in the village a couple of nights earlier. She'd followed the woman, studying her style of clothing so she could reproduce it at will. Everything seemed strange to her, but that was part of the excitement of discovery. She wanted tactile learning, not just pulling information from another's mind.

She made her way through the forest, enjoying the way the fog wrapped around her legs and made her feel as if she was walking through clouds. She remembered at the last moment to add shoes, something that was still very uncomfortable for her. She felt as if the shoes weighed her down and felt very foreign on her body.

The wind rushed through the trees, kicking up leaves and swirling mist around tree trunks. The mist began to rise from the floor as she walked toward the only light at the forest's edge that she could see. Music poured from the building, singing to her, beckoning, but this time she knew she wasn't going just to hear those beautiful notes. She normally chose a different location every night to glean more information to share with her sister.

This place called to her every rising now. The feeling was so strong it was nearly a compulsion. She had resisted for a few days, but she couldn't stop herself another night. She drew closer to the building. The windows were lit with that same yellow glow, two eyes staring at her through the thick mist. A chill went down her spine, but she kept walking toward it.

The Wild Boar Tavern sat on the very edge of the forest, surrounded on three sides by heavy brush, trees, and plenty of cover for anyone needing to hide quickly. Providing shelter and camaraderie as well as easy exits should the law happen to venture near, the tavern offered regulars comfort by the fire, warm food and plenty to drink. The crowd was rough, no place for the timid, and even the law generally avoided the place. No one asked questions and everyone was careful not to officially notice anything.

Fenris Dalka came to the tavern nearly every night, so why did he feel such a fool sitting at the bar, slowly nursing a beer, pretending to drink it like he often did? He huffed out his breath and kept his gaze forward, using the mirror to keep an eye on the door. From his vantage point, he could see every corner of the tavern as well as the door. He'd scoped out the perfect place to sit some time ago and now, if he came in and someone was sitting there, he just stood over them, staring, until they got up and vacated his seat.

Fen knew he was intimidating and he used his rough, dangerous looks to his advantage. He was tall enough, but it was his broad shoulders and thick chest, his roped arms and five o'clock shadow, the piercing glacier-blue eyes he used to look right through someone into their soul that usually intimidated people. He rarely had to speak and he preferred it that way. The regulars knew him and knew to leave him alone.

Music played in the background and laughter occasionally rang out, but for the most part, the patrons spoke in hushed whispers. Only the bartender ever spoke to Fen when he entered. A few of the regulars lifted a hand, or nodded, but most avoided his eyes. He looked nearly as dangerous as he was. A man with no friends, trusting only his brother and always hunted or hunting. He was even more ruthless and brutal than the whispers said.

His hair was long, very thick and distinctly silver with black strands woven into the waves falling down his back. Most of the time he secured it at his nape with a leather cord to keep it out of his eyes. He had large hands, and his knuckles were scarred. There were scars on his face, one up near his eye and another that ran from his eye halfway down his face. There were far more scars on his body. Centuries of defending himself, every battle and every victory was stamped into his bones.

Whispered conversations were easy enough to listen in on with his acute hearing, allowing him to glean a tremendous amount of information. But tonight was different. He wasn't here for information . . . he was drawn . . . compelled by something altogether different this time.

Uncomfortable, he played with his beer mug, moving his fingers over the handle, gripping with his fist and forcing himself to let go before he shattered the glass. He wasn't a man to do another's bidding. He didn't trust anything he couldn't understand—and he didn't understand the urgent need that kept him coming back night after night, waiting.

This was a tavern for the lawless. For clandestine meetings. He and his brother had discovered the tavern when he'd first arrived back in the Carpathian Mountains. It had been necessary to find a safe place, out of the way, where they could spend time and talk unseen by anyone who might know either of them. He wanted to make absolutely certain that his younger brother was safe. No one could know they were brothers. No one could ever associate the two of them, or he would be putting his sibling's life on the line—something he wasn't willing to do. So many years had passed that everyone had forgotten him—or thought him dead—and for his brother's protection that falsehood had to remain.

He knew every face in the tavern. Most had been coming even longer than he had. The newest patron was the most suspect. He had arrived in the area only a couple of weeks earlier. He had the stocky build of a hunter—a woodsman—yet he dressed more refined. He was not someone to take lightly. Anyone could see by the way he moved that he would be good in a fight.

He was definitely armed. He went by the name of Zev, and clearly he was new to the area. He hadn't disclosed his business, but Fen would bet his last dollar, he was hunting someone. He didn't look like the law, but he was definitely pursuing someone. Fen hoped it wasn't him, but if it was, he took every opportunity to study Zev, the way he moved, which hand he favored, where his weapons were carried.

Zev wore his hair longer than usual, just as Fen did. His hair was a deep chestnut color and very thick, much like a rich pelt. His eyes were gray and watchful, always moving, always restless, while his body remained quite still. Fen found it significant that no one in the bar had yet challenged him.

The wind picked up, rushing through the trees, capricious and playful, pushing branches against the sides of the tavern so that they creaked and scraped, a heralding of danger if one could read the information the wind provided. Fen let out his breath and glanced through the window into the dark forest.

The mist snaked through the trees, stretching out like greedy fingers, winding in and out of the trees, closeting the forest in a thick veil of gray. He needed to go—now—he had only five days before the full moon—that gave him two days to find a safe place to ride out the threat to him. The three days before the full moon, the full moon and the three days after were the most dangerous for him. Yet he didn't move from the barstool, not even when self-preservation screamed at him. Every hair on his body was raised, both in alarm and extended as antenna to catch the smallest of details.

He smeared cold beads of sweat on the glass, his gaze drawn to the mirror once again. He did not have the full range of the color spectrum, but the dimmer the light, the more shades of gray he could see. He couldn't tell the difference between yellow, green or orange, they all looked the same to him—a dull yellowish color. Red looked brownish gray or black, but he could detect blue. What he lacked in his abilities to distinguish color, he more than made up with his acute hearing, sense of smell and his long-range eyesight.

Her scent reached him as she opened the door. A woman. *The* woman. Was she bait to catch him? If so, he was hooked. That scent of hers—fresh earth, the forest, wild honey, of dark secret places and the night itself, drew him as no expensive perfume ever could. She'd been coming on and off to the tavern for the last week. Three visits, and yet he was already under her spell.

She'd captured him effortlessly, without doing anything but walking through the door. He'd never seen a woman so beautiful or alluring. She literally stopped all conversation the moment she entered, but she never seemed to notice. And that was the trouble. She was far too young and naïve, far too innocent-looking to come unescorted to a place like this one.

He'd heard the whispers of some of the men and he knew she wasn't safe. The two barmaids glared at her, aware that the moment she came in, they no longer had the attention of the men. Again, the woman seemed completely unaware. She walked with confidence, but she seemed to pay no attention to the predators surrounding her—and they were predators. The only reason she hadn't been attacked so far was because he'd made it very clear she was under his protection. When one of the men had started to make his move on her, Fen had stood up. That was all. He just stood up.

The man subsided instantly and no one had dared make another move, but it was only a matter of time. From what he heard, three conspirators planned to follow her when she left the tavern and Fen wouldn't be around to protect her. Well, that was unfair. Two conspirators and one friend trying to talk sense into them. He could have told them not to put their money on that plan and that listening to their friend was the better idea, but he didn't bother. He rolled his shoulders slowly, opened and closed his fists, stretching out his fingers and looking down at the hands that could be such deadly weapons. He needed the exercise.

He watched her in the mirror. He'd seen her try a drink each time she came in, one she'd obviously seen someone else drink, and each time she made a horrible face and spit the liquor back into the glass, shook her head and moved away from the bar to the tiny area where she could dance. Again she seemed completely oblivious to those around her, losing herself in the music. Fen was certain she came to the tavern only because she loved the music.

She never spoke, not even to the bartender, and Fen wondered whether or not she could speak. Her skin was porcelain white, as if she never saw the sun. Her hair was beautiful, falling far past her waist, long enough that she probably could sit on it, as if she'd never cut it in her life. She wore it in a braided rope that was as thick as his wrist. The silky fall was a color he couldn't quite define, but when the light hit it just right, the color seemed to change, although it could just be the way he perceived color.

Her eyes caught at him. He couldn't stop staring at them, and as she danced, she suddenly lifted her lashes, her eyes meeting his in the mirror. His heart nearly stopped and then began pounding. Women didn't have that kind of effect on him. His mouth didn't go dry. His jaw didn't ache and his canines didn't grow sharp. He was always—*always*—in control. And yet . . . He heard thunder roaring in his ears, and breathed deep, calling on centuries of discipline.

Emotions dulled and disappeared in time. What little he felt, he felt as the other, not in this form. Sometimes he forgot what it was like to be in his present form. Yet now, looking into her eyes, he found he couldn't look away. She mesmerized him. Captivated him. He didn't trust her. He didn't trust his unfamiliar, very strange reaction to her.

A gust of wind hit the tavern hard, blew down the chimney and sent sparks rising in the fireplace. A log fell from the iron grate and rolled toward the opening, coming to an abrupt halt, but flames leapt and danced, while cracks inside the log glowed brightly. Fen swung his head toward the window. The thick mist spun out of the forest, threads of gray, wrapping itself around the tavern, enclosing the entire building in a giant glistening spiderweb.

The woman stopped dancing, drawing his attention back to her. She stared at the fire, as if every bit as mesmerized by it as he was by her. She moved closer and he found himself frowning, watching her closely in the mirror. Her eyes reflected the leaping flames, almost as if the lenses were multifaceted, reminiscent of the cut of a diamond. She stepped closer, too close. The fireplace was open. Mountains of ashes glowed, flames leapt hungrily. Fen slipped off the barstool.

She slowly extended her hand toward the flame. The path would take her palm right into the center of the fire. He moved, using blurring speed, coming up behind her, reaching around and catching her wrist, pulling her hand back away from the flames before the flames could blister her soft skin.

For a moment she stiffened as if she might fight him. He felt a brush, the lightest of touches along his mind, which shocked him. Who was she? What was she? He held his barriers effortlessly and kept his touch gentle, taking care not to convey a threat of any kind. She relaxed and he inhaled the scent of her, his head near her shoulder, so that the thick braid of silky hair brushed his skin and her feminine scent enveloped him. He drew her deep into his lungs. She smelled like sin. Like sex. Like paradise and everything he didn't—and would never—have.

"It's hot. Fire will burn you," he said softly, making certain no one else in the tavern would hear.

She was intelligent, he could see that, but something had happened to her and clearly, there were things she'd never experienced and had no knowledge of. Amnesia? Trauma? There was no other explanation. Everyone knew about fire, and her lack of knowledge just made her all the more vulnerable.

She turned her head slowly to look up at him over her shoulder, frowning slightly, a puzzled expression on her face. Up so close, she appeared ethereal, mysterious, her skin silky smooth, touchable. He'd never been so drawn to another being in his life.

"Your skin will burn," he explained patiently. "It would be extremely painful to you."

She continued to look at him, confused. He tried repeating the warning in several languages. She just looked at him, and they were drawing far too much attention. Every time she moved she had the eye of everyone in the tavern and he didn't want anyone to think she was easy prey because of her lack of knowledge of the most basic necessities such as fire. In the end, there was nothing else to do. He pressed her arm down to her side, stepped around her and extended his hand, palm down, into the flames.

She watched, her eyes widening as his skin blistered and the scent of burning flesh rose. She caught his arm and jerked his hand from the fireplace.

"Do you understand?" he asked, showing her the damage.

She turned his hand over, her palm covering his burned one, not quite touching, yet he still felt her energy vibrating through his skin. Soothing coolness slid over the blisters. She lifted his palm toward her mouth. His breath caught in his lungs, the air trapped there. He couldn't move or even speak as she bent her head toward his palm. Her tongue touched the blisters, lightly, barely there, a slow brush that actually made his hand tremble and his knees just a little weak. Worse, his body reacted with a hot surge of blood, rushing and pooling in wicked demand.

She let go of his hand slowly, almost reluctantly. He lifted his palm to inspect it, still feeling that soothing coolness, as if she'd spread a healing gel over the blistered skin. The blisters were gone. His palm was no longer burned, nor was it even red.

Fen drew in his breath sharply. He knew what she was. No other species could heal with just their saliva so easily. She had to be Carpathian—a race of beings who called the Carpathian Mountains their home. Few knew of their existence. He frowned, trying to wrap his brain around the idea. In truth, it made no sense. He doubted that a Carpathian female would come to a tavern alone, especially a rough place like the Wild Boar. She would not only have knowledge of fire, but she would be well-schooled in all things. No one lived as long as Carpathians without acquiring a great deal of knowledge along the way. What had happened to her? And why was she unescorted?

He felt the weight of a stare and glanced up to meet Zev's gaze. Zev was looking at the woman. Instinctively, Fen shifted his body slightly, blocking Zev's view of her. Her gaze jumped to his face and then she peeked around his broad body to look at Zev and then moved back behind him.

"You aren't safe here," Fen said, reluctant to admit it. "This crowd is rough."

She smiled at him. Smiled. His heart shifted. His stomach tightened and blood surged hotly in his veins. Her teeth were very white, her lips full, red and the thing of fantasies. He took a breath, knowing it was a mistake, but drawing her into his lungs anyway. He took her deep and left her there, swirling around, twisting up his insides until he knew he could—and would—find her again.

He tipped her chin up so that she could look at his mouth. "Zev in particular is dangerous." He mouthed the words rather than made sound, fearing Zev had the same extraordinary hearing as he had. "The others, too, but not like him. Do you understand?"

Tatijana nodded. Of course she understood, although she was more concerned with the effect of his touch on her than the warning he gave her. She was definitely drawn to this man—Fen was his name. He appeared human when she brushed his mind with light contact—as did everyone else in the tavern—and yet Fen puzzled her. He had moved with blinding speed. Preternatural speed. How could he be human and yet move with the speed of a Carpathian? More—she hadn't felt any energy preceding him, and she should have.

He was far more muscular than most Carpathian men, but he had the height. His eyes were different and she'd spent an inordinate amount of time secretly studying them as he sat at the bar, nursing his drink. He wasn't really drinking it, yet over time, the liquid disappeared. She hadn't figured out yet how he was accomplishing that particular feat, but she knew she wanted to learn it.

Why had he singled out Zev in particular as dangerous? He felt like every other human in the tavern. "Why Zev?" She was adept at reading lips. She'd learned long ago, as a child, encased in ice, watching the cruelty of her father as he sacrificed animals and humans alike. No one was safe. Mage, Carpathian, Jaguar, Lycan—no species was left unharmed. Even the dead were not safe from Xavier.

She mouthed the question to Fen, making certain that no sound accidentally escaped, just in case he was Carpathian. She was so inexplicably drawn to Fen, and he was definitely a question mark in her mind, so she wasn't about to take any chances. She was not ready for any male to claim her. She needed time on her own and she'd been told all about lifemates and how a male could take over her life even without her consent. That *couldn't* happen—not to her. Not now. She was actually, for the first time in her existence, enjoying her life. The path of discovery was exhilarating. She felt so alive, and she didn't want anything or anyone to take that away from her.

Truthfully, she wasn't altogether certain she could have a relationship with anyone—at least a healthy one. That would require trust, and she simply didn't have that. She trusted only Branislava, her sole ally. They'd been together so much, it was difficult to think of being apart, yet Tatijana knew she needed this time alone desperately. How did one find out who they were and what they liked if they didn't ever have the time to find out?

"I just know," Fen mouthed back. He reached out and tucked a stray strand of hair behind her ear.

Her breath caught in her throat. His touch did something strange to her entire body and it was alarming. She stepped backward, unable to pull her gaze from his.

The sound of a wolf howling outside, a distance away, had both of them simultaneously turning their heads toward the window. Out of the corner of her eye, she saw that Zev had also turned toward the sound and Fen definitely noticed his movement as well. She couldn't see that anyone else had heard that spine-chilling sound.

This was no wolf howling at the moon, it was the sound of one calling others to the hunt. At least three others answered, even more distantly, but they didn't sound like the local wolf pack. They sounded aggressive and eager as if they had prey already in sight. More than that—to her ears—the call sounded just a little off, as if the wolves were off.

Her gaze jumped to Fen's face. He was quite still. Completely motionless. His expression hadn't changed at all, but she felt the difference in him. He appeared relaxed, but she felt him coiled and ready.

"I have to go," she mouthed to him, and backed up another step.

His attention immediately returned to her. He frowned and glanced out the window again. "I'll walk you." He said it aloud this time.

Heads turned in the tavern toward them. Two of the men scowled, the ones, he noted, who had whispered together that they would follow her. Clearly their friend hadn't convinced them, although he still seemed to be arguing.

Tatijana had expected it to happen sooner or later, but all she had to do was dissolve into mist and she'd be gone. The men would never know what had happened to her. She had every confidence that no matter what, she'd be safe.

Tatijana knew Fen had announced his intention to walk with her because he was attempting to ensure she was safe from the men in the tavern—and maybe whatever was outside of it as well. Her first inclination, one of self-preservation, demanded she decline his offer. But there was that compulsion pushing at her, wanting just to be in his company for no apparent reason.

She took a chance and scanned his mind a second time. He seemed an ordinary man . . . Maybe it was the intriguing contradiction he represented, or maybe it was the way he drew her like a magnet, but she gave a slight nod of her head to let him know she'd walk a bit with him. In any case, she knew she could protect him if there was trouble.

Zev pushed away from the bar, buttoned up his coat and stepped outside without so much as looking their way. As if Fen's word had been a signal, the three men huddled together, whispering their conspiracies, stood up and pulled on their coats and hats, to shuffle out of the tavern as well. One of the men glanced a little nervously at Fen while the other two leered at Tatijana.

Her heart sank. Clearly she was putting Fen in danger by agreeing to walk with him. She opened her mouth to tell him she'd go by herself but he took her hand and tugged her toward the door. The moment the warmth of his hand closed around hers, her heart shifted and a million butterflies winged across her stomach. His hands were much larger than hers and he completely engulfed her smaller hand, making her feel feminine and very much a woman—a brand-new concept for her.

She didn't want that incredible feeling to go away. In any case, she was certain she could protect Fen without him knowing what she was. If necessary she would remove any bad memories. She also needed to feed. It wasn't that hard to convince herself that she had very good reasons for allowing Fen to walk her through the forest.

"Where's your coat?" Fen asked.

Coat. Everyone was wearing a coat. Carpathians regulated their temperatures. She didn't feel hot or cold, which was why she didn't feel flames, but they went out of their way to fit in with humans. That was one of the biggest rules that governed their society. No one could know of their existence. Before she and Bronnie had been placed in the earth to heal, that tenet had been drilled into her. She'd forgotten a coat.

She glanced toward the rough pegs at the door where many of the patrons hung their jackets and hats. At once a long, hooded coat appeared there. She sneaked a quick look in the mirror, grateful no one had seemed to notice. She indicated the coat with a small jerk of her chin. If Fen was startled, he gave no indication. He simply removed the long coat from the peg and held it up.

She hesitated, unsure what she was supposed to do. Fen stepped closer and slid her arm into one sleeve, wrapping the coat around her back. He waited patiently for her to put her other arm into the remaining sleeve. He turned her around and buttoned the coat for her. The entire time, while he slipped each button into the loops, she held her breath and stared up into his face.

He was beautiful. Scarred, rough, totally masculine but beautiful all the same. She memorized his bone structure, the shape of his nose, the cut of his mouth and his strong jaw. She wanted to remember him for her entire life—to remember this moment. She might never have such a moment or feeling again, and this was one that needed savoring.

Fen reached around her and opened the door. A blast of cold air rushed in. She raised her chin, inhaling the night, allowing the wind to bring her information. Fen took a deep breath and stepped outside just ahead of her, retaining possession of her hand. His body partially blocked hers from the elements while he took a careful look around.

Gray mist churned and spun, blocking the tavern's view of the forest. The trees rose eerily above the worst of it, still obscured and slightly misshapen, the tops looking as if they floated without trunks above them.

"Which way?" Fen asked.

Tatijana indicated to the left, into the forest. The wolves had gone quiet and she hoped that they were still a great distance away. Fen tugged just a bit on her hand to bring her closer to him, and they set off. She smelled Zev's scent, a rugged, ancient forest smell, which clung to Fen as well. She quite liked it. The scent was all about running free, something she wanted more than anything.

There was the night in that enticing fragrance—a cool dark midnight-blue night, with stars overhead and a round full moon as well. That elusive aroma conjured up everything that she had come to love in the short time she'd been freed from her prison. More, she wanted to stay close to Fen and just inhale him into her lungs, to take him deep so she would never forget him.

"Tell me your name. I'm Fen. Fenris Dalka." He didn't break stride, walking with absolute confidence into the forest. He seemed a man without much fear.

She looked up at him. Studied him carefully and did one more scan just to be certain she was safe. She opened her mouth to tell him, but she just couldn't. Something stopped her. There was far too strong of a compulsion to be with him. Maybe it was all new to her, this attraction between a man and a woman, but it had never happened before. She hadn't been the least attracted to anyone else in the tavern, not even a single spark. She shook her head and smiled at him.

He flashed a grin at her. "You do know that mystery is very intriguing in a woman, right? I'll be more enamored than ever. I can read lips," he added.

She wanted him to know her name. She mouthed "Tatijana," exaggerating every syllable so it would be easier for him. He got it on the first try.

"Tatijana is a beautiful name. Do you live close?"

She shrugged, happy to just be walking with him. His body gave off unexpected heat and she allowed herself to feel it. She *needed* to feel every moment with him. She knew she should pull her hand away from his. She didn't know him. She didn't know proper etiquette between a man and a woman, but for just this moment, for the first time in her life, she felt normal. Real. She wasn't Carpathian. She wasn't Dragonseeker. She wasn't a mage's daughter. She was a woman enjoying the company of a man.

"I lived here long ago," Fen volunteered. "I've only returned for a short visit and must leave again." He looked around at the dark shapes of the trees rising from the mist. "I'd forgotten how beautiful it is."

Tatijana agreed with him silently. She wanted to dance there in the deep forest just because she was so happy. Just something so simple as walking in the woods at night flooded her with joy, and Fen was an added bonus. She nodded her head, feeling a little foolish that she wasn't speaking aloud, but maybe he thought she couldn't. She didn't even care if that meant he pitied her, although when she scanned his thoughts, she didn't find pity. She found . . . attraction.

"Have you lived here long?" he asked.

She glanced at his face. He wasn't looking down at her, although his tone made her feel as if she was the most important person in the world and he wanted an answer. His gaze was restless, moving constantly, up in the branches of the trees, down along the ground, his vision trying to pierce the heavy veil of mist.

Had she missed something? Some warning? She took a careful look around, sending out her senses, scanning carefully to try to detect a threat. Just up ahead and slightly to her left, concealed in the trees were the three men who had left the bar after Zev. She sighed. Of course. She'd known they were going to make their try for her. She'd allowed herself to be swept away into a magical world that had no threats in it. Everything and everyone who could possibly threaten her just seemed trivial in comparison to Xavier.

She touched Fen's arm. "I have to go," she mouthed. "You can turn back now."

She wasn't going to involve him. She wasn't certain he was human, but if he was, three against one, even when he looked big and lethal, wasn't fair. She could dissolve into mist and they'd never find her, but Fen had to be protected, even if it was from his own gallantry.

Fen stopped abruptly. "You know they're there, don't you?"

Tatijana nodded reluctantly. She was giving herself away, but then so had he. The three men were in the distance, impossible to see with the heavy mist and the cover of the dense trees and brush.

"I'll take care of them. You get out of here."

She shook her head. She'd been afraid that he would be the protective male. She sent him a small "push" to leave. He scowled at her, shaking his head. Tatijana knew she'd made a terrible mistake. Fen was much more than he seemed, and that push she'd just tried had given him far too much information about her.

What was he? Mage? She didn't think so. She'd been held prisoner for centuries by the most powerful mage the world had ever known and Fen was in no way similar physically nor did his brain scan that way. Jaguar? She didn't think so. That left Carpathian or Lycan. If he was Carpathian, she would have known by his energy field. Lycans were the only species who didn't produce that energy field readable to others.

She took a chance. "I am quite capable of defending myself. You need to leave. Those men are after me, not you."

2

F en went very still while the earth under his feet seemed to tremble and the trees surrounding them shook. He had all but forgotten being Carpathian. He had lived so long as an abomination—the most hunted of the Lycan kind—considered worse than any rogue wolf or pack who had to be hunted and destroyed. His kind could not be tolerated in the Lycan world.

He was both Carpathian and Lycan, and the combination made him an outcast. He had lived under a death sentence for centuries. There was no question of having a lifemate, no chance for him. He had long ago given up on that fairy tale. His lungs burned and he realized he was holding his breath. She was looking up at him with her amazing green eyes. The color changed, going from that deep emerald to a fascinating multifaceted aquamarine.

She knew. The signs for both of them had been there all along but they'd ignored them, misread them, or just plain didn't believe them. On some impractical level he'd been waiting for this one moment his entire life. She existed. His lifemate. The one woman who held the other half of his soul. She was the light to his darkness. She brought back real color and real emotions.

Everything hit him at once, all of it. Feelings. Vivid color. Her hair was red gold yet changed in the shadows to deeper hues or streaks of color blending together. For one moment, he just let the emotions wash over him. He wanted to go where love would be, with this woman, this incredible miracle standing in front of him, staring up at him with wide, shocked eyes.

There was fear in her eyes and if she knew the half of it, she would run for her life. Fen cupped the side of her face gently, rubbing the pad of his thumb over her satin-soft skin. His heart stuttered and thunder roared in his ears.

"My lady," he said softly. Regretfully. "I would give anything to bind you to me, but your protection must come first. You can't be anywhere near me. I'm under a death sentence and anyone giving me safe harbor or aiding me will be killed with me. If they find you and know who you are, they will not take chances. They will kill you, too."

Tatijana blinked up at Fen. His declaration was the last thing she expected. She'd braced herself for the claiming, the words that she knew would bind their souls for all time. There would be no living without him, and no precious freedom—the thing she wanted above all else.

"Why would someone want to kill you?" She sounded just a little accusing, a little miffed. She glanced toward the three men secreted in the trees in the distance. They were waiting to ambush the couple and wouldn't creep through the brush—at least not until they got a lot more courage. "What did you do?"

A faint smile appeared on his face at the slight accusation in her voice. "Don't pretend you wanted me to claim you. You did everything in your power to keep me from knowing that you're my lifemate. I don't think outraged feminine ruffled feathers are the appropriate response. You should be jumping for joy."

"Well I'm not. Jumping for joy, I mean, that you're my lifemate. I can't have a lifemate right now. I've got issues."

His grin turned into a smile that warmed his eyes and that made him all the more attractive. His eyes were amazing. In the tavern they'd been ice-cold blue, like the ice in the caves that had been her home for so long. She'd been drawn to his eyes. Now they were even a deeper, richer blue, like the glittering sapphires that she'd seen in Xavier's cache of gems and artifacts he'd used for his magic. She didn't feel in the least that it was her fault she was acting like a ninny, not when he had those blue eyes.

She held up her hand. "But, here's the thing, Fen. I'm not going to leave my lifemate, or any Carpathian in trouble. So why are you under a death threat and from whom?"

He shook his head. "Woman, you do know how to complicate things, don't you?"

She liked the idea that she did. She liked the idea of complicating his life. She'd never had that experience before and she found she was quite proud of her abilities.

His smile widened, and she realized she hadn't taken care to guard her mind from him. He was there before she realized, pouring warmth into her, filling every barren lonely place, fusing with her mind, joining them together. She caught glimpses of his memories, but she found them strange, not Carpathian.

"You like messing with me," he accused, but the laughter in his voice and the warmth in his incredibly blue eyes belied any anger.

She'd never "messed" with anyone before. It took a moment to translate the modern jargon in her mind, but yes, she quite liked "messing" with him. He was providing several new and exhilarating experiences. "I do, yes." The smile faded from her face. "Those three men waiting to jump me don't really present a threat to either one of us, but you're very serious about this death threat. Is Zev hunting you? Is that why you said he was so dangerous?"

He sighed and tucked her hand against his chest. "You're really going to insist on an explanation, aren't you? If anyone finds out you know, they would come after you."

She lifted her chin. "I'm not afraid, Fen. I've faced monsters you cannot conceive of . . ." She studied his rugged features, the lines in his face. "Maybe you can. But the point is, I will not run from trouble. I'm not going to hide. Just tell me why."

"Centuries ago, I was hunting a particularly savage vampire. I'd never run across one so powerful and brutal. He was destroying entire villages, killing everyone in them, and for some reason I couldn't feel him at all, not his energy, or any of the usual means of finding a vampire. Sometimes, when hunting vampires it's what's not there that gives them away, yet I was always one step behind. I could track him by his destruction, but I couldn't get ahead of him."

Fen turned his head toward the three men waiting. Tatijana immediately realized he had been listening to them the entire time. Carpathian hunters had enormous skills, aware of their surroundings at all times, even when they seemed totally focused on one thing—one person.

She was a little disappointed that she hadn't kept his entire attention when he'd kept hers. "Seriously, those men are annoying me now." She marched toward them, forgetting that Fen was on the other end of her hand. She managed three steps and came to an abrupt halt. She swung around, scowling at him. "What *are* you doing?"

"Wondering what you're planning," he replied, one eyebrow raised.

She swung back to face the threat. "I'm so disgusted with the three of you," she called out. "If you're planning on jumping us, get it done already. I'm trying to have an important conversation and Fen here is having difficulty concentrating. So either gather up your courage and come out into the open where the two of us will annihilate you, or slink on home."

Fen burst out laughing. The rich, husky tone was so unexpected, so masculine that the sound seemed to reverberate through her body, sending little shock waves of electrical current sizzling through her bloodstream.

"I'm not having difficulty concentrating," he said, his voice dropping an octave. "I'm hanging on your every word."

She gave a little delicate sniff. "You're supposed to be explaining yourself. When one's lifemate *refuses* to claim his woman, there should be a reasonable explanation."

"You have no desire for me to claim you," he pointed out.

"That's beside the point."

Fen found himself grinning. The three humans waiting in the brush were discussing what to do next now that the element of surprise was gone. The one continued to try to persuade the other two that they were drunk and going to get into trouble. That he couldn't have them hurting a woman.

Fen didn't care one way or another if they attacked, but he was truly fascinated by the woman who all but stamped her foot at him. As a rule, Carpathian women were tall with dark hair. Tatijana was on the diminutive side, with light ever-changing hair and her amazing emerald eyes.

The vivid colors, after centuries of no color and then spotty, muddy hues, were almost blinding. The joy of feeling filled him even as the intensity of emotions nearly overwhelmed him.

"I want the explanation and I think, as your lifemate, I deserve to hear it." She sounded both snippy and regal if that combination was at all possible.

"And no matter what, you aren't going to do the practical thing and leave me, are you?" he asked.

She had him. The mystery and intrigue surrounding her drew him almost as much as the call of her soul to his. The pull between them was very strong, and he wasn't certain, in the end, he would have the strength to watch her walk away.

"Of course not. Do you think I'm a coward?" She tossed her head like a fractious filly, indicating the three men now arguing in low tones they thought couldn't be overheard. "Like them? I am Carpathian. I may not have practical experience in a battle, but I certainly have knowledge of every kind of enemy and how best to defeat them. I will never run from a fight, nor will I accept another's command over me."

She was . . . magnificent. The moon was mostly obscured by the veil of mist, yet her long braid seemed to give off sparks.

"How did you get your knowledge?" Fen asked.

She shrugged. "Perhaps you know the name of my father. He was the most powerful mage ever known, Xavier. He was a false friend to the Carpathian people, tricking them for years into thinking the alliance between mage and Carpathian was strong. He wanted immortality and the Carpathians did not give him their secret. He killed my mother's lifemate and held her prisoner, as only the most powerful mage could. He forced her to have his children, triplets, two girls and a boy. My sister, Branislava, my brother, Soren, and me. He needed us for our blood."

Fen was shocked and he knew it showed on his face. "I studied with this man, centuries ago. We all did. No one knew of his treachery?"

She shook her head. "My sister and I were held from birth in his lair deep beneath the ice where he fed from our veins, keeping us weak. Our mother had turned us completely when she realized what Xavier meant to do, in the hopes that we would find a way to escape. He killed her the moment he felt we could provide the blood he so craved."

Fen had been centuries gone from the Carpathian Mountains and his brother hadn't had time to give him much news. To know that a mage as formidable as Xavier had betrayed them and committed heinous acts against a Carpathian woman and his own children chilled him to the bone. He'd seen deceit in the form of vampires, but someone his people had considered such a friend and ally—Xavier's betrayal seemed far worse. They had all trusted him.

"How long were you held captive?"

For the first time he saw her hesitation. Her hand trembled when she reached up to push back stray strands of hair. Fen covered her hand with his.

"My entire life. Centuries. We never left the ice caves until nearly two years ago. We've been in the Earth healing," Tatijana admitted.

"And the prince allows you to go unescorted? Unprotected by his hunters?" He didn't bother to conceal the edge—or disgust in his voice.

Tatijana hastily shook her head. "He has no idea that I've awakened. None of them know. My guardians believe we are safe beneath the ground. I needed to feel freedom." Her gaze met his. "I *needed* this."

He understood what she was trying to convey. She hadn't slipped away out of spite, or because she frivolously wanted to outwit her guardians, she really did need to feel freedom—and he understood that. In a way, Carpathian hunters lost their freedom when they lost all emotion and color. They had one purpose after that—to find their lifemate. If they didn't manage to do so, as the years went by, they would run the risk of becoming nosferatu— the undead. The only thing left for hunters was to hunt and destroy the vampire and search for their lifemate.

"I told you about me," she said. "Now it's your turn."

"I think we're about to have company. Two out of three. The third one chose to abandon his friends when he couldn't talk them out of their drunken idiocy—and I must say—he definitely tried." He wanted to laugh at the expression on her face. She looked absolutely pained—and adorable. He'd never considered using that word, but now he knew what it meant.

"You have got to be kidding me." She threw her hands into the air and whirled to face the two men creeping out of the bushes. "Are they really that stupid? What's wrong with them?"

"It's called alcohol. You spit it out when you tried it, but many humans like and are very affected by it. The more they drink the less inhibited they are, and they make really stupid decisions sometimes."

"They aren't even coordinated," she pointed out. "One can barely stand. Do they really think they would have a chance against you? I can see them making the mistake about a woman, but they have to have seen you in the tavern."

"Alcohol impairs the ability to think straight." Fen turned to face the two men coming toward them, shifting position to place his body just a little in front of hers.

Tatijana pressed her lips together, an ominous warning. Fen caught the look on her face out of the corner of his eye. She suddenly looked both irritated and determined. He felt the burst of energy, and then she moved with blurring speed.

You must appear human! he warned quickly, moving with her as he pushed the warning into her mind.

At the last moment she emerged out of the mist as human, leaping through the air to land a perfect roundhouse kick, her foot slamming into the most aggressive man's gut, doubling him over so that he folded in half. He swayed and slowly sank down onto the ground, blinking up at Tatijana.

Fen whistled softly as the second man staggered to a halt and stood swaying, staring at his companion with blurry eyes.

"Nice," Fen commented. "I'm impressed." He held out his hand to Tatijana. "Get along home, boys. The woods can turn dangerous very fast at night."

Tatijana took his hand and went with him into deeper forest. He took the narrow path leading back toward the village. She wouldn't show him her resting place, but she would be much safer in the village than the forest. His last glimpse of the two attackers was of one trying to help the other off the ground.

The mist enfolded them once again. Tatijana cleared her throat. "You said you were chasing a particularly violent vampire. Please continue. I'd really like to hear."

Fen glanced down at the top of her head. She didn't come up to his shoulder, but already she was a force to be reckoned with. She hadn't put any compulsion in her voice, yet there would be no resisting her. He had no experience with lifemates, so he had no idea if the spell she'd cast was one any woman could easily place on her Carpathian lifemate.

"The vampire was named Vitrona and I could not get ahead of him no matter what I did. I never felt him. Not once. I could only follow in the wake of his total destruction. Entire villages, so many people and mostly Lycans. He was wiping them out. More than once he doubled back and caught me off guard, something that had always been impossible. I have hunted the vampire long centuries and even back then I was no beginner."

"I have seen vampires and the cruelty they exhibit," Tatijana admitted. "Xavier had an alliance with one."

Fen shook his head. "Centuries ago, vampires did not make alliances. They have evolved into even more of a threat, but this one, Vitrona, killed not only for the rush, but for pleasure. It seems he was not only vampire but Lycan—well—not Lycan—werewolf as well."

She gasped, one hand going to her throat. "Lycans can walk in sunlight. They can go undetected by Carpathians and Mage. Lycans are the one species Xavier had difficulties obtaining because it was so hard to locate them."

"The Lycans kept to their own villages back then, but that policy changed when Vitrona tore through their ranks, killing everyone, man, woman and child. No one could stop him." Fen ducked his head, the memories of finding so many brutally murdered families washing over him. "Not even me." For a moment, sorrow choked him—sorrow he hadn't been able to feel until his lifemate had brought intense emotions back to him.

Tatijana's fingers tightened around his. "I didn't think when I asked you to tell about this that you might have to relive it with emotion this time. Please forgive me. You don't have to continue."

Fen was a little shocked at how the psychic connection between them continued to grow stronger with each passing moment in her company. He touched her mind, brushing lightly, and found she was distressed at the thought that she had caused his discomfort. No one had ever been upset on his behalf that he could remember.

He brought her hand to his chest, pressing her palm close over his heart even as he continued walking with her toward the village—and safety. The veil of mist blanketed the forest now, making it nearly impossible to see the trees until they were right up on them, but he could feel them through the hair on his body and the energy radiating from the living plants.

He guided her unerringly along the path, cutting through the interior and picking up his pace. His warning system was beginning to give off little ripples.

"You gave me a gift beyond measure, my lady. Walking with you is both peaceful and exhilarating. Just to have your interest in my past is a miracle I did not expect."

She gave him a glance from under long lashes, a brief glimpse of her astonishing green eyes. "I have an interest in your future as well, Fen. From what I've gleaned about lifemates, one does not do well without the other for long."

"Then I will continue with my story. I followed Vitrona for a full, very long year, and during that time, I became aware of another hunter tracking him—a Lycan. He was an elite hunter, one who tracks down and kills rogue werewolves, those who kill humans and their own kind, just as we destroy the vampire who preys upon humans. The Lycan's skills were formidable. I found myself having great respect for him. He came closer than me on two occasions and yet, he, too, missed Vitrona."

"How awful for both of you," Tatijana said. "What was so different about this vampire?"

"When one hunts the undead, there are certain signs to look for, but this vampire was nearly impossible to find by any of the usual means. There were no scorch marks in his passing unless he deliberately made them. There were no blank spaces indicating he was hiding. The Lycan, his name was Vakasin, eventually hunted him solely by scent. We joined forces, knowing that would double our chances of executing the monster. Many times we engaged him in battle, and both of us sustained terrible life-threatening wounds." Fen hesitated, uncertain how to tell her the rest—fearing her reaction.

Tatijana stopped walking and turned to stand directly in front of him, blocking his path, forcing him to halt. "I told you about Xavier. He was the most hated criminal the Carpathian people had. Women lost their babies and eventually couldn't have children. The high mage who committed such

treachery against the Carpathian people was my own father. I think whatever your secret is can't be as bad. Whatever happened, you need to tell me."

The only person Fen had trusted enough to tell his secret to was his
brother. He had just met Tatijana, but she was his lifemate, and one couldn't
lie to one's lifemate. She could slip in and out of his mind at will, just as he
could hers, making it impossible to hide anything.

He found it strange that he was already so comfortable, as if they'd been
together for a long time, yet the mystique surrounding her was as strong as
ever, drawing him with a magnetic pull as strong as their obvious connection.

"I often needed blood and there was no one else to provide it but Vakasin. I sometimes provided blood for him when our hunt took us places where
there was no sustenance for either of us, or our wounds were too many and
we had to wait to heal. In a battle, we both sustained life-threatening injuries and we had to have large amounts of blood to survive."

Tatijana continued to look up at him, wide-eyed. Unblinking. Holding
him captive so that he could not look away from her even though his next
words might turn her against him.

"Vakasin and I both became an abomination—what the Lycans refer to
as the *Sange rau*, which is literally *bad blood*, a mixed blood. We became like
Vitrona. Both Lycan and Carpathian. We had no idea how it happened,
probably over time, our blood mixing, yet not mixing, changing us, yet not
really changing us." He confessed his sin quickly, in a rush to get it over.

She didn't change expression or step away from him. She just looked at
him as if expecting more. He cleared his throat. "Perhaps you don't understand what I said. I am not Carpathian and I am not Lycan. I am both. An
outcast that cannot be tolerated by either species. The Lycans have elite
squads that hunt and kill someone like me on sight."

Tatijana frowned. "Why would that be? Lara is lifemate to Nicolas, and
his brother Manolito is lifemate to MaryAnn. Manolito and MaryAnn are
as you are, and no one is hunting them."

Fen shook his head. "That cannot be."

"I heard Nicolas telling the prince that MaryAnn was Lycan and they
were as you describe. No one seemed upset by it."

"No one can know. They cannot. This has not been made common
knowledge or my brother would have told me. They are in terrible danger.

If the Lycans hear of this, they will send their hunters. They hunt in packs and once set on a trail, they do not stop until they kill their targets."

Tatijana drew in her breath. "If the Lycans killed or attempted to kill MaryAnn and Manolito, his brothers would start a war. As I understand it, the De La Cruz brothers would take on the world for one another. Lara and Nicolas gave us quite a bit of information when they would come to give us blood while we were healing in the earth."

"It is important, Tatijana. You have to warn them. Once the death sentence is handed down by the council, the elite hunters will spend centuries, if necessary, to find and destroy them. There are only a couple of us. Vakasin was killed by his own kind after he helped me to rid the world of Vitrona. They were savage with him when he had done nothing wrong. He tried to tell them that Vitrona had turned vampire, that he didn't represent what we could be, but they wouldn't listen."

"Could Vakasin have turned vampire?" Tatijana asked. "That's what they were afraid of, wasn't it?"

Fen nodded slowly with a small sigh. "He didn't have time to find out. Like Carpathians, Lycans live long lives. I don't know what the consequences of a Lycan-Carpathian cross would be. Obviously, I could turn without my lifemate, but staying in Lycan form helped throughout the long, empty years." He hesitated. "The gifts grow stronger over time, mutating, and as one grows more powerful, that aid disappears and the call to darkness grows."

He shook his head, sorrow nearly overwhelming him. He had respected Vakasin as a hunter and a man, but until this moment he hadn't realized he'd felt affection for him. Camaraderie. The bond between two men who shared battles and watched each other's backs. He'd been unable to feel those things until Tatijana. Emotions, he found, were both a blessing and a curse.

"From the Lycan's point of view, I can see why they would condemn such a powerful being. It took years to bring Vitrona to justice. During the long centuries he nearly single-handedly destroyed the Lycan world. He killed pack after pack in brutal and vicious ways."

"He was vampire," she pointed out. "It's unreasonable to think every single Carpathian-Lycan cross would do the same, any more than it would be reasonable to think every mage is evil because Xavier was."

"Surely there must be some suspicion when Carpathian meets mage,"

Fen replied. "You know there would be. The Lycans are fully integrated into the human world. They take jobs in the field of law enforcement and they keep small packs within the cities, all with jobs of humankind. They are ruled by a shadowy government of their own and those who rule use human resources. Nearly all the elite hunters are considered wildlife experts or specialists and they travel the world secretly hunting rogue werewolves."

"How many are like you?"

Fen hesitated. He didn't know exactly what that answer was, and he feared the truth. "As far as I know for certain, there is only me, and now Manolito De La Cruz and his lifemate." He had a small suspicion that his brother might have already crossed into his world as well, but he didn't know for certain.

"So few," Tatijana mused. "That does present a problem. If there were more, perhaps the Lycans would think twice before they decided to try to kill all of you, but with only three, they could strike and no one would know."

"You are kin to this Lara?"

Tatijana nodded. "She is the daughter of my brother's son, Razvan. My brother, Soren, was killed by Xavier and Xavier held Razvan and Lara prisoner as well."

"Get word to the De La Cruz family through Lara to be very careful and do not let anyone know of their cross-species."

"Did you think that I would leave you to face this alone?" Tatijana asked. "What kind of a lifemate would I be if I abandoned you?"

He felt an unexpected urge to laugh. "The kind of lifemate who does not want to be claimed."

"That was before I knew you were in trouble." She tossed her long braid over her shoulder, her eyes glittering like emeralds. "I am Dragonseeker. We do not run."

"I'm beginning to understand how true that is," Fen conceded. "Still, the Lycans have existed for centuries, adapting and evolving with each new generation, and they are well integrated into human society. They use their human counterparts to aid them in investigations and tracking down those they deem criminals."

"Like you."

"Vakasin did not tell his slayers about me and they have not discovered my identity. Elite hunters tracking a rogue pack came across me when I was hunting the rogue pack as well, but they have no knowledge of my identity. Perhaps Zev suspects what I am, but he doesn't know. There is only a short window of opportunity for hunters to find me. They can identify me only one week out of every month. It's only during the weeklong cycle of the full moon that my energy feels different to the Lycans and they know immediately what I am."

Tatijana frowned, her delicate eyebrows drawing together. "Why are you here? In the Carpathian Mountains? You didn't come back to inform the prince of your duality. And you didn't come back to swear your allegiance to him. You're a hunter. You hunt the vampire. Ancient hunters don't change their ways."

Fen sighed. Tatijana looked a fragile flower but she had a spine of steel, and she was highly intelligent. She might not know about fire, but she hadn't wasted her time during her centuries-long incarceration. She had studied each of her father's victims carefully. She had learned to read them and draw on their abilities and experiences. She had looked for hunters and those who knew how to fight in order to further her chances of escaping. He could almost feel her brain putting the pieces of a puzzle together with lightning speed.

"You suspect there is another—the one you call *Sange rau*," she said, shrewdly. "You followed him here, didn't you? By doing so you put yourself directly in the path of that hunter, the one from the tavern you said was dangerous."

He took her hand and turned her back toward the village. They had to get out of the woods—at least she had to. The blanket of mist had begun to churn and roil—fast-spinning eddies within the heavy fog. He held still for a moment, listening, his every sense tuned to the threads of information whirling in the mist.

"It is a suspicion, no more, but yes, I suspect Zev is here hunting the same rogue pack I was trailing when I ran across a strange, but familiar pattern. I believe Zev is Lycan and very lethal—especially to one such as me."

"This week of the month wouldn't be during the full moon would it?" she asked.

He found himself grinning in spite of the seriousness of the situation.

His lifemate had a little bite to her tone. She had just a bit of an attitude. He nodded his head. "Why, yes, my lady, it would."

She shook her head. "If the big bad wolf is coming for you, do you really think it's a good idea to be walking through the woods with me?"

Fen did laugh. Her coat was red and had a fleece-lined hood. "Where in the world did you hear the story of Little Red Riding Hood?"

"We had reading materials. Scrolls. Skins. Thin parchment. And then books. In the beginning, he thought we would become like him, only subordinate to him. He didn't realize that our mother had also left us a legacy before he murdered her. She made certain we were fully Carpathian but she concealed what she had done from him. We had the ability to communicate telepathically and to draw memories from Xavier's victims. When he realized we were not going to aid him in his efforts to wipe out the Carpathian species, he kept us drained and weak so we had no chance of escape."

"He made a mistake educating you."

"Yes he did, and we learned far more than he realized. His spells, the ability to counter them, shifting, the strengths and weaknesses of each species. We acquired a great deal of knowledge and waited for the moment we might be strong enough to strike at him—or defend ourselves. In the end, we were able to get Razvan's child free. Lara was so young, and we had hoped to go with her to protect her, but Xavier used Razvan to stab Bronnie and I couldn't leave her there, although she begged me to go without her. We were imprisoned for many years again until Lara came back for us."

The wind shifted again, sending the mist spinning around them. They both stopped abruptly and looked at one another.

Blood, Fen identified. *Human.* Death. The rogue pack was there in the forest. *He's just ahead, but I fear he's dead.* He used telepathic communication and the moment he was in her mind, he felt flooded with warmth—complete. All those empty places were filled with her. The terrible blackness receded and light poured in.

He's the third man from the tavern, the one who left when I called out to them. She was intelligent enough to follow his lead. There was sorrow in her voice, guilt even. *This is the man who tried to talk sense into his friends.*

The pack smelled like wolves, animals, tearing at their prey for fun, not food, and then rushing on their way to wreak more violence just because they could. Real wolves would be blamed and human hunters would destroy entire innocent packs because the rogue werewolves took joy in killing.

He squeezed her hand hard. *You are not responsible for this.*

I drove them out into the open and he left the safety of the others.

Fen's gut twisted. *Take to the sky. Get out of here. I need to go back and find the other two. The pack will sniff them out and kill them just for the fun of it.*

I will go with you.

The resolution in her voice had him swinging around rather than trying to dissuade her. He could feel the absolute determination in her mind. Perhaps if he wasn't basking in her company, enjoying everything about her, he would have been far more firm—not—he was certain—that it would do him any good.

They broke into a run, using blurring speed to retrace their path back to the two drunken men. It took only minutes. The two sat beside a tree passing a flask back and forth, one occasionally bursting into song.

Tatijana instinctively broke away from his side, moving to his left and allowing him to approach the two men alone. Fen was grateful to her. Already, he knew the pack was hunting. The rogues had both heard and smelled the men. They knew both men were physically impaired, drunk from the alcohol they'd consumed, and would be easy prey. Tatijana and he could take to the skies if necessary, but the two men were extremely vulnerable.

He muted his appearance, blending with the mist until he was directly in front of them, sending a swirl of mist ahead of him so that he could emerge naturally out of the fog. Both looked up at him.

"Fen, what are you doing out so late? You want a drink?" One held out the flask.

"You're Enre," Fen greeted. "Do you live far?" He projected his voice directly at the two men, although there was really no hope that the pack wouldn't know Tatijana was in the forest. He had known, from the moment the werewolf pack leader had given his hunting cry and the others had answered that the rogue pack was close by and hunting. To them, he would smell human.

"Gellert here, too," the other said drunkenly, opening his eyes and removing the flask from Enre's hand. "What are you doing here?"

"Let's get you two home," Fen encouraged. "It's too cold to stay out all night. Your families will worry."

"My woman kicked me out," Gellert said, his words slurred. "She said I drink too much." He was indignant. "I don't drink too much. She accused me of sleeping with the barmaid, Faye."

"You did sleep with Faye," Enre said.

Gellert took a long pull from the flask. "There was no sleeping," he said slyly.

"He's staying with me," Enre admitted. "I've got no family."

He didn't sound quite as drunk as he had been earlier. He struggled to his feet and reached down for Gellert. Gellert groaned and let both Fen and Enre help him up.

"You shouldn't have let your friend talk you into attacking the lady," Fen said to Enre.

Enre shrugged. "It was all just talk. I wouldn't have attacked her. I would have just given him a good clout upside the head and dragged him home if he'd really gone through with it."

"The redhead wants me," Gellert slurred. "She comes back night after night, and dances for me."

"The redhead is my woman," Fen said. "It isn't a good idea to say those kinds of things in front of me."

Gellert peered up at him with red, runny eyes. He burped loudly, the smell wafting toward Fen like a green cloud. "Sorry man. Didn't know. Come on, Enre, let's get on home."

A sound broke the night. Chilling. Close. Too close. The howl of the werewolf on the hunt. Enre, the more sober of the two, shivered and looked around warily. That joyful, frightening note floated on the wind, full and round-bodied, different from that of a normal wolf, far more unnerving.

"We have to go now," Fen urged, gripping Gellert on one side while Enre took his other arm. "Tatijana, leave us now while you can. Defending against a pack, even for one such as you, is not easy."

She lifted her chin, but her eyes stared out into the night. Like Fen, her senses had reached out far beyond the immediate area in an effort to locate the pack individuals—something he knew would be impossible. "I will not leave you to this fight alone. They won't be of any help." She indicated the two men with a jerk of her chin, still not looking at them.

"Do either of you have a weapon?" Fen hissed. He glanced toward

Tatijana. They weren't going to make it out of there without a fight. Depending on the pack size, they could be in real trouble.

Above them, a large owl landed in the branches of the neighboring tree. He folded his wings for a moment, surveying the small group below him. A burst of mist rose around the tree and out of it, a man emerged. He strode toward Fen, tall, his shoulders broad, and his eyes every bit as piercing, intelligent and ice-cold blue as Fen's. Hair as black as midnight flowed down his back, and he moved with a smooth, fluid step.

Fen stepped forward and they clasped forearms in the centuries-old greeting of warriors.

"*Kolasz arwa-arvoval*—may you die with honor," the tall warrior greeted. "I would not want to miss such a battle with you, *ekäm*—my brother."

"*Kolasz arwa-arvoval*—may you die with honor, Dimitri, *ekäm*—my brother," Fen said. "You are most welcome to this battle."

3

"We fight together then," Fen agreed. He held out his hand to Tatijana. "This is my lifemate, who remains unclaimed and quite happy about it. Tatijana, my brother, Dimitri."

Dimitri's gaze, glacier-cold, swept over her. "You are Dragonseeker."

Tatijana's answering nod was regal. Fen hid his grin in spite of the graveness of the situation. She looked like a royal princess.

"Have you ever battled the werewolf?" he asked Tatijana, already certain of the answer. She'd given him enough of her history to know she had no practical experience.

Tatijana made a face at him. "Of course not. I've been locked in ice my entire life, but I can help. Just tell me what to do."

"They mask energy easily. You will not feel the attack before it is on you. They move as fast as Carpathians and they cannot be killed without a special silver stake or bullet. Heads are removed and bodies burned."

Tatijana nodded solemnly, taking him seriously.

"Dimitri, remember our war games. Fight as if you are fighting the *Sange rau*."

"That makes it difficult without special silver stakes," Dimitri pointed out a little drolly.

"I always carry a few weapons," Fen admitted. "One has to, when rogues are in the vicinity." He reached into the pockets of his jacket and pulled out several very small stakes. They were made of pure silver, shaped like a unicorn horn, a gleaming spiral worth a fortune.

"How do you kill them?" Tatijana asked.

"You must penetrate all the way through the heart with silver," he warned her. "Unfortunately, they will be close enough to bite you and they tear chunks of flesh, going for arteries. They'll try to gut you with their claws. Again, they're fast."

"I flew over the forest and counted thirteen. There may have been more, they were difficult to spot," Dimitri said. "We can't abandon the humans, but we could fly them out of here."

"Rogue werewolves will kill everyone they come across. They're worse than vampires because they hunt in packs," Fen said. "Tatijana, perhaps you should fly the two humans out of here."

"I will not leave you. I can fight, better than you know. There were a few Lycans brought into the ice caves. I learned their strengths and weaknesses and I've looked into your mind as well. With what you told me, I know I can do this."

"They're close," Fen said.

"How can you tell?" Dimitri turned in a circle. "I cannot feel them."

"I can smell them. Get Enre and Gellert into the tree and throw a shield around them," Fen instructed.

Zev, from the tavern, strode out of the mist and brush. He looked cool, and confident, his long trench coat open, his hair gathered at the nape of his neck, much like Dimitri and Fen wore theirs. His eyes blazed a mercurial gray, sheer steel. He looked around the small circle of fighters.

"You cannot stay here."

"There's no safe passage," Fen said. "Carpathians will fight with Lycans to bring this rogue pack to justice." He nodded toward his brother. "This is Dimitri, and that is Tatijana."

"Zev," the newcomer identified himself. "This pack is my problem. I've sent for the hunters, but they are still twenty-four hours out."

Dimitri waved his hand toward the two drunks to take over their minds, spinning his fingers to encase them in the safety of a shield before wedging them in the higher branches of the trees.

Zev studied Fen's face. "Dimitri and Tatijana are Carpathian, but you are Lycan." It was a statement, the tone strictly neutral.

There was no hint of distrust in Zev's voice, but Fen knew Zev was suddenly very suspicious of him. Why would a Lycan be friends with two Carpathians? There was no way not to notice the resemblance between Dimitri and Fen. Zev was an elite investigator, which meant he had gone from an elite hunting pack to pursuing rogues on his own for the shadowy government behind the Lycans. He seemed more than confident.

"Have you any idea of the size of the pack?" Fen asked.

Zev nodded. "It's large. The largest I've ever run across. I've been tracking them for months."

"Dimitri counted thirteen, and that was just with a single pass."

"It's more like fifty to seventy. I've identified that many individual tracks, and I'm not certain that's all of them. They tend to divide, each unit hunting separately and then coming back together."

"That's why they've been able to do so much damage," Fen said.

Zev shot him a quick glance. "You've been tracking them?"

Fen nodded. He wasn't about to admit that he thought Zev was wrong, or at least partially wrong. He was fairly certain the rogue pack killed often, but a vampire either trailed them, doing far more of the brutal destruction than the pack had done, or traveled with them as a Lycan. The vampire was intelligent. He covered his tracks well, making certain the pack took the blame for his work. Of course, that was conjecture, Fen had no real proof.

"I ran across their kills a few weeks back and trailed after them," Fen admitted. *Dimitri, they're coming at you from your left. Three of them. Tatijana, go to mist or take to the skies. You've got two targeting you. They'll rush you from opposite sides and they're unbelievably fast.*

Mist swirled, a thick gray fog. The wind rushed through the trees and the rogues were on them, tall wolves running at them on their hind legs, each leap crossing thirty feet or more with blurring speed. The wolves poured into the circle from every direction, a silent, eerie attack made all the worse by their red glowing eyes, shining through the mist.

The three wolves leapt at Dimitri before he could move, or dissolve, all three sinking their teeth deep, ripping through muscle right down to the bone. Claws dug at his belly, trying to slash him open.

Claws raked Tatijana from her shoulder to her hip, even as she tried to turn to mist. They got to her far faster than she ever conceived possible. Fen rushed past the ones coming at him from every direction, his speed and momentum allowing him to knock over the one directly blocking his path to Tatijana. As he passed the werewolf, he slammed the silver stake deep into the chest wall. The sound of the rogue's heart was his beacon. The werewolf went down, and he kept going, blowing past the other three as they tried to close in on him.

He reached Tatijana, pulling one werewolf off her, spinning him around and staking him through his heart so hard he nearly drove the silver dagger all the way through the man. Tatijana punched the second werewolf hard in his throat as he drove teeth, dripping with saliva, at her face. She used the enormous force of the Carpathian hunter, staggering the werewolf. As he stumbled back, she dissolved into mist and tried to take to the sky.

Droplets of blood mingling with the mist led another werewolf straight to her. He leapt high and hooked claws into her dissolving ankle, yanking her down to the ground. Fen caught the movement out of the corner of his eye as two others tried tackling him. He felt the burn of teeth snapping down, the bite pressure, an enormous tearing at his calf and thigh. He ripped both wolves off of him, knocking their heads together with tremendous force, just needing a few seconds to get to Tatijana.

Out of the corner of his eye, he could see Zev, in the form of a huge Lycan, half man, half wolf, whirling in the midst of several werewolves, his body torn and bloody, but he moved with grace and precision, ducking attacks, coming up under one of the werewolves to plunge a silver stake in his heart and whirling away again.

Fen caught the werewolf who had his claws in Tatijana's ankle, snapping his neck and yanking Tatijana back up to her feet in one smooth motion.

Go, he hissed. *Take to the air.*

A werewolf landed on Fen's back, sinking teeth into the nape of his neck. Tatijana put on a burst of speed, darting into the skies, shifting as she did so, taking the shape of a blue dragon. Fen shifted into the shape of a Lycan, using the strength and muscular form to throw off the werewolf ripping at his body.

The second wave of the pack rushed in. Fen spun around toward the new threat, saw them engulfing Dimitri and Zev, who were back to back. He moved fast, using the double speed of the Carpathian/Lycan blood flowing in his veins. He plunged a silver spike deep into one werewolf's heart and rushed past just as an enormous werewolf came out of the mist.

Instantly, Fen knew. This was no ordinary werewolf. This was the vampire masking his presence in the midst of a rogue pack, no, not just a vampire, this was far more. "Zev, Dimitri," he shouted the warning. "Behind you. *Sange rau.*"

He was already leaping across the werewolves, trying to get to his brother before the newcomer did. His burst of speed put him directly in the vampire's path. Eyes glowed red, settling on him. The wolf/vampire charged him. They came together with terrible force, shaking the ground around them. The impact was so hard, Fen felt his very bones rattle. He felt as if a freight train had hit him, but if he felt that way, he knew his adversary did as well. He punched through the chest wall, his last silver stake in his fist, driving for the heart. To kill a *Sange rau* was far more difficult than killing either a Lycan or a vampire. He'd had a lot of experience on what didn't work.

Around him, the battle waged, Zev and Dimitri fighting off the werewolves, while up above them, the dragon came in low, breathing fire on the wolves she could without harming Fen, Dimitri or Zev.

"I see you," the *Sange rau* hissed, his voice low. "I know you."

Fen knew him, too. He'd been in a pack for a few months a century or so ago and this Lycan had been the pack alpha. His name was Bardolf and he'd been particularly mean, ruling his pack with an iron hand. He'd disappeared on a hunt, and when they'd tracked him, there had been a bloody battle between him and what Fen had been certain had been the undead. Neither were anywhere to be found, nor were there bodies. Now, Fen knew what had happened. The Lycan had torn into the vampire, gulping his blood, and he'd consumed enough to transform himself.

"I see you, too," Fen said, ducking under the wolf/vampire's reaching arm to come in close to slam his fist hard into Bardolf's chest.

He had no more silver stakes. To kill Bardolf he would need the silver spike as well as to remove the heart from the chest and destroy it with fire. Few knew how to kill one such as Bardolf, but Fen had plenty of experience in trial and error when he'd tracked the *Sange rau* centuries before. He knew destroying the monster would be very difficult.

He plunged his fist deep, twisting his body to avoid the muzzle full of teeth rushing toward his throat. The teeth grazed him, ripping through flesh. He felt the flash of pain an instant before he blocked it, his fist moving deep in the chest of the undead, fingers seeking the withered heart. He couldn't kill the beast, but he could slow it down, giving Tatijana time to destroy a number of the rogue pack from the sky.

Bardolf wrenched his body backward, pushing himself off of Fen with tremendous force so that Fen was flung backward as well, his fist pulling free of the vampire's chest. Bardolf, instead of following up his advantage while Fen staggered, trying to recover his footing, leapt for the air, for the small dragon skillfully wielding flame.

"Fen!" Zev yelled. "Catch."

Dimitri and Zev took the brunt of the attack on the next wave of werewolves as Bardolf clearly directed his rogues toward Fen. The two hunters, Carpathian and Lycan, quickly leapt between Fen and the oncoming assault.

Fen had his hand in the air almost before he turned around. A silver sword spiraled toward him. Fen caught the glittering handle and leapt into the air as a Lycan would, almost in one motion, slicing cleanly through Bardolf's body just as the undead werewolf reached for the dragon's spiked tail. Bardolf's scream shook the trees below him, the discordant note an assault on every ear.

The werewolves set up a terrible cacophony of howls. The brush shivered. Leaves withered and tree branches shifted away from the body of the *Sange rau* as it dropped like a stone in two pieces to the ground with an ugly splat. Acid fell like rain, burning everything in its path.

Fen raced toward the head and chest. A large werewolf intercepted him. Fen swung the sword as another werewolf leapt on his back. The sword sliced through sinew and bone, cutting off an arm. The scent of blood and burned flesh made the werewolves nearly crazed so that they renewed their attacks in a mad frenzy, rushing at Dimitri and Zev, and dragging them to the ground.

Tatijana! Circle back.

Fen had no choice but to go to his brother's aid. He turned away from the severed body of the undead, leapt over a fallen werewolf and landed in the middle of the frenzied pack. He picked up a large werewolf who ripped open Dimitri's belly with his teeth and clawed at his insides in triumph. Fen snapped the werewolf's neck and threw him into another one so that they both went crashing down, one on top of the other. He waded through more of the werewolves, it seemed a wall of them, trying to get to his brother and Zev.

Tatijana burst overhead, fire raining down, a long sweep of flames so that fur blackened, singed and then curled into ashes. Werewolves screamed in panic and pain. Fen took advantage of the assault from the sky, breaking through the mass of wolves to yank Dimitri up and away from the frenzied mob. Blood sprayed into and over the thrashing wolves.

Dimitri staggered back, pain etched into his face. He righted himself and the pain was wiped from his expression. He held up his hand for the silver sword. Fen tossed it to him and went back for Zev.

Fen spared a quick glance toward the two halves of Bardolf's body. Already the hands and legs were dragging the pieces closer together, digging in the dirt to reach each half.

Tatijana, flame the Sange rau *cut in half. Burn that carcass before it's too late.*

Even as he told her, the two severed halves merged and instantly disappeared into the mist. Cursing in his native tongue, Fen snapped another neck. Dimitri charged the thrashing werewolves, one hand holding his belly together, the other slashing through bodies with the silver sword.

A sharp call from the sky had the werewolves retreating, fighting their way past Dimitri while Fen fought off any of them trying to finish off Zev. The pack was gone into the mist almost instantly and silently. Only those with the silver stakes in them lay on the ground.

Dimitri folded in half, went to his knees and sank into the dirt a distance from Fen. Fen caught up the silver sword and cut the heads off the staked werewolves before turning to his brother.

Zev half sat, blood running down his face and chest in steady streams. Fen shifted back to completely human form as he bent over Dimitri. His brother was in bad shape. He'd had the brunt of the attack, the pack pouring out of the forest straight at Fen. Fen had gone after the *Sange rau* while Dimitri and Zev had drawn the others to him to give Fen his chance at destroying the ultimate threat.

Tatijana. See to Zev. Dimitri is close to passing.

He would save his brother first, no matter how valiant the Lycan had been. He had told Dimitri of his fear that there was such a powerful predator closing in on their homeland, and it was Dimitri who had paid the price because he believed his brother's suspicion in spite of the lack of proof.

Tatijana might have healing skills, but he couldn't take the chance. Better that she practice on the Lycan than Dimitri.

Hang on, ekäm—my brother, Fen whispered telepathically. He had to maintain his link with Dimitri at all times so that the light of life would not leave his body. *Tatijana, I have need of you now. Shield us from Zev's sight. He cannot see what I do.*

There was so much blood lost. Far too much. He felt her presence almost immediately. Tatijana. His own private miracle. She brushed her hand along his shoulders as she moved toward Zev.

Mist stands between you and the Lycan.

Thank you, my lady.

Fen didn't hesitate, but plunged his hands into the jagged opening of Dimitri's belly, searching for the main source of the blood pumping from his brother's body.

I will not be aware of my surroundings. You are our only protection, he warned Tatijana.

I've got your back.

Believing her, he didn't wait for her reply. He didn't have time. He had to trust that she would be alert for the return of the pack. He doubted if the rogues would return, their alpha was nursing his own wounds and would need to heal himself before he could kill again, but it was always possible.

He shed his body fast, becoming healing light, pure spirit to sink into his brother. *I am with you. My soul calls to yours,* he whispered.

He traveled through Dimitri's body to the mass of destruction in his belly. The werewolves had clawed and bitten, tearing great chunks from his body. The first thing he had to do was repair the damage to arteries and veins and stop the flow of blood. It seemed Dimitri's entire belly was filled with blood and nothing else.

Ot ekäm ainajanak hany, jama—My brother's body is a lump of earth, close to death.

It had been long since he'd used the great healing chant, but this was no small wound. If he was to succeed he would need time, patience and blood. Powerful blood.

That light in Dimitri was very dim, moving down the tree of life, far away from Fen. Fen redoubled his efforts. Time was running out fast. He found the places where teeth had bitten through the lifelines in Dimitri's body—so many places—the damage far worse than he'd seen in centuries. Dimitri had given much to give him the time to keep Tatijana from the *Sange rau*.

He resisted the urge to hurry, taking his time to repair each severed or torn artery or major organ with great care. As he performed the task he continued to chant softly in his mind.

"We, the clan of my brother encircle him with care and compassion. Our healing energies, ancient words of magic and healing herbs bless my brother's body, keep it alive."

When he was certain he had done enough of the repairs that Dimitri's body would hold blood, he tore at his own wrist with his teeth and pressed the wound to Dimitri's mouth. Dimitri made no attempt, even when Fen dripped the blood into his mouth, to take it in. Often times, a warrior so badly wounded, when he'd lived long centuries holding darkness at bay, preferred to slip away, but Dimitri had someone to live for. He'd told Fen of his lifemate, too young to claim, surviving a horrendous childhood. Fen had no compunctions against using the information Dimitri had confided.

Drink for your life and the life of the girl you told me about. Young Skyler who has suffered so much and deserves happiness. Do not let that happiness end here, my brother.

The light had retreated so far Fen feared he was too late. *You are strong, my brother. Think only of your unclaimed lifemate. She will live out her days sad and lonely without you. Come back.*

The dim light halted. Faltered. Stayed still. He felt the smallest movement at his wrist and instantly aided his brother in swallowing the liquid of life. Even as Dimitri took in blood, Fen knew it wouldn't be enough. He was weak himself from blood loss. Healing took tremendous energy. He would have to feed quickly and return to draw his brother's life light back. He gave Dimitri as much blood as he dared before returning to his own body.

The act of being in two places at one time, feeding his brother and healing him, aiding him in sending the blood through his body took a tremendous toll. Normally, with a wound so grievous, there were many Carpathians participating in the healing ritual. Fen had to remain a Lycan in Zev's eyes. There was no controlling Zev's mind. Tatijana could shield them using the mist, but at all times, Zev had to believe that Fen was Lycan, not a mixture of wolf and Carpathian.

He rose quickly, staggered, regained his footing and, after making certain the mist remained thick enough to hide his actions, took to the trees where the two drunken humans were cocooned in the shield Tatijana had provided for them. Before using them to replenish the blood he'd given his brother, he drove as much alcohol from their systems as possible through their pores. As a rule, Carpathians rarely touched tainted blood, but this was an emergency and he'd take anything he could get.

He took even more than he needed, knowing Dimitri would need much more. *Tatijana, how long before you can aid me?*

I put him into a healing sleep with his permission, but he won't be in it long.

Bring down the lightning and burn the bodies. Make certain you get every last bit of fur and hair. Do not remove the silver spikes from their hearts otherwise they can regenerate. Let the fire burn everything and we'll recover the stakes after that. Once that's done, come help me. I need to find my brother in the other world and guide him back. He's stuck between two places.

He caught Tatijana's shocked gasp. Both knew it was difficult to bring someone back when they were so close to death. The only thing that had stopped Dimitri was knowing what his unclaimed lifemate would suffer without him.

Fen hurried back to his brother and knelt down, this time mixing his saliva with dirt, rich with Lycan blood, and packing it into the worst of Dimitri's wounds. He took a deep breath and once more left his body behind to become pure light.

He took up the great healing chant of his people from centuries earlier. He spoke in his native tongue, using his most charismatic, commanding, persuasive voice.

"My brother's soul is only half. His other half wanders in the nether-world. My great deed is this: I travel to find my brother's other half."

Tatijana sank down beside him. "We dance. We chant." She pulled the words of the mystical song from his mind. "We dream ecstatically."

"To call my spirit bird and to open the door to the other world," Fen continued.

He felt the cold of that other place. He'd been there more than once after a battle, but Dimitri had traveled farther than he ever had to the other side.

"I mount my spirit bird and we begin to move. We are underway." He suited action to words. He was going down that long tree into the dark and cold to find Dimitri and bring him back whole. "Following the trunk of the Great Tree, we fall into the netherworld."

His very breath felt like ice. "It is very, very cold." Worse than cold. He'd never been this far into the other world before. He could hear wailing in the dark. Teeth gnashing. He continued, unmoved by what might be stalking him in a place he had no business being in.

He was connected to Dimitri. They were brothers and their minds were tuned to one another. "My brother and I are linked in mind, heart and soul. My brother's soul calls to me. I hear and follow his track."

As he approached that dim light he knew to be Dimitri's, another approached as well. Something dark and terrible. Something familiar. Some-thing also calling softly, sweetly to Dimitri. "Encounter, I, the demon who is devouring my brother's soul."

Fen knew that sweet, deceiving voice all too well. He would recognize it anywhere. Fen was oldest, Dimitri youngest, but in between there had been Demyan and almost from the beginning, Demyan had shirked duty. He'd been a man of little honor, and it was no surprise to Fen when he had, early on, chosen the path of the undead. Still, it was difficult to discover that his own brother had chosen to give up his soul and become the undead.

After that, Fen had checked on Dimitri often. Over the long centuries, he'd learned that his youngest brother was a force to be reckoned with and he never swerved from his duty, no matter how difficult. It had been Dimitri he had turned to when he realized he was both Lycan and Carpathian, and it had been Dimitri who had provided a sanctuary where he could go when he needed rest and healing. Fen had been the reason Dimitri had chosen brotherhood with the wolves in the wild by setting up sanctuaries for them.

Demyan called to Dimitri's weary soul, promising him rest. Peace. No pain. Demyan was so busy focusing on ensnaring Dimitri's light that he never saw Fen coming at him through the darkness. He never suspected Fen would travel so far after his brother.

Anger swept through Fen. Shook him. To think that Demyan had waited all this time, crouched in the darkness, still refusing to accept his responsibilities, waiting for one of his brothers to come in death, angered Fen more than he ever thought possible. Dimitri had fought long with honor in the world, and now, when he was at his most vulnerable, the light in him slowly fading, his own brother planned to steal that honor.

Furious, Fen struck out of the darkness, just as Demyan reached for Dimitri's flickering light. Dimitri must have sensed danger, even so near death. The spirit light jerked inches from Demyan's outstretched greedy fingers. Fen caught at his disgraced brother, and wrenched him backward. Demyan felt insubstantial, yet he cried out, a long wail of terror when he spun around and saw his oldest brother Fen ready to do battle.

Nenäm ćoro; o kuly torodak.—In anger, I fight the demon.

He whispered the words into Dimitri's mind. Into the mind of Demyan. He spoke the greater healing chant in the language of the ancients.

O kuly pél engem.—He is afraid of me.

He stared into Demyan's eyes. *You should fear me. How dare you think to steal our brother's soul.*

Tatijana, call down the lightning, give it to me, Fen whispered into her mind. He felt her immediate reaction, the hot energy sizzling through her.

Staring into Demyan's eyes he repeated the next line of the healing chant. *Lejkkadak o kaŋka salamaval.*—I strike his throat with a lightning bolt.

Demyan tried to run but it was too late—the lightning bolt followed

Fen down the tree of life and struck with precision at Demyan. For a moment the world below lit up and Fen could see the other shadowy beings, red greed-filled eyes, watching nightly as pure souls of light passed beyond their reach. They waited, as Demyan had, for one who would recognize their voice and was not yet into the next realm, one so near death, but not yet dead.

The creatures had drawn close—too close—drawn not by Dimitri's waning light, as they could not call to him, but pulled by the scent of Fen's blood. He had open wounds he had not yet cared for. How bad the wounds were he didn't know, nor at that moment did he care.

The spear of lightning sizzled through the darkness and Demyan fell back as did the other hungry creatures, blinded by the shocking white sword of pure electrical energy cutting through absolute blackness.

Fen caught the paperlike form of Demyan in his powerful hands. With the force of both Lycan and Carpathian, Fen held his disgraced brother still, face-to-face, looking into his eyes. "I break his body with my bare hands."

Demyan shook his head, knowing what came next in the healing chant, but no sound escaped. There would be no mercy. Fen had none for him.

"He is bent over and falls apart." As Fen chanted the words, he wrenched the paper figure in two, tore him into shreds and let the pieces fall. "He runs away." He whispered the words into darkness as Demyan shrieked and wailed, trying to recover the pieces and shrink away before the creatures hovering close turned on him with all their greedy hunger.

Fen turned back to Dimitri's waning light. The life force was almost gone. "I rescue my brother's soul," he said, continuing the healing chant.

As he neared his brother's life-light, surrounding him with his own much brighter, stronger light, he heard a soft female voice, not Tatijana's, whispering to Dimitri.

Don't leave me. Stay. Stay with me. I know you're weary. I know you're hurting. I know I'm asking for so much, but don't go without me. Dimitri. My love. My everything. Stay.

The soft plea was so intimate, Fen felt guilty hearing her. Skyler. Dimitri's young lifemate, fighting for him across the continent. How strong was she that she could reach so far? Very few Carpathians could reach such a distance. A human. A child by the terms of Carpathian society. Yet she fought for her lifemate as courageously as any fully grown Carpathian would do.

The light grew a bit stronger, as if for her, Dimitri made a valiant effort.

Skyler must have sensed Fen's presence. He felt her suddenly go still, studying him. Assessing him. She didn't feel like a child to him, she felt like a woman. A warrior. One prepared to do battle should it be necessary. She clearly weighed him, friend? Foe? He actually felt her ready herself to do battle, and her strength was enormous and unexpected.

I will bring him back from this dark place. I am Fenris Dalka, Dimitri's eldest brother. I will not leave him in this place of darkness. I have fought long and hard for him. He will not die this night.

She was silent a moment, assessing not his words, but the feel of him. She was indeed, strong. He liked her. She was a fitting lifemate to a warrior who had survived centuries hunting the undead and keeping darkness at bay.

Thank you, Skyler said simply.

He felt her move through Dimitri's mind, brushing up against that fading light, stroking caresses, giving strength to him. She faded away, the distance too far to maintain for long.

"I lift my brother's soul in the hollow of my hand," he whispered, holding Dimitri's life close to him. "I lift him onto my spirit bird. Following up the Great Tree, we return to the land of the living."

Fen came back into his own body, swaying with weariness. He looked around him. Time had passed and he hadn't known. He shivered. The ice of that place, even for a Carpathian, got into one's bones and stayed. Tatijana had held the mist. He could hear Zev calling out to her. His voice sounded stronger.

"Give me another minute. We're trying to save Dimitri," Tatijana said. "The rogues have not returned. I'm aiding Fen in closing these wounds."

She waited for Fen to turn his head and look at her. Immediately she knelt beside him and put her hands on his shoulder, leaning in close to expose the beautiful line of her throat to him. His heart clenched. Even there, under such dire circumstances, Tatijana was calm, thought ahead, and provided for him.

Fen didn't hesitate. He enfolded her close to him, stroked his tongue once over that pulse calling so strongly to him and then he sank his teeth deep and drank. He had used up precious energy in his fight to save Dimitri, to bring him back from the brink of death. He needed to give Dimitri more blood and continue to heal his wounds before putting him in the welcoming earth.

Tatijana cradled his head as he drank. Stroked his hair. Her fingers caressed his temples. She tasted like heaven. Like a miracle. He had never considered taste before. She lingered on his tongue and filled every vein with a rush. He felt her spreading through his body claiming every part of him, organs, bone, tissue. All of him. Strength burst through him at the influx of ancient Carpathian blood. She was from a strong linage and she gave to him freely. He was careful to close the small wound on her throat, to heal it so that Zev's sharp eyes wouldn't discover his secret.

"You have many wounds of your own, Fen," she said, kneeling beside Dimitri. She closed her eyes and put her hands over the lesser lacerations while Fen concentrated once again on his brother's open belly.

"As do you, my lady," Fen said, looking her over with sharp eyes.

"I healed most of them while I was in the air," she said. "Have no worries about me. Keep Dimitri alive."

Fen leaned over Dimitri, one hand hovering over the open gashes while he fed his brother more blood from his other wrist. *Drink freely, my brother. And then you can rest.*

Warmth burst from Tatijana's hands. She spread it over Dimitri's body while Fen concentrated healing light over his belly. When Dimitri had taken enough blood from him to satisfy Fen, Fen took his time packing each separate wound on his brother's body with Lycan blood-stained soil and his own saliva.

Keep Zev occupied while I find a resting place for my brother, he instructed Tatijana and lifted Dimitri's body into his arms.

Tatijana nodded. She looked a little tired and very pale. She hadn't fed and yet she'd fought a battle, was wounded as well and she'd worked to save Zev.

I will return swiftly to see to you, my lady. Forgive me for not putting you first.

I would have liked you less had you done so, she replied. She raised her voice. "Zev, I'll be right there. I'm sorry this has taken so long."

Mist swirled thickly around them. He felt Tatijana's feminine hand in the renewed veil of fog.

Fen took to the air. It had been long since he had used his Carpathian abilities. Staying in Lycan form, thinking like a Lycan, living as one had allowed him to keep the ever-present darkness at bay. Now he needed his Carpathian skills. He searched for a safe resting place where his brother could remain. He would return and give him blood when needed, but it could not be a place another might rest. No cave.

He found a field rich with life and knew the soil was extraordinary. A dog barked near the small dilapidated house and he silenced it automatically. Fen opened the earth for his brother. He went deep, weaving safeguard upon safeguard. Dimitri would be vulnerable should any enemy find him. He floated down with his brother in his arms, placing him carefully in the rich soil. Almost at once, he felt *her* presence again, that young-old soul that was Dimitri's lifemate. He waited while she moved through Dimitri's mind, assuring herself he was still alive, although still so close to death.

He won't die, she declared. *Will you, Dimitri?*

When Dimitri stirred as if he might answer, she painted brushstrokes, small caresses over the cracks and fissures where the darkness had seeped into his mind. *Be still. I will come to you soon, when you are healed and strong again. For now, rest. Take my love with you and wrap yourself in it while you sleep, just as I did yours for so many troubling nights.*

There was such a simplistic honesty in her voice. A directness. And love. He heard it. She felt the emotion deeply for his brother. The connection between Dimitri and Skyler was strong. They were already intertwined although so far apart.

Mother Earth, I call to you. Skyler's voice once more slipped into his mind through her connection to Dimitri. *This is Dimitri, my lifemate. The other half of my soul. I ask a favor for your daughter. Hold him close in your arms. Heal him of every wound. He is a great warrior and has served his people well. Protect him from all things evil while you hold him close. I ask this humbly.*

Fen actually felt the small shift of the earth around them. Richer soil pushed up from beneath him, to form a bed for Dimitri to lie in. *Sleep well, my brother. I thank you for your aid this night. Without your intervention, I might not have gotten to Bardolf in time to save Tatijana.*

He waited until the earth was filled in and the field was exactly back as it had been before he returned to the battlefield in the forest.

4

"Great battle," Zev greeted as Fen came out of the thinning mist toward him. Zev half sat, half laid on the ground, his back against a tree.

"You look a little worse for wear," Fen said.

Zev was covered in wounds from teeth ripping at him and claws tearing him open. He was obviously in pain, but stoic about it.

"You might want to take a look in the mirror yourself," Zev suggested with a show of his white teeth.

By the way he didn't move, Fen knew Zev was in bad shape. Like Dimitri, he had taken the brunt of that last attack in order to give Fen time to save Tatijana from the *Sange rau*.

"Honestly, I'd rather not. Tatijana dealt with the carcasses. I still have to get those two home." Fen jerked his head toward Enre and Gellert still shielded in the tree. "I have to admit, I'm tired." He sank down, his legs a little rubbery. He'd given a great deal of blood to Dimitri and he hadn't attended his wounds.

"You knew he was here, didn't you? The abomination? You tracked him here."

Fen shrugged. He didn't mind Bardolf being called an abomination.

The undead had chosen to give up their soul, but he knew that Zev would think Fen was *Sange rau*—bad blood as well, if the Lycan knew the truth about Fen's own mixed blood. Fen respected Zev, so it was just a little disconcerting. "I suspected. I came across the rogue pack and thought I'd better try to do damage control, pick them off one by one if possible. But then I saw the destruction, and even for a rogue pack, it seemed too brutal."

"I didn't know," Zev admitted. He sounded disgusted with himself. "I should have suspected. You called him by name."

"My pack was destroyed by the *Sange rau*, years ago, and I went to a neighboring pack," Fen explained. "Bardolf was the alpha. He was . . . brutal with the younger members. I had a hard time with him and knew I wouldn't be able to stay long."

Zev looked a little amused. "I can imagine. You're pure alpha. One would think you would have a pack of your own." There was a mixture of speculation in his voice as well as the laughter.

"A few months after my pack was destroyed, Bardolf's pack was attacked by the same *Sange rau* that had killed most of my pack. The demon wreaked havoc, killing everyone in his path. He targeted the women and children first and then began killing the men. Bardolf's mate and his children were killed in the first attack. Bardolf went a little crazy and went hunting on his own while we were burning the dead. No one noticed at first that he was missing. We tracked him to a cave deep in the mountains."

Fen leaned his head back against the tree trunk and closed his eyes as Tatijana knelt beside him. Rather than the battle with blood and death, she smelled of the forest, fresh rain and wild honey, that elusive scent he found enticing. She passed her hands over his face. At once a soothing calm came over him. He looked at her face, so beautiful, her skin flawless, her lashes long and feathery. She smiled at him, lighting up her glittering emerald eyes.

"You need healing, Fen," she said gently.

"So do you, my lady," he answered, his fingers finding the wound on her shoulder.

The wind ripped through the trees, sending a shower of leaves and swirling fog rushing between Zev and Fen, hiding the glow of warmth and Fen's mouth moving over the wound with healing saliva.

"It's nothing," Tatijana said aloud for Zev's benefit. "Let me see to your wounds. They're far worse. I will have to go to ground soon and any injury will heal fast."

Fen couldn't help but be proud of her. She never missed a cue. As far as Zev was concerned, Fen was Lycan. Tatijana had gone a long way to keep his secret safe. She bent over his wounds, her body partially hiding her actions from Zev, but Fen wasn't too concerned. Carpathians were known for their healing abilities.

Her tongue stroked over the wound. His body clenched, reacted unexpectedly. Her eyes had closed, and she looked so incredibly sensual she took his breath away. He'd never thought in terms of sensuality, that was a new experience for him, and he was a little shocked at how intense his reaction to her was.

For me as well.

Her voice was soft, brushing along the walls of his mind, almost with the same sensuality as her tongue. She didn't attempt to hide her wonder or her need from him.

"You said you'd tracked Bardolf to a cave in the mountains," Zev prompted.

Fen couldn't help himself. He touched Tatijana's face with gentle fingers. She smiled, but she didn't stop her work. She took soil from between them, where Zev had no chances of seeing what she was doing, and mixed it with saliva to press into the worst of the bite marks and lacerations.

"What was left of his pack went with me to find him—to aid him. There weren't very many of us, and we had wounded along so we couldn't go as fast as we would have liked. We didn't dare leave them alone, not with the *Sange rau* so close, and none of us wanted to take the chance of Bardolf finding him and taking him on alone. I couldn't leave them to go ahead. I knew none of them had the skills to deal with a monster like we would be confronting. That gave Bardolf a good head start on us."

Fen was tired. Much more exhausted than he had been in a long, long while. Fighting in the other world, without his body and only using his mind and spirit, had been draining. Tatijana seemed to know, her hands moving over him with sureness, taking on some of the burden. Zev shifted position and groaned softly. It occurred to Fen that Tatijana had performed the same healing rituals on the Lycan.

Not the same, she denied. Her breath was warm against his skin as she knelt up and pushed the hair from his face to find a particularly nasty claw rake.

His body tightened unexpectedly. *No, it's not the same, my lady,* he agreed, filling her mind with his warmth. It was the only thing he could give her without betraying who he was.

He glanced at Zev before he could help himself, afraid to put Tatijana in any more danger. He was tired and it would be easy enough to make mistakes.

Zev's eyes were closed. Lines were etched into his face. He looked every bit as exhausted as Fen felt.

Fen laughed softly. "We're in great shape, Zev. I'm not looking forward to another dance with this bunch, at least not tonight. Aside from getting our two drunken friends home safely, there's a body in the forest the rogues killed. Tatijana and I found it on our way to the village. That's what brought us running back."

Zev stirred as though he might rise. Tatijana whirled around and held up her hand to stop him. He groaned and subsided.

"I don't know what the healing rate is for Lycans," Tatijana said, "but it isn't this fast. If you don't want those wounds to open again, give yourself a few minutes. I'll get you back to the inn so you can rest. Let me take care of Fen first. But don't you dare move."

Zev laughed. "Are all Carpathians as bossy as you?"

Tatijana gave a little sniff, her eyes alight with amusement. "Only the women. We have to be. Our men are difficult, you know. We have no choice." She turned her emerald eyes back on Fen. Laughter made the green facets glitter. She looked more beautiful than ever.

"If your men don't treat you right, they don't have brains in their heads," Zev said. "You're a beautiful woman, Tatijana, and hell on wheels in a fight. You didn't even flinch."

Fen felt himself go still. He looked around Tatijana to Zev. The man clearly wasn't flirting, just stating a fact. Everything in him settled, when two seconds before, he'd been coiled and ready.

Tatijana nudged him. "Pay attention, wolf boy."

Zev snickered. "That's a good one. You fight like the elite."

It was a probing question delivered in a casual tone.

Fen forced a smile, showing strong white teeth. He'd lived as a Lycan so long it was second nature to him now. He wouldn't make a mistake, not unless Tatijana was in danger. He thought like a Lycan. Zev was cunning, intelligent and fierce, a very skilled fighter. He had walked into their circle and told them to leave, and had they, he would have fought the entire rogue pack alone.

"I've been around and without a pack, I tend to hunt more than most," Fen admitted carefully. "Once I suspected Bardolf was running the rogue pack, I've spent most of my time tracking them, trying to pick them off one at a time." He shot Zev a grin. "They've turned on me a couple of times and I got my butt handed to me."

Zev studied him, eyes too old—too shrewd. "I doubt that. But you've seen your share of battles. You're every bit as skilled as I am, maybe more, and that's saying a lot."

He hadn't hid as much from Zev as he would have liked. Zev was one of the elite, and they were few. They were born that much faster, that much stronger and that much more intelligent than the rest of the Lycans. They regenerated at much more rapid rates. When a pack discovered a child with such attributes, he or she was sent to a special school for education.

"You must not have been very old when your pack was destroyed," Zev ventured.

Tatijana sank back on her heels. "There you go, gentlemen. Both of you should live, although next time I suggest you move just a little faster. If you notice, I have very few bites on me." She flashed a saucy grin at them both.

You healed them, my lady, and that is unfair, he teased her privately.

The Lycans looked at one another and then both of them laughed. The tension between them seemed to evaporate with Tatijana's observation.

"Finish telling me about Bardolf and the cave," Zev prompted again. "If you really think that he's the alpha for this pack, I need to know everything about him."

"We found massive amounts of blood. Scorch marks. A sign of a terrible battle. No bodies, but we knew Bardolf had met up with the *Sange rau*. All of us believed Bardolf had been killed by him, but there was no body."

There was a small silence. Zev shook his head. "The others believed Bardolf died that day. You knew he was still alive." He made it a statement.

"Bardolf did die that day, whether he appears to be intact or not. He tangled with the *Sange rau* and somehow he became just like the one he fought. I wasn't certain, but the more I studied the battlefield, the more it looked wrong to me. Staged. The burn marks, the withered plant life, blood everywhere, but no body. Something wasn't right."

Very slowly, Fen could feel his strength returning. Tatijana's powerful blood and healing magic was already working miracles and soon, his Lycan blood would kick in to aid in even faster healing.

"Where are you staying, Zev?" Tatijana asked. "I can take you there. Have you ever ridden on a dragon?"

"I can't say that I have," Zev admitted. "I've been around a few Carpathians over the long years, but only to hunt with them and not once was any of them polite enough to offer me a ride home." He flashed a tired grin. "Of course, they weren't nearly as beautiful as you are, and I might have had to object to them insinuating I couldn't make it home on my own."

"Of course you could," Tatijana said. "But I'm not turning down an escort."

You are amazing, Fen said. *Zev has a lot of pride.*

He's hurt pretty bad. Even with his blood, and mine, it will take him several days to heal.

Alarm spread. *Is he aware you gave him blood?*

Centuries ago, the Lycans didn't know what caused the combination of Lycan/Carpathian. Or for that matter, Lycan/Vampire. Clearly the Lycans didn't distinguish between the two. They saw both as a powerful threat. So few crosses had been made that maybe the Lycan council still was unsure, but they must have guessed. They had access to laboratories and they studied and researched. Most likely they had to suspect a mixture of blood in this century.

I was careful, Tatijana soothed. *Rest until I return. And be watchful. Don't go to sleep on the job.*

Fen found himself laughing. She was one smart woman. He had explained the danger he was in and she was going to be able to tell him exactly where Zev stayed. She'd taken Zev's blood as well as given him blood. She could monitor him even from a distance.

"How do you both manage to wield silver?" Tatijana asked curiously. "Wouldn't it harm you the same way it does the rogues?"

"We get used to using gloves," Zev answered. "Or we coat our hands and arms with sealant. That wears off fairly quickly. I prefer gloves, and clearly Fen does as well." He nodded toward Fen's protected hands.

Fen had lived so long as a Lycan it was second nature to him to don gloves and he was grateful he'd done so the moment they had been threatened by the rogue pack.

"Are you strong enough to hold on by yourself?" Tatijana asked Zev.

Fen winced. That would hurt Zev's ego. A hunter of rogue packs? A skilled warrior? To be asked by a woman if he could hold on all by himself? He nearly groaned out loud. He didn't dare look at Zev's face.

"I think I can manage. What about you, Fen? Are you safe here until she returns for you?"

Fen looked around the battlefield. There were several silver stakes lying on the ground in the ashes of the burned carcasses. He had enough energy to draw them to him after they left. He lifted one eyebrow. "You can leave me that silver sword. I covet that."

"I made it," Zev said. "It comes in very handy in tight situations."

"What other weapons have you made?" Fen asked curiously.

Zev hunted with an elite pack. He'd been chosen, above all other hunters in his elite pack, to be the scout. He went ahead, investigating rumors and sifting through evidence before calling in his pack to clean up. Scouting put him in continual danger. Rogue packs could be as few as three but as many as thirty. The fact that he was still alive was a testimony to his skills.

"I'll have to show you. Have you considered being trained?" Zev asked.

Fen shrugged. "Honestly no. Since my pack was destroyed—and it's been a very long time—I've been on my own. I'm an independent thinker. Following an alpha would be difficult." That much was the truth. That, and the pack would turn on him the first full moon.

"I'd welcome you into my pack anytime," Zev said. "Elite packs are different. Every member is an independent thinker, they have to be. Our alpha is more the counsel than one individual within the pack, although generally, the scout has a lot of clout. I imagine you would be more suited to the life of a scout." He grinned suddenly, the weariness and pain etched into his face gone for a moment. "And think of all the cool toys you get to have."

"I'd be very interested in seeing those toys," Fen admitted. He was just a little envious. That sword had come in handy. He needed time to study it, to figure out how best to forge one himself. Silver was natural—of the earth—which meant he could easily produce one, as he did the silver stakes, but one didn't just fashion a fine weapon from thin air without having knowledge of how it was made. He really did covet that extraordinary sword.

"Come by my room at the inn."

"You know you're deep in Carpathian country," Fen pointed out. "Everyone in that village is friends with the prince. He's close by and his hunters are probably already aware of you. They'll be watching closely. And there's no way you can keep a rogue pack under wraps here."

Zev nodded. "They won't be able to detect what I am, although they may become suspicious. They're very astute."

"Hello. Did you both forget I'm right here?" Tatijana demanded. "Of course the prince will know you're here. I have every intention of ratting the both of you out immediately. We don't take kindly to rogue packs and vampires killing anyone, human, Lycan or Carpathian. Did you think I'd be a good girl and just forget to report this?"

"We could only hope," Fen said good-naturedly.

"You fought so well," Zev added. "For a minute there I forgot you were Carpathian and believed you were Lycan."

"Ha, ha, ha, Zev," Tatijana sniffed. "As if a Lycan can fight as well as a Carpathian. Who saved your butt today? That was me."

"Don't tease her, Zev," Fen said with a small groan. "She's sassy enough without making her think she has to defend the entire Carpathian species."

Zev flashed him a knowing grin. "Come take me on my first dragon ride," he said to Tatijana. "I'll let you deal with dead bodies and Carpathians this night, Fen. Come see me and I'll show you those weapons. I might even have an extra or two." The smile faded and he lifted his head and sniffed the forest.

Fen did the same. The scent of blood and death and burnt flesh permeated the entire area. The scent of rogues in battle was already present, and if they were creeping close again, they would have made certain their scents would remain hidden. Zev was worried about leaving him there alone.

"How long will it take Bardolf to regenerate?" Zev asked. "I've never actually fought the *Sange rau*. I've never come across one before," he admitted.

"Longer than he'll like." Enough time that Fen planned to go looking for his lair. But he'd do that alone. Neither Tatijana nor Zev needed that information.

Silly wolf man. You think to protect me from the vampire thingie, whatever he is. I learn fast. I am not going to leave you to fight this battle alone.

There was soft, sensual affection growing in her voice, enough that the low note turned his heart to mush. He was supposed to be the big bad warrior and she seemed to reduce him to melted goo with just a few words. That didn't bode well for his future.

Tatijana threw back her head and laughed aloud. "You two are priceless. I'm collecting the silver stakes and giving them to Fen. Do you want to loan him your silver sword as well while he waits all alone like a sacrificial lamb in the forest for the wolves to return?"

That was a good one. No way would Zev want to part with his sword, but she'd made it nearly impossible for him to do anything else. If he insisted on taking it with him, when an injured man was waiting alone and vulnerable, he would look pretty petty.

Zev shook his head. "I want this back, Fen." He held the sword out to Tatijana.

"I'll see to it," Fen promised. "You said your pack would be here to help in another twenty-four hours."

Tatijana might be the one giving the sword back. Fen had only another day before he entered the time of great danger. Zev would recognize his mixed blood. By the full moon, every Lycan in the vicinity would sense his presence and try to kill him. Once Zev's pack of elite hunters arrived, Fen would be in real trouble. They would put the rogue pack on the back burner and make him their primary mission.

"It amazes me that the silver would be strong enough to cut through bone."

Zev's smile was distinctly wolfish. Clearly he had a few secrets when it came to making his weapons. Fen needed those secrets. He glanced at Tatijana. She nodded.

"Let's go, Zev, before it gets much later. Unlike you, I have to be aware of time," Tatijana reminded gently. "I'm going to shift and you'll have to climb up my wing to get onto my back." She looked around. "I'll need a little room."

She didn't wait. Tatijana was so fast at shifting into the form of a blue dragon, and so completely engulfed, mind and body, immediately, that Fen realized she was far more comfortable in that form than in her own.

By dragon standards, she might have been considered small, but there in the forest and so close to them, she seemed enormous—and beautiful. Her scales were iridescent blue, shimmering in the surrounding mist. Spikes ran along the ridge of her back down her long tail to end in a lethal-looking spear. Her eyes were large and emerald green, faceted like sparkling diamonds.

"Magnificent," Zev said. "Tatijana, that's incredible." He glanced at Fen. "Did you see how fast she was? I would have thought a dragon would take a few minutes." He attempted to rise, holding on to the tree trunk for support.

Fen could see the extent of Zev's injuries. He'd been badly wounded in dozens of places. Deep chunks of flesh had been torn from him. His face was etched with pain. Beads of sweat dotted his forehead. He didn't make a sound, as stoic as ever, but his skin looked a little gray.

"Hang on," Fen ordered, using his most compelling voice. Low. Velvet soft. A sneaky compulsion that slipped in on an alpha when the most commanding voice would never work. He stood up himself, blocking out the rush of pain as he got to his feet.

His respect for Zev was growing with every passing minute spent in his company. He'd met many tough Lycans, good men who knew how to fight in a battle, but clearly Zev was a cut above the rest. Lycans couldn't cut off pain the way Carpathians could. They endured it and fought on. The really great ones, like Zev, stayed in the battle even when others would have passed out.

Fen crossed the distance between them, one hand sliding over the body of the dragon in a long caress. "You're a lucky man, Zev," he observed.

"A privilege," Zev agreed. "I never thought I'd ever get this close to one. They're long gone now from this world."

He didn't protest when Fen slipped an arm around him to aid him. That told Fen more than anything, that Zev was badly injured. Tatijana extended her wing toward Zev. Fen helped him cover the ground to get to the wing.

He can't walk up your wing, Fen told her, using their telepathic link. He was beginning to worry about Zev's condition. *Just how bad was he?*

He'd been so concerned with Dimitri's horrendous wounds he hadn't considered that Zev had borne the brunt of the attack right along with Dimitri. He'd known, but Tatijana hadn't really told him just how bad Zev's injuries were. She'd been concerned with protecting Fen's secret as well as getting to him quickly to see to his wounds.

He didn't have intestines hanging out like Dimitri, Tatijana said. *But it was very bad. A lesser man would be unconscious right now.*

If I use my abilities as a Carpathian to get up on your back he'll know immediately that I am more than Lycan.

Tatijana made a little sound in his mind, a very feminine humph of annoyance. *All you had to do was ask.*

He found himself smiling. Maybe he did try to annoy her just a little bit on purpose. He liked her fiery little temper. He could feel each time that temper flared, bursting across his mind like stars across a sky on a hot summer's night, warming him. He found comfort in her explosive reactions, small as they were, but still directed at him. Engulfing him. Surrounding him. Sinking into his bones. His blood. She was his.

You wish.

She gave a little delicate sniff, but there was growing affection in her teasing tone. He felt surrounded by her warmth. She seemed to pour into his mind, liquid fire, filling every empty, dark place with light, laughter and her incredible natural sensuality.

Why is your dragon blue when you burn so hot?

Have you never seen a blue flame? Tatijana asked. *When I was a little girl I would see the flames dancing blue in Xavier's secret caverns. I could never touch or feel them because they were always far away and I was often encased in ice, but they looked so beautiful.*

Which was why she had been so intrigued with flames earlier in the tavern.

The blue dragon looked at Zev with worried eyes. She projected her voice through the great beast. "If you will allow me, Zev, I can float you up to my back. It will be easier on both of us."

"Thank you, of course I don't mind if it's easier for you. You're already doing me a huge favor." He looked up that long wing. The climb would be quite difficult with his wounds.

He was weak from loss of blood. *I gave him blood, but was careful it wasn't so much that he would know. He was in and out of consciousness for a few minutes until I got enough blood in him.*

I could kiss you for making it easy on his pride, Fen told her.

There are much better reasons for kissing, Fenris Dalka. Perhaps you might consider one or two in my absence.

Tatijana floated Zev up to her back and waited until he was seated comfortably.

And wolf man . . .

Her voice had turned dark. Sensual. The blue dragon turned that wedge-shaped head, lowered her neck until her multifaceted emerald eyes were on the same level as his. His breath felt trapped in his lungs. His heart stuttered. Every muscle in his body tensed.

You haven't seen just how hot I can burn yet.

Fen nearly choked. He watched the dragon maneuver its long body through the trees until the mist swallowed them up. He let himself sway, one hand on a tree for support, just for a moment until the world stopped spinning. He kept pain at bay, even though that also cost in strength, uncertain whether or not Tatijana would touch his mind.

He still had the dead body to take care of, and he needed to find a warm body to provide enough blood to sustain and heal him. He would provide sustenance for Dimitri. It would take his brother a longer time to heal due to the extent of his injuries.

Fen had always, always stayed as a Lycan, thinking and acting as one, which helped him to keep the darkness at bay until this last century or so when his mixed blood began to add to the pull of darkness. Now he needed to go back to being Carpathian, at least until this night was over. He was going hunting, wounds or no. That was what Carpathian hunters did.

He took to the air, a long trail of mist streaking through the denser fog.

What do you think you're doing? Tatijana's voice was deceptively mild.

He wasn't buying it. *My lady, I have duties to perform this night. As do you. Make certain your prince is aware of what is happening in his homeland.*

Tatijana's amusement burst through him like sparkling fireworks. *Our prince, Fenris. You can change your name to anything you want, your blood may be different, but you were born Carpathian and you will always be Carpathian. You may have left your homeland when another prince was ruler, but you have returned and you owe your allegiance to Mikhail, just as we all do.*

She had a point. He had been alone so long he had forgotten there was an entire society attempting to rebuild itself. He had long ago resigned himself to being completely on his own. He'd never even heard of Mikhail or his second-in-command, Gregori, until Dimitri had filled him in on the news of the past few centuries there in the Carpathian Mountains.

It is so, my lady.

Wait for me. I'll only be a few more minutes.

She was tenacious—and worried about him. While it warmed his heart and made him feel alive and exhilarated, it was also a very bad combination.

Tatijana, what I do is dangerous. I can't do this and worry that you will be harmed.

Again she surprised him. There was no petulant woman, upset with him for brushing her aside when she'd aided him in battle and was still aiding him. She stroked a gentle caress through his mind. *You do not know your lifemate. I absorb everyone's knowledge when I come into contact with them. Enemy and friend. It is a habit I acquired from my childhood when I had no other life than an intellectual one.*

I hunt rogue and the Sange rau *this night. Bardolf will not expect it and he will be weak, trying to repair himself.*

And that is why your lifemate will be an asset to you on the hunt, she replied complacently. *I am Dragonseeker. No vampire could hide from me, which essentially, that's what he is. He can sink into the wolf and I would still know he was there. I made a mistake tonight. I felt his presence and dove to protect you. I would have flamed him but you were too close. You were his target, Fen.*

He had heard, down through the long centuries, that Dragonseekers could ferret out vampires when no others could. They were the only lineage in the history of the Carpathian people who had never had a single family member turn. Tatijana was Dragonseeker. More, she had been honed in the fires of hell, more precisely, in the glacier ice of the mage world. He couldn't discount what she said.

Fen had come across the rogue pack's trail of destruction and he'd begun to suspect that a monster, the combination of wolf and vampire, traveled with them or at least near them, but he hadn't known until Bardolf had come to kill him. If Tatijana said she had known immediately Bardolf was vampire and not werewolf, he believed her. It was difficult to tell an untruth to one's lifemate when you often shared the same mind.

Her laughter was soft and warm. *So now you are thinking I just may come in handy on this hunt of yours after all, aren't you?*

The difficulty as he saw it, would be letting her go. She was already deeply entrenched in his mind. He had been so alone for so long in a shadow world of violence and darkness, and with just one evening in her company she had brought laughter, emotion and companionship into his life. He hadn't even realized he'd missed such things. He could barely remember having them. He was under a death sentence and it was only a matter of time—this century or the next—but it would happen. He would be hunted down and killed.

He couldn't give Tatijana the most basic thing between lifemates—the blood of life. His blood was no longer pure Carpathian. He would never have given Dimitri his blood had there been an alternative, and in any case, Dimitri and he had shared so much blood over the centuries his brother was already well on his way to becoming a mixed blood.

That is not your choice, Fen, Tatijana reminded. *I am no young child as Dimitri's lifemate is. I am centuries old and no one will ever make my decisions for me again. If my choice is you, then I will share all things a lifemate does, including exchanging blood. I am a woman. A warrior in my own right. I am an asset to you on the hunt and I refuse to be relegated to the role of a child with you making decisions for me.*

There was no defiance, only implacability. Tatijana was not a woman to be pushed around and he found he admired her all the more for that. She was a fitting partner for him, which made it all the more difficult to protect her from his life—and herself.

She gave an inelegant snort of pure disdain. *If I choose to be claimed by you, then I will share your blood with open eyes. This is not your decision alone, Fen. It is a mutual decision. My lifemate is my partner, not my keeper.*

Again there was truth in what she said. He was both Carpathian and Lycan. If he claimed her and shared his life with her, there could be no half measures. *I understand, Tatijana,* he replied. What else could he say when she had a point he couldn't refute.

She was his miracle and he wanted to wrap her up in a safety net and always make certain she was protected.

Have you considered that I might think you're a miracle? That I want to make certain that you're safe at all times? Why should that be only your prerogative?

Below him was the body of the man who had been killed by the rogue werewolves. His body was torn almost beyond recognition. If it was found in its present state, all real wolves in the vicinity would be threatened. There would be an outcry for justice and hunters would be overrunning the forest and mountains to wipe out the dangerous packs. In the meantime, the rogue werewolves would move on to new territories or begin killing the villagers.

They don't know they are in Carpathian territory, do they?

I doubt it. Not even Bardolf would know. If he's the one who stirred the pack in this direction, he certainly didn't. He was Lycan, not Carpathian, and he would have no knowledge of this culture or the fact that the prince is in residence here.

Fen dropped down to the forest floor. The body was exactly where he and Tatijana had stumbled across it earlier, but something about it caught his attention. He circled warily. He needed to conserve his strength in the event he managed to track Bardolf to his lair. Even in his present condition, the vampire would be lethal. After meeting Fen, recognizing what Fen was, Bardolf would move on as soon as he could. Now would be the optimum time to destroy him.

What is it?

That tinge of worry in her voice warmed him, showing him more than ever that he was no longer alone. She might not want to be claimed, but she was his.

Concentrate on what you're doing or you're going to get yourself killed, wolf man. *We'll never find out about this lifemate business if you keep trying to play the hero.*

Trying? He gave her a male smirk. The branches above his head tapped together in the wind. There was no wind. The air had gone still, yet that tapping persisted—a consistent, steady, very rhythmic beat. *I was the hero tonight, my lady. You clearly weren't paying attention, which makes it necessary to repeat myself.* He let her hear the clacking of the branches.

I see. You think it necessary to impress me. She listened to the rhythm. *That sound is one Xavier used to ensnare his victims. It's hypnotic on a subtle level. Whoever is using it was once trained by the mages. It is not natural.*

What is going on here? A rogue pack has entered Carpathian territory with Bardolf, a wolf/vampire combination. And now another enemy? This makes no sense.

Perhaps it does, Fen, Tatijana mused. *The prince's lifemate, Raven, has a son. His daughter, Savannah, has twin girls. She is lifemated to the prince's second-in-command. These children will grow into great power. Would it be so farfetched to think that enemies of the Carpathian people would be drawn here?*

Fen circled the torn body. The werewolves had nearly pulled the man apart in their initial attack. Rogue packs enjoyed torturing and killing their victims and often fed on them even while their victims were still alive. The elite hunters, much like Carpathian hunters, had no choice but to destroy them. This body had been left as bait. It wasn't an unusual tactic. Humans, as a rule, went looking for their lost loved ones.

Fen made it a point not to look above him at the clacking branches. An attack could come from any direction. Was it possible Bardolf had lesser vampires under his control? That had become more and more of a popular thing for master vampires to do. They took newly turned vampires and used them as pawns, sometimes building a formidable army.

I saw no evidence of vampires massing here, Fen told Tatijana, *but get word to the prince this night that there might be a problem.*

Tatijana sighed. *If I let the prince know what is happening, instead of waiting for them to find out, they'll know I've been out on my own.* There was regret in her voice. *The tapping is growing faster. You'll have to be careful, Fen, and block the sound. As the rhythm changes, the hypnotic affects really take hold.*

I don't feel it all. He was more than Carpathian and more than Lycan.

Things that worked against other species didn't work on him—which was why the Lycans had outlawed his kind.

Please be careful. Don't get all cocky. I'm on my way.

He read the growing anxiety in her voice. She had more experience with mage traps than he did and she clearly was worried.

5

Tatijana approached the house built into the side of the mountain cautiously. She was under surveillance. She could feel eyes on her, and when she scanned, allowing her senses to flair out, she knew she wasn't alone outside the home of the prince. She had no idea of protocol and how one approached him, or even if he was accessible. She'd met him briefly, but both she and Branislava had been so weak and injured they barely knew what was happening to them.

She stopped a few hundred meters before she reached the large verandah. She had plenty of room to defend herself if need be. Spreading her arms out away from her body to show she had come in peace, she waited while Mikhail Dubrinsky's second-in-command, and protector, looked her over.

"Tatijana of the Dragonseeker clan," Gregori Daratrazanoff strode out of what appeared to be thin air. He looked impressive with his wide shoulders and glittering silver eyes. "To what do we owe this honor? We had no idea you had risen."

There was no censure in his tone, but she knew he wasn't pleased she was unescorted. He was a great believer in their women being protected at all times. She'd gleaned that much about him before she'd gone to ground to heal. He was an excellent man to protect the prince, but he was not her keeper.

"I've stumbled across something I think is important for you to know, if you don't already. I actually hoped to see you rather than disturbing the prince, so I'm grateful you were close. There is a rogue pack of werewolves hunting in this area and they answer to an alpha by the name of Bardolf. He is a mixture of both wolf and vampire blood and very difficult to kill, Lycans refer to such a mix as the *Sange rau*."

"*Bad blood*," Gregori translated.

Tatijana nodded. She was aware of time passing. Fen was on his own and wounded. She didn't like leaving him so long. "Not only does his heart have to be removed from his body, but the silver stake must be inserted completely through the heart and then both body and heart burned. He can regenerate very quickly. It's possible, but I don't know, that he's traveling with lesser vampires as well as the rogue pack."

She turned to go, but then turned back. "An elite Lycan hunter by the name of Zev is staying at the inn. He fought them this night and was badly injured. I did my best to see to his wounds. I was forced to give him blood, although I didn't allow him to know. MaryAnn and Manolito De La Cruz could be in danger."

She hesitated. She had no idea what the Carpathians thought of mixing the blood of a Lycan and Carpathian. For all she knew they could consider it just as taboo as the Lycans. She had been told by Lara, her niece-kin, during one of the times Lara had given her blood while she was still healing, but that didn't mean it was common knowledge that MaryAnn and Manolito were both Lycan and Carpathian.

"Why would they be in danger?" Gregori prompted.

She shrugged. "I only know that they are. I trust that you will warn them." Tatijana turned around and began to walk away, holding her breath, afraid he would stop her. She nearly ran into him, trying to listen for him behind her. She had to stop abruptly, almost bouncing off his chest. He had moved unbelievably fast—and silently—and had blocked her way.

"Where did you get this information?" His voice remained pleasant, matter-of-fact even, but she could tell he was used to intimidating those he questioned and that he expected an answer. Those piercing, intelligent eyes moved over her, dwelling on the streaks of blood she'd forgotten to clean when she was so busy trying to heal both Zev and Fen.

"I ran across the pack. They killed a man who had been drinking earlier in a tavern I'd visited. We found his body in the forest as I was returning."

He didn't take his eyes from her face. "As you can see, we have heightened security around the prince, but it was more that I had a feeling and the fact that Raven and Mikhail's son has survived his first two years than any real knowledge of a threat to the prince and his family. Lycans are extremely difficult to sense."

"These are *not* Lycan," Tatijana reiterated. "They're considered a rogue pack, and the Lycan elite hunters have been called in to exterminate them. It would be a grave error to mistake the two."

His eyebrow shot up. "I suppose it would. Who is 'we'? Who was with you when you ran across this dead body?"

"That's not relevant." Because she was uncertain of how Carpathians reacted to the mixed blood between Lycans and Carpathians she had to protect Fen at all costs. She didn't want to make an enemy of Gregori, but Fen was her lifemate. "I told you what I know because I felt as the protector of the prince you should be aware of the rogue werewolf pack. I'm still very uncomfortable in the presence of others. I need to leave."

That much was true. She feared he would attempt to detain her, and she knew she would fight. The fight-or-flight syndrome was engrained in her. She couldn't be held prisoner ever again. Her decisions, right or wrong, had to be her own. Gregori, with his impressive set of shoulders, implacable expression and glittering silver eyes was standing in her way and showed no indication that he would move.

"You are a Carpathian woman, Tatijana." Gregori's voice turned gentle. "Why would you think I would harm you in any way? I am sworn to protect you. There is no need to fear me."

"I fear myself and my reactions to situations," she replied honestly. "I must feel free. I do not want, nor can I have, guardians who watch my every move. I'm sorry if I appear to be difficult, but I have to be in charge of my own life."

"Yet you ran into a rogue pack." He indicated her lacerations. "You were in a battle, and you could have been killed. Our women are cherished. We protect them out of both love and respect. Along with our children, they are our greatest treasure."

She could hear the sincerity in his voice. She took a step back and attempted to still her wild heartbeat. Perhaps he wasn't threatening her. She had given him disturbing news and she had been in a battle. She wasn't used to anyone but Branislava caring about her well-being.

"I wander on my own in order to learn the things I need, and sometimes I stumble across things I shouldn't. I'll be more careful." She tried to placate him, if only just a little.

"Tatijana, do you really think I should let you go, bleeding from a battle, without escorting you back to your resting place and healing you properly?"

"It is my choice. My wish. You would have the freedom to go your own way. Why shouldn't I?"

A strange urgency was beginning to take hold of her. Fen was alone and wounded. Not only was the rogue pack after him but the wolf/vampire called the *Sange rau* had joined the hunt. She had been gone far too long.

Gregori inclined his head. She didn't like the way his eyes never left her face. He saw far too much.

"You have a point. But you are one of our greatest treasures, Tatijana. I would be remiss in not aiding you. Allow me to heal you."

No way could she let him touch her. He was too powerful. He might be able to get inside her mind and discover Fen. She didn't wait for him to make a move and she was through arguing. She was Dragonseeker. She knew every mage spell ever conceived. She dissolved and streaked up toward the clouds, deliberately leaving behind a nearly translucent trail of vapor. The moment she'd laid that false track, she called on the elements to aid her.

That faint, barely there stream moved away from the prince's home, its trajectory heading up the mountain into deeper forest. She doubled back, leaving no trace, not even the smallest molecule that would allow a hunter such as Gregori to pursue her. For a moment she had considered asking for his aid, just in case, but not knowing how Carpathians viewed mixed blood, she wasn't going to risk Fen any further.

She might have just come out of the ice caves, but over the centuries, more than one Carpathian hunter had been taken by Xavier and tortured before he was put to death. The male Carpathians especially found it distressing to see the twin females encased in their ice prison. The hunters had willingly shared their experience and knowledge with both women in the hopes that eventually they could use the information to escape.

She left no trace of herself behind. No scent. Nothing at all Gregori could track. More, she knew he wouldn't leave the prince for long, not with the news she'd brought. Lycans were elusive. They could be standing next to you and you would never know. The thought of a rogue pack so close to the prince and his son had to be disconcerting.

Tatijana made her way in the opposite direction of her false trail, going into deep forest, winding through the trees, staying low, close to the ground so she could see any evidence of the rogue pack passing. Wolves were very good at moving through an area and leaving few telltale signs, but twice she saw droplets of blood and twisted grass. The pack had passed through quickly, moving away from where the battle had taken place.

Still, something seemed off to her. It seemed more a discordant note, something unnamed, unseen, that jangled her nerves and set off warning bells.

Fen? Are you safe? I'm very close to you but something's not right.

Tatijana, this place is not for you. Let me spring this trap before you join me. If I get into trouble, you will be close to give me aid.

If she was in any form with teeth, she would have ground them in sheer frustration. She didn't know much about men and even less about lifemates, but why would he think she would worry less about him than he did about her? The pull between them was very strong, and the more time she spent in his mind, the more she came to know his honor and integrity. She found it impossible to just leave him to fight the battle alone.

She stayed quiet, not wanting to distract him as she moved through the trees with much more care. Fen bent over the dead body, removing evidence of the wolf pack's attack. It was important that locals thought he died accidentally and that none of the wildlife was responsible. He appeared to be wholly absorbed in his work.

The clacking of the branches was constant, the sound working its way through every living creature for miles. She braced herself when she heard it. She wasn't in a physical form, but still, the rhythm preyed on her nerves, threatening to consume her. She found it difficult to think straight. Her mind felt fuzzy and thick. She'd seen the trick work on countless victims in Xavier's cave of horrors.

She reached out to Fen's mind, terrified for him. His mind was calm.

Clear. He was very aware of his surroundings and every tiny detail. The hypnotic effects didn't work on his brain pattern. There was something about the mixture of Carpathian and Lycan that repelled the notes, bouncing it back away from him.

Stay in my mind, Fen warned softly, brushing against her brain with a gentle touch. *You'll be safe with me.*

Xavier had mutated species on purpose, but his results had always been grotesque and frightening—beings that ate human flesh or were mindless, violent puppets. He had never considered what it would be to cross Lycan with Carpathian.

She allowed herself to sink into Fen's mind, surprised that he had invited her so deep into his memories. She was still protecting herself, holding most of her past away from him, yet he was completely open to her, hiding nothing from her. She felt warm and protected, not at all like she thought she'd feel—claustrophobic—a prisoner even.

She heard the soft whisper of a footfall because he heard it. His hearing was far more acute than she'd realized. A soft murmur accompanied the clacking branches. Her heart jumped, began to thud wildly.

That's a holding spell. If he completes it, you will not be able to move. He'll control your every movement.

The spell is tied to the rhythm, my lady, Fen reminded gently. *I do not feel the effects of either. I want to see who or what is driving these attacks.*

This is mage. I recognize the work of one of Xavier's favorite protégés. He was much younger than Xavier, but a true psychopath. Xavier was very proud of him and his sadistic nature. His name is Drummel. He is evil and very, very dangerous.

Can you counter his spells without revealing yourself?

Tatijana took a deep breath, allowing Fen to wrap her in his confidence. His calm was amazing to her. He had to have nerves of steel. He didn't turn around to face the threat, or indicate in any way that he knew he was being stalked. His hands were as gentle and reverent on the dead man as always. No trembling. Nothing at all to give away that he was well aware of the danger coming up behind him.

The chanting increased, more rhythmic than ever, matching the increasing beating of the branches together. One step. Two. A slight rustle and then there was only the sound of the hypnotic notes. Tatijana tried to stop up her ears and settle deeper into the safety of Fen's mind.

Fen exploded into action, whirling around, still in a crouch, going in low, using his Lycan form, half man, half wolf, enormously strong. He knocked Drummel onto his back and was on him in an instant. Tatijana would never have believed anything could move as fast as Fen had. He struck so hard he knocked the wind from Drummel's lungs, leaving him gasping for air.

Fen wrapped his hand around his assailant's throat, cutting off his air supply. With his lungs already burning, Drummel's eyes bulged out of his head. He drew back his lips in a gasping snarl. His teeth were stained brown and pointed.

Fen shook him, never lessening his grip. "I see you, Bardolf," he hissed. "You knew your possession had no chance of capturing me with his holding spell. Why sacrifice a pawn of value?"

He's shadowed. How would Bardolf know how to split himself and implant a shadow in another? Tatijana asked. *Very few mages can do this. It's extremely difficult and very frightening. Shadows are lethal, Fen, and they can enter anyone close to them. Be careful.*

Fen didn't need to be told Drummel was shadowed. He could see Bardolf staring back at him through the eyes of the man's body he'd commandeered. He had found a way to possess a mage as skilled and as powerful as Drummel. What did that say about Bardolf?

Drummel's mouth moved several times, his lips struggling to form words. "I will take my pack and move on, Fenris Dalka."

There was power in speaking another's name. Every instinct Fen had immediately put him on guard. He stretched his senses, scanning the area around him. It was nearly impossible to detect Lycans when they wanted to remain hidden. Werewolves had a more difficult time as they couldn't contain their energy and their eagerness for the kill, but they were still adept at hiding from the average hunter.

Be on the alert, Tatijana. There is more going on here than meets the eye.

"Why do you say this to me, Bardolf? Why not just take your pack and go?" Fen demanded.

"I want your word you will no longer hunt us." Drool and spittle ran in long strings from Drummel's mouth to his chin

That made no sense. Fen was a hunter. A Carpathian. Bardolf had recognized that he was both Lycan and Carpathian, which meant he had to know Fen was Carpathian first, an ancient hunter of the vampire. It was his duty, a matter of honor to hunt the undead. Bardolf was definitely the undead. He might have werewolf mixed in, but he was vampire and had to be destroyed.

"It is my sworn duty to my people to bring justice to those who have given up their souls for the rush of adrenaline they get for the kill." Fen's hold on Drummel's throat was relentless. He wasn't about to allow Bardolf's shadow to escape and try to slip inside him. "I think you already know that."

I will watch for the shadow. If he tries to enter you, I can repel him, Tatijana assured. *I didn't spend centuries in Xavier's lair without learning every spell he ever made. Bardolf had to learn from Drummel. Yes, he was very good, but I am better.*

There was no bragging in her tone. Tatijana was afraid of what was happening. She knew just how dangerous the mage was and now doubly so with Bardolf's shadow in him. She had confidence in herself, but she didn't want Fen to be overly confident.

Have no worries, my lady, he assured. *What he is saying to me is pure drivel. He knows I will hunt them. I am well aware this is a stalling tactic.*

He inhaled, using Lycan-heightened senses, the acute hearing and smell, but he didn't take his eyes from Drummel.

"I offer you a deal."

"Justice does not make deals, Bardolf. I am the one appointed to bring that justice to you."

Drummel spit and snarled, the red eyes spinning wildly with hatred and malice before Bardolf made a tremendous effort to recover. Just that alone put Fen further on edge. Vampires were not known for their control. Why would Bardolf make such an effort?

Fen, I am telling you, if Bardolf was Lycan before he became vampire, he could not possibly have placed a shadow of himself inside of a mage of Drummel's importance. An ancient Carpathian might know. Even a vampire might have run across

a mage willing to trade his soul for immortality, but how would a Lycan even know about such things? Tatijana asked.

If Tatijana was right, and she was the daughter of the most powerful mage in history, then Bardolf couldn't have placed his shadow in Drummel. Fen didn't wait to find out what Bardolf had to say next. There was no reasoning with madmen, and he saw no reason to wait for the attack he knew was coming any moment. He struck hard and fast, breaking Drummel's neck.

The mage's eyes opened wide, Bardolf staring in shock and horror. The body seized, convulsed. Poisonous sweat burst from his pores, out his eyelids and mouth.

Look out. Get back, Tatijana warned. She withdrew from her refuge, streaking to the battlefield to aid him. *The sliver of Bardolf will seek another host.*

Fen spun around, more worried about what he couldn't see or hear than that small piece of Bardolf. *Keep it off me,* he commanded, certain of her now, knowing she would guard his back. *And stay hidden. Do not reveal yourself no matter what happens,* he added, cautioning her. They were not alone and he knew it.

The dead body jerked. Coughed. Fen didn't spare it a glance. That was Tatijana's territory and he could already hear her murmuring an ancient spell directed at the sliver of a shadow, so small but deadly. His was to find the unseen threat. He moved away from the dead body where Bardolf's shadow sought a new host.

On the ground, small insects swarmed over rotting vegetation and Fen leapt into the air, just as creatures in the form of half man, half wolf, poured out of the trees in all directions. Directly beneath where he'd been standing, the ground erupted into a dark geyser of contaminated soil, spraying high, and with it, another large figure burst into the air after Fen, his long wolflike arms extended, claws tipped with glistening poison.

Fen reversed direction, hurtling toward the newcomer with blurring speed, slamming into him with such force they both tumbled back toward the ground. In his fist, he had a silver stake. This was the vampire/wolf Bardolf had tangled with and supposedly killed. Bardolf had exchanged life for servitude under a master killer.

Fen plunged the silver stake through the chest wall, deep into the heart of the vampire. He barely recognized him, a Carpathian male only a few years younger than him, one he'd played with as a boy. Abel, his parents called him. He'd been a boy with a sunny personality. Always smiling. Fen would never have thought Abel would choose to become vampire. He actually felt a pang of sorrow when he drove that silver stake into his chest and twisted the spiral in deeper.

Black blood poured over his fist, wrist and arm, burning like acid down to his bone. Abel's eyes widened, but he didn't pull away as expected. He was not only vampire, he was also werewolf. The long snout rushed at Fen, the razor-sharp teeth sinking into his neck and shoulder, slicing down to the bone as Abel ripped chunks of flesh away. Blood streamed down Fen's body, and the vampire lapped at the ancient treat, gulping to get as much as possible.

Fen shoved him away as they both hit the ground hard. The scent of his rich, Carpathian blood set up a frenzied mass hysteria. The werewolves howled and rushed at him. Fen dissolved as they all leapt on him. As he streaked away, one arm emerged, fist holding a silver stake, which he plunged into the nearest werewolf's heart. He moved quickly to get out of that crush of werewolves, a trail of ruby red blood giving his path away.

He pushed the pain to another dimension as he worked furiously to stop the blood flow. Tatijana was immediately beside him, a mere translucent image. Her hands became flesh and moved over his open lacerations. The sound of her soft healing chant filled his mind. For a moment the ice cold of his injuries burned hot. She'd stopped the blood by cauterizing the area.

You cannot be here. It's too dangerous. If he spots you, he'll go after you in order to get to me.

I can scatter the werewolves, and hunt them from the sky.

There was no time to argue with her. *Watch for tricks and stay high. Lycans can leap enormous distances.*

The tree limbs shook. Trunks split with a terrible boom, a heralding of great danger. Tatijana streaked for the sky, shifting into her blue dragon, answering the echoing blast with a roaring challenge of her own.

Abel followed the trail of red blood, and was on Fen just as Tatijana took to the air. The undead leapt after her, but Fen blocked his path with his body, so that the vampire slammed into him and they both landed on their feet in the middle of the werewolf pack.

"Take him, my hungry wolves," Abel commanded, his voice filled with compulsion. "Do not let him escape. He is my gift to you with his hot, rich blood, fresh and flowing in his veins."

Howling, the wolves surrounded Fen. He moved in a circle, keeping his gaze on the *Sange rau*, but his senses waiting for the attack from the werewolves. The rumbling growls grew louder, indicating the pack was working itself up to attack mode. Abel smirked, his black-stained, serrated teeth were stuck deep into his receding gums as he pulled the silver stake from his heart and tossed it to the ground at Fen's feet.

"I have come to join this party," a voice announced.

A Carpathian hunter strode out of the trees into the midst of the frenzied werewolves, drawing them away from Fen. Silver eyes slashed as he moved fast through their ranks, breaking necks and backs and then tossing the bodies aside.

I'm sorry. That's Gregori Daratrazanoff, second to the prince and prime protector of the Carpathian people. He must have followed me here. I can't flame the werewolves from the sky without burning Gregori alive.

As fast as Gregori was, the werewolves were faster, seeking new blood, hot and alive. They swarmed him, sheer numbers taking him down until he was buried beneath the frenzied bodies.

Cursing under his breath, Fen had no choice but to share his knowledge of all things rogue and the vampire/wolf combination with the hunter through the common Carpathian telepathic link. He knew he was putting himself at risk—the Carpathian could glean a tremendous amount of information about him as well in seconds. He had used the common pathway so rarely, he couldn't be certain he had conveyed the speed and strength of the rogues, or the immense power of the *Sange rau*. As he passed on the information, Fen leapt into the fray, hurtling bodies off the prince's guardian.

As Gregori struggled to stand, Abel struck hard and fast, rushing Fen, hitting him from behind and knocking him off his feet. Fen called on his Lycan blood, twisting in midair as he went down, shifting with lightning speed so that it was Lycan claws grasping Abel's neck and yanking him down with him. His claws dug deep into the vampire's neck, anchoring himself, his own muzzle growing to accommodate the expanse of teeth.

They rolled on the ground, Fen taking them away from the writhing mass of werewolves, his teeth tearing at Abel's throat.

Gregori, get out of there! he warned as he tore into the *Sange rau* with the strong bite of the Lycan. Black blood poured over him, his muzzle, and down his neck and chest, burning like acid. The scent of burnt flesh permeated the air.

Abel screamed in horror and fear as Fen relentlessly held him, uncaring that the undead ripped at his flesh and tore at his chest to get to his heart. He had to hold out until the undead became so terrified that he called to his pack. It was the only way to save Gregori from the vicious, voracious pack.

Fen drove one fist deep into Abel's chest, claws searching for the withered, blackened heart, even as he continued to bite chunks of rotted flesh from the vampire/wolf.

"Kill this one. Leave the other. All of you, kill this one," Abel screamed.

His voice was high-pitched and hurt the sensitive ears of the werewolves. They set up a terrible din, howling and screaming, as they reluctantly obeyed their leader. Out of the corner of his eye, Fen could see Gregori on the ground, still fighting off a particularly large werewolf who didn't want to give up the rich blood of the Carpathian.

Above him, the blue dragon soared across the sky, circling around above the canopy to suddenly drop down with a steady stream of fire that engulfed several of the werewolves. She took great care to stay clear of Gregori. The tall werewolf ripping and tearing at him leapt without warning, without so much as turning his head, claws catching the underside of the blue dragon's belly where he hung by his curved long nails alone.

The blue dragon retaliated with a curling of her long, spiked tail. It swept beneath her to hit the werewolf with a tremendous slap, the spikes driving in deep even as her great wings drove hard to lift her high above the canopy. The force of the blow knocked the rogue's claws loose. For a moment he teetered, desperately raking at her belly for a better grip. The tail slapped him a second time, and with a sharp cry, he fell back to earth.

Blood dripped steadily from the wounded dragon, but she dove after the werewolf as he hurtled toward the ground, righting himself in order to better land on his feet. The werewolf looked up just as the wedge-shaped head shot toward him, bellowing fire as she trumpeted her pain and rage. Flames engulfed the wolf as he fell to the ground, landing hard. He leapt to his feet, legs clearly broken, but still, he ran screaming through the remaining pack, fanning the fire as he did so that the orange-red flames roared and grew larger.

The moment the werewolf had leapt to claw at the blue dragon, Gregori staggered to his feet, bleeding in dozens of places. He thrust his hand toward the rest of the rogue pack, setting a barrier between Fen and the werewolves, preventing them from rushing the hunter as he fought the powerful vampire/wolf cross. Some of the rogues turned back toward Gregori while others tore at the shield in an effort to go to the aid of their master.

The dead body of the drunken human jerked and moved, inching across the ground toward Gregori, the shadowy sliver of Bardolf working to find a live host to help his master.

Behind you! Tatijana warned.

The blue dragon circled back, large globs of blood falling from the sky as she banked and came in low. Gregori swung his head around, seeing the abomination of dead flesh digging fingernails into the earth to pull the body toward him.

I'll burn it, but you have to get out of there, Tatijana warned.

Gregori made a valiant effort to get out of the line of fire, stumbling toward the pack trying to tear down the barrier between them and Fen. Fen and the *Sange rau* rolled across the shivering ground, neither letting go of their hold on the other. As Tatijana made her approach, the ground shifted and rocked, throwing Gregori down.

The earth shuddered, trembled and then beneath the surface, one side drove the other upward. Great cracks appeared. Trees split in half.

From her vantage point in the sky, Tatijana could see the huge zigzagging crack, a great yawning abyss opening and rocketing toward Fen and the vampire/wolf as their fierce battle continued.

Fen! Tatijana screamed his name in her mind, half warning, half sobbing.

She flamed the dead body jerking and clawing its way toward Gregori and continued diving straight down. Tucking her wings and dropping like a stone, she hurtled toward that widening crack just as it engulfed Fen and the *Sange rau*. Gregori leapt after them, just as the werewolves broke through the shield to get to their master. They tumbled into the narrow crack in their rush to get to the rogue leader.

Fen dropped through the crack, shoulders scraping on either side of the walls of dirt, roots and rock. He hung grimly onto Abel, claws digging deeper into the chest, determined to get to the heart even as he tore chunks from the vampire's neck and throat. Neither could dissolve into vapor as their claws prevented the other from getting away.

Tatijana blasted past Gregori, wings still tucked tight against her body, as she dove after Fen. As she approached the two combatants, she stretched her neck as far as it would go, her giant, wedged-shaped head shoving itself up against the side of Abel's head. She let loose a blast of fire, taking great care even as they were tumbling, to make certain she concentrated the exhale of flames only over the vampire's skull.

Fen couldn't help but admire her skill. She was still diving, moving fast, and he felt the blast of heat, but not one hint of flame touched him. Abel screamed, the sound horrible. The smell was worse. The earth began to close below them with ominous groans and creaks. The very planet seemed to shudder.

Let him go, Tatijana ordered. *Right now, you have to let him go or we'll all be killed. All three of us.*

He was so close. His fingers were around that withered heart. He couldn't quite yank it free. *Abel's too powerful to leave alive. I just have to get a better grip . . .*

Tatijana used her triangular head to knock the vampire/wolf out of Fen's hands. Abel dropped away, the wind fanning the flames totally engulfing his head. Tatijana used her long neck to wind around Fen, catching him before he could drop away. He caught the spines and pulled himself around until he could slide onto her back. Her wings braked their fall.

Fen looked up to see Gregori dropping fast, his bloody body ravaged and torn. He held out his hand. *Gregori!*

His hand caught Gregori's wrist, Gregori's fingers wrapped tightly around his. Fen dragged him onto the dragon's back. He heard Gregori grunt in pain, but the hunter gripped him hard as the blue dragon made her valiant effort to outrun the closing of the earth. The walls scraped her wings, tearing chunks of skin from her. She cried out, but she continued the ascent.

Every werewolf she passed, most clinging to the dirt walls of the deep fissure, tried to claw and scrape at her, sometimes driving teeth into her in a desperate attempt to either impede her progress or hitch a ride. They were all trying to climb fast up those dirt walls before the crack closed all the way. Below them, both sides of the abyss accelerated the speed with which they were slamming closed.

Tatijana burst into the air above the gaping hole in the ground and nearly toppled from the sky. She landed awkwardly, her sides heaving just as the two sides of the crevasse jolted together with a terrible grinding sound. The blue dragon staggered forward in an effort to keep her passengers safe, leaving behind a thick trail of blood. She shuddered, stumbled and went down, the wedge-shaped head slamming hard and plowing through the soil as her body continued driving forward.

Tatijana! A woman's cry filled Fen's mind using his lifemate's path to him. Torn. Frightened. Shocked. *Is she dead? I'm coming to her.*

He knew at once that voice was Branislava, Tatijana's sister. *Do not. I can heal her and protect her. Gregori is here as well, but not both of you. Trust me to do this.*

Fen leapt from the dragon's back, landing on his feet, the long distance jolting him hard. He glanced down at his body and was shocked to see the blood and chunks of gaping flesh where Abel had clawed, bit and raked him.

Branislava was in his mind for a moment drawing as much information about him as possible before she abruptly acquiesced. *If you let anything happen to her I will hunt you for all your days until I destroy you.*

I accept that.

He broke the connection between them as he rushed around the dragon's body to the head and caught it in his arms, bringing it up so the huge eyes stared into his.

"Shift, Tatijana. Shift right now. If you never ever obey me again in this lifetime, you do it this once. Shift for me *now*." He poured everything he was into that command. His fear for her. His anger that he had allowed her to get hurt. His growing love. His respect. His need that she stay alive and stay with him.

Gregori jumped from her back, landing heavily, barely managing to stay on his feet. He staggered around the large body of the dragon to the head as well.

The great eyes of the dragon blinked and then closed, but Fen felt her body shudder with the effort to obey. He slipped into her mind. Consciousness was fading fast. *Come to me, sívamet—my love. Give yourself to me. I will hold you safe.*

There was one moment of uncertainty, as if she might not trust him enough to place herself so fully into his hands. He waited for her to make up her mind, although there was no time and his heart pounded so hard in his chest it sounded like thunder to him. She capitulated suddenly and he felt her let go, giving her spirit essence into his care.

Immediately the great blue dragon was gone and Tatijana's body was in his arms. He didn't wait. He tore open his wrist and pressed it to her mouth. He sank to the ground, holding her to him. Gregori went to his knees beside them. He immediately shed his wounded body and became pure light. He entered Tatijana's body and began to work feverishly to stem the flow of blood. He didn't stop, not even when two more hunters dove from the sky to aid them.

Jacques Dubrinsky, brother to the prince, and Falcon Amiras, an ancient hunter, looked around the battlefield. Some werewolves were beginning to stir. Some bodies were already regenerating.

"Tell us what to do to kill them," Jacques said. "Nothing like coming late to the party."

"Silver spikes. Drive them completely through their hearts and then remove the head of the rogue. Burn the bodies with the spikes in them," Fen said.

He was tired. Exhausted. He kept his focus on Tatijana, holding her close while he fed her life-giving blood. He was grateful to Gregori, so torn up, but selflessly healing Tatijana, putting her before his own injuries.

Falcon came to stand beside Fen. "You and Gregori need a little healing of your own," he pointed out, offering his own wrist. "I offer freely," he added in the tradition of the Carpathian people.

Fen hesitated. It had been long since he'd trusted anyone but Dimitri.

"You need it," Falcon told him. "For her. Do you remember me? You were a few years older. You helped to hone my fighting skills."

Fen inclined his head. He had to shift Tatijana in his arms, propping her against his chest while he continued to give her as much blood as he could. It was slow going, as he basically had to swallow for her. He bent his head to Falcon's proffered wrist. The ancient blood hit him with a rush of strength, in spite of his horrendous wounds.

He could feel the difference in Tatijana, the way Gregori meticulously repaired the damage done to her belly and sides. Her arms were torn with bite marks and multiple lacerations. Gregori's body was ravaged and torn as well, but he took his time, ensuring he missed nothing.

The moment he was back in his own body, swaying with weariness, Jacques was there, one arm going around the healer and the other offering him blood. "This looks like one heck of a battle," he said. "In all my years, I've never run into a rogue pack."

Fen politely sealed the small wounds in Falcon's wrist. "This is a big pack. Two vampires/wolves called the *Sange rau* by the Lycans who run with them."

All three Carpathians exchanged long looks and then turned their full attention on Fen. He shifted Tatijana in his arms. "The vampires are crosses, both Lycan and vampire. I knew Bardolf, an alpha Lycan. That was many years ago. A vampire cross had torn through packs, completely destroying entire packs, and I joined the hunt for him. Evidence looked as though Bardolf had killed him. Instead, they must have joined forces. I tracked them here."

"Who is guarding the prince with both of you here?" Gregori demanded of Falcon and Jacques. "He sent you after me, didn't he?"

Fen hid a smile at the sheer frustration in Gregori's voice.

"At least he didn't come himself, this time," Jacques pointed out. "That's a first for him. Must be his son mellowing him out." He grinned down at Gregori. "You're a little worse for wear. I can't let you go home this way. Savannah would have my head. Let me see what I can do to heal you while Falcon works on . . ." Deliberately he waited.

"Fen. Fenris Dalka," Fen stated. He pinned Falcon with a steely gaze.

"It's imperative I remain Lycan to those in this area. The elite hunters are on their way. A man by the name of Zev is staying at the inn. He's the scout sent out ahead of the hunters. To do that, he has to be the elite of the elite. Believe me, I saw him in action, and he's even better than I could describe. They're hunting their own killers just as we hunt ours."

"Why would you want them to think you're Lycan rather than Carpathian?" Gregori asked. He ignored the fact that Jacques hadn't waited to get his permission to heal his wounds.

Fen shrugged. "Lycans do not tolerate a mix between Lycan and Carpathian. They believe once they turn vampire, they are far too destructive and too difficult to kill. I have no idea how Carpathians weigh in on the issue."

Gregori frowned at him. "I have never really seen or heard of a Lycan/Carpathian cross until MaryAnn and Manolito De La Cruz sent us word that she was Lycan and their blood mixed rather than one taking over the other. Is there some reason why we should have a problem with a Lycan/Carpathian cross? We've always been friends with the Lycan and vice versa. Carpathians and vampires are not the same, they know that."

"Master vampires are extraordinarily difficult to kill," Fen said. Already the influx of Falcon's blood and the healing the Carpathian had done had given him more strength, but he was utterly exhausted. He needed to go to ground. And he needed to get Tatijana to ground. "A vampire/wolf cross is a hundred times that difficult. The destruction and damage, the savagery of their kills is also a hundred times more. They are rare to come across, so few hunters know how to kill them."

"But you do," Gregori stated.

Fen sighed. "Knowing isn't always enough, as you well know, hunter."

"Gregori," Jacques interrupted gently. "All three of you need to go to ground. Perhaps this discussion would better take place in my brother's home at a later time."

Gregori nodded his head. "Forgive me, Fenris, you do need to take Tatijana, who is clearly your lifemate, and go to ground."

"I thank you for coming to our aid. I didn't know about Abel at the time I tracked them here. And I only suspected Bardolf's involvement with the rogue pack when I crossed their path and began tracking them. Also"—he frowned—"the pack is much larger than we first thought."

Gregori stood up slowly, his body still reluctant to work properly after the terrible savagery of the rogue pack attack. "Please come to Mikhail's home on your first rising to give us more information. We'd be grateful."

Fen sighed. By rights, if he met the prince, he should swear fidelity, but he had to think like a Lycan. Be a Lycan. And the cycle of the full moon was starting. If he crossed paths with Zev, or his elite hunters, they would kill him and ask questions later. Life had gotten far more complicated.

The Carpathians were silent, waiting his decision. In the end, he simply nodded and took to the air, Tatijana in his arms. He made certain no one was following him before he circled around to the spot where he'd left his brother. He opened the earth above Dimitri—better to guard him—and settled in with Tatijana. Above him the soil poured in, covering them both. Leaves and debris swirled above their resting place and fell softly, naturally, covering the area as if it had never been disturbed.

6

F en woke three risings beneath the earth, still sore, feeling bruised and battered, but he left Tatijana and Dimitri to find sustenance for them. He'd reassured Branislava each rising that Tatijana was mending well and would come to her as soon as she was properly healed.

He was well aware on his third night that he was now in the most perilous time where any Lycan would know immediately he wasn't wholly one of them. He took care to conceal himself. As a rule, during this time, he stayed in the ground, avoiding any possible confrontation, but he didn't have that luxury—and he knew the elite team would have joined Zev by this time.

He was a little surprised that, although it had been centuries for him, the Carpathian Mountains still felt like a home to him. He had traveled throughout the world, rather than remaining in one place, so he'd never truly found another environment to call home. The soil was extraordinary, and he'd forgotten what that mineral rich loam could feel like. Still . . .

He was worried about Dimitri. Dimitri's belly wasn't healing as well as he would have liked. He concealed himself in the fog, moving through the forest until he came upon the outskirts where a small farm had been carved out of the marsh. The farm backed up to a swampy area, but was neat and tidy. Stacks of hay were piled in the field farthest from the water. Horses tossed heads nervously and stomped hooves as he passed, the Lycan scent spooking them.

The farmer came out of his house, glancing toward the corral where the horses began to half rear and gallop around as if that would save them from a pack of wolves. The man disappeared back into his house and reemerged with a shotgun, looking over toward the nervous horses. Fen stayed in the mist as it circled through the field, swirling around the haystacks so they appeared as disembodied towers in the clouds.

The farmer stepped off the porch and again cautiously looked around. The horses trumpeted their distress over and over. Fen moved slower, allowing the wind to carry him above the corral. There was no way the horses would be in such a state over his scent. There was something else there, stalking the animals—or the farmer. There was no wolf pack closing in on the horses, or he would have seen them.

Fen kept his gaze on the farmer even as he moved cautiously in the midst of the dense fog creeping around him. Something moved along the ground. Something dark, twisted and ugly. The thing had crawled out of the swamp and dragged itself over the field, first toward the horses, then, when scenting the farmer, turned toward him.

Fen saw the disgusting creature huddled beside a boulder, positioning itself for the attack as the farmer drew near. Hastily, Fen shifted, to come striding out of the mist straight toward the owner of the farm. "Look out, man, step back," he called, pushing compulsion into his tone.

Startled, the farmer did as Fen commanded. The twisted creature struck at him, fangs hooking his boot. It wiggled and growled, hissing its impatience. That small sliver of a shadow, a part of Bardolf, was still without a host it could influence to do evil. Animals could sustain its life, but certainly could never be used for the purpose Bardolf intended.

"What is it?" the man asked, shaking his boot and trying to knock the animal loose with the shotgun.

"A deadly creature," Fen answered honestly. "A vampire's familiar." He knew most of the folks living around the village were superstitious—they believed in vampires—mostly because they'd had encounters with them even though the rest of the world made fun of them. They knew evil existed and they did their best to guard against it. The farmer made the sign of the cross and slammed his shotgun down on the wriggling creature.

Fen kicked it away from the farmer, produced a silver knife and plunged it into the ghastly creature, a cross between an eel and a snake. The creature screamed and writhed, black blood pouring from it. With it came the elusive shadow—a sliver of Bardolf. The sliver leapt toward the farmer, determined to live, to make its way back to its master.

Fen withdrew the knife from the twisted creature and threw it. The blade sliced cleanly through the shadow, pinning it to the ground. A great eye formed in the middle, staring at them with hatred and malice—a combination of Bardolf and Abel. The eye was evil, vertical rather than horizontal. The silver knife penetrated exactly in the middle of the eye. Black blood burst around the pupil and dripped on the ground, forming a dark pool.

The eye squealed, the pitch rising to a horrendous shriek as it wriggled and fought to become free. Fen swept the farmer behind him protectively, as the two vampires fought with concentrated strength to free the shadow. The eye convulsed, and a puff of black smoke burst the pupil and the light began to slowly fade as the shadow lost its life. With one last fading cry the shadow went limp and completely dark.

The farmer stepped around Fen and spit right in the middle of the pool of black blood before turning to face the hunter. He bowed awkwardly. "Thank you. You saved me. I've never had the honor of meeting one of our guardians." He smiled, his eyes lighting up. "We hear the rumors you know, but we can go lifetimes without ever knowing if they're true or not."

"For your own safety," Fen pointed out. "Stand way back. I have to incinerate this quickly. You don't want infected vampire blood anywhere near your fields."

Fen waited until the farmer moved off to a safe distance and he stared up at the sky, drawing in churning dark clouds. Thunder rolled ominously. Lightning forked, sizzling, spreading out, nearly blinding them with the bright flash of light. He felt the ground charging, the energy flowing through his body. He extended his arm toward the black blood, hideous creature and malevolent eye. Lightning leapt from ground to sky and back again. The stench nearly choked them both. Black tendrils of smoke rose and dissipated in the air, leaving a clean, fresh scent. The creature, eye and pool of blood incinerated as if they never had been.

Fen turned toward the stunned farmer. The man stood there with his mouth slightly open, curved in a half smile, clearly totally shocked and awed. He flashed Fen a quick grin.

"I know I will have to go to my grave with this memory secret, but I thank you for the experience."

Bardolf and Abel had both seen the farmer. They might very well decide to attack and kill him, just to get back at Fen. At the very least, they would send members of the pack to kill his livestock as well as his family. Ordinarily there were few humans left with the knowledge of the Carpathian people, even there in the Carpathian Mountains.

"These vampires are extremely dangerous. They run with a pack of rogue werewolves they control. You and your family will be targeted. Is there a possibility of taking your family to safety and perhaps a neighbor would take your livestock?"

The farmer looked scared, but he shook his head. "I can send my wife and children to her mother's, but I'll have to run the farm myself. If I lose my livestock, or leave, we'll lose everything." He swept his arms out. "This is all we have. A man takes care of his family."

Fen sighed. He could see the farmer's point, but he wouldn't be taking care of his family if they were all dead. "Send them away tonight. Pack light and tell them not to return until you send for them. Forgive me, but in order to safeguard you as much as possible, I will have to take your blood, and give you a very small amount of mine. You will be able to reach me in an emergency. Even if I am too far away, I can send aid to you. The choice is yours."

If the farmer refused, Fen would have to allow him to be on his own. He would have no choice but to remove his memory of Fen's visit, which would make him ten times more vulnerable.

The farmer bowed formally a second time, this time with a deeper bow. "It would be an honor." He paused. "Does it hurt?"

Fen shook his head. "You won't feel anything at all."

The farmer stepped close, shotgun in his hands, exposing his throat. Fen gently removed the shotgun just as a precaution. He slipped into the man's mind. Costin Eliade had grown up on a farm as had his father before him. He was a good man, worked hard, was devoted to his wife and family. He was frightened, but hiding it well, determined to do whatever it took to protect his family and farm.

Fen was both careful and respectful in the taking of the farmer's blood. He took enough to feed and then soothed the man's anxiety, keeping him from being aware as Fen gave him a small amount of his own blood. Any time he reached out to Costin, he would know where the farmer was, what he was thinking or doing. He would know the instant there was betrayal— or trouble. He put a strong barrier in his mind, a warning that if he tried to give up the information about the incident to anyone—including his wife— he would be forever on his own.

Costin's intentions were admirable and he seemed a very honest man. Fen could find no hint of duplicity in his mind whatsoever. He meant to keep the Carpathian's secrets. Fen made certain there was no evidence on the man or his clothes that blood had been taken before stepping away, although one hand remained on the farmer to steady him. Perhaps he'd taken a little more blood than necessary, because he had both Tatijana and Dimitri to provide for.

"Get your family out of here tonight. I'll send aid to watch over your farm, both day and night until we locate and destroy the rogue pack and vampires. The moment that deed is done, I'll let you know," Fen assured the farmer.

The wind came in from the north, blowing with it a heavy fog. Gregori strode out of the dense mist, his shoulders wide, his silver eyes blazing. His sharp glance went from the farmer to the blackened ground and then to Fen. He raised a single eyebrow.

Fen managed to stop his grin just before it emerged. Of course Gregori would be suspicious of him. He was a stranger and with him had come two *Sange rau* and a rogue werewolf pack. Gregori didn't want those enemies anywhere near the prince. No matter how severe his wounds, he wouldn't trust his prince's safety to anyone else.

Clearly Gregori was already scanning the farmer's mind. He found the data needed and how Fen had destroyed the sliver of evil Bardolf and Abel had used to gain information. It was far easier and much more polite to pull the information from the farmer's mind. He wasn't questioning Fen or demanding why he would break a very hard rule, leaving memories of the Carpathian people in Costin Eliade.

He held out his hand to the farmer. "I'm Gregori. I understand you may need a little help protecting your farm."

Costin nodded. "Very much so. They sent a familiar, and he killed it." He gestured toward Fen.

"You'll need protection during the day as well," Fen said. "Rogue packs can be out in the sun. They'll usually come at you at dusk or dawn, but in this case, the alpha will send them in during the part of the day our people are unable to protect you."

"We've got a few people who can aid you," Gregori assured.

They can never, under any circumstances, be here if the Sange rau *show up. The combination of vampire and wolf is powerful beyond belief, and killing them is extremely hard.* Fen sent the information on the common Carpathian mental path.

Gregori didn't look at him or give it away they were in communication. *I am certain you will be coming this rising to give us the information we need to destroy these vampires of mixed blood.*

"I would be most grateful for anyone you can send," Costin admitted.

"At night, you will be protected by a couple of us, but your real danger is during the day," Fen said. "Should you have need, reach for me. Use your mind, even if you have to use your fear. I will hear you."

Gregori turned slashing silver eyes on Fen. *You can walk in the sunlight?* There was no mistaking the edge of alarm in his voice. He didn't exactly try to cover it up.

Fen barely inclined his head. *If necessary, although it is not easy.* He was not giving out any more information until Gregori shared more data with him. He turned to leave.

"Are you returning with me?" Gregori asked aloud.

Fen shook his head. "I need to attend my brother. He isn't doing as well as I would like. In the first battle, he and Zev fought off the rogues in order to allow me to get to the *Sange rau*. His belly was ripped open, his wounds severe."

Immediately he felt Gregori's sympathy as the Carpathian fell into step with him. "Do you have need of a healer?"

"I don't know yet. Allow me to examine him. Should I need your aid, I will call." Fen was reluctant to disclose Dimitri and Tatijana's resting place to anyone.

Gregori nodded. "I will tell Mikhail to expect you, unless, of course, you call for my aid."

Fen studied Gregori's face. He was pale, with lines etched deep. He wasn't completely healed from the battle, yet he had come himself to ensure the prince was safe. Fen's respect for him went up another notch.

"Thank you. Should Dimitri require your skills, I will call. I'll come to speak to the prince as soon as I can."

Should Gregori have to aid him in healing his brother, Fen would move Dimitri just as a precaution. Gregori would discover Dimitri's blood was different. How could he not if he entered the body to heal it? Dimitri was too vulnerable, and with the elite hunters either drawing close, or already there, both Fen and Dimitri were already at great risk. Fen preferred not to take chances with his brother's life.

As if reading his mind, Gregori touched his arm to slow him down. "There are six strangers in the village. All of them met with the man you call Zev. They're all staying at the inn. They look . . . tough."

Fen nodded. "They are best left alone. I cannot be anywhere near them over the next few risings."

Gregori frowned. "This has to do with your Carpathian blood mixed with their Lycan blood?" He made it more of a question than a statement.

Fen shrugged. "When you first came upon the battle, were you certain I was Carpathian?"

"No," Gregori admitted.

Fen knew that was most likely the reason Gregori remained suspicious of him.

"It is the same with the Lycans. Until the week of the full moon, they cannot detect me, but during this phase, they know exactly what I am. They call a vampire/wolf cross a *Sange rau* and they do not distinguish between that monster and me."

"The strangers who have come to our village?"

"They are the elite of the Lycans. Their best hunters with superior speed and gifts. Zev is their true alpha. They have a leader, but all of them answer to him. They were summoned to hunt and destroy the rogue pack, just as we send our hunters out to kill the vampire. Zev is aware that there is one *Sange rau* running the pack. He doesn't yet know about the second."

"They'll need the information to successfully hunt them," Gregori pointed out.

Fen nodded. "I cannot deliver it to them, at least not for a few more risings. You will have to find another way." He turned his face toward the forest. His unease had been growing. "I need to get to my brother."

Gregori stepped away and lifted a hand to him. "I'll see to it that this farmer gets his family to safety."

"Thank you." Fen inclined his head and then leapt for the sky. He shifted in midair, sprouting the feathers of an owl, the talons and curved beak. He circled the farm and the outlying area just to double-check that no more threats were close, before winging his way back to the forest.

Again, he was very careful, making certain no one had followed him, before he dropped down, shifting again as he opened the earth beneath him. Tatijana lay in the rich soil, her face pale, skin nearly translucent. She looked like an ice princess, elusive and beautiful. Her hair was very long and thick, still twisted into that flowing endless mass of an intricate braid. Ribbons woven into her hair bound the long length, adding a touch of the dramatic.

He gathered her into his arms, inspecting her body carefully to ensure the wounds were healing properly. The dragon had sustained heavy damage to her belly, just as Dimitri had. The dragon had, for the most part, protected Tatijana. Dimitri hadn't had his body encased within dragon skin and scales. The werewolves knew to rip softer underbellies, and they'd done their damage, but she would be fine.

Fen woke her with a single word, pressing her mouth to his chest. She moaned softly, her eyelashes fluttering before awakened fully and he found himself staring into her multifaceted emerald eyes. He smiled at her. "There you are. I was beginning to think you were going to sleep your life away."

She smiled back at him, relaxing into his arms. "Not a chance." Her cheek rubbed along his chest, sending little darts of fire racing through his bloodstream.

His entire body reacted to that small move. As he pushed back stray tendrils of hair from her face, he thought it a miracle to feel such deep emotions. The experience was unexpected, new and exhilarating. Everything about her was exhilarating. "Aside from being courageous and a warrior, you're a truly beautiful woman, Tatijana Dragonseeker," he whispered. "I'm honored to be your lifemate, claimed or unclaimed."

"I must say, sir, I am beginning to feel much the same, which is rather a surprise to me," she admitted.

The honesty in her voice and that low, sultry tone added to the hot surge of his blood, racing to pool low and wicked. He savored his ability to feel such a new extremely exhilarating flood of feelings, both physical and emotional. He knew immediately the two things were tied together inexorably. Even the Lycan blood mixed with his Carpathian blood had not dampened his drive to find the other half of his soul. No other woman would do. He'd never felt such an urgent desire. He'd learned about sex, who couldn't after so many centuries, but he'd never understood the rush. The joy. The urgent hunger.

He smoothed his hand over her hair. "Drink from me, my lady. I need you at full strength this rising. Dimitri is in desperate need and I fear it will take two of us, if we have any chance at all of saving him."

She looked into his eyes—into his mind. He hid nothing from her. She reached up to smooth away the line of worry on his brow. "You did not ask the healer to aid you."

"I am a skilled healer as is Gregori. Dimitri is beyond both of our abilities. I know this. He lingers, but he still slips an inch at a time toward the other side. Gregori is severely wounded, and yet he rises to do his job guarding the prince. His job is too important to risk his life needlessly. His skills—and mine—will not save Dimitri. He needs Mother Earth to intervene on his behalf."

He will be saved if possible.

Tatijana whispered the words into his mind as her teeth sank deep into his chest. The flood of need was so strong, the hunger for her almost out of control. He closed his eyes and breathed, as his rich blood filled her veins and rushed through her body to every wounded organ, helping to accelerate the healing process.

He'd fed hundreds of Carpathians wounded in battle. He'd given his blood to a trusted Lycan friend who fought with him over and over to defeat a common enemy. He'd taken blood from men, women and his own kind, both Lycan and Carpathian. Never had there been a sexual component until now. He breathed in and out. Listened to his heart beating hard in his chest. Heard the roaring sound of thunder in his ears. Felt his cock grow, lengthen and harden with a never before felt *desperate* urgency.

He was alive for the first time in his life that he could remember. Fully alive. The claiming words, imprinted upon him long before his birth, pounded through his mind. He heard those ritual binding words, that fateful chanting that would forever bind them, but he refused to speak them to her. He would never make such a decision for her, not until he knew for certain she wouldn't be at risk if she became what he was. Even this small exchange was a little frightening for him. There was no knowing how much blood it took before the recipient became as he was.

With one last sensual sweep of her tongue, Tatijana opened her eyes again and smiled at him. "This one would be honored to become as you are. Stop worrying so much." Her expression changed, going solemn as she sat up. "Let's save your brother. I would never want to lose my sister."

"She doesn't want to lose you. When we're finished here, you must go to her and reassure her that you still live." Fen couldn't help himself. "I'm going to kiss you again. If you need a reason this time, it won't sound reasonable, but I can't help myself."

"Well, then, certainly you must."

He closed the gap between their mouths, half lifting her in his arms and bending his head to hers. Her lips were warm and soft. He stroked his tongue across that small seam and she opened her mouth in invitation. His heart nearly exploded in his chest as he sank into her. He poured himself into her like liquid gold.

Her mouth was warm honey. Dazzling diamonds. A sky filled with brilliant sapphires and just sheer paradise. It made no sense at all—he wasn't a poetic man—but the world around him exploded in an amazing array of the most beautiful natural caves he'd ever seen with their gem-studded walls glittering behind his eyes. How could she do that? So simple it seemed. All she had to do was open her mouth and let him kiss her.

He reluctantly raised his head, shaking it, a little bemused. If her eyes were anything to go by, she was feeling the same. He hadn't shared her mind because he was already so hungry for her, the ritual words pounding at him, that he feared he wouldn't stop and his duty was to his brother. Kissing once was perfectly fine, but he needed long, endless nights with Tatijana to do her justice.

Her hand crept into his as she sat up all the way. "We can save him, Fen. Together."

He nodded, and they floated just above where they had rested and once again peeled back the earth to reveal Dimitri. He lay as still as death. His skin was almost pure white. He looked already long gone from their world. Fen felt his heart plummet, knowing, for the first time in his life, he'd put off the inevitable.

"He has a lifemate, Fen," Tatijana reminded. "There is always hope. What cannot be done for one's self, can often be done for one's lifemate, no matter how extraordinary it seems."

"Or miraculous?" He could barely get the words out, a lump in his throat threatening to choke him.

"Especially miraculous. Isn't simply finding one's lifemate a true miracle?" Tatijana smiled at him. "At least that is how Lara explained it to me, and she would know. She is my nephew's daughter and is very wise. Call to his lifemate."

"She is young. Far away. Another country it felt. A great distance."

"And yet she came when needed. Gain entrance to his mind and follow the path back to her. She will answer your summons. She has to be strong if she can bridge the distance you speak of." Tatijana knelt on one side of Dimitri's body and waited.

Fen slowly sank to his knees on the other side. Placing both hands on his hips he reached for the strong telepathic connection he'd had with Dimitri since Dimitri's birth.

Warrior. My brother and friend, hold steadfast for me. For your people and most of all, your beloved lifemate. He spoke formally, using their ancient tongue, relying on the Carpathian past as well as present memories so carefully imprinted upon them. He had a lump in his throat, something hard threatening to choke him.

He felt the smallest of flickers, and took advantage, slipping into Dimitri's mind. He found darkness and cold, as if light after light had slowly faded away, leaving only shadows of memory, but that was enough to work with. He quickly found the one he needed most. She was the brightest of the fading lights. The starlight beacon was still pulsating, although much dimmer than Fen had hoped, but brighter than he believed possible. He followed the path for endless time, a narrow comet lighting the dark as he arced across cold space. The distance was far longer than he'd ever traveled telepathically.

She is Dragonseeker. Tatijana breathed the words into his mind, a propulsion of warm air and peace in the terrible, stunning cold. *This child. This human, she is Razvan's daughter, yet she is human and so powerful? I am in awe of her.*

He felt Tatijana's breathless surprise and welcomed the added boost of strength to his mind as it crossed that space on its journey. He found her almost abruptly, one moment in that arcing cavern of cold and the next in a warm, magical mind.

Little one. Lifemate to Dimitri. I have urgent need of you. Fen did his best to slowly pour into his brother's mate's mind, afraid of scaring her. It was always uncomfortable to know another had access to your every thought, word and deed—unless that man or woman was one's other half.

She surprised him. No, more than mere surprise. Shocked him. Even humbled him. There was no hesitation. *Tell me.*

He is slipping away from us and I cannot alone save him. I know the journey is long, but you must help me keep him in this world.

Tatijana's whisper in his mind was soft. Awed. *She is . . . amazing. Strong.*

Tatijana's entire attitude had gone to one of absolute respect. She heard, maybe even felt, more of the steel in the woman/child than he had—she shared the same bloodline.

I can maintain my own path. Save your strength for healing him.

She made it a command, every bit as confident as Tatijana had been. And she was only nineteen—and a human at that. Fen was amazed all over again.

I will need to see him through your eyes.

That, at least had been a plea rather than a demand. She even understood the concept of possessing one's body enough to share vision, hearing or other senses. That gift, too, was rarely used. One had to have complete trust and faith to allow another to possess their physical body.

I have much to learn about you, little sister, Fen said, allowing his awe to show as he opened himself more fully to her. *You show remarkable skill and training in a woman so young.*

He caught glimpses of her family in her memories. There was a strange young man with black hair and wild blue tips spiked all over his head, and then she abruptly pulled from his mind and he felt her connect to Dimitri. Through Fen, Tatijana was also connected. Both heard her gasp of alarm.

Beloved. Heart of mine. I know you are weary. Forgive me. I cannot let you go. There is no other for me. You can do this—for me. For us. Fight for us, beloved.

Fen glanced at Tatijana. Skyler hadn't actually seen Dimitri's horrific wounds and yet she was already fully aware of what they faced. He heard the raw love. The softest of intimate whispers only true lifemates could establish between them. He feared once she saw the wounds, the daunting sight would shake her confidence.

Still, Dimitri responded more to that soft little confession and flow of pure love washing through his mind, than anything else Fen had tried so far. Fen felt a small portion of that darkness and cold recede.

Please.

This time, she had found her way into his mind without any assistance at all. Skyler poured into his mind and nearly instantly found his connection to Tatijana—was well aware she was there as well.

I greet you as sister-kin, though I am more than your aunt, Tatijana identified herself. *I am lifemate to Fen.*

Yet unclaimed, as am I, Skyler said. *Thank you for your aid.*

He felt Tatijana wince just a little that Skyler should find her unclaimed when her lifemate was right there, yet there had been no accusation in Skyler's voice. In fact, he felt it helped her identify with Tatijana and make her more comfortable.

A flood of reassurance washed over him. He glanced at Tatijana kneeling across from him, there in the soil, her hands already moving into Dimitri's horrendous wounds. He placed his hands there as well when she flashed him a very small, reassuring smile.

Look at his wounds.

Slowly, reluctantly, he allowed Skyler to "see" through his eyes. He focused his vision wholly on the extent of Dimitri's wounds. She understood instantly.

The pain went far beyond what any physical body could tolerate, human, Lycan or Carpathian. Now there was no denying what she was dealing with.

Skyler showed no hesitation. *I am in the library of the university where I am studying. I will need my friend to come to me. When we are done here, I will no longer be able to maintain my own body. Give me just one second to contact Josef. I am fortunate that he came to visit me this evening. I didn't even know he was in town.*

There was a moment's pause. *He will come to me right away.*

She joined closely with Tatijana and Fen. He felt her take a deep breath. *We call upon the power of the Earth—she who creates us all.*

Tatijana and Fen answered. Fen, only because he knew the words through his lifemate. *Hear our call, Mother.*

We beg you for clear sight, the ability to be seen, that which seeks not to be seen. Guide us, Mother, take our hands, make them your own.

Use them as your tools to mend that which has been broken and torn.

Guide us, Mother. Provide rest and healing to a tortured soul.

Skyler's voice nearly cracked, but she took another deep breath and continued. *Embrace him as your own, Mother. Heal him of all injuries. Guide him, Mother.*

Her voice did waver, and Fen heard her tears for the first time. He felt her terrible growing sorrow even as she tried desperately to hold herself together. He couldn't imagine her all alone in the college library, yet not alone. She had to be surrounded by human students studying. She couldn't portray emotion, or her draining strength to anyone. The distance was nearly incomprehensible, and yet she persisted.

We three, your daughters and son, call upon the higher power. Use us as your vessel. See through our eyes.

Look into our souls. Use us as your tools. Guard him, great one. Take him fully into your care. Nurture him as you would your child, this great gift we bring even as we humbly beg your service. He will serve you as we do and rise once again to fight. Guide us with your knowledge.

Around him, the soil began to move on its own. So rich the loam looked as if it was ebony in color, Fen could see minerals glittering throughout, like gems. Before he could identify any of the properties, the soil rose to cover Dimitri, pouring into him.

Fen's hands moved of their own accord. He nearly jumped out of his skin. Nothing possessed him. He knew possession. Skyler hadn't taken over their bodies, but the loam itself pushed their hands and fingers in the directions needed.

The soil began to churn and tiny shoots broke through the surface. Fascinated, he tried to figure out if it was Skyler who fed that churning soil with all of the energy from Tatijana and him as well as what she could provide from such great a distance. He couldn't distract either of the two women by asking questions so he let the power and strength of his body flow into his brother and focused wholly on the artistry of the healing.

The tiny shoots came from every direction and moved into his brother, as if burrowing into the gaping wounds—arteries—he realized, providing some kind of much-needed nutrition. More soil poured in and around his brother's body.

Give him blood. One at a time. As much as either of you can spare, Skyler directed.

By every right she should have collapsed long ago, but her voice held steady and the warm flow of energy never ceased in that continuous current. The movement of Tatijana's wrist toward Dimitri's mouth caught his attention.

Beloved. Take this gift offered so generously and freely from my sister-kin. It is strong, ancient blood of the Dragonseeker lineage. Hear me, Dimitri. Do this thing for me.

Fen was no longer even astonished that Dimitri managed to move his mouth against Tatijana's wrist. He helped his brother take in the life-giving sustenance. All around them the soil continued moving and churning. The sprouts and veins twisting through Dimitri's body reached for the nutrients so old and ancient and pure from Tatijana's lineage and pushed them through his brother's unresponsive organs.

Fen counted the minutes slowly, fearful that in her effort to save Dimitri, Skyler might forget that they were vulnerable there in the forest and couldn't be drained to the point of weakness. He shouldn't have been. For a human child, she certainly understood the needs and ways and dangers of the Carpathian life.

Enough, beloved. Rest before you take from your brother. Allow our Mother Earth to guide you. Do not fear her. She is granting a tremendous favor and has accepted both you and your brother as her sons. Just sleep and let her repair your body.

Again, that soft tone was so intimate, Fen almost felt as if he'd slipped into a private encounter between Dimitri and his astonishing lifemate. She gave of herself so freely, and yet he could feel her energy beginning to wane. She did then have her limits. She must have been afraid that she would not complete this healing in time before she gave out, but if she did feel that way, she didn't betray herself.

Tatijana closed the wound on her wrist herself, with a single swipe of her tongue. She glanced up at Fen, her eyes meeting his. His breath caught in his throat. Her eyes nearly glowed, changing color until they were such a deep shade of green he felt the very coolness of the forest blowing over him.

Now from your brother, Dimitri. He is strong. Ancient. Like you, he is a good man and has survived long against nearly impossible odds without his lifemate. He is patient and kind and holds you dear to him. Take what is freely and so generously offered.

Fen rejoiced when this time, Dimitri turned his head toward him. For one moment those long, dark lashes, two blackened crescents against the stark white of Dimitri's skin, finally opened. He saw him there, present, his spirit back in his own body. The lashes drifted down as Fen pressed his wrist to his brother's mouth. Again he had to help Dimitri take in the blood, but at least he knew Dimitri was alive and fighting.

Fen began to hear a sound, much like the cavernous boom of a drum below them, around them, surrounding them. He recognized the rhythm as that of a heartbeat. Each single beat vibrated through Dimitri's body, his every organ, sinew and bone. Because all four were connected, each of them felt that strong pulsation. Each beat seemed to send pain crashing through his body, but Dimitri didn't fight.

Mother Earth has accepted you, beloved, as her son. You are now a part of her. You are hearing her heart beating through your body, making you one with her, one with all nature. We are bound together now, the four of us.

With every ounce of energy he possessed, Dimitri reached toward his lifemate. The two spirits brushed against one another and Dimitri's light spread and grew brighter.

It is enough, I think, beloved. I cannot stay. Be strong for me. Skyler's voice was already fading, her strength draining fast.

Dimitri stirred, lashes once more lifting, almost in a panic that he hadn't seen her. Fen closed the wound on his wrist and watched the momentary heat in his brother's eyes fade when he realized Skyler was present only in spirit.

Rest, beloved. I must go. Josef is with me. He'll keep me safe. You live, Dimitri. Stay alive. Just live for me.

The moment the soil stopped churning, Skyler was gone abruptly. She'd given everything she had and must have passed out there in the library so far away from them. Fen could only hope that her friend Josef knew what he was doing.

"Sleep my brother," he whispered to Dimitri and smoothed his hand over his brother's forehead. There was raw love in the gesture and he was grateful only his lifemate witnessed his vulnerability.

"We've done what we can here, my lady." He offered his hand to her. "We must safeguard his resting spot, revive ourselves, reassure your sister and then, I suppose, we must go see a prince."

7

Mikhail Dubrinsky's home was so well-crafted and the safeguards so strong, that even with Carpathian eyes Fen found it difficult to see at first. Deep in the forest, higher up toward the cliffs, the house was both mountain and wood. The air shimmered around the home, a veil not so easily pierced. Abruptly that veil dropped away, and Gregori strode toward them.

Tatijana's fingers brushed his and he caught her hand without looking down at her. Jacques Dubrinsky jumped out of the uppermost branches of the trees and landed easily on his feet. On their left, Falcon Amiras did the same, essentially creating a funnel—a polite chute—but one all the same.

"Welcome, Fenris Dalka," Gregori said formally. His silver eyes slashed over them both, taking in far more than either would have wished. "You are much later than anticipated, but I see why. Dimitri?"

"He is alive," Fen said.

He didn't know these people. He had never sworn loyalty to this prince, nor would he until he knew the heart and soul of Mikhail Dubrinsky. He certainly wouldn't trust any of them with the life of his brother without knowing the truth.

"How many weapons do you carry on you?"

"Enough to take down a rogue pack," Fen answered vaguely, his eyes steady on Gregori's. He never once turned away. If necessary, Tatijana could fend off the two men flanking them, but he would have to defeat the prince's second if this was a trap.

"That is not really an answer," Gregori pointed out mildly, a slight edge creeping into all that charm.

"In truth, I do not know. When an elite hunting pack is in the area during a full moon, I am always fully armed if I am not beneath the ground." Fen accompanied his answer with a casual shrug. If they wanted him to speak with the prince, it was going to be on his terms. He was exhausted, still not fully healed and was risking his life just to come there. If they wanted him to leave, he'd be more than happy to oblige.

Tatijana's soft laughter slipped into his mind. *I think wolf man has a chip on his shoulder. I will have to remember that when you're tired, you're a little bit grumpy.*

They invited me. But his mood was slipping away with her teasing. It was impossible to keep a Lycan's foul temper around her, even if he wanted to. He sent her a small glimmer of a smile and when her eyes met his, his heart reacted with a hard bang. *You do get to me, woman.*

She looked smug. And pleased. Her eyes took on a sparkle. *I know.*

Gregori led the way to the large wraparound porch, shaded by a roof held by strong stone columns. The moment he set foot on the exquisite wooden planking, the heavy door opened, and Mikhail filled that entrance.

There was no mistaking the prince of the Carpathian people. His power was raw, yet controlled. The energy burned in and through him, barely contained. Fen had often met his own prince, and yet never had that raw power been so strong in him. Mikhail looked princely with his wide, straight shoulders, tall physique and eyes that held the weight of their world in them. He had seen battle on many occasions. He had seen the decline of his people and had turned them around to grow anew.

"Fenris Dalka," Gregori provided. "And his lifemate, Tatijana Dragonseeker."

The prince's gaze moved to Tatijana. For the first time Fen felt her tremble. It was slight, but it was there. She was just a little nervous to face her prince after she had struck out on her own. Maybe feeling a little guilty even, that she had tried to escape Gregori's care.

"I see that. You both are welcome. Please enter of your own free will." He stepped back to allow them both the decision to enter his home.

The house was suspiciously quiet. He was given entrance, but Mikhail's lifemate, Raven, and their son were conspicuously somewhere safe. He didn't blame the prince or Gregori. He expected nothing less of them. He was, after all, completely unknown to them and he was bringing a battle right to their doorsteps.

"Thank you." He stepped across the threshold and knew instantly the house itself was tied in some way to the prince and his powers. With one hand he swept Tatijana behind him, his hand staying there in warning to her as he advanced.

He felt the weight of stone and wood. The walls breathed in and out. The curtains fluttered, drawing his eye. They twisted. He felt the urge to put out his arms and spin in a slow circle, allowing the house to see his cache of weapons. He held firm against that slow continuous push and stood, feet slightly apart, upright, arms loosely at his sides.

Gregori's laughter was soft. "I told you he was a warrior through and through. He isn't a man I want to tangle with."

But he would in spite of everything he was saying so smoothly. Gregori was laughing. Looking comfortable. Luring Fen in, making him feel comfortable. Fen had met a few like him. There was nothing humorous whatsoever about a man like Gregori Daratrazanoff. He would have already gone through the kill a hundred times in his mind, planning every move out in his mind until he would be smooth, fast and deadly should Fen prove to be treacherous. His backup plans had backup plans. He was dangerous and anyone who couldn't see that was an imbecile. Fen didn't count himself among the imbeciles.

Fen made no attempt to approach the prince or anything else in the house. The game of high stakes chess had begun. Their move. The prince waited courteously for Tatijana in the open doorway. She remained motionless, waiting for Fen's signal. If it was a trap, she could better aid him from outside.

Time seemed to stand still. Somewhere an owl hooted. A wolf called. A slight breeze moved through the forest, sending leaves quivering.

Mikhail sighed. Extending his hand to Tatijana, he gave her a small, old-world bow along with a charming smile. "Come, my dear. There seems to be posturing going on and I would very much appreciate your help in defusing this situation."

Tatijana kept her gaze on Mikhail, but stirred in Fen's mind. *Yes? No?* It was his decision. He barely inclined his head. She took Mikhail's hand, smiled up at him and stepped over the threshold into the house. There was no reaction from the house and Mikhail led her over to a ring of comfortable chairs and gallantly seated her.

"Thank you, Tatijana." He waved his hand toward the chair beside Tatijana's in invitation to Fen.

The location of the chair was the least vulnerable seat in the room, positioned for the best defense, designed no doubt to make Fen feel even more comfortable with them, but it had been long since he'd been enclosed in a room with four walls meeting. He was, however, used to meeting with many possible enemies—but this time, he had a woman to protect.

Worry about protecting yourself. I can take care of me, Tatijana assured.

She had that little mischievous tone he found himself listening for. *I'm becoming quite partial to you, my lady.*

I know. Smug.

He wanted to laugh, but he kept his expression pure stone. "How can I be of use to you?" he asked the prince.

Mikhail sank into the chair opposite him. Jacques and Falcon both took their seats, but Gregori stood, and from his angle, he had a commanding view of nearly every window in the house. The house reminded him of an eagle's nest, perched up high, where weather could protect it, yet they could see anything—or anyone—coming at them.

The house was warm and felt friendly, but Fen knew it was designed for a single purpose—to protect those residing in it. There was a faint scent he couldn't quite place, a blend of something that confused his Lycan senses. He couldn't quite smell Mikhail's true scent, an interesting form of protection. He would be hard-pressed to distinguish the prince from the others if tracking him.

"This is the first time in my lifetime that the Lycans have openly entered our territory." Mikhail sat back and carefully folded his hands together. "You have been long gone from our people. While you have been gone, our women dwindled until there was no longer hope of lifemates for our males. What few women we did have could not carry a child, or, if by some stroke of luck, one did, they could not nurture the child. We lost nearly all babies in that first crucial year."

Fen frowned. Dimitri had shared that the Carpathian ranks had fallen well below safe numbers. The fear of extinction was always present, but he hadn't described the problem. Most likely, Dimitri feared if he told Fen that finding a lifemate was nearly impossible, Fen would give up and choose to meet the dawn.

Mikhail continued in a low, even voice, almost musical, a very powerful weapon should he choose to use it as such. "We have discovered, over time and with a great deal of blood-spill, heartache and tears, that Xavier, our greatest mage, had secretly and over centuries worked to bring about our downfall. He even went so far as to introduce microbes into our soil to contaminate it and kill our women and children before they were born. Each time we find one threat and destroy it, another has arisen."

"I had no idea this was happening," Fen admitted. "I have been gone from these lands for centuries. My only contact has been my brother, and then only when I sought a safe haven in the refuges he created for my wolf brethren when I needed to rest."

Mikhail inclined his head. "Your brother's wounds are healing?"

Fen couldn't stop himself from glancing at Tatijana. For comfort? He didn't know the answer to that question—only that having her with him made it easier to bear the idea of Dimitri's pain and suffering. "We have hope." There was nothing else to say.

Mikhail leaned toward Fen suddenly, his dark eyes penetrating deep. "We've had a period of relative peace after the De La Cruz brothers and Dominic defeated the vampires in South America. The vampires scattered with few leaders to direct them. I'm certain they will rise again, or perhaps they have been waiting to see if our children survived beyond their first year."

Silence filled the room and with it came tension, stretching nerves tight. Fen could feel his every Lycan sense activating. His muscles ached. His jaw. He felt threatened in some primal way, but wasn't certain what they expected of him.

"I don't understand." He made the statement without a hint of fear, but he was beginning to wish Tatijana had remained outside the four walls where he knew she had a chance of being safe. They weren't safe locked in a relatively small space with four lethal predators.

"My son is now two years of age. And my brother, Jacques's boy is growing and thriving at three. Gregori's twins survived those critical first years. Gregori's brother Darius has twins, a boy and girl, both healthy and past the two-year mark. I am certain you must have grown up with Gabriel and Lucian, two other of Gregori's brothers. Gabriel has a little daughter, again, she is healthy."

"This is the first time in centuries such a thing has happened," Gregori added.

Mikhail gestured toward Falcon. "You crossed paths as children with Falcon. His lifemate, Sara, has announced she is once again pregnant and the pregnancy appears to be a healthy one. There are others and perhaps ones not yet known. The point is that in over five hundred years we have never had it so good." His eyes went steely, pupils dilated and pitch-black. "And now, at this time when all is beginning to look up, the Lycans have shown up in my backyard. I would like you to tell me what that means."

Fen could see the damning arrow. How could he not? Carpathians finally beginning to recover and suddenly they are overrun with a species so elusive one nearly forgot their existence. Had it been just coincidence that the rogue pack had run this way? Led by Bardolf, Fen might have believed the choice had been a random one. But Abel, not Bardolf, really led the pack.

"Fen?" Mikhail prompted.

"I don't honestly have an answer for you. I ran across werewolves committing murder and knew I'd discovered a rogue pack. A single hunter can't take on a small pack by himself, let alone a large pack. And this is a very large pack. I followed them and began picking them off one at a time. It's dangerous and time-consuming, but believe me, it's the only way if you want to survive."

Fen sighed, shaking his head slowly. "I traveled this way only to be close to my brother once again. I felt drawn here. In doing so, I ran across the kills." He looked at Tatijana. "I had resisted for well over eighteen months. I found I had to come, although I felt it dangerous to do so."

"Did you think we wouldn't welcome you? Gregori tells me you are of mixed blood. You thought this would matter to us in some way?" Mikhail inquired, his tone deceptively mild.

Fen spread his hands out in front of him, fingers wide. "People like me are called *Sange Rau,* literally *bad blood* in the Lycan world. We are hated and hunted the instant it is known we exist." He shrugged. "I could live with that from the Lycans. I understand their reasoning. The only mixed bloods they have known have been vampire-Lycan. To them, that is what I am should I be discovered. The idea of my own people condemning what I've become did not sit with me so easily."

Gregori turned his head, those pale silver eyes moving over Fen in a careful study. "You are not so easily killed, even by one of us."

Fen gave him a slight nod in response to the compliment. Gregori only stated the truth, he wasn't out to flatter Fen. Clearly Gregori had made a show of Jacques and Falcon's presence because he knew they would need more than one hunter to try to kill him. And then whose side would Tatijana come down on? She had sworn her allegiance to the prince, and no Dragonseeker would ever break their word after giving it.

He took another slow look around the room. There were others. There had to be more than just these three warriors protecting the prince. He had allowed the house to confuse his senses while they distracted him with talk. He was happier to be in his homeland, surrounded by his own people, than he'd let himself believe. That had also thrown his guard off a bit. And then there was Tatijana . . .

He sighed. "You may as well tell the insect in the rafters to come on down. The mouse in that tiny hole over there"—he indicated his left—"and the knot directly behind me is concealing a beetle of some sort. If there are others, they certainly are adept at hiding, but being in the body of something so small for so long, makes for slow fighters."

The flying insect in the rafters responded first, shimmering into the form of a tall, broad-shouldered male with strange-colored, nearly aquamarine eyes. His hair was very long, nearly to his waist, thick and tethered with a single long leather cord winding all the way down to secure even the ends, a typical way to bind hair for battle. Fen recognized him immediately and to his shock, relief spread through him. Mataias had been a childhood friend.

Fen had known Falcon, but he'd grown up close to Mataias and his brothers. They'd run wild together in the mountains, learned battle skills and shifting on the run. They'd been like family, and he'd lost track of them. He came to his feet and clasped Mataias's forearms in the age-old traditional welcome between two warriors.

"*Arwa-arvo olen isäntä, ekäm*—honor keep you, my brother," Fen greeted.

Mataias's answering grip was strong. "*Arwa-arvo pile sívadet*—may honor light your heart."

"It's good to see you," Fen said, meaning it. He truly felt as if he had come home, seeing Mataias, knowing he hadn't succumbed to the ever-present darkness.

The fact that Mataias was there meant the other two guarding the prince had to be his brothers. The siblings were never far from one another. Coming from a long line of respected warriors, they had traveled together to see each other through darker times. They were lethal hunters, calm, experienced, and coordinated their attacks with expertise, much like the packs of Lycans. A master vampire had killed their parents when their mother was pregnant and they'd hunted the vampire across two continents, with a ruthless, implacable purpose, never stopping until they had found and destroyed him.

"Lojos and Tomas may as well show themselves," Fen added.

"Did you smell them?" Gregori asked.

Fen glanced over at him. Clearly he'd been testing something new. He shook his head. "No, not even with my Lycan senses heightened."

Gregori nodded. "Good. We've got a couple of brilliant researchers working for us, and this was one product I thought would be good to use if the Lycans are invading."

Fen shook his head. "They aren't like that. They've never been like that. They remain in the background, working quietly to keep their packs as strong as possible, but they've integrated into human society well. I can't see them making a decision out of the blue to suddenly go to war with Carpathians."

The small mouse grew and kept growing fast, until another Carpathian male, looking very much like a clone of the first one, came forward to greet Fen with the traditional forearm clasp. His eyes were as brilliant aquamarine as his brother's. His hair was identical as well as body frame, but Lojos had a web of scarring running down his left shoulder and arm, all the way to his hand. It was very unusual for any Carpathian to scar. The wounds had to be near fatal, the suffering great.

"Well met, brother," Fen said, meaning it. "*Veri olen piros, ekäm.*" Literally the greeting translated to blood be red, my brother, but figuratively, it meant "find your lifemate."

They stood eye to eye, staring into each other's pasts. Fen knew what it was like to struggle against the darkness, to be alone in the midst of others— even those you could only cling to the memory of loving.

"This is your lifemate? A Dragonseeker?" Lojos shook his head. "You are a very lucky man, Fen. This Lycan hunter you call Zev, the one so badly wounded, with his belly ripped open. I have watched him, and he is healing at a remarkable rate for the extent of his injuries."

Fen knew they all were listening for every detail. "Lycans regenerate very quickly, which is one of the reasons, when you take them on, you have to know how to properly kill them. They aren't easy. Zev is an elite fighter, one of the best I've ever seen. He was willing to take on the rogue pack alone in order to allow me to get Tatijana out of harm's way."

The men looked at one another, secretly amused that a Lycan thought to protect a Carpathian, especially one who was Dragonseeker.

"Obviously he didn't know what, or who she was," Fen said.

"You admire this man." Gregori made it a statement.

"Yes, very much. You don't get to his position without seeing hundreds, if not thousands of battles with packs. The moment he and Dimitri realized the one leading the rogues was one of the *Sange rau*, they held off the pack in order to allow me the opportunity to destroy the demon. Zev didn't hesitate to put himself in a very dangerous situation. He knew he could die, but he didn't back down."

The small beetle fit snugly in the knot landed on the floor and grew with alarming speed into the shape of the first two brothers. When he clasped Fen's forearms in the warrior's greeting, Fen could see the droplets of scars down the right side of his face, almost like tears, all the way to his jaw. The same strange scars ran up his temple and disappeared into his hairline.

"*Bur tule ekämet kuntamak*—well met, brother-kin," the third brother greeted Fen. "It is good you found your lifemate. I have thought often of you over the last centuries, and hoped I would never have to meet you in battle."

"I felt the same, Tomas," Fen admitted honestly. "So many of us have been lost to the darkness."

He took another careful look around. The prince had these three experienced warriors, Gregori, Falcon and Jacques to protect him against an unknown Lycan/Carpathian combination. *In his house.* Close quarters. Gregori had an inkling of what he could do. There was another somewhere. Someone extraordinary, their ace in the hole. There was one other from his childhood. A little older, only by a decade or so, which was nothing in the years of Carpathians. He'd always been a little odd, but he'd been a source of vast knowledge. Andre. Some called him the ghost. He often passed through, wiped out any vampires in an area and was never seen or heard from. But he left his mark, and Fen had tried to keep track of him. He'd heard that he often was near the triplets, banding to hold on in order to keep the darkness at bay.

The Carpathians had prepared for a war. They'd spent the last two years of peacetime getting ready for anything that might threaten them as a species. He was just seeing the tip of the iceberg.

"Fen." Mikhail's cool voice brought him back to the business at hand. "The Carpathian people know the difference between a Carpathian and a vampire. You are no threat to us. In fact, your added speed and abilities as a Lycan only serve to aid our cause."

Fen frowned and sank back into the comfortable chair. "The Lycans' fear of the combination of blood is so deep that they would go to war should they find you are giving aid and harboring one of us. My presence here puts you all in jeopardy."

He dropped the bombshell quietly, knowing he didn't need to embellish. The stark truth was enough. Mikhail Dubrinsky was no one's fool. He would grasp instantly the enormity of what Fen was telling him. He would hear the ring of truth and know Fen had brought a problem of an alarming magnitude to him.

"I see," Mikhail said, steepling his fingers. "We're going to need to know everything you know about the Lycans. Everything. The smallest detail."

"There are very few like me," Fen cautioned. He certainly didn't want to be the cause of a war. "The Lycans are essentially good people," he added. "I like them and respect them. As fighters there are few who could surpass them. They don't look for power or glory as a rule. They live their lives within their small packs, happy with their families."

"I am certain they are good people," Mikhail agreed. "However, they have come to my lands without contacting me, a general courtesy, which I find unusual. A rogue pack with two of these creatures you refer to as *Sange rau* have also come when it simply has not happened before. We have several children who have survived into their second year. Are these coincidences? I am not such a fool as to believe that. I cannot afford to be that foolish."

Fen had his own doubts that the timing was coincidental.

"What is your experience with becoming Lycan? What do you know of them?" Mikhail asked.

"I can tell you as the wolf gets older so does the integration between wolf and man. In the beginning the wolf is separate—a guardian so to speak, protecting the host body as soon as the other half feels its presence. The wolf brings with it history and facts it has known throughout its lifespan and that of its ancestors. He passes that information to the man half and he moves to protect that man when necessary."

"As you grow older and more comfortable, the two, wolf and man, become one entity?" Mikhail reiterated to make certain they all understood.

Fen nodded. "Yes, that's as close to an explanation as possible. All senses, even when in the form of a man, are heightened beyond all reason. A young wolf often cannot control the transformation—usually before the full moon. He's clumsy and the pack watches him closely to make certain he or she doesn't get into trouble. It's an awkward stage."

"One of our males has a lifemate who was Lycan but didn't know it," Falcon said. "How is that possible?"

"Sometimes members leave the pack, falling in love with an outsider. Their children can carry the Lycan gene, but often it doesn't develop. Females in particular don't always know because their wolf doesn't come forward right away." Fen shrugged again. "I didn't stay with packs for long periods of time. It was too dangerous for me. They couldn't detect the difference most of the time, but during the week of the full moon, any of them could have figured it out. I spent the full moons in the ground as often as possible. Over the last century I traveled outside of packs."

"When do they begin training?" Gregori asked.

"In a pack, all children are trained almost from the moment they can talk. Education is all important, world affairs, the politics, cultures and running of every country. They are also taught fighting techniques and of course tracking and shifting. They're fast. Really fast. And they're taught battle strategy as well, training with all kinds of weapons."

"Much like what we do with our youth," Jacques said.

Fen nodded. "They work in the human world. They take jobs and actually serve in the militaries of whatever country they're in. Always, always though, they answer to their pack leader, and the pack leader answers to the council."

Mikhail got up and paced restlessly across the room. The stone fireplace was enormous and drew one's eyes. Fen was still looking for the last warrior's hiding place. The ghost. He was there somewhere in the room. The house was interesting in that no matter how many tall, broad-shouldered men were at the windows and close enough to guard their prince, the room felt spacious and open. Sometimes he almost felt as if the stone and wood were alive, and breathing, and watching them all.

He studied Mikhail out of the corner of his eye. The man moved with fluid grace and absolute control. Power radiated from him. He was definitely a man to lead and he took his duties very seriously. As did Gregori. Fen kept his eye on Mikhail's second-in-command at all times.

"You have not sworn your allegiance to our prince," Gregori said quietly.

Fen felt the familiar coiled readiness of the Lycan, but outwardly he remained stoic.

"Nor will he," Mikhail said in that same low tone. "Did you ask him why he didn't send for the greatest healer the Carpathian people have for his brother? He loves Dimitri, and he's fought hard to save his life. You were close, yet he didn't send for you, Gregori. What does that tell you?"

Gregori's silver eyes slashed at Fen. "I do not know that answer, Mikhail."

"Really?" One aristocratic eyebrow rose. "He tells himself he is protecting his brother, but more, he is protecting me. He believes no other will guard me as you will. He is just as concerned that we have not one, but two of these *Sange rau* suddenly close to me and our children. He did not want you to leave my side. Isn't that the truth, Fenris Dalka?"

One couldn't very well lie to the prince, but he sure didn't want to admit he was protecting the man. He said nothing.

"That doesn't explain why he will not swear his allegiance to you," Gregori pointed out.

"Doesn't it?" Mikhail turned cool dark eyes on Fen. "He believes if he swears his allegiance to me, that if the Lycans insist on destroying all like him, he'll put me in a position of having to go to war with them."

Fen felt the brush of Tatijana's hand down his jaw in a small caress. He didn't glance at her, knowing she hadn't moved. She saw too much inside of him and that was bad enough. He could share his innermost thoughts with a lifemate but . . . He would have preferred Mikhail didn't know anything at all about the way he thought. It only made him believe Mikhail Dubrinsky was a worthy leader. He could look into the eyes of a man and know his truth.

You're just embarrassed because he recognizes you're not nearly the bad wolf boy you present to the world.

Tatijana's intimate whisper in his mind twisted his heart. She added so much to him, without even knowing it. After centuries of being utterly alone, continually holding the whisper of temptation at bay, keeping the shadows back, to have her light pouring into his heart and soul was nothing short of a miracle. In his darkest hour, her light would always be there for him.

"Fen, you are not the only Carpathian who is of mixed blood now," Mikhail reminded in that same, low compelling voice. "I would never give up a single one of my people to make a treaty with any other species. Clearly we will have to address the council and make them understand the difference between a Carpathian/Lycan mix and a vampire/wolf mix. They are intelligent people and once it is made clear, they will see reason."

"You are looking at centuries of prejudice, Mikhail," Fen said. "I watched them condemn a great man, an elite hunter, one who had spent years battling and suffering to destroy the *Sange rau* preying on their packs. They condemned him to a slow torturous death they call *Moarta de argint*."

"Death by silver," Gregori translated.

Fen nodded. "It's the most painful way a Lycan can possibly die. It takes days. They place hooks of silver through the body and hang them upright. Every move the victim makes trying to get away from the pain of the silver only embeds the hooks deeper. The silver spreads through the body, burning everything it touches until eventually the heart is pierced through. I'm whitewashing this for you, but it's an ugly brutal way to go. Vakasin had given up his life to protect his pack, yet when they realized he was *Sange rau*, his own pack turned on him. They killed him knowing he had battled the *Sange rau* time and again for them."

Sorrow welled up—the sorrow he'd never been able to truly feel for the man who had been his friend and partner for a full century as they battled the most difficult enemy they'd ever taken on. Vakasin had been a good man. One of the best hunters Fen had ever known. He had found it shocking and unbelievable that his own pack could turn on the elite hunter and condemn him to the Lycan's most torturous, brutal death imaginable when they knew he was a good man.

Fen nodded toward Tatijana. "She saved Zev a few nights ago and extracted the information on weapons and how to make them properly. I would suggest arming every single warrior and, if possible, even the women just to be safe. Once you know how to kill the rogues, don't be fooled into thinking you're safe. They hunt in packs. This rogue pack is the biggest I've ever run across in all my centuries of hunting. However many silver stakes you think each person should carry on them, double the number."

He was uncomfortable within the four walls and getting more uneasy by the moment. Healing and going out of one's body took its toll. So, apparently, did emotions. "The wolf you see is not the one you're in danger from. They have a pack mentality and they've been hunting all their lives with packs. They'll go for the belly, rip you open and spill your insides out just to incapacitate you. No matter how high you think they can jump, double it and know it's still probably higher. You're never safe just because you take to the air."

"I can see why the Lycans would worry about a blood mix between the two species if you gain the assets from either species." Gregori's voice was thoughtful. "That's what happens, isn't it? That's why the vampire/wolf mixture is so deadly."

Now someone finally understood. He looked up slowly until Gregori's strange silver eyes met his. They stared at each other in complete understanding. Fen hadn't claimed his lifemate. He was still a threat and would be up until the moment he bound Tatijana to him with the ritual binding words imprinted on his Carpathian brain far before his mother had given birth to him. Even then, if he were being honest with himself, he didn't know if he would still be safe.

"You need to claim your lifemate," Gregori advised. "It would be much better for everyone."

Tatijana squirmed. She didn't move, but Fen felt her reaction to the healer's reprimand.

No one can tell us when the time is right for us, my lady, he assured. *We'll know. I'm not in danger of turning. Now that I have you close, your very light keeps the darkness at bay. Don't let him make you feel bad. I would not want you to come to me until you are ready. In any case, I was the one who said I wouldn't claim you. If there is blame, it is mine.*

Tatijana turned her head and looked at him, her large emerald eyes glittering with many facets. She could rob him of his breath so easily. One look. One touch. Her lips parted slightly, drawing his attention. Everything in him stilled. She was amazing. A miracle. Sitting only a scant few inches from him, the scent of her surrounding him and her warmth filling every cold space in his mind.

He smiled at her. Not outwardly of course, his smile was far more intimate, brushing across her mind to reassure her she was the most important person in his world and he didn't want anyone to make her uncomfortable.

"I am not in danger of turning, Gregori, if that's what you're implying," he said, perfectly calm. "I'll be hunting both Abel and Bardolf as soon as I'm back on my feet. They should have moved the pack fast, but they haven't. While Tatijana was checking on her sister, I picked up their trail. The majority of the pack headed south. They hit a farm just on the other side of the ridge, close to the ravine. No one was home, but the animals were slaughtered."

"And the farmer you helped earlier?" Mikhail prompted.

"He will be attacked." Fen sighed and resisted pushing his hands through his hair. He feared the farmer would be killed. He'd taken measures to try to protect him, but if Bardolf or Abel accompanied the pack, the farmer wouldn't have a chance. "He's a good man."

"So Gregori tells me. Perhaps, if we know the pack will attack this particular farm, we should find a way to use that to our advantage," Mikhail mused.

"Or better yet, allow the elite hunters Fen has spoken of to get this information. We can watch them in action and help prepare our own warriors," Falcon offered. "Although, I could never sit out when there is work to be done."

"It is necessary for me to avoid Zev's pack a few more days. He'll be looking for me soon," Fen said.

Mikhail nodded. "He made inquiries at the inn. His pack appears to number six. Five men and a woman. Is it common for a woman to be a hunter?"

"Any child, male or female, who shows promise in the packs as being above average in intelligence and faster in reflexes is sent to a special school as soon as the pack deems them old enough to go. It's a great honor for a pack to have elite hunters emerge from its ranks," Fen said. He looked around the room. "Don't underestimate the female hunter. She wouldn't be traveling with them if she wasn't just as capable of a fighter as the men. Each one often has to take on several rogue pack members alone."

"Do any of them have experience killing a *Sange rau?*" Lojos asked.

"I doubt it. I came across the first one several centuries ago and then when Bardolf's pack was decimated by Abel. Until now, I've never heard of or come across any other."

"Zev recognized that the vampire was of mixed blood?" Gregori asked.

Tatijana nodded. "Immediately. He and Dimitri both knew, at least I think so. Fen shouted out *Sange rau,* but they were already sacrificing themselves to give Fen a chance at killing it. Of course, at the time, we didn't realize there were two of them working together."

"There's a feel to them," Fen said. "You'll know immediately as well. I can't describe it, but in the way you know a vampire is foul, you'll recognize that the *Sange rau* is more. They have the capability of hiding themselves. Vampires leave a distinct trail most of the time. The very plants and trees shrink from them. They leave blank spots in their wake when they try to conceal themselves, but the *Sange rau* don't. They also don't give off energy before they attack, but if you come across one, you'll know," he reiterated.

"And yet you can track them and know they are present before they attack," Gregori said.

"I am also considered *Sange rau*. I am of mixed blood."

8

F en was very happy to get away from the four walls of the living, breathing house. He never had spotted Andre, the ghost among Carpathian
warriors, but was satisfied that he knew his old friend was there. He
inhaled the night air. Tatijana and he had to return quickly to their resting
place, but before they did, he needed to breathe the fresh air once again.

Tatijana slipped her hand into his as they turned up a trail to climb
higher into the mountains. "I guess that went as well as could be expected."

"Between the two of us, you with the information on weapons and me
with what I know about Lycans and rogues, I think we gave them enough
to protect themselves," Fen said. Already the surrounding trees cut them off
from all civilization, making him feel as if it were just the two of them, alone
in the night.

"You were very uncomfortable," she observed.

"It is long since I've been inside a house for any length of time," he
conceded. "I felt the more time I was in the company of the prince, the more
danger I exposed him to. Even with his hunters gathered around him, and
they are some of the best, they have never experienced this kind of threat
to him. I can tell them what the *Sange rau* is like, but until they actually
witness one in action, they'll never really understand."

Tatijana's eyebrow shot up. "You believe the threat is to the prince, then. Not the children?"

"Of course. Don't you?" Fen chose a route that would take them even farther up the mountain. More than anything, he needed to be with Tatijana and just savor every moment alone with her that he could have.

The night sky glittered with stars, although darker clouds floated lazily, occasionally blocking out the sparkling diamonds overhead. "If they kill Mikhail, the little prince at the age of two is far too young. His daughter might be able to take his place, but if not, there is no vessel for power. If you wish to wipe out Carpathians, the best way to do so would be to kill the prince now while his heir is young and vulnerable."

"His brother? Jacques?"

Fen shrugged. He threaded his fingers more comfortably through hers and brought her hand to his heart as they walked. Her hand felt small in his and made him feel all the more protective over her. "Maybe. Not all those in a lineage make good leaders. I know little about his brother, but Jacques is as protective over his brother as Gregori is and that tells me Jacques does not believe he can lead our people."

"Or does not want to," Tatijana added thoughtfully.

He glanced down at her, amazed that such a beautiful woman could be his. She moved with fluid grace, in complete silence. She fit into his body so perfectly. He was aware of everything about her. Her breasts moved beneath her shirt, a delicate enticement he'd never noticed on another woman. Her hips swayed gently, and the stars seemed to have settled in her eyes. The wind teased her long hair, trying hard to loosen it from the long thick coil she bound the mass of silk with.

His heart felt lighter than it ever had. He could hear the blood coursing in his veins. His teeth were sharp, and the need to taste his woman was nearly overpowering. With that hunger came rising lust, sharp and terrible yet tempered with such an intense love for her, he knew she was safe. Just walking with her up in the mountains, far from everyone else, he felt as if they were the only ones in the world. The beauty of the night and their surroundings seemed to have been crafted for them alone.

They followed a deer path winding upward through the thick stands of trees. So many varieties of trees, branches reaching upward for the dark, midnight blue sky. The forest was thickest here. Higher, the tree line became more scraggly as the mountain jutted toward the sky. Fog rolled around the upper mountain range, closing it off almost permanently from below. The white veil looked much like a cloud formation, as if the mountain simply disappeared into the heavens.

He inhaled the scent of brush, flowers and trees. The vegetation making up the forest floor had its own distinct odor. Wildlife was abundant. This was home to him as both Lycan and Carpathian, yet it was the scent of the woman walking with him that made him feel most at home. She crept into his heart, filled his mind with her brightness and found a way to make him forget every bad thing he'd ever done or seen.

The world around him took on her beauty. Deep, vivid colors he hadn't seen in so long he didn't remember them ever being so vibrant. The leaves rustling in the trees took on hues from a deep forest green to a particularly beautiful shade of silver. Ribbons of water bubbled over winding paths of rock, streamers of shiny diamonds cutting their way downhill to feed the large marshes.

He was content with just walking with her. His body might demand more, and the Carpathian male in him had such a drive to bind her to him that it shocked him, but none of that mattered. Not when she accompanied him and listened to the wealth of information the wind provided just as he was. For the first time in his life he felt he belonged somewhere. He found the ability to want her, that constant demand coursing through his bloodstream, the roar in his ears and drum beating in his pulse only added to the serenity of the moment. Feeling physical need and hunger for her in itself was a miracle.

Tatijana looked up at Fen. The moonlight spilled over him, illuminating every rugged feature, the lines etched deep, his unusual eyes and strong jaw. He looked more Lycan than Carpathian with the moon pulling at his wild side. She found him irresistible with his blend of elegant, charming Carpathian with old world manners and the much rougher, feral, dangerous wolf lurking just under the surface.

He looked the ultimate predator. There was no hiding the wolf blood, not under the moon. She knew if she could see it, so could other wolves. Still, the wildness in him made him that much more appealing to her. She knew Carpathian males were dominant and their counterparts in the Lycan society had to be as well, yet his dominance was tempered with restraint. Fen knew what she needed—freedom.

He accepted her just the way she was. He didn't try to mold her into anything different. She found she wanted his company and his sense of humor. He didn't reveal himself to anyone else, and that made her feel special. He clearly would protect her with his life and he made her feel precious, cherished even. It was in the way he looked at her. The touch of his hand, the tone of his voice, and there, in the thoughts he couldn't hide from her.

She'd been restless since she'd awakened from her long, healing hibernation, looking for something, but she hadn't known what. She'd thought it was information, but it hadn't been so mundane. She'd known almost from the first time she'd entered the tavern at the edge of the woods. She'd been drawn back time and again even though she tried to fight the compulsion. She'd known it was Fen. She couldn't stop thinking about him. She couldn't stop dancing for him, trying to get his attention. She'd avoided asking herself why, but deep down, she'd known he was her lifemate.

She hadn't wanted him, fearing his dominance, but something had changed inside of her. Whatever wall she'd built up had come tumbling down when she watched him fight for his brother, for her and for Zev. He had placed himself in harm's way knowing the consequences, but he'd been unflinching. He hadn't once chastised her, and he seemed to value her opinions and abilities.

He fascinated her. Everything about him fascinated her. She found herself slipping more and more into his mind. He never closed himself off from her, no matter what memories she examined. She knew his newfound emotions could be intensely painful when he recalled the death of his friends. His Carpathian unemotional nature had protected him to some extent, now he was wide open to every feeling, a flood of them all at once.

Fen didn't flinch from his memories. He met them head-on. He processed the sorrow and moved on. He held tight to her in his mind, and that made her feel as if he truly needed her. He didn't ask for anything from her though. Not a single thing. She could feel the need and hunger beating at him, but he never tried to make her feel guilty. In fact, he fully supported her decision. The problem was . . . she wasn't at all certain about her decision anymore. She'd changed her mind. He was her lifemate and there seemed little reason to avoid the claiming. She would follow him no matter what happened, claimed or unclaimed. She knew that her commitment to him was already there.

The scent of flowers hit Fenris as they approached a large open meadow. He tightened his fingers around Tatijana's. She felt small to him, fragile even, yet he knew a core of steel ran through his lady. He enjoyed the way they walked in step together. She fit perfectly with him, not just her height, but her mind, the way she seemed to pour into every dark place, wiping out the battles and the hunting and the destroying of childhood friends. She seemed to be able to bridge the cracks in his soul from too many kills.

Fen's eyes widened. "Night star flower. Did you know they were here? I haven't seen them in centuries. As far as I know they don't grow any-where else."

The blossom was large, shaped like a star, but the petals and texture were much like a lily. The inside filaments were striped and the ovary was ruby red. The stigma was definitely a perfect replica of the male organ, large and erect. The flower was beautiful beyond belief and the scent seemed to burst over both of them.

Tatijana blushed. "The fertility flower. My understanding is the flower was brought back from South America by Gary Jansen, a human researcher. He and Gregori are very close friends. He's done so much for our people, and this flower is thought to have been part of one of those rituals needed to aid in producing children. Gary did so much research and he found ref-erences to this flower several times and he began looking for it. He was the one who found a reference to it on a volcanic range in South America."

Lara had given both Tatijana and Branislava as much information as she could about what was happening in the Carpathian world each rising that she came to give blood before she had returned to South America with her lifemate. Sara had taken over until she got pregnant, and then it was Falcon who gave them blood and snippets of knowledge.

"The ritual is beautiful," Fen said.

Tatijana slipped between two rows of the milky white flower. "The scent is intoxicating."

"It's meant to be," Fen said. "Every ritual between lifemates only brings them closer together."

"I want to try it, Fen," Tatijana said. She made it a casual statement, but there was nothing casual about her prompting. She wanted to perform the fertility ceremony with him. She'd never thought about bringing a child into the world, not after her horrendous childhood, but the thought of a boy with Fen's nature and character made her long for things she didn't have. She could feel her body reacting to the stimulating scent.

"It smells like you," she added.

He stayed very still as if his body might shatter if he moved. "Each blossom takes on the scent of one's lifemate, enhancing the addiction to their taste and smell." He looked as if he were made of stone. "This could be very dangerous, Tatijana."

Fen's voice dropped low. Husky. Velvet soft. Oh, yeah, the fragrance rising from the field of flowers affected him just as much as they did her. He actually looked strained.

"We are lifemates, Fen," she reminded, placing one hand on his chest. She stepped close to him so that her scent enveloped him along with the blossoms. She was blatantly seducing him and she realized she wanted him with every breath in her body.

"You persist in thinking I'm strong, Tatijana. When it comes to you, that is not so." He shook his head, but he didn't step away from her. She could feel the beat of his heart and hear the blood rushing through his veins. His body betrayed him, hard as a rock, his skin hot with need. Even his teeth had sharpened.

"What do I do?" Tatijana asked with a little satisfied smile. This man was her man. *Hers.* Her eyes met his, a little shy. A little tempting. Completely sensual.

Fen knew there was no way to resist her. In truth, he didn't want to. If there was a woman made for silk sheets and long nights, he was certain it was Tatijana.

He selected a blossom, picked it and cupped it in his hands, lifting it up to her mouth, his gaze holding hers captive. "Taste it."

Tatijana, gaze locked with his, slowly took the sexy blossom and stroked her tongue along the bulbous head. Immediately her mouth watered with the addictive taste of spice and forest. Wild. Almost feral. A taste like nothing she'd ever experienced. Fen. Fenris Dalka, her lifemate. It was sex and sin and the ultimate temptation all rolled into one.

She couldn't stop herself from licking along the stigma, determined to get every drop. Clearly the taste had taken on that of her lifemate. She kept her eyes on Fen, hunger for him growing with every passing moment. The fertility ritual wasn't going to be nearly enough for her. Fenris Dalka was going to claim her this night.

She couldn't honestly say when she'd changed her mind. Maybe it was his care of his brother. She knew it wasn't just the pull between lifemates; she liked him, even enjoyed his company, preferred it to being alone. Everything about him appealed to her, when she thought he would be the last thing she wanted.

Even the soft velvet petals seemed to hold his scent. There was no way to control her desire, not for his taste and not for him. Hunger grew with every drop she consumed. The more she drew that spicy nectar into her mouth, the more she craved Fen. When she'd managed to get every single drop, she licked her lips.

"Now what?" Her breath came in little ragged, needy gasps. She knew he could scent her siren's call. Her heart found the rhythm of his and pulsed in time to that strong, steady beat. Deep in her veins, a distinct throbbing began, a drumbeat of need and hunger only he could assuage.

Even as she asked the question, she instinctively cupped her hands around the bloom and offered it to him. She could barely breathe, watching the way he took the blossom from her as if it was the most sacred thing in the world. His soft groan sent a shiver down her spine, and deep inside she felt her body turn hot and needy.

Eyes still holding hers captive, Fen lowered his head to the fragrant petals, nuzzling them with his strong jaw before dipping lower, his tongue stroking sensuously along the ovaries and filaments.

She couldn't tear her gaze from him. It was the hottest, sexiest thing she'd ever experienced. Her breasts actually ached and she could feel the welcoming liquid gathering at the junction of her legs. In that moment, watching him devouring the nectar, his eyes burning over and into her, she realized there was no going back from this, nor would she want to.

Fenris was her lifemate. Pure and simple. She wanted him to complete the binding ritual. She felt her heart was already his. Clearly her body wanted his. She could taste him in her mouth, but she needed their souls bound together in the way of their people.

She had set out to prove something to herself and maybe to everyone else as well. She wanted freedom above all else. But freedom was choice. Fenris Dalka, surrounded as he was by danger, was her choice. She couldn't even say for certain it was the pull of lifemates. She liked him. She respected him. He didn't waste time on useless arguing. She was in his mind and knew he respected her vast amount of knowledge when it came to all the species and their fighting abilities. He didn't relegate her to a safe corner somewhere, although her protection and safety was uppermost in his mind. He made her feel beautiful and special, as if she were the only woman in the world. He listened to her. He liked hearing her talk. He had a sense of humor. And right now, in this moment, he was the sexiest man alive to her.

He took his time with the flower, his gaze growing hotter and wilder as he savored every single drop of nectar. "I love your taste," he murmured.

Her entire body seemed to clench in anticipation. "I am beginning to think it might not be so bad to have you claim me," Tatijana ventured. "I'm getting used to the idea."

His gaze grew hotter. More intense. He lowered the blossom, his eyes moving over her in a slow, possessive manner that left her mouth dry.

"Don't tempt me, Tatijana. Not now. I don't think I have the strength to resist and we both know it isn't the right time."

"I think it's exactly the right time. There's more to this ritual, and I want it done right. Binding us together is logical. This feels like the perfect time to me."

Fen's breath came in a long rush, which added to her happiness—and her certainty that she was right. He tried not to be affected by the fertility ritual, or by her close proximity, but he was. He was just as hungry for her as she was for him.

Fen's eyes devoured her even as he tried to reason with her. "I've been showing restraint because I won't be able to resist sharing blood with you. Over time, you'll end up like me—the *Sange rau*—and until we know what agreement the Lycans and Carpathians come to, mixing our blood could be dangerous to you."

She stepped close to him, a mere breath away, one hand going to his chest. She could feel his heart, rock steady beneath her palm. His skin was hot beneath the thin shirt he wore. "I am your lifemate, claimed or not, Fenris Dalka. What happens to you will happen to me."

"Not so, my lady," he denied. "Should I be killed, claimed or unclaimed, you could choose to live out your life. It would not be easy, but easier if unclaimed."

"I would follow you as most lifemates would, Fen. It does no good to pretend our lives are not woven together. I'm in your mind every bit as deep as you're in mine. My sister, Branislava, has always been my world, yet I follow you wherever you go. We are lifemates. Our blood will mingle and I will become as you are. No matter what you choose, I will follow you. I prefer to be a claimed lifemate, but if you insist I follow you into the next life unclaimed, so be it."

He shifted on the balls of his feet, a slight movement both fluid and graceful that sent her heart racing all over again. His gaze held hers captive.

"Tatijana, it's important to me that you want me for who I am, not because Gregori or any other sought to shame you for being unclaimed. I need you with every breath I take. My body hungers for yours. The more I share with you, the closer I feel, but I will not let any Carpathian tell us what we have to do. This is our life, and I want us to do things our way, at our pace. You have reservations. I feel them in your mind, and until they are resolved and I feel strong enough to protect you from even me, then we will just have to be careful."

Tatijana placed both hands on either side of his head to frame that beloved face. She loved him all the more for wanting the time to be right. He didn't rush her. He never had. "I am your lifemate. I would bind you to me if I had the power, not because Gregori or any other decrees it, but because I know you now. My life is safe with yours. You do not expect me to change or be any other than Tatijana. I want this for myself."

Beneath her hand his heart seemed to burst. Joy crept into his hungry gaze. His eyes had gone from glacier blue to hot cobalt. "You're certain, my lady? Once it is done, it cannot be undone."

"Here, in this field of flowers, right now, before the sun comes up and we have to go to ground. Bind our souls together, Fen." Tatijana didn't feel in the least bit shy. She knew what she wanted and she told him in bold, certain terms. "The moon is full and never again will we have a time like this one. I know you're not safe above ground during a full moon, but tonight is ours. I think it is meant to be, don't you? We have this one chance, Fen. Let's take it together and never look back."

Fen studied her face, loving her all the more for her declaration. Her emerald eyes never once flinched away from his stare. He slipped into her mind and found implacable resolve. She had every intention of becoming *Sange rau*, just as he was. There was no fear of a future with him, only contentment now that she'd made up her mind. If he refused, he would hurt her to no end.

And how could he refuse her? Not when every cell in his body demanded hers. Not when his soul cried out for hers. The ritual words pounded through his veins with the force of a jackhammer.

Fen took control immediately, setting the blossom carefully aside for later, wanting to complete the fertility ritual, but the need and hunger surging so hotly through his body had to be assuaged first. He swept his hand along the rows of flowers lifting their faces to the night sky. Velvet soft petals rained from the sky as the rows parted to allow a soft cushiony bed of sheer fragrance. The scent was a mixture of both of them, heady and intoxicating.

He bent his head to hers, wrapping his arms around her and drawing her into the heat of his body. She fit perfectly, breasts tight against his chest and the vee between her legs riding his thigh as he kissed her, pouring the intensity of his hunger into the haven of her mouth.

Who knew that kisses could be so heady? So intoxicating? She swept him into paradise where there was no way to get enough. Not in this lifetime and certainly not in the next. He craved that soft, hot mouth, full of raw wild honey, lavender and clover mixed together. He kissed her over and over, pulling her closer until her body was imprinted on his. Still, it wasn't enough.

He shed his clothes even as she removed hers, the Carpathian way, with just a thought. Both needed to be skin to skin. He felt as if he couldn't get close enough to her. In her mind, in her body—he wanted to wrap his heart around hers.

They floated to the bed of velvet petals, the fragrance sinking into their lungs, so that blood heated and tension coiled. Need lived and breathed between them. Fen could feel the blood pounding in his veins, whispering at first, then drumming louder, demanding he claim what was his. His soul reached for hers.

He laid her down into the bed of white so that her hair spilled around her face, the thick braid falling across the petals. He loved her hair, that ever-changing color, vivid and bright and as thick as his arm. Before he could stop himself, he unwound the cord binding it, fanning the luxurious length across the velvet petals, and buried his face in the waterfall of silk.

The sensuous feel of her hair against his skin only added to the building hunger. Her voice in his mind whispered to him, filling his mind with her. She felt like warm molasses pouring into every dark crack and fissure, repairing damage, bridging the gaps, until all darkness was gone and there was only his lady with her soft skin and sinful mouth.

He kissed her over and over while the ground seemed to shift and tremble and thousands of stars glittered above them like comets streaking overhead in a rare display. His pulse thundered in his ears, and a drum beat hard in his veins. He could feel his teeth sharpening, hungering for the taste of her.

Her mouth was delicious. Hot. Velvet soft. The roaring in his ears grew as the wind danced gently over their bodies. The embers burning so hot in the pit of his stomach became a roaring conflagration, spreading fast like a wildfire out of control.

Fen lifted his head, pressing his forehead against hers, staring into those beautiful multifaceted eyes. "*Te avio päläfertiilam,*" he whispered. The moment he uttered the words, he knew he had waited his entire life to say them. Nothing in his life had ever felt so right.

He kissed her again, needing to taste that exclusive spice and honey that was only Tatijana. She was cool on the outside like water, blue and green and soothing to the touch, yet a wealth of hot springs deep inside. She moved against him, her body melting under his, her arms sliding down his back to his narrow waist, her hands shaping his hips, pulling him even closer. She turned her head and licked at the pulse pounding in his neck.

"You *are* my lifemate," she murmured against that rhythmic hammering beat, translating the ancient language.

He nudged her knees apart with one thigh, wedging his hips in the tight junction of her thighs. His heavy erection pressed into the heated entrance, bathed in her slick welcome. He wanted to take his time, but his body burned from the inside out, his Carpathian/Lycan blood demanded his mate. Her teeth scraping seductively back and forth over his pulse nearly drove him insane.

"*Éntölam kuulua, avio päläfertiilam.*" The words came out in his ancient language, all Carpathian male, claiming his lifemate. "*Ted kuuluak, kacad, kojed.*"

"You do belong to me," she reiterated, showing him she understood every word he uttered binding their souls with unbreakable threads.

"*Élidamet andam.*"

"I offer my life back to you," she whispered, nuzzling his neck.

Flames licked at his skin. He was all too aware of her teeth so close to his veins. His blood called to her. His lifemate. His lady. The one. "*Uskolfertiilamet andam. Sívamet andam.*"

Tatijana lifted her head to look him straight in the eye. "I give you my allegiance," she answered back. "I give you my heart." The ring of truth was in her voice.

He had never known tenderness, nor gentleness, but it was there inside of him—for her. She was turning him inside out with her generosity and her acceptance of who he was. He'd killed hundreds, maybe far more than he ever wanted to remember and each kill had brought him closer to that hovering darkness. In truth, he had been close more times than he'd ever care to admit, and she saw those terrible moments when only the thought of his brother kept his honor intact.

"*Sielamet andam.*"

"I accept your soul, Fenris," Tatijana whispered into his throat, "and I give you mine to make us complete."

"*Ainamet andam.*"

Even as the words broke from somewhere deep inside him, Tatijana made her own demands. She began a slow assault, moving her hips enticingly.

"I give you my body," she whispered back. "I want you inside me, Fen. I want your blood in my veins, and your heart entwined with mine. I want our souls bound together, but most of all, right this minute, I want you and I to share the same skin."

Even had he wanted, he wouldn't have the strength to deny that breathless, ragged plea. He entered her scalding hot sheath slowly—so tight she robbed him of breath and reason. Her cool skin was in such contrast to his heat, and yet deep inside, those snug velvet muscles were on fire, surrounding and gripping, slowly submitting to his invasion. The sensation was so exquisite he could barely bite out the next words in the ritual.

"Sívamet kuuluak kaik että a ted." He took her body into his keeping for all time.

He could feel her surrounding him, squeezing and milking his cock, her muscles scorching and tight, strangling him with pleasure. He felt her barrier, thin, almost insubstantial. His fingers tightened around hers.

Take a breath. Breathe for me. He wanted only pleasure for her, not even a small bite of pain. He surged forward, making her his, burying his body deep inside hers. He swallowed her gasp and stayed still, allowing her body to adjust to the invasion of his. To him, she was a haven of pleasure.

Her heart found the rhythm of his. Her hips moved, a small telling sign that she wanted, even needed more. Only then did he begin to move, a slow pull to the very verge of her entrance and then burying himself in a long, equally slow assault on both of them.

Tatijana moaned softly, her hips rising to meet his, urging him to move faster. He kept the pace slow and languid, savoring every moment of being inside her.

"Ainaak olenszal sívambin." Her life would be cherished by him for all time. He meant those words. She was his miracle and she always would be.

He found the longer he was in her, that exquisitely tight sheath creating such friction as her muscles clung and dragged over his shaft, it was becoming increasingly harder to concentrate. Her hands stroked his hair, his back. Nails dug into him, sharp little pinpoints of pain that only added to the pleasure building, always building. Her breathless moans and soft little pleas seemed music like none other than he'd ever heard.

"Te élidet ainaak pide minan. Your life will be placed above my own for

all time," Fen said softly. How could that not be the truth? She was everything to him, with her sweet body and generous heart. Even more, she was
a warrior in every sense of the word, unafraid and willing to enter into a life,
that of both Lycan and Carpathian, knowing fully the danger they would
always be in.

As if reading his mind—and she probably was—her teeth sank deep.
His entire body shuddered with erotic pleasure. Through his telepathic connection with her, he felt a scorching hot burn traveling through veins and
arteries and spreading to every organ. His blood merging with hers—the
most basic and sacred of all rituals between lifemates. His body reacted with
a hard surge forward.

"*Te avio päläfertiilam.* You are my lifemate." He had been so certain it
would be best to protect his lady from becoming the *Sange rau*, yet he had
never considered the actual bond between lifemates. He couldn't imagine
continuing without her. Why should their bond be less for her?

Flames moved through him, over him. He could have sworn that the
entire meadow was on fire, yet Tatijana's skin remained cool to the touch.
That sensation of fire and ice added to the scorching heat sheathing his heavy
erection. The night air played over his body and overhead the moon bathed
them both in beams of light. He couldn't have asked for a more perfect
moment.

Ainaak sívamet jutta oleny. The whisper filled his mind, moved to hers.
"You are bound to me for all eternity."

They had been bound together long before he invoked the ritual words
imprinted on him before his birth. She enhanced everything in his life, made
every moment that much richer and more vibrant. More, there was the
solace of her sweet body, a refuge when the world around him didn't make
sense.

Tatijana used her tongue to seal the small pinpricks in his neck and
slowly opened her eyes. His heart leapt, and then shuddered in his chest.
Those multifaceted eyes glowed at him, brilliant emeralds, glazed with desire.
She had never been more beautiful.

"*Ainaak terád vigyázak.* You are always in my care."

With the ritual binding completed, Fen could concentrate on every
nuance, every pleasure point in Tatijana's body. He wanted this night to be

engraved in her mind for all time, just as it would always be in his. He took his time, holding her hips rigid, so that she was unable to move as he surged in and out of her body, sheathing himself over and over in her tight channel. Nothing could have been more pleasurable.

Her little frantic moans and pleas added to the rising tension, the way both bodies built and built toward a soaring crescendo. Still, he kept the pace slow, drowning them both in the swirling wash of ecstasy.

Tatijana felt as if she were burning from the inside out. She was surrounded by heat and fire. His skin—so hot to the touch. His body—so firm, like an oak tree with little give. His hands—strong where he gripped her hips and pinned her so effectively. His hips never ceased their rhythm, long, slow, tantalizing surges that only seemed to inflame her more.

She wanted more. Needed more. Was desperate for more. She heard herself moaning. Pleading. She couldn't stop writhing beneath him. Attempting to lift her hips to meet his. None of it helped. He didn't stop. Didn't speed up. Didn't slow down. Her entire world seemed to be centered on the joining of their bodies. Every nerve ending was inflamed, the tension building higher and higher until she thought she might go insane.

She became aware of his teeth, a subtle pinpoint to that leisurely rhythm that was driving her so crazy, tiny nips along the swell of her breast. With each slow thrust, his teeth scraped over her frantic pulse and her body reacted, clamping hard around him, holding on for life, providing a fresh flood of joyous liquid. Each scrape of his teeth took what little breath she had so that her panting moans became staccato.

He was driving her slowly crazy with need. She couldn't tell which was worse, the waiting for him to bring her over the edge or the anticipation of his bite. She was right there, so close, yet couldn't fall. He stretched her out on a rack of pure pleasure, building, always building until fear that the intensity would kill her skittered down her spine. The scraping of his teeth, the little nips as he worked his way from her breast to her neck limited her ability to breathe properly. Her entire body seemed to shudder and writhe in anticipation.

Fen, I can't breathe. I won't survive.

Then we'll both die right here, just like this.

She heard herself give a strangled scream as his teeth sank deep, right over her pounding pulse, the scorching burn between her legs matching the one at her neck. Pain gave way instantly to pleasure. She writhed under him, arched her back and rubbed her breasts along his chest. She couldn't stay still, moving continually, unable to release the burning, scalding heat and the tension coiling tighter and tighter.

She could feel his pleasure, the mind-numbing pleasure was all pure feeling as he took in the very essence of her. He was everywhere, deep in her body, inside her mind and her blood flowed into him. It was too much and not enough. His pleasure only added to hers. Only took her higher and higher until she was nearly thrashing under him. Pleading with him.

He lifted his head and looked at her, those eyes burning over and through her. Marking her. Branding her. As if he wasn't already stamped into her very bones. He lowered his head to follow that trickle of ruby red drops down her neck to her left breast with his tongue and then closed the pinpricks.

Her heart pounded even harder in anticipation. His eyes burned with such intensity, such hunger and such love for her she couldn't believe she had ever gotten so lucky. Her past, all the years in captivity, all the horrendous things she'd seen, were gone when she looked into his eyes. His fingers gripped her hips hard. She had time for one breath and then he thrust into her hard and her world went up in glorious flames.

His body moved hard and fast and deep, over and over and the flames made her feel like the phoenix, burning clean and pure so that her past and the memories of her father and his malicious experiments, the scars she thought would never be gone were reduced to a fine ash and she was remade—reborn. Stronger. Better.

He dragged both legs over his shoulders, driving into her again and again, so deep, those hard thrusts filling and stretching her with every thrust. His face above her, that beautiful face, was carved with such sensuality she found herself staring, loving, shocked at the intensity of emotion when her body was inflamed and writhing with such need.

It was the most beautiful moment of her life. The complete coming together. His love for her. Her knowledge that she loved him every bit as much. That she could wipe out his past as effectively as he wiped out hers.

And this . . . this rapture. This insane place only Fen could take her was beyond anything she'd ever known or conceived of.

The pleasure was almost too much, the tension building so fast and hard that she couldn't catch her breath. He didn't stop and this time he didn't slow down, his body moving in hers with purpose, deeper and harder as if he would live there always. Flames rose, she could feel his heat engulfing her, burning her from the inside out. She heard her pleas, her calling his name, her fingers dug into his arms seeking an anchor when she felt as if she might not survive the absolute beauty and pleasure.

Her breath came in ragged gasps, her eyes glazed over, but still he continued at a furious pace, the friction building and building, until she felt the first explosive tremor. A series of waves followed, so strong the sensations shook her entire body, running from breasts to thighs, the epicenter in her very core, so that her sheath clamped down on Fen's heavy shaft, taking him with her on a wild, erotic ride she'd never forget. One she would need to repeat often, and even then she doubted if she would be sated.

They lay together beneath the moon, gasping for breath, clinging to one another, savoring every aftershock. She had no idea how much time passed. She was content to lie in his arms, her ear pressed over his heart, happier than she'd ever been in her life.

Fen stirred first, kissing her several times, and then he whispered into her ear. "We have to finish the ritual."

He knelt up, making a vee between his legs for her to fit into. He indicated for her kneel as well, facing away from him. Tatijana did as he asked, kneeling in the soft bed of fragrant white petals. Her body felt flushed and achy, completely alive and vibrant.

"Sit back on your heels and open your thighs," he whispered.

Tatijana felt flushed all over. She'd just made love to her lifemate, but this was way sexy, even after he'd possessed her so thoroughly. She knelt up in front of him, opening her thighs to the night air. Instantly her body reacted with more liquid heat. She felt it trickle down her thighs and felt more sensual than ever.

His arms came around her, palms cupping the weight of her breasts, his fingers and thumb rolling, and tugging her nipples. She gasped as the nerve endings went crazy, sending shocks of electricity straight to her channel. A deep shudder set off another strong ripple.

He urged her to lean back so her head lolled against his shoulder and her breasts jutted even more into his hands. One hand left her breast and made its way slowly down her narrow rib cage to her belly. He pressed his fingers to her shuddering muscles.

"You are so beautiful, Tatijana," he whispered, "so sensitive to my touch."

His touch inflamed her. She couldn't imagine being any more sensitive. She wanted his hands on her always. He was in her mind and knew exactly how every tug and roll of her nipples sent more heat coursing through her veins. She was all too aware of his fingers slipping lower, tracing the dragon over her ovary with a reverent fingertip before continuing the journey lower still.

She closed her eyes, gasping, arching her back when his fingers penetrated deep. Her muscles clamped around him and again delicious strong aftershocks shook her.

"*Tied vagyok.*" He whispered the words against her neck, his teeth grazing over her pulse. "Yours I am."

She loved that he was hers. There could never be another. No other man would ever measure up to him. He reluctantly pulled his fingers from her body and carefully took the blossom he'd set aside earlier, and placed it tight into the junction of her leg so that the soft petals teased her ultrasensitive body. She knew her body was weeping and the flower collected every drop.

"*Sívamet andam.*" His hands were at her breasts again. "My heart I give you, Tatijana."

He had all of her, heart, soul, mind and body. She felt almost as if she was melting with heat. She wanted him all over again. Whatever ceremony with the flower he was completing was a potent one. As she leaned her head back against his shoulder, her hair covered both of them, a long cascading waterfall of silk that felt sensuous against their bodies. Her skin was cool against the heat of his, only adding fuel to the fire of need.

"*Te avio päläfertiilam*—you are my lifemate."

The way he said the words in his own language, a language so ancient and long gone from the world but for a very few, added to the mystique and beauty of the ritual.

"Now you place the flower, as a symbol of optimum fertility for me and say the words to me. We are bound and asking—pleading—with Mother Nature to bless us with our own children during our time in this world or the next."

Her hands shook as she carefully picked up the blossom and turned to face him. Kneeling up as he was, his body rock hard, his face carved so masculine, he was beautiful to her. The moonlight spilled over him, streaking his hair with dancing light. Moistening her suddenly dry lips with the tip of her tongue, she placed their night star flower directly under his very heavy erection. Her hands brushed his sac, fingers lingering a little too long on his thick shaft while the back of her hands slid over the insides of his thighs.

"*Tied vagyok.*" She placed her palms on his bare thighs and looked into his eyes. "Yours I am. *Sívamet andam.* My heart I give you." She meant every word. She couldn't imagine anything more right than giving her heart into his keeping. "*Te avio päläfertiilam.* You are my lifemate."

9

The first few streaks of dawn's light poured over the large field, turning haystacks into small hills of gold. The wind touched the sheaves still in the ground, setting them swaying gently, like a softly rolling wave. The air was crisp and cold, but the sky clear.

Costin Eliade yawned as he stepped outside onto his porch to look over his farm. Satisfaction appeared in every line of his body. His farm had been in his family for two generations, and his father as well as his grandfather had done their best to improve the conditions. He'd been the first to seek a higher education and put the procedures he'd learned into practice. He had been the first to bring cattle to the farm and successfully sell his beef to the outside world.

Farming was hard work, but he was a man who took great pride in doing for his family. His animals always had the best of care. His fields were planted with rotating crops, and his irrigation system was up to date and served him well. He was also proud of the house. Many farmers took great care of the land and the livestock, but neglected their dwellings. His wife had no complaints with her indoor bathroom and year-round running water. He made repairs instantly to anything that she pointed out.

In his area, he had become the first to introduce cattle and procure a large contract. His cattle made up most of their income and had elevated them to a decent living. Losing the steers would be devastating not only to his family, but to several other families who had thrown in with him as well. His dogs guarded the cattle, three of them, and they were fiercely protective.

Costin reached for the walking stick he kept on the porch just behind the column. It fit neatly into the palm of his hand, worn from use. The ground was uneven and being the sole provider for his family, he didn't take chances on accidents. A turned ankle could mean no one feeding the livestock.

Two small goats bleated at him and raced each other around the yard. One leapt up on a small boulder and lifted his nose to the air. The other rushed toward the larger of the two goats, head down in an attempt to butt it off the boulder. The slightly larger goat sidestepped so that the smaller one was forced to jump playfully past. The smaller goat sent his brethren one laughing look and then lowered his mouth to snack on grass just to the left of the corral. Occasionally both looked toward the horses, and then back out to the field.

In the distance, several yards away, most of the cattle still lay in the cushioned grass, sleepy and not quite ready to face the day. A few birds circled above in the sky, a lazy early morning flight before settling in the field to catch any worms not burrowing into the earth.

Costin took a deep breath of the dawn air. This was the time he liked the best. Just between night and day. Everything was always peaceful. There was such beauty surrounding his farm and he was a man who most of the time was far too busy to notice such things, but not at dawn. Dawn was his time to relax and enjoy what he had.

He watched as the wind playfully tugged at the grass in the field, creating a rippling effect and pushing small tornadoes of dirt playfully into the air. The field rolled gently, the smallest of lifts, as if far below, the ground shifted. The soil lifted slightly almost in the middle of the field, no more than a couple of inches. He wouldn't have noticed but for the horses.

He'd left his best four in the corral, close to the small covered shelter he'd built three winters ago. He had six horses, but two were older and he used them mainly for pulling the cart going into the village to the store. A neighbor had taken them for him, just in case his farm came under attack.

The chickens began to fuss. The horses stomped nervously, sensing something he didn't. He stepped off the porch and walked a few feet away from the house, his eyes on the field. There it was again. A subtle movement beneath the soil, picking up speed and racing straight at the corral.

The horses tossed their heads, eyes rolling nervously. His horses weren't the nervous type, but they were eyeing that strange lift in the soil coming straight at them. A hen flew down to the ground, pecking lazily. She cocked her head to one side and then, wings flapping, gained a few feet of air. The shift was so fast it was nearly impossible to see, although the small hen became a full-sized blue dragon, slamming deep into the earth, burrowing fast.

Tatijana came up out of the ground, a raging, clawing werewolf in her dragon's mouth. She shook him hard and dropped him at the farmer's feet. Fen shifted from the farmer's form back to his own, pulling the silver sword from the walking stick and slicing cleanly through the werewolf's neck, severing the head. He slammed a silver stake through the heart.

As if Fen revealing that Costin was merely an illusion and the warrior was waiting for them, the werewolves poured into the farm out of every conceivable cover. Clearly they'd circled the farm and now closed in fast. They came over the roof of the house and barn, converging on the animals, determined to slaughter everything.

Two raced over the house to drop on Fen as he straightened up, the wolves clawing and biting, tearing at his flesh. He reached behind him with one hand and caught one wolf around the neck, jerking him down and off, throwing him toward the porch where the invisible silver net hung between the columns. The wolf slammed into the netting and screamed, hanging there on the slender silver wires.

The second wolf reached his muzzle around and sank teeth into Fen's side, ripping and gnawing in an effort to incapacitate him. Fen snarled, cutting off the pain, stabbing down with a silver stake, driving it deep into the rogue's eye. The werewolf howled and dug his claws deeper. Fen was more worried about the ones he didn't see than the one he did. He spun in a circle, using his sword to cut a wide swath around him, fending off the second wave leaping at him from the horses' shelter.

Wolves flung themselves at the corral with astonishing speed, determined to gut the horses. One wolf threw himself on top of the nearest horse, sinking his teeth into the neck, tearing out great chunks of flesh while a second ripped at the horse's belly. They worked with blinding speed, almost too fast to comprehend.

The horses shifted, revealing the Carpathian warriors Tomas, Lojos and Mataias. The three brothers immediately went back to back, swords at the ready, silver stakes in their other hands. They'd fought wars together and they moved in complete synchronization. The werewolves howled their rage, circling, feinting attacks to keep the attention centered on them while three others leapt up on the corral itself.

The three rogues screamed as the fence flashed silver and sparks accompanied the scent of burned fur and flesh. Tomas nodded his head. "Electricity is a marvelous invention."

"Come on, furball," Lojos added, beckoning with his sword hand to the nearest werewolf.

"Time for a little justice," Mataias added.

The remaining rogues rushed them, using blurring speed, sliding beneath the blades to fling themselves onto the three brothers, ripping with razor-sharp claws at their arms to try to dislodge the weapons.

Gregori shifted back to his own shape, shedding the form of the fourth horse. He came out fighting, trying to unseat the werewolf tearing at him with powerful jaws and teeth. The second wolf, clawing at his belly, dug faster and deeper, trying to eviscerate the Carpathian.

"These furballs are fast." Lojos spat on the ground as he threw a rogue off of him. He was bleeding in half a dozen places even as he stepped up to slice off the head of the werewolf. He had barely started his downswing when his arm was ripped backward.

Mataias tried to wade through the line of werewolves to go to Gregori's aid, but one managed to leap over Tomas and land on his head, strong hands attempting to twist his head off.

The billy goat on the boulder launched himself into the air, ripping at his own horns as he shifted, driving feet first into the wolf on Gregori's back, knocking him back and off the Carpathian warrior. The billy goat's horns morphed into a long silver sword and stake as Jacques took his true form. He sliced through the werewolf's neck cleanly before the body ever hit the ground. Landing on his feet, he straddled the torso, driving a silver stake deep through the heart with his enormous strength.

The werewolf ripping at Gregori's belly spun around and caught Jacques's head in powerful claws, his gaping mouth closing over the Carpathian's shoulder. He tore out a great chunk and went for the throat and a quick kill.

The other goat shifted in midjump, landing behind Jacques and the rogue wolf. Falcon slammed the silver stake through the werewolf's back straight into his heart. The wolf went down hard, taking Jacques to the ground with him.

Falcon reached down and yanked Jacques up. "Not safe down there, bro. These boys came for a fight."

"Bloodthirsty, aren't they?" Jacques acknowledged with a little grin. He wiped blood from his face. The wolf had bitten him numerous times in a few short moments, tearing out great chunks of flesh.

Gregori cut down another leaping for Jacques's back. "Fen wasn't kidding when he said it's the ones you don't see."

As ten of the werewolves had rushed the horses, a good dozen had gone for the all-important cattle. The cattle lying in the grass didn't move. One raised his head, but simply looked bored as the large wolves descended on them. The fastest rogue bore down on the lazy steer fast, saliva dripping from its gaping jaws. Still the cattle didn't move, even when the wolf landed on the steer's back and lowered powerful jaws to take a bite out of the placid animal's neck.

The other wolves followed, leaping upon the sleepy cattle, sinking claws and teeth into the unsuspecting animals. Teeth clamped down hard on rock. The entire field was filled with boulders, the cattle mere illusions. The three cattle dogs shifted into their natural forms—that of three Carpathian hunters.

Nicolae Von Shrieder, a renowned vampire hunter, wielded his silver sword, the blade flashing scarlet as he removed the head of the nearest rogue. Even as he did so, before he could plunge his stake in the chest of the still clawing creature, two leapt upon his back and tackled his legs, taking him to the ground. They were so fast, these werewolves, leaping higher and moving quicker with no warning than even the vampires he'd hunted for centuries had given.

Traian Trigovise hit the ground running as he shifted. The werewolf coming at him was huge, seemed to be all muscle, teeth and claws and lightning fast. He dove under the wolf's reaching claws, sliding along the ground, hooking his arm around the wolf's knees to bring him down. He slammed the silver stake into the heart before the rogue could recover. Two more were on him before he could make it to his feet. He tried to dissolve, but the claws digging into his flesh prevented escape.

The third cattle dog shifted fast. The Carpathian known simply as Andre was as elusive as a legend could get, moving fast, a shadow only, streaking through the air and literally ripping the wolf from Traian's back. He didn't slow down at all, moving continuously, his sword flashing in the early dawn's light, wreaking havoc with the number of werewolves attacking.

Andre's swordsmanship was superb. He'd fought in centuries past and the sword felt right at home in his hand. He seemed to flow, his feet smooth and sure. The blade gleamed bright red, blood dripping onto the ground and spraying through the air as he calmly cut through the raging wolves.

Traian and Nicolae followed in his wake, slamming silver stakes into hearts as Andre cut the rogues down. The three made short work of the werewolves who had attempted to attack the cattle. Costin Eliade and his cattle were safe on a neighboring farm, leaving the Carpathians to build their trap for the rogues.

It took a few moments to realize they had successfully destroyed the twelve werewolves bent on killing the livestock. Both Traian and Nicolae were surprised at the lacerations and chunks of flesh missing from their bodies. Blood streamed down their chest, necks and backs. Nicolae had slash marks across his belly. Andre had bite marks on his legs, but other than that, he'd remained unscathed.

Traian grinned at Nicolae. "What did we learn from this?"

"That Andre needs to give us both sword lessons," Nicolae acknowledged. "We had to do all the grunt work and look at us. Next time, I want to be the one dancing with the sword while you two do mop up."

Stop congratulating yourselves and get over here. We could use a little help. Gregori used the common Carpathian telepathic communication, his voice dripping with sarcasm.

Traian, undaunted, flashed another quick grin and winked at Nicolae. "We also learned werewolves fall for illusion and we had the advantage here."

Nicolae, Andre and Traian moved quickly across the field to go to the aid of the other Carpathians just as a second wave of werewolves leapt over rooftops to drop down on the warriors fighting off the rogues.

I don't like this, Fen said uneasily to Tatijana. *Get into the air and see if you can find who is coordinating their attack. They have to have a leader directing them. This is too organized.*

He fought his way toward Gregori. He'd dealt with rogue packs throughout the centuries and none were this large. He'd never seen a single pack this large.

How many dead? he asked Andre.

Twelve. Andre's answer was short and clipped. *I have come across smaller packs of rogues, but none this size and none this well organized.*

Just the fact that Andre added anything at all to his statement further alarmed Fenris. Andre conveyed tension in his terse sentence. Like Fen, he realized something was definitely not right about the attack. It was too well orchestrated, especially that second wave of werewolves sent to join their brethren.

Tatijana immediately took a running start and leapt into the air. As she did so, a werewolf launched himself from the horse shelter rooftop and swatted her out of the sky. Her body tumbled toward the ground, the rogue catching her around her rib cage between his teeth. Fen leapt to meet him, driving his silver sword through the werewolf's gut. As the rogue opened his mouth in a gasp, Fen yanked Tatijana to him, streaking upward to avoid hitting the ground. The werewolf hit hard, rolled and came to his feet howling, holding his ripped belly with one hand while his red eyes tracked Fen and Tatijana.

Drops of bright blood fell to the ground, almost on top of the wolf. Tatijana clamped her hand over the bite marks. She could feel Fen's building rage that she had been bitten. He was anxiously trying to examine her as he went airborne.

I'm all right, Fen, she assured. *They're so fast and they jump so high, it's hard to judge a safe distance from them.*

I can feel your pain. Don't tell me an untruth, Tatijana, I need to know how you are.

It hurts like hell, but nothing's broken. I thought for a moment he was going to snap my ribs like twigs, but you were on him so fast.

I am Sange rau. *Faster than they are.* His voice was grim.

Even as he replied, telling her the strict truth, she felt the warmth of healing energy slipping into the wounds on her rib cage. There was instant relief. *Thank you.*

Always.

The Carpathians were seeing for the first time the damage a rogue pack could have on them. When they realized just how difficult it would be to destroy the *Sange rau*, they might change their minds about allowing such a mixture of blood to live. It was tantamount to having a nuclear weapon aimed at one's head.

Fen reversed his direction and this time aimed for the ground, moving like a speeding bullet straight toward the werewolf he'd knocked from the sky. The wolf leapt to meet him. At the last moment, Fen pushed Tatijana back skyward, giving her the opportunity to shift into her dragon as he met the wolf head-on. He was moving so fast, a mere streak in the sky, that when he hit the rogue, he nearly went through the body. His fist shot through the chest wall, the silver stake he held in it slamming through the heart so that the wolf was dead before both ever hit the ground.

You play rough. Gregori had observed the encounter in spite of fighting off the latest wave of attackers. His voice was thoughtful. Wary.

Now they begin to understand, Fen said to Tatijana. *He will be more concerned that I keep my distance from his prince.*

Tatijana sighed. *Our prince. Don't pretend you would not guard him with your life. I am in your heart and soul, remember, wolf man? I see what you are doing. You want Gregori and the others to realize what they're up against. Mere words are not enough. They have to see for themselves.*

No one Carpathian hunter will ever be able to defeat the Sange rau *alone,* Fen told her. *Only if a miracle occurred. The combination of Lycan and Carpathian abilities is lethal. The Lycans know it, because they have seen thousands of their kind killed, nearly wiping out their species, by only one or two of these monsters. The Carpathians have not faced them, and their arrogance will get them all killed—and possibly their prince if they don't process the information fast. Even now, they can't fathom an enemy like the* Sange rau.

Gregori, the prince's primary guardian, would be the first to grasp the enormity of what they were up against. His natural instincts already made him suspicious and wary of Fen. Fen didn't blame him any more than he could blame Zev, who was the Gregori of the Lycans. He was directly responsible for the welfare of the council and it was his duty to keep the Lycan people safe no matter what part of the world they resided in.

Rough is the only way with werewolves. You can't ever underestimate them, Fen answered Gregori.

This pack is well organized. Too well organized.

That is so, but the master is not here. I would know. The Sange rau *has left this battle to those he commands.* Fen knew Gregori would catch the worry in his voice.

The fighting near the corrals was fierce. Gregori was wounded, and yet he displayed no emotion when he answered. He could have been having a picnic in a park instead of fighting for his life. *You believed this master would be close.*

I had hoped. Fen thought Abel might throw Bardolf under the bus in order to weaken the Carpathian fighters. It would be a sound strategy, especially given the endless supply of rogues he'd acquired along the way to do his bidding. *I need to find the one who has their master's ear. There is a way I can perhaps get information on either Abel or Bardolf, maybe both. At least find out what they are up to. It's risky, but if I get what we need, well worth it.*

He felt Gregori's instant rejection of the idea. Tatijana echoed him with her distress.

How risky? We will need you to continue to educate our fighters . . . obviously.

From where Fen was, he caught occasional glimpses of Gregori. The werewolves had definitely targeted him for termination. Fen's vision narrowed as he watched for a moment, the way the wolves circled Gregori. The prince's guardian had been made known to them. He'd been involved in the fight earlier, but why such sacrifices? The bodies of werewolves lay sliced and staked around the prince's guard, and yet still they came after him.

The nagging fear in Fen began to blossom into urgency. Something else was going on here, and he was missing it.

I think it's worth the risk. I need to know that you and the others can finish this.

We've got this, Gregori assured, even as he fought off two more wolves driving straight at his throat and belly. He knew how they fought now, gutting their prey and tearing great chunks of flesh away to make their victims weak from blood loss.

Zev and his hunters will come quickly, Fen advised. *It's important that all Carpathian hunters know the difference between Lycan and werewolf.*

Gregori ducked a leaping rogue, so that the creature sailed over his head and right onto Andre's flashing blade. *All of us know exactly what the Lycans look like. We have their scent as well. Each of us visited the inn where they were staying. There will be no mistakes,* he said with certainty.

The elite may sense my presence, but they cannot identify me. I doubt they are that sensitive in the midst of blood and death, but Zev is more than elite, he is their best. It is possible. Fen had already located his entry point. He needed to use the ground so whoever was directing the battle from his safety zone wouldn't see him coming.

Gregori grunted in pain, quickly cut off, as a great beast landed on him, driving him to the ground. The moment he was down a frenzy was triggered among the rogues. They threw themselves at him, piling on in spite of the other Carpathians racing to Gregori's aid. The Carpathian hunters realized Gregori was the prime target and they redoubled their efforts to fight their way to him. It was Jacques who cut the head from the wolf tearing the flesh from his back and Nicolae who sliced through the one burrowing beneath him to rip at his belly.

The moment Fen saw the others going to Gregori's aid he whirled around and indicated the ground in the middle of the field where the werewolves had tried to surprise the farm. *I need a tunnel to follow back to the original source without him seeing. I'll cast an illusion while you burrow quickly for me.*

Tatijana waited until Fen sent images of her and her lifemate rushing to aid Gregori, entering the intense fighting near the corrals. The moment the illusion was strong and intact, she shifted to her dragon, trusting Fen to keep her from being seen. Tatijana's dragon followed the trail beneath the soil, burrowing through the earth fast, leaving behind a nice-sized tunnel for Fen to follow in.

Fen left the Carpathian warriors to it. He had one purpose—to track the attack back to its source. He had to find the captain directing the battle, and that meant trusting that the Carpathian warriors would defeat the werewolves at the farm.

Tatijana had paid great attention to detail and the weapons the Carpathians had made were truly exceptional. The Carpathians had shared the information he'd given them on the rogue wolves attacking in packs and they were prepared for the fight. They'd lured the pack to Costin Eliade's farm and coordinated the defense. They'd done everything they could do to decimate the pack and give Fen the chance to find the lair of at least one of the *Sange rau.*

He knew without a doubt that with two *Sange rau* so close to the prince, it was only a matter of time before disaster struck. Fen plunged into the hollow tunnel Tatijana's dragon had carved out and moving with his Carpathian/Lycan speed began the race to ferret out the hiding place of the pack's captain.

Tatijana, nothing is adding up. The Sange rau *should have led their pack away from Carpathian territory immediately on realizing they were so close.*

She was quick on the uptake, following his train of thought. *You believe they have an agenda.*

Absolutely. I've gone over it a million times. There are only three reasons I can think of that would keep them here. The best would be if either Abel or Bardolf or both were badly wounded and couldn't leave. But that wouldn't explain sacrificing a good part of their pack.

The dragon burrowed back toward the surface once she hit the beginnings of the marsh.

So something much more sinister.

The drive for a lifemate doesn't always end when a Carpathian turns vampire. I've seen cases where they believe a woman would somehow restore their soul and yet they can keep to their ways. Abel may have returned with that idea in mind.

Tatijana already knew him far too well. *But . . .*

That might be a secondary issue, but more likely Mikhail is the intended target. Did you see the wolves going for Gregori? The prince and a Daratrazanoff have a special bond that creates an unstoppable power. Gregori was specifically targeted.

No matter the reason, the *Sange rau* had to be dealt with. None of them could afford any more time passing before ferreting the masters out and destroying them.

You'll get them, Tatijana said firmly, every confidence in her voice.

Fen wished he had that same confidence. The nagging worry had grown to a full-blown alarm going off. He *had* to find the captain directing the werewolf pack's attack on the farm.

The tunnel beneath the ground ended abruptly in the marsh. Reeds choked the water. Waterfowl ducked heads beneath the surface and rose to flutter wings peacefully, as if no abomination had passed near them. There was no telltale shriveled greenery to mark the way of a vampire, but then he hadn't expected any. He had known all along neither Abel nor Bardolf would be close.

That nagging, growing alarm blared at him. He reached for the prince's guard. *Gregori, I need to know where the prince is.*

He got the immediate impression of fierce battle. The Carpathian hunters, despite as many as there were and with the traps set for the rogue pack, had not found it so easy to destroy a ferocious and well-trained pack on the offensive.

He is safe.

The voice was clipped. Gregori would not disclose the location of the prince to anyone. Fen could tell by that implacable tone. Gregori was severely wounded. He would need care and blood and the ground to heal him. If the pack couldn't kill Gregori, wouldn't this be the next best thing? Wounding him so badly that he had no choice but to go to ground? The alarm, rather than quieting with Gregori's assurance blared even louder.

The children? he persisted.

They are safe. Gregori was terser than ever.

Fen cursed in his native language. *Tatijana, with the main force of Carpathian warriors concentrated here on the farm, the prince, and the all-important children are left with little protection.*

Gregori would never leave them without protections, Tatijana said. *He's overboard when it comes to the prince's protection. He doesn't even listen to Mikhail at times. He would never leave the prince unguarded with a rogue pack near. And don't discount the women. Your* Sange rau *and the Lycans might, but many of them are good fighters.*

Fen didn't reply. He wasn't about to tell her he didn't find the information reassuring. He emerged out into the open, although he took care to mask his presence. He stood on the edge of the swamp, taking a careful look around, seeking the best vantage point above them, where the captain direct-ing the battle would be able to see the entire farm.

Tatijana shifted into her human form and slid beneath his shoulder, standing close so that her scent enveloped him. It always amazed him that the huge blue dragon could be his lifemate, this woman with her shapely figure in human form.

"Can you find the location of the prince?"

She shook her head. "No one, not even Dragonseeker, can get into Gregori's mind."

"Then we'll have to do this the hard way."

The way he said it alerted Tatijana instantly. "What are you planning?"

He sighed. She wasn't going to like it. He didn't like it, but he felt there was no other choice. "The pack was sent out, but neither of the two main leaders came here with them, not even to ensure the orders were carried out effectively. That tells me Bardolf and Abel have plans far beyond the destruc-tion of Costin Eliade's farm. And we need to know now what that is."

Tatijana tipped her head up to look at him. She was already in his mind, but she didn't understand what it was he planned to do. "I don't like where this is going," she admitted, looking him straight in the eye.

He slipped his arm around her. He didn't like where it was going either. "I think Abel or Bardolf plans to hit the prince while the pack distracts the Carpathians and Lycans by hitting the farm."

There was a small silence while she turned the idea over in her mind. "That would mean they would know about the trap at the farm and delib-erately sacrificed some of their pack as a distraction."

"Or they didn't know it was a trap but sent them to devastate the farm no matter what, believing warriors would come to defend it. Certainly the elite Lycan hunters will come," Fen said, but he didn't believe that was the case.

Abel was Carpathian. He knew how Carpathians thought and how they fought vampires and other enemies. Abel also knew Lycans, or at least rogues. He'd always been known for his intelligence. He'd orchestrated the attack. Fen would bet everything he was on that.

Across the marsh, a boulder jutted out from the mountain. He was certain he would find the wolf put in charge of running the attack on the farm. He indicated the spot to Tatijana. "Over there, that's where we're going to find him. I'll need you to stay close to me, but out of his sight at all times, even when you think he's dead."

Tatijana frowned at him, placing a cautionary hand on his arm. "Are you going to tell me what you're going to do?"

"There has to be something more at play here then a rogue pack over-running a farm in retaliation for my interference. Bardolf might make the mistake of underestimating the Carpathians, he was Lycan before he embraced the vampire, but Abel was not only Carpathian, but a successful and a valued vampire hunter. He would know what he was running into by coming here."

"That would mean he's deliberately sacrificing the rogue pack." She shook her head. "It doesn't make sense, Fen. I just think you're wrong."

Her tone of voice told him she wasn't certain of the truth of what she was saying aloud. She wanted him to be wrong, but none of it made sense to her. She was also very aware he had sidestepped her earlier question.

"We don't know how big this pack is. I think we're dealing with an enormous pack and if so, he's got pawns to spare. He sent out twenty-five or thirty to the farm, figuring he might lose over half. What are the others doing? Where has he sent them? These wolves were a sacrifice for a greater end. There is no other explanation."

"You have to tell me what you're going to do." For the first time, fear crept into Tatijana's voice. She tightened her fingers around his arm. "Fen, don't throw your life away."

"Gregori isn't going to reveal where the prince is to anyone else, certainly not to me, and I don't have time to try to persuade him. He doesn't yet understand the difference between a vampire and the *Sange rau*. The combination of mixed blood adds to the cunning and intelligence as well as physical capabilities."

Now she was really alarmed. Her green eyes grew multifaceted, brilliant with color. He had no words to reassure her. Instead he bent down and brushed a kiss along the corner of her mouth.

"Bardolf believes he's in a full partnership with Abel, but there is no such thing among vampires, and ultimately, Abel and Bardolf are both vampires. Abel will sacrifice Bardolf in a heartbeat."

"You're telling me these things in case you don't survive. I'm your life-mate, Fen. My fate is tied to your fate. I will follow wherever you lead."

He shook his head. "The prince must not die. Above all else, Tatijana, every Carpathian must put the life of Mikhail Dubrinsky first. Our kind will not survive his passing. Not at this time. If something happens to me, you must convince Gregori it is Mikhail they will try to kill. Everything else they do is secondary, no matter how it looks."

She shook her head, but he could feel her conceding he was right.

"I have seen signs from the beginning that Abel is the master *Sange rau*, clearly orchestrating every detail of the attacks. It was Bardolf's shadow sliver at risk, not Abel's. Although there was no risk to Abel, he was the one using the familiar Bardolf created."

He dropped another kiss on the top of Tatijana's silky head and then glanced at the sun. It was barely making its appearance. "Perhaps you can give us cloud cover. Bring it in slowly, make it natural," he suggested.

Tatijana swallowed hard, but nodded. "No problem."

"Abel is the key here. I need to remember everything I can about him. His friends and allies. I think he was a first or second cousin to the prince," Fen mused aloud. "Abel always seemed a decent sort. I was surprised that he had turned."

"What are you going to do?" she demanded.

This time there was no denying her. In any case she had to know, because in the end, she was his only real chance at succeeding.

"There is a reason why we sever the head from the shoulders, Tatijana," he said. "The silver stake through the heart takes time for the werewolf's body to recognize and the brain continues to function. That brain contains all information the wolf has acquired over his lifetime and sometimes, others as well. It also contains the hatred and bloodlust the werewolf feels in a lethal, concentrated amount. Enough to kill any who has harmed it and dares to try to acquire its knowledge."

"Are you crazy? No. Absolutely no. We don't even know for certain that Mikhail is in danger."

"We do know that there are two *Sange rau* close and everyone, human, Lycan and Carpathian alike are in danger. This has to be done."

She heard the absolute implacable determination in his voice and took a deep breath. "Alright then. Tell me what to do."

"That's my lady. I can do this, Tatijana, because I have you." He glanced up at the sky. The cloud cover she'd promised had drifted in slowly, pushed by a gentle wind. She had such a skill, her touch light. He doubted if even an elite Lycan would have detected the clouds were not natural. He was lucky to have her and he would treasure this memory of her straight spine, straighter shoulders and clear eyes.

"Tatijana, you cannot show yourself by word or deed. No emotion. You will be tempted time and again to step in, but you cannot. If you do, all will be lost. But"—he took both her hands—"you are Dragonseeker and there are none greater or with more honor. That moment when I call to you, come for me, pull me back. Do you understand?"

She turned to face him completely, grasping his forearms as a warrior would. Her green eyes stared directly into his. "I will not lose you, lifemate. I will come for you."

He believed her.

10

F en had learned at a very early age just how fast fights began and ended. The battle at the farm might be ferocious, but it wouldn't last long. He didn't have a lot of time to find out the information he needed. He took to the sky, rocketing through the air, using his *Sange rau* speed, leaving Tatijana behind. He couldn't afford to take the chance that Abel's captain would see and identify her, not with what Fen intended to do.

The rogue paced along the edge of the boulder, his gaze intent on the scene below him. He wasn't happy with the losses of his pack members. Unlike the vampire, the werewolf still retained some emotion for his pack. Unfortunately the lust for blood overcame every civil behavior learned over hundreds of years.

Fen recognized him. He'd been a young member of Bardolf's pack. He'd been smart even as a young pup. The pup had been called Marrock. Fen could well believe that he was a great strategist when it came to running a battle.

He blocked out everything good he knew about the werewolf. Marrock had long ago succumbed to the need to kill for fresh blood, believing he was superior to all other species and his wants came first. In essence, he was the Lycan vampire—a murderer.

Fen came out of the clouds with blurring speed and was on Marrock almost before the wolf knew he was under attack. The body recognized it before the brain. Eyes narrowed and went bloodred. The muzzle began to take shape, teeth exploding in the mouth in a desperate attempt at self-preservation. Fen drove the silver stake deep into the heart, taking the werewolf to the ground, watching the hatred and need for retaliation concentrate in those red, glaring eyes.

Fen could feel regret now, thanks to his lifemate, and once again he had to acknowledge bringing justice to murderers one knew was easier without emotion. He shook his head, pushing all emotion aside so he could do his job. He couldn't hesitate, or feel fear. He had to be absolute in his quest. In control. He was *Sange rau*, both Carpathian and Lycan and there was little in the world stronger than him—or his will.

He thrust his mind into the mind of the dying rogue. Hatred. Rage. Bloodlust. For a moment those things threatened to consume him as they had consumed the mind of Marrock. His entire world went red, the intensity of the bitter emotions pouring into his mind, infecting him, as if the wolf had a disease that transferred from one brain to the other. Feelings of superiority crept in. He was more intelligent. He could think faster than others, size up situations and figure out before the others what they were going to do. Physically he was faster, stronger, his body rejuvenated faster.

Fen hung on and breathed away the worst of the intense emotions, knowing Marrock was trying to trap him. The danger of being infected with the bloodlust was the worst and that pushed at him harder than anything else. He craved blood. Was addicted to it. Why shouldn't he have the right to take what he was designed to take? He was born to be a predator. There was no taming what or who he was.

That much was true. Every Carpathian male he knew was a predator. Every Lycan. And he was a combination of both. The drive was already in him. Why should he pretend to be someone else? He could take what he wanted or needed and no one would be able to stop him. Their leaders had all become victims, afraid of who they were, ashamed even.

The whispers began, another voice promising riches, promising to live the way they were meant. He could have anything at all he wanted, money, power, women, and blood, as much fresh, rich blood as he desired.

Fen latched onto the memory in Marrock's mind, striking hard and fast, pushing open the door so that a flood of memories assailed him at once. Marrock's induction into the pack of rogues. That first taste of a kill, so unforgettable and never to be repeated, no matter how many times one killed or how. Marrock's rise to captain.

Fen pushed down the rising fear when he saw the enormity of the pack. He couldn't get exact numbers because they were broken down into smaller groups, but they all answered to Bardolf and Abel. Few actually met them, but all were sworn to be loyal to them.

He had to get past the older remembrances Marrock had offered up as a wall to conceal the information Fen was after. Marrock snarled and fought, trying to ensnare him in a muddle of recollections, pushing the need for fresh, adrenaline-laced blood on him, sharing the taste of hot blood, anything to keep Fen out of his most recent memories.

Fen pushed harder, using more strength, careful not to tip his hand, but slipping past those memories that wouldn't help him. Marrock still had options that could be harmful to him. He didn't want to trigger any of them until he got the information he needed.

Fen found the most recent orders from Bardolf. Marrock was to keep the Carpathians busy, kill as many as possible and inflict as much damage as possible to force them to go to ground to heal. A second force would find the humans who aided in protecting children, destroy them and grab any Carpathian women helping to protect the children. The two forces were to attack simultaneously and keep everyone busy, allowing Abel and Bardolf to slip in and assassinate the prince.

The moment he accessed the memory, he knew he had only seconds before Marrock would try to warn Bardolf or Abel and also bury Fen in a quagmire of poisonous emotions to prevent him finding his way out. Red and black poured into his mind even as he reached out.

"Lifemate." One word. Everything. The miracle.

She was there instantly, his own dragon lady, and she knew exactly what to do without him telling her. She poured into his mind, driving everything else out, and as she extracted him from Marrock, she swung the silver sword and removed the head, making it impossible for the wolf to warn the *Sange rau*.

Fen took the time to drag her into his arms and hold her tight against him for just a moment, breathing in her sweetness and steel after the blood-lust and mayhem in Marrock's poisoned mind. She was a breath of fresh air.

"You make a pretty good partner, my lady."

She smiled at him, rubbing her hands over his back. "It's nice to know you have such faith in me. That was horrible. Never do that again."

"You'll have to get to the village, Tatijana, and warn the others at the farm that they're being detained there on purpose. I'm going to try to stop the *Sange rau*. I'm the only one with a chance."

She shook her head. "Not two of them. Not alone, Fen."

"Go, Tatijana," he said gently. "Hurry. The rogues decimate entire villages."

Fen brushed a kiss against the corner of her mouth and took to the air, streaking back toward Mikhail's home. He had been in that house and knew it was designed to help protect the prince. There had to be more, a complete protection system Gregori was confident would stop any attack on the prince—but they believed the attack would come from a vampire—perhaps even a master vampire. They hadn't designed their defense system to deal with the *Sange rau*.

Tatijana took a deep breath and stepped off the jutting cliff, streaking toward the village. She didn't want to imagine what the werewolves would do to humans barely waking in their homes.

Gregori, Mikhail's in danger. Fen has gone to try to stop the Sange rau *from getting to him. But there are two of them.*

There was a short silence. Pain exploded in her skull—Gregori's pain—quickly cut off. *Fen does not have to worry. Mikhail is completely protected.* There was utter confidence in Gregori's voice.

Mikhail's guardian would check anyway, no matter how arrogant or confident he sounded. Tatijana knew Gregori would fight his way to Mikhail with his last breath.

The Sange rau *sent another group of rogues to attack the village, specifically targeting women and children of our kind.*

Again there was a short silence, but this time, Gregori kept the pain from his terrible wounds from touching her. *I wondered why the Lycans didn't show up. They must be defending the village.*

Of course. She'd been in Zev's mind. He was every inch the man

Gregori was. His confidence. His abilities. His complete determination to defend others. He would definitely wade straight into battle and shield human and Carpathian alike.

As she approached the outskirts of the village, she felt the disturbance almost immediately. The scent of blood was overpowering. She shifted into her dragon form flying high enough, she thought, to keep any rogue from leaping on her as she circled the battle scene.

She spotted Zev in the middle of what looked like twenty werewolves. He was whirling around in a circle, his silver sword crimson red, his long hair flying as he cut a path to a single dwelling that appeared under siege. His long coat flared out as he spun, the sword never stopping, his boots placed perfectly and fluidly as if he was dancing, not in deadly peril. He seemed to flow, confidence in every line of his body. He looked almost beautiful there in the early morning light. Had it not been for the blood spraying through the air, she would have thought she was watching a ballet.

Around the back of the house, four others fought with swords and silver stakes, while another was on the rooftop of the house. That was a woman, and her form was every bit as good as her male counterparts. A sixth Lycan was down in the corner of the yard, two rogues tearing at him. Two Carpathian women were fighting their way to him.

Use the silver stakes, Tatijana advised the woman with thick dark hair who slammed her fist into a werewolf's face, driving him back and off her. Tatijana was amazed at the woman. Clearly Carpathian, she was used to fighting vampires, it showed in every line of her body. Women rarely fought the undead, not like this woman. Tatijana wanted to meet her immediately.

The clouds above had gone black and lightning veined the one directly over the house. Destiny Von Shrieder glanced up to make certain the blue dragon was out of harm's way. *Dragonseeker, I'm about to bring down the lightning.*

Tatijana circled back around, giving the dark-haired woman plenty of room. From her vantage point she could see the fierce fighting in the front of the house where Zev fought alone. Out of the house came two men. She recognized both of them. Gary Jansen and Jubal Sanders rushed without hesitation into the mass of werewolves attacking Zev. Gary shot a crossbow with silver arrows very accurately, firing rapidly while Jubal used some strange weapon she'd never seen before.

The two humans were fast and confident, and had obviously seen battle before. The werewolves outnumbered them and were extremely fast, ducking the flashing sword Zev wielded and using the house itself as a springboard to leap onto their backs in an effort to take them to the ground. Zev seemed to be directing the two men in their efforts, but their constant movement prevented her from aiding them. She couldn't flame the werewolves without harming the defenders.

The rogues were extremely aggressive. One lit a torch and flung it at the house. Zev cut him down, but two wolves waiting their moment leapt from the roof and landed squarely on his shoulders, their combined weight driving him to the ground. Immediately the rogues surrounded the fallen Lycan, determined to kill him fast.

Gary hit one of the wolves in the head with a silver arrow, and then smashed another out of his way with the crossbow as he ran toward Zev.

"Go, go, keep going," Jubal called out. "I'll cover you."

The wolves leapt on Zev, tearing at him, biting great chunks of flesh from him. One very aggressive rogue went for the kill, going for Zev's throat, while the others seemed determined to eat him alive. Zev fought back, using silver stakes and a shorter knife, but the rogues quickly pinned him with their numbers and weight.

A wolf managed to claw Gary's arm as he raced past, leaving four long bloody furrows. Gary didn't slow down or falter. He ran through the double line of wolves determined to get to Zev before the rogues killed him. The wolf got a second hold on him, spinning him around. Gary stabbed an arrow deep into the wolf's thigh and broke free, jumping over a downed werewolf and putting on a burst of speed.

He'd broken through the double circle of rogues surrounding the elite hunter and now they were between him and the house.

Jubal let loose with the weapon on his wrist, a strange spinning very sharp tool. The edges of each of the four blades must have been tipped with silver because as the spinning blades struck a wolf, cutting through his arm, the veins in his body seemed to grow rigid and turn color on his skin.

Gary fired off two more arrows, downing two of the wolves in a fighting frenzy over Zev. "Can you get up?" he yelled.

Zev slammed a silver stake into the leg of the wolf pinning him down while the second rogue tore at his belly, determined to rip it open and yank out the insides. Zev threw himself away from the wolf, rather than covering his belly, sacrificing his body by giving the rogue time to rip him open, but giving himself the room to swing his sword, lopping off the wolf's head.

Blood spurted from Zev's belly and the wolves behind them seemed to go into a frenzy the moment they scented the weakness in the elite hunter. The headless wolf fell across Zev in a deliberate attempt to pin him to the ground as well as to protect his own heart from being staked.

Gary yanked the body away from Zev, slamming a patch over the deep laceration in Zev's belly. Clearly the Carpathians were more prepared this time for the way the rogues fought. He followed the body of the headless wolf down to the ground, driving an arrow through the heart, using sheer strength fed by adrenaline.

The moment he bent over to punch the arrow deep, a rogue slammed into Gary's back, driving him away from Zev and deeper into the front yard. The circle of wolves howled their approval and rushed the two men cutting them off from the house. Now that the three men were separated it would be easier to pick them off.

Zev staggered to his feet, found his sword still in his hand and was already in motion, flowing through the yard toward Gary, while Jubal fought with his strange weapon as well as a silver machete.

Tatijana saw Gary go down under the weight of several wolves and she dove fast, the dragon streaking down out of the sky, her touch delicate in spite of her size and speed. She blew a steady stream of flame across the werewolves' backs as they bent, ripping, biting and tearing at Gary's body. Zev swore—she heard him over the howling growls and screams of the burned rogues—as he fought his way toward Gary.

The rogues whose backs had been burned by Tatijana leapt away from the downed man, looking to the sky, more angry than hurt. She tried to pull up fast, knowing the giant leaps they were capable of. One leapt from ground to fence and then was nearly on her.

Out of the corner of her eye, Tatijana saw the dark-haired woman run with long, confident strides over the rooftop and leap to intercept the rogue in midair. She held a knife in one hand and a silver stake in the other. The werewolf and woman slammed into one another hard, the momentum helping to bury the stake deep in the chest of the wolf. He howled, falling, reaching for her, and the woman simply dissolved in the air.

Who are you? Tatijana asked as her dragon streaked for the clouds. *And thanks, I've had my belly ripped open already by one. It's no fun, I'm Tatijana.*

Of course. Clearly she'd heard of Tatijana and Branislava. *I'm Destiny, lifemate to Nicolae Von Shrieder.*

Tatijana had met Vikirnoff Von Shrieder and his lifemate, Natalya. Natalya was related to Tatijana—she was Razvan's sister and a Dragonseeker as well. She guessed Vikirnoff and Nicolae were brothers. Where one was, the other probably wasn't far behind. She was grateful to see a woman like Destiny joining aggressively in the battle. Tatijana wasn't a woman to stand by and let others do the fighting if it was necessary. She didn't know a lot about the policies of the Carpathian people, but it had been impossible over the last two years when others brought blood to Branislava and to her not to become familiar with a few of them.

Can you tell how bad Gary is? From her vantage point, Tatijana's dragon could usually see far better than any human or Carpathian, but there were so many wolves fighting around him, she couldn't get a clear look at him.

I'm trying to get to him now, Destiny confirmed. *These things are fast. If the Lycans hadn't joined the fight, we'd be in real trouble. We only had a couple of men here to help defend the children. They hit us only a few minutes ago, but the casualties are high. If it wasn't for the Lycans, especially the one they call Zev, we'd have a few losses.*

They hit the farm at the same time and they targeted Gregori, Tatijana informed her.

Her dragon made another circle high above the combat zone. The fighting was furious in the front, with only Destiny, Zev, Gary and Jubal trying to combat the number of wolves. In the back, there were six Lycans battling a larger force of rogues.

Is Mikhail's son in the house? Gregori's daughters? Tatijana was worried the sheer number of rogues would overrun the small defenses they had.

No. Sara's children. Sara is on bed rest and Gabrielle is there with her. Gabrielle and Shea are in the house to be the last line of defense for the children.

Vikirnoff and Natalya? They had to be somewhere close and yet they weren't in the middle of the fray. Tatijana couldn't imagine either of them sitting out a battle.

Destiny ducked under one of the beasts, slipped past another and got to Gary. She plunged a silver stake through the back of the wolf tearing at Gary's insides. Crouching, she got an arm around his back. He was a mess, his belly ripped open and great chunks of flesh removed from his chest. Once the wolves got a victim down, they tore him apart. Gary made an effort to rise, but he had to clamp both hands over his open belly, and he'd lost so much blood so fast that he was weak. The blood made him slippery and trying to lift him was impossible. The patch didn't begin to cover the mess.

"Come on," Destiny hissed. "We're not out of trouble here."

They were ringed by snarling wolves. She was bleeding in dozens of places. Zev was in nearly as bad a shape as Gary, and Jubal couldn't get past the wall of werewolves to get to them.

"Get out of here," Gary urged. "You can make it through without me."

"That's not an option." Destiny looked to the sky. *Tatijana, flame these bastards. I've had enough of them.* She raised her voice. "Jubal, Zev take cover now!"

With that, completely trusting Tatijana to do as she asked, she took Gary back to the ground. Before she could cover him, he was covering her, hands over her head, his body on hers, pinning her down.

"You're crazy, you know that," he whispered in her ear, laughter in his voice in spite of the pain he had to be in.

Without hesitation, both Jubal and Zev hit the ground. Jubal, still close to the porch, managed to roll partially beneath it. Zev went down where he was trusting several wolves would follow him to the ground, which they did, effectively covering his body.

The world around them erupted into flame as the dragon blasted out of the clouds, neck extended, wings creating a windstorm to help fan the white-hot flames as they burst in a steady stream from the dragon's gaping maw to the ground below. Rogues, half wolf, half man, found fur and hair on fire, and dropped, rolling, desperate to try to put it out.

The temperature in the front yard went from crisp and cold to instant searing heat. The roar of the flames thundered in their ears. The wind rose to a fever pitch as the great wings fanned those flames so that they jumped from one rogue to the next. She hovered overhead another moment or two after she quit spraying fire, her enormous wings acting like bellows and then with a loud trumpet, she once more gained altitude.

"Now, now," Destiny hissed. "This is our chance."

Zev leapt to his feet and began slamming home silver stakes, heedless of the flames, uncaring of any injury to himself. Jubal rolled out from under the porch and followed his example, staking as many as possible.

"Use the sword," Zev called out, tossing his sword to Jubal. "Any that's been staked, sever the head."

Jubal caught the sword easily with one hand and swung at the head of a rogue charging at him who had remained relatively unscathed.

Gary made a huge effort and rolled off of Destiny, coming up to his knees, careful to keep his hands over his ripped belly. The rogues were adept at their chosen fighting method—to incapacitate their opponent by eviscerating them. It took only seconds. Gary had saved Zev, but he hadn't escaped the pack and their relentless, tireless thirst for blood and the kill.

Destiny didn't think any of them had escaped. Every Carpathian and Lycan had very bad wounds. Once again she got her arm around Gary. He made a valiant effort and struggled to his feet, going completely pale, black blood pouring from his gut. She knew those signs, and they weren't good. Gary obviously knew it as well, but he said nothing, breathing deep to try to make it through the burning yard, back to the house.

Gregori. We have great need, Destiny called to their healer on the common telepathic path. *Gary won't live out the hour if you cannot make it to us. No other has the skill to save him, not even Shea.* She did not say that she doubted even Gregori could save him, but it was in her mind and he would know.

Zev moved with astonishing speed, so efficient and skilled at killing the rogues, Tatijana from above couldn't help but watch him. He flowed through the yard, making his way toward Destiny and Gary, even as he cut down numerous wolves. Those wolves rolling to put the flames out were in danger from both Zev and Jubal. Jubal wasn't waiting for the stakes—he sliced through bodies and then staked them as he went.

Tatijana's dragon had turned the tide in the front yard. She circled back for another view of the furious fighting in the backyard. The wounds were severe. The largest group of wolves had attacked the backyard, probably because there was more cover, trees, brush and even a fence the wolves could use as springboards.

Zev, Gary and Jubal had taken on the entire pack in the front, while most of the Lycan elite hunters were defending the back. Destiny clearly floated between, lending her skills to either side, depending on who needed her the most.

Tatijana studied the scene below her, trying to find where she could come to the aid of the Lycans. The Carpathian woman was small, but she was a powerhouse, mixing it up with wolves, blood streaking her body. Some of the blood belonged to the enemy, but clearly she'd been bitten several times and those claws tore open great lacerations.

Tatijana couldn't communicate with the Lycans, but she could with the Carpathian woman. This was Joie Trigovise, Traian's lifemate and Jubal's sister. Several times it had been Joie who had given blood to both Tatijana and Branislava as they healed their minds and bodies in the rich soil of the Carpathian Mountains.

Joie had a cap of thick glossy dark brown hair. Her features were strikingly beautiful, yet at times she blended in with her surroundings, so, like now, it was difficult to keep an eye on her.

If there is a way to get all the Lycans under shelter, I could flame the were-wolves, Tatijana offered. *It certainly turned the tide in the front.*

Joie didn't answer right away. She rolled beneath a wolf, slashing at the back of his knees as she gained the back porch, where it looked as if six or seven werewolves were tearing at the back door.

Tatijana heard a child scream, a high-pitched frightened sound and then another younger one began to cry. The pitch of the roof over the back porch prevented her from seeing exactly what was going on or how close the wolves were to breaking into the house, but the cries of the children made her heart pound and spurred her into action.

The female Lycan leapt the wooden railing of the house. "Over there." She indicated the corner of the porch where three more of the rogues were rushing to gain access.

Her name is Daciana. She's a heck of a fighter, Joie informed Tatijana as she angled her approach to intercept the three wolves hoping to break into the house with their other pack members.

Are they into the house already? If they were, it was time to let her dragon form go and get into the fray with Joie, Daciana and the other Lycans. The werewolf pack couldn't be allowed to breach the house and get to the children.

Tatijana knew Shea, Jacques's lifemate, was inside. She was a doctor, a healer, not a fighter, but she would defend the children. Joie's sister Gabrielle was in the house as well. She was a researcher, not someone who engaged in battles, but she would fight fiercely to protect the children. Sara had to be inside, Falcon's lifemate. They had adopted these children and Sara was pregnant with a child. She'd miscarried her first pregnancy and was on bed rest with this one, but no doubt she would fight with the others in spite of everything.

Stay in the sky, Joie said, clearly reading her concerns. "Daciana, we've got a dragon on our side. If we can drive these wolves back into the open and get our people under shelter, Tatijana will flame them."

Daciana glanced upward toward the dragon circling above them. As she did, one of the werewolves leapt from the railing of the porch up to the roof and launched himself skyward at the exposed underbelly of the dragon.

Oh no you don't. Tatijana hissed the words in her mind.

She'd had her belly ripped open once and wasn't about to have it happen again. As the wolf rose, his claws outstretched, she swung her neck around, using her wedged-shaped head as a bat to knock him away from her. He sailed end over end into the canopy of the trees several yards away from the house. He landed hard, snarling, raging and grasping at the branches to keep from falling.

He yelled threats at her, shook his fist and began climbing down fast as she swooped over his head. Tatijana knew it was reckless of her, but even inside the dragon's body, she felt the rush of adrenaline. The little scream of a child, the sound of crying, had gotten to her as the blood and wounds hadn't.

The werewolf reversed direction with astonishing speed. She didn't even see him, just the furious shaking of the branches as he rushed back up the tree to the very top of the canopy and flung himself at her a second time.

His claws hooked in the dragon's softer belly just as Zev came over the top of the roof. Tatijana could see the Lycan moving as if he didn't have a hundred deep lacerations, as if his belly hadn't been sliced open. He flowed over the peaked roof, his eyes nearly glowing, the metallic gray color so intense they could have been gems.

He never took his gaze from the rogue attacking her, never looked down to make certain his footing on the pitched roof was solid. His eyes were penetrating, piercing, totally intimidating and unblinking, fixed on his prey. He launched the silver stake. It spun through the early morning light, gleaming, spiraling, rocketing toward its target.

Zev continued running over the roof even as he threw the stake, down the other side and then dropping into the backyard. He landed in a crouch right in the middle of the swarm of werewolves, sword in hand, already drawing another stake from his belt.

The stake spinning through the air flew straight and true, slamming deep into the chest of the rogue clawing at the dragon's soft underbelly, driving through the heart. The wolf went rigid, dropping like a stone from the sky. Droplets of blood followed him down from where he'd torn the dragon open.

Zev fought his way through the wall of werewolves to get to two of his hunters who were fighting back to back, ringed by the rogues. Both were slashed, bitten and wounded, but neither wavered for an instant. Zev joined them.

"Work your way back to the house," Daciana called to them.

Daciana and Joie cut between the wolves and the back door, each coming in from a different side, presenting a united front and a barrier to the entrance of the house. Destiny burst out of the back door, joining them. She was covered in blood.

Joie frowned. "You all right?"

"It's mostly Gary's. He's in bad shape. I called in Gregori, but I doubt he'll get here in time." Destiny's voice was grim. "Shea's doing what she can."

The wolf directly in front of her leapt over her, crashing into a window, shattering the glass. A child's wail came from somewhere inside. Daciana leapt after the rogue, landing on his back, driving him down to the ground. He was strong, pushing himself up fast with both hands and legs, trying to shake her off of him.

"To the house," Zev directed his hunters.

"Lykaon is down," Daciana yelled. "North corner."

Zev and the two other hunters with him aggressively began fighting their way to their fallen brethren. The other two Lycans both made their way toward the corner as well. Lykaon was on the ground, more dead than alive.

Tatijana could see blood spraying into the air and three wolves tearing at the body. Frustrated, she circled again. If the Lycans would just get to the porch, she knew she could lay down a stream of flames that would take the fight out of the remaining wolves. As hard as they fought, the pack kept the hunters back from their downed comrade.

Tatijana couldn't stand it. She wasn't going to sit up safe in the sky while one of the Lycan fighters was being torn apart or eaten alive right under her nose. She dove fast, folding her wings close to her body and sped toward the yard. Trees were close and she was forced to shift to tiny molecules and streak down to the fallen Lycan.

She shifted again just before she landed, her dragon breathing a steady stream of red-orange flames to clear out the wolves as she hovered just above Lykaon. The wolves tearing at him caught fire. The scent of burnt flesh and fur filled the air.

Tatijana was extremely vulnerable on the ground. The moment the wolves were off the body, she gathered the fallen warrior in her front talons and took to the air with him. A dozen rogues leapt at her. Most hit her scales and dropped off, but one flung himself onto her back and sank teeth into her neck—or tried to—the spikes and scales prevented him from harming her.

She had to work hard to get airborne with the injured Lycan in her talons and the wolf on her back. Two more tried to grip her tail, but she thrashed it hard and they fell away. Again, it was Zev who came to her aid. He threw a knife, and just like the stake, the throw was done with deadly accuracy. The wolf on her back grunted hard and fell away, leaving her to rise easily. She circled, watching for her chance as the Lycans fought their way to the porch.

With so many defenders, the few werewolves who had tried to gain entrance into the house abandoned the small confines for the yard. Tatijana tucked Lykaon close to her body and once more dove, spraying a steady stream of flames through the pack, setting most on fire. Just as in the front yard, the burning wolves retreated, rolling to try to put out flames while the hunters emerged and did their best to destroy as many as possible.

Tatijana landed in the front yard, grateful that Daciana and Destiny ran to take the fallen Lycan from her. She was weak, exhausted and bleeding. The moment she shifted, her knees nearly gave out.

Destiny glanced at her over her shoulder while she and Daciana half carried Lykaon toward the house. "You all right? Can you make it?"

Tatijana nodded. The werewolves were on the run, but it wasn't safe. Nearly every defender had been wounded, many of them seriously. She knew many members of the rogue pack would linger to try to get in as many kills as possible. She forced her shaky legs to work and made it to the porch just as Gregori and Jacques emerged, startling her. Jacques immediately reached his arm out her to steady her.

Both men looked as if they'd been in a war zone. They were covered in wounds and blood, Gregori especially. She couldn't see how he could still be standing. He had to be in pain, but there was only purpose etched into his face.

Gregori flung open the door to the house. "Where is he?"

The wounded lay, sat or stood waiting for Shea's attention. Joie, Destiny and Daciana began to help her attend them. Shea looked up the moment they entered. Jacques helped Tatijana to a chair and went immediately to his lifemate.

"Are you all right?" Zev asked.

Tatijana nodded. "I lost a little blood. I'm not nearly as bad as the rest of you."

"We got our asses handed to us," Zev said with a sigh. "This pack is very large. Too large. It doesn't make sense." He looked around the room. "Where's Fen?"

Tatijana let out her breath slowly. "They hit us in three different locations. At first we thought just the farm, but then when we discovered the pack had been divided into thirds, we divided our forces. Fen has experience fighting them, so he went on to the third location."

Zev nodded. "Makes sense." He looked around at the wounded. "Where's Gary? He saved my life and I wanted to thank him."

There was a small pregnant silence. Shea looked at Gregori and shook her head. "I did what I could. He's holding on to see you."

Gregori strode into the room Shea indicated. It smelled of death and blood. Gabrielle, Joie's sister, sat beside Gary, holding his hand. There were tears on her face. Gary was gray, pain edging every line.

His eyes met Gregori's.

"You look like hell," Gregori greeted.

Gary tried a smile that didn't quite come off. "You look the same." Even his voice was no longer his own, but a mere thread.

Gregori stood over Gary, his silver eyes nearly liquid. "You have accepted our way of life, my brother. You are jaguar, which means you can become one of us."

Gary shook his head.

Gabrielle gasped. "I don't understand. Why are you even hesitating? Gregori can save you this way."

Gregori gently moved her away from the fallen man. He put his hand over Gary's very gently. "He knows the human perspective will be lost once he becomes Carpathian and so far, that perspective has served us well." He knelt beside Gary, leaning close. "I will do what I can, and give you my blood, but know this, you are my brother-kin. I do not lose kin easily. If I see this will not work, protest or not, I will convert you. Do you understand?"

Gary managed a nod. He closed his eyes and slipped into unconsciousness. Gregori sank to the floor beside him and quickly shed his body to begin the work of healing the man who had been more of a brother to him than his blood brothers.

II

From his vantage point above the Dubrinsky home, Fen studied every detail carefully. There was a feel to the mountain that made him uncomfortable, but he couldn't tell if it was an actual defense in place, a safeguard, or the *Sange rau* were already well ahead of him. He allowed his senses to flare out, reaching beyond the boundaries he'd always imposed on himself.

Being *Sange rau* could be dangerous, much more so the more often one used the incredible gifts. Arrogance and superiority were treacherous, insidious traits, threatening the very moral fiber of one's beliefs. Without Tatijana to keep him grounded, Fen knew the things he had done and would do this day were inherently risky.

Carpathians were born of the earth. Most of their safeguards were woven from natural things and reinforced with spells from the mages when the two species had been close. There were always psychic footprints. No one could move or breathe without expending some energy, and Carpathians were very good at feeling or seeing it.

Lycans were born of the earth as well. Both species epitomized both ends of the spectrum. They were predators, fast and ferocious. They enjoyed the battle and both had a taste for blood. On the other hand, they were loyal and dedicated to their mates and children. Both species put honor and integrity high on their list of attributes. They were willing to sacrifice for the better of their species.

Both species embraced the night. Both read the wind. And both were gifted with tremendous powers. There had always been a balance. As many gifts that both species had, each had weaknesses. The *Sange rau* didn't have such a balance and that could be a very bad thing.

Fen continued to scan the mountain behind the Dubrinsky home as well as the surrounding forest and clearing around it. He took his time, patient as always. Often in a battle, the first to move was the first to die. He was facing not one, but two *Sange rau*. It was often the little things that gave one an advantage. He knew from experience nature spoke to him if he just listened.

His connection to Mother Nature was stronger than ever and each small shift of the wind brought him information he might not have picked up on. Small nuances, but now they told such stories. There were ripples running over the ground leading to Mikhail Dubrinsky's home. He could see them, as if they were tides ebbing and flowing in the sea.

Around the house itself, up and down the stone walls and even beyond to the mountain where the structure was built into it, thousands of symbols and patterns ran like an endless loop. It looked a bit like the code on a computer, moving fast and changing rapidly. It would be impossible for a vampire or a Carpathian or even a Lycan to read it that fast. But he was none of those things and neither was the enemy he was hunting. The *Sange rau* could process that fast.

Scattered throughout the ground surrounding the house from every direction, he spotted disturbances in the earth. He wasn't certain whether he saw those because he had mixed blood and heightened senses, or if his connection to Mother Earth provided the information. Nevertheless, the traps were revealed to him and he had to believe they would be to his enemy as well.

Another small shift in the wind brought another scent he recognized instantly. *Dimitri. Are you insane? You cannot come here. You should be in the earth, healing.*

Little brothers were the very devil. Dimitri had always gone his own way, even as a child. He was stubborn and made up his own mind about things. It wasn't that he ever argued. He was quiet about his stubbornness. He simply did what he thought was right.

Did you really think I'd let you come here alone and face these killing machines? Dimitri asked, taking the offensive, which was another trait Fen remembered from when his brother was a child.

Dimitri materialized out of the sky, right beside him. He looked pale, almost translucent, but as tough and as implacable as ever. When Dimitri made up his mind to do something, it took a miracle to change it.

"You never did have any sense," Fen answered, but he was secretly proud of Dimitri. His brother was the type of warrior to find a way, no matter how injured, to come to his aid, especially when the battle looked hopeless. "You know we'll be lucky to come out of this alive."

"When has it been any other way?" Dimitri asked.

"They're after the prince," Fen pointed out. "This place is a death trap for vampires, but it isn't going to stop either of the *Sange rau*. If I can see the traps and safeguards, they will be able to as well."

Dimitri studied the ground below him. "Just how much of your blood is running in my veins?"

Fen frowned. "Why? Can you see the traps, too?"

"Not exactly. I know something's there. And I feel the mountain's off. Different. It feels like a living, breathing sentry to me."

Fen pressed his fingers to his eyes. "I didn't trust anyone else to heal you properly. I should have had Tatijana give you her blood. Mine is . . . tainted. Over the centuries, we've shared blood so many times . . ."

"Your blood is just fine," Dimitri said. He shrugged his broad shoulders. "I've always known I would end up like you. Lycan and Carpathian. It's meant to be. I run with the wolves. I understand them. I always have."

"The Lycans will condemn you to death. You know I have to go to ground each full moon to avoid detection. And what of your lifemate?" Fen turned to look his brother in the eye. "That woman is the most powerful psychic I've ever encountered. She crossed a continent to heal you. I don't know very many powerful ancients who can do that."

Dimitri smiled for the first time. "She's amazing."

"Yet you haven't claimed her."

"Her father wants me to wait until she's at least twenty-five."

Fen raised an eyebrow and then turned back to studying the Dubrinsky stronghold for signs Abel and Bardolf had already unraveled the safeguards. He couldn't imagine his brother living by anyone else's rules. "And you're abiding by that?"

"Skyler and I have an understanding. When she's ready, she'll let me know. If she isn't twenty-five, well, hopefully her father and uncles will let me live." There was only the slightest trace of humor in Dimitri's voice. "She was adopted by Francesca and Gabriel Daratrazanoff."

Fen swung around to stare at his brother in shock. "The legends? As in Gabriel and Lucian Daratrazanoff? They're alive? And Gabriel is her father?"

"That would be the one."

"Any chance he's not all that fond of her?" Fen asked.

"He adores her."

"Of course he does." In spite of the perilous situation they were in, Fen found himself grinning. "You shouldn't worry about this little fight we're about to enter, because your woman's daddy is going to tear you limb from limb."

"Don't sound so pleased." Dimitri nudged him. "You're my brother. You're supposed to be on my side."

"Maybe your only chance is to become fully *Sange rau*," Fen said, half meaning it. He nodded toward the eastern side of the mountain behind the Dubrinsky's house. "Do you see that? A shadow slipping along the cracks. He's moving fast, too, but staying in the crevices and cracks. That's Bardolf. So where's Abel?"

"Someone's just emerging out of the forest. It looks like Gregori's here to defend Mikhail," Dimitri announced. "Over there, he's stopped and is looking around. The man has always been careful when it comes to Mikhail's protection. I'm not surprised he's here."

Fen didn't answer. He turned his attention to Gregori and the minefield in front of him. Gregori was a striking figure in anyone's war. Tall, with broad shoulders and a thick muscular chest, with his long black hair drawn back and his strange silver eyes, he looked a frightening figure with his immaculate clothes and his confident air.

Where was Abel? Would the *Sange rau* allow Mikhail's guardian to remain unharmed? Mikhail and Gregori had a powerful bond. Together they could destroy nearly any enemy, even a mixed blood if they were allowed the time to initiate their complete sovereignty together. Abel would know that and he would move heaven and earth to stop Gregori.

Gregori walked toward the house. Except he didn't walk, he floated, avoiding the traps on the ground. He veered away from the structure and advanced toward the mountain the back of the house was built into. That had to be where Mikhail was. A mountain could provide all kinds of securities and ways to escape. Gregori went straight to the entrance and began the complicated unraveling of the safeguards so he could enter.

Fen found himself frowning as he shifted his gaze to the shadowy figure of Bardolf a few hundred feet above Gregori. He should have been leaping on the guardian, but instead, he was still keeping to the cracks and crevices as he made his way down.

Something's not right, Dimitri, he whispered into his brother's mind.

Alarm thundered in his very blood. He could hear it roaring in his ears. His heart beat even harder. He *knew* something was wrong.

Other than the shadow you've already spotted, everything is as it should be. There was a question in Dimitri's tone. If Fen said something was off, he believed him, he just couldn't see it.

It's Gregori.

Dimitri narrowed his eyes and focused on the Carpathian. *He looks fine to me.*

Exactly. And he shouldn't look fine. He was attacked at the farm. Viciously. Totally targeted by the pack. He's torn up. No one, not even Gregori could recoup this fast.

So I'm looking at?

That has to be Abel. Fen caught his brother's forearms in a tight grip. *Bardolf is fast. You won't be able to kill him, but do as much damage as fast as you can. Use everything you have in your arsenal and stay out of his reach. He's not only vampire, but he's werewolf. Stay alive, brother.*

Dimitri gripped Fen hard. *I expect to see you in one piece when this is over.*

Fen couldn't let himself think about his brother and how terribly injured he'd been. Dimitri was a grown man, an ancient warrior who had been in countless battles. He was courageous and he definitely was skilled. Fen had passed every bit of knowledge he had on the *Sange rau* to his brother in the hopes that would aid him should he ever have to fight one. Dimitri already had heightened senses, proving Fen had given him a good amount of mixed blood. Now it was up to fate.

Like we practiced. Exactly like we practiced. You know how to do this.

Dimitri nodded. *Like we practiced.*

Fen had to trust he'd prepared his brother for this day. He stepped off the cliff and shifted, his Carpathian/Lycan blood masking all energy as he streaked through the sky to drop down behind Abel just as the safeguards came down. Abel stepped cautiously into the entrance to the mountain. As he did, a Carpathian male came down the wide tunnel leading deeper under the mountain to greet the prince's guardian.

"Gregori, I thought you were at the house healing Gary. We expected you'd stay with him."

Gregori didn't reply, but kept quickly striding toward the Carpathian.

Fen struck hard, driving his hand, silver stake firmly in his fist, through Abel's back, seeking the heart. The Carpathian male raced down the corridor to come to Gregori's aid.

Abel, using the enormous speed and strength of the *Sange rau*, leapt forward, dislodging Fen's fist. He spun around and attacked, dropping the façade of Gregori, aggressively slamming his fist into Fen's chest. As he did, his muzzle grew and he clamped his teeth over Fen's shoulder, the bite pressure enormous, tearing through muscle down to the bone.

Vikirnoff Von Shrieder was shocked by few things, but the monster attacking was no ordinary vampire. He'd gotten through intricate safeguards as if the locks weren't even in place. He'd looked and smelled just like Gregori. Carpathians had such an acute sense of smell they could place one another by blood alone, and Vikirnoff would have sworn he had been talking to Gregori.

He'd never seen anything move as fast as the two men fighting in the corridor. He felt like he was watching a fight scene on television in fast-forward. Hands and feet, shifting, and moving, the two combatants slammed into the rock walls and hit the high ceiling with neither giving an inch. He couldn't help. There was no way to get off a weapon, they were moving too fast.

Mikhail, are you seeing this? Vikirnoff had never been afraid in a fight, not even when facing a master vampire. He always figured he had even odds.

He was a skilled fighter and had been battling for centuries, but he'd never in his life seen opponents like these.

I believe you are looking at the true Sange rau *Fen told us of.* Mikhail studied the two combatants. *He was correct in saying we have never faced an enemy such as this one.* Mikhail's voice had little inflection in it. He was merely stating a truth.

Vikirnoff drew his bow and pulled out a silver arrow. All of them were armed against an attack by the rogue pack. He doubted he could get the arrow off where it could do any good, but just in case the monster got through Fen, he was determined to stand between it and the prince.

Mikhail, he had a perfect image of Gregori in every way. He even smelled like Gregori's blood. And he blew through the safeguards as if they weren't even there.

Clearly our safeguards are for the vampire and not this new enemy. Again, the prince's tone was matter-of-fact. He had to have known that the *Sange rau* had come for him, but he seemed more interested in studying the way the creature fought. *They are almost too fast for even our eyes to keep up with.*

Natalya. Vikirnoff reached for his lifemate. She was in the corridor ahead, closer to the prince, waiting just in case something got past her lifemate and endangered the prince. *Do not attempt to fight this creature if he gets past me.*

If he gets past you that means you are no longer in this world, she answered. *I will do my duty and defend my prince and join with you as soon as possible.*

Neither of you will sacrifice your lives uselessly, Mikhail decreed. *If he should get past Fen, fall back and let us see if any of our defenses work against him. The sun is climbing in the sky. Surely even the* Sange rau *will be affected as we are. After all, he is vampire,* Mikhail reasoned.

The fight between Abel and Fen raged on. Neither seemed to get the upper hand and both bore terrible wounds, but that didn't slow them down. Most vicious fights were over in a matter of minutes, but the two seemed to sustain the physical energy necessary to continue the battle indefinitely.

"Join me, Fenris Dalka. You can see we are the superior race. We can command the wolves and the Carpathian people alike. The humans will be our cattle. You will die here defending a species that should be extinct," Abel proposed as they broke apart.

Blood ran in streams from both of them. Abel wiped at his chest and licked his fingers, smirking as he did so.

"Stalling isn't a good idea, Abel. If you're waiting for Bardolf to join you, you'll be waiting a long time," Fen said.

The smile faded from Abel's face. His eyes turned wholly black. Fen didn't wait for the attack, but launched himself fast, going low, sweeping the legs out from under the *Sange rau*. He stabbed down hard with a silver stake, missing the heart, but opening another hole in Abel's chest. Blood poured out, hopefully weakening him more.

Abel rolled, his legs locking around Fen as he lifted up and slammed him down on the hard ground, trying to drive the air from his lungs. As he forced Fen into the ground, the hard rock beneath them rose in sharpened spikes. Fen grunted as he landed on his back, the spikes driving deep. Just that fast, the spikes dissolved, although the damage had been done to Fen's back. Fen rolled up, punching his fist through Abel's ribs. The snapping sound was audible.

As Fen regained his feet, Vikirnoff could see blood pouring from the deep punctures on his back. Just as he was certain he would lose so much blood that the vampire/wolf cross would have the advantage in spite of the broken ribs, the wounds in Fen's back appeared to close and the blood stopped flowing.

Abel and Fen crashed together again, this time, Fen spinning Abel around to slam him face first into the side of the tunnel. The walls of the tunnel had grown thick crystals, thousands bursting out of the rock. The mountain shivered. The force Fen used to drive Abel into the wall was so enormous the crystals shattered into thousands of razor-sharp pieces.

Abel pushed back, slamming his head into Fen's forehead. Fen staggered back, giving Abel room to turn. His face was a mask of hatred and blood. Fen looked cool and confident, no expression, not of anger or pain. They both moved with breathtaking speed, Fen firing several rapid punches into Abel's face, driving the crystals deeper into the flesh so that Abel wore a mask of bloody gems.

The two combatants moved so fast Vikirnoff found himself standing a few yards away, his bow lowered and his mouth opened. Not only were they blurred, but they were also changing the landscape around them into weapons so fast he could barely catch it all. As fast as one would create a weapon, the other would neutralize it.

Vikirnoff, fall back. You and Natalya join me.

Vikirnoff hesitated. He had one purpose in that moment—to protect his prince. He had been assigned a position by the prince's primary guardian . . .

Now. You can both serve me best from behind our safeguards.

There was pure command in Mikhail's tone. Vikirnoff abandoned his position and hurriedly made his way down the corridor to the prince. Natalya joined him. Both could still see the furious fighting taking place.

Mikhail brought down the last and most intricate of their safeguards to allow Natalya and Vikirnoff through. Immediately he resurrected them again, all the while watching the two *Sange raus'* furious battle.

"Fen is slowly moving his opponent backward. It's slow," Mikhail pointed out, "but clearly he's trying to get him out from under the mountain. There's a disturbance outside as well. I can feel a second battle taking place."

"The man fighting with Fen is Abel, an ancient. I believe he's connected to your family in some way," Vikirnoff said. "It took a few minutes to place him."

The mountain shivered again as Fen and Abel crashed into the ceiling. Great spikes of spun silver burst from the walls, burning into Abel's body from every direction. Abel screamed with pain. Fen was on him instantly, driving one of the stakes deep into the chest by using his fist. He grabbed Abel's shoulders and hurled him out of the corridor, back into the early morning sunlight.

"I can see why the Lycans have forbidden the cross of blood between Lycan and Carpathian," Mikhail mused. "There seems to be no stopping them. Abel didn't slow down, not even when he was pierced with silver stakes."

"I feel like we should be trying to help Fen," Vikirnoff said. "But I'm not certain how we can go to his aid."

For the first time he knew what Mikhail, as the prince of their people, must feel like when he couldn't go out and join in a fight. Carpathians were warriors. It wasn't in their nature to sit back and watch another battle, especially if that person was one of their own. He had never considered how

Mikhail must feel when he was relegated to the sidelines, always having his people standing between him and danger.

Vikirnoff knew he was the prince's last protection, but still, everything in his body, mind and very soul needed to be out there helping Fen. He felt cowardly, crouched behind a safeguard while another hunter was outside alone with a killing machine.

"You'd just be in his way," Mikhail pointed out, reading his mind. "He can't look after you and fight this monster. Besides, it appears as if Fen is a killing machine as well."

Vikirnoff nodded. Natalya moved up beside him, close, not touching, but offering him comfort, fully aware of his frustration. He was grateful to her. He couldn't help feeling better when she was near. "Still, there should be something we can do for him."

"He'll need blood," Mikhail pointed out. "The patches he applies when Abel tears him open appear to be temporary."

"Gregori needs to see this."

"He's busy at the moment trying to make certain we don't lose Gary, but I'm passing on to him everything about the *Sange rau* that we observe."

Fen was aware of the unease of his fellow Carpathians, but grateful that they used good sense not to join in the battle. He couldn't watch out for them and anticipate Abel's moves and react at the same time. As it was, part of him was engaged in the battle taking place outside.

Overhead, the clear early morning rays were gone, replaced by a ferocious storm. Black clouds churned and roiled overhead, a giant cauldron of boiling nature. White lightning laced the edges of the clouds, flashing and sparking, great forks veining each of the dark clouds. Few were better than Dimitri at creating the ultimate storm.

A whip of lightning lashed the mountainside, hitting directly into a thin crack. Sparks rose up, and Bardolf yelped. He sprang into the air, furious that Dimitri had struck him again with the whip of lightning. Once was bad enough, but the Carpathian hunter was playing a game of hit and run. Dimitri had planned for the anger. Fen had counseled him that Bardolf didn't have the control Abel did.

I can see why you serve a master, Dimitri taunted.

He shifted into the form of a smaller hawk, streaking through the branches of the high canopy in the forest, making certain to stay close to the edge of the meadow, certain Bardolf had been ordered to stay close to the tunnel to keep any Carpathian from interfering.

I serve no master. Bardolf blasted into the sky after the small hawk. He chose the form of a great harpy eagle, talons as large as bear claws. He was fast, very fast and he caught up fairly quickly.

Dimitri and Fen had played many war games over the last few centuries, and Dimitri used the same tactics that had been successful on his brother. He lengthened the branches, and this time changed the leaves and needles to spikes. The smaller hawk was able to maneuver through the dense foliage, but the larger eagle crashed into the lengthening branches, the spikes driving into the body and wings of the bird.

A little slow for a Sange rau, *aren't you?* Dimitri taunted.

Vampires and werewolves definitely had egos. Getting Bardolf angry was a good tactic in that if he was mad, he might make mistakes. Dimitri had been trained for centuries in fighting the *Sange rau*. The practice sessions with Fen might have been games, but he'd learned what worked and what didn't. He wasn't as fast, but his tricks would work once, just enough to hurt his opponent and hopefully slow him down.

Bardolf's echoing cry reverberated through the trees as the body of the eagle tumbled, bleeding from several wounds. Feathers floated to the ground, but Bardolf recovered midair, shifting to a smaller owl and streaking toward Dimitri once more.

Dimitri waited until he was very close and blasted him with a sudden downdraft, driving the owl straight toward the earth. Bardolf went down fast. As he fell to earth, the ground rose to meet him. Bardolf hit hard.

Dimitri deliberately snickered, digging at him again. *I thought you were supposed to have been an alpha, a leader of the pack. You don't fly so well, do you?*

Bardolf yelled, a ferocious sound making the trees shiver. He launched himself again, this time streaking straight at Dimitri, shifting as he did so, slamming into the Carpathian before Dimitri could move, claws ripping at his chest and belly, digging deep.

Dimitri shifted out from under him the moment Bardolf drew back for another assault. Bardolf made his grab but his hands went through empty space. Dimitri couldn't afford to allow the *Sange rau* to actually catch him.

The idea was to hit and run, not get caught. He'd been a little slow and he paid the price. Bardolf was so fast, he'd sliced Dimitri's body in a dozen places before Dimitri could actually shift.

He became tiny molecules, and instead of doing what Bardolf anticipated, he attached himself to the *Sange rau*'s clothing, allowing the wolf/vampire to take him up to the storm where he was expected to be. Bardolf sniffed around, his acute sense of smell telling him Dimitri was near, but he couldn't find him in the roiling, spinning clouds.

Dimitri had practiced the move on his brother hundreds of times, but he hadn't been wounded. Blood hadn't been leaking from his body to give his position away. He didn't have much time to control the bleeding and slip off Bardolf. Ahead of him, he wove four different strands and sent them out into the storm, forcing the wolf/vampire to make a choice of which would be Dimitri.

Bardolf took the bait, hesitating for a moment, using his enhanced vision to try to choose the one element he believed was his Carpathian opponent. He made up his mind and flew after the strand leading back toward the opening to the mountain. Dimitri abandoned him, moving into a dark, spinning cloud, catching his breath and preparing his next move.

The *Sange rau* suddenly changed direction as if he'd been summoned. Dimitri's pulse jumped. *Fen? You okay? Bardolf is headed your way fast.*

Can you stop him? Slow him down?

His brother sounded the same way he always sounded. Matter-of-fact. But Dimitri touched his mind for a moment. There was pain. Exhaustion. Blood loss. *No problem. I'm on it now.*

Dimitri studied the trajectory of the wolf/vampire hurtling recklessly toward his master. In his hurry to obey, Bardolf forgot the cat and mouse game they'd been playing, dismissing Dimitri as of little consequence. After all, Dimitri hadn't actually engaged in a fight with him.

Dimitri used the storm he'd built. Superheating a pocket of air was easy enough. Placing it exactly where Bardolf would choose to fly was the much more difficult part, but Dimitri had spent lifetimes running with the wolves. The real thing. He'd spent time with his brother, who had become Lycan.

Bardolf thought as a wolf first. He was comfortable in that skin. He was familiar with it and seemed to hesitate before he used the gifts his vampire blood gave him. Dimitri thought like a wolf as well. He'd run with them for centuries and studied their behavior. Bardolf was comfortable with a pack. He fought in a pack. Fighting alone was completely foreign to him.

His master had only perpetuated that weakness in order to keep the wolf from wanting to usurp his leader. Bardolf would go straight to his alpha, taking the fastest line of flight to obey. Dimitri chose a spot just ahead of the wolf/vampire and built the searing heat. Bardolf burst into the small section and screamed as the scalding heat burned his skin.

Bardolf backpedaled, desperate to get away from the heat burning right through him. Dimitri blasted out of the sky behind him, driving straight for him. The force of the two coming together at such a speed helped drive the stake deep into Bardolf's back. Dimitri knew immediately he'd missed the heart. Something must have warned the *Sange rau* because at the last moment, he turned slightly, just enough to throw off Dimitri's aim.

Bardolf spun, claws whipping across Dimitri's face, knocking him back so that he tumbled. Before he could shift, Bardolf was on him, ripping at his belly, pushing the silver stake from his body and catching it in his palm, reversing and throwing it hard at Dimitri.

Dimitri twisted hard, trying to present the smallest target possible. The stake entered his shoulder high. The force of Bardolf's throw drove it straight through so that the shaft left a large hole behind. Bardolf immediately pursued the injured Carpathian, following up on his advantage. Dimitri had suspected all along that he was close to becoming the *Sange rau*, and the terrible, relentless burn of the silver confirmed it for him.

Get out of there! Fen called out urgently, seeing his brother falling out of the sky, a spray of blood surrounding him and the *Sange rau* streaking toward him.

Fen had thrown Abel out of the tunnel and into the meadow where he knew the traps Gregori had prepared for a vampire were waiting. He was counting on the sun, but the storm overhead kept the harmful rays from reaching Abel. He had a choice—follow up on his advantage—or to go the aid of his brother. He was protecting the prince and that had to be his first priority . . .

He drove both feet hard into Abel's face, smashing the crystals deeper into the skin. Abel fell back into a fine net of silver. Fen launched himself skyward, intercepting Bardolf before the *Sange rau* could get to his brother.

Fen was faster and much more skilled. He'd been *Sange rau* for centuries, long before Bardolf had been, and he'd been an ancient Carpathian hunter. The wolf wasn't comfortable in the sky, in the midst of a violent storm, but Fen was right at home. And he was protecting his brother. More, he felt aggressive toward Bardolf, enraged even that he'd dared to try to kill Dimitri. That emotion had never once been with him in battle.

He hit Bardolf hard, slamming him down with air pressure as well as physical force. Bardolf hit the ground and rolled, trying to get to his feet as Fen dropped on top of him.

Dimitri, get out of here now. You need blood fast. His tone brooked no argument. In any case, Dimitri had a lifemate. He wouldn't throw his life away, and anyway, he was too wounded to help.

Fen drove a stake deep into Bardolf's body as he landed on him, straddling him, pinning him down. Still, Bardolf's immense strength as both wolf and vampire came into play, allowing him to once again avoid the stake to the heart. He was bleeding in dozens of places, but he still squirmed away from the deadly silver stake.

He shifted, falling back on his wolf, tearing at Fen's body, biting hard on his thigh, nearly going to bone, refusing to let go, pulling at the flesh and sinew, determined to get to the artery. Cursing, Fen had no choice but to let him go. Bardolf immediately shifted again, taking to the air, streaking like a comet away from the battleground, self-preservation uppermost in his mind. He abandoned his master, running for his life, leaving behind a trail of blood in the sky.

Fen had to choose to follow him or go back to stop Abel. Every cell in his body wanted to follow Bardolf for daring to put a hand on his brother, but honor and duty demanded he protect the prince. With another snarl and curse, he streaked back to the tunnel. He could see the blood where Dimitri had chosen to go inside. He could get blood from Vikirnoff and Mikhail and yet still help to defend the prince. That was his brother. Always choosing the right path in spite of the danger to himself.

Dimitri paused as he swept past Abel. If he had been one hundred percent he would have tried to engage with the *Sange rau*, but he had lost too much blood and the silver netting clearly wasn't going to hold Abel for much longer. Fen would have to take care of him. The best Dimitri could do to aid his brother was to clear the storm so the sun could break through and help to guard the prince.

He sent word ahead that he was coming in fast and would need blood. He didn't want to get caught in any of the traps set for vampires as he rushed down the tunnel to the back of the cavern. Mikhail had the safeguards down and immediately he offered his wrist. Dimitri didn't hesitate. Mikhail's blood was powerful and would aid in healing him.

Both Vikirnoff and Natalya began attending his wounds, trying to stop the flow of precious blood. He hadn't realized just how many deep lacerations Bardolf had managed to inflict in the few brief encounters when they came together.

"You're a little crazy," Vikirnoff told him. "You know that, don't you?"

"He's coming," Mikhail announced.

Dimitri nearly stopped taking blood, but Mikhail indicated to continue. "We need you as strong as possible."

Dimitri politely took a little more blood and then closed the wound on the prince's wrist. He watched Abel approach. The vampire looked terrible. Bloody crystal covered his face, producing a grotesque mask. His eyes looked black, surrounded by flaming red rather than white. He was covered in blood. Veins stood out starkly on exposed skin. The netting strands, as fine as they were, had been burned into his skin so that he was crisscrossed in raised welts.

He walked right up to the sheet of amber that prevented him from reaching the prince, and slammed his fist against the plate. The mountain shook. Dirt and rock fell from the ceiling. Mikhail didn't so much as blink. He stood straight and tall, his dark eyes staring straight into Abel's. He appeared totally confident.

Vikirnoff and Natalya stepped up to the amber, as expressionless as their prince. Neither flinched when Abel began the complicated process of unraveling the safeguards. He did so with astonishing speed, proving he could see the coding. He made short work of the intricate guards that would have stopped even a master vampire. Next he began systematically tearing at the thick amber sheet. The amber stuck to his claws and muzzle when he leaned in to tear at it with his teeth. Still, he made steady progress.

Dimitri saw his brother materialize directly behind Abel, plunging his fist once more into the *Sange rau*'s back. Clearly Abel had been so focused on tearing down the amber guard that he hadn't detected Fen's approach. His mouth opened wide in a silent scream, blood trickled from his mouth. He shifted immediately, his body jerking and twisting as he did so, trying to dislodge the stake.

Fen streaked after him as Abel abandoned the tunnel and emerged out into the early morning sunlight. His high-pitched shrieks reverberated through the cavern, shaking loose more crystal, dirt and rocks. The debris fell on Fen, smashing him to the tunnel floor. Several larger boulders crashed down around him. He was pinned for just one moment before he dissolved the rocks and was up and after Abel. The scent of burning flesh was unmistakable. Abel had pushed his limit of being outside in the sun.

He's gone, Fen, Mikhail said. *You need blood and care. Dimitri needs the earth.*

Both still live. Fen was deeply disappointed that he hadn't killed at least one of them.

We've learned more than we ever could have expected. You and Dimitri took them both on and yet you still are alive. They are not invincible. Come back and let us attend your wounds. The sun rises and soon we'll need to go to ground.

Fen sighed. He could feel Dimitri's exhaustion and weakness. Dimitri's lifemate Skyler was going to get angry with him soon if he didn't take better care of his brother. Mikhail was correct, they both needed to go to ground and allow Mother Earth to heal them. He would gladly take ancient Carpathian blood to help heal his wounds. And he intended to give Dimitri more of his mixed blood. The Lycan would repair him at a much faster rate.

He frowned up at the sky for a few moments and then turned back to join the others.

12

The cave of warriors was the most sacred place the Carpathian people had. Fen had come here only a few times in his youth, and the power of the caves had been felt deeply then, but even more now. He walked with Dimitri on one side and Tatijana on the other, through a series of smaller caves, each descending deeper into the earth. Each time they moved into the lower tunnels, that great labyrinth of caverns and chambers, he felt the absolute majesty of the place.

Few could take the heat in the lower caves. Carpathians could control body temperature so they were immune to the searing heat, but few other species found their way into the environment. The cave they moved through had crystalline flows draping the high ceilings. Overhead the formations appeared as great chandeliers, some with long white fringe hanging from nature's masterpieces.

Fen hadn't been in many cathedrals, but in his travels, he'd seen a few, and the series of subterranean chambers he moved through, undisturbed, untouched, the natural artistry of nature itself, seemed just as much or more places of worship.

Great columns, sculpted and beautiful, stalactites and stalagmites, grouped together in various shades of color formed a jungle as they went deeper.

Tatijana stumbled a few times on the uneven surface, busy looking in awe at her surroundings. "I lived in ice caves and didn't think anything could be more beautiful, but this is amazing," she whispered.

Fen found it interesting that when speaking, all of them, even the warriors during a meeting, tended to lower their voices out of respect for raw nature.

"As we go lower, it's even more beautiful," he confided.

They made their way through another long chamber, nearly four hundred feet long and almost as wide filled with more towering columns draped with various colors and shimmering shallow pools that reflected back the startling crystalline flows overhead and the sculptures surrounding them.

Fen knew part of the mystique of the cave of warriors was this long walk to gain entrance. The deeper into the earth one went, the more they felt at home. They were creatures of the night. Places like this massive maze of caverns felt like part of them.

They traveled farther down into heat. At first, Tatijana forgot to regulate her breathing and body temperature she was so busy staring in awe at the curtains and draperies, all different colors, some translucent and some dark with impurities, constructed out of calcite. Long fringe gave the illusion of shawls carefully woven, while other sculptures appeared to be capes or scarves. Overhead and dropping near the wall like great coverings were long, wide sculptures of breathtaking flowing stone, so that the entire chamber looked like a theater with thick, intricate drapes.

"How could you not come here every day just to look at this?" Tatijana asked. "My form is a blue dragon, so I need the cooler water, but Branislava would totally love this. Not that I don't. It's so beautiful, but I have to keep remembering to keep my temperature regulated."

Fen brought their joined hands to his face and rubbed the back of her hand against his jaw. "Your skin is always so cool, *sívamet*. No matter how hot it gets in these caves your outside temperature remains quite cool. I find that . . ." He waited until her eyes met his. *Sexy.*

Tatijana laughed softly. "You're such a flirt, wolf man."

Dimitri groaned. "Enough of that. My woman is too far away for me to hear this kind of talk from you two."

That distracted Tatijana immediately. "She's so powerful! I couldn't believe her strength. I've never actually experienced that kind of healing power from a distance by anyone else. And she's so young. A child really."

"In Carpathian years, a child, yes," Dimitri said. "In terms of human years and what she's been through, she's years ahead."

"Whatever the case, she's amazing. I can't wait to meet her." Tatijana narrowed her eyes. "Which means you can't go near the *Sange rau* again, not for any reason. It took all of us to heal you the first time, along with Mother Earth. I think Fen nearly drained every drop of blood out of his body replacing yours. And now this time. Three days in the ground and more blood . . ."

"Hey now, *all* of us took a few days to heal," Dimitri protested.

Tatijana flashed him a grin. "Perhaps some of us heal faster than others."

"Perhaps you think you're safe, sister-kin, because my badass brother is looking out for you, but he isn't so tough."

She laughed softly. "You're as crazy as your brother, aren't you?"

Dimitri and Fen exchanged a long, pleased look.

They were coming to the end of the long theater. The draperies only became more intricate and translucent. The smiles on their faces faded, leaving them all sober. There was a change in the feel of the caves. Where before they felt like a series of inspiring cathedrals, the atmosphere surrounding them as they neared the most sacred of places—the warrior's cavern, became much heavier.

They stepped inside the worn passage, centuries old, carved out by their ancestors, the rock smooth where feet had trod over so long. There was no doubt it was a little like stepping back in time. The stalagmites and stalactites were everywhere, hanging from the ceiling and thrusting upward from the floor. The circumference of the bases was quite large and there were many of varying sizes and color. Each was sculpted and one could make out faces up and down the stone as if each was a totem pole hand carved rather than fashioned by nature itself.

Tatijana stopped just inside the chamber and looked suspiciously around. The oppressive silence was far different than the other caverns. Not even the three pools of water made her feel better. One was crystal clear, lined with stone, and looked deep and cool, almost an ice blue. The second pool gave off a cloud of steam and was slightly tinged red orange. The third bubbled with mud.

"The stalagmites and stalactites used to hum as we entered," Fen said. "Our ancestors greeting us. I wonder when that stopped."

"They hummed the last time I was here," Dimitri said.

The moment Fen had entered the chamber, he had the sense of being weighed, judged, not by the few living who had gathered, but by the dead whose spirits gathered at every meeting. The presence of his ancestors, warriors long gone from the world, was heavy there in that chamber. The fact that they hadn't greeted him boded ill.

Tatijana tightened her fingers around Fen's. "I don't like the feel of this," she whispered. "They know what you are, and some of them feel antagonistic. We should make certain we have an exit plan."

Fen glanced down at her. There was genuine worry in her voice. He was a little worried about the outcome of this meeting, but he was certain he hadn't passed that on to his lifemate.

She's got a point, Fen. The air is heavy in here, Dimitri told him. *With judgment.*

Fen couldn't say the two didn't have a point, but he didn't want Tatijana to worry. He was grateful Dimitri had used their private telepathic path.

"They got their butts kicked royally," Fen said. "They're used to being at the top of the food chain. They aren't too happy to discover they have an enemy out there who is just that little bit faster than they are."

"You mean superior to them when it comes to fighting," Tatijana corrected. "You're one of those *Sange raus* who can kick their ass. Do you think they all aren't aware of that? They resent it, Fen. Egos can get out of hand."

Fen shook his head. "That's where I think the misconception comes in, my lady. The *Sange rau* is not necessarily as skilled in battle as most of these hunters. They are faster, but that doesn't necessarily mean that with a little training, a skilled hunter can't beat them."

He tried to avoid Dimitri's telling glance and focus only on Tatijana.

She stopped moving, tugging at his hand until he stopped directly in front of her. "You mean like Dimitri." She indicated his brother. "You taught Dimitri how to fight them."

Dimitri snickered in his mind. *You have an intelligent lifemate, Fen. She's quick on the uptake.*

Don't I know it.

He ducked his head, avoiding Tatijana's eyes. "I taught him how to hunt and defeat me. Just in case."

Tatijana's fingers tightened in his. "That's my point. You have always acted with honor. I feel as if you're being accused of something."

Fen had been around Lycan society for centuries and had grown accustomed to viewing himself as an outsider who had to hide what and who he was. It was a way of life, and in the end he'd chosen to remain with the Lycans. He found it endearing that Tatijana had become so protective of him.

I agree with her, Fen. Maybe this isn't a good idea, Dimitri advised.

Fen did look at his brother then. Dimitri was an ancient, a skilled hunter of the vampire, but he'd spent centuries giving his brother a refuge when the traits of the *Sange rau* became particularly difficult to overcome. He knew, more than any other, that becoming what Fen was, was highly dangerous. Worse, Dimitri's blood was already changing. Both knew it. The Carpathian council could become aware of it as well.

Dimitri had not claimed his lifemate and he could very well be in double the danger. Fen kept his fingers firmly threaded through Tatijana's. He had expected the chamber to be filled with a good number of Carpathian males, but there was only Mikhail and his brother Jacques, Vikirnoff and his lifemate, Natalya, and, of course, Gregori.

He felt Tatijana hesitate. She lifted a hand as if she might try to straighten her hair. All eyes were on them. He gently caught her wrist.

You have nothing at all to prove to these people. You look beautiful. You are my lifemate and we've chosen to live our lives our way. If they do not like it, it will be no different than we have known our entire lives.

It was the truth. Tatijana's life had not been one of acceptance. Her father had kept her prisoner, not even allowing her to be in her natural form for most of her years. Those captured and tortured by Xavier didn't always understand that she was a prisoner just as they were. She'd spent lifetimes outside the norm.

Fen had spent centuries apart from his kind. Had the Lycans known what he was, they would have killed him immediately, without question. He was used to being an outcast, and in truth, it no longer bothered him. He never wanted Tatijana to feel less than what she was—a beautiful miracle.

Mikhail came forward to greet them. He stepped close to Fen, nearly toe-to-toe, a deliberate move that placed him in a vulnerable position. Gregori, who stepped with him, didn't flinch, but his silver eyes had gone to steel. Mikhail gripped Fen's forearms tight, in the traditional greeting of one respected warrior to another.

Fen gripped the prince's arms tightly, surprised at the raw power he felt surging beneath the surface. It was impossible to be so close to the man and not feel the power emanating from him, so great there was no way to contain it.

"Thank you for coming, Fenris Dalka," Mikhail said. "May your heart stay strong, hunter," he added in the language of the ancients, a more traditional Carpathian greeting. He turned to Dimitri and repeated the formal welcoming. He took Tatijana's hands in his. "Thank you for the aid you gave to our warriors, Tatijana. You definitely turned the tide of the battle in our favor."

He stepped back and paced away from them, his quick energy flowing rather than nervous. When he turned back, his dark eyes seemed to look right through Fen. "You have indeed brought us an interesting problem."

Fen looked around the great chamber. "You did not call a council of warriors as I expected."

Mikhail nodded. "I gave this great thought. The only ones among us who actually witnessed the fight between you and the one you call *Sange rau* are here in this chamber. I thought it was important to know more about what we're actually dealing with. There are many questions that have come to mind."

"May I ask why we are having this conversation here in this sacred place rather than the convenience of a house?" Tatijana asked.

Gregori turned his piercing stare on her.

Her chin went up, Tatijana refusing to be intimidated. Fen could have told him her Dragonseeker blood didn't seem to allow her to be overawed by anyone, not even her own lifemate.

Fen could have told her why. Mikhail Dubrinsky was no one's fool. He'd thought long and hard over the problem of the *Sange rau*. He had witnessed up close what a mixed blood was capable of. By now he would have gone over all the pros and cons, just as the Lycan council had so many centuries earlier. Nothing had really changed down through the centuries. The solutions were every bit as bad as the problem itself and Mikhail no doubt had come to that conclusion, just as Fen had.

"She asks a fair question, Gregori," Mikhail said, his tone mild. "The truth is, Tatijana, I'm disturbed by the abilities of the *Sange rau*. They present a real threat to not only our species, but to the Lycans and humans as well. One way to put it is that they have the nuclear weapon and we don't."

"That's what Fen said," Tatijana acknowledged.

"The immediate solution seems obvious," Mikhail said. "And certainly it was proposed that many of our most skilled hunters become the *Sange rau* in order to better destroy the ones who have turned vampire."

Fen tried not to react. He could feel not only the stare of the prince and the others, but also the weight of the warriors long past. Everything in him rebelled against the idea the prince was suggesting. He had known all along that this would be one of the proposals. If every warrior went out and became the *Sange rau*, their skill as fighters should give them an advantage when fighting those who had turned vampire—but it didn't work quite like that.

"One does not become *Sange rau* in one step. The wolf comes to you to protect you. You are not both together and it takes some time before you merge with your wolf. I was living with the Lycan on and off and I think it may have happened faster than normal, but it took time. In that time you're going to lose a lot more warriors to the other side. They will choose to be vampire much faster with their blood mixed."

Fen shook his head, disturbed that he might sound like he didn't want anyone else to be like him. It was a fine line he walked, giving what he felt was pertinent information and not sounding arrogant.

Mikhail seemed to recognize his reluctance. "You do not have to hide what you feel from us," the prince said. "We've asked you here to help us find a viable solution to this problem—and it is a problem. A complex one, the more I study it. I looked at it from every angle and something occurred to me. There is great power in my family, but it comes with a terrible price. I think there has to be a balance, and with the gifts given to us, there is always a price to pay, so I had to ask myself, what is the price of being a *Sange rau*? Only you can answer that question for us, Fen."

Fen felt the ancient warriors waiting for his answer. The air grew heavier as silence descended in the chamber. A few of the great columns vibrated, darker colors swirling through the stone giving the illusion that the chamber itself was alive.

He sighed. He had come here knowing that Mikhail would be intelligent enough to ask the right questions. He'd seen it in him. They all had to know the truth—especially Tatijana and Dimitri.

"The price is far too high, Mikhail," Fen answered honestly. "Especially for a warrior without a lifemate, but even those of us who have a lifemate are not necessarily as safe as our Carpathian counterparts. At first, yes, the wolf helps. You can see as a wolf does, the colors are dull, but better than nothing. But as time passes, the pull of darkness grows until it crouches like a monster above you and whispers continually."

He didn't look at his lifemate or his brother. He looked around the great chamber at the vibrating columns—ancient brethren who had lived their lives honorably—no matter the difficulty.

"I think every Carpathian who lives a long time and battles the vampire successfully, comes to a place where he believes in himself. He has to. He has to have absolute confidence in himself. Confidence can lead to arrogance. Carpathian males lose emotion and in some ways it is both a blessing and a curse. To feel, when you destroy old friends and family, to live year after year in darkness, is pure hell. To be *Sange rau* is to fight feelings of arrogance and superiority every rising, lifemate or no. I believe that if you give into these feelings, even with a lifemate, you can become vampire/wolf. Obviously I haven't tested this theory."

Again there was a silence. He could feel Tatijana's horror rising. *You understand now my reluctance to bind you to me.* There was shame in knowing he hadn't disclosed the worst of his fears to her before claiming her for his own.

Again, Tatijana surprised him. Soft melodic laughter filled his mind. *I do not feel horror at your admission, my love, only at your belief that you would ever succumb to the darker impulses of our kind.*

We do not know that. There is no way of telling what I would do in a moment of madness. You saw into my mind when I fought with the werewolf to get information from him and again, when I was battling Abel and Bardolf. I believed myself superior even to them. Fen made the confession to her reluctantly.

Silly wolf man.

He was shaken by the love in her voice. She could bring him to his knees so easily.

We have spent most of our time in battle or in the ground healing since you claimed me. How can you possibly know how having a lifemate will affect the feelings of superiority? I can assure you, my love, that Dragonseeker women are superior and therefore, you won't have a leg to stand on.

Her teasing note soothed him as nothing else could. And she had a good point.

Of course I have a point. You knew it was dangerous to access the rogue were-wolf's memories, but you did it anyway. Of course there were repercussions. You expected that. And every single warrior facing a vampire must believe that he can defeat him. Acknowledging that you are smarter and faster and more skilled than a vampire is the only intelligent thing to do. You did what every Carpathian hunter does. You're so worried about it that you are not remembering what it is like to be a hunter.

Fen hadn't considered it, but she was right. Every Carpathian male who hunted the vampire did so believing he could destroy the undead. He reached his hand out to her, telling her without words that he loved her.

Mikhail frowned as he paced with restless energy through the great columns of his ancestors while he thought about what Fen said. No one interrupted him. Fen was grateful that Mikhail was the kind of man who didn't simply react to information. He digested it carefully, looking at it from every angle before he made decisions.

"Another concern I have is evolution itself," Mikhail said, coming back to stand in front of him. "Our species is near extinction. Could this be a more evolved species? The combination of our blood with the Lycans?"

Everything in Fen rebelled against the idea that his species was doomed and another would rise in their place—and certainly not the *Sange rau.*

"Then there is the question of children. For the first time in a long while we have had multiple children who survived their first year," Mikhail continued. "We have no idea if the *Sange rau* can have children. Manolito and MaryAnn are the only pair we know of and MaryAnn has not become pregnant. That, of course doesn't mean anything, but it could be worrisome.

What would this change in the blood do to a child? Do we want to take chances when we're just now rebuilding our population?"

Fen hadn't considered that particular point. He glanced at his brother. Dimitri was not fully *Sange rau*, but he was well on his way. Had he condemned Dimitri and his lifemate to a life without children because centuries ago he hadn't known what caused mixed blood and they'd shared blood in the battlefield? When he'd healed his brother himself, he had given Dimitri his own blood. Fen knew the blood would aid Dimitri in healing faster if they could keep him alive, and he'd made that choice for Dimitri.

I would much rather live and know Skyler will live as well, even if we cannot have children. She deserves a life of happiness and I intend to make her life as wonderful as possible. So thank you for saving our lives.

Fen felt humble in the face of his brother's adamant revelation, mostly because he and Dimitri had been in and out of each other's minds for centuries and he could feel the honesty in Dimitri's statement.

"Throughout the centuries," Fen said, "I have lived on and off with the Lycans. During that time, I have come across only two other *Sange rau*. The first I hunted with Vakasin and the second was Abel. I, of course, didn't know that at the time. Abel turned Bardolf for whatever reasons. But I never once met a pair, not in any country I traveled in. At one time I speculated that perhaps a woman couldn't have mixed blood. Tatijana told me about Manolito De La Cruz and his lifemate. I was worried they wouldn't know the danger they were in from the Lycans."

"So to your knowledge, worldwide, only you, MaryAnn and Manolito are *Sange rau* who have not succumbed to darkness. Bardolf and Abel are the only ones you know of alive, who have," Mikhail reiterated.

Fen nodded. "That doesn't, of course, mean there aren't others. Worldwide, I can't imagine there wouldn't be others."

"Lycans have avoided Carpathians for centuries," Mikhail pointed out.

"Their council has discouraged interaction between the two species, probably for this reason. There was never any animosity that I heard," Fen replied.

"That would explain the small numbers," Gregori said. "MaryAnn was Lycan already. Do we know what happens when a Carpathian woman changes?"

Tatijana shrugged. "I'll let you know when it happens. It's my choice to be what he is. I doubt that Lycan blood can overpower Dragonseeker to the point that I would be in any danger."

"We hope not," Gregori said, his voice dry. "If something happens to you, what guarantee would we have that Fen would follow you?"

Dimitri scowled at him. "There is never a guarantee for any of us. You included, Gregori, should something happen to Savannah. All Carpathian males are at risk without a lifemate."

"True, but we are not the *Sange rau*. Our hunters will find us and destroy us before we can inflict too much damage on the other species around us. Can you imagine an army of *Sange rau*? Your brother told us a single one decimated the ranks of the Lycans. We are few. They could wipe us out entirely very fast," Gregori said.

"There is truth in what he says," Fen agreed. *You do not need to stick up for me, Dimitri, although I greatly appreciate it. I knew when I went to Mikhail the enormity of the problem I was bringing to him. The* Sange rau *are as much a danger to Carpathians as they are to Lycans and humans. We don't have any answers to the questions he's raising. I've had centuries to consider these problems and I still haven't come up with solutions.*

We are not Lycan, Dimitri hissed in his mind. *I refuse to believe that Mikhail will outlaw the* Sange rau *without discrimination and sentence you and anyone else who becomes such a mixture to death.*

Fen had lived with the Lycans a long time. *Do you believe we're more civilized then?* He couldn't help the note of amusement in his voice. The Lycans were well entrenched in every high society and public office in nearly every country. They served in the military, and most were highly educated. While the Carpathians had withdrawn from the world of humans for the most part and become silent guardians, the Lycans had done just the opposite—they embraced that world and protected humans just as aggressively.

Dimitri, the rogue pack isn't indicative of Lycans. They've reverted to the animal just as vampires embrace the darker side of Carpathians. Zev and the elite hunters represent the Lycans far better. Don't be fooled into thinking we're superior to them.

"I don't believe we have to worry about Fen turning vampire," Mikhail stated in his usual soothing, calm voice. "We need to come to some decision on what we're going to do. Clearly we need to meet with the Lycan council. We've discussed it at length for several years. We need them as allies, not enemies. This is our best opportunity to invite them to a sit-down meeting and come to some kind of terms."

"Zev is your best man for that," Fen advised. "The elite scout sent ahead of the pack is normally the most intelligent and their best man. He'll report directly to the council and they'll listen to him. His word carries the most weight."

Mikhail inclined his head. "He was severely wounded and had lost a good amount of blood. To ensure he lived, Jacques gave him blood."

Fen closed his eyes, suddenly feeling weary. Tatijana had given Zev blood as well. In his travels and many battles, had Zev received blood from any other Carpathian? It was possible—and dangerous. Fen knew no matter how honorably Zev served his people, should he become the *Sange rau*, they would turn on him and condemn him to death without a second thought.

"I have no idea how much blood has to be shared before the mixture converts one into something else," Fen admitted. "When Vakasin and I battled the *Sange rau*, both of us had countless wounds and both of us lost blood often. I don't know how often we'd given one another blood before I began to feel the wolf inside of me, but I felt it long before he felt the Carpathian traits, or maybe he simply didn't recognize that he was any different."

"You're afraid Zev may be in trouble," Mikhail guessed.

Fen nodded. "He's a good man. His ability in a fight is unsurpassed by most hunters. He reminds me of Vakasin. I would hate to see him killed by his own people after the service he's given them."

"That makes it all the more important to talk with their council," Mikhail said. "If they understand the difference between a vampire and Carpathian, we can convince them to look at the *Sange rau* in another light. We might distinguish the two by providing our own name for a Carpathian/Lycan cross."

Fen sighed. "I wish you every success, but I can tell you the Lycans will fight you on the issue of the *Sange rau*. Not only do they have legitimate reasons to fear the mixture of Carpathian and Lycan blood, but you're fighting centuries-old prejudices. There are fanatics who belong to a secret society that's not very secret and they dedicate their lives to ferreting out the *Sange rau* and destroying them. They draw in every misfit there is and brainwash them. The *Sange rau* gives them a target for their fanatical hatred. Not of course that they ever actually find one, but every sin is blamed on them."

"Surely cooler heads prevail on the council," Mikhail said.

Fen shrugged. "I would hope so, but I've seen some of these fanatics. They've become a religion and they preach to the packs and they're very persuasive. You have to remember, this has been going on for centuries, so the prejudice is well established." He tried to find another way to explain it. "This belief of the *Sange rau* is at the very heart of their traditions. He represents everything evil. He is their demon, the epitome of every sinful thing."

"Like a religion," Gregori said.

Mikhail shot him a look. Gregori didn't believe in any religion, where Mikhail was a devout worshipper.

"One that is very sacred to them and if not an actual spiritual belief, certainly one that is woven in the very fabric of their existence," Fen said.

Mikhail let out his breath. "All right then. It's good to know what we're up against. Still, I believe we have to try. In the meantime, how do we fight them? How did Dimitri fight such a creature when our warriors sustained so much damage?"

"The Lycans and werewolves are pack fighters. Carpathians are used to fighting lone monsters."

"Lately vampires have been banding together," Gregori said. "Vampires, as unnatural as that sounds, actually put an army together to attack us. For a little practice run, they hit the De La Cruz compound in South America."

"That must have been like stirring up a hornet's nest. Of all the hunters in the world, I think I would prefer any other to come after me," Fen said.

"It was personal," Dimitri explained. "The Malinov brothers decided they were going to rule all Carpathians, and the De La Cruz brothers refused to join them."

"You can see why we would want the Lycans as allies," Mikhail said. "There are too few of us for an all-out war with any enemy."

"If your warriors embrace the *Sange rau* and deliberately seek to become one, the Lycans will attack you," Fen said. "The war would be endless, and no one would win in the end other than vampires. You have to go into a meeting knowing their prejudice is ingrained in them and will be difficult to change."

Mikhail nodded. "I do believe we need to have our own name for those Carpathians and Lycans who have not turned vampire yet have mixed blood, something to indicate they are very different than the demon the Lycans believe them to be. That must become part of our vocabulary before I even meet with Zev. Which means we should come up with it immediately."

"Do you really think changing a name is going to change their minds?" Vikirnoff asked. It was the first time he'd spoken, and Fen could tell by his tone that he didn't like the situation at all. Had the situation not been so grave he would have smiled. Mikhail Dubrinsky fully understood the problem. He wasn't going to throw his hands in the air and walk away, he was going to actually try for resolution. More than anyone there, other than Fen, it was Mikhail who knew what he was facing.

Many of his Carpathian warriors would be tempted to become *Sange rau*, just to make them better fighters. They would want to ignore the potential problems and they wouldn't recognize that MaryAnn and Manolito and Fen and Tatijana as well as Dimitri would become experiments. They would be watched closely by both Lycans and Carpathians if Mikhail was successful in convincing the Lycan council that there was a difference. If not, what then?

Would the Lycans be willing to go to war to force the Carpathians to hand over those who were *Sange rau*? Sadly, Fen considered that a big possibility. Even if Mikhail convinced the council, that didn't mean all the packs would agree, not over something that had been so ingrained in them. If the council agreed, their decision could very well cause a split among the packs.

"We need a lot more information before we allow any of our people to voluntarily choose this path," Mikhail said. "I am counting on the three of you to supply us with that information."

Fen nodded. "I have no choice but to follow the rogue pack if it moves. I have to hunt both Abel and Bardolf."

"After seeing Abel's return to his homeland, I believe he has one purpose in mind, and he won't be going anywhere very soon," Mikhail said. "He has returned in order to kill me. In the meantime, our hunters need to know how to fight Abel and Bardolf. You obviously trained Dimitri, who has known about this for some time."

There was the smallest hint of a reprimand in Mikhail's voice.

Dimitri shrugged, unrepentant. "The rogues never came near our homeland. I chose to set up sanctuaries for our wolf brethren knowing Fen needed a place to rest and heal at times. It gave me a chance to be with him. What he was, during those centuries, had no impact on our people."

Gregori stirred, his silver eyes slashing at Dimitri, but Mikhail held up his hand to prevent Gregori from speaking.

"There has never been a question of Dimitri's allegiance to our people," Mikhail said. "Until this rogue pack came to our homeland, the Lycans avoided us."

"True," Gregori admitted, "but had we known of such a potential enemy, we could have been better prepared. As it is, many of our hunters were badly wounded."

"They fought the pack, not the *Sange rau*," Dimitri pointed out.

Why are you engaging in this argument with him? Fen asked. *You know he is right. We both should have brought this enemy to light long before this. You were protecting me, Dimitri, we both know that.*

Dimitri frowned. It was unlike him to take exception to someone pointing out the truth. It was Gregori's job, above all else, to guard their prince. Why did he feel this unsettling restless, almost feral, resentment?

Your wolf is rising to protect you, Fen explained. *Can you feel him? You're in a place where our ancestors can judge us. He feels that and is urging you to leave.*

Mikhail waved his hand and hundreds of candles along the walls sprang to life. Instantly the giant columns and crystals radiated muted colors. In the very center of the room was a circle of crystal columns. They were the shortest in the chamber, the middle one coming up to Mikhail's shoulder. It was bloodred, formed of rich minerals and crystals. The tip was razor-sharp.

Mikhail spoke in their ancient language, the ritual words to call to their long gone ancestors. "Blood of our fathers—blood of our brothers—we seek your wisdom, your experience and your counsel. Join with your brother-warriors and lend us your guidance through the blood bond. We pledge to our people our unwavering loyalty, resolve in the face of adversity, compassion for those in need, strength and endurance through the centuries and above all, we will live with honor. Our blood connects us."

Mikhail brought his palm down over the tip of the column so that it pierced his flesh and droplets of blood coated the top of the column. "Our blood mingles and calls to you. Heed our summons and join with us now."

13

Mikhail's blood mingled with the long dead warriors. At once the crystals were illuminated, throwing off colors, deep emerald, rich ruby red swirling and banding throughout the room and over the walls. The display was much like the aurora borealis, many colors dancing through the chamber.

The swirling colors actually hurt Fen's eyes. He was used to gray and white and sometimes the duller colors the wolf could distinguish until Tatijana had given him back the ability to see such things, but he wasn't used to it yet. Still, the display was extraordinarily beautiful. Their native language was comforting to him and made him feel a part of his people after so many centuries of being alone.

Fen glanced at his brother. Dimitri was tall with broad shoulders and a face that could have been etched from stone. He was handsome, but aloof, a man apart. He had a lifemate he couldn't claim. She had restored his emotions and color to his world, but that made hunting vampires all the more difficult. Now he had to contend with a wolf prowling inside him, battling for supremacy. Fen hoped that the sacred chamber would ease his suffering just a little.

The columns hummed, each with a different note, a perfect pitch so that the totems with faces appeared to be chanting musically. The colors swirling over them gave the faces life and expression. Fen had been careful not to swear allegiance to the prince. It was important to make certain he didn't put Mikhail into the position of having to go to war to defend him. But . . . There was MaryAnn and Manolito. He knew Zacarias De La Cruz. Zacarias was pure hunter. He was pure Carpathian. Top of the food chain. Uncivilized. Untamed. The real thing. No one would touch his family without swift and brutal retaliation. He would be relentless, and he would never stop until he annihilated anyone or any group who targeted his family.

Fen knew Zacarias had found his lifemate, but he would bet his life that the eldest De La Cruz hadn't changed much. Fen was a hunter. He knew no other way of life. Zacarias would be the same. That meant Mikhail would have to protect the couple from the Lycans.

If Tatijana were to become like him, and eventually she would, he wanted the Carpathian people to protect her. The same with his brother. Dimitri was well on his way to being *Sange rau*. They had given one another blood in the past, over the last few centuries when they had hunted together, and now Dimitri was feeling the effects of his wolf.

Centuries ago his blood had been added to the column of warriors, when he had sworn his allegiance to a prince long dead. Adding his blood again would allow the warriors to weigh in on the decisions Mikhail would be making. They would know what it was like to think and feel as a *Sange rau*. He was not ashamed of who and what he was. He had lived as honorably as he could. He had engaged the enemies of Lycan, human and Carpathian every time he came across one.

"You do not have to swear allegiance," Mikhail said. "But if you are still hesitant because you fear you will force a war between Lycan and Carpathian, I can assure you, I will never agree to indiscriminately hunt those Lycans referred to as *Sange rau*. Any Carpathian who has this extraordinary and difficult gift will be referred to as *Hän ku pesäk kaikak*, or *Paznicii de toate*, which translates in either language to *Guardians of all*, and I will not give up any of them."

Mikhail's voice was compelling. Mesmerizing even. He could persuade most anyone to do anything he wanted with his voice, yet he was careful to keep his tone neutral.

Hän ku pesäk kaikak, Guardian of all. Mikhail Dubrinsky saw him that way, or he wouldn't have bestowed such a name on what he was. Fen couldn't believe what a difference such a small thing meant. He had been the hated *Sange rau,* and yet with just one small declaration, the prince had elevated him to Guardian of all.

Mikhail gave him and others like him purpose and status.

He was definitely born to lead, Tatijana whispered into his mind. *Just changing the name changes the feel of who and what you are.*

I can see why you gave him your allegiance.

Don't do this for me.

I wouldn't. This has to be a personal choice, and I choose to be part of his world.

Fen didn't hesitate further. It had been too many centuries where he was a man without a country. His people were Carpathian no matter what his blood had become. He loved the Lycans and respected them, but his heart was here, with his people. He wanted to be part of the Carpathian community again. He wanted to ensure that Tatijana was always accepted.

He glanced at his brother. Dimitri was a respected warrior among the Carpathian people and held in great esteem. Whatever changed inside of Dimitri, whatever the wolf brought, it would benefit the Carpathian people, not take away from them; Fen was certain of that.

Fen stepped up to the bloodred crystal. He lowered his palm slowly. Before he ever reached that sharpened tip, he felt power emanating from the large crystalline column. He knew it was a calculated risk. If his ancestors rejected him, Mikhail and certainly Gregori might reject him as well, but it was a chance he felt he had to take.

He allowed the totem of minerals to pierce his flesh and draw his blood. At once his blood mingled with the blood of those who had gone before. His soul stretched and called to the warriors who had gone before him. He felt them, so many, their presence strong, ringing him, filling him, making him feel a part of a community that dated back to ancient times. The flood of camaraderie and belonging, of acceptance, was overwhelming.

Every cell in his body responded. He became aware of everything, the smallest detail. He heard the steady drip of water, drumming like a heartbeat deep within the chamber so that his own heartbeat took up that collective rhythm. The ebb and flow of blood in his veins, in the veins of those surrounding him, matched the endless flow of the ancient's blood within the crystal. Deep below the chamber floor, hundreds of feet below the forest of giant columns, he felt the pool of magma feeding the heat throughout the labyrinth of multilevel caverns.

He heard whispers, ancient words spoken in the Carpathian language, warriors greeting him. *Bur tule ekämet kuntamak.* He could hear old friends, calling to him—well met brother-kin.

He whispered back in his mind, reaching for them . . .

Without warning the entire atmosphere of the chamber turned somber and sorrowful. The low humming in the chamber took on a completely different melody—a death chant—the dirge unmistakable although ancient. It was a melody reserved for a fallen warrior held in extremely high regard, a man of legend.

Fen found himself holding his breath. The ancient warriors were paying tribute to him—the highest tribute a fallen warrior could receive—but he wasn't dead. The column went from dark red to a darker, somber purple, a color of sorrow for a fallen comrade. The flickering flames on the candles lowered, throwing more shadows into the room, adding to the feeling of sadness.

It was the last reaction Fen expected—to have his ancestors mourn and give tribute to him as if he'd died in battle. He kept his features absolutely expressionless, but Tatijana had merged her mind with his and the instant his heart felt heavy, she stepped up behind him and circled her arms around him, laying her head against his back to comfort him.

The moment she pressed close to him, her arms encircling him, the mournful humming came to an abrupt, confused halt. There was a startled silence as if the ancestors didn't know what to think. The crystalline column began to pulse a deep rich red through the dark purple. The voices whispered greetings and encouragement.

Fen put both hands over Tatijana's, pressing her palms into his waist. He wasn't certain what to think. One moment the ancient warriors had been mourning as if he'd died in a great battle and the next moment they were calling to him in camaraderie again. It was very confusing.

It's your Dragonseeker blood they sense, he told his lifemate.

It mingles with yours. They should have sensed it before I came near them, Tatijana said with a little sniff of disdain.

They call to you, sister-kin. Fen still wasn't quite certain how to react. He told the simple truth. *She is Tatijana—keeper of my heart and soul*—hän ku vigyáz sívamet és sielamet.

Murmurs of approval hummed through the chamber. It wasn't as if they rejected Fen, in fact just the opposite. The ancient warriors embraced him, but they thought him gone from the world until Tatijana had surrounded him with herself.

The display of lights given off by the stalactites above their heads changed colors, throwing lavenders and pale pinks, with bursts of soft greens and blues. All of the colors, Fen was certain, represented his Dragonseeker woman. The stalagmites, great sculpted columns with faces and eyes swirling through them, came to life again, staring openly at Fen and Tatijana.

Why are they so surprised? We're lifemates. Can't they see that?

Fen's eyes met Mikhail's. What did it all mean? Only the prince might be able to decipher the meaning of the mourning and then the change.

"Can you tell me why they thought I had passed?" Fen asked, not entirely certain he wanted to know.

It doesn't matter what they think, Tatijana insisted, circling around to stand protectively in front of him, placing herself between Fen and the short column used for communication with the ancients long since passed.

It matters, my lady, Fen said gently. *We have to know the consequences of becoming* Sange rau *before any other Carpathian decides with the misguided notion that he will help to save his species from extinction, or just from the worst of monsters that we've faced by becoming a mixed blood.*

Not Sange rau. *You are* Hän ku pesäk kaikak, *Guardian of all,* Tatijana disputed firmly.

Fen found his heart doing a strange, slow somersault. Even his belly felt that same peculiar roll at her fierce protective streak. *I am lucky in my lifemate.* He meant every word. She had changed his life and would always be at the center of it. She made him feel alive and gave him his first taste of joy and real laughter.

"The ancients greeted you warmly because they recognized your heart and soul as Carpathian, Fen," Mikhail said. "Some of them knew you and celebrated that you kept your honor throughout such a long and difficult journey."

Fen nodded. He had felt them welcome him and the camaraderie had made him feel as if he were part of a much larger circle. After having been alone for so many centuries, Fen felt connected to his ancestors. He would have given anything to feel that way before he met and claimed Tatijana. He had needed that connection, but once she had poured into his mind with so much fluid grace and light, he found he really didn't need anymore. She had given him peace.

He had come here with the idea that he needed and wanted acceptance, not only for him but for his brother and any other who shared the same mixed blood, but now that he was in the sacred cave of warriors, he felt comforted by the traditional rituals, but it was Tatijana that made him feel complete, not the warrior circle itself.

"What happened? Why would they think I had died?" he asked curiously.

"When your blood first touched the sacred stone, they felt what they expected to feel. I woke them with the invocation. But as they processed it, as your blood touched their blood, they realized it was far different and you, as a Carpathian, were no longer there. They had already judged your heart and soul and knew you were honorable and that you'd fought long and hard for our people, so they awarded you the warrior's highest honor as they mourned your death."

"They believed he was dead because his blood is different?" Dimitri asked, wanting clarification. "Or they named him dead to the Carpathian people?"

"They believed him dead," Mikhail explained. "Couldn't you feel their genuine sorrow? Your blood, Fen, must be completely different at this point from that of a Carpathian."

"Yet I can give blood to anyone just as a Carpathian can," Fen said.

"You said the transformation happens in stages. Probably had you come here in the beginning stages, there would have been enough of a resemblance to Carpathian blood that few would notice the difference," Mikhail said.

"But then they sensed Tatijana. Her Dragonseeker blood is powerful."

"Yes it is. And already, because you're lifemates, that strain must be in you as well. But I felt something else, something equally as powerful. Not your Lycan—his presence was formidable—but something very subtle and equally as dominant."

Mikhail looked from Fen to Dimitri and then back at Fen, speculation in his eyes. "Tatijana is Dragonseeker, one of our most powerful lineages. She has a strong connection to Mother Earth, but this still feels different, as if it isn't her connection but yours."

"Tatijana does have a very strong connection to Mother Earth," Fen admitted.

Mikhail shook his head, his piercing, intelligent gaze moving back to Dimitri. "Aw. I see now. Young Skyler. We do underestimate that girl. She helped to heal you. How is that possible from such a distance? Isn't she in London?"

"I believe she is," Tatijana answered for both men.

"And yet you know her and can speak to where she is," Mikhail said. "How is it that a young girl, a child really, a human at that, can cross over two thousand kilometers and reach out to heal someone near death?"

Tatijana shrugged her shoulders. "It must have something to do with her being part of the Dragonseeker lineage. You said yourself it is a powerful line."

"Have you been able to do such a thing?" Mikhail asked.

Tatijana hesitated. She shook her head. "No. Both Bronnie and I tried to reach our niece when she escaped the ice caves, but the distance was too great."

Mikhail raised an eyebrow at Gregori.

Gregori shook his head. "I've never covered that distance. I've come close, but I doubt I could sustain it long enough to heal someone."

Dimitri remained silent. His expression never changed. Fen touched his mind. His brother was crazy in love with Skyler, but he hadn't claimed her, respecting their decision to wait until she felt ready. He would not give her up, not even to the prince and his enquiries in the sacred cavern.

Dimitri had been his own man for centuries. He might be Fen's younger brother, but he had hunted the vampire on his own for centuries. He was respected and held in some circles as a legend. His relationship with Skyler was private. He rarely spoke of her. Fen had gotten more information about her from their brief healing encounter together than in all the years Dimitri had given him safe havens to rest and heal in.

Mikhail seemed to be more amused than upset that none of them were forthcoming about Dimitri's young unclaimed lifemate. He simply nodded his head. "I'm certain that young woman somehow managed to seal both Fen and Dimitri to Mother Earth, a privilege to say the least."

"Did the ancients accept Fenris as he is?" Dimitri cut to the heart of the matter.

For the first time Mikhail hesitated. He let out a soft sigh. "I can't give you the exact answer you're looking for, or that I was looking for, Dimitri. The ancients acknowledge Fen as a great warrior who has lived with honor, but his blood is no longer the blood of a Carpathian."

Dimitri didn't flinch, but Fen was close to him and felt the inner blow like a punch to his gut. Mikhail had raised questions both men needed to think about. Tatijana was already tied to Fen and she would accept their fate together as his lifemate. It was different with Skyler. She was young, a human at that. Did Dimitri have the right to sentence her to a life so unknown, surrounded by enemies at every door?

"How long does it take before a hunter has the speed you have?" Gregori asked.

Fen shook his head. "It took me nearly a year to begin to merge with my wolf. I think you'd get a better answer from Manolito De La Cruz. You said he was recently changed. You have to remember when this happened to me we didn't even realize the cause was the blood. I'd been bitten numerous times in battles with rogue packs and the *Sange rau* we were chasing. In those days, no one knew about genetics. I recall the wolf and then gradually merging with it."

Fen shrugged. "Over the years, when Dimitri sometimes joined with me in battle, we gave each other blood when one of us was wounded as Carpathians do. Again, that never raised a single red flag."

Vikirnoff, who had remained silent throughout the ritual of the ancients, stepped forward to offer a greeting. "I gave you blood after your battle with Abel and even after what I saw, I didn't think anything of it. Giving blood is part of our everyday lives. No one would have considered not saving a fellow Carpathian."

"Or Lycan," Fen agreed.

"The Lycans stayed away from us because they didn't understand how the process of becoming a *Sange rau* worked all those centuries ago," Mikhail ventured. "If this started centuries ago then what you say about ingrained prejudice has to be very true."

Fen nodded. "Each new council renewed their decree to avoid Carpathians when possible. To fight alongside them when needed and there should be no animosity toward them."

"Why did you choose to live as a Lycan and stay close to their packs rather than come home?" Vikirnoff asked.

"In the beginning I wanted as much information as possible," Fen said. "But then I realized when I allowed the Lycan to be more dominant, it wasn't as difficult to fight the temptation of darkness swallowing me."

Gregori sent him one look from slashing silver eyes. "You said it was much more difficult to resist the call of the vampire."

"Much later," Fen said. "Not in the beginning. In the beginning the wolf at first protected me from the temptation, and later while I lived in the packs as a Lycan I realized the darkness wasn't as oppressive. Over the centuries it really aided me as I hunted. I was very . . . active as a hunter."

Dimitri nodded. "He was extremely proficient hunting rogues. When he was severely wounded, or during the full moon, he stayed in the ground and some of that time I guarded his resting place until he was fit again."

"Why is it you can be detected during the full moon and not any other time?" Mikhail asked curiously. "There has to be something there we can use against the *Sange rau*."

"It's all about energy with Lycans. When a pack hunts, they can't have much success if prey knows they're coming for them, so they've evolved to mask their energy," Fen explained. "Unfortunately, during the week cycle of the full moon, it's impossible. The pull is too strong on Lycans. I'm Lycan enough that the effect is the same for me. My energy feels different to the Lycans and if I'm in close proximity, they know immediately what I am."

"That's why you wanted Tatijana to warn MaryAnn and Manolito," Gregori said. "You knew they wouldn't know any of this and if they came across Lycans during a full moon, they'd immediately be targeted for death."

"I have evolved as the *Sange rau* . . ."

"The *Hän ku pesäk kaikak*," Tatijana and Mikhail corrected simultaneously. "Guardian of all." They looked at one another and smiled.

"I have evolved as the *Hän ku pesäk kaikak*, Guardian of all," Fen corrected, "over centuries. For warriors to choose to become a Guardian, thinking they will be able to fight the existing *Sange rau*, is ludicrous. It takes centuries to build the speed and understand the gifts. Not to mention, if they have no lifemate, the danger to their soul increases every passing year."

Mikhail nodded. "I think I have enough information to come to some decisions that will guide our people as well as help me persuade the Lycan council to agree to stop the hunt for those who are *Hän ku pesäk kaikak*—Guardians of all, rather than *Sange rau*. Once I determine our course of action, I'll call a meeting here in these sacred chambers with as many of our warriors as possible to let them know what we are up against."

Gregori nodded, but he didn't look happy about it.

"Word will be sent to MaryAnn and Manolito. Once I contact Zev and ask for a meeting with the Lycan council, if they agree, I'll call in our warriors to be here for that summit." Mikhail gave a slight bow, a gesture of respect toward Fen. "Thank you for coming today and allowing me the opportunity to learn."

"My lifemate, Tatijana, has sworn her allegiance to her prince. My brother, Dimitri, has as well," Fen said. "Although my blood is no longer Carpathian, my heart and my soul are. I would swear allegiance to my prince, if he would choose to accept me as I am."

"You are and always will be Carpathian first," Mikhail said. "I would be honored to have you among my warriors."

The hum in the crystals began again, swelling in volume, each tuned to a perfect note. Colors swirled, the deeper hues of dark reds and purples, as if the ancestors still were a little confused as to what Fenris really was, but were in agreement with his decision to swear allegiance to the prince; after all, they did recognize he had served their people with honor for centuries.

Fen opened the vein in his wrist and held the offering out to Mikhail. "I offer my life for our people. I pledge my loyalty to them through our blood bond."

Mikhail, Gregori cautioned.

He is one of us.

His blood isn't. I'll take his blood.

Mikhail's eyes darkened even more, and Gregori stepped back reluctantly.

Mikhail took the offered wrist, accepting the blood bond with Fen. He closed the wound carefully and gave Fen a slight bow. "As vessel of our people, I accept your sacrifice."

You could be the most stubborn man alive, Gregori hissed. *There are times I'd like to lock you in a dungeon and throw away the key.*

Mikhail's laughter was soft in Gregori's mind. *My daughter would not be very happy that her husband has such thoughts.*

You can't play the Savannah card whenever you want. Seriously, Mikhail, I'm responsible for your safety and you refuse to listen to me.

Mikhail sighed. *I listen. I always take what you say under careful consideration before I make my decisions, Gregori. I don't try to make your job more difficult but I still have to go with my instincts. Fenris Dalka will be a huge asset to our people. I know he has a place in our future. The ancestors know it as well.*

Fen wrapped his arm around Tatijana. He knew no one else had really noticed the instinctual move on Gregori's part to stop Mikhail from taking his blood. He couldn't blame Gregori. The more he was around Mikhail, the more respect he had for the man. The fate of an entire species rested on Mikhail's shoulders. He was thoughtful, intelligent and his own man—a bodyguard like Gregori's worst nightmare.

Fen was absolutely certain there had been an exchange between the two men, although neither Dimitri nor Tatijana seemed to notice. His awareness was extremely heightened and he'd felt a small current of energy going back and forth between the two men. He shouldn't have felt anything. They were used to communicating telepathically and had centuries of experience. Psychic communication was effortless for them.

Fen let out his breath slowly, not wanting to alert or alarm Gregori. They were deep beneath the Earth in the most sacred of caves, surrounded by the spirits of their ancestors, all warriors who would protect Mikhail, and he was aware of a telepathic conversation between the prince and his most trusted man. That was not good. If he'd been guessing, that would have been one thing, but Fen knew, and that meant he was still evolving. He would have to tell either Gregori or the prince at some point, but not here, not where he couldn't sufficiently protect Dimitri and Tatijana should the ancestors suddenly withdraw their acceptance.

What's wrong? Tatijana asked. She stroked a caress through his mind.

Instantly he felt peace stealing into him. He couldn't change what he was and she accepted him, problems and all. *I've got you, my lady, there can be nothing wrong.*

She laughed softly in his mind, filling him with that strange emotion he now thought of as joy. *Have I told you this rising that I am madly in love with you and you're clearly the most beautiful woman in the world? Because if I haven't, it is very remiss of me.*

You covered that nicely when we were feeding this evening. Remember? You picked me up and we made love? In case you've managed to forget that, I wrapped my legs around your waist and hooked my ankles so I wouldn't fall and just lowered myself right over you. Nice and slow. Is it coming back to you? Her voice smoldered, as sultry as ever.

There was no forgetting any moment of making love to her. He preferred to have that experience as often as possible. *It would be impossible to forget, my lady. It's burned into my soul.*

Vikirnoff waved his hand in front of Fen's face. "Are you still with us? Mikhail takes a little blood, and you're turning pale."

"He doesn't look pale to me," Dimitri drawled. "He looks a little overheated."

Fen sent his brother a fierce scowl, but Dimitri didn't look at all intimidated.

"I'd really like to get back to how to fight the *Sange rau*. There must be a way. Dimitri successfully managed to battle with the one you call Bardolf," Vikirnoff pointed out. "He's Carpathian. Was he able to do that because he has some of your mixed blood, or because he used some kind of special strategy?" Curiosity and a hint of eagerness edged his tone.

"I feared turning, just as most ancient Carpathian hunters do," Fen said, "so we practiced with war games each time we got together. Dimitri found the things that worked as well as the things that didn't."

"Hit and run is always the best approach," Dimitri said. "I had a few tricks I devised, but they could be used only once, at the most twice and only if I spread them out. The *Sange rau* learn and adapt very quickly, so the name of the game is always to change things up."

"Fortunately," Fen continued, "a vampire is a vampire is a vampire. The same with a rogue werewolf. They don't always have the patience they should. The *Sange rau* definitely take longer to anger, but they're actually more puffed up with ego than the vampire, so you can rile them enough that they make mistakes."

"It's definitely better for hunters to go after them in pack form," Dimitri added. "A single hunter doesn't have nearly the chance a group would have."

"But to fight pack-style takes skill. Bardolf will know every pack move, while Abel less so," Fen continued. "The thing you have to know about each *Sange rau* is where they came from, what they were before they mixed blood. Bardolf is comfortable as a wolf and when pressed, he goes back to what he knows best. The same holds true for Abel. Clearly in this relationship, Abel is the master and has acquired more skills because he's been *Sange rau* much longer."

"We'll need a crash course in fighting these bad boys," Vikirnoff stated. "Are the two of you willing to stick around and help us out?"

"That would be the idea," Dimitri said. "That and devising a strategy for destroying both Bardolf and Abel. If they do move the pack, we'll have to track them."

"Don't discount the pack. We don't have exact numbers and many were killed during the two battles. But even if we killed thirty or forty of them, if the pack is a hundred strong, as I'm afraid it may be, they still have a large army they can throw at you," Fen said. "They'll come at you during the day because Abel knows that's when they can do the most damage to you."

"Another good reason for the two of you to stay and help us out," Gregori said.

"They fight like a well-synchronized army. They strike fast, do as much damage as possible and kill as many as they can before they disappear. They nearly always go for the belly, ripping their adversary almost in half," Fen told them.

"I've got the scars to prove it," Dimitri said with a small self-deprecatory shrug.

Gregori smiled at him. "You're not alone. I think half our men had their bellies ripped open, me included. They definitely made us look like amateurs."

"I knew better than to let him get that close," Dimitri admitted.

"Packs are dangerous fighters and very skilled," Fen said.

"Think about the wolf packs in the forests," Dimitri added. "The Lycans are even more of a threat than an animal pack when they come at you because their very best strategists lead the hunt."

"But the Lycans don't hunt humans or Carpathians," Mikhail said quickly. "When you talk about pack hunting you're actually talking about the rogue, werewolf packs."

"True," Fen agreed, "but they start out as Lycans. Most of the time individuals within a pack drop out to become rogue. The rogues form their own packs."

Natalya, Vikirnoff's lifemate suddenly frowned. She was Tatijana's niece, daughter of her long dead brother, Soren, but the Dragonseeker features were there, including the changing eye and hair color. Having come to know Tatijana as he had, Fen wasn't surprised to see Natalya fighting by her life-mate's side or entering the cave of warriors with absolute confidence.

"What is it?" Fen asked.

"The elite hunters like Zev. Everyone's talking about him and how skilled he is."

"I saw him in action," Gregori said. "He's every bit as good as our best."

"So I've been hearing," Natalya said. "Do they ever go rogue?"

"It's possible," Fen said. "But I've never seen it happen. Our best hunters eventually succumb to the darkness and become vampires. Our species aren't that different. We're both born predators and we do have to submerge that part of our natures in order to keep our honor."

"You're part Lycan," Natalya persisted. "Do you have to fight the incli- nation to allow the animal side of you to take over?"

She knows the right questions to ask. Can you imagine Zev being a Sange rau? There was pride in Tatijana's voice.

She'd never had the chance to know her niece while she was growing up. In a way, Fen knew, she was grateful for that. She'd endured watching her father torture his own grandson and use him in horrendous experiments.

Tatijana was firmly merged with him as she had been since the moment they'd entered the cavern. She'd been so determined to protect him from the slightest insult, but it left her open to Fen reading her thoughts. She wanted a relationship with Natalya. Natalya had helped to rescue her aunts, but both Tatijana and Branislava had been so frail they'd been put in the earth almost immediately. She hadn't had the time to get to know her relatives.

She certainly does ask the right questions, Fen agreed. *She's definitely a Dragonseeker.*

"On the other hand, my friend, Vakasin, became *Sange rau* while we were hunting." Fen paused, shook his head and corrected himself. "Not *Sange rau*, he was a Guardian of all."

Once again Tatijana filled him with—her. Pure love. Closeness. The moment he felt sorrow for his lost comrade, she was there, sharing the emotion with him, comforting him. She was such a miracle.

Each rising, I hope to give you happiness. He didn't know how else to put into words his feelings for her. He could only hope that she felt that overwhelming emotion he had for her each time she merged with him.

Wolf man, don't get too romantic on me with your brother eyeing us both like he is.

You started it, he teased, but she had a point. Dimitri was sharp and he was watching both of them with a faint, knowing grin.

"We have to be far more creative and prepared for attacks during the day," Mikhail said. He'd been quiet through most of the discussion on fighting the packs. "Sara and Falcon's adopted children are human and they must be protected. We have only Jubal and Gary to help fight off the packs if they come while we're at our most vulnerable, and Gary is not in a position to help us at all for some time."

"Zev and his pack will defend them as long as the rogues are in the vicinity," Fen said. "They're sworn to hunt the rogues and bring them to justice."

"Will they be more interested in actively hunting the werewolves, or protecting our children?" Gregori asked.

Mikhail shrugged. "We will protect our own children with or without them. I have much to consider before we call a full council of warriors. I want to meet with Zev as soon as possible, meet his pack and get them to take an invitation back to their council to meet with us. As soon as we have an answer, if it's positive, I'll call in the others."

Mikhail turned back to the thick bloodred crystal, still pulsing with light. "I thank my ancestors for their kindness in making the journey to be with us and help guide us through these difficult times. Be well and go with honor."

The giant columns sang for a moment, colors shifting throughout the strange aurora borealis effect, shimmering and slowly fading away.

Fen heard the dripping of water and bubbling of the hot mud, and the breathing of his companions. More, he could feel the pulse and heartbeat of the mountain itself. Below them, he felt the pull of the magma pools. There was a rhythm here he felt in his own veins. Something about the sacred cave had only added to his acute senses, heightening them even more. Was he still evolving as he'd considered earlier?

Or your connection with Mother Earth has granted you even more gifts.

Why had he ever thought Tatijana wouldn't catch those alarmed thoughts? He took her hand, pulling it to his chest over his heart. Her explanation was delivered in her casual, matter-of-fact tone.

"My lifemate, Raven, would love to meet you, Fen. After battles and solemn ceremonies and rituals, it would be good for everyone to just relax. She thought it would be nice to bring everyone together for a celebration of sorts," Mikhail said. "I realize you're probably exhausted, but she rarely asks for anything so . . ."

"A celebration sounds lovely," Tatijana said instantly.

Her fingers tightened around Fen's. He could feel her eagerness.

A celebration. A party. I can visit with Natalya and get to know her. Bronnie might even rise for this. She's not as outgoing as I am. She's a better warrior, but she's shy around so many people. I'm afraid she won't ever come out of the earth. Tatijana smiled at him. *Wouldn't it be great if there was music? Dancing? I love dancing.*

"Will it be safe for everyone with two of the *Sange rau* so close? And a werewolf pack?" Natalya asked.

"I doubt if even Abel would be crazy enough to attack the Carpathians when all are present," Mikhail said. "But we will certainly hold our celebration in a safe, well-defensible place and have safeguards."

Natalya and Tatijana smiled at each other. Above their heads, Vikirnoff and Fen sent one another a quick grin.

"It's settled then," Mikhail said. "Next rising, we'll have a little fun."

14

Rain had fallen during the daylight hours, but that steady fall had only freshened the night air so that colors appeared vivid and clean. Leaves on the trees shimmered as Fen and Tatijana walked through the forest together toward the cave where the celebration was to be held. Fen found himself looking around him in a kind of wonder as if everything was new and he'd never seen it before.

Walking hand in hand with Tatijana always made him feel amazing, somebody—a family man. She would always know him like no other, and yet for him, he knew she would be a mystery he would take centuries to try to solve. How could one woman wipe out centuries of utter loneliness? How could she take away all the deaths, the friends he'd had to kill?

He walked with her slowly, savoring every step. Moss grew in chartreuse and lime curls up the tree trunks and over stones. He marveled he could distinguish the difference between the colors. The sky was so clear it appeared midnight blue, the scattered stars a wondrous collection of thousands of gems sparkling overhead. As they passed scattered bunches of flowers, Tatijana's sandal-covered feet skirting the edges of the beds, the night flowers unfolded their petals in tribute to her.

"You're magical, my lady," he said. "Absolutely magical."

Tatijana moved closer to him, fitting beneath his shoulder. "There's nothing magical about me, wolf man, but I'm glad you think there is."

He brought her fingers to the warmth of his mouth. She looked especially beautiful, dressed in a long flowing gown for dancing, just in case, she'd told him laughingly. She was definitely dancing tonight even if he was the one providing the music.

"I'm sorry you couldn't persuade your sister to come with us," Fen said. She'd tried hard to talk Branislava into rising just for a few hours, but to no avail. Tatijana had accepted her sister's decision, but she'd been disappointed. She missed her. He could feel that ache in her growing.

"She'll come out in her own good time. She's much fiercer than I am in a lot of ways, and yet she's always had a difficult time talking to others. Xavier, our father, really worked at keeping us afraid and under his thumb. He had a lot of psychological tricks. Bronnie always tried to shield me and she got the worst of everything."

"She was genuinely happy for you. Finding your lifemate. I could feel it," Fen said.

"She would be. She's like that. She may still come tonight. She didn't exactly say no. Bronnie does things her way. She wants to see Natalya and Razvan, that's my nephew, Natalya's brother. I told Bronnie I didn't think Razvan was close by, but just getting to know Natalya is a priceless gift."

They slowed their steps as they approached the edge of the forest, just at the base of the mountain, drawing out their time alone together.

"I gave her as much information on the rogue packs, elite hunters, Mikhail's concerns and everything else I could think of when she asked for it," Fen said. "She was adamant that I give her my blood."

"I expected her to insist," Tatijana said. "She's protective of me. All we had was each other for centuries." She gave him a little nervous half smile. "Do you really think I look all right?"

She had dressed with such care and changed her mind twice before settling on the long gown. She'd put her thick hair in a long braid and then put it up in an intricate knot. She'd taken that down and now it was partly up and partly down, in a knot but with loops of braids.

"You look so beautiful you take my breath away," he said sincerely. "You have no need to be nervous tonight, Tatijana. No one can hold a candle to you."

He was surprised at her vulnerability. She'd never really shown that side of herself before. She fought the rogue pack with him, stood up to Gregori and entered the sacred cave of warriors fully prepared to do battle on his behalf. She had even seemed sure of herself in the tavern, dancing and ignoring the rough crowd. Now, going to a celebration with her fellow Carpathians, she was anxious.

He slipped his arm around her, halting her, tipping up her chin so he could look into her brilliant ever-changing eyes. "I love you very much, *sívamet*. I would never want another woman . . ."

"Of course not, because I'm your lifemate."

He shook his head. "Silly woman. I fell in love with you long before I claimed you. It's impossible not to love you when I'm in your mind and see your kindness and compassion. When I see who you really are at your very core. I'm more than honored that you're my lifemate, but my love for you is all consuming. My heart and soul, my mind and body, all belong to you."

He slipped his palm around her neck, his thumb tipping her head up to his. Her eyes, so startling green, looked like deep pools of emerald. "I know this sounds silly to say out loud, Tatijana, but you take my breath away."

Her lips curved into a smile, beautiful beyond his wildest imagination. Her lower lip was perfect, inviting, a temptation he couldn't ignore. He bent his head to hers, brushing small, light kisses over her chin and up to the corner of her irresistible mouth. He teased her lower lip, drawing it into his mouth, tasting the sweetness of her, before settling his mouth over hers.

He was gentle, tender even, something he hadn't known he could be. When he kissed her, the world seemed to stand still. Time simply stopped. She became the entirety of his world. The texture of her skin, the cool feel of it against the heat of his. The silk of her hair falling around her face and brushing his. His hand seemed so large framing her face, as he deepened the kiss, stroking her neck with the pads of his fingers.

He found himself lost in her taste. In the rising passion between them. Love was in his kiss. How could it not be when she was truly everything? He kissed her again and again, reluctant to stop. "I could kiss you forever," he admitted.

Tatijana reached up with her slender arms and pulled his head down to hers, kissing him one more time. "I love kissing you. Kissing forever sounds like a good idea."

"But . . ." He heard that laughter in her voice.

"We'll miss the party and I want to dance. I really, really want to dance."

"More than kiss?" Fen raised his eyebrow and looked as stern as possible, daring her to choose the wrong answer.

"I was hoping for both," Tatijana admitted. "I'm very good at multi-tasking."

"Very diplomatic. You also think on your feet. I'm going to have to work to stay ahead of you." He took her hand. "Come on. We won't miss the party."

"Is Dimitri coming tonight?" Tatijana asked as she walked with him.

Fen let out a sigh. "Dimitri hasn't claimed his lifemate and he's very close to the edge. We knew some time ago that over the last few centuries our blood exchanges from the battles we shared with vampires had begun the change in him. The change can ease the terrible toll of the centuries of darkness and the constant whispered temptation, but Dimitri has emotions and colors restored."

"But doesn't knowing he has a lifemate help? And he has his emotions and color back."

"You would think so," Fen said, "but it can drive a Carpathian male mad. The centuries close in on you, all those deaths, all that darkness and still no light to guide your way. For some time now, Dimitri has had the infusion of my blood as well, but not enough to change him—just enough to add to the fight he's had."

She frowned. "I don't understand."

"I don't think any of us understand, Tatijana, it's imprinted in our DNA. Our men are driven to find and bind our mates to us. It's primal. The drive is very strong and we don't like other men around our woman, especially if she is unclaimed. Modern society and the fact that many of our lifemates are another species have added to the danger of waiting."

She sighed. "Before becoming your lifemate, I only had Bronnie to worry about. Now I have relatives as well."

He laughed. "I never thought about it like that." He gestured toward the cave. "I think you have far more relatives than I do."

She started laughing as well. "Uh-oh. Relatives. I've probably got a lot more than either of us know. We may have to run from all this."

He leaned down to kiss her again just because she looked so radiant there in the night. Her skin looked flawless, her mouth generous, seductive, oh, so alluring he couldn't possibly resist her.

"I think kissing you while dancing is a very good idea, my lady," he murmured when he lifted his head. "Are you certain you don't just want to have a private dance right here?"

Tatijana laughed. "We're just feet from the entrance. I'm certain eventually someone will come along."

"We'll be doing them a favor, properly educating them in the ways of love," Fen persisted with another stolen kiss.

"You are going to properly dance with me," she said.

He laughed and took her hand, walking her right up to the cliff side of the mountain. The cave entrance was narrow, a mere crack between two jutting boulders. Carpathians had no trouble slipping through to the wider corridor leading down to the well-lit chamber where the gathering was being held. Torches were lit high up along the cathedral ceilings, casting glowing, dancing lights around the enormous chamber. Steam rose from a warm pool in one corner of the room where water spilled from a series of cracks in the wall above it.

The sound of children laughing tugged at Fen. He hadn't been around a Carpathian child in centuries. His heart did a curious somersault the moment he walked into the room and saw two identical twin girls playing with a little boy near a miniature playhouse inside of a jungle gym for toddlers. Another little boy with a riot of chestnut curls hurried over to the other three, a bucket in his hand. Wolf cubs followed the four children everywhere they went.

Several older children were grouped together around a fire pit, their eyes bright as an adult male told them a story. The boy who looked the oldest wrapped his arm around the youngest little girl when she gasped and drew back at whatever the storyteller said. The sight brought back memories of his youth, when Carpathians gathered together and stories were a big part of the night entertainment.

He hadn't realized then how much history was being handed down to him. It was only later when he needed information on fighting vampires or suddenly he'd remember how an ancestor had flown between two close rocks that he realized the stories had been a way to teach him. Clearly that tradition was still in place.

Tatijana slipped her hand into the crook of his arm, her body sliding closer to his as if for protection, bringing his attention back to her. Most of the adults in the room turned to look at them as they entered. The atmosphere was welcoming and celebratory. That also felt familiar to him, the faded memory suddenly leaping to the surface. Carpathians had taken many opportunities to come together for a night of fun.

"I'm so glad you came," Mikhail greeted them. He had his arm around a short woman with clouds of dark hair and unusual, almost violet eyes. "This is Raven, my lifemate. My son, Alexandru, is over there." He gestured toward the toddler playground. "Raven, you remember Tatijana, of course, and this is Fenris Dalka, Dimitri's older brother."

"Tatijana," Raven exclaimed, holding out both hands. She also wore a long gown that swirled around her curvy figure. "You look lovely tonight."

"She's hoping for dancing," Fen said.

"So am I," Raven admitted.

"Thank you, Raven," Tatijana answered. "I'm so glad you thought of this. I love the entire idea of the community coming together for a party."

"I thought we all could use a little fun after . . ." She trailed off and looked at Mikhail.

He shrugged. "You can say it, we got our butts kicked."

"You've been saying it often enough to Gregori," Raven teased. "He so loves to tweak our son-in-law."

"It's good for him," Mikhail was unrepentant.

Raven just laughed, her hand sliding down Mikhail's arm to his wrist in an intimate gesture. She turned to Fen. "I wanted to thank you for tracking the rogue pack. We would have been in far worse shape if it wasn't for you."

"I'm glad I ran across them," Fen said honestly. He looked at Tatijana. "I might have missed meeting my lifemate."

Raven laughed. "I honestly think if it's meant to happen, it does. Fate or destiny must put us on the right path. When I came out here all those years ago on my own, just to get away, I never dreamed I'd meet a man like Mikhail. He was very intimidating to a woman who knew nothing about Carpathians."

Tatijana joined in her laughter. "He can still be intimidating when he wants."

"Not so much to me anymore," Raven said. "Come meet our daughter, Savannah. She's lifemate to Gregori. Our two adorable granddaughters are right over there, and they definitely have their daddy wrapped around those little fingers of theirs."

The love and affection for her family was obvious in her expression, her tone of voice and the tenderness in her eyes when she looked at them. Fen turned to see Gregori scoop up a little girl just as she made a daring leap from a slide to the top of the playhouse.

"*Isä*"—*father*. She scowled at him, yet somehow managed to pout at the same time. "I coulda made it."

"Anya." Gregori used his sternest voice. "I told you to stop trying to jump from the top of the slide to the playhouse."

Fen pressed his lips together to keep from laughing. The slide was no more than two feet off the ground and the playhouse roof wasn't much taller. Little Anya didn't seem intimidated by her father at all, not even when he was holding her high off of the ground, his silver eyes glaring directly into hers. Her dark, curly hair bounced around her head like a halo, framing her little pixie face. Her eyes, as light as her father's, grew stormy. She lifted her chin defiantly.

"I'm not a baby like Sandu. I can do it."

Mikhail lowered his voice. "The girls call Alexandru, Sandu." He said it just loud enough that Gregori could hear and know they were watching. Amusement was uppermost in the prince's tone. "The twins are only a couple of weeks older than he is, but they like to think they're years ahead. He's bigger than both of them."

"*Isä*," the second little girl said. "If we can't jump, can we float? You know we're really good at floating."

Gregori cast a glare over his shoulder at Mikhail, turned back to his daughter and sighed. He reached down and picked her up. "Anastashia, I thought we talked about this. You need adult supervision when you're trying things, even floating. It's dangerous."

"How can they talk already?" Tatijana asked. "Isn't that advanced even for our children?"

"They were born very gifted," Raven admitted. "They speak ancient Carpathian as well as several other languages. Well . . . I should clarify. They understand the languages and know many words and use sentences. As far as what they can do at such a young age, they're giving us gray hair."

Mikhail tugged on Raven's hair. "I don't see any gray."

She laughed softly. "Lucky for me I'm Carpathian and I don't turn gray, although with those two little girls I just might anyway." She gestured toward the twins. "They were born early and were in separate incubators. Barely alive, they floated from one to the other, determined to stay together. In the end, there was nothing we could do so we let them stay together. Gregori's had his hands full ever since."

"That Anya, she's a little daredevil," Tatijana said.

Fen could tell she was proud of the little girl. He imagined Tatijana would have been like Anya, wanting to try everything.

Raven nodded. "If she was a boy, Gregori wouldn't have any problem allowing her to try to jump from the slide to the playhouse roof, but he has this thing about his girls."

"How's that working out for him?" Mikhail asked, nuzzling the top of Raven's head.

"You aren't going to find it so funny when our son starts defying you to do dangerous things," Raven pointed out, but she laughed softly when she said it and rubbed her head along his chest affectionately. "Little Miss Anya is far too adventurous. I think she'd try shapeshifting if anyone gave her half a chance."

"She probably already has," Mikhail pointed out.

"Bite your tongue," Raven said.

Fen found himself genuinely laughing at Gregori's predicament. He was tall, broad-shouldered and much respected in the Carpathian world. When he spoke everyone listened. Next to Mikhail, Gregori's word was law, yet his twin girls, barely two, defied him. With them, he was patient and gentle, although firm, not that it seemed to do him any good with little Anya. She was obviously adventurous.

"Aren't they beautiful?" Tatijana asked.

"Terrifying, though," Fen said. "If we have children, *sívamet*, let's try for boys. If the girls turn out like you, I'll definitely have a heart attack before they're grown."

Tatijana laughed, turning to Raven. "Men. They're such babies when it comes to children. What's your Alexandru like? You've given him a fine name. It means defender of all mankind, doesn't it?"

Raven nodded. "It's a lot for a little boy to live up to."

Fen was curious about the prince's son as well. His gaze continually went to the four little ones, Gregori and Savannah's twin daughters who were planting kisses all over their father's face, the curly-headed boy slightly older and the little boy with big eyes the color of his mother's and midnight black hair just like his father's. Fen noticed that even though both girls were in Gregori's arms, the twins kept an eye on the prince's son, as did the curly-headed boy. "The twins are very interested in Alexandru," he observed aloud.

Raven nodded. "They've already established a bond. Gregori's a little worried about it. It isn't a normal child's bond, but the Daratrazanoff/Dubrinsky bond. As far as we know, no woman has ever been second to the prince. Anastashia has already shown very early signs of being a natural healer like Gregori. If anyone gets so much as a bump she rushes over and takes care of it. Even the older children go to her. Anya is Gregori all over again. She's exactly like him right down to her fierce protectiveness of Alexandru. Anastashia actually is equally protective but in a far gentler way.

"Alexandru is already thoughtful, like Mikhail. He seems to think problems through before he makes a move," Raven said. "He's serious most of the time."

"And who is the little boy who looks so much like him?" Fen asked.

"That's Jacques and Shea's son, Stefan. He's only about nine months older but he definitely thinks he has to watch out for the others. He's a little jokester, although he takes his job of protecting the twins and Alexandru seriously," Mikhail said. "He's like Jacques was when he was young. I suspect he'll be playing pranks on all of us in a couple of years. No one will be safe."

Raven laughed. "He'll definitely enlist the aid of the twins and they'll be happy to help."

A small, curvy woman who looked a lot like Raven approached them. Mikhail held out his hand to her and pulled her to his side. "This is my daughter, Savannah. I don't know if you had the chance to meet Tatijana yet, but she is Dragonseeker, Razvan and Natalya's aunt."

"It's such an honor to finally meet you," Savannah said instantly, taking Tatijana's outstretched hand. "Gregori and my father think so highly of you."

"She saved several of our warriors nasty wounds with her quick thinking," Mikhail said.

"I think everyone was helping out," Tatijana said.

"And this is Fenris Dalka, Dimitri's older brother," Mikhail continued with the introductions. "No doubt Gregori has spoken of him as well." His tone turned droll.

Fen couldn't help but laugh. "No doubt."

Savannah joined in Fen's laughter. "Actually he has spoken of you at great length," she admitted, "but it was all good. My father replayed the entire battle for him and Gregori was very impressed with your skills. I'm so glad you're here. Sara and Falcon's children"—she indicated the small group of older children gathered together to listen to the storyteller—"are all human with psychic abilities. They were living in sewers when Sara found them. They'd already banded together and formed a family, working together for survival before she found them and brought them here."

"Who takes care of them during the daylight hours?" Fen asked. "How would something like that work?"

"Gabriel and Francesca also adopted a human child," Mikhail pointed out. "Young Skyler, and they've done quite well."

"Aidan and Alexandria are raising Alexandria's younger brother, Josh," Savannah added.

"Colby and Rafael De La Cruz have Paul and Ginny," Raven said. "It can be done with a little help and being creative about the hours you spend with them. Sara and Falcon rise as early as possible and the children sleep in and start their day later so they can stay up later."

"Who watches them?" Fen persisted. More than once he'd run across a child he would have liked to help, but it was necessary to go to ground. Who would ensure their protection when he was immersed in the soil as if dead?

Tatijana brushed his mind with love. *You are so compassionate, Fen. Few men think of taking in a child when they live a lifestyle like yours.*

Sadly, vampires, rogue packs and the Sange rau *leave behind a number of orphans.* He looked down at her. *If we can't have our own children, would you consider a family such as Sara's?*

Even if we have biological children, I would love to incorporate other children who need us into our family, she assured.

Even if they are human or Lycan?

I would expect that they would be human or Lycan as Carpathians have so few children.

Tatijana's voice was so loving it took discipline not to lean down and kiss her. Instead, he brushed a kiss over her mouth in his mind.

"Sara and Falcon have a few people who help them out during the daylight hours when they can't be there. There's Maria, who is their full-time nanny. Slavica and her daughter both help as well. Slavica and her husband, Mirko, own the local inn and she's very busy as a rule, but when there's need, she comes. If there's trouble during the afternoons, we have Jubal and Gary and Slavica's husband to guard them," Savannah explained.

"The oldest boy, Travis, is eleven now. He's the oldest of the seven," Mikhail said. "He's Falcon's shadow and he's already learning how to fight. Falcon and the other adults work with all the children. They have to know our enemies, just as all of us were taught. Travis looks out for the others. The little girl he has his arm around is Emma. She's the youngest girl."

Fen could see the boy was older beyond his years. Even while he seemed to be taking in every detail of the story, he was watching his siblings. When two of the boys began punching each other and then knocked into one of the girls, he pinned them with a very adult look and both stopped their antics immediately. One whispered an apology to the girl seated beside him.

He indicated the byplay with his chin. "He definitely has their attention."

"That's Peter and Lucas. They're both ten and a handful. Jase, the youngest boy, is sitting very close to him and keeps scooting closer," Raven told them with a little laugh.

As the story progressed, Fen could see the littlest boy with a mop of blond hair inch closer and closer to Travis. "Chrissy is the one Lucas bumped into and Blythe is sitting beside her. They're all human, but the psychic talents they possess are extraordinary."

"Where in the world did Sara find them?" Tatijana asked.

"She read an article in a magazine about children living in the sewers

Vikirnoff, who had been talking to his brother Nicolae, turned around abruptly and instantly was at her side as if sensing her distress. He wrapped his arm around her waist and pulled her back into the shelter of his body.

"What is it?" Tatijana asked gently. "I'm your sister-kin. There is nothing you can tell me that would make me love you less."

"Were you aware Xavier was the one possessing Razvan's body against his will and forcing him to do such terrible things, or did you think my brother did them?" Natalya took a deep breath. "I mean, they were such hideous crimes. All those women giving birth to children Xavier wanted to use just for their blood. And if they didn't measure up to his standards he threw them away. Like poor little Skyler being sold to that awful man she thought was her father."

"We were there in the caves and observed firsthand Razvan taking blood from his own child, and of course, he stabbed Bronnie so she couldn't escape the ice cave. But we knew it was Xavier using his grandson as a puppet in his never-ending quest for immortality and power."

"I wouldn't believe the things I heard about him, or even saw with my own eyes for so long, but in the end, I stopped believing in him," Natalya said, sorrow in her eyes. "When he needed me most, I wasn't there."

"Natalya." Tatijana took both of her hands. "You must know Razvan would never hold such a thing against you. He loves you very much. How could he not? The thought that you were free and happy somewhere in the world kept him going all those years. We spoke of it often in the beginning, when he hadn't been so worn down. Before Xavier murdered the little mage, Lara's mother, in front of him and left Razvan chained there with her body. After that, Razvan rarely communicated with us."

"Xavier was so hideous, so evil," Natalya said with a small shudder. "I have a hard time with the idea that he's actually my grandfather."

Tatijana touched Fen's mind, almost as if she needed reassurance. Those little moments, when his warrior woman was vulnerable tugged at his heart-strings.

"Xavier is my father," Tatijana said. "He tried to destroy an entire species. He created children using his own son, just for their blood. He tortured and killed well over a thousand individuals of several species, including my mother and brother for his experiments. The list of his heinous crimes could go on for hours, but I refuse to feel shame or guilt for the terrible things he did. I was tortured and imprisoned by him just like his other victims. Bronnie, Razvan and I survived by relying on one another and through Razvan, you, Natalya. In a way, you saved us all. That's what you need to always keep in your heart."

Fen was more proud of her in that moment than when she'd fought off the rogue pack so fearlessly. The moment she'd reached out to him telepathically, he had merged his mind with hers, and he felt her response to Xavier's name. Just his name. She had slammed the door on the memories welling up, but his name made her feel ill.

Tatijana?

Merged so deep with her, Fen heard Branislava's voice when she reached out to her sister. Clearly Tatijana's distress and that glimpse of a horrific childhood and the ensuing years had been enough to cause alarm in Branislava.

You have need of me?

At once Tatijana soothed her sister. *No. No. I'm sorry I disturbed you. I was talking of difficult times with Natalya. But it is fun here and nice to see the children. The prince has a son, Gregori has twin daughters and Jacques has a beautiful little boy as well. Sara and Falcon have seven amazing children. The world seems a different place with children in it, Bronnie.*

He didn't manage to wipe out our people, did he, Tatijana?

No, my sister, he did not. All those times you fought to slow his experiments down, all the times you ruined them and he had to start over, were for good. You risked your life and in the end it paid off.

There was pride in Tatijana's voice, and Fen caught glimpses of her past, vignettes of memories where she laid, heart beating fast, fist jammed in her mouth to keep herself from making any noise while her sister crawled to Xavier's laboratory and sabotaged his latest work. Tatijana had been terrified Xavier would kill Branislava or enact one of his terrible punishments.

She's amazing, he whispered to Tatijana. *Her courage is terrifying.*

Tatijana beamed at him. *She was always the brave one. She defied Xavier at every turn and when he threatened me, she always got between us. I was always a little more timid when I was young. I learned to take a stand and fight for the things that are important from her.*

"Thank you so much, Tatijana, for saying those things to me," Natalya said. "I can't seem to forgive myself for losing faith in my brother."

"You know I was the one who convinced you Razvan was evil," Vikirnoff said. "You never would have thought it, even for a moment."

"You were just protecting me," Natalya said. "You didn't know him. How could you think anything else? But I'm his sister, and he sacrificed so much for me. For all of us."

Tatijana shook her head. "The future lies in front of us. We have each other now. Razvan escaped and found his lifemate. He feels happy to me whenever I touch him, even from a distance. I'm very happy with my lifemate as you are with yours, Natalya. Razvan is incapable of holding grudges. He's seen so much and been through so much there is little that can ever be done to him that would ever shock or hurt him. He would want you to be happy, Natalya. Think of it like that. If you think you owe him, then be happy. That's all that ever mattered to him."

"I think that's an excellent idea," Fen said. He took Tatijana's arm and drew her a little away from the others, out toward the center of the cave, right in the middle of the crowd. "And now if you don't mind, I have something important to say to my lifemate."

15

There was something mischievous about the way Fen pulled Tatijana into the center of the crowd that warned her he was up to something. He had both laughter and something else in his expression, something that totally melted her heart. When Fen looked at her like that—so playful and carefree, Tatijana was lost. How could she not be? The lines in his face eased. There was merriment in his eyes when he looked at her. There was peace in his heart. And love in his mind.

He had seen so many horrific things over the centuries. He had fought endless battles that had resulted in mortal wounds. She was the one who had brought light and hope and peace to him. She brought joy and laughter. Companionship and most importantly belonging. She couldn't help but fall deeper in love when he was looking at her like that.

When they reached the middle of the room, he stepped away from her and gave her an old-world, very courtly bow.

He looked the perfect gentleman and she couldn't help dropping a small curtsey back to him. His smile told her it had been the right thing to do. The cavern hushed. Even the children. From somewhere behind her, music began to play.

You caught a forest scent by fate's strange chance,
and found me—though you had not sought romance.

He sang the words to her, his voice shocking her with its perfect pitch and a sexy rasp to it that sent a chill down her spine. He held out his hand to her, continuing in song.

Still I sing; lady, may I have this dance?

Tatijana felt tears burning behind her eyes. Music grew louder, taking on a rhythmic beat. She didn't know where it came from, and she couldn't look away from Fen to see who he'd enlisted to help him make this night special for her. She placed her hand in his. He took it gently and brought her in close to him. She actually was shaking as she put her other hand on his shoulder.

Music swelled in the cavern as he began to move with his fluid grace until she felt as if she was floating. His mouth moved against her ear. "This is for you alone, my lady," he whispered. "I wrote it for you."

He began to sing again while they moved in perfect synchronization, their bodies close while her heart found and followed the rhythm of his.

I roamed the lonely centuries in the dark,
This Fenris wolf near famished for the light.
Then you appeared—a sudden brilliant spark,
My miracle who banishes my night.

Tatijana laid her head against his chest and closed her eyes, savoring the feeling of floating and the way his body felt so warm and hard against hers as they moved together. His arms were strong, holding her safe in a world where she knew madness and monsters often lurked.

You, too, knew loneliness while trapped in ice.
Set free, you swore you'd not be bound again.
Then may you never feel my arms a vise!
And may you willingly enter my den!

Above their heads, stars swirled around the high ceiling of the cavern and the torches dimmed, giving the illusion that they were dancing beneath the sky itself. Tatijana held herself closer to him. The night felt magical, a wondrous surreal moment as they drifted together, their bodies close while she felt love for him rising, swamping her.

Your eyes . . . they shift in color like your hair.
They gleam like emeralds,
Fascinate with light.
You dance as though with wings upon the air.
You match our greatest warriors in fight.

Tatijana knew the words of his song to her were heartfelt. How could she not? She was in his mind, feeling what he was feeling. He made no attempt to hide his love, respect and admiration from her—or anyone else. She felt beautiful, loved and as if she was the only woman in the world.

My dragon flame, you set my heart aglow!
Above all else, these ancient words hold true . . .
My Tatijana, these words hold true:
You are my lifemate.
I belong to you.

Fen really had written the song for her. He sang it to her in front of their people, and their prince, uncaring who heard as he poured out his heart to her. She hadn't known a man, a fierce independent warrior, could make himself so vulnerable in front of others the way he was. He didn't seem to care that everyone could see how much she really meant to him. His voice, when he sang the lyrics, rang with raw honesty. His emotions were totally exposed for all of those present to see.

The music began to fade and she lifted her head, tears in her eyes as she looked up at him. She had fallen so deeply in love with him, and yet she didn't even know when her emotions had grown so intense. Out of the corner of her vision she realized other couples had been dancing as well. She hadn't even known they were there, she'd been so completely wrapped up in her magical dance with Fen.

To make her dance happen, not only had Fen written a song for her and sang it publicly, he had to have enlisted the aid of other Carpathians for the music and the show of stars on the ceiling.

"Thank you," she whispered almost shyly, slipping her arms around his neck and leaning into the shelter of his body. "I don't know what to think about you, sometimes, Fen. This was such a beautiful, amazing gift and I'll always treasure the memory of it."

"I wanted you to know how I feel about you, Tatijana. You need to know how truly extraordinary you really are. You love to dance and I thought this would be a good way to let you know how much you mean to me."

"This was perfect, Fen. Just perfect. I'll never forget it."

Fen brushed his mouth gently over hers. She was more radiant than ever. For him that was enough. He had wanted to give her something special. He had poured his heart and soul into his music for her. He had no idea what the future would bring for them. His life was one of battles and secrecy. Every moment that he could, he wanted to give her laughter and joy.

"Fen." Gregori came up behind them. "Thank you for that. Savannah has wanted to dance for some time. We haven't had a lot of celebrations and this has been fun for her."

"Is she leaving already?" Tatijana asked, swinging around to see Savannah holding Anya in her arms. Destiny held Anastashia. Neither of the little girls looked happy.

"We've invited Zev and the others to join us," Gregori explained, "but we thought it best if the children went home. It's late for them to be out."

Fen knew Gregori was protecting the children, using the guise of lateness. It was still fairly early for Carpathians. All of the youngsters had to be used to staying up nights, even Sara and Falcon's human children. There was no danger from Zev and his pack. If anything, everyone would be that much safer with them around. Still, he couldn't blame Gregori. There were only a handful of Carpathian children. If he was in Gregori's shoes, responsible for their safety, he would have spirited them away from strangers as well.

"I'm so glad I had the chance to see them," Tatijana said. "They bring us hope."

Fen slipped his arm around her waist as they waved good-bye to the children. Several of the unlifemated males escorted them as they left. Gregori went to work changing the entrance of the cavern so the Lycans could easily slip inside and yet would never find the entrance again when it was changed back to the natural formation.

"The children have plenty of protection." Fen made it a statement. He was uneasy with the rogue pack so close and two *Sange rau* in the neighborhood. Surely by now, after all the discussions and the casualties the pack had inflicted on the Carpathians, Mikhail and Gregori were taking the threat as very real.

Gregori nodded. "We've enlisted the aid of our ancestors as well. This night no harm will come to these children."

Fen frowned. The temperature in the labyrinth of sacred caves was far too much for a human child. "What of Falcon's children?"

Gregori suddenly smiled and it transformed his face completely. He looked younger and more relaxed. "A word of advice, Fen. With your soft heart you'd better never have daughters."

Fen scowled at him. "I don't have a soft heart."

"You'd be a complete pushover."

Mikhail had quietly come up behind him. "He says that kind of thing to all of us to make himself look better. Everyone knows his twins rule his life." His laughter was very genuine. He nudged Gregori. "Poor man. Brought down by babies."

Gregori gave Mikhail his deepest, forbidding scowl. "I'm very firm with those girls. They know better than to mess with me."

Fen couldn't help but join in Mikhail's laughter. Clearly Gregori didn't care if he was firm with his daughters or not, they were everything to him.

"Gregori even told my adorable granddaughters to call him *Isäntä* out of sheer desperation." Mikhail continued to give Gregori a hard time.

"Master of the house," Fen translated. "And did they?"

"It might have worked," Gregori said, "if Savannah hadn't laughed hysterically every time they called me master."

Tatijana's laughter joined the men's. "I'm sorry, Gregori. What a blow. Your little girls are adorable, and quite frankly, I'd probably give them anything they wanted and Fen would be even worse. Don't deny it, Fen, you would."

Fen had to admit she was right. "Your daughters are just too beautiful, Gregori, with their sassy attitudes and their adventurous streaks. I'd be lost."

Gregori smiled and shrugged his shoulders as if finally giving up. "Her mother doesn't know it, but Anya has already tried shapeshifting. I caught her two risings ago. Took a hundred years off my life. Forbidding her isn't going to work. And what she does, Anastashia does. I'm going to have to start working with them. I promised Anya I would, but only if she promised not to try on her own."

"Savannah is going to kill you." Mikhail made it a statement.

"I know. I haven't figured out how to tell her. There isn't any stopping Anya," Gregori said, running a hand through his hair in the first sign of agitation Fen had ever seen him make.

"She's a miniature you," Mikhail pointed out. "You were just like that as a boy."

"I can't believe I started this early. She's barely two," Gregori said.

"I was your friend, you maniac," Mikhail told him. "We got in so much trouble together, and you were always the instigator. Even at two."

"Don't believe him," Gregori said. "He's never followed anyone in his life. Especially when any advice given was for his own good."

The deep affection and easy friendship Gregori and Mikhail had for one another was very clear. Fen believed Gregori. Mikhail definitely was born to lead. He listened to those around him, but in the end, he made his own decisions. He'd most likely been that way since birth, and his son probably was a great deal like him. Little Anya would have just as difficult a time trying to protect young Alexandru as her father had with Mikhail.

"The children are tucked away for the night," Jacques announced. "Shea's going to join us for a short time." His voice lightened when he uttered his lifemate's name. "We've got to get the food right. Fen, that's your department. You know more about the Lycans than any of us."

"You're going to serve food?" Food certainly wasn't the forte of Carpathians.

"We want them to feel as at home with us as possible," Mikhail said. "The more they see us as they are, the better chance we have of their council coming here for a summit meeting. I also want to start the process of subtly changing their view of a Guardian versus the *Sange rau*."

Fen nodded. He could see how Mikhail's plan was a good one. The elite hunters, especially Zev, had the ear of the council. If they could be persuaded, they would be advocates for an alliance with the Carpathians.

"I'll handle the food," he agreed. "Everyone here has to view me as a Lycan. That's how Zev knows me. If he suspects any different, there will be trouble." He pulled on thin, almost invisible gloves.

Mikhail raised his eyebrow.

Fen shrugged. "No Lycan ever goes anywhere without his gloves or his silver. Zev's weapons are amazing, but most just have stakes. Silver can't touch their skin either, so they have to protect themselves. They'll be wearing their gloves, or they'll have them, and they'll definitely notice if I don't."

"I didn't think about that aspect of what they do," Gregori said. "During an intense battle they have to occasionally touch it."

"Silver burns like nothing you've ever felt," Fen said. "Every elite has scars from it, but that's one of the hazards of fighting the rogue packs. They accept it just as every Carpathian hunter accepts he's going to get torn up fighting the undead."

"I covet Zev's weapons," Jacques admitted with a grin. "Totally cool."

Mikhail groaned. "My brother has become very modern with his language."

"I was always very modern," Jacques said. "You're a dinosaur, but we're working on dragging you into this century."

"Go recheck the entrance with Gregori so everything is ready for the Lycans to come inside," Mikhail ordered. "And when your lifemate arrives, send her my way. I'm going to tell her tales of you as a boy."

"Big threat." Jacques shrugged his shoulders at his brother. "You've already done that." Laughing, he followed Gregori toward the main entrance to the cave.

The large cavern took on another look entirely. All playthings for children were gone. The stars were left in place as if their celebration was out in the open, but the torches were changed to soft lighting. On one side, Fen set up tables with food and drink. Tables and chairs were strewn around the area. Soft music played and a few of the couples danced under the scattered stars.

The chamber took on the atmosphere of a long ago ballroom, elegant and warm. Destiny and her lifemate, Nicolae, had returned from escorting the children and he spun her around the dance floor. Destiny laughed like a child herself, clearly enjoying the simple pleasure. Vikirnoff and Natalya danced alongside them, laughing with them and trying to outdo each other's intricate dance steps.

Looking around the room, Fen realized most of the single hunters weren't present, at least not openly. He allowed himself to use his Guardian senses, scanning the chamber. Of course. He should have known how Gregori thought by now. Mikhail and Raven were present and they were inviting strangers into their midst. In spite of all the Carpathian hunters present, Gregori would have an ace or two in the hole—in this case four of them.

Tomas, Lojos, Mataias and Andre were concealed somewhere in the chamber. Each guarded a key position. He knew them all well, those ancients, and they were dangerous predators. The elites had amazing skills, but Gregori knew how they fought now. He was very fast at learning and he wouldn't get caught unawares again. He was prepared for any act of treachery.

Zev came through the door first, which didn't surprise Fen at all. Zev was so much like Gregori they could have been brothers. Neither would probably ever admit it, but they thought alike.

Mikhail immediately crossed the chamber to greet him, Gregori and Jacques on either side of him. Fen moved just as quickly to join the greeting party. As a Lycan, it would be expected. Zev was of the highest rank, above any of the packs and would never be ignored by any Lycan once he had revealed himself as an elite scout.

Mikhail shook Zev's hand. Out of respect, Zev had removed his gloves, something Fen knew elites rarely did. Some slept with them on their hands, especially during a hunt. A rogue pack could attack at any time.

"Thank you for coming," Mikhail greeted. "More, again, thank you for coming to our aid when the rogue pack attacked. We would have suffered far more causalities and perhaps even losses."

Zev gave him an easy smile. Fen noted that smile never reached his eyes.

Zev had the eyes of a man who had lived long and saw far too many horrific things.

"Thank you for inviting us. My pack needed a break. They've been traveling and fighting battles with rogues for weeks now. We knew something big was happening, but we had no idea the trail would lead us here."

He turned as the others entered. "This is Daciana."

Mikhail bowed over her hand. "Welcome and thank you. Destiny tells me you were very instrumental in protecting our children. There are no words for how grateful we are."

Daciana smiled at him. "It's what we do. And Destiny certainly did her fair share of fighting."

"I hope you enjoy yourself," Mikhail added.

Zev continued with the introductions to his pack. "These four are Convel, Gunnolf, Makoce and Arnou."

The four Lycans were extremely polite as Mikhail greeted them, but held themselves stiffly as if they weren't certain what they were getting into.

The last elite hunter limped a little as he came up to be introduced. Zev touched his shoulder briefly. "This is Lykaon."

Lykaon bowed slightly toward the prince but looked at Gregori. "I would not have survived without your aid or Shea's. I thank you."

"It was the least I could do after what you did for us," Gregori said.

Mikhail graciously thanked each of the Lycan hunters for their help. Vikirnoff and Natalya along with Destiny and Nicolae immediately came over. Destiny had fought with the Lycans and she introduced her lifemate, his brother and Natalya as she led the other pack members over to the tables of food and drink.

Fen knew immediately that Mikhail had planned for just that move. The pack respected Destiny's abilities and would relate to her and her family. Out of the corner of his eye he could see other Carpathian couples going up and introducing themselves to the pack members and engaging them in conversation.

Mikhail inclined his head toward Fen. "I believe you two know one another."

"We've certainly fought a few battles together now," Zev said, holding out his hand to Fen.

Fen was glad he'd thought to put his gloves on. Zev accepted him as Lycan but found his relationship with the Carpathians suspect.

"I see you've come prepared," Zev acknowledged.

"Always. With two of the *Sange rau* in the area, running such a large pack, I figure no one is safe," Fen said, opening the subject up immediately.

"I agree," Zev said. "It doesn't make sense that they're staying here when they know the hunters have arrived and there are so many Carpathians to fight them off."

Mikhail chose to inch toward a corner where the five of them could talk privately. Tatijana discreetly slipped off to talk with the pack members and Natalya's family. Zev walked with them to the small alcove where there were comfortable chairs. Once Mikhail sat, they all did, even Gregori, although Fen noticed that the way he'd positioned his chair, he could get in front of Mikhail instantly.

Fen didn't tell him it wasn't needed. No one in the room was faster than he was, and he would defend Mikhail, but he'd bet, Zev was every bit as quick as Gregori.

"One of the *Sange rau* is Bardolf, who had been a Lycan I thought long dead," Fen explained. "The other had been a Carpathian named Abel, an ancient hunter who turned vampire some centuries ago."

"We believe that they built a large pack with the intention of sacrificing them in order to distract the hunters while one of the leaders comes in to assassinate Mikhail," Gregori said.

Zev frowned, bringing the fingers of his hands together in a steeple. "They're intelligent enough to come up with such a plan, but what would they gain?"

"If I'm killed, it very well could end our species," Mikhail admitted. "My son is far too young to take over and we've been at a crisis point for centuries, barely holding on as a species."

Zev nodded. "The *Sange rau* decimated our ranks centuries ago. We had to completely restructure to build and we're still fragile."

"I believe it's time for our two species to become close allies. Whatever the problem that occurred between us certainly doesn't exist anymore," Mikhail said, leaning forward. "We could learn so much from one another, and I believe we can be of mutual aid to one another."

"The problem is what happens when, if by some chance, the blood between your species and mine mix. The *Sange rau* is what happens," Zev pointed out.

"Not exactly," Mikhail countered, his tone matter-of-fact as well as carrying a hint of surprise as if he expected Zev to already know. "A lifemated Carpathian could not become the *Sange rau*. Only a Carpathian who chooses to give up his soul could. The *Sange rau* is a vampire, not a Carpathian. Should a Carpathian become mixed blood, he would be *Hän ku pesäk kaikak*, or *Paznicii de toate*—Guardian of all. They aren't the same. They are the ones capable of matching the *Sange rau* in battle."

Zev shook his head. "I've never come across such a fighter, although, to be honest, the *Sange rau* is so rare few hunters ever run across one even with the longevity of our lives. If what you believe is true and you are the target of these two, then perhaps there is more to it than we know. What benefit would it be for them to destroy an entire species?"

"That's the question, isn't it?" Mikhail said. "I've been turning it over and over and it has occurred to me that there is another master somewhere, one we haven't discovered. One with an agenda that might be the demise of both our species."

Zev was an intelligent man and saw the reasoning. "I can get word to the council and ask if they would be willing to meet with you."

"If they agree, I'll call in my warriors for their protection as well," Mikhail said. "Hopefully you can stick around to help us ensure their safety."

Zev nodded. "First we have to destroy this pack. We've been picking them off, but I'd like to really get an idea of their numbers. They've broken the pack in smaller units to help hide them from us."

"We can help with that," Mikhail said. "We can use the sky to see their numbers."

"That would be extremely helpful," Zev said. "This is a big area with so many places to hide, and you know it where we don't. If they aren't aware that you've seen them, and we get their locations, we can destroy them."

"I don't think," Fen contributed, "even if we destroy their enormous pack, that Bardolf and Abel will leave without another attempt at Mikhail. They want him dead."

"Then we have to come up with a battle plan," Gregori said simultaneously with Zev.

The two men looked at one another, each with a grim smile.

"I don't want to take up more of your time tonight," Mikhail said. "I'd like you to have fun and meet some of my people. We can plan our battle this next rising." He stood and once again shook Zev's hand.

"I'll get word to the council," Zev promised. He looked around the room at his scattered pack. They were definitely enjoying themselves, talking animatedly with the Carpathians surrounding them, making them the center of attention, listening to their every story. "Thank you for this, Mikhail, my pack needed a little downtime."

Mikhail gave a small old-world bow from the waist and moved away with Jacques and Gregori, leaving Fen and Zev alone.

"He's cool under fire," Zev said. "I've got to give him that. With two *Sange rau* after him, he's in mortal danger, and he knows it."

"We managed to fight one off, but the other got through the safeguards and went right for him. He didn't move a muscle, didn't flinch. He just watched to see how fast they were and how good they were at unraveling the safeguards set in place," Fen said. "We were lucky, but next time we'll have to be better prepared."

"Do you think there is another masterminding—" Zev broke off in midsentence, looking over Fen's shoulder.

For a moment Zev looked as if he'd been hit over the head with a club. Those eyes, so empty and cold before, lit up as if with a flame. The light transformed the hunter's entire face. His edgy, tough features softened a little, leaving him younger and more approachable.

"She's stunning. Who is she?"

Fen turned his head as a hush fell over the room. Branislava stood at the entrance. Her thick fiery red hair fell to her waist in soft waves framing her face. Her skin was pale, but seemed to glow as if a furnace burned inside her and there was no containing the scorching heat. Her eyes—Dragonseeker eyes—dazzled. Her lashes were long and feathery, shading her emerald eyes. She looked as if two gemstones had been pressed into her face and a fire had been lit behind them so the brilliance shone at all times.

She wore a vintage gown reminiscent of days gone by. The style suited her. The sleeves were long and the bodice clung to her full breasts and narrow rib cage, dropping to her small waist and then flared over her hips so that the full skirt fell to the floor.

Fen drew in a breath and looked over at Tatijana. The joy on her face and in her heart swamped him so that for a moment he experienced the overwhelming emotion with her. Tatijana rushed over to her sister and they embraced one another tightly.

"That is Branislava, Tatijana's sister. She's been . . . recovering. We didn't expect her tonight, although we'd hoped she could come."

"She's truly beautiful," Zev reiterated.

"Don't let her looks deceive you," Fen warned. "She's Carpathian, from a very powerful lineage, and she is a warrior born and bred."

Zev nodded his head. "She moves like water flowing over rock, so fluid and graceful," he said. "I have to meet her, Fen." He looked over his shoulder at his pack. Some were eating. A couple of the hunters were drinking, and Daciana danced with a Carpathian male. "Now, Fen," he added urgently. "I want to meet her now."

Zev wishes to meet Bronnie, Tatijana. I know she came here for you, to make certain you were all right, and she's terribly shy around so many people, but would it be okay to bring him over?

We're trying to make a good impression on the Lycans, Tatijana said, *so I guess we can hardly refuse. I'll let Bronnie know you're bringing him over.*

I heard, Branislava said. *I'm not that fragile. Truly.* She turned her head and looked over at them.

"Sure," Fen said. "Let's go before everyone swamps her. She'll be surrounded in another minute."

Zev let out his breath. "I'm not exactly suave with the ladies."

"That's just as well. Look around you. Every one of those men will be defending her if they think you're a player. This is a tight-knit group."

"I'll chance it," Zev said, once more pulling off his gloves and tucking them inside his jacket pocket. "That's a woman worth getting killed over."

Fen knew both Branislava and Tatijana heard the whispered remark. Their hearing was far too acute even with the wealth of conversations and music around them. Tatijana's sudden grin gave them away as they exchanged a quick telling look.

"Bronnie," Fen greeted.

She turned fully to face him. Fen took her into his arms, grateful that she had come for Tatijana. He hugged her close. "It's so wonderful to see you like this. You made the evening complete for Tatijana. She really wanted you with her."

"I'm happy to come," Branislava said. "I could feel her happiness, Fen."

Be careful, Bronnie. Zev is Lycan and must believe Fen is as well, Tatijana cautioned.

I may have been recouping beneath the earth, sister, but I can assure you, I have a good grasp on what these people would do to my brother-kin should they find out what he is.

Fen wanted to smile at the fierceness in Branislava's tone. She was ready for combat should anyone attack her sister's lifemate. Yet she turned to Zev with a smile that could melt entire glaciers.

"Branislava, this is my friend, Zev," Fen introduced them. "He's an elite hunter for the Lycans."

"How lovely to meet you," Bronnie said, extending her hand. "Any friend of Fen's is certainly welcome here."

Zev took her fingers in his hand and gallantly lifted them to the warmth of his mouth. Lycan sense of smell was very acute and Branislava's enticing scent was so alluring he found himself entranced by her. Nearly hypnotized. It shocked him that he could be so completely mesmerized when he had been shaped and trained from the time he was a child to be a killer.

He'd been taught a woman could be a warm body or comfort, but was of little use to his role as a hunter. His entire focus was on hunting and destroying the threats to the Lycans.

"I'm honored to meet you," he said, looking into her eyes.

Staring into those deep pools of emerald green, he felt himself falling. A man could get lost there. He knew better than to spend one more moment in her company, but he couldn't resist that sensual allure. The feel of her bare skin, even if it was her fingers, set his heart racing. Her skin was satin-soft, but so warm in the coolness of the evening it shocked him. She seemed to burn from the inside out, which only made him wonder just how hot she would burn for a man she loved.

"I am not the most elegant of dancers, but I would love to dance with you," he said.

The words came out of their own accord. Frankly, he was shocked at the invitation. He certainly hadn't come over to her with the idea of asking her to dance. He'd make a fool of himself the moment he stepped out on the dance floor, but the thought of holding her in his arms, her body close to his, was more than he could resist.

"I would love that," she answered, with an elegant nod of her head. "But I must warn you, sir, I do not dance either. I have never danced."

You don't have to do that, Fen said. *You're a great ambassador for the Carpathians, but you aren't required to dance with him.*

I think I will enjoy it, Branislava admitted, astonished.

She really does want to do this, Fen, Tatijana added. She seemed as surprised as her sister.

"Never?" Zev's eyebrow shot up.

What the hell was wrong with the Carpathian males? He couldn't imagine why this woman was unattached. He hadn't been able to bring himself to let go of her hand. Afraid she might change her mind, he led her to the dance floor. The moment he wrapped his arm around her waist and brought her in close to him, he knew he was lost.

She fit into him perfectly, melting into his body, so that when they moved they appeared to be one body, not two. She matched his steps intuitively, as if they had been dancing forever together. Her hair was silk against his face, strands catching in the dark shadow along his jaw, tangling them together, and he found he wanted them to stay like that. He swore, even the beat of his heart matched hers.

He knew he shouldn't hold her so close, or so possessively, but he felt possessive of her. He didn't want the music to ever end. His life was one of battles, of killing, cold nights out in the open, horrendous wounds, blood and death. It wasn't holding a beautiful woman in his arms, drifting around the dance floor in a mixture of desire and pleasure.

"I thought you didn't know how to dance," he murmured against her ear. Even her little shell-like ear was beautiful. He had it bad, whatever "it" was. He wanted to sweep the hair off her neck and press featherlight kisses all over her soft skin.

"You apparently are a very good leader," she whispered. "You're so very easy to follow."

Her voice wrapped him in intimacy, making him forget for a moment that they were not alone and other couples—including Tatijana and Fen—danced on the same small dance floor. Branislava was lethal and he had no defense against her. If it was possible for a Lycan to fall for a Carpathian, he was well on his way, and it was forbidden, especially for an elite hunter.

He pulled her closer until her body imprinted on his. Hot. So hot. She burned through his clothes—his skin—every muscle in his body until she was branded in his very bones. No, deeper still. Like molten lava she flowed into him through his pores, until her brand found his heart and then his soul. Until he belonged to her. Body. Heart. Mind. And his lost soul.

The music ended and his heart nearly stopped. She smiled up at him and he had no choice but to wrap his arm around her waist and escort her from the floor, back to the corner where he'd first found her talking to her sister. The far corner. Farthest from where the Lycans held casual conversations with the Carpathians.

"Thank you, Branislava," he said. "You certainly can cast a spell."

She blinked several times and he wondered if he'd said something wrong.

He doesn't know about our mage background, Bronnie, Tatijana hastily explained. *He means he finds you very attractive.*

Strangely, I find him very attractive.

"I really enjoyed dancing with you," Branislava admitted. "Tatijana told me it was like floating. I could hear the music right through my body."

And his heart, matching the rhythm of mine, Tatijana, she added in wonder.

Branislava searched his face. It was a strong face. Lines etched deep, telling her he'd seen war. His eyes fascinated her. They were wolf eyes, pure and simple. They showed his piercing intelligence. There was no disguising the predator in him. When he locked onto his prey he would be merciless and unswerving. Right now, in the room with Carpathian hunters only feet away, those eyes were wholly focused on her.

She should have been frightened, but she was more intrigued. She might be shy around people—she'd never been around them before—but she would defend herself and her family with everything she was, every weapon in her arsenal.

"You're a beautiful dancer," Zev said. "I hope we get the chance to do this again soon."

"Me, too," Branislava said, meaning it.

She slipped away from him, back to her sister. At once the Carpathians seem to close ranks around her. Zev observed her for a few minutes, all too aware Fen was watching him.

"I understand now, why you have chosen to become friends with these people," Zev said with a sigh. "Tatijana and her sister are beautiful women."

"Yes they are," Fen agreed.

"You know it is forbidden. We are to avoid the Carpathian people just for this reason. We can't take the chance of falling in love with one."

Fen not only heard the reluctance in Zev's voice, but felt it as well. "Carpathian men and women don't have the luxury of falling in love until they meet their lifemate," he explained. "A Lycan might fall in love with a Carpathian, but he or she couldn't or wouldn't reciprocate. There is only one."

"I still don't understand."

"I've learned that they are literally two halves of the same whole. The soul of the male contains the darkness needed and the soul of the female the light. The ritual binding words are imprinted on the male before birth. When he finds the woman with the other half of his soul, he recognizes her, says the words and they are bound. There are no others. If one dies the other follows."

"So even if it wasn't forbidden, you're saying she's out of reach," Zev said with real regret. "She's definitely out of my league." He was afraid she'd taken his heart and soul away with her, but then one didn't need those things to kill.

"Let's get you something to drink. You're here to have fun." Fen clapped him on the shoulder and led him back to the rest of the pack and the Carpathians there.

16

"Either we have to keep a Carpathian with us at all times so the women can communicate from the air, or one or all of you has to be brave enough to allow them to exchange blood with you," Fen explained for the third time.

It was one thing to eat and be merry with the Carpathians, but a blood exchange was repugnant to every Lycan. They gave one another blood in battle, but to them, that was entirely different than what Fen was asking of them.

"Fine," he said with a small sigh. "I'll have to be the one to do all the communicating with our squads in the air. I'll ask Tatijana to exchange blood with me." They'd done so just this rising when he'd made passionate love to her, but he wouldn't mind the rush before they set off to try to pick off the pack one small unit at a time.

"The woman will take your blood?" Zev asked, his gaze shifting to where Branislava and her sister were laughing together beneath the forest canopy.

"Her name is Tatijana," Fen said, beginning to feel annoyance that he had to continue the charade of being fully Lycan. They were wasting time while the pack could be moving into position to attack.

The women were going up into the air because their energy output was far less than the men's in any shape they chose. Tatijana, Branislava, Destiny and Natalya were all going, each taking a different direction. It could be dangerous if the *Sange rau* detected them and chose to defend their pack. Fen would be undetectable by any of them, yet he had to keep up appearances. It was frustrating to know Tatijana might encounter trouble.

"Would Branislava be the one taking my blood?" Zev asked.

Silence fell on the pack. His pack mates looked at him as if he'd lost his mind. Convel shook his head, his expression grave. "You can't, Zev. We don't know what could happen."

"What will happen," Fen said, gritting his teeth, "is we can get to work. We have four riders and four groups of hunters. I'm volunteering, but just in case we have another pack discovered, we need someone else able to hear. Destiny and Natalya are communicating with the Carpathian hunters."

Zev didn't continue to argue. He crossed the ground between Branislava and him, hoping she wasn't as mesmerizing as she had been the night before. He could feel the gaze of his pack mates boring holes into his back. The weight of their disproval was heavy in the air. Still, his feet kept moving, striding now, covering the ground faster.

She turned and watched his approach, her emerald eyes a deeper green than he remembered, nearly glowing. And then she smiled and the very air left his lungs in a rush. He couldn't decide if it was her hair, all that fiery red contained now in a fancy braid as thick as his arm, or her amazing eyes that sometimes, like now, appeared to be multifaceted, or her mouth with her full, inviting lips, that drew his gaze the most.

She let him come all the way to her. He was aware Fen had followed him and Tatijana had gone to meet him. They had stepped into the shadows and were shielded from sight by a large tree. Branislava simply stood motionless, waiting for him.

"My dancer," he said, wishing he had some elegance to him, "I was told it was possible to communicate telepathically with you if you took my blood and I gave you mine. Would you be willing to exchange blood with me?"

"Yes, of course," Branislava said. "Telepathy is the easiest form of communication. You can rest assured that I would never pry into your mind. I will simply relay information."

"You could do that? See things in my mind?"

"Perhaps," she answered, "but there is no need for such a thing, and you are Lycan. Lycans have different brain patterns and most of us can't read your thoughts easily. I would think you have a rather good shield."

He didn't want to think too much about the consequences. "Let's do it then. Tell me what to do."

She took his hand and led him deeper inside the trees where the shadows would keep them safe from prying eyes. "Would you prefer not to feel anything at all? Or taste anything at all?"

"I've tasted blood. I'm a Lycan. I want to know what's going on at all times," Zev said firmly. He wouldn't mind tasting her blood. Everything about her intrigued him.

She stepped close to him. So close. There wasn't more than a scant inch between them. Her scent wrapped him up in velvet and left him reeling just as it had the night before. She put her arm around his neck and drew his head down to her. Her mouth moved over his skin, featherlight, but oh, so sensually. His entire body reacted, going hard with urgent need, blood surging hotly, every nerve ending alive and aware of her.

"You'll feel the bite. A sting of pain but it will be gone quickly," she whispered in his ear. "Trust me, I would never do anything to harm you."

He didn't even care. His every sense was fixated on her mouth and the way it moved over his pounding pulse so seductively. Her lips touched his neck and his gut clenched into knots of anticipation. His cock jerked strong, hard and alert. Her teeth sank deep and pain added to the intensity of his desire, and then it eased, giving way to pure pleasure. The way she took his blood was the most erotic thing he'd ever experienced.

He wrapped his arms around her, holding her to him, feeling his blood pounding hotly in his veins. His pulse thundered in his ears. He didn't want her to stop. He wanted more, so much more. His hands moved beneath her shirt to find bare, satin skin. He slid his palms up her rib cage to cup the weight of her breasts, thumbs seeking her taut nipples beneath her shirt. He was so inflamed he would have taken her right there, in the deep shadows of the trees, but she lifted her head, closing the pinpricks with her tongue.

Their eyes met. The amazing green emeralds pressed into her face looked glazed, as if she'd just been made love to. She also looked a little confused.

"Sir, I believe you are trespassing into areas we never discussed in our negotiations."

Shocked, Zev slid his hands from beneath her shirt. Her skin had been so hot to the touch that he actually felt the cold of the night on his fingers.

"I'm sorry. I don't know what happened. Every time you take someone's blood do they feel like I do?" If so, he was just a little bit jealous, although he wasn't familiar with that particular emotion and was guessing at it.

She shook her head. "No. It's never been like that before."

"Good." He wanted to be her first. Maybe she'd remember him the way he knew he'd always remember her. "Do I get to bite your neck?"

She laughed, breaking the slight tension between them. "I think it would be safer if we just use my wrist."

"Safer, but not as much fun," Zev pointed out.

She bit into her wrist and offered it to him. Bright drops of blood seeped along the laceration. He took the proffered wrist and raised it to his mouth. Even her wrist gave off that beckoning scent of wild honey and citrus that he'd come to identify as Branislava. He licked at the ruby droplets. She tasted as good as she looked—better even. She could be addicting, and that was dangerous for his species. Hot, fresh blood this good was a temptation none of them dared have.

Lycans always had to be cautious ingesting blood. They were predators. Feral. Civilization had come to them, but deep in their hearts, they would always be wild. Blood sang to them. Called to them. Whispered and cajoled. Her blood was exceptional—the taste exquisite.

Branislava put her other hand on his shoulder, her eyes meeting his. The feeling was nearly as erotic as it had been earlier when she'd taken his blood. He let himself fall into her unusual eyes, let himself feel that moment fully. He would never again have a chance to be this intimate with her—and it was intimate.

Fen had said she couldn't fall in love with anyone else but her lifemate, but she felt that same magnetic pull toward him as he did to her. He saw it in her eyes and felt it in her mind. Her blood was rich and hot. So hot. So good. It energized him.

"Enough," Branislava cautioned. "I can't be weak when I'm in the air." She tugged at her wrist.

Zev let go immediately. He was rough and crass compared to her, but still, she didn't take her gaze from his and she closed the wound in her wrist with her tongue.

"It's done then?" he asked. "You can talk to me telepathically?"

Yes.

Her soft voice whispering so intimately in his mind was shocking. Maybe it hadn't been such a good idea to allow her to take his blood. He could barely breathe and he damned well couldn't walk.

You try it. Talk to me.

There's not much I can say without making a fool of myself. My attraction to you has been unexpected.

"Are you all right, Zev?" Convel called, anger edging his voice.

He should have known his pack would be worried. The moment Branislava had led him into the privacy of the trees, his pack mates must have become anxious that the Carpathians might be ambushing them in some way.

"I'm fine. We were just making certain it worked," Zev called back. He smiled at Branislava. "Thank you, Miss Branislava, I think we'll be able to hunt together."

"I think we will, too," she said. "My friends and family call me Bronnie."

He gave her a little salute and strode out of the trees to meet his fellow elite hunters.

Tatijana and Fen joined Branislava the moment he left.

Fen took her hands. "You're certain you're up for this, Bronnie? Tatijana and I both gave you every memory we could of the *Sange rau* and how they fight, how fast they are. Any werewolf will go for your belly every time, and don't underestimate how high they can leap."

"I think I've been hibernating a long time and I need to jump right into the fray. Right now, I can be of use and I need that, Fen, to help push me to start living. Being a prisoner for so long and trapped in the ice can make one long for what's familiar to them and certainly that isn't the best thing for me."

"Just promise me you'll be careful," Fen said. "Nothing can happen to either of you. I can be in the air in seconds and I travel fast. Just call for me."

"Don't you dare give yourself away to the Lycans," Tatijana said. "I mean it, Fen. They'll turn on you so fast. Mikhail gave Zev something to think about, but not the others. And you can't count on him for protection. We'll be fine. We know what to do."

"Is everything all right?" Zev asked, coming up behind them. "We're all ready."

"I'm just making certain they know how the rogue packs work," Fen said. "I don't want them to take any chances with their lives."

"You're just giving us information," Zev cautioned the women, adding to Fen's warnings. "That's all, just find them and tell us. The Carpathians will transport us if it's a great distance."

"We need the field," Tatijana said. "Move your pack back into the trees."

Zev nodded, glanced at Branislava, shook his head and walked away. Fen wrapped his palm around the nape of Tatijana's neck and pulled her in close to him.

"He might look back, wolf man," she hissed, but she didn't pull away.

"I could care less," he said, and kissed her. "Don't you dare get hurt. Not a single hair. Do you understand me?"

"I understand you," she said, and kissed him back. "I love it when you go all wolfie on me."

Branislava burst out laughing. "Come on, Tatijana, let's show them what Dragonseekers can do."

The two women walked out of the trees, into the open. Both looked elegant in spite of their jeans, shirts and boots. They came out holding hands, but in the middle of the field they embraced and each turned and walked into the center of their quadrant.

"What are they doing?" Zev asked.

"Shifting," Fen said. "And they need room."

The two shifted almost simultaneously, their small curvy figures shimmering one moment and becoming something else altogether. Fen was used to Tatijana's blue dragon. She was beautiful to him, with her long, spiked tail and wedge-shaped head. She could dive into water and swim beneath the surface for long periods of time. In her human form, after centuries in dragon form, her skin was always cool.

Branislava was just the opposite. She was a fire dragon, her crimson scales nearly glowing. She looked as if her dragon had been born in a live volcano, a part of the fiery blast, all red and orange. When she expanded her wings Fen heard gasps from several members of the pack.

She stood on her hind legs and flapped her wings, creating a windstorm. Tatijana followed suit. Fen looked around him. There was shock and awe on the faces of the pack as the two dragons took to the sky.

"You saw her in battle," Fen reminded them.

"She was in the sky mostly," Arnou defended. "I was looking out for my skin, killing as many of the werewolves as possible. I guess I didn't think too much about it, but seeing them up close like that after seeing the women as they really are . . . it's just . . ." he trailed off. "I have no words."

"Amazing," Daciana seconded. "I wouldn't mind being able to shift shape."

The pack burst out laughing. "You can, Daciana," Zev reminded. "You're Lycan. You feel like being a wolf, just shift."

She shrugged. "It's not the same. I've always been a wolf."

"Tatijana and Branislava were born into the Dragonseeker lineage, a very ancient and honored line. They were actually in the form of dragons for several centuries and it's far more familiar to them than their natural human form."

He reached for Tatijana. *How's it going up there?*

It's been two minutes, Fen. I couldn't possibly get into trouble that fast. Her laughter teased at his body, soft and intimate. *The night is fairly clear and that will help. We're flying high though and using the existing clouds to mask what we are. From below, we just look like clouds in strange shapes.*

Good idea, my lady.

I do have them occasionally, but I can't take credit for that one. Bronnie thought of it.

It's her first flight in a very long while, Tatijana. Are you certain she's strong enough for this?

Branislava was family now. They were bound by Tatijana. More than that, he liked and respected her. He'd seen the glimpses of her courage when Tatijana inadvertently opened the door on her past and he couldn't help but admire her.

She's excited. She really does need this. When you've never been in the open before, or around others, it's easy to stay away and hold yourself tight, not move for fear of falling, so to speak.

Tatijana spotted a small opening in between two massive boulders. Brush grew right up to the side of the mountain and those jutting boulders, but right between them was an opening, a dirt floor no more than two feet by two feet. If there was an actual cave there, it would make a perfect den for wolves. The werewolves might be attracted to such a place.

She sent the image to Fen. *Is there a cave here? What other signs should I look for?*

There's definitely a cave there, Fen said. *I'd marked it earlier as suspicious, but when I checked it out, there was no one there. That doesn't mean the pack hadn't targeted it as a possible place to hide if they needed to lay low for a few days. If they're there, even a small number of them, look around in the surrounding brush, they'll have at least two lookouts outside. They'll be concealed well. Think wolves. The werewolves think like their animal counterparts in terms of protecting their pack.*

Tatijana didn't want to drop lower, especially if the rogue pack had lookouts that might spot her. She moved from cloud to cloud, appearing to be drifting with a slight wind. Her dragon's eyesight was very keen. She could see miles away if she chose to use the superior vision.

At once the look of the world changed around her. It was a little disorienting to concentrate on such visual acuity, but her dragon was quick to pick up movement. Below them and just to the south, she spotted the leaves of a bush waving against the wind. Once her dragon had found a potential target, she stayed high in the air, drifting, her dragon only occasionally having to circle back.

The third circle confirmed there was a creature, half wolf, half man lurking in the brush. *I see one of the guards. He's in the form of half man and half wolf.*

That's what we're looking for, Fen said. *Send me the coordinates and just keep an eye on them until we arrive. If any come out of their hiding spot, count so we get some idea, but do not, under any circumstances engage with them.*

"We've got one of the units," Fen said. "Let's go."

Eight Carpathian males had agreed to transport the elite hunters to cut down on time as well as the chance of the *Sange rau* spotting them.

They took the form of giant birds and, although the hunters looked at one another as if they might balk, the moment Fen and Zev stepped forward and swung onto their bird's backs, the others followed suit. They were hunters and there was a rogue pack to destroy. That job came before anything else, even fear of the unknown.

The Carpathians took them in soundlessly, dropping out of the sky a distance from the cave to allow the elite hunters to get their feet on the ground again. Jacques, Vikirnoff and Nicolae went with Lykaon, Arnou and Fen, spreading out a couple of feet apart to the left. Falcon, Dimitri and Tomas went with Zev, Daciana, Convel and Gunnolf to the right, again spreading out so that they made less noise as they stalked the rogue pack.

Dimitri, the lookout on that side is just a little over nine meters from you, to your left. He hasn't spotted you yet, Tatijana warned.

Take care that you don't do anything to tip Zev off that you're anything but a Carpathian, Fen warned hastily, cursing himself for not maneuvering Dimitri to stay in his group.

Dimitri didn't answer him. Instead, he held up a clenched fist. Immediately all members of his hunting party dropped low and stayed completely silent. Dimitri went to his belly and shifted to a small squirrel, covering several meters before determining he might give off too much energy the werewolf would pick up.

He halted, assessing the situation. He wanted a silent kill so the lookout couldn't warn his fellow guard or those hiding inside the cave.

You no longer give off energy, Fen reminded. *You haven't for a long time. After these last two nearly mortal wounds and all the blood given to you, you're more mixed than Carpathian. He won't feel you coming.*

Dimitri took his brother at his word. The little squirrel easily made his way through the brush until he nearly ran into the werewolf's foot. Just as the wolf looked down with greedy eyes, Dimitri shifted, driving the silver stake straight through the heart of the rogue. Simultaneously, he silenced any cry the man could give, by simply cutting off his windpipe. He eased the body to the ground.

It's done. Can you get to the other one, Fen?

I see him. Going after him now.

Above their heads, Tatijana stayed in the clouds. She watched Fen creep forward, easing his body through the brush. She knew there wouldn't be a whisper of movement and he knew exactly what he was doing, but still, she wanted to plunge down and wipe out the threat to her lifemate. Her bond with Fen seemed to be growing with every passing hour. She didn't think it could get any stronger, but her love for him just seemed to deepen.

Fen palmed the silver stake. Insects sang all around him, undisturbed by his presence. He took a breath and let it out as he eased closer. He smelled the rancid odor of the werewolf. The rogue hadn't washed and old decayed meat and blood clung to his fur.

Don't move. Don't move. Tatijana's warning froze him. *Dimitri, another coming your way as well. I think the guards are being changed.*

Fen allowed his gaze to encompass the pack spread out behind him. Lykaon's fist was clenched, a sign for them all to freeze. Apparently that had been meant for him as well. He preferred the Carpathian form of communication between hunters. Telepathy made things so much simpler.

Fen, he's going to walk right over the top of you. Do you want me to help?

I've got this, sívamet. No worries. Just sit tight. Dimitri? Can you take the second guard out?

Yes. They'll come looking when the first two don't come back, Dimitri pointed out.

That will be to our advantage. Fen glanced around to see if any member of the pack could see him. He would have to use the speed of the *Hän ku pesäk kaikak*—Guardians of all—if he was going to kill both guards and keep them silent as they died.

Zev was the only one within eyesight of him to see his blurring speed. *Tatijana, have Bronnie distract Zev just for a moment. I need enough time to take both guards out simultaneously. She'd better be quick. I'm running out of time.*

He could hear the other werewolf breathing in short, ragged pants. He'd been injured recently and hadn't completely healed. Fen could smell the wound. He kept his eye on Zev even as he planned the moves out in his mind.

He could reach out and touch the first guard. The second was two steps away, cursing as he got hung up on a thorny branch. The moment Zev looked away, Fen rose up fast, slamming the silver stake through the rancid werewolf's heart with his right hand, silencing him as he did so. He turned, using his left hand to take out the second guard. The rogue never actually saw him, he was too busy trying to get brambles out of his fur when the stake went through his heart.

He felt Tatijana's relief. She poured into his mind just for a moment, letting him feel her love before she quickly turned back to her job. Fen eased across the distance separating them until he was beside Zev.

"The others will have to use their swords to cut off their heads. I'm not hacking them off with my knife."

Zev grinned at him. "What a wuss. All this time I thought you were so tough you carried a spare knife in your teeth just for hacking off heads." He signaled the pack forward again.

"I trust you have a plan for entering that cave," Fen said.

"Not exactly. I thought we'd let them come to us."

Fen raised his eyebrow.

"That blue dragon up there came up with an idea and sent it to me through Branislava. She thought it might be fun to fill the cave with insects. The biting kind. If you've got your eye on her, Fen, you might reconsider. She's intelligent and has sass. You're old enough to know to stay away from that kind of woman."

"Not a bad plan," Fen agreed. His lady did have sass. *You could have shared your plan with me.*

I had to give Bronnie something real to distract him. He's too smart for any-thing else. In any case, I didn't want you charging in there. You and Dimitri seem to get into trouble every time I turn around. I'm in your mind, wolf man. You planned on leading the charge, didn't you?

He shared his amusement with her. *I'm faster.*

You've been fighting other people's battles for too long, Fen, and you can't stop. You use your body as a shield for the others, and Dimitri is just like you.

That much was true. Dimitri was more like him than he wanted his brother to be. Dimitri was fearless in a fight. Fen would rather have him than any other at his back.

Zev signaled his pack to move forward into place. He nodded to Fen.

We're ready down here. Do you want to do the honors, my lady? Or should I? he teased, already knowing her answer.

I lived in a cave my entire life, wolf man. I know insects. And what I don't know I can imagine, Tatijana added with a little laugh.

The wind drifted over them, a soft, gentle touch that sent a ripple through the leaves around them. Above them, the clouds changed shapes as they lazily floated across the dark sky. A slapping sound suddenly disrupted the silence of the night. Inside the cave, a muffled yell, quickly silenced, was heard.

Suddenly at the entrance, men in various stages of shifting began pouring out of the cave, nearly falling over one another, slapping at their clothes and fur. Two stumbled and fell, creating chaos for those still inside. The two downed werewolves were trampled as those inside, desperate to vacate, simply ran over them. Swarms of red ants covered their bodies so that they looked as if their clothes and skin were alive and moving.

That woman is a terror, Zev observed, hardly able to contain his laughter. *We may as well go home and let her handle this.*

Fen couldn't help but find the situation amusing. His lady did have a scary imagination, sending revved-up fire ants swarming over the werewolves. *Make certain none of us get bit,* he warned her.

Don't be such a baby. She gave a little sniff of disdain, but he felt her laughter. She did have a nasty little sense of humor.

I believe in retaliation, he warned, although his threat was an empty one and they both knew it.

Tatijana laughed softly and he felt her fingers brush down the side of his face.

I brought them out of there, now it's your turn. And check on your brother, after. Something's not right.

What does that mean?

If I knew I wouldn't have said to check on him. Again there was that soft laughter.

Fen shook his head, but he did locate his brother. Dimitri appeared to be like the rest of them, waiting for Zev's signal to move in on the werewolves. He touched Dimitri's mind, just to assure himself. Dimitri blocked a merge with him, shocking him, but he turned his head toward Fen and gave him a thumbs-up.

Fen sighed. He couldn't worry about Dimitri in the middle of a battle with rogues. Fen counted fourteen werewolves exiting the cave. If the *Sange rau* were breaking the larger pack into smaller units, their numbers were definitely depleted. The units before had been much bigger, twenty-five or thirty.

Zev signaled the hunters forward. They had formed a loose semicircle around the entrance and they went at the werewolves, springing out of the brush to attack. Fen moved fast, using the silver stakes as quickly as possible, wanting to get it over with. It felt like a massacre, the screams and blood and smell of death.

He'd had several lifetimes of hunting and destroying those preying on others. He knew it was the only thing they could do, but it still was difficult at times. The rogues were caught unawares and only a handful managed to fight back. The elite hunters used silver swords to remove the heads before the bodies were gathered and burned. The scent of burning fur and flesh made him feel sick.

Tatijana, did you find any trace of Abel or Bardolf? he asked to distract himself.

Well . . . she hesitated, clearly unsure. *When I was flying around the mountain of mist, I felt a sudden shiver, an awareness of danger. It was there for just a moment, but it occurred to me that one of them, or both, could be holed up there. The mountain is above the one where the prince resides and it is possible someone could spy on him from up there. But, Fen, honestly, I don't know, it was just a weird, scary feeling.*

"Zev, Tatijana is going to land and pick me up. She may have found the lair of the *Sange rau.* I'd like to take Dimitri and check it out," Fen said.

Zev looked up at that sky. He could see the blue dragon circling above them. "I'll never get used to that sight. It's amazing. Dragons." For a moment he searched the sky, and Fen was fairly certain he was looking for the fiery red dragon. Zev sighed. "I can't stop you, Fen, but you and I both know, even two of you have little chance of killing one of them. If they're together . . ."

"I doubt they'll be together. Vampires don't trust one another that much. It just doesn't seem to me like they'd share resting quarters."

"You've got the best instincts I've ever seen for hunting them," Zev said, "and you certainly know more than I do about fighting one. You've clearly had more experience, just don't get yourself killed."

Fen nodded. "Good luck hunting the other packs. I'll join you if nothing comes of this."

Dimitri, let's go hunting. I've had enough of these rogues and their masters invading our homeland.

I was just waiting for you.

Shift to a dragon and I'll go up with you. Once we're out of sight, I can stop this pretense. We have to find them, Dimitri. I have a sense of urgency growing in me. I can feel a real battle coming.

Dimitri made his way to a small clearing and shifted without preamble, changing to the form of a dragon, politely extending his wing to his brother. Fen climbed up to the dragon's back, settling himself before giving the go-ahead. Dimitri was never showy. His dragon was brown, but the spikes were razor-sharp. Beside the red and blue dragons, he looked drab and could be easily overlooked.

Fen knew that was Dimitri's way. He was nearly always quiet, rarely putting in his opinion, but he was lethal and his dragon would be as well.

Tell me what's going on with you, Dimitri.

Dimitri's dragon stayed close to Tatijana as they winged their way through the night sky. *Fen, the wolf is present. He's strong. Very strong. He's been with me a long time now.* He spoke abruptly, without any warning, dropping the bombshell into Fen's mind.

Fen let out his breath in a little rush. He'd known all along that his brother was well on his way to becoming what he was. Still, the wolf's presence was undeniable.

He'll protect you. The more you work with him, the faster you'll merge, Dimitri.

Long before we came here, I had already felt him rising. Now, though, he's different, as if we're becoming one. All those years we hunted together. You giving me blood. Me using some of the Lycans for a food source when we were hunting with a pack. It never bothered me. I wasn't afraid of the Lycans hunting me. I figured I could go to ground the way you do.

But now you realize it might not be such a good thing. Fen had realized the same thing some time ago, but he'd suspected it was too late for his brother. A male who spent lifetimes killing and living in darkness was extremely susceptible to the pull of the *Sange rau*, more so he thought than the Carpathian to the vampire.

There's Skyler.

There it was. Fen had wrestled with that very problem. Did one have the right to expose his lifemate to such a thing when there was no data on a Carpathian/Lycan cross? The more questions that had been brought up, the less of an answer he had. He'd been selfish giving in to Tatijana's demands. He had wanted to be persuaded, and he'd let her seduce him into it.

On the other hand, Dimitri would not survive without Skyler. Now, more than ever, he needed her.

I'm sorry I got you into this, Dimitri. Centuries ago, he hadn't a clue what caused the change, although even then he'd suspected. He should never have gone to Dimitri, but the fight to stay honorable had become nearly impossible.

I went into it with my eyes open. You explained even then what the danger was in exchanging blood. I have to talk to Skyler about this, but before I do, I have to figure a few things out.

Don't make her decision for her. Tatijana was adamant that she had the right to make her own choice, and I have to believe that's true.

Skyler's young.

But she's powerful. And intelligent. Your instinct is to protect her, but don't just discount her because of her human age. She's not yet Carpathian . . . Fen broke off.

There was the real dilemma. Fen hadn't even considered the real problem. Skyler wasn't Carpathian. She was human. She hadn't been converted. If Dimitri converted her with his mixed blood, what would happen? Could he even convert her? Would it work? They didn't have an answer to that question. As far as they knew, it hadn't been done.

Now you see.

Still, there are ways around that. Gabriel or Francesca? Fen suggested her parents. He knew even as he made the suggestion that it wouldn't work. If Gabriel was already insisting Dimitri couldn't claim Skyler until she was much older, he would never aid Dimitri into bringing his daughter into an unknown, uncertain world. *Okay, not either of them, but someone will help us. Perhaps Bronnie. She's Dragonseeker and I know Skyler has Dragonseeker blood in her. Isn't her birth father Razvan?*

That would be a possibility. There was a grain of hope in Dimitri's voice.

There's always a solution, Dimitri. When you're too close to the problem and it involves someone you care about . . .

Love, Dimitri corrected. *I love her with everything in me. I'd rather meet the dawn then expose her to something dangerous.*

I hate to be the one to tell you: she was exposed to danger long before you knew she was your lifemate. The moment Gabriel and Francesca adopted her, they brought her into our world. Fen frowned. *How did you manage to hold silver with the wolf already in you?*

I burned my palm the first time I tried to use it, so I just coated my hands. That way Zev and the others wouldn't suspect anything.

That was Dimitri. Smart. No fuss.

We're making the approach, Tatijana warned. *Do you want to change shapes just in case? We're very close to where I felt the warning.*

17

Fen touched Tatijana's mind. She didn't know. Didn't realize. The dragon had flown high into the misty clouds surrounding the upper part of the mountain. The dread was there, a feeling of revulsion, the need to leave. Tatijana had spent her life deep under this very mountain, in the ice caves of her father, Xavier, the high mage. She had never seen the outside of the mountain, only the inside. The mage spells were still intact and working to keep every species away from Xavier's laboratories.

He signaled to her to take her dragon to the ground. *Dimitri, you know what this place is, right? The ice caves where she was held are below.*

I knew that, but how did you know?

In the old days, Xavier was considered a friend to the Carpathian people. We all studied with him. That was how we first began weaving safeguards. I studied with him for years. No one had any inkling he was plotting against us, Fen explained.

I'm only a century behind you. I studied with him as well, Dimitri said. *It was shortly after that he kidnapped Rhiannon of the Dragonseekers and killed her lifemate. Of course we didn't know Xavier had committed such treachery for some time.*

Dimitri settled his dragon beside Tatijana's and Fen leapt off, landing in a crouch.

I cannot imagine Abel choosing to set up a lair in the caves of Xavier.

What of Bardolf. Although . . . do you think Bardolf would have been affected by the warning emanating from the mist? He would have no idea just how dangerous that entire labyrinth of caves really is.

Dimitri shifted into his own form as did Tatijana. Fen went to her immediately and put his arm around her. He leaned in to brush a kiss over the top of her head.

"Did you feel it?" she asked.

"Tatijana, there is every possibility that Bardolf might have chosen those caves to retreat into. Look at the mountain. Really look at it. Those caves were your prison for centuries." He held her while he delivered the blow, his mind firmly in hers.

For a moment she rejected the idea, her mind trying to protect her from the memories of the torture and death of so many she'd been forced to watch.

"Breathe, *sívamet*," he encouraged. "We're here with you. Xavier is long gone from this world and can't hurt you. You don't have to go in with us to check. You can monitor us from right here."

Tatijana had heard the screams of the dying, felt the weight of the dead—so many; Xavier had never discriminated between species. The only things that mattered to him were immortality and power. He thought himself above every other species and he wanted to rule. He wanted for himself the gifts each had and would stop at nothing to get them.

She had been forced to feed her blood to Xavier for centuries. When she and Branislava grew too strong and even keeping them anemic didn't help, Xavier kept them encased in ice in the form of dragons. They were his laboratory wall decorations, forcing them to watch every heinous crime he committed against humanity, Carpathians and every other species. They were helpless to stop him.

He had possessed the body of his grandson and violated women, impregnating them in order for him to find new sources of Carpathian blood. If the child was deemed unsuitable, as in Skyler's case, he sold them into a life of misery or simply abandoned them. He kept his grandson prisoner as well, torturing him with the foul things Xavier used his body for.

Tatijana could hear her own silent screaming and abruptly stopped, knowing her distress would pull Branislava to her. She had to gain control.

Fen was right. She was safe—but he and Dimitri wouldn't be if they went into those caves. Xavier might be gone, but his traps and evil spells remained behind. She knew every mage spell ever conceived by him, as did Branislava, as well as where most of the traps were in areas visible to where she'd been held, but Fen and Dimitri wouldn't know.

She lifted her chin. "I'll go."

Fen slipped his hand down her arm until his fingers tangled with hers. "Perhaps you could fly your dragon for us and keep guard, just while we explore the outer caves for signs of Bardolf. If he's not there, there's no need for any of us to enter what was Xavier's domain."

She didn't know if it was being cowardly, but, relieved, she took that way out. "That makes sense. But, if you think he may have gone in, give me your word that you will call to me right away. There can be no untruth between lifemates. I need to face this with you, if Bardolf has gone in. With you and Dimitri, I know I can. If you leave me out and something happens to either of you, I would for all time feel as if I caused it through my cowardice."

"You have my word, my lady. The moment I suspect, you will know."

She put her arms around his neck and leaned into him, needing to feel how solid and strong he was. "I know both of you are worried about what the change in your blood will do to a woman and our future children, but in this moment, I'm grateful both of you have the mixed blood. And Dimitri"—she turned in Fen's arms to look directly into Dimitri's eyes—"I guarantee you, Skyler would feel exactly the same way."

Dimitri nodded. "I'm certain of it. Let's do this, Fen."

His form shimmered and he took to the sky streaking for the mist that veiled the top of the mountain.

Fen sighed. "You be careful, Tatijana. Don't think because you're in dragon form that you're safe from him. If Bardolf is here and he realizes you're out there circling around, looking for his trail, he could attack you."

"You do your job, I'll do mine. Believe me, even the outside of Xavier's mountain will have a few traps," she cautioned. "Try not to trigger any of them."

He leaned down and kissed her upturned lips, shifting as he pulled back.

He followed his brother up the steep, snow-topped mountain and into the veil of mist. The mountains looked peaceful, ringed as they were with the swirling, dense fog, but the upper peaks were inhospitable. Very little plant life managed to grow amid the boulders and rocks, just a few scraggly flowers and grasses. Above the boulders was the glacier itself.

The locals knew to avoid the peaks, and the few travelers ignoring the mountain's warnings often were victims of falling rocks or avalanches. The mountain trembled and rumbled continually when anyone set foot on those upper peaks hidden within the white veil of mist.

Fen felt the energy concealed inside the bank of fog itself. No wind ever disturbed it or blew it away. The swirling veil acted like a force field of sorts that made anyone approaching the peaks uneasy. Things moved subtly in the dense fog. Shapes. Nothing substantial, but Fen could make out various threats. Voices echoed those threats, warning any and all to stay away.

Fen had seen such things many times in his travels. Xavier had been the father of all safeguards and this one was classic. It was meant for any species exploring the mountain. The first layer would simply make anyone coming close uneasy. Most turned back right there. If that didn't succeed and an explorer kept coming, actually walking around the entrances to the maze of caves, voices would begin to be heard, warnings, and if that failed, traps would be sprung.

"Anything?" he asked Dimitri.

Neither set foot on the mountain, but rather floated along its side to study the ground for tracks, for anything at all that might tell them Bardolf had come this way.

"Maybe. It's small, but he was Lycan. He has skills. Take a look over here." Dimitri indicated a rock that was smashed with others piled high around it. "This entrance was closed by our people a short while back, but in closing this, the area next to it was pushed up. See right there where those small flowers are growing."

Dimitri moved closer, almost crouching as he peered down. Fen moved up beside him to see the struggling flowers growing in the cracks of the rocks scattered all over the ground. He spotted the small telltale sign Dimitri had. One tiny flower and a leaf had been crushed by something heavy as it passed.

"Pretty slim," Fen said.

"Very," Dimitri agreed.

They both looked at the pushed-up rocks, which could have been used to form a cave.

"He's in there," Fen said.

"I'm certain of it," Dimitri agreed. "Let's go get him."

Tatijana, we think he's made himself a cave up here, off to the side of the entrance to Xavier's cave. We're going to check it out.

I'll join you.

She didn't hesitate. Clearly she'd made up her mind that she could face her prison.

"She's a strong woman," Dimitri said.

"She's Dragonseeker. I expect nothing less of her," Fen admitted.

He took the lead, keeping his feet from touching the mountain, careful not to brush up against a boulder. When they got to the newly formed cave's entrance, he shifted to mist. In that form he could move through the air without fear of triggering any trap.

The entrance had been artificially widened, but not by much. Bardolf could shift just as any Carpathian could, but clearly he preferred his wolf or human form. He found a lair and he'd covered the entrance just enough that if anyone got through the veil of mist, they might not notice his cave. The rocks scattered around on the ground helped to camouflage the cave.

Fen slipped into the cave itself. It was dark and much colder than any wolf would like. He knew the moment he entered that Bardolf had been there. His scent was everywhere. The small space reeked of him.

Fen went all the way to the back of the cave—and it was small. It seemed to dead-end. That didn't feel right to Fen. No self-respecting Lycan would ever get caught with no way out.

He's here somewhere. I know he is. Fen felt him. As if they were connected. Maybe by the blood, or the battles, but he felt him—and Bardolf was close by.

He has to have an escape route, Dimitri said. *We'll find it.*

The three of them inspected every inch of the cave walls and ceiling. It was Fen who found that incongruous little crack that ran from the floor midway through the cave up about knee-high. He came back to it twice, drawn not by the crack itself, but the feel of it.

It's here. But this wall is the outside wall to Xavier's cave, he cautioned.

If he found Xavier's caves, Dimitri said, *he won't be able to resist exploring.*

He's a wolf, and if he sees any weapons, he'll definitely try to figure out how to use them.

He'll trigger traps in there if he hasn't already, Tatijana said.

Fen had no choice but to shift enough to allow his hand to run over the crack. His acute senses told him there was a way to trigger the opening, but how? He moved his palm slowly up and down. It would have to be fast, no safeguard to keep anyone out on this side. Bardolf would want to come and go without trouble.

Tatijana leaned over him and studied the entrance. *This opens to the tone of his voice. Can you re-create the sound? You've both heard him. Just say "open," but only if you can get his exact pitch.*

You're good at pitch, Fen, Dimitri encouraged. *And you knew him before he turned wolf/vampire.*

Fen pulled up the memory of Bardolf's voice, listened intently and then tried. "Open."

The crack obeyed, separating without a sound. Of course Bardolf would need his escape hatch to be completely silent. Icy cold air blew into the cave, swamping them with a bitter chill. Fen went through first. They didn't need the light as all of them were able to see in dark, but Bardolf had used torches to light the way.

They were in a passageway rather than an actual chamber. It was narrow and curved, and led only one direction as the entrance had been closed. Fen moved downward quickly, flowing as a stream of vapor. Bardolf had begun his exploration of Xavier's cave. Whatever traps lay in wait that he might trigger might catch the hunters as well.

The actual floor had broken away in several places, making it impossible for anyone who couldn't travel as they were to proceed. The narrow tunnel gave way to a chamber where originally there had been a large hole where one could descend to the ice city below. The chambers and caves sprawled for miles, and Xavier held rule over the entire underground lair. A great chunk of ice had pushed through that hole, making descent impossible.

Bardolf went this way, Fen said following the scent of the wolf.

There were no real tracks; Bardolf was, like them, streaming through as vapor, but he couldn't hide his stench after so many clashes between them. Fen led the others to a far wall where a large lava tube rose up from below.

He went down there.

There are guardians. Hideous creatures, Tatijana warned. *He mutated vampire bats. They're larger and prey on deer and other victims. He fed them humans and even mages who had displeased him. They live in the walls of the lava tubes and anything disturbing them will be attacked immediately. As you descend they'll drop on top of you and begin eating you alive.*

Great. Fen looked down the tube. It was pitch-black and he couldn't see a thing, nor did he really want to. *How did Bardolf go down unscathed?*

Maybe they're all dead, Dimitri suggested. *I heard when they left these caves they tried to burn them out, isn't that right, Tatijana?*

There is no way a single pair didn't make it through that holocaust. They've been breeding again. I feel them. When you live so close to that kind of danger, you know the feel of it and your body reacts. Mine, right now, is shuddering with fear.

Fen immediately poured warmth and strength into her mind. He didn't dare assume his body to hold her, but he wrapped his arms around her telepathically and let her lean on him for a moment of support. When he could feel she had steadied herself, he turned to the lava tube.

Lighting the tube to see what we're facing might awaken the creatures, he decided. *I think Bardolf just flowed down without knowing they were there. He didn't trigger their feeding frenzy or we'd smell blood.*

He took another cautious sniff, just to be safe. Tatijana was right. He smelled the odor of rotting meat. Something had been torn apart and feasted on down in that hole. Still, Bardolf had gone that way.

I'll lead. If I go down safe, Tatijana, you follow next. I can protect from below and Dimitri can protect you from above. Don't touch the walls, even with a single molecule. We don't know enough about these creatures and the danger they represent to us.

He sent another wave of reassurance to Tatijana. Going deeper into this maze of ice caves had to be her worst nightmare. Merged as he was with her, he felt the absolute determination that overrode the fear bordering on terror.

If it's possible to fall in love with you more, my lady, I am.

He didn't wait for a reply but turned and streamed into the lava tube, dropping straight down, moving slow enough that he wouldn't disturb the air. It was wretched inside the tube. He used the vision of his mixed blood to try to see what was inside. There were honeycombs in the walls, round holes that were stained with blood, fur and a few feathers. He was certain the mutated bat creatures lived in those holes.

I think I'm just past the halfway point. Tatijana, start down, but don't make the mistake of going fast. You want to keep from disturbing the air so anything living in these walls just stays there. Dimitri will be right behind you.

They didn't have bodies for the creatures to leap upon, but he wasn't taking chances, not with his lifemate or his brother. He continued to drop, fighting off the need for speed. It was necessary to keep his sense of smell from being so acute. The farther down he got, the worse the stench was. He wasn't particularly happy about that aspect as so far, he hadn't spied an opening from the tube to the cavern floor. If the bottom was closed off and the creatures ate their prey inside the tube, where did that leave them? He should have gone all the way down before calling to the others.

His superior vision was what saved them. The hole in the side where the tube had crumbled away had to be the entrance to the chamber. He drifted through and immediately the sounds of ice creaking could be heard. Now and then there was a tremendous roar as a great chunk shot out, driven from the ice wall from the tremendous pressure. The chunk hit the opposite wall and dropped to the floor below.

In the distance, from the opposite side of the chamber, near a door, a torch had been lit and soft light spilled into the cavernous room, turning the ice a deep blue. It was beautiful. He had forgotten that Xavier's school had also been a place of beauty with ice sculptures, fountains and intriguing formations.

You're coming up on the entrance now, Tatijana, he said, guiding her through.

He waited until his brother followed and then he set out after Bardolf. He moved much more quickly now that they had actual chambers large enough that they didn't have to worry about touching the walls or floors. He followed the trail of torches Bardolf had so conveniently lit . . .

Conveniently lit, Fen repeated for the others. *He knows we're following him. How?* Tatijana asked. *We haven't made any mistakes.*

No, that was true, but they were dealing with a *Sange rau.* Bardolf couldn't feel energy from Dimitri or Fen, but he could from a Carpathian.

As sensitive as a mixed blood was, Bardolf had felt Tatijana's energy, perhaps even when they had returned and she was in dragon form.

Me. I've endangered you.

That's what he thinks, Fen agreed, *but you're our ace in the hole. You might despise the fact that you were here for centuries, but that's what's going to save us all, Tatijana. He doesn't know mage spells or any of the dangers here like you do. We don't know them either. He'll come at us, but it's you that's going to bring him down.*

Fen could feel her turning what he'd said over and over in her mind. If she wanted to go back, he would have Dimitri . . .

No. No way am I deserting you. Her voice turned strong. *You're right. I do know these caves. I do know spells. Bardolf was Lycan and he never studied at Xavier's school. I can trap him even if he doesn't trigger one of the older snares left behind by Xavier.*

Let's do this then, Dimitri said into their minds.

It was Dimitri's mantra—get it done no matter how repulsive the task. Fen proceeded, allowing his senses to flare out to explore every aspect of the chamber as they moved through it toward the torch. Dimitri, he knew, was doing the same. Tatijana looked for any hidden tricks the high mage may have left behind.

They got through the chamber to the entrance itself. Fen studied that carefully before he streamed through. He nearly ran straight into webs of fire spiders. The thin threads glowed with flames. They were woven tight, layer upon layer, so had he even in his present form touched a strand, he wouldn't be able to get loose.

He's using fire spiders.

Fen felt Tatijana's instant rejection of his assessment. *Fire spiders would never allow themselves to be used by Bardolf against a Dragonseeker.*

How would they know who follows him? Dimitri asked with a little smirk in his voice.

The insects in this cave know everything. They aren't mere insects. Each species was mutated to some degree. The fire spiders, in fact most species of spiders, were our allies.

Fen had to believe her. *How did Bardolf get through?* He studied the glowing web. Bardolf had led them to the fire spiders in the hope that they would be trapped.

He couldn't have, Tatijana answered. *He couldn't have gotten past that web. It's too big and thick. The spiders have been here for years, spinning that web. There are no tears in it and they couldn't have repaired a tear this fast. He didn't go through this entrance.*

I smell him.

Then he went through it, stopped and came back. He had some time to explore this cave. This can't be the first time he's been in it. He probably found his lair the first night he was here, she insisted. *I'm right about this, Fen. I am. If there's one thing I do know, it's fire spiders.*

I believe you. We need to figure out where he went.

There were two other ways to leave the cave, each leading into another, larger cavern. One way dropped lower, leading to another level. The floor of the last entrance seemed even with the chamber they were in. Fen wasn't especially keen on exploring the maze of caves beneath them. The lower they went, the more likely it was that they would run into Xavier's safeguards.

The moment he neared the entrance to the next chamber, warnings rippled through him, yet he couldn't see any obvious trap—it just felt wrong to him. He approached cautiously.

I've got multiple warning signals going off all over the place, Fen, Dimitri said.

Me, too, Tatijana added. *Maybe we should try door number three instead.*

Fen waited a moment, thinking it through. Bardolf didn't have a lot of time to prepare for an attack. He had to have noticed Tatijana's dragon and had exited his cave into the ice caves for safety. The other alternative would have given him even less time to prepare—if he felt her energy as she'd joined the two hunters at the entrance to his cave.

Wait a minute. He went this way. He's trying to herd us that way. He didn't have enough time to set up many traps. He's using what he knows is already here.

Fen didn't wait for the others to agree; he knew Bardolf was close. Misdirection was an easy escape if the *Sange rau* could make it happen. Bardolf didn't want to fight them. He would if he was cornered, but if he could escape them, that would be his first choice. He was running.

He streamed through the arched opening into the next, cathedral-ceilinged chamber. The walls were covered in ice balls, great glops clinging to the sheets of ice, looking for all the world as if someone had thrown huge popcorn all over the walls to decorate them. Hanging from the ceiling were enormous icicles.

Good God, Fen, Dimitri hissed. *This is a massacre waiting to happen.*

Tatijana, don't come through to this chamber yet, Fen cautioned. *If he's using your energy to track us, I don't want him to know we chose this way. Let me see what I can find before you enter.*

But, little sister-kin, Dimitri cautioned, *don't go exploring. Stay right by the entrance where we can see you.*

Now I have two of you worried about me. I'm perfectly fine right here. I'm really not all that fragile.

She felt fragile to Fen, but he wasn't a stupid man and he didn't say that to her. He wanted to take her out of there and just hold her tight, but there was no turning back. He kept close to the walls of the room, moving slowly to keep from disturbing the air. He matched the temperature of his molecules to the chamber's so that even that couldn't give him away.

He's here, he cautioned Dimitri. *In this room. Hiding. Tatijana, move back a little more from the entrance. If he felt you there, he would think you were retreating toward the other chamber.*

He's got a lot of weapons in here, Dimitri reminded, *but so do we.*

Tatijana moved away from the door and they lost sight of her. Both stilled, waiting. Patience was needed in the hunt. No one moved. Time passed. Water dripped and the continuous creaking of the ice became a strange music. More drops ran down the west-facing wall. Small. Like tiny beads of sweat. Hardly noticeable. Both hunters noticed.

The droplets rolled halfway down the sheet of ice before they froze there. Still, the hunters didn't take the bait. They waited in absolute stillness. Again time passed. The creaking of the ice gave way to a thunderous roar from a chamber quite close as the pressure pushed a giant-sized chunk out of a wall and flung it hard into the room. The chunk crashed to the floor with a resounding boom, shaking several adjoining caves.

With the strength of the vibrations, a few of the round balls clinging to the walls close to Fen broke free and fell to the floor, crashing and splintering into fragments like glass. A soft chuckle added to the music of the ice.

He believes we fell for his ruse and went to the next chamber, Fen said. *He's going to be fast, Dimitri, he's fighting for his life and a cornered wolf is a very dangerous one.*

His brother knew as much about wolves as he did, but still, he worried. He wasn't about to get Dimitri killed, and his younger brother always was patient about Fen giving him advice. He was quiet, often shaking his head, but he never seemed offended.

Both hunters focused on the corner, up by the ceiling where the drips had originated.

Don't reveal yourself to him, even if it looks as if I've staked him. He won't know you're close by and we'll get that second chance at him, Fen instructed. *Tatijana, if he slips through, conceal yourself, don't try to take him on alone.*

I would never consider taking him on alone.

She had that little snippy voice that told him she might be up to something, but he had to trust her word and know she would put her safety first.

The ice at the corner of the wall began to ripple as if it was coming alive. More water dripped and then ran down the side of the wall in a little stream. Bardolf didn't bother to keep his body temperature the same as the chamber. He preferred his comfort, and ice caves weren't for wolves.

Fen had never tried to kill a *Sange rau* without its body. He didn't even know if it could be done. At best, he might be able to force Bardolf into another form, giving Dimitri the chance to kill him. Nevertheless, he planned to try. He began drifting up toward the corner of the ceiling, keeping his movements slow, so there was no chance of his disturbing the air.

Bardolf was pleased with himself. He continued to chuckle out loud as he slowly removed his shelter. He had surrounded himself with a thick sheet of ice, blending it seamlessly into the wall, so it was impossible to detect. He just hadn't been able to force himself to be as cold as he needed to keep the ice from melting.

Fen remembered when he'd first come upon Bardolf's pack so long ago, when the Lycan had been the alpha. Even then he liked his comforts. His mate served him first and would massage his feet and back for him no matter how tired she was or what she'd done that day. He liked a hot fire waiting in his house and if it wasn't lit, there was hell to pay.

The ice in the corner shimmered. Slowly, Bardolf emerged. He had chosen to stream through the ice cave in the form of vapor as well, but because he needed warmth, steam rose around him, giving Fen a target to lock onto. As Bardolf moved forward, Fen attacked, shifting at the last possible second, a silver stake in his fist. He plunged it into the center of the mist, hoping to hit the heart, but knowing it would be nearly impossible. As he pushed the silver stake into the vapor, he melted all but the point so that the silver spread fast, coating every molecule.

Bardolf screamed in agony as the silver invaded his body, working its way through him. He shifted immediately, hands grabbing at the melting stake, trying to pull it from his body, even as he directed the icicles above their heads to fly at Fen.

Icicles rained down, sharp missiles seeking targets, hundreds of them, so that the chamber was filled with the sounds of cracking ice as they broke away from the ceiling to hurtle toward Fen. He threw up a shield around his body, but that split second it took to do so allowed Bardolf to shoot away from him, across the room, racing toward the arched doorway he had come through earlier.

Dimitri waited in absolute stillness, positioning himself directly in front of that door, Bardolf's only way to escape. The *Sange rau* ran straight into a silver stake, impaling himself on it. Bardolf had been moving fast and with Dimitri's enormous strength, the stake went deep, piercing the heart, but not going through.

Bardolf wrenched himself away at the last moment, just enough to keep the stake from penetrating through his heart. Cursing, blood pouring from his wound to drip on the floor of ice, he used both hands to pull the stake from his body and slam it hard into Dimitri's shoulder, to drive him back.

Fen streaked across the room while the hail of icicles followed him, heat-seeking drones locked on to him specifically. Bardolf was already on the run, racing through the door to the next chamber. He uttered a cry of alarm, but then slammed a block of ice into the entrance, trapping Fen and Dimitri on the other side.

Tatijana, get out of there. Don't reveal yourself to him.

Tatijana watched Bardolf burst through the door. She was not alone. Branislava had felt her rising distress upon entering the ice caves and she had come, as she always had.

Spiders, spiders of firespun ice, hear my call, spin and splice. Create a web of finest thread to protect your sisters from harm or dread.

Thousands of tiny spiders raced down the wall, slipping out of cracks and crevices, coming up from the floor and down from the ceiling, weaving and spinning fine webs of silken orange-red flames. There were so many of them, coming from every direction that the density and sheer size of the web was astounding.

Neither Tatijana nor Branislava moved, remaining directly behind the fiery protection, facing the wounded *Sange rau* without flinching.

Blood poured from his chest, and he roared with fury, the sound reverberating through the ice chamber. Great cracks appeared in the walls, crackling and groaning. Bardolf shifted, his muzzle elongating, making room for his teeth. His eyes went red and fur sprang around his upper body and arms. Huge sharp claws burst from his hands. He stood tall on two legs staring at the two women with hatred and malevolence.

"Take it down and I will spare your lives," he bargained, his voice mostly growls. Saliva dripped from his muzzle in long strings.

Tatijana smiled serenely. "We are Dragonseeker, and we have faced a monster far worse than you. You will not pass."

Both women lifted their hands and began to weave a pattern in the air.

Air, Earth, Fire and Water, hear my call. See your daughters . . .

The force of the elements coming together, spinning into a tight woven power, sent energy crackling through the room. The air itself grew heavy with the intensity of the combination.

Air unseen, seek that which is closed. Earth that does hold open, unfold. Fire that burns, eat that which would harm, water that flows, break open this door.

Air whistled as it gusted around the block of ice preventing Fen and Dimitri from following Bardolf into the chamber. The mountain rumbled, shaking the block, loosening the edges as the wind continually battered the seal. Spiders raced to spin their fiery strands around the entire block of ice so that water ran in streams to unseal the door.

Bardolf raged at them. His blood, tainted with the vampire's acid blood, dropped in great globs on the floor, causing the two women to look uneasily at one another. The cave was Xavier's domain and blood would call evil to it

Bardolf clapped his great claws together and chunks of ice fell on the thick fiery web. Instead of destroying the fire spider's web, the chunks melted as they dropped through, the silken strands glowing and leaping with fiery flames.

Behind him, Bardolf could see the door melting away. He chose the fire rather than facing the two hunters. Using his speed, he rushed into the web, expecting to break through. The webbing wrapped him up, trapping him while thousands of fire spiders leapt on his body, biting and feasting on his flesh. Flames raced through his fur, engulfing him as he fought to break out of the dense web.

Behind him, the door fell from a combination of the elements and the two men working on it from the other side. Fen and Dimitri rushed into the room so fast they nearly ran into the fire web themselves. Both stopped abruptly, shocked at the sight of the two women standing together, side by side, while the *Sange rau* struggled in the fiery webbing. It wouldn't kill him, but it certainly would slow him down.

The floor rippled, the ice pushing upward in places as if the cave had become unstable.

"Hurry, Fen," Tatijana said. "We can't stay here. There's evil coming for us."

She lifted her hands into the air, stepping closer to the web. *Spiders, spiders, friends of ours, ensure your flames do my lifemate and kin no harm.*

"Fen, now." Desperation edged her voice.

Muffled sounds came from beneath them, a booming, like a heartbeat, striking dread in all of them.

Seeing Bardolf covered in thousands of spiders, being eaten alive and burned at the same time, gave him pause, but he trusted Tatijana and he forced himself to step forward into that fiery web. He caught hold of Bardolf, trapped in the fire, expecting the flames to burn him, but when he touched the web, he felt only sticky silk against his skin.

Spinning Bardolf to face him, he slammed the silver stake in his fist straight through the heart. Lifting his hand, he caught the sword Dimitri threw to him and in one motion, sliced through the neck, so that the *Sange rau's* head rolled onto the shifting floor.

At once the fire spiders leapt on that as well, covering the head until there was only a sea of moving spiders and fiery flames and Bardolf was swallowed beneath them.

"We have to go fast," Tatijana said.

She stuck her arm into the web and Branislava did so as well. A narrow opening appeared. Both men shifted and streamed through. The women shifted as well and all four moved through the chambers as fast as possible until they came to the lava tube, their only exit.

Whatever evil had been awakened below them had roused the creatures inside the tube. They could hear the bats squeaking in alarm.

We have no choice, Fen said.

Tatijana and Branislava looked at one another. Their hands went up simultaneously. *Spiders, spiders of crystal ice, spin your web of strongest light. Spin and dance, surround and form, prevent these creatures from doing us harm.*

Tiny white spiders swarmed up the tube, spinning crystalline silk, all the way up the cylinder in one continuous web of light. The inside of the tube began to glow as the spiders spun and danced, more and more slipping out of cracks to join in a glorious display of shocking light. The creatures couldn't stand the light and wailed, moving back hastily into their dens.

Quick, the effects won't last long, but Bronnie says they can't see when the light is so bright. We have to hurry, Tatijana advised.

Fen went first. As he rose, he could see into the darker holes where the creatures resided. Bits of bone and fur and dark blood stained the entryways and walls inside the honeycombed dwellings. He streamed past, knowing speed mattered this time, not finesse.

Tatijana followed close behind him and Branislava was on her heels. Dimitri brought up the rear. The moment they were all out, Fen and his brother both turned back to lean over the tube. Already the light was fading and the bats began to swarm up the tube after their prey.

Fen and Dimitri together waved their hands and murmured a firm command.

"Go, run. The moment you're out, get in the air fast and away from here," Fen snapped.

The women didn't argue; both streaked through the narrow tunnel back to Bardolf's cave and then out into the open air. They leapt straight up, shifting as they did, the two dragons banking and then, wings flapping hard, shooting out of the mist.

Fen and Dimitri followed them, practically on their heels. Behind them, the world blew apart. The lava tube detonated, a fiery blast that shook the entire mountain. The shock waves from the explosion followed them through the caves, blowing a hole just to the side of Bardolf's chosen lair.

Fen and Dimitri flung themselves skyward, shifting as they did. The concussion sent both of them reeling through the air and out of the mist as if the mountain threw them away. Tatijana raced back, her dragon diving beneath Fen, while Branislava managed to seat Dimitri on her fire dragon.

I'm ready for a long sleep in the ground again, Branislava said. *Your adventures are very exciting, but too much of a good thing is exhausting.*

Fen had to agree with her.

18

Fen wrapped his arm around Tatijana. Branislava was safely beneath the earth, well fed and ready for sleep. Dimitri's wound had been attended to. He'd been given blood and he, too, was in the ground rejuvenating. Tatijana and Fen walked through the forest—their favorite place—and just breathed in the crisp air. He knew she'd been traumatized all over again entering the ice caves and he didn't want her to go to ground until they had talked it out.

He stirred her toward a spot where a series of natural pools had developed. The sound of water was calming and he knew the night sky would help to make her feel less claustrophobic. Going to a place of such natural beauty with waterfalls and pools, so entirely different than her prison had been, he hoped would ease the tension from her. He knew she was drawn by the sound and feel of water. He wanted to turn the rest of the night into something beautiful to erase what had come before.

"You were amazing," he said, meaning it. "I know you were frightened."

"Anyone would be afraid, knowing the traps and the hideous creatures locked away in that mountain," Tatijana said, "but more, I was sickened. I couldn't believe how nauseated I was. My stomach was in knots and a couple of times the smell actually made me gag. I locked away most of those memories so I could survive."

"I'm sorry our fight with Bardolf led us to the ice caves," he said as gently as he could. He tightened his arm around her shoulders. "I know I've got a lot of rough edges, Tatijana. You deserve a man who is gentle and always considerate, but know that I love you above all else and I will do anything to make you happy." He regretted that he hadn't figured out a way to keep her out of Xavier's labyrinth of evil. He'd brought all those terrible memories crashing down on her. Where Branislava took to the ground, allowing the healing soil to keep the trauma at bay, Tatijana embraced the night, needing the freedom of the open air.

Tatijana frowned up at him. She lifted one hand to trace the lines in his face. "Why would you think I would want any other? Your words are sweet enough when I need to hear them. I feel surrounded by your love, enveloped in it and I need no one else. I chose to go back to that cave with you. It was my choice, and I appreciate that you understood it had to be my choice. More than anything, Fen, I fell in love with that trait in you. You let me be me."

He took her deeper into the forest, listening for every sound. He wanted them safe and after the hunt for the werewolves, he was certain they would be. Branislava had found another unit of sixteen and Zev and the others had wiped them out. Abel was slowly losing his army. He would be much more wary of sacrificing his pawns until he had a concrete plan to carry out his mission.

More and more, Fen feared that Abel was working with someone else— someone far away. It would be rare for a master vampire to take orders from another, and in spite of being the *Sange rau* that Abel was.

"Where are we going?" Tatijana asked as he lifted her over a fallen tree trunk covered in moss. "I've never been out this way."

"I'm glad. I wanted to surprise you."

Already the sound of the falls was beginning to be heard. She turned her head toward it. "A waterfall? I had no idea."

He felt the lightness in her heart lift away some of the shadows pressing down on her. "A series of waterfalls. They fall into natural pools. Two of the pools are fed from underground springs that are hot. The others are very cold."

"Temperature matters little to a Carpathian," she said.

He grinned at her. "Unless your lifemate can surprise you and toss you into a cold pool before you can regulate."

"You wouldn't dare," she said, her emerald eyes beginning to sparkle.

"Probably not," he soothed, "but you never know. I am a wolf man, after all, and they do like their pranks."

The sound of the falls grew louder, water cascading down the mountainside and dropping several meters into the pools formed below by rock. Over time the pounding water had smoothed the boulders and bottom of the pools until they were polished and even.

"Strange that I didn't notice that jokester trait in the Lycans," Tatijana said. "They looked like a sober lot to me." She sent him a warning from under her lashes, but her eyes couldn't contain her amusement.

He pushed aside fronds from a fern as tall as he was so she could get her first look at the waterfall and pools. They were hidden from view by a grove of old-growth trees whose trunks were as wide and thick as a small car. He watched her face as he held the lacy leaves back. Her entire face lit up. Her hair actually streaked with deeper shades of red. Her emerald eyes deepened in color until they were nearly the same as the deepest pool.

Tatijana gave a little gasp as she stepped forward. "It's so beautiful, Fen. Truly beautiful. You couldn't have found a place I would like more."

She turned into his body, circling his neck with her slender arms and bringing his head down to hers, leaning into him until she was pressed tight. "I love you, Fenris Dalka. Everything about you, but especially that you always seem to know exactly what I need. This is perfect."

Fen framed her face with his large hands. She looked up at him with her incredible, dazzling eyes and he let himself fall into the deep depths. He wanted to live there inside her, with her, be one with her.

Her fingers brushed his mouth, and then, featherlight, traced his lips. He felt the jolt of shock go through his body straight to his groin. As gentle as her fingers on his face were, the lightning bolt slamming through his body was exactly the opposite, a punch hard and mean.

The intensity of his love for her was terrifying. Wonderful. A miracle. He had never envisioned that emotions could run so deep. Love and lust were a potent combination, heightening every sense and inflaming every nerve ending.

He was aware of every breath she drew. The subtle rise and fall of her breasts beneath her clothing. He inhaled her fragrance, the wild of the forest and clean of the rain. His hand bunched in the thick silk of her hair.

Fen pressed his mouth close to her ear. "I don't want a single stitch of clothing between your skin and mine."

Her long lashes swept down, veiling her expression, but her lips curved and her clothes disappeared, leaving her standing in front of him completely naked. He took a breath. Her body was beautiful to him. The full curves, the tucked-in waist, her flaring hips and the small dragon low and to the left below her waist, just faintly visible. She had shapely legs and small, bare feet. Her hair, usually kept in a braid, tumbled passed her waist like a riot of fine silk.

He removed his own clothing, suddenly finding the material too tight to contain his hard body. He leaned his head down to hers and took possession of that oh-so-incredibly-generous mouth. Soft. Cool against the fire of his. Everything he could possibly want was right there in his arms.

Her mouth moved under his, giving him everything he asked of her. His fingers tightened in her hair, burying deep to anchor her to him, to hold her still. In spite of the blood surging hotly in his veins and his cock hard and thick and making its own demands, he was patient, savoring each moment of time with her.

He felt her lips tremble as he deepened the kiss, exploring all that cool sweetness that was his alone. His skin felt burning hot, hers cool and soft. A whip of lightning cracked and snapped through his bloodstream, sending flames licking at his groin. The rush was all encompassing.

She gave herself to him as generous as always, pouring herself into his mind and heart, her mouth giving him everything he craved. He tasted passion. Love. A world he hadn't known existed opened up the moment he'd met her, and this, her mouth, her kiss, was his passport there. His belly tightened, every muscle hardening, yet he wanted slow and gentle. He wanted to savor every moment, imprint the feel and taste of her into him for all time.

He lifted his head, pressing his forehead into hers. His lungs burned, whether for air or just the miracle of finding her after centuries of loneliness—after believing his world would always be one of darkness, killing and a continuous struggle.

"You saved me. You did, Tatijana. No matter what you think, you saved my soul. I still can't believe what a perfect miracle you are or what I ever did to deserve you."

She ran both hands up his flat belly to his chest, her mouth following, kissing every defined muscle until she was teasing his flat nipple with her tongue. "Perhaps, wolf man, you saved me," she murmured, licking at his pounding pulse.

Before he could answer, her teeth sank deep. He threw his head back and growled in ecstasy. Her hands smoothed his shoulders, traced his ribs and dropped lower to find the girth of his burgeoning cock. She danced her fingers over his sensitive skin, then wrapped her fist tightly and slid the length of him from base to head in that firm grip. Her other hand dropped a little lower to find his heavy sac. She rolled and caressed, squeezing gently.

The sensations she created, between her hands and her mouth, turned his brain to absolute mush. Thunder roared in his ears. Blood pounded through his body. He had set out to give her a night of pleasure, only to have her turn the tables. She licked across the small wound in his chest her teeth had caused, her eyes nearly glowing as she lifted her lashes.

"I need more of you, lifemate," she said softly.

If it was possible, his cock hardened even more.

She tugged very gently, not relinquishing her hold on him. "I think you'd better come with me."

He did. How could he not? She got as far as the first pool where the rocks were smooth all around it and stepped into it. The water came to her waist.

"Sit right here." She patted the edge where the rock was the smoothest.

He complied with her command, sitting right on the edge. His cock was rock hard against his stomach, but his sac hung down toward that steaming water. Standing so much lower than him, her head was perfectly aligned with his groin.

"This night was meant for you," he said, his voice raspy and raw.

Tatijana gave him a siren's smile, one that made him hotter than ever.

"Exactly. I want more of you, and it's time I got what I wanted. Ever since our night in the field, tasting you on that flower, I've been craving that exact taste. I could be addicted."

Her mouth slid over him like a silken glove. His entire body shuddered with pleasure. He was hot, his skin, his blood, his desire. Her mouth was cool silk, wrapped tightly around him, drawing him deeper into her with every movement she made. She didn't take her eyes from his, so that he could see her pleasure.

Fen cupped her breasts, his fingers finding her nipples. He rolled and tugged, watching the glaze come into the very depths of her eyes. Her hands moved over his groin, soft hands, but her touch drove him wild.

Tatijana had butterflies in her stomach. She'd never been nervous, but this time, she wanted to give Fen as much pleasure as he always gave her. More, she wanted this for herself. She wanted to make her own demands of him and know he found everything as pleasurable as she did.

She looked up at Fen's rugged features. He was a man who had seen more in life than he ever should have. There was the stamp of confidence, of dominance, an alpha who took control when necessary. He was beautiful to her, wholly masculine, his face sensual. She loved his eyes. Those amazing, glacier-blue eyes. When he focused on her, there was no one else in the world and she knew it. He made her feel alive and vibrant and beautiful herself.

She loved the control she had, driving him wild, and she knew he was nearly crazy with pleasure. Her mouth and tongue teased and tortured, and clamped around him, tighter, urging him deeper, his hands on her breasts making her just as wild for him. She hadn't known she was so sensitive there, but every tug on her nipples sent fresh, welcoming liquid between her legs.

Fen bunched Tatijana's hair in his fist, groaning, his body swelling more. He tried to keep his hips still, giving her the control, but her tongue teased his most sensitive spot under the head of his cock and then suddenly flicked back and forth. Fire sizzled through his veins, settling in his groin, roaring as it grew out of control. She used the edge of her teeth, scraping gently, and then her tongue danced again. She slid her lips up and down his shaft, over his tight sac and the very base of his cock and then swirled her tongue around the head.

She sipped at the pearly drops leaking almost continually, keeping him so off balance he knew he would be lost. She took him deeper, her mouth constricting around him, and he took over, thrusting into her, giving her what she wanted most. Both hands gripped her hair, holding her still, drawing her into him as he thrust upward. She braced herself with one hand on his thigh while the other cuddled his sac, her hold intimate.

His body tightened, the fire roaring. He could feel flames from his feet to the top of his head. Blood pounded through him. His pulse thundered in his ears. She flattened her tongue, keeping her mouth tight while he thrust deep over and over. He felt the blast coming and there was no way to stop, not when she felt like heaven.

Nothing prepared him for the way she suckled him, the constriction and the feel of her silken mouth clamped around him. He threw back his head and howled like a wolf as he poured down her throat. His hands gripped her hair hard, but she didn't pull away, only licked gently at his shaft and the exquisitely sensitive head until he felt thoroughly loved.

"Yep. That's definitely the taste I remember," Tatijana said. "Definitely addicting."

He couldn't breathe. He wasn't certain he could ever breathe again. She smiled her siren's smile and swam away from him, her bare buttocks flashing white. She rolled over and leisurely floated, her breasts thrust up toward the sky. The mist had come in, so soft and light, it was barely noticeable, or he'd been preoccupied and hadn't observed it.

Now it was becoming thicker, denser, falling lightly into the steaming pool. He watched her for a few minutes, clearly enjoying the feel of the water against her skin. Even in the heat of the pool, Fen knew her skin would feel cool and inviting against his. He leaned back and let the mist fall on his face, watching the tiny drops fall like glittering diamonds from the sky.

He would always associate Tatijana with fresh rain, with the feel of cool water against hot skin. There was a sensual feeling he couldn't deny with the mist falling softly over him. He'd never connected rain or fog to sensuality, but would forever more.

Tatijana sent a wall of water shooting at him. He ducked under it using the speed of his mixed blood and did a shallow dive into the water. The heat after the cool rain was shocking. He gave chase, catching her just near the far side, nearest the mountain where icy cold drops from the waterfall splashed over them to hiss in the heat of the pool.

Standing, he pulled her to him, catching her legs to wrap them around his body. The vee between her legs nestled over his already thickening cock. Her skin was cool, just as he suspected, but that sweet invitation was hotter than ever. She linked her fingers behind his neck and leaned in to kiss him.

"Thank you. I love this place, Fen. My beautiful wolf man. First you write me a song, and then you give me this wonderful night." She threw her head back, allowing the mist to fall into her face. "I think it's going to rain. Wouldn't that be lovely?"

He laughed, enjoying how happy she was. "Only you would say that, my lady. Most women would prefer to be indoors when it rains."

"They don't know how good it feels on their skin." She leaned down to lick droplets off his neck. "Or how good rain tastes on skin."

"Lean back. I'll hold you," he promised. "Just enough that I can get a taste of you."

When she complied, stretching her arms to full length, the movement pushed her body into his. She moved, a subtle circle, rubbing against him, so that his cock jerked with demand. Her breasts swayed invitingly and the silk of her hair fell in waves like a bright cape. Behind her, the waterfall spilled continuously down the mountainside, long crystal streaks of water racing toward the pools below. Wind moved through the trees, so that the tops swayed as if to music. Steam rose around them, creating even more of an intimacy.

"There is music to the rain," Tatijana confided. "Haven't you ever heard it?"

"No," he admitted, nuzzling her breast. "When it rains, I'll listen," he promised.

The temptation of her taut nipple was too much for him. She was a redhead and her nipples were more of a pink than dark—and very sensitive. Each time he stroked his tongue over and around her breast, he felt her body's reaction. He used his teeth, tiny little nips, before he drew her nipple into the heat of his mouth and suckled strongly.

The mist turned to a light rain, the drops feeling cool against his body heat. Cool, like Tatijana. His mouth was burning hot. His skin. His cock.

His blood, surging, rushing, inflamed in the midst of such temptation. He couldn't leave her other breast unattended and took his time paying tribute to her soft flesh until she was crying out his name, cradling his head and arching into him.

Her body squirmed against his, each delicious movement sliding over his shaft, rubbing and teasing, inflaming him more. He still had trouble believing that such a beautiful woman had chosen him, and each time he reached for her, gave herself again and again so generously. He touched her mind often, and she always was as eager to explore his body as he was to explore hers.

He kissed his way up her breast, over the creamy slope, his teeth nipping along the way, just to feel the hot liquid response of her body against his shaft. Using his tongue, he eased each sting and then found her pounding pulse. The frantic rhythm beckoned and called seductively to him. He felt the pull of her blood as deeply as he felt the need of her body. The taste of her burst through his mouth even before he actually sank his teeth deep.

Tatijana cried out, sweet music to his ears, as he drank from her, taking the essence of her into his own body. The rain fell over the both of them— small, gentle droplets cooling the heat of his skin, making his core burn hotter than ever. She cradled his head to her, holding him close, her body writhing against his. Twice she lifted her hips, trying to impale herself on him, but he held her firmly in place, drawing out the need, building it in her.

"Fen. What are you doing?"

She gasped his name. Chanted it again and again. Adding to the music. He was beginning to hear the rain's song through the pounding of his own blood. Small little drops plopping in the water. The random hiss of droplets from the waterfall accompanying the steadier fall of the rain. Her ragged breathing. His pulse thundering in his ears like a drum.

He took his time, savoring the taste of her and the response of her body, before he finally closed the wound over her breast.

Her breathing became part of the symphony. The drops hitting the leaves produced a different sound than when they fell on the ground. He heard it now, the music the rain made, that same music she heard, and it became part of their night, part of them. His hands slid down her body to grip her buttocks, lifting her so that the head of his cock lodged just inside of her.

Tight muscles closed around him, gripping and squeezing, trying to drag him inside of her, desperate for him to move hard and deep. Her panting gasps and desperate pleas added to the melody of the rain, that perfect song. He would always love her soft little cries, the way she said his name over and over.

Very slowly he lowered her body over his, burying his cock in her scorching hot feminine sheath, such a contrast to the cool of her outside skin. Her body was tight, reluctantly giving way for his invasion. Her breath hissed out against his neck, a long sigh of pure rapture.

"At last," she whispered, her fingers locking at the nape of his neck. "I feel I've waited a lifetime for this moment."

"Clearly I've been remiss in attending to your needs," he said, lifting her hips so that her body rode his.

She moved in a small, intriguing circle as she rode his cock down, her tight muscles locking over him so that the friction sent streaks of fire racing from his core up to his head and down to his toes.

Tatijana laughed softly, throwing her head back so that fine rain could touch her face. Her hair fell in long waves and her breasts jutted up, swaying temptingly. She looked so beautiful, wild, and obviously happy. He loved that about her, that inhibition, showing him how she felt about him every moment.

"Do you hear the music now, Fen?" she asked, her hips shifting to a faster rhythm.

The raindrops felt like little tongues against his skin. The concentration on her face added to her beauty as she rode him, her muscles a fiery velvet fist wrapped tightly around him. Yes, he heard it. The plinking of the drops in the water. The wild beating of their hearts in complete synchronization. The creaking of the trees and the little sounds she made that drove him completely and utterly mad with love for her.

He tightened his hands on her hips and took over, lifting her, picking up the pace so that he drove hard and deep while he held her still. He thrust over and over, surging into her, a piston out of control, listening to her gasping breath, her little cries, watching the glaze come into her eyes and the flush come to her body. The slap of the water just added to the crashing crescendo as he took them both right to the edge, teetered there, and then both fell together in a long erotic free fall.

Tatijana collapsed over him, her head on his shoulder, fighting for breath, pressing little kisses along his collarbone and neck.

Fen carried her to the edge of the pool before sinking into its warmth, keeping her on his lap as he sat, stretching out his legs, stone behind him and his woman a soft bundle in his arms. The soft rain fell on them both and Tatijana turned her face sideways so she could feel it.

"This has been such a beautiful night, Fen. A gift. Thank you. I love the way you love me. I was—" she broke off, searching for the right way to tell him. "I was having trouble closing the door on my past. I accepted what happened to me. One has to learn acceptance in a situation like ours, but it becomes a way of life. The terror of being outside that cave was almost as bad as being inside of it."

He brought her hand to his mouth, kissing her knuckles and nibbling on her fingers. "Yet you've done so well, Tatijana. You set out exploring on your own, learning things you wanted to learn."

She nodded. "But I avoided people. I observed them, but I still didn't want to be part of anything else. I'm not explaining this very well. But I want to be a part of us. You and me. More than you and me. We have family. Branislava, Dimitri. Razvan and Natalya. Their lifemates. Young Skyler. My niece Lara who led the rescue of us. You've done that for me. You've given me the ability to go beyond just Bronnie and me."

He nuzzled the top of her head with his chin. "You loved them all before I came along."

"From a distance. I didn't want any interaction with them. I avoided them, just as Bronnie is doing now. We both retreated underground where we were safe. Where we didn't have to figure out the rules of the new world we lived in. Where no one could ever get to us again. We had no measure of trust. How could we? It was our own father who tortured us and held us prisoner. You made me realize just how honorable a man could be."

"I'm glad then, that it was me, Tatijana. For me, you're a complete miracle."

"That's it, right there. You think I'm the miracle, Fen, but really it's you." She caught his face between her hands and kissed him hard. "I love you with all my heart. You, Fen. You're my lifemate and that means everything, it means we're bound together. One. But I want you to know, I love *you*, my wolf man. I would follow you anywhere."

She had followed him—into the labyrinth of evil her father had held her captive in. She had supported his every decision, following him into danger and fighting alongside him.

He kissed her again, savoring the taste of her, a part of him wondering how he got so lucky. His world had changed almost overnight. "I love you more than life itself, Tatijana," he murmured. "Inadequate words but heartfelt."

Tatijana laid her head on his shoulder again, closing her eyes, her body relaxing into his. Sometimes, like now, for Fen, it felt as if she simply melted into him. Soft. Cool. His lady.

"Fen." Tatijana lifted her head from his chest to look into his eyes.

He felt the familiar tightening of his gut, the strange slow somersault of his heart the moment their eyes met.

"What's next? What are you planning to do?"

"I've got to stop Abel. He's after Mikhail. He plans to wipe out the entire species. We're all connected through the prince. I don't know what Abel stands to gain from killing Mikhail, but he's dead set on it."

"Maybe he's moved on," she said hopefully. "He's lost most of his pack and now Bardolf. It would make sense for him to run."

Fen sighed, his fingers at the nape of her neck, massaging gently. Tension was creeping back in when she'd been limp and relaxed only moments earlier. "I don't think he's going anywhere. I think his mission was to kill Mikhail, and unfortunately for him, I ran across his tracks, as did Zev. He wasn't expecting either of us."

"Do you really think you can kill Abel? How long has he been a *Sange rau?* Isn't it true that your abilities grow with time?"

He felt the anxiety in her mind, heard the note of worry she tried to keep from her voice. "I've seen him in action, and I think we're fairly evenly matched. So, yes, I believe I can kill him. It may take a little bit of luck and I know I'll probably need recovery time after, but I'll get the job done."

He didn't need to pretend confidence for her, and in any case he doubted if he could deceive her. He was confident. He brushed another kiss on the top of her head for reassurance. "No matter if Abel moved on or not, I would have to hunt him down. It's what I do. It's who I am. I can't let him kill whoever he pleases. He lives for that now. The rush. The blood. No one is safe, no species. He has to be destroyed."

"I know. But isn't Zev supposed to hunt rogues?"

He couldn't help but smile. "Abel is no rogue. He's far more than that and you know it. The key to killing Abel is to remember what he's like, I think. I grew up with him. I knew him as a child. The memories are vague, but I'm slowly pulling them up. He was a good man. Honorable. He didn't have the character flaws one associates with those who choose to lose their souls. I have no idea what would make him choose to become the very thing he hunted so successfully for centuries. I ran across him once in a rare while. He was unswerving, even relentless in carrying out his duties."

"What usually tips someone over the edge?" Tatijana asked, curiosity in her mind. "You all start out with honor."

"I think it has to do with character. I've met Carpathians who crave power. Who enjoy killing. Remember, we are predators. We're born to hunt. The darkness is in all of us, but just like everyone, we have character strengths and weaknesses. There were some whose paths I crossed that I was certain would turn if they didn't find their lifemate very quickly. Abel wasn't one of them."

"Would he turn if he did find his lifemate and she was killed somehow?"

That gave him pause. There was always that danger. In the midst of grief, of wrenching intense sorrow when the other half of one's soul had been ripped away, insanity could ensue. Tatijana may have hit on something, although he didn't like the idea. If Abel had become vampire upon losing his lifemate, and it was known, that would make it much more difficult for Mikhail to convince the Lycan council that any Guardian who had a lifemate would be safe from becoming the *Sange rau.*

"It's possible. That's definitely one of the most feared moments for any Carpathian. Males refer to that moment as the madness thrall. You hold light in you, Tatijana, but we're all darkness until you provide us with that light. You've given me life," he tried to explain. She might be able to understand, because she had to have felt hopeless in those long, barren years prisoner in the ice caves.

"The centuries go on endlessly. There's nothing but the kill. After a while a hunter begins to look forward to the kill because there is nothing else for him. There is no beauty in the world." He looked around him. "Look at this. The falls, the pools and forest. The colors, so vibrant. Without you, I couldn't see any of this. I wouldn't even notice it. You provided that for me. I had no ability to feel for others. I hunted. I killed. I fed. That was my life. That's the life of a Carpathian male. I was luckier than most because I found the Lycans. For a long while I could see as a wolf sees, but as my abilities as a . . . Guardian grew, so did the darkness in me."

Tatijana pressed closer if it was possible, holding him tight in her arms.

"Can you imagine what it would be like for me, having been given these incredible gifts, this miracle of a lifemate who allows me to see such beauty in the world, to feel so intensely, such emotion and then have it ripped away? A madness grips, takes over. Most get through it, but not all."

"Is it really a choice then, to become the vampire?" Tatijana asked.

"I haven't been in that situation, but because the decision has to be made, give up one's soul or follow your lifemate, it is decreed that it is a choice. I believe, in a moment of madness, anyone can make a bad decision."

"How sad. How tragic."

"It's both," he agreed. "But once he's vampire, then there is no choice for the hunter. He must destroy the undead, even if it's one's father, brother or best friend. Vampires are wholly evil. Believe me, Tatijana, over the centuries, I've tried to reach one or two and pull them back."

She nuzzled his throat. "Of course you did. You had little or no emotions, but you still had it in you to try."

"We have memories. That is one thing we don't lose. That is the one gift left to us. Our memories are vivid and very much alive. They do fade as the centuries go by, but we hold them close to us. Dimitri and I aided one another, keeping those important memories alive in one another. If not for him, I would have met the dawn a century ago. The pull of evil is so strong in a mixed blood. I think the predator is strong in both species, and when they come together it is far worse as time goes by and the gifts develop."

"I feel sorry for Abel if he did lose a lifemate. I can't imagine losing you. But Fen, if something happens to me, follow me. I don't want to think of you lost without me and I can't get to you to save you."

She frowned up at him and he tried not to melt. It seemed a ridiculous thing to do for a Carpathian hunter and worse for a Guardian. One shouldn't find their lifemate's frowns adorable.

"I'll do my best to always stay honorable, my lady," he assured her.

"You're worried about Dimitri, aren't you?"

"I don't worry that he will turn," he said slowly. "The connection between Skyler and Dimitri is very strong. Intense. I've never seen anything like it, but, having said that, he puts himself in harm's way more than I would like."

She laughed softly. "In other words, he's just like you. You throw yourself in front of people when there's danger. Is that what you mean?"

He tugged on a strand of her hair. "He took me in even when I explained the dangers of what I was to him. He went into battle with me over and over and when we gave each other blood to survive, he knew the risks and still did it anyway." He caught her chin and lifted it, forcing her to look up at him. "As you're doing now."

"And always, my Guardian, you have to know it is my choice. Just as it is Dimitri's choice. None of us have control over what another does, we can only control ourselves. Dimitri is a strong man. He's one of the best in any battle. He's known for some time that he's becoming as you are . . ."

"Yet he didn't tell me until this evening."

"He's a man who handles his own life, just as you do," Tatijana said. "He may be your younger brother, but he caught up with you many centuries ago. He has a need to protect you, just as you protect him. Skyler returned his emotions to him and he feels deeply. You can't fault him for being a man."

She spoke the truth and Fen knew it. Dimitri would always be his own man. He'd make his own decisions. Fate had given Dimitri the skills of a hunter and he'd excelled at his job.

"I love that the two of you are so close. I don't know what I'd do without Bronnie. We definitely relied on each other all those centuries. It's nice to know you understand that unbreakable bond we have."

Fen sighed. The sky overhead was becoming lighter in spite of the rain-clouds drifting across. "We have to go to ground, my lady."

"I know." She kissed his throat again. "I wanted this night to never end. I know you're going to hunt Abel this next rising." She paused to look up at him. "Aren't you?"

"It has to be done. I can't take the chance of waiting. He's got a plan to kill Mikhail and he believes he can do it. That means the plan is already in place. I can't wait for him to put it into motion and maybe get away with it. If I push him, actively hunt him, and he knows I'm coming for him, that might throw him off his game."

Fen stood up, taking her with him, cradling her in his arms, close to his chest. He didn't bother with clothes, there seemed no need. Both could regulate their body temperatures and she loved the feel of the rain on her skin. He was coming to love it as well.

"When it's over, will we stay here? Make our home near the others?"

She was asking if they would remain close to her sister. Again she tried to hide that little anxious note from him, but he felt it would be impossible for him not to recognize when his lady was upset.

He leaned his head down and fastened his mouth to hers. She tasted like the rain. Like wild honey. Like Tatijana. She always made him hungry for more.

"I would never take you far from your sister, *sívamet*," he assured when he had kissed her thoroughly. "I would never do anything that would make you unhappy."

Tatijana's eyes searched his. She nodded her head and tightened her hold on his neck. "Let's go back to our little spot in the forest. I want to lie close to you for a while before we go to sleep. I need you to hold me."

"Always," he said, and took to the air.

19

Tatijana woke before Fen. She lay curled in his arms, her head on his shoulder, just as she had when they'd finally closed the earth over them. They'd made love two more times, and she knew part of that terrible hunger in her was sheer fear. The *Sange rau* terrified her. There would be no stopping Fen, or Dimitri for that matter. Both had sworn loyalty to the prince and the Carpathian people. They would defend Mikhail Dubrinsky with their lives.

She waved her hand to open the earth. It was dark in the forest, although still rather early in the evening. Tree branches swayed and danced to the wind. The rain had stopped, but gray clouds spun in the sky. A storm was coming. A big one. She pressed a hand to her wildly beating heart. She would not lose her lifemate to this monster. Strangely, last evening, when she thought it was possible Abel had turned because he'd lost his lifemate, she'd felt compassion for him. That was gone this rising. She only cared that Fen came home safe to her.

She took a deep breath of the fresh air. The rain always left behind a fresh, clean scent. Now, it was mixed with the soothing aroma of forest—trees and rich soil. She arranged her surprise for him, the candles set in a protection circle around soft blankets right out under the canopy so they could look up and see the night arriving through the beauty of the trees. Fen hadn't seen much beauty these past centuries and she was determined to make up for lost time. She'd awakened early just for that purpose.

When she was ready, Tatijana floated him out of their sleeping quarters and over to the blanket, ensuring his body was clean and free of all rejuvenating soil. She knew he was aware, but he didn't stop her or try to take over. That made her love him all the more. Fen always provided what she needed most. Right now, she needed to feel his strength and know they were both alive and well.

She crawled over the top of him, kissing her way up his thigh, his groin, the erection that was already becoming heavy and thick, his belly and chest with all that beautiful muscle definition. She traced the muscles with her tongue, exploring him, imprinting him into her bones, in her mind so there wasn't a single inch of him she didn't know.

His hands tangled in her hair as she took her time with her exploration. He turned his body over and let her do the same to the back of him and then each side. He never said a word, but she felt completely surrounded by his love. She'd never felt so close to anyone in her life. She knew he was telling her silently that he belonged to her. Whatever she needed, whatever she hungered for, he provided.

When she turned him back over and took his face between her hands, her body stretched out over his, so that every inch of her was pressed into him, she kissed him long and hard. Taking her time. Telling him she loved him with her mouth, with her hands.

When she lifted her head, Fen smiled at her. He traced her mouth with the pad of his fingers. "My turn," he said abruptly and catching her in his arms, rolled her beneath him.

She couldn't help the little thrill that burst through her. He was so strong, his body fit and hard, yet he never hurt her. Fen repeated her actions, exploring every inch of her, but she was certain he was far more thorough than she had been, he had her squirming and mewling like a kitten, her hips bucking at times when he used his tongue and teeth on her most sensitive nerve endings. He paid no attention, but took his time, making certain he didn't miss a single spot.

He pulled her to her hands and knees, wrapping his arm around her waist and jerking her body back into him as he knelt up behind her. His hands massaged her buttocks, his finger slipping into her to make certain she was ready for him.

The position allowed him to go even deeper, to take her harder and faster. He started slow and gentle, giving her body time to get used to his invasion as he almost always did. Her sheath always seemed reluctant at first, so tight she strangled his cock, but then opening for him like a sensitive flower to allow his deeper penetration.

He seemed to know without words what she needed and he pounded into her, showing no mercy, taking her up fast and hard and then stopping just before her release. Over and over he built the tension, stretching them both out on a torturous rack of pleasure until she was nearly sobbing. Still he was relentless. Merciless.

Fen waited for her pleas. The chanting of his name. The music that always accompanied their lovemaking. He didn't stop until he heard it, surging deep, his cock swelling gloriously, while her feminine sheath gripped and milked him. He heard his own hoarse cry blending with hers as jet after jet of hot seed filled her. The ripples went from her core to her breasts and down her thighs, the aftershocks nearly as strong as the orgasm itself and he felt them all, merged deep as he was in her mind.

Fen leaned over her, wrapping his arms around her waist and nuzzling her back. "There is no better way to wake up, my lady, than with you like this."

Tatijana didn't say anything at all, but he felt her heavy sorrow pressing down on him.

Very gently, reluctantly, he withdrew, pulling her back onto his lap. She wouldn't look at him and he had to grip her chin and turn her face up to his. There were tears on her face. "I will not die. I know you're afraid, but I will not die."

"I have a terrible feeling of dread." She traced her finger over the faint image of the dragon over her ovary. "Sometimes, I know something bad is going to happen before it does. I don't know what, but when I woke, I could barely breathe."

"I will not die," he reiterated. "I have battled the vampire for centuries and I have sustained many mortal wounds. It could very well happen again in this fight with Abel, but I survived without my lifemate. How much easier will it be for me this time? You are Dragonseeker. Mother Earth has accepted me as her son. We have Gregori close, a great healer, and young Skyler, who we both know is exceptional. I do not fear this. I don't want you to be afraid either."

Fen brushed at the tears on her face, and then leaned down to take one into his mouth, tasting her fear.

Tatijana knelt up in front of him, taking his face between both hands. "You are everything to me, and know this, wolf man. Should you go into the next life, I will follow. Look for me only minutes behind. I will not give you up."

"There will be no need. Unless you see my body and know I am dead, do not even consider such a thing," he cautioned. "I've come back from wounds worse than Dimitri's. The wolf in me is strong and regenerates fast."

Tatijana sat back on her heels. "Like the *Sange rau*. Abel can regenerate very fast, can't he? Like everything else it speeds up with the length of time you've been a mixed blood."

Fen wasn't surprised that she was aware Abel would be a far cry from Bardolf. "True. But silver will still kill him. I just have to figure out where he set up his lair."

"I woke you early so you would have time to prepare," Tatijana admitted. "And feed from a Carpathian ancient, one with pure line. I will give you my blood, but seek out Jacques Dubrinsky. You need to be as strong as possible."

She stood up, clothing herself as she did so, but she left the candles burning. "This is a circle of protection. I was careful setting it up and as long as you're in it, no harm can come to you. More, if you and Dimitri use this circle to figure out what Abel might do and where he might be, no other can accidentally overhear words, thoughts or telepathy."

As frightened as she was for him, she had still taken the time to give him such a gift. He stood up as well, clothing himself, his hair tied back with a cord, his boots and long coat ready for war. He called his weapons to him, a multitude of silver stakes slipping into the loops made for them, as well as a long sword. He didn't bother with gloves as he had no intention of running into any member of the pack. Instead, he coated his hands and arms with sealant as Dimitri had.

My brother-kin. Let us come together with a battle plan. Fen wasted no time at all waking his brother.

Tatijana stepped close to him and offered him her neck, sweeping back the long length of hair. Her arms went around his head, bringing it down to the warmth of her neck and throat where he nuzzled her.

"Take what you need, Fenris Dalka, and come home to your lifemate."

"I will take that as a command, my lady," he said.

She smelled so good. He'd just had her, but that woodsy scent, fresh honey and rain aroused him all over again. He folded her into his arms and took her offering without hesitation. He was already addicted to her taste, and Dragonseeker blood would be invaluable in his pursuit of the enemy. For a moment, he lost himself in the sensual, intimate act of taking his lifemate's blood, but still, he was aware the moment Dimitri approached.

He closed the small wound on her neck and held her a moment longer. Tatijana smiled up at him, waved at Dimitri and shifted, using a small wolf to move through the forest to the edge of the village where she would find sustenance.

Fen wrapped her up in warmth, pouring his love of her into her mind for a moment, before he had to turn his attention to business.

"She made us a protection circle," Dimitri said as he stepped inside. He was dressed very similar to Fen, his weapons concealed but easily accessed.

"She's worried and wanted us to be as safe as possible. We're going to have to remember at all times we have more than one enemy. Should the pack become aware of what we are, they will turn on us," Fen cautioned.

Dimitri nodded. "I had hoped to avoid them."

"We know Mikhail is the target. I'm almost certain Abel has come here on a mission to assassinate the prince. It can't be personal, Mikhail is far too young and I doubt Abel ever crossed paths with him. He would gain nothing from destroying an entire species."

"But you believe someone else has something to gain?" Dimitri asked. "You've mentioned this before, but whom?"

"I don't have that answer, and at this point, we have to deal with one thing at a time. Try to remember Abel as a young man. He was closer to my age than yours, but he would have been around. Anything might help."

Dimitri frowned, trying to call up old, faded memories. He shrugged. "The only thing I remember of him, other than that he was a good man who answered questions when I asked him about various weapons, was the one time he took me out to the lake to show me how to fight in the water."

Fen swung around. "The lake. He was obsessed with that lake. When anyone needed him in the old days, they would find him there. That's where he is, Dimitri. He's found a lair somewhere near the lake."

"There's a small island in the lake; it's actually close to the shore and he might be able to use it," Dimitri suggested. "It would be unusual for a vampire to do something like that. Wouldn't he have to have a retreat, an exit? There's not much on that tiny island, some trees and a few rocks."

"I say we check it out," Fen said. "He would have safeguards. No Carpathian will go to ground without safeguards and he was a Carpathian for centuries. He'll fall back on what he knows best."

"Let's do this," Dimitri said.

The moment both stepped from the circle, it disappeared as though it had never been. Before either could move, an owl settled into the tree above them. They spread out, moving quickly so that the owl was in the middle. Jacques Dubrinsky shifted, leaping to the ground to land closer to Fen.

"Tatijana sent me to you. She said you were going to hunt the *Sange rau* and you would need blood. She sent your message, that the prince needed to be guarded and we've got him protected. Have you sent word to the Lycans?" As he spoke he used his teeth on his own wrist and extended his arm toward Fen. "I offer freely," he added, using the ritual between battle mates.

Fen took the proffered wrist, ingesting a small amount, making certain there would be enough to sustain his brother and yet not taking so much Jacques would grow weak.

While Dimitri fed, Fen answered. "No. The Lycans would handicap us at this point. They would do better guarding the prince with you. If Abel gets through us, I doubt he'll stop trying to go after Mikhail. Better to have all of you there. We'll have to fight as Guardians, not Lycan or Carpathian, and we can't worry whether or not we're observed."

Jacques nodded. "That makes perfect sense."

Dimitri politely closed the laceration on Jacques's wrist. "Good luck this day."

"Good hunting," Jacques replied. He gripped Dimitri's forearms hard and did the same with Fen before shifting and taking to the air.

They waited until Jacques was out of sight and then both brothers shifted to owls and took to the sky in the opposite direction, heading for the lake. The forest was thick, the canopy hiding the ground below, but twice, Fen sensed wolves below him. Not animals, but small groups of werewolves making their way toward Mikhail's home.

We could be wrong, Dimitri ventured. *He could be making an all-out assault on the prince's home.*

He has to believe the prince would never be left in his home. We already found out the safeguards wouldn't hold up against Abel, Fen said with confidence. *He knows the prince isn't there. He wants everyone to think that's what he's doing.*

I hope you're right, Dimitri said. *I've got this feeling . . .*

One person with a feeling was bad, two was far worse. Fen believed in instincts. His gut told him Abel had made his lair somewhere near the lake. He would be sending what was left of his army as a diversion, but he would have another plan altogether.

Tatijana had a feeling as well. We'll have to be doubly careful. Abel knows that realistically, we're the only ones standing between him and Mikhail, Fen said. *His plans include us. He'll want to wipe us out first.*

He plays chess or at least he's studied it. Take the King's Queen, his best defense. In this case, we're his Queens, Dimitri speculated. *He's left with Bishops, Rooks and Knights.*

Fen, in the body of the large owl, flew out of the forest into open air, flying over the meadows and farms. He saw the marsh below and in the distance, the glacier mountain where Bardolf had established a lair. *Dimitri, from Bardolf's position, could see both Mikhail's home and the lake.*

You have to be right. Bardolf was his lookout. He used him for information. Bardolf would have told him if anyone was poking around the lake, Dimitri agreed.

Reeds choked the shoreline of the lake on the west side. The island looked deserted and had little to offer in the way of shelter, but Fen knew better than to take chances. There was a mud bank to the left of the reeds with a suspicious looking slide on it, as if a heavy body had been dragged from the tall grasses growing on shore, down the embankment and shoved into the lake.

The lake seemed placid enough except the few ripples the wind caused. The water was murky, but tinged with blue. It was fed by the glacier and very cold, if Fen remembered correctly.

The island first? Fen suggested. *Watch my back. Let's see what he's got.*

The owl circled the island and then dropped down fast, talons extended, in hunting mode, as if it had spotted a mouse and was homing in for the kill. Several meters from the largest rock, the bird hit an invisible force field and bounced backward. Squawking, feathers floating toward the ground, it flapped its wings hard to get airborne again.

He's down there all right, Fen said. *And that hurt. He used silver against us. He's managed to make it so thin it's impossible to see.*

We did that at the farm and again at Mikhail's, Dimitri reminded. *He stole the idea from us. So where on that tiny island is he? Where could his lair be?*

Fen studied the island from every angle. *That might be part of his escape route somehow, although I can't figure out how.*

Or it's simply a trap or diversion, Dimitri suggested.

Dimitri, what if he's in the water. Underneath the water. Is that possible? He was so obsessed with the lake and learning to fight beneath the water. Most of the others ignored him, thinking he was a little strange. After all, what vampire would choose the water as a battleground? Fen asked, as he looked at the large beaver lodge built close into the reeds.

Dimitri studied the lake. *A beautiful trap. That would appeal to a vampire. He could kill anyone fishing, or bringing their animals close, he would have a wealth of victims to choose from. They would simply disappear beneath the water and no one would ever find them.*

Fen indicated the slide. *A body could have been dragged along there, but why? He wouldn't need to do that.*

Unless they were alive and he wanted the adrenaline rush when he killed them. He might deliberately torture his victims just for fun, Dimitri added. *Certainly that's a favorite pastime of vampires.*

Alright, we'll have to check it out, Fen said. *The minute I hit that silver, if he was close by, he probably knew that was no owl. He's smart. Forget pretense. Let's just straight up hunt.*

The brothers dropped through the air fast, shifting just before they touched the grass-lined shore. The moment their boots stepped onto a clump of greenery, both felt the ground shift beneath them. Their boots sank just an inch, but it was enough to give the lurking mutated leeches the chance they needed to swarm up their boots to their legs, biting and sucking in a feeding frenzy.

Dimitri swore under his breath in ancient Carpathian. "I really detest these things. Did he have to put giant teeth in them?"

Both men leapt back away from the edge of the lake and the leeches swarming to the top of the muddy holes their boots had made in the grass. They began to peel the creatures off of them, killing them and throwing their bodies into the swarm.

"I wouldn't worry too much about the giant teeth," Fen said, "but more about what they're injecting into our bodies." He felt the difference in his bloodstream almost with the first bite. "Can you track the virus? The poison? It's already in your bloodstream. It can't get to your heart." He was already circling the foreign strands he could feel with white energy to keep them from taking over his cells.

Dimitri nodded. "I wouldn't have if you hadn't caught it. It's subtle. I've contained it. It tried to spread very fast."

"He was banking on us not catching on," Fen said. "Can you feel that tiny trace of silver inside the strand? He sent in a silver needle to pierce the heart. Talk about subtle."

"Would it work?" Dimitri asked.

Fen shrugged. "I don't know, but we'd be in agony and probably wish we were dead."

"We knew he'd have traps."

This time when they approached the water's edge, they did so without actually allowing their feet to touch any part of the shore. Fen gave a small sigh. "I've got an idea that might work. Let me try this."

Tatijana, I have need.

I am here.

Visualize your dragon for me. It must be exact.

She didn't question him, but immediately did as he asked. Fen sent her a telepathic salute and turned to his brother. "There's nothing else for it, Dimitri, watch my back."

He didn't hesitate, rather simply floated over the top of the water a distance from shore, turned upside down and dropped his head and shoulders beneath the surface of the water, shifting as he did so. He used the head of Tatijana's water dragon. It would have the best vision beneath the water.

It took a moment to adjust and then he turned his head, rotating around so that he could see as much as possible. Near the island, over by where the reeds were the thickest, was a strange underwater lodge built of tree branches and downed tree trunks—a beaver lodge—yet he doubted there were beavers in the lake. They'd been reintroduced to some parts of Romania, but this wasn't one of them. The structure was huge, and part of it was above water, hidden by the reeds. If it was built like a beaver's lodge, it would have multiple entrances and exits.

Fen, get out of there now! Dimitri warned.

Fen backed straight out of the water, shooting into the air, using his mixed blood speed. The jaws driving at him from below missed him by a scant quarter of an inch. He felt the hot breath on his face and smelled decaying, rotten meat. The monstrous crocodile dropped soundlessly into the lake but not before Fen saw those eyes, ringed in red but with solid black pupils staring at him malevolently.

I think it's safe to say there have never been crocodiles in this lake, Fen said.

He definitely wanted you for dinner.

How did you spot him? I was looking under the water and didn't see him, Fen asked.

He was just under the surface, swimming out from the direction of the island. I could see the ripples in the water and then spotted his eyes.

Fen returned to shore, avoiding getting near the water's edge. "That was a rush. It was definitely Abel. He simply took the form of a crocodile. He's got some kind of den beneath the water and it's tied to that island. It's also partially in the reeds."

"He's going to have the advantage in the water, Fen. He deliberately showed himself to lure you in."

Fen sighed. "I figured that much, but it has to be done."

Dimitri shrugged. "Then let's do it."

Both men once more took to the air, the only safe place they had left to them. Fen looked down at the mass of logs, muds and sticks below him, studying the structure from every angle. There was a definite link to the island, but he still couldn't figure how Abel could use the island for an escape. A good part of the structure had been constructed in the reeds, so that the giant green stalks hid a portion of the lodge.

Fen glanced up at the clouds overhead. Most had turned from gray to black. They spun and churned as the storm moved closer, the wind driving them overhead. He lifted one hand, directing the energy to gather into a great fireball. Lightning edged the clouds. Thunder rumbled. The fireball streaked down to smash in the middle of the lodge, blowing it apart. Logs exploded outward, twigs and mud scattering across the lake, into the reeds and even edging the island.

Below the waterline a room was exposed. Two bodies floated to the surface, bobbing in the aftermath of the explosion. Abel had made kills and anchored his victims in his lodge to keep his lair from being exposed. Neither hunter moved, both inspecting the damage below, looking for signs of Abel.

Movement near the edge of the reeds sent Fen plunging deep, rocketing through the water toward that telltale flash. Straight toward him, out of the reeds, hurtled a goliath tigerfish, one of the most feared freshwater fishes found in the world—but not in a lake in Romania. With thirty-two teeth as long as those of a great white, the monster opened its jaws wide and powered through the water straight at Fen.

Lightning fast, it streaked toward Fen, the olive-colored back barely visible. All Fen could see was the dagger-sharp teeth coming at him. The aggressive, powerful goliath was known to attack and kill crocodiles. With barely any lips and teeth set into the jaw, the fish was deadlier than the smaller piranha and once its teeth clamped down on its prey, the cut was so clean it was almost surgical.

Fen, using his Guardian speed, managed to just slip sideways out of its way. The huge body drove passed him by a few feet before the enormous fish could stop its charge. Fen dove below it, coming up under its softer silver belly, reaching around it to take a good grip.

His upper arm and shoulder, chest and side, every part of his body coming in contact with the fish, instantly burned like fire, the pain excruciating. He tried to pull away, but that soft underside was not the tigerfish's own belly, but a solid sheet of thin silver. Already the metal burned into his skin, so that he was attached and unable to break loose.

The fish tried turning its head to snap at him with dagger teeth, but Fen stayed well under the body, fighting off the pain. He tried to push pain aside as Carpathians did when wounded severely, but the silver seemed to be melting, finding his pores and working its way into his body. The more he fought, the worse the pain and the deeper the silver went. Abel had come up with another form of *Moarta de argint*—literally—death by silver.

Fen forced himself to remain absolutely still, while the tigerfish whirled in circles snapping at him. Suddenly it streaked straight through the water as if it was as anxious to dislodge Fen and get away.

Dimitri saw the fish rocketing through the deep lake with his brother attached somehow to the underbelly. The goliath swam directly toward the reeds and the lodge that was partially dismantled. He spotted a single flash of movement and instantly dove deep, intercepting the second tigerfish head-on, his body between his brother and the new threat. He drove his silver sword through the massive, open jaws.

Dimitri, the underbelly is pure silver, don't touch it, Fen warned. *Take off its head, but keep a distance.*

The werewolves are attacking, Tatijana reported. *They're coming at us in great numbers, maybe forty strong. Three hunters and Zev have spotted Abel. He's commanding them himself.*

Fen removed his sword with his free hand. If it was possible beneath the water while one was being rocketed across a lake, he felt as if he might be sweating. Between the pain that seemed to grow worse with every passing second and the thought of what was to come, he had to keep up a shield to prevent Tatijana from knowing just how bad it really was. She would come to him no matter the danger.

Abel has sent a clone. Gregori will know what to do.

You're certain? He appears real enough.

It was all Fen could do not to snap at her. He snapped his teeth together instead and forced calm. *Abel is here.* He broke the contact abruptly. He couldn't be in two places at one time, not when Abel was doing his best to kill the two biggest threats to him.

Without waiting he took the sword and sliced upward in one motion, removing his own skin from elbow to shoulder that had adhered to the tigerfish. He forced himself not to feel the pain, but managed a second slicing motion, stripping the skin from his waist, up his rib cage to just below his arm. Blood poured into the water. The tigerfish went crazy and began snapping at itself, the teeth missing him by inches. It took every ounce of discipline he possessed to make the last cut to free himself from the monster before slicing the head off the goliath.

Something's happening above us, Dimitri said as he withdrew the sword from the tigerfish's mouth, spinning to the side of the large fish and slicing down to cut the head off. *Near the shore, there's a disturbance.*

Go. I've got this.

Fen stopped the flow of blood and dove deeper, ignoring the small bits of silver still burning through his body. He found an entrance to the underwater rooms in Abel's lodge. To enter the lair of a vampire was a very risky thing. There was water in the first room. Part of the wall had been blown away. The *Sange rau* had stored his food there and the bodies had risen to the surface.

Fen swam through it to the entrance to the second room. Immediately he felt the resistance blocking him. He waved his hand and at once the safeguards symbols and code flowed in front of his vision, a little blurry at times and very fast. He unraveled them just as fast, but was far more careful going into the second chamber.

Abel slept here. It was dark and dank and snug, warm even, all the comforts of a cave. Fen looked around carefully. There was no one there, but he hadn't expected Abel to make it easy for him. This was a cat and mouse game. He was the mouse, the bait to bring Abel out. He made his way slowly across the room. He hadn't gone more than three steps when his warning radar shrieked at him. Screamed. Flashed. He wasn't alone in the close confines of that room.

Abel dropped down on him from above, driving him to the floor of the lodge. The curved claws dug deep, tearing at him. The moment his body hit the floor, the walls of the room came alive, bats, clearly carnivorous, abandoning their resting place to join their master.

Feast. Feast my brothers, Abel commanded.

The bats dropped to the floor, coming from all directions, leaping on Fen and biting deep.

Dimitri surfaced, going straight out of the water, to see two of the elite hunters, Convel and Gunnolf, tangled up in the reeds. Clearly Zev had sent them scouting and the dead bodies in the lake had attracted them to the shore. They both had fallen into one of Abel's traps. Thick vines burst from the reeds, wrapping the two Lycans up tightly in the stranglehold of an anaconda.

Cursing under his breath, Dimitri rocketed across the sky, dropping down behind the first Lycan, making certain not to touch any of the reeds. "Stop struggling. You're only making it worse," he advised.

Both Lycans, elite hunters, stopped moving instantly, although it had to have been difficult to obey when the vines continued to wrap them tighter, squeezing until their very bones were in danger of snapping.

Dimitri tried his sword, but the moment he touched the vines, others sprang up around him to try to cage him in. He could hear a quiet hum, the faintest of sounds, and knew the reeds and vines communicated with one another.

Although he didn't move, Gunnolf began to make a sound of distress. Dimitri had run out of time. Using the strength and speed of the Guardian, he caught at the vines with his bare hands and yanked them away from the hunter, crushing the wood in his bare hands. The vines disintegrated into sawdust from the sheer strength he used. He pulled the hunter free and took him to a safer spot away from the reeds before going back for Convel.

The reeds had come alive, swaying and stretching, trying to find a target. Again, he dropped down fast from above, coming in behind Convel, grasping the thick vines, crushing them in his hands and snatching their prey from them to rise just as quickly into the air. It was his speed that saved them both. The vines shot up from all directions, but he had Convel safe and away. He set him down beside Gunnolf.

"Thanks," Gunnolf said, holding out his hand. "You saved our lives."

Dimitri was impatient to get back to Fen, but he gripped Gunnolf's extended hand. Gunnolf slapped loops of silver around his wrist, a long chain like a leash attached. From behind him, loops of silver chain were flung over his head to drop around his body. The chain was pulled tight and agony shot through him. Before he could call out to Fen, something hard struck his head and everything went black.

⁓

"Let's see what's inside a hunter, my pets," Abel said. Smiling, exposing his brown-stained teeth, he reached down in slow motion and deliberately ripped open Fen's belly. The vampire/wolf took his time, wanting Fen to feel the pain as he eviscerated him. The bats uncovered the raw flesh where his missing skin should have been and tore into him.

"Eating people alive is what they do best and I so enjoy watching," Abel taunted. "You weren't quite as good as you thought, now were you?"

Fen felt a burst of pain that was not his own. That agony galvanized him into action as nothing else could. He was Carpathian before all else and he could shut off the pain from battle wounds. He'd done so for centuries. The silver was a different matter, but he could endure until something could be done.

"What happened to her, Abel?" Fen asked, forcing himself to lie quietly beneath the assault on his body. He stayed absolutely relaxed so Abel unintentionally relaxed as well. "Your lifemate? What happened to her?"

Abel went still. For one moment the malevolent lines disappeared from his face and he looked like the hunter Fen had known so long ago. The change in the *Sange rau* was fleeting, but it gave Fen that split second that he needed.

He slammed his empty fist into Abel's chest wall with the incredible strength of a Guardian. He drove straight through with astonishing speed, his fist wrapping around the heart and extracting it before Abel even realized Fen had attacked him. As he extracted the heart, Fen rolled right over some of the bats, uncaring that they still bit at his flesh. All that mattered was destroying Abel.

A roar thundered through the lodge, shaking apart the structure that was left above them so that logs and debris rolled into the lake. Holes sprang in the walls. Fen palmed a silver stake with one hand, the heart in the other. Abel went insane, thrashing and screaming, his terrible claws reaching into Fen's belly, pulling and tearing through everything he could grasp. His face contorted at the same time and he bit down on Fen's shoulder and neck, tearing out chunks of flesh and wolfing them down whole.

"Get it, take it from him, my pets," Abel screamed. "My heart!"

Fen didn't dare drop the heart on the floor. Already Abel's bats had begun biting at his clenched fist to try to retrieve what the *Sange rau* had lost. He palmed a silver stake with his other hand, opened his fist and slammed the dagger home, driving it all the way through the heart, his own hand and into the floor.

Abel's wail rose to a screech. He slapped both hands over the hole in his chest, shock and horror on his face.

"Go to her, Abel. Seek her forgiveness," Fen said. With his other hand, he used a downward motion, slicing through Abel's neck with the silver knife he carried. He was forced to use the strength of the Guardian to remove the head.

There was so much blood. His. Abel's. He was tired. So very tired. He expected the bats to leap upon him and tear him to shreds, but as Abel toppled to the floor, more water poured into the lodge, faster now, rising quickly and the bats retreated. With his last effort, he looked up at the sky through the holes in the roof. Lightning continued to edge the clouds. He called it down, directing it over Abel's body and head, watching it burn in spite of the rising water. It seemed to take a long time and a tremendous amount of effort to finish burning the body, but finally, there was nothing left but ashes.

Fen looked around him, a little astonished that it was over. The water was more red than brown. He closed his eyes. *Tatijana, my lady. I may not be able to keep my promise to you, but know that I love you with all my heart.*

20

Fen, you have to open your eyes. Wake for me. Tatijana called to her lifemate for the seventh straight rising.

In all honesty, he slept as one dead, and his wounds had been so horrific had not Gregori found him when he had, Fen would have died within another few minutes. It had taken everyone to save him, all Carpathians, participating in the healing chant. The people had come together providing strength and much needed blood, while Gregori, Tatijana, Branislava and Mother Earth fought for his life.

"I don't understand why he doesn't wake up." Tatijana looked to Gregori, her eyes welling with tears.

Gregori reached over and covered her hand gently in a rare gesture of compassion. "He's alive. He's rejuvenating far faster than I expected. I will tell you now, Tatijana, I did not expect him to survive at all. You must have patience. His spirit seems far away, but he hangs on."

"I can touch him sometimes, but then he slips away again," she said. "I just need him to let me in, just for a moment, and then I'll feel like I can breathe."

"That is simply a reaction of lifemates," he advised matter-of-factly. "When you're separated too long, the effects can be damaging. You know he lives. You know he will come back to you."

She knew he was giving her a warning. It was difficult to keep her mind steady and focused when she feared Fen had already slipped too far away from her. She'd made a promise to him though, and she would keep it. No matter how much sorrow weighed on her, she would find a way to hang on as he was doing.

The cave of healing was a peaceful place. The soil was dark and rich with minerals. Fen had been brought directly there by Gregori and the Carpathians had hastily gathered to try to save him. Tatijana had been horrified when she saw him. His skin had been peeled from his body in numerous places and he had chunks of flesh missing along the long raw patches. Larger chunks of flesh were missing from his shoulder and up close to his neck. The worst was his belly. Gregori had to keep his insides from falling out as he transported him back to the cave.

"Tatijana," Gregori said sharply, and then gentled his voice. "He grows stronger with each passing rising."

"Then why isn't his spirit where I can touch it?"

"I don't know. Perhaps he is traveling on his own while he heals. Look at his body. He rejuvenated far faster than I expected."

She nodded her head. "You're right. I know you're right." It was just that she wanted to hold Fen in her arms close to her body, feel his heart beating the same rhythm as hers. Just for a moment and then she knew she could breathe easier. Right now, it felt as though she couldn't draw a full breath into her lungs.

"What are you going to tell him about Dimitri?" Gregori asked, clearly to distract her.

Tatijana forced herself to respond. Distraction was exactly what she needed. Still, she put her hand on Fen's chest, right over his heart. "Even young Skyler has been unable to reach Dimitri, and their connection is unbelievably strong. I don't know how to tell him that Dimitri was taken by the Lycans, and no one, not me, not his lifemate or any of you can reach him."

She swept back her hair, although there was really no need. No stray strands had escaped, but she felt shaky and in need of covering it. "I feel as if I failed him. The moment we knew Dimitri was missing—that Vikirnoff found evidence he'd been taken by the Lycans, both Bronnie and I took to the sky, but even with dragon vision we couldn't find him. I was so worried about Fen, I felt so *desperate* to save him, that I just didn't take my dragon up fast enough."

"Our best and fastest hunters raced after them," Gregori pointed out. "Nothing has ever escaped so many hunters, and yet they came up empty, Tatijana. Dimitri's disappearance is not your fault."

"Zev told Mikhail that two of his elite hunters had taken him," Tatijana said, shaking her head. "Do they want to start a war? Don't they realize Fen will never stop until he gets Dimitri back? Never, Gregori, he'll be relentless in his pursuit."

Gregori nodded. "I'm well aware of that and so is the prince. Zev has given Mikhail reassurances that Dimitri will be safe for the time being. The Lycan council has sent word that they will come to a meeting with Mikhail. The Lycans don't want a war with us. Neither species will win. We all know that. They won't harm Dimitri while this summit takes place."

"Why can't we reach him? Why can't Skyler?" With her hand still over Fen's chest, for a moment, she thought she felt his heart flutter, and her heart jumped for joy, but when she looked down at him, he hadn't moved.

"She's little more than a child," Gregori said dismissively. "You say they have a particularly strong connection, but look at you and Fen. He's right here, close to you and yet he doesn't awaken at your request. Sometimes the spirit travels on its own while the body heals."

"Are you saying you suspect Dimitri is so hurt that he *can't* respond?" Tatijana asked. "Because if that's the case, time is of the essence and we need to go after them. Zev must know where the Lycans would take him."

"I'm certain he does. Dimitri is probably on his way to their council. He is *Hän ku pesäk kaikak*—Guardian of all to us, but *Sange rau* to them and they fear the *Sange rau* more than anything else," Gregori answered.

"Do they fear the *Sange rau* more than they fear war with us?" Tatijana asked.

Gregori sighed. "I wish I knew the answer to that, but Mikhail has called in all Carpathians for this summit. We've made it very clear to the Lycans the summit doesn't happen if they kill Dimitri. They're still coming, which they'd be insane to do if he wasn't alive."

"He's alive," Tatijana said. She was tired of explaining to both Mikhail and Gregori that she knew he was alive because Skyler knew. They insisted on viewing Dimitri's lifemate as a child and didn't really give credence to her abilities.

"Mikhail has quietly begun putting together some of our best hunters. Once you wake him and we know he's strong enough, the hunters trying to track Dimitri will slip away with Fen leading them. We know that a couple of the Lycan hunters are nearby, watching to see that we don't launch an attack on their people or try to retaliate, so we have to do this under their noses without getting caught."

Tatijana couldn't imagine Fen caring one way or the other that the Lycans knew that he was coming for his brother, Dimitri. He probably would want them to know. He would be absolutely merciless, implacable and maybe the Lycans needed to see that.

Gregori must have caught her thoughts. He leaned forward and shook his head. "You can't let him go off after his brother without thinking of the consequences. If they know we're coming for him, they very well could kill Dimitri. We don't know where he is. They've found some way to silence him."

"That's more frightening than anything else," Tatijana admitted.

Again there was that strange fluttering beneath her hand. She leaned over Fen and brushed a kiss over his mouth. *Come back to me, my love. I need to know you're alive.*

"I believed Zev when he said he had no part in taking Dimitri, but more importantly, Mikhail believed him. He knows when people speak the truth. Zev didn't give the order to take Dimitri prisoner, he didn't even know he was of mixed blood," Gregori said. "I suspect the two Lycans observed Dimitri in the battle and he gave himself away out of necessity."

"Does he know Fen has mixed blood?" Tatijana strained to keep her voice even, but she thought it quivered a bit.

Thankfully, Gregori pretended not to notice. "He doesn't know Fen and Dimitri are brothers. No, I think he believes Fen stays close because he's fallen in love with you. He spoke to Mikhail and said such a match would be forbidden by the Lycans. It is obvious he both admires and respects Fen and wants him to join his pack as an elite hunter."

Tatijana frowned. "It's forbidden for Fen to fall in love with me just because I'm Carpathian? Isn't that just a little archaic?"

"They know Carpathians exchange blood."

"They were happy enough to have our blood when they were wounded," Tatijana hissed. Again Fen's heart fluttered. She pressed her palm hard over his chest, nearly crying out. That had to be a heartbeat. She wasn't mistaken. She felt tears burning behind her eyes and clumping in her throat. He was alive. He was coming closer to the surface.

Beside them, Fen stirred, his body still covered in the rich healing soil of Mother Earth. Tatijana let out a cry of joy. His lashes fluttered and he looked up at her. His face was very pale and there were lines that hadn't been there before, but he smiled just for her.

"You're a beautiful sight to wake up to, my lady."

"I think you're rather beautiful yourself." She was *not* going to cry. She kept her palm flat over his chest, needing the reassurance of his steady heartbeat. It was music to her.

"You're back with us," Gregori observed, his silver eyes missing nothing. Fen was breathing a little shallow and was still in some pain, but he was very aware of everything around him. "How much of our conversation did you get?"

"Enough to know that"—Fen had to reach for his voice—"we need to find out why the two Lycans were at the lake in the first place. How did they know where we expected the last *Sange rau*'s lair might be? Dimitri and I found it because we knew Abel when we were young."

"A very good question," Gregori agreed.

"If Zev didn't know where we were, and he didn't send those hunters to aid us, why weren't they with their pack, fighting the rogues?" Fen asked. "Zev is dominant over the pack alpha, he's the big boss. No self-respecting alpha would ever allow his pack to desert a fight and go off without a word."

"Zev left in a hurry. I wonder if he was asking himself the same questions," Gregori mused. "He wasn't happy."

"I'm sure he wasn't. If members of his pack took someone prisoner and didn't even report back to him—that's mutiny in the pack. That's challenging leadership. Those two would have to fight Zev for the position of leader," Fen explained. "The best hunter is always the scout and therefore the dominant alpha."

"You heard us?" Tatijana exclaimed, still stuck back on the original point. "You heard our conversation?"

"You called to me and you sounded distressed," Fen said. "I came, of course."

"Fen, I've called you to me for the last seven risings."

He frowned. "Really? I'm so sorry, Tatijana. I had no idea of time passing. When your spirit wanders there's no concept of time. I went looking for my brother."

"You knew Dimitri was missing?" Tatijana asked, her eyes wide and a little accusing. She couldn't stop herself from raining kisses on his face. "You scared me to death."

"I'm sorry. I couldn't be in two places at one time, I was too weak. My body needed to heal. I thought I was gone a short time only." He covered her hand with his. "I would never wish to cause you distress."

He tried to sit up, and Gregori put a hand on his chest. "Not yet. I'd like to make certain everything is healing properly."

Fen looked around him. "You brought me to the cave of healing. I must have been pretty torn up this time."

"You've been out for *seven* risings," Tatijana reiterated.

"I was looking for Dimitri," Fen explained again, his voice growing stronger. "When I was there in the lodge with Abel, I felt Dimitri's pain, just for a moment, and I knew it was his pain. I've felt the agonizing burn of silver many times and this was all encompassing. I knew immediately they wrapped him in it, which could only mean one thing—they had taken him prisoner."

"You could have let me know," Tatijana said. "I'm your lifemate, Fen."

"It wasn't easy on her," Gregori added. "Your spirit was far away and appeared at times to fade completely."

"I'm sorry." Ignoring Gregori's warning, Fen pulled himself gingerly into a sitting position. His belly protested, but he managed. He took Tatijana's hand and brought it to his mouth to kiss her fingers. "I didn't mean for you to worry. I thought once my body had healed, my spirit would have found him and we could go get him."

Tatijana managed a smile. Now that he was alive and talking to her, all the tense nights and heavy sorrow pressing down on her lifted. "You're alive, Fen. That's all that really matters to me. That and getting Dimitri back."

"I have to go after him, Tatijana," Fen said.

"How will you track him if you couldn't find his spirit?" Gregori asked. "We sent Tomas, Andre, Mataias and Lojos after them. We couldn't find a trace of them. Do you have any idea where they would take him?"

Fen sighed and shook his head. "No, and the council is very secretive. If they are taking him before the council, finding them would be extremely difficult."

"The council is coming here," Gregori assured. "We don't think they would allow anything to happen to Dimitri before or during the summit, so we have time. Zev is carrying the message to them for us. And it's a rather stern one. Mikhail didn't pull any punches."

The healer stood up and stretched. It was one of the few times Tatijana had ever seen him look tired. "I'll leave you two alone, but Tatijana, don't let him stay up long. I've given him blood, but he needs to let his body do its work. You heal remarkably fast," he added.

"Thank you," Tatijana said, standing as well, giving Gregori a hug even though his body felt rather like she might be hugging an oak tree. "You saved him."

"It was a group effort," Gregori said, "but it was probably one of the most difficult battles I've ever fought."

He gave her an awkward pat on her shoulder. Clearly he was used to being around his lifemate and daughters but few other women. Still, she was grateful. He had come to the cave of healing every day and sat with her waiting. Bronnie spent time with her as well, and when she wasn't physically present, she soothed and comforted Tatijana telepathically.

When they were alone, Tatijana put her hand on Fen's shoulder, urging him to lie back. As soon as he was comfortable she eased down beside him, taking care that she didn't put pressure on any of the places he'd been so horribly wounded. She put her hand over his heart, needing to feel that steady beat.

"Next time, if there is one, although I'm not letting you out of my sight for some time, promise me before you go wandering around in the dark, you'll let me know you'll be coming back to me," Tatijana said, closing her eyes.

She wanted to savor the feel of him beside her, alive and awake. He felt solid to her. She allowed her heart to find the rhythm of his and follow that steady beat, just to reassure herself.

"I really am sorry, *sívamet*," he reiterated sincerely. He turned his head to stare into her eyes. "I would never knowingly cause you any grief. There was no sense of time for me. I could have been gone months or a few minutes. I did come when I heard you call."

She felt the jolt of those glacier-blue eyes, his love intense, real, so raw, right there for her to see. He never tried to hide his emotions from her. His love was something she had grown to count on without even realizing it.

"I didn't know I'd feel this way, Fen," she admitted. "When I first saw you and felt the pull toward you, I didn't want to take any chances. When we met and I said I didn't want to be claimed, it never in a million years ever occurred to me I would feel this way about you."

He leaned close to brush a kiss along her temple. "Wolf men can be very persuasive."

"We'll get Dimitri back, you know." She made it a declaration.

He nodded his head. "I know we will. You're Dragonseeker. I'm a Guardian. We'll find him together."

She threaded her fingers through his and held on tightly. She believed him. She believed in him. Dimitri would be found because Fen would never give up, and no matter where the hunt took them, she intended to be right by his side.

"Go back to sleep, Fen," she said, her voice soft with love for him. "The faster you heal, the faster we can get started. I'll be right here watching over you."

Fen gave her a faint smile, but he didn't protest. She watched his lashes come down and within moments, his heart seemed to have stopped beating and his breath no longer ebbed and flowed from his lungs.

Tatijana was content to just lie beside him. She knew he was alive and that was all that mattered. Fenris Dalka. Her lifemate.

Keep reading for an excerpt from the next
exciting Carpathian novel by Christine Feehan

DARK WOLF

Available January 2014 from Piatkus Books!

S kyler Daratrazanoff pulled the long black shawl closer, making certain her hair was covered and there was little to see of her face. Her heart beat so hard she was afraid anyone close would hear. Everything hinged on making the official believe her. Josef had forged the papers, and he was the best. He could hack any computer, provide information or get it. She didn't doubt for a minute that the papers he created would be in order and would pass close scrutiny, but she still had to make the official believe her.

The tin building was rusted and looked as if it might fall apart at any moment. A man came forward to meet her, looking solemn as the casket was wheeled ahead of her into the shade of the building. Fortunately the sun was setting and shadows fell around her, helping to make it more difficult to see her clearly.

"Your papers?" he said. His voice was kind. The name on his badge identified him as Erno Varga.

She glanced back toward the small plane she'd flown to the airport and then handed her papers to the official, making certain her eyes were downcast and she looked weepy. She had taken care to use drops to make her eyes red and watery, just in case she couldn't pull off acting on her own.

Varga looked over her papers and then up at her several times with sharp, disbelieving eyes. "You're young to be bringing home your brother's body alone. No one else is traveling with you?"

She shook her head, trying to look more tragic than ever. "My father is dead and now my brother." She choked back a sob worthy, she was certain, of an Oscar performance. "There is no one else to bring him home to our mother."

The official looked at her again and studied her papers closer. "He died of a broken heart?" There was skepticism in his voice.

Skyler nearly choked. *When I get my hands on you, Josef, you're going to die of more than a broken heart.* She used her telepathic connection with Josef to let him know he was in huge trouble.

A terrible tragedy. Josef was unrepentant as always. There was amusement in his tone. No matter how serious a situation, he didn't mind in the least being mischievous.

She managed to keep a straight face and gave Varga a solemn nod. "He just wasted away when his girl left him. He refused to eat." She had no choice but to go with it, even if it meant twisting her fingers together hard in order to prevent the official from seeing she was shaking. "It's a terrible tragedy. Nothing could save him."

Okay, even to her ears, that sounded totally lame. But a broken heart? Only Josef would come up with something so dramatic and unbelievable. How else could she explain he'd died of a broken heart? There was *definitely* going to be another cause of death after they opened the casket.

She could feel Josef's laughter. *Of course you're laughing. You're safe in the coffin, the tragically dead brother, while I'm lying my ass off to this man who could put me in prison for the rest of my life.*

She knew Josef would never let that happen. If necessary he'd give the official a "push" to believe her. Right now, Josef was having too much fun listening to her squirm—and she supposed she deserved it. She was making him do something highly dangerous and he would be blamed far more than she would be if anything went wrong. Her father would probably just kill him on sight.

He will too, Josef said. *He'll rip me from limb to limb.*

You should be worrying about me *ripping you from limb to limb*, she threatened.

"How old are you?" The official stared at her passport and papers and then back up to her face. "Did you pilot that plane?"

She lifted her chin, trying for older and much sterner. She knew she looked young, but not her eyes. If he looked her directly in the eye, he would believe what those forged papers said. And they were great forgeries. Josef had many talents, although making up stories was clearly not one of them.

"I'm much older than I look," Skyler replied. It was partially the truth. She felt older, and that should count for something. She'd been through more than most women—okay, teens.

"Twenty-five?" he said skeptically.

Josef had insisted she be twenty-five if she was going to pilot the plane. Piloting planes had come easy to her and it was something she especially loved, so her adopted father, Gabriel, had allowed her to learn.

"I have to open the coffin," he said, watching her closely.

Skyler managed a little sob and covered her mouth, nodding slightly. "I'm sorry. Yes, of course. They said you would. I was expecting you to." She straightened her shoulders and spine courageously.

He looked at her much more kindly. "You don't need to watch. Stand over there." He nodded to a corner of the building just a few feet away.

She felt a little sorry for him. If she knew anything at all about Josef, she knew he would put on some kind of show.

Don't you dare blow this by scaring him, she warned. *I mean it, Josef.*

You're no fun. I can always remove his memories. Wouldn't it be so delicious to do an impression of Count Dracula? I've watched the movie a million times. I've got the look and accent down perfectly.

He sounded far too eager. It took a lot of discipline to keep amusement from her mind where he could read it. She didn't doubt for a moment that Josef could do a perfect Dracula impression.

Resist the urge. We aren't out of the woods and we can't afford to take any chances. We're in Carpathian territory. Or at least close enough that someone might be near us to sense the use of energy. Restrain yourself, Josef.

He heaved a sigh. *No matter what the outcome, your father is going to kill me, a slow and painful death too. I should be able to have a little fun.*

That was hitting very close to the truth. Gabriel was going to murder all of them, but if their planned worked, it would be well worth it.

She gave Varga a small, grateful smile and moved away from the coffin. Standing in the open door, her arms wrapped around her middle for comfort, she stared outside into the gathering darkness, holding herself very still. Their plan *had* to work.

Behave, Josef, or else. Gabriel's in London and I'm here. She had never been on the receiving end of Gabriel's wrath, but he and her uncle Lucian were legendary vampire hunters. The Carpathian people, most extremely powerful, whispered their names in awe.

You've got a point. Laughter bubbled over in Josef's voice. *What a sorry waste of a good coffin.* Now there was disgust in his tone.

Skyler couldn't tell if he was going to behave or not. It was impossible with Josef. He marched to his own drum. She sent up a silent prayer, hoping for the best.

Right now, Francesca and Gabriel were probably awake and would soon be preparing to fly to the Carpathian Mountains. They thought she was a continent away, safe with her human college friend, Maria, using her vacation to help build homes and run irrigation to farmers in South America. She had never lied to them before. Not once. And it hurt her to do it now, but there was no other way.

She knew her parents had been summoned to the huge meeting between Lycan and Carpathian to discuss an alliance between the two species. Most of the Carpathians had been called home. Gabriel and Francesca had been more than happy to receive a call from her from school asking to go with Maria. They didn't want her anywhere near the Carpathian Mountains.

She would never think of repaying their extraordinary kindness, the love they had given her from the moment she'd been taken into their home, with lies and betrayal—not for anything or anyone accept Dimitri. Dimitri Tirunul was her unexpected miracle. A man beyond any she'd ever dreamed of. She was human. He was Carpathian—nearly immortal. She was nineteen years old. He was an ancient, centuries old. She held the other half of his soul, the light to his darkness. Without her, he would not survive. She was his lifemate—his savior. Yet she knew just the opposite was true: Dimitri was the one saving her.

He knew she was his lifemate when she was just a child and he had given her time. Space. Unconditional love. He never demanded anything of her.

He never told her how difficult it was for him—that she was his salvation, just out of his reach. He had always been there for her, in the middle of the night, when her violent past was too close and she couldn't sleep, when nightmares haunted her to the point where she couldn't breathe. He was there, in her mind, holding all those terrifying memories at bay. Dimitri. Her Dimitri.

Dimitri was caught in the middle between the two species. The Lycans had taken him and planned to kill him. No one had gone after him to save him. He had spent centuries hunting the undead to keep his people safe, as well as humans. He had survived honorably when others had chosen to give up their souls. Yet there was no rescue party. No hunters were rushing to save him. He was badly injured. She felt that much before he cut himself off from her to protect her from his pain—or his death.

Dimitri was stoic about life or death. He was a Carpathian hunter and he'd been around for centuries, protecting innocents from vampires. Her lineage was complicated, but for all intents and purposes, she was human. The Lycans would never expect a teenage, human girl to mount a rescue operation for a Carpathian. She had the element of surprise on her side. That, as well as good, trustworthy friends and her very powerful but untested abilities.

Skyler had faith in herself. She knew her every strength and every weakness. Like Josef, she was extremely intelligent and most of the time underestimated. She believed the Lycans would underestimate her—she was counting on it.

No one would start a war over a Carpathian hunter, it seemed, but she knew her father would come after her, and if anyone harmed one hair on her head, the Lycan world would be in for a nightmare it couldn't possibly conceive. Not only would Gabriel come after her, but so would her uncle Lucian. She was fairly certain her biological father, Razvan, and his lifemate, Ivory, would join the hunt for her. They were extremely lethal as well. There was satisfaction in knowing that if she was injured or killed, she would be avenged. No one, not even Mikhail Dubrinsky, the prince of the Carpathian people, would be able to stop a war if the Lycans harmed her.

She lifted her chin. Dimitri would never leave her in danger. He would rush to her side the moment he knew there was trouble; he had—more than once—just to soothe bad dreams when she had too many in a row. She couldn't do less for him.

Holding her breath, she turned back to watch the official gingerly open the coffin. It creaked ominously. Hideously. Just like in the movies. The sound sent a chill down her spine. The lid raised slowly and, darn Josef anyway, it looked as if it was lifting all by itself. Varga stepped back, one hand going up defensively.

There was silence as the lid came to a stop. Nothing moved. She could hear the sound of a clock ticking loudly. Varga coughed nervously. He glanced at her. Skyler put her hand over her mouth and lowered her eyes.

Josef! Behave yourself. Skyler was somewhere between laughing and crying with nervous tension.

Varga stepped back to the coffin and peered in, beads of sweat visible on his forehead. He cleared his throat. "He certainly looks robust for a man who starved himself to death."

The least you could have done was make yourself look emaciated, if you wanted him to believe your preposterous story, she scolded.

Skyler pressed a handkerchief to her mouth. "They did such a good job at the funeral home. I particularly asked them to make certain he looked good for our mother."

Varga pressed his lips together and studied the body. He was suspicious, but she wasn't certain of what. Clearly there was a dead body in the coffin. Did he suspect her of running drugs? Guns? If so, that didn't bode well for what she had planned. She needed to look like a naïve, a young teenager who might be slightly ditzy.

She held her breath as he reached for the door of the coffin and slowly closed it.

"Is someone coming for you?" Varga asked as he locked the coffin door and glanced at his watch. "I can't stay. You were the last plane coming in."

"My brother's friend arranged for a truck to pick us up. He'll be here any minute," Skyler assured him solemnly. "Thank you so much for all your help."

"You can wait in here," Varga said in a kind voice. "I'll come back in a couple of hours and lock up." He looked around the dilapidated building. It was nothing more than four metal walls, mostly rusted, some so badly there were holes. "Not that there's much to lock up." He glanced again at his watch. "I would wait with you, but I have another job to go to."

She sent him a wan smile. "It's all right. Really. He'll be here any minute."

Varga gave her one last look and exited the rickety building, leaving her there alone with the locked coffin. Skyler waited until she saw his car drive off and the lights disappear completely down the road. She took a careful look around. She appeared to be alone.

"Josef, you can quit playing dead," Skyler said, her voice dripping with sarcasm. She banged on the coffin lid with her fist. "Died of a broken heart? Really? You couldn't think of anything else, anything, say, more realistic?"

The lid of the coffin opened with the same series of ominous, horror-film creaks he'd used when Varga had opened the lid. There was silence. Skyler's heart beat steadily. She leaned over the coffin and glared at the young man who lay as if dead, his arms crossed over his chest, his eyes closed. His skin was pale porcelain and his black spiky hair with the dyed blue tips stood out starkly against the white backdrop.

"You look amazingly robust for a man who starved himself to death," she said sarcastically, mimicking the official. "You could have blown everything with your absurd story."

Josef's eyes snapped open dramatically. He faked an accent as he slowly sat up. "I could use a drop of blood or two, my dear."

She smacked him over the head with her papers. "The customs official didn't believe I was twenty-five."

Josef flashed a cocky grin. "You're not. You're barely nineteen, and when Gabriel and Lucian find out what we've done, we're both going to be in more trouble than either of us has ever known." He paused, the smile fading from his mouth. "And I've been in a lot of trouble."

"We have no choice," Skyler said.

"Don't kid yourself, Sky, there's always a choice. And you aren't the one they're going to kill. I'm going to be their prime target. When Gabriel and Lucian come looking for you—and they will," Josef said. "They'll find you. They have a reputation for a reason. If we really do this, every Carpathian hunter will be out looking."

Her father, Gabriel was extremely powerful, a legendary Carpathian hunter. Her uncle Lucian, Gabriel's twin, had helped to create that legend among the Carpathian people, and when they discovered her gone, *of course* they would come after her.

"Isn't that the point?" Skyler replied with a small shrug. "By the time they wake and realize we're gone, we'll have a good head start. We should be able to find Dimitri."

"You do realize," Josef said, floating out of the coffin, "this could very well cause an international incident. Or worse, war. All-out war."

"You agreed to help me," Skyler said. "Have you changed your mind?"

"No. You're my best friend, Sky. Dimitri probably despises me and wishes I was dead, but he's your lifemate and he's been literally thrown to the wolves." Josef sent her a little grin, pleased with his pun. "Of course I'm going to help you. I helped you come up with this plan, didn't I? And it will work."

"Dimitri doesn't despise you, in fact he's glad you're my friend. We've talked about it. He isn't like that." Skyler made a face at him. "You know very well he knows I think of you like a brother. He'd defend you with his life."

Josef grinned at her. "Forgive *me* for despising *him* just a little bit. He's good looking, intelligent, an ancient hunter and your lifemate. He destroyed all my dreams and fantasies about you. I don't dare even think along those lines or he'd know."

Skyler rolled her eyes. "As if. Even I know you don't think of me that way, Josef. You can hide a lot of things, but not that. There's no fantasy and no destroyed dreams. Your lifemate is either not born yet or," she smirked at him mischeviously, "she's probably one of Gregori's daughters."

He groaned and slapped his forehead with his palm. "A curse on you forever for uttering those words, for putting that thought out into the universe. Don't even think that, let alone say it aloud. Can you imagine Gregori Daratrazanoff as a father-in-law? Sheesh, Skyler, you really do want me dead."

She laughed. "It would serve you right, Josef. Especially after putting that you died of a broken heart on those papers!"

"It could happen. I'm a romantic, you know. Dimitri thinks I'm a little kid, just like they all do, which is probably just as well, because otherwise he'd see me as a rival."

"You take great pains to keep them all thinking you're a kid," Skyler pointed out with a small smile. "You like them to underestimate you. You're a genius, Josef, and you don't let any of them see the real you. You deliberately provoke them."

His grin widened until he looked positively mischievous. He blew on his fingertips. "That is very true. I don't deny it." His smile faded. "But this is very different than the pranks I pull on them. This is big, Skyler. I just want you to understand what's at stake."

"Of course I know what's at stake."

"Your family is one of the most powerful, legendary families of our people." He frowned. "Which reminds me, why don't you ever refer to Gregori as your uncle? He's a brother to Lucian and Gabriel, so technically, he is your uncle."

"I guess I never thought about it. I don't know him. We're in London and he's here in the Carpathian Mountains and he's never shown a tremendous amount of interest in me."

"He's a Daratrazanoff—believe me, Sky, he's interested in you. If you disappear, your family is going to come looking and they'll be on the warpath. *All* of your family, especially Gabriel."

"Are you afraid of my father?" Skyler asked.

"I've got news for you, Sky—*everyone* is afraid of your father, and if they aren't they should be, especially when it comes to you. Haven't you noticed how protective he is of you? Your uncle Lucian is just as bad if not worse, and if anyone messes with one of those men or anyone they love, they answer to both of them."

Skyler bit her lip. "I'm sorry, Josef, for putting you in this position. I can't turn back. I have to find Dimitri. I know I can do this. This plan is flawless. And we both knew—and counted on Gabriel and Lucian coming after me. I can go from here by myself, I really can."

Josef burst out laughing. "Now you really have lost your mind. If I let you do this alone, they'd *really* kill me. No, we're here and we have to see it through. I think you're the only one who could pull this off. But

Skyler, if you get into trouble, this really will start a war. Lucian and Gabriel are not going to back off if someone hurts you, or if you're captured. They won't care what the prince says. They'll go after you and no one will stand in their way. You'd better go into this knowing that. You have to know the consequences and be willing to face them."

Skyler pressed her lips together. She'd thought about little else since she and Josef had come up with the plan. "Dimitri is a good man. He could have claimed me, taken me away from my home and the only stability I'd ever known. I wouldn't have been able to resist him, the pull of lifemates is just too strong. But he didn't, Josef, no matter the terrible cost to him. He didn't insist on claiming me or binding us together. He wasn't afraid of Gabriel. He was never afraid of Gabriel."

Josef waved his hand at the coffin and the lid creaked closed. "I know," he admitted softly.

"He knew I wasn't ready, that I needed time to find myself and overcome . . . everything in my past." Skyler ducked her head, so that her wealth of silky hair covered her expression.

"Don't, Sky," Josef said. "We're best friends. What happened to you wasn't your fault and you should never feel ashamed."

"I'm not ashamed—well, not like you think. I believe Dimitri is a great man and he deserves a lifemate who can match him in everything. I'm not that woman yet. I want to be with him; I feel that need nearly as strongly as he does. It grows in me every single day."

"Do you think he would hold your past against you?" Josef asked.

Skyler shook her head. "No, he often is close enough to talk to me at night when I can't sleep. We talk a lot at night. I love his voice. He's very gentle with me, never demanding. I know it's difficult for him. I can feel his struggle, although he hid it from me at first. You can't be in someone else's head without eventually seeing everything. Darkness threatened to swallow him all the time, yet he never said anything to me, he never tried to hurry me. He certainly didn't condemn me because I was too young—and afraid. Dimitri doesn't judge me."

"No one does, hon," Josef pointed out. "You're the one who's so hard on yourself. I especially loved the stage when you dyed your hair constantly. It took you a little while to find yourself and be comfortable with who you really are."

Skyler's eyebrow shot up. She stared pointedly at Josef's black spiked hair tipped with blue.

His grin was contagious, revealing twin dents near his mouth. "This is who I am. I found that out a long time ago. I like my hair with blue tips."

"Because no one will ever guess just how smart you are. They're too busy looking at your hair and the piercings you occasionally put in just to bug them all," she accused, laughing softly. "I love you, Josef, you know that, don't you?"

"Yep. That's why I'm here, Sky. I don't have all that many people who care about me. If you say you need me, I'll come." He looked away from her.

Skyler put her hand on his arm. "There are many people who care about you, Josef, you just don't let them get close. If you gave Dimitri a chance, he would be a good friend to you. I know he would. I've talked to him many times about you."

"I thought you hadn't seen him since you'd been to the Carpathian Mountains."

"He thought it best if we stayed away from one another. I knew it would be too difficult for him with me being physically close to him, but he came to London on and off when he needed to hear my voice."

"Did Gabriel know?" Josef asked.

"Probably. He didn't ask me, but I noticed when Dimitri was close, Gabriel stayed closer. And when Gabriel wasn't with me, Francesca was close by. There were times when Uncle Lucian and Auntie Jaxon hung around. They're busy so I knew it was because they were afraid Dimitri would come and claim me."

"But he didn't."

"Of course not. He's a man of honor. I'm not old enough in the Carpathian culture, which is funny because in the human culture I could marry easily. No one would think twice about it."

"Did you want him to claim you?" Josef asked curiously.

Skyler shrugged. "Sometimes. I dream about him. I don't ever think about other men, or even look at them. It's always Dimitri. He calls to me and isn't even aware of it. When we're talking, mind to mind, I see things. How alone he is. How dark his world is. How hard it is to struggle against the constant pull of the darkness. He endures so much for me. So much for all of us. When he hunts, it has become harder for him. Every time he has to kill. I see all that, and the terrible sacrifices he makes for me."

"He wouldn't want you to see those things, Sky," Josef said gently. "You know that, don't you? Carpathian males, especially the hunters, they're like stone, total warriors. And if he thought he wasn't protecting you from that creeping shadow, he'd be very upset."

Skyler smiled at Josef. "I can't help what I see, Josef. I'm not exactly like everyone else. What kind of a concoction am I? Psychic. Mage. Partly Carpathian. Daughter of the Earth. Dragonseeker. I see things I'm not meant to see. I feel things I shouldn't. I know he was nearly taken from me. I felt him. I called to him. Sang the healing chants I've heard Francesca sing. I lit candles and I cried for days when he was so far away I couldn't reach him."

She looked into his eyes, letting him see her grief. Josef was definitely underestimated by most people, but she saw his genius, and she valued their close friendship. She could talk to him, tell him anything, and he never betrayed her confidence.

"I need him," she admitted simply. "And I have to find him."

Josef slung his arm around her shoulders. "Well, little sister, that's exactly what we're going to do. Paul should be here in any minute. He texted me and said he had everything ready."

"Did he cover his tracks? Didn't he tell you once that Nicolas took his blood? If he did, he can track Paul."

"Baby, any of them can track us, and they'll be hot on our trail the moment they realize you're missing."

"I know that. I'm just saying it can't happen until we're ready." Skyler glanced again at her watch. "He's late."

"His cover is perfect," Josef assured. "He flew over with the De La Cruz families and he told them we were going to go exploring the mountains on the Ukraine side. We're camping for a couple of weeks. Of course they were happy to get rid of us and no one is going to question that we'd want to do something together. We've talked about it endlessly for the last couple of years. This would be the perfect opportunity for us to get together, so they bought our story easily."

Skyler gave a little sniff. "Of course they don't mind if you two go off camping in the wilds together. Remember when I wanted to go on one of your camping trips? The world almost came to an end."

Josef laughed and lazily leaned one hip against the coffin. "Gabriel turned into the big bad wolf and nearly ate Paul and me for dinner just at the suggestion. I was surprised he allowed you to go off to college. You were so far ahead of your age group in school."

Skyler shrugged. "I went home at night the first year. I needed to. That had nothing to do with Gabriel and Francesca. I don't know what I would have done without them. I needed them so much in the early days. And they really came through for me." Tears shimmered in her eyes. "I hate to repay their love and kindness with lies, but they left me no choice."

"You tried talking to them about Dimitri?" Josef asked.

Skyler nodded. "I knew something was wrong, that Dimitri was troubled, the last time we talked. He left abruptly for the Carpathian Mountains a few weeks ago and then he was in a terrible battle. I felt him slipping away from me. He was so far away and I almost couldn't reach him. By the time I did, he was nearly gone. I could feel his life force fading." She looked up at him. "You remember that night? I called you to come and help me."

"You were in the college library and fortunately I'd come to visit you, so I wasn't far away," Josef said. "But you didn't tell me what happened. Only that Dimitri needed you. You were wiped out."

The memory of that night shook her. Dimitri had been badly wounded. Mortally wounded. She was far from him, studying in the college library—so mundane—the distance dimming their connection. She'd reached for him, knowing he was in trouble and it was his brother she found. When she touched Dimitri, he had grown so cold, ice cold. She shivered, the coldness still in her bones. Sometimes she didn't think she'd ever get it out.

"His brother was there, fighting for him, following after his fading light and trying to bring him back. I called to Dimitri and begged him not to leave me. I did my best, even across such a great distance, to help his brother bring him back to the land of the living. I just couldn't let him go."

She caught her lower lip between her teeth, biting down hard. Even now her heart ached. She pressed her palm tightly over the pain. "I can't lose him, Josef. He has always been there for me, as long as I've needed him, any way that I've needed him. It's my turn now. I won't let him down. I'm going to find him and I'm going to help him escape."

"Before, when he was dying, you could reach him," Josef ventured carefully, knowing full well he was walking through a minefield. "Why do you think you can't now?"

"I know what you're getting at, Josef," she snapped. "And it isn't true. Dimitri is alive. I know he's alive."

Josef nodded. "I hear you, Sky, but that doesn't answer my question. Maybe we'd better figure out why you can't reach him when the two of you have always been able to communicate telepathically. You're extraordinarily powerful. More so than some Carpathians. Many of us can't cover the kinds of distances you've been able to. So what's different now?"

She frowned at him. Josef was incredibly brilliant, and even if she didn't want to hear it, she needed to listen to him. He had a point. She'd been able to cross great distances to connect with Dimitri—and he with her. She had known when he was in trouble, when he had fought in a battle with a rogue pack and took the brunt of the attack in order to give his brother the opportunity to destroy a very dangerous vampire/wolf cross.

She had felt Dimitri's pain, so terrible she could barely breathe. Right there, in the college library, she had nearly fallen to the floor, with that flash of pain that wasn't hers. She had followed that trail back to him unerringly despite his fading light. Over the years of talking telepathically, the connection between them had grown strong and she found him even as his life force was fading away, traveling to another realm. If she could do that, Josef was right, why couldn't she find him now? It didn't make sense—and she should have figured that out on her own.

"You're too close to the problem," Josef said, proving he was so tuned in to her he could practically read her thoughts.

"I don't like it when I'm not thinking straight," Skyler said. "He needs me to be one hundred percent on this."

"I think it's called love, Sky, as much as I don't want to admit you could love anyone but me." Josef winked at her.

"Something's really wrong, Josef. I know it is. How could I find him when he was already technically dead, but I can't do it now?"

"Perhaps he's unconscious," he ventured.

She shook her head. "I thought of that. I could still find him. I know I could. There's something about our connection. It's so strong, I can follow him anywhere. I could touch him when he was underground, rejuvenating in the soil."

Josef's eyes widened. "No way, Sky. No one can do that. We stop our hearts and lungs and we can't move. That's our most vulnerable time. How could he be aware?"

"I don't know, but whenever I reach for him, day or night, he's always been there for me. Always. I can't remember a single time that I couldn't find him. Mother Earth always sang to me, a vibration I could feel, and I would know where he was."

"Did you tell Gabriel and Francesca you could do that? Could you do it with them? With me?"

Skyler paced across the floor, looking once more at her watch a little impatiently. "I never thought to tell anyone, not even Dimitri, the how of it. But no, I never tried to wake anyone else. Francesca and Gabriel get very little time alone together these days, so I never considered waking them. It seemed natural to turn to Dimitri. I knew that he needed me as much as I needed him."

"All this time I thought you were afraid of a relationship with him," Josef said.

Skyler's smile held little humor. "I was never afraid of a relationship with him. How could I be? We have a wonderful relationship. He treats me like I'm the greatest, most desirable woman in the world. He's intelligent, we can talk about anything together for hours. He's kind and gentle. He's everything a woman could want in a partner."

"I'm hearing a 'but' in there."

"I am not certain I can be the lifemate he truly deserves. I'm great at the emotional relationship and the intellectual relationship, but I have no idea if I can ever be what he needs physically. That's an entirely different matter."

Josef shook his head. "Skyler, don't get all psycho about that. It will happen when it's supposed to. Dimitri will never want another woman. Not ever. He'll give you all the time you need."

"I know. I do. Dimitri would never push me and he never has. It isn't him that's worried. I just get anxious thinking about it. I want to be the best lifemate possible to him and my mind just can't go to a physical relationship yet."

She glanced again at her watch. "Paul had better get here soon. Are you certain he got away without anyone being suspicious?"

"Yeah, he's on his way. Only a few minutes out. You said Dimitri was alive. If he is, we'll find him."

Skyler let her breath out slowly. "I don't like any of this. I detest the fact that the prince, along with everyone else, has abandoned him."

Josef slung his arm around her and hugged her tight. The smile faded. "We'll find him. We will."

Skyler clung to him for a moment and then nodded, straightening her shoulders and stepping away from him. "I don't like the only explanation I can think of for not being able to connect with him."

"What is it?" Josef asked.

"He's blocking me." There was hurt in her voice. "He has to be. There's no other explanation that makes sense."

APPENDIX I

Carpathian Healing Chants

To rightly understand Carpathian healing chants, background is required in several areas:

1. The Carpathian view on healing
2. The Lesser Healing Chant of the Carpathians
3. The Great Healing Chant of the Carpathians
4. Carpathian musical aesthetics
5. Lullaby
6. Song to Heal the Earth
7. Carpathian chanting technique

1. THE CARPATHIAN VIEW ON HEALING

The Carpathians are a nomadic people whose geographic origins can be traced back to at least as far as the Southern Ural Mountains (near the steppes of modern-day Kazakhstan), on the border between Europe and Asia. (For this reason, modern-day linguists call their language "proto-Uralic," without knowing that this is the language of the Carpathians.) Unlike most nomadic peoples, the wandering of the Carpathians was not due to the need to find new grazing lands as the seasons and climate shifted, or the search for better trade. Instead, the Carpathians' movements were driven by a great purpose: to find a land that would have the right earth, a soil with the kind of richness that would greatly enhance their rejuvenative powers.

Over the centuries, they migrated westward (some six thousand years ago), until they at last found their perfect homeland—their *susu*—in the Carpathian Mountains, whose long arc cradled the lush plains of the kingdom of Hungary. (The kingdom of Hungary flourished for over a millennium—making Hungarian the dominant language of the Carpathian Basin—until the kingdom's lands were split among several countries after World War I: Austria, Czechoslovakia, Romania, Yugoslavia and modern Hungary.)

Other peoples from the Southern Urals (who shared the Carpathian language, but were not Carpathians) migrated in different directions. Some ended up in Finland, which accounts for why the modern Hungarian and Finnish languages are among the contemporary descendents of the ancient Carpathian language. Even though they are tied forever to their chosen Carpathian homeland, the wandering of the Carpathians

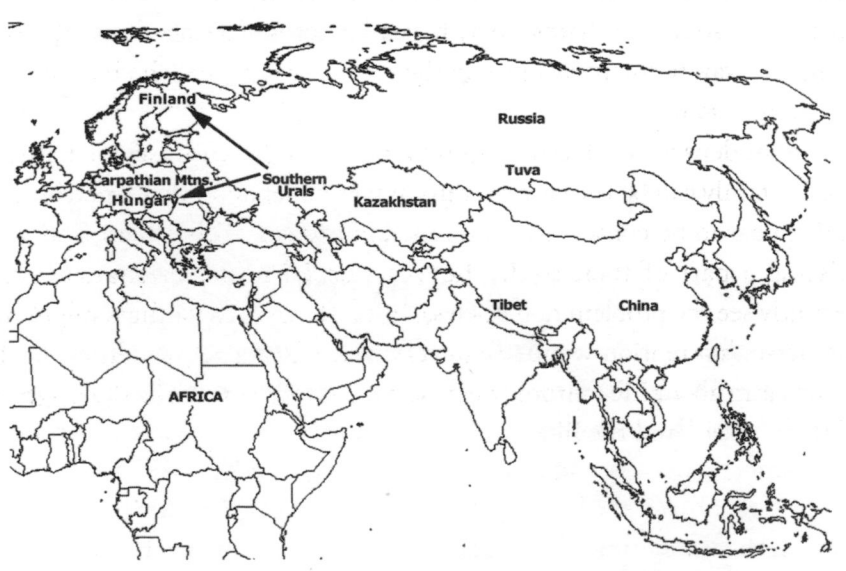

continues as they search the world for the answers that will enable them to bear and raise their offspring without difficulty.

Because of their geographic origins, the Carpathian views on healing share much with the larger Eurasian shamanistic tradition. Probably the closest modern representative of that tradition is based in Tuva (and is referred to as "Tuvinian Shamanism")—see the map on the previous page.

The Eurasian shamanistic tradition—from the Carpathians to the Siberian shamans—held that illness originated in the human soul, and only later manifested as various physical conditions. Therefore, shamanistic healing, while not neglecting the body, focused on the soul and its healing. The most profound illnesses were understood to be caused by "soul departure," where all or some part of the sick person's soul has wandered away from the body (into the nether realms), or has been captured or possessed by an evil spirit, or both.

The Carpathians belong to this greater Eurasian shamanistic tradition and share its viewpoints. While the Carpathians themselves did not succumb to illness, Carpathian healers understood that the most profound wounds were also accompanied by a similar "soul departure."

Upon reaching the diagnosis of "soul departure," the healer-shaman is then required to make a spiritual journey into the netherworlds to recover the soul. The shaman may have to overcome tremendous challenges along the way, particularly fighting the demon or vampire who has possessed his friend's soul.

"Soul departure" doesn't require a person to be unconscious (although that certainly can be the case as well). It was understood that a person could still appear to be conscious, even talk and interact with others, and yet be missing a part of their soul. The experienced healer or shaman would instantly see the problem nonetheless, in subtle signs that others might miss: the person's attention wandering every now and then, a lessening in their enthusiasm about life, chronic depression, a diminishment in the brightness of their "aura," and the like.

2. THE LESSER HEALING CHANT OF THE CARPATHIANS

Kepä Sarna Pus (**The Lesser Healing Chant**) is used for wounds that are merely physical in nature. The Carpathian healer leaves his body and enters the wounded Carpathian's body to heal great mortal wounds from the inside out using pure energy. He proclaims, "I offer freely my life for your life," as he gives his blood to the injured Carpathian. Because the Carpathians are of the earth and bound to the soil, they are healed by the soil of their homeland. Their saliva is also often used for its rejuvenative powers.

It is also very common for the Carpathian chants (both the Lesser and the Great) to be accompanied by the use of healing herbs, aromas from Carpathian candles and crystals. The crystals (when combined with the Carpathians' empathic, psychic connection to the entire universe) are used to gather positive energy from their surroundings, which then is used to accelerate the healing. Caves are sometimes used as the setting for the healing.

The Lesser Healing Chant was used by Vikirnoff Von Shrieder and Colby Jansen to heal Rafael De La Cruz, whose heart had been ripped out by a vampire as described in *Dark Secret*.

Kepä Sarna Pus (The Lesser Healing Chant)
The same chant is used for all physical wounds. "Sívadaba" ["into your heart"] would be changed to refer to whatever part of the body is wounded.

Kuńasz, nélkül sívdobbanás, nélkül fesztelen löyly.
You lie as if asleep, without beat of heart, without airy breath.

Ot élidamet andam szabadon élidadért.
I offer freely my life for your life.

O jelä sielam jörem ot ainamet és soŋe ot élidadet.
My spirit of light forgets my body and enters your body.

O jelä sielam pukta kinn minden szelemeket belső.
My spirit of light sends all the dark spirits within fleeing without.

Pajńak o susu hanyet és o nyelv nyálamet sívadaba.

I press the earth of our homeland and the spit of my tongue into your
heart.

Vii, o verim soŋe o verid andam.

At last, I give you my blood for your blood.

To hear this chant, visit: http://www.christinefeehan.com/members/.

3. THE GREAT HEALING CHANT OF THE CARPATHIANS

The most well-known—and most dramatic—of the Carpathian healing chants was **En Sarna Pus (The Great Healing Chant)**. This
chant was reserved for recovering the wounded or unconscious Carpathian's
soul.

Typically a group of men would form a circle around the sick Carpathian
(to "encircle him with our care and compassion") and begin the chant.
The shaman or healer or leader is the prime actor in this healing ceremony.
It is he who will actually make the spiritual journey into the netherworld,
aided by his clanspeople. Their purpose is to ecstatically dance, sing, drum
and chant, all the while visualizing (through the words of the chant) the
journey itself—every step of it, over and over again—to the point where the
shaman, in trance, leaves his body, and makes that very journey. (Indeed,
the word "ecstasy" is from the Latin *ex statis*, which literally means "out of
the body.")

One advantage that the Carpathian healer has over many other shamans
is his telepathic link to his lost brother. Most shamans must wander in the
dark of the nether realms in search of their lost brother. But the Carpathian
healer directly "hears" in his mind the voice of his lost brother calling to
him, and can thus "zero in" on his soul like a homing beacon. For this reason, Carpathian healing tends to have a higher success rate than most other
traditions of this sort.

Something of the geography of the "other world" is useful for us to
examine, in order to fully understand the words of the Great Carpathian
Healing Chant. A reference is made to the "Great Tree" (in Carpathian: *En*

Puwe). Many ancient traditions, including the Carpathian tradition, under-stood the worlds—the heaven worlds, our world and the nether realms—to be "hung" upon a great pole, or axis, or tree. Here on earth, we are positioned halfway up this tree, on one of its branches. Hence many ancient texts often referred to the material world as "middle earth": midway between heaven and hell. Climbing the tree would lead one to the heaven worlds. Descending the tree to its roots would lead to the nether realms. The shaman was necessarily a master of movement up and down the Great Tree, some-times moving unaided, and sometimes assisted by (or even mounted upon the back of) an animal spirit guide. In various traditions, this Great Tree was known variously as the *axis mundi* (the "axis of the worlds"), Ygddrasil (in Norse mythology), Mount Meru (the sacred world mountain of Tibetan tradition), etc. The Christian cosmos, with its heaven, purgatory/earth and hell, is also worth comparing. It is even given a similar topography in Dante's *Divine Comedy*: Dante is led on a journey first to hell, at the center of the earth; then upward to Mount Purgatory, which sits on the earth's surface directly opposite Jerusalem; then farther upward first to Eden, the earthly paradise, at the summit of Mount Purgatory; and then upward at last to heaven.

In the shamanistic tradition, it was understood that the small always reflects the large; the personal always reflects the cosmic. A movement in the greater dimensions of the cosmos also coincides with an internal movement. For example, the *axis mundi* of the cosmos also corresponds to the spinal column of the individual. Journeys up and down the *axis mundi* often coincided with the movement of natural and spiritual energies (some-times called *kundalini* or *shakti*) in the spinal column of the shaman or mystic.

En Sarna Pus (The Great Healing Chant)
In this chant, ekä ("brother") would be replaced by "sister," "father," "mother," depending on the person to be healed.

Ot ekäm ainajanak hany, jama.
My brother's body is a lump of earth, close to death.

Me, ot ekäm kuntajanak, pirädak ekäm, gonul és irgalom türe.
We, the clan of my brother, encircle him with our care and compassion.

O pus wäkenkek, ot oma śarnank, és ot pus fünk, álnak ekäm ainajanak, pitänak ekäm ainajanak elävä.
Our healing energies, ancient words of magic and healing herbs bless my brother's body, keep it alive.

Ot ekäm sielanak pälä. Ot omboće päläja juta alatt o jüti, kinta, és szelemek lamtijaknak.
But my brother's soul is only half. His other half wanders in the netherworld.

Ot en mekem ŋamaŋ: kulkedak otti ot ekäm omboće päläjanak.
My great deed is this: I travel to find my brother's other half.

Rekatüre, saradak, tappadak, odam, kaŋa o numa waram, és avaa owe o lewl mahoz.
We dance, we chant, we dream ecstatically, to call my spirit bird, and to open the door to the other world.

Ntak o numa waram, és mozdulak, jomadak.
I mount my spirit bird and we begin to move, we are under way.

Piwtädak ot En Puwe tyvinak, ećidak alatt o jüti, kinta, és szelemek lamtijaknak.
Following the trunk of the Great Tree, we fall into the netherworld.

Fázak, fázak nó o śaro.
It is cold, very cold.

Juttadak ot ekäm o akarataban, o sívaban és o sielaban.
My brother and I are linked in mind, heart and soul.

Ot ekäm sielanak kaŋa engem.
My brother's soul calls to me.

Kuledak és piwtädak ot ekäm.
I hear and follow his track.

Saγedak és tuledak ot ekäm kulyanak.
Encounter I the demon who is devouring my brother's soul.

Nenäm ćoro, o kuly torodak.
In anger, I fight the demon.

O kuly pél engem.
He is afraid of me.

Lejkkadak o kaŋka salamaval.
I strike his throat with a lightning bolt.

Molodak ot ainaja komakamal.
I break his body with my bare hands.

Toja és molanâ.
He is bent over, and falls apart.

Hän ćaδa.
He runs away.

Manedak ot ekäm sielanak.
I rescue my brother's soul.

Alǝdak ot ekam sielanak o komamban.
I lift my brother's soul in the hollow of my hand.

Alǝdam ot ekam numa waramra.
I lift him onto my spirit bird.

Piwtädak ot En Puwe tyvijanak és sayedak jülleen ot elävä ainak majaknak.
Following up the Great Tree, we return to the land of the living.

Ot ekäm elä jälleen.
My brother lives again.

Ot ekäm weńća jälleen.
He is complete again.

To hear this chant, visit: http://www.christinefeehan.com/members/.

4. CARPATHIAN MUSICAL AESTHETICS

In the sung Carpathian pieces (such as the "Lullaby" and the "Song to Heal the Earth"), you'll hear elements that are shared by many of the musical traditions in the Uralic geographical region, some of which still exist—from Eastern European (Bulgarian, Romanian, Hungarian, Croatian, etc.) to Romany ("gypsy"). Some of these elements include:

- the rapid alternation between major and minor modalities, including a sudden switch (called a "Picardy third") from minor to major to end a piece or section (as at the end of the "Lullaby")
- the use of close (tight) harmonies
- the use of *ritardi* (slowing down the piece) and *crescendi* (swelling in volume) for brief periods
- the use of *glissandi* (slides) in the singing tradition
- the use of trills in the singing tradition (as in the final invocation of the "Song to Heal the Earth")—similar to Celtic, a singing tradition more familiar to many of us
- the use of parallel fifths (as in the final invocation of the "Song to Heal the Earth")
- controlled use of dissonance
- "call and response" chanting (typical of many of the world's chanting traditions)

- extending the length of a musical line (by adding a couple of bars) to heighten dramatic effect
- and many more

"Lullaby" and "Song to Heal the Earth" illustrate two rather different forms of Carpathian music (a quiet, intimate piece and an energetic ensemble piece)—but whatever the form, Carpathian music is full of feeling.

5. LULLABY

This song is sung by women while the child is still in the womb or when the threat of a miscarriage is apparent. The baby can hear the song while inside the mother, and the mother can connect with the child telepathically as well. The lullaby is meant to reassure the child, to encourage the baby to hold on, to stay—to reassure the child that he or she will be protected by love even from inside until birth. The last line literally means that the mother's love will protect her child until the child is born ("rise").

Musically, the Carpathian "Lullaby" is in three-quarter time ("waltz time"), as are a significant portion of the world's various traditional lullabies (perhaps the most famous of which is "Brahms' Lullaby"). The arrangement for solo voice is the original context: a mother singing to her child, unaccompanied. The arrangement for chorus and violin ensemble illustrates how musical even the simplest Carpathian pieces often are, and how easily they lend themselves to contemporary instrumental or orchestral arrangements. (A wide range of contemporary composers, including Dvořák and Smetana, have taken advantage of a similar discovery, working other traditional Eastern European music into their symphonic poems.)

Odam-Sarna Kondak (Lullaby)

Tumtesz o wäke ku pitasz belső.
Feel the strength you hold inside.

Hiszasz sívadet. Én olenam gæidnod.
Trust your heart. I'll be your guide.

Sas csecsemõm, kuńasz.
Hush my baby, close your eyes.

Rauho joŋe ted.
Peace will come to you.

Tumtesz o sívdobbanás ku olen lamt3ad belső.
Feel the rhythm deep inside.

Gond-kumpadek ku kim te.
Waves of love that cover you.

Pesänak te, asti o jüti, kidüsz.
Protect, until the night you rise.

To hear this song, visit: http://www.christinefeehan.com/members/.

6. SONG TO HEAL THE EARTH

This is the earth-healing song that is used by the Carpathian women to heal soil filled with various toxins. The women take a position on four sides and call to the universe to draw on the healing energy with love and respect. The soil of the earth is their resting place, the place where they rejuvenate, and they must make it safe not only for themselves but for their unborn children as well as their men and living children. This is a beautiful ritual performed by the women together, raising their voices in harmony and calling on the earth's minerals and healing properties to come forth and help them save their children. They literally dance and sing to heal the earth in a ceremony as old as their species. The dance and notes of the song are adjusted according to the toxins felt through the healer's bare feet. The feet are placed in a certain pattern and the hands gracefully weave a healing spell while the dance is performed. They must be especially careful when the soil is prepared for babies. This is a ceremony of love and healing.

Musically, the ritual is divided into several sections:

- **First verse**: A "call and response" section, where the chant leader sings the "call" solo, and then some or all of the women sing the "response" in the close harmony style typical of the Carpathian musical tradition. The repeated response—*Ai Emä Maye*—is an invocation of the source of power for the healing ritual: "Oh, Mother Nature."
- **First chorus**: This section is filled with clapping, dancing, ancient horns and other means used to invoke and heighten the energies upon which the ritual is drawing.
- **Second verse**
- **Second chorus**
- **Closing invocation:** In this closing part, two song leaders, in close harmony, take all the energy gathered by the earlier portions of the song/ritual and focus it entirely on the healing purpose.

What you will be listening to are brief tastes of what would typically be a significantly longer ritual, in which the verse and chorus parts are developed and repeated many times, to be closed by a single rendition of the final invocation.

Sarna Pusm O Mayet (Song to Heal the Earth)

First verse
Ai Emä Maye,
Oh, Mother Nature,

Me sívadbin lañaak.
We are your beloved daughters.

Me tappadak, me pusmak o maγet.
We dance to heal the earth.

Me sarnadak, me pusmak o hanyet.
We sing to heal the earth.

Sielanket jutta tedet it,
We join with you now,

Sívank és akaratank és sielank juttanak.
Our hearts and minds and spirits become one.

Second verse
Ai Emä maγe,
Oh, Mother Nature,

Me stvualbin lañaak.
We are your beloved daughters.

Me andak arwadet emänked és me kaŋank o
We pay homage to our mother and call upon the

Põhi és Lõuna, Ida és Lääs.
North and South, East and West.

Pide és aldyn és myös belső.
Above and below and within as well.

Gondank o maγenak pusm hän ku olen jama.
Our love of the land heals that which is in need.

Juttanak teval it,
We join with you now,

Maγe maγeval.
Earth to earth.

O pirä elidak weńća.
The circle of life is complete.

To hear this chant, visit: http://www.christinefeehan.com/members/.

7. CARPATHIAN CHANTING TECHNIQUE

As with their healing techniques, the actual "chanting technique" of the Carpathians has much in common with the other shamanistic traditions of the Central Asian steppes. The primary mode of chanting was throat chanting using overtones. Modern examples of this manner of singing can still be found in the Mongolian, Tuvan and Tibetan traditions. You can find an audio example of the Gyuto Tibetan Buddhist monks engaged in throat chanting at: http://www.christinefeehan.com/carpathian_chanting/.

As with Tuva, note on the map the geographical proximity of Tibet to Kazakhstan and the Southern Urals.

The beginning part of the Tibetan chant emphasizes synchronizing all the voices around a single tone, aimed at healing a particular "chakra" of the body. This is fairly typical of the Gyuto throat-chanting tradition, but it is not a significant part of the Carpathian tradition. Nonetheless, it serves as an interesting contrast.

The part of the Gyuto chanting example that is most similar to the Carpathian style of chanting is the midsection, where the men are chanting the words together with great force. The purpose here is not to generate a "healing tone" that will affect a particular "chakra," but rather to generate as much power as possible for initiating the "out of body" travel, and for fighting the demonic forces that the healer/traveler must face and overcome.

The songs of the Carpathian women (illustrated by their "Lullaby" and their "Song to Heal the Earth") are part of the same ancient musical and healing tradition as the Lesser and Great Healing Chants of the warrior males. You can hear some of the same instruments in both the male warriors' healing chants and the women's "Song to Heal the Earth." Also, they share the common purpose of generating and directing power. However, the women's songs are distinctively feminine in character. One immediately noticeable difference is that, while the men speak their words in the manner of a chant, the women sing songs with melodies and harmonies, softening the overall performance. A feminine, nurturing quality is especially evident in the "Lullaby."

APPENDIX 2

The Carpathian Language

Like all human languages, the language of the Carpathians contains the richness and nuance that can only come from a long history of use. At best we can only touch on some of the main features of the language in this brief appendix:

1. The history of the Carpathian language
2. Carpathian grammar and other characteristics of the language
3. Examples of the Carpathian language (including The Ritual Words and The Warrior's Chant)
4. A much-abridged Carpathian dictionary

1. THE HISTORY OF THE CARPATHIAN LANGUAGE

The Carpathian language of today is essentially identical to the Carpathian language of thousands of years ago. A "dead" language like the Latin of two thousand years ago has evolved into a significantly different modern language (Italian) because of countless generations of speakers and great historical fluctuations. In contrast, many of the speakers of Carpathian from thousands of years ago are still alive. Their presence—

coupled with the deliberate isolation of the Carpathians from the other major forces of change in the world—has acted (and continues to act) as a stabilizing force that has preserved the integrity of the language over the centuries. Carpathian culture has also acted as a stabilizing force. For instance, the Ritual Words, the various healing chants (see Appendix 1), and other cultural artifacts have been passed down through the centuries with great fidelity.

One small exception should be noted: the splintering of the Carpathians into separate geographic regions has led to some minor dialectization. However the telepathic link among all Carpathians (as well as each Carpathian's regular return to his or her homeland) has ensured that the differences among dialects are relatively superficial (e.g., small numbers of new words, minor differences in pronunciation, etc.), since the deeper, internal language of mind-forms has remained the same because of continuous use across space and time.

The Carpathian language was (and still is) the proto-language for the Uralic (or Finno-Ugrian) family of languages. Today, the Uralic languages are spoken in northern, eastern and central Europe and in Siberia. More than twenty-three million people in the world speak languages that can trace their ancestry to Carpathian. Magyar or Hungarian (about fourteen million speakers), Finnish (about five million speakers) and Estonian (about one million speakers) are the three major contemporary descendents of this proto-language. The only factor that unites the more than twenty languages in the Uralic family is that their ancestry can be traced back to a common proto-language—Carpathian—that split (starting some six thousand years ago) into the various languages in the Uralic family. In the same way, European languages such as English and French belong to the better-known Indo-European family and also evolved from a common proto-language ancestor (a different one from Carpathian).

The following table provides a sense for some of the similarities in the language family.

Note: The Finnic/Carpathian "k" shows up often as Hungarian "h." Similarly, the Finnic/Carpathian "p" often corresponds to the Hungarian "f."

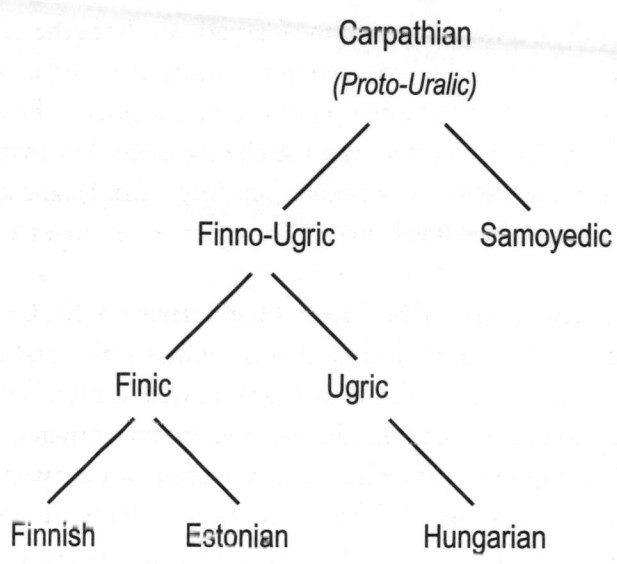

Carpathian	Finnish	Hungarian
(proto-Uralic)	*(Suomi)*	*(Magyar)*
elä—live	*elä*—live	*él*—live
elid—life	*elinikä*—life	*élet*—life
pesä—nest	*pesä*—nest	*fészek*—nest
kola—die	*kuole*—die	*hal*—die
päl<u>ä</u>—half, side	*pieltä*—tilt, tip to the side	*fél, fele*—fellow human, friend (half; one side of two) *feleség*—wife
and—give	*anta, antaa*—give	*ad*—give
koje—husband, man	*koira*—dog, the male (of animals)	*here*—drone, testicle
wäke—power	*väki*—folks, people, men; force	*vall-vel*—with (instrumental suffix)
	väkevä—powerful, strong	*vele*—with him/her/it
wete—water	*vesi*—water	*víz*—water

2. CARPATHIAN GRAMMAR AND OTHER CHARACTERISTICS OF THE LANGUAGE

Idioms. As both an ancient language and a language of an earth people, Carpathian is more inclined toward use of idioms constructed from concrete, "earthy" terms, rather than abstractions. For instance, our modern abstraction "to cherish" is expressed more concretely in Carpathian as "to hold in one's heart"; the "netherworld" is, in Carpathian, "the land of night, fog and ghosts"; etc.

Word order. The order of words in a sentence is determined not by syntactic roles (like subject, verb and object) but rather by pragmatic, discourse-driven factors. Examples: *"Tied vagyok."* ("Yours am I."); *"Sívamet andam."* ("My heart I give you.")

Agglutination. The Carpathian language is agglutinative; that is, longer words are constructed from smaller components. An agglutinating language uses suffixes or prefixes whose meaning is generally unique, and which are concatenated one after another without overlap. In Carpathian, words typically consist of a stem that is followed by one or more suffixes. For example, *"sívambam"* derives from the stem *"sív"* ("heart") followed by *"am"* ("my," making it "my heart"), followed by *"bam"* ("in," making it "in my heart"). As you might imagine, agglutination in Carpathian can sometimes produce very long words, or words that are very difficult to pronounce. Vowels often get inserted between suffixes to prevent too many consonants from appearing in a row (which can make the word unpronounceable).

Noun cases. Like all languages, Carpathian has many noun cases; the same noun will be "spelled" differently depending on its role in the sentence. Some of the noun cases include: nominative (when the noun is the subject of the sentence), accusative (when the noun is a direct object of the verb), dative (indirect object), genitive (or possessive), instrumental, final, supressive, inessive, elative, terminative and delative.

We will use the possessive (or genitive) case as an example, to illustrate how all noun cases in Carpathian involve adding standard suffixes to the noun stems. Thus expressing possession in Carpathian—"my lifemate," "your lifemate," "his lifemate," "her lifemate," etc.—involves adding a particular suffix (such as "*-am*") to the noun stem (*"päläfertiil"*), to produce the possessive (*"päläfertiilam"*—"my lifemate"). Which suffix to use depends upon which person ("my," "your," "his," etc.) and whether the noun ends in a consonant or a vowel. The table below shows the suffixes for singular nouns only (not plural), and also shows the similarity to the suffixes used in contemporary Hungarian. (Hungarian is actually a little more complex, in that it also requires "vowel rhyming": which suffix to use also depends on the last vowel in the noun; hence the multiple choices in the cells below, where Carpathian only has a single choice.)

person	Carpathian (proto-Uralic)		Contemporary Hungarian	
	noun ends in vowel	**noun ends in consonant**	**noun ends in vowel**	**noun ends in consonant**
1st singular (my)	-m	-am	-m	-om, -em, -öm
2nd singular (your)	-d	-ad	-d	-od, -ed, -öd
3rd singular (his, her, its)	-ja	-a	-ja/-je	-a, -e
1st plural (our)	-nk	-ank	-nk	-unk, -ünk
2nd plural (your)	-tak	-atak	-tok, -tek, -tök	-otok, -etek, -ötök
3rd plural (their)	-jak	-ak	-juk, -jük	-uk, -ük

Note: As mentioned earlier, vowels often get inserted between the word and its suffix so as to prevent too many consonants from appearing in a row (which would produce unpronounceable words). For example, in the table on the previous page, all nouns that end in a consonant are followed by suffixes beginning with "a."

Verb conjugation. Like its modern descendents (such as Finnish and Hungarian), Carpathian has many verb tenses, far too many to describe here. We will just focus on the conjugation of the present tense. Again, we will place contemporary Hungarian side by side with the Carpathian, because of the marked similarity of the two.

As with the possessive case for nouns, the conjugation of verbs is done by adding a suffix onto the verb stem:

Person	Carpathian (proto-Uralic)	Contemporary Hungarian
1st (I give)	-am (andam), -ak	-ok, -ek, -ök
2nd singular (you give)	-sz (andsz)	-sz
3rd singular (he/she/it gives)	— (and)	—
1st plural (we give)	-ak (andak)	-unk, -ünk
2nd plural (you give)	-tak (andtak)	-tok, -tek, -tök
3rd plural (they give)	-nak (andnak)	-nak, -nek

As with all languages, there are many "irregular verbs" in Carpathian that don't exactly fit this pattern. But the above table is still a useful guideline for most verbs.

3. EXAMPLES OF THE CARPATHIAN LANGUAGE

Here are some brief examples of conversational Carpathian, used in the Dark books. We include the literal translation in square brackets. It is interestingly different from the most appropriate English translation.

Susu.
I am home.
["home/birthplace." "I am" is understood, as is often the case in Carpathian.]

Möért?
What for?

csitri
little one
["little slip of a thing," "little slip of a girl"]

ainaak enyém
forever mine

ainaak sívamet jutta
forever mine (another form)
["forever to-my-heart connected/fixed"]

sívamet
my love
["of-my-heart," "to-my-heart"]

Tet vigyázam.
I love you.
["you-love-I"]

Sarna Rituaali (**The Ritual Words**) is a longer example, and an example of chanted rather than conversational Carpathian. Note the recurring use of *"andam"* ("I give"), to give the chant musicality and force through repetition.

Sarna Rituaali (**The Ritual Words**)

Te avio päläfertiilam.
You are my lifemate.

Éntölam kuulua, avio päläfertiilam.
I claim you as my lifemate.

Ted kuuluak, kacad, kojed.
I belong to you.

Élidamet andam.
I offer my life for you.

Pesämet andam.
I give you my protection.

Uskolfertiilamet andam.
I give you my allegiance.

Sívamet andam.
I give you my heart.

Sielamet andam.
I give you my soul.

Ainamet andam.
I give you my body.

Sívamet kuuluak kaik että a ted.
I take into my keeping the same that is yours.

Ainaak olenszal sívambin.
Your life will be cherished by me for all my time.

Te élidet ainaak pide minan.
Your life will be placed above my own for all time.

Te avio päläfertiilam.
You are my lifemate.

Ainaak sívamet jutta oleny.
You are bound to me for all eternity.

Ainaak terád vigyázak.
You are always in my care.

To hear these words pronounced (and for more about Carpathian pronunciation altogether), please visit: http://www.christinefeehan.com/members/.

Sarna Kontakawk (**The Warriors' Chant**) is another longer example of the Carpathian language. The warriors' council takes place deep beneath the earth in a chamber of crystals with magma far below that, so the steam is natural and the wisdom of their ancestors is clear and focused. This is a sacred place where they bloodswear to their prince and people and affirm their code of honor as warriors and brothers. It is also where battle strategies are born and all dissension is discussed as well as any concerns the warriors have that they wish to bring to the Council and open for discussion.

Sarna Kontakawk (The Warriors' Chant)

Veri isäakank—veri ekäakank.
Blood of our fathers—blood of our brothers.

Veri olen elid.
Blood is life.

Andak veri-elidet Karpatiiakank, és wäke-sarna ku meke arwa-arvo, irgalom, hän ku agba, és wäke kutni, ku manaak verival.
We offer that life to our people with a bloodsworn vow of honor, mercy, integrity and endurance.

Verink sokta; verink kaŋa terád.
Our blood mingles and calls to you.

Akasz énak ku kaŋa és juttasz kuntatak it.
Heed our summons and join with us now.

To hear these words pronounced (and for more about Carpathian pronunciation altogether), please visit: http://www.christinefeehan.com/members/.

See **Appendix 1** for Carpathian healing chants, including the *Kepä Sarna Pus* (The Lesser Healing Chant), the *En Sarna Pus* (The Great Healing Chant), the *Odam-Sarna Kondak* (Lullaby) and the *Sarna Pusm O Maγ et* (Song to Heal the Earth).

4. A MUCH-ABRIDGED CARPATHIAN DICTIONARY

This very much abridged Carpathian dictionary contains most of the Carpathian words used in these Dark books. Of course, a full Carpathian dictionary would be as large as the usual dictionary for an entire language (typically more than a hundred thousand words).

Note: The Carpathian nouns and verbs below are word stems. They generally do not appear in their isolated, "stem" form, as below. Instead, they usually appear with suffixes (e.g., *"andam"*—*"I give,"* rather than just the root, *"and"*).

a—verb negation (*prefix*); not (*adverb*).
agba—to be seemly or proper.
ai—oh.
aina—body.
ainaak—forever.
O ainaak jelä peje emnimet ŋamaŋ—Sun scorch that woman forever (*Carpathian swear words*).
ainaakfél—old friend.
ak—suffix added after a noun ending in a consonant to make it plural.
aka—to give heed; to hearken; to listen.
akarat—mind; will.
ál—to bless; to attach to.

alatt—through.

aldyn—under; underneath.

alə—to lift; to raise.

alte—to bless; to curse.

and—to give.

and sielet, arwa-arvomet, és jelämet, kuulua huvémet ku feaj és ködet ainaak—to trade soul, honor and salvation, for momentary pleasure and endless damnation.

andasz éntölem irgalomet!—have mercy!

arvo—value; price (*noun*).

arwa—praise (*noun*).

arwa-arvo—honor (*noun*).

arwa-arvo olen gæidnod, ekäm—honor guide you, my brother (*greeting*).

arwa-arvo olen isäntä, ekäm—honor keep you, my brother (*greeting*).

arwa-arvo pile sívadet—may honor light your heart (*greeting*).

arwa-arvod mäne me ködak—may your honor hold back the dark (*greeting*).

ašša—no (*before a noun*); not (*with a verb that is not in the imperative*); not (*with an adjective*).

aššatotello—disobedient.

asti—until.

avaa—to open.

avio—wedded.

avio päläfertiil—lifemate.

avoi—uncover; show; reveal.

belső—within; inside.

bur—good; well.

bur tule ekämet kuntamak—well met brother-kin (*greeting*).

ćaδa—to flee; to run; to escape.

ćoro—to flow; to run like rain.

csecsemõ—baby (*noun*).

csltrl—little one (*female*).

diutal—triumph; victory.

**el...

ekä—brother.

ekäm—my brother.

elä—to live.

eläsz arwa-arvoval—may you live with honor (*greeting*).

eläsz jeläbam ainaak—long may you live in the light (*greeting*).

elävä—alive.

elävä ainak majaknak—land of the living.

elid—life.

emä—mother (*noun*).

Emä Maɣe—Mother Nature.

emäen—grandmother.

embɛ—if, when.

embɛ karmasz—please.

emni—wife; woman.

emnim—my wife; my woman.

emni hän ku köd alte—cursed woman.

emni kuŋenak ku aššatotello—disobedient lunatic.

én—I.

en—great, many, big.

én jutta félet és ekämet—I greet a friend and brother (*greeting*).

én maɣenak—I am of the earth.

én oma maɣeka—I am as old as time (*literally: as old as the earth*).

En Puwe—The Great Tree. Related to the legends of Ygddrasil, the axis mundi, Mount Meru, heaven and hell, etc.

engem—of me.

és—and.

ete—before; in front.

että—that.

fáz—to feel cold or chilly.

fél—fellow, friend.

fél ku kuuluaak sívam belső—beloved.

fél ku vigyázak—dear one.

feldolgaz—prepare.

fertiil—fertile one.

fesztelen—airy.

fü—herbs; grass.

gæidno—road, way.

gond—care; worry; love (*noun*).

hän—he; she; it.

hän agba—it is so.

hän ku—prefix: one who; that which.

hän ku agba—truth.

hän ku kaśwa o numamet—sky-owner.

hän ku kuulua sívamet—keeper of my heart.

hän ku lejkka wäke-sarnat—traitor.

hän ku meke pirämet—defender.

hän ku pesä—protector.

hän ku piwtä—predator; hunter; tracker.

hän ku vie elidet—vampire (*literally: thief of life*).

hän ku vigyáz sielamet—keeper of my soul.

hän ku vigyáz sívamet és sielamet—keeper of my heart and soul.

hän ku saa kuć3aket—star-reacher.

hän ku tappa—killer; violent person (*noun*). deadly; violent (*adj.*).

hän ku tuulmahl elidet—vampire (*literally: life-stealer*).

Hän sívamak—Beloved.

hany—clod; lump of earth.

hisz— to believe; to trust.

ho—how.

ida—east.

igazág—justice.

irgalom—compassion; pity; mercy.

isä—father (*noun*).

isäntä—master of the house.

it—now.

jälleen—again.

jama—to be sick, infected, wounded, or dying; to be near death.

jelä—sunlight; day, sun; light.

jelä keje terád—light sear you (*Carpathian swear words*).

o jelä peje terád—sun scorch you (*Carpathian swear words*).

o jelä peje emnimet—sun scorch the woman. (*Carpathian swear words*).

o jelä peje terád, emni—sun scorch you, woman. (*Carpathian swear words*).

o jelä peje kaik hänkanak—sun scorch them all. (*Carpathian swear words*).

o jelä sielamak—light of my soul.

joma—to be under way; to go.

joŋe—to come; to return.

joŋesz arwa-arvoval—return with honor (*greeting*).

jŏrem—to forget; to lose one's way; to make a mistake.

juo—to drink.

juosz és eläsz—drink and live (*greeting*).

juosz és olen ainaak sielamet jutta—drink and become one with me (*greeting*).

juta—to go; to wander.

jüti—night; evening.

jutta—connected; fixed (*adj.*). to connect; to fix; to bind (*verb*).

k—suffix added after a noun ending in a vowel to make it plural.

kaca—male lover.

kadi—judge.

kaik—all.

kaŋa—to call; to invite; to request; to beg.

kaŋk—windpipe; Adam's apple; throat.

kać3—gift.

kaða—to abandon; to leave; to remain.

kaða wäkeva óv o köd—stand fast against the dark (*greeting*).

kalma—corpse; death; grave.

karma—want.

Karpatii—Carpathian.

Karpatii ku köd—liar.

käsi—hand (*noun*).

kaśwa—to own.

keje—to cook; to burn; to sear.

kepä—lesser, small, easy, few.

kessa—cat.

kessa ku toro—wildcat.

kessake—little cat.

kidü—to wake up; to arise (*intransitive verb*).

kim—to cover an entire object with some sort of covering.

kinn—out; outdoors; outside; without.

kinta—fog, mist, smoke.

kislány—little girl.

kislány kuŋenak—little lunatic.

kislány kuŋenak minan—my little lunatic.

köd—fog; mist; darkness; evil (*noun*); foggy, dark; evil (*adj.*).

köd elävä és köd nime kutni nimet—evil lives and has a name.

köd alte hän—darkness curse it (*Carpathian swear words*).

o köd belső—darkness take it (*Carpathian swear words*).

köd jutasz belső—shadow take you (*Carpathian swear words*).

koje—man; husband; drone.

kola—to die.

kolasz arwa-arvoval—may you die with honor (*greeting*).

koma—empty hand; bare hand; palm of the hand; hollow of the hand.

kond—all of a family's or clan's children.

kont—warrior.

kont o sívanak—strong heart (*literally: heart of the warrior*).

ku—who; which; that.

kuć3—star.

kuć3ak!—stars! (*exclamation*).

kuja—day, sun.

kuŋe—moon; month.

kule—to hear.

kulke—to go or to travel (on land or water).

kulkesz arwa-arvoval, ekäm—walk with honor, my brother (*greeting*).

kulkesz arwaval—joŋesz arwa arvoval—go with glory—return with honor (*greeting*).

kuly—intestinal worm; tapeworm; demon who possesses and devours souls.

kumpa—wave (*noun*).

kuńa—to lie as if asleep; to close or cover the eyes in a game of hide-and-seek; to die.

kunta—band, clan, tribe, family.

kutenken—however.

kuras—sword; large knife.

kure—bind; tie.

kutni—to be able to bear, carry, endure, stand, or take.

kutnisz ainaak—long may you endure (*greeting*).

kuulua—to belong; to hold.

lääs—west.

lamti (*or* **lamt3**)—lowland; meadow; deep; depth.

lamti ból jüti, kinta, ja szelem—the netherworld (*literally: the meadow of night, mists, and ghosts*).

laña—daughter.

lejkka—crack, fissure, split (*noun*). To cut; to hit; to strike forcefully (*verb*).

lewl—spirit (*noun*).

lewl ma—the other world (*literally: spirit land*). *Lewl ma* includes *lamti ból jüti, kinta, ja szelem*: the netherworld, but also includes the worlds higher up *En Puwe*, the Great Tree.

liha—flesh.

lõuna—south.

löyly—breath; steam (*related to lewl: spirit*).

ma—land; forest.

magköszun—thank.

mana—to abuse; to curse; to ruin.

mäne—to rescue; to save.

maγe—land; earth; territory; place; nature.

me—we.

meke—deed; work (*noun*). To do; to make; to work (*verb*).

mića—beautiful.

mića emni kuŋenak minan—my beautiful lunatic.

minan—mine; my own (*endearment*).

minden—every, all (*adj.*).

möért?—what for? (*exclamation*).

molanâ—to crumble; to fall apart.

molo—to crush; to break into bits.

mozdul—to begin to move, to enter into movement.

muonì— appoint; order; prescribe; command.

muonìak te avoisz te—I command you to reveal yourself.

musta—memory.

myös—also.

nä—for.

nâbbŏ—so, then.

ŋamaŋ—this; this one here; that; that one there.

nautish—to enjoy.

nélkül—without.

nenä—anger.

ńiŋ3—worm; maggot.

nó—like; in the same way as; as.

numa—god; sky; top; upper part; highest (*related to the English word: numinous*).

numatorkuld—thunder (literally: sky struggle).

nyál—saliva; spit (*related to nyelv: tongue*).

nyelv—tongue.

odam—to dream; to sleep.

odam-sarna kondak—lullaby (*literally: sleep-song of children*).

olen—to be.

oma—old; ancient; last; previous.

omas—stand.

omboće—other; second (*adj.*).

o—the (*used before a noun beginning with a consonant*).

ot—the (*used before a noun beginning with a vowel*).

otti—to look; to see; to find.

óv—to protect against.

owe—door.

päämoro—aim; target.

pajna—to press.

pälä—half; side.

päläfertiil—mate or wife.

palj3—more.

peje—to burn.

peje terád—get burned (*Carpathian swear words*).

pél—to be afraid; to be scared of.

pesä (n.)—nest (*literal*); protection (*figurative*).

pesä (v.)—nest (*literal*); protect (*figurative*).

pesäd te engemal—you are safe with me.

pesäsz jeläbam ainaak—long may you stay in the light (*greeting*).

pide—above.

pile—to ignite; to light up.

pirä—circle; ring (*noun*). to surround; to enclose (*verb*).

piros—red.

pitä—to keep; to hold; to have; to possess.

pitäam mustaakad sielpesäambam—I hold your memories safe in my soul.

pitäsz baszú, piwtäsz igazáget—no vengeance, only justice.

piwtä—to follow; to follow the track of game; to hunt; to prey upon.

poår—bit; piece.

põhi—north.

pukta—to drive away; to persecute; to put to flight.

pus—healthy; healing.

pusm—to be restored to health.

puwe—tree; wood.

rambsolg—slave.

rauho—peace.

reka—ecstasy; trance.

rituaali—ritual.

sa—sinew; tendon; cord.

sa4—to call; to name.

saa—arrive, come; become; get, receive.

saasz hän ku andam szabadon—take what I freely offer.

salama—lightning; lightning bolt.

sarna—words; speech; magic incantation (*noun*). To chant; to sing; to celebrate (*verb*).

sarna kontakawk—warriors' chant.

śaro—frozen snow.

sas—shoosh (*to a child or baby*).

saɣe—to arrive; to come; to reach.

siel—soul.

sieljelä isäntä—purity of soul triumphs.

sisar—sister.

sív—heart.

sív pide köd—love transcends evil.

sívad olen wäkeva, hän ku piwtä—may your heart stay strong, hunter (*greeting*).

sívamet—my heart.

sívam és sielam—my heart and soul.

sívdobbanás—heartbeat (*literal*); rhythm (*figurative*).

sokta—to mix; to stir around.

soŋe—to enter; to penetrate; to compensate; to replace.

susu—home; birthplace (*noun*). At home (*adv.*).

szabadon—freely

szelem—ghost.

taka—behind; beyond.

tappa—to dance; to stamp with the feet; to kill.

te—you.

Te kalma, te jama ńiŋ3kval, te apitäsz arwa-arvo—You are nothing but a walking maggot-infected corpse, without honor.

Te magköszunam nä ŋamaŋ kać3 taka arvo—Thank you for this gift beyond price.

ted—yours.

terád keje—get scorched (*Carpathian swear words*).

tõd—to know.

Tõdak pitäsz wäke bekimet mekesz kaiket—I know you have the courage to face anything.

tõdhän—knowledge.

tõdhän lõ kuraset agbapäämoroam—knowledge flies the sword true to its aim.

toja—to bend; to bow; to break.

toro—to fight; to quarrel.

torosz wäkeval—fight fiercely (*greeting*).

totello—obey.

tsak—only.

tuhanos—thousand.

tuhanos löylyak türelamak saye diutalet—a thousand patient breaths bring victory.

tule—to meet; to come.

tumte—to feel; to touch; to touch upon.

türe—full, satiated, accomplished.

türelam—patience.

türelam agba kontsalamaval—patience is the warrior's true weapon.

tyvi—stem; base; trunk.

uskol—faithful.

uskolfertiil—allegiance; loyalty.

varolind—dangerous.

veri—blood.

veri-elidet—blood-life.

veri ekäakank—blood of our brothers.

veri isäakank—blood of our fathers.

veri olen piros, ekäm—literally: blood be red, my brother; figuratively: find your lifemate (*greeting*).

veriak ot en Karpatiiak—by the blood of the Prince (*literally: by the blood of the great Carpathian; Carpathian swear words*).

veridet peje—may your blood burn (*Carpathian swear words*).

vigyáz—to love; to care for; to take care of.

vii—last; at last; finally.

wäke—power; strength.

wäke beki—strength; courage.

wäke kaða—steadfastness.

wäke kutni—endurance.

wäke-sarna—vow; curse; blessing (*literally: power words*).

wäkeva—powerful.

wara—bird; crow.

weńća—complete; whole.

wete—water (*noun*).

Do you love fiction with a supernatural twist?

Want the chance to hear news about your favourite
authors (and the chance to win free books)?

Keri Arthur
S. G. Browne
P.C. Cast
Christine Feehan
Jacquelyn Frank
Thea Harrison
Larissa Ione
Darynda Jones
Sherrilyn Kenyon
Jackie Kessler
Jayne Ann Krentz and Jayne Castle
Martin Millar
Kat Richardson
J.R. Ward
David Wellington
Laura Wright

Then visit the Piatkus website and blog
www.piatkus.co.uk | www.piatkusbooks.net

And follow us on Facebook and Twitter
www.facebook.com/piatkusfiction | www.twitter.com/piatkusbooks

piatkus